MONETARY POLICY IN SUB-SAHARAN AFRICA

Africa: Policies For Prosperity Series

Series Editors

Christopher S. Adam and Paul Collier

For the first time in more than a generation, sustained economic growth has been achieved across much of Africa—even despite the downturn in global economic fortunes since 2008—and in many countries these gains have been realized through policy reforms driven by the decisive leadership of a new generation of economic policymakers. The process of reform is continuous, however, and the challenge currently facing this new generation is how to harness these favourable gains in macroeconomic stability and turn them into a coherent strategy for sustainable growth and poverty reduction over the coming decades. These challenges are substantial and encompass the broad remit of economic policy. Each volume in this series brings leading scholars into the policy arena to examine, in a rigorous but accessible manner, the key economic challenges and policy options facing policymakers on the continent.

BOOKS PUBLISHED IN THIS SERIES

Kenya: Policies for Prosperity
Edited by Christopher S. Adam, Paul Collier, and Njuguna Ndung'u

Zambia: Building Prosperity from Resource Wealth
Edited by Christopher S. Adam, Paul Collier, and Michael Gondwe

Tanzania: The Path to Prosperity
Edited by Christopher S. Adam, Paul Collier, and Benno Ndulu

Monetary Policy in Sub-Saharan Africa
Edited by Andrew Berg and Rafael Portillo

Monetary Policy in Sub-Saharan Africa

Edited by
ANDREW BERG AND
RAFAEL PORTILLO

OXFORD
UNIVERSITY PRESS

Great Clarendon Street, Oxford, OX2 6DP,
United Kingdom

Oxford University Press is a department of the University of Oxford.
It furthers the University's objective of excellence in research, scholarship,
and education by publishing worldwide. Oxford is a registered trade mark of
Oxford University Press in the UK and in certain other countries

First Edition published in 2018

Published in the United States of America by Oxford University Press
198 Madison Avenue, New York, NY 10016, United States of America

British Library Cataloguing in Publication Data

Data available

Library of Congress Control Number: 2017953556

ISBN 978–0–19–878581–1

"Nothing contained in this Work should be reported as representing the views of the
IMF, its Executive Board, member governments, or any other entity mentioned herein.
The views in this Work belong solely to the Editors and Contributors."

To Katie, Sarah, and Noah
A.B.
To Filiz and Deniz
R.P.

Foreword

Contemporary perspectives on the role of monetary policy emphasize three core functions: to deliver low and stable inflation; conditional on this, to moderate fluctuations in the path of domestic output by tightening or loosening monetary conditions as circumstances dictate; and to support the smooth functioning of the payments system and the financial system more generally, so as to promote the efficient market-based allocation of credit and pricing of risk.

How these broad objectives are best met is a subject of extensive and active debate, not least as central banks around the world seek to navigate the low interest rate environment that has prevailed since 2008. Nonetheless, a strong consensus has emerged from this debate in favour of systems of 'constrained discretion', usually framed in terms of inflation targeting and commonly found in the industrialized economies and amongst an increasing number of middle-income countries. The 'discretion' reflects central banks' operational independence in the deployment of their policy instruments, while the 'constraint' is manifest in an explicit, verifiable, and credible target for inflation (and possibly other economic outcomes), typically set by government. A credible inflation target of this form serves to anchor inflation expectations and to tie the authorities' hands in a way that minimizes their incentives to act in a time-inconsistent manner. With expectations anchored, space is created for the authorities to pursue output stabilization.

The demands of these frameworks set the bar high and in practice only a few emerging market countries currently clear it. This small band includes a mere handful of African countries although, as described in this book, many more are modernizing their monetary frameworks. The economic history behind this move provides the context both for understanding this journey and for framing the analysis presented in the chapters that follow.

The journey starts in the early post-Independence decades when many Sub-Saharan African countries conducted economic policy in ways that placed infeasible demands on their fledgling central banks, burdening them with broad-based 'development' mandates that not only over-powered central banks' limited instruments and operational capacity but also severely compromised their ability to deliver on their core price stability mandate. Being asked to do 'too much' resulted in monetary instruments being deployed to target both the exchange rate *and* the money supply; to target interest rates; and to direct credit to preferred sectors. Moreover, as serious macroeconomic imbalances emerged, especially during the 1980s, many central banks were drawn into attempts to sustain this dis-equilibrium with the result that official exchange rates became progressively overvalued and interest rates increasingly repressed. The resulting anti-export bias, excess aggregate demand, and extreme credit-rationing placed enormous pressure on current accounts, which in turn drew the authorities into ever more distortionary capital- and current-account controls on the balance of payments. In the end, monetary policy neither delivered sustained development outcomes nor did it provide a nominal anchor for inflation.

As the need for deep economic adjustment became increasingly clear and broad-based economic reform and liberalization programmes were put in place through the 1990s, the monetary policy pendulum swung sharply to the other extreme, away from broad development mandates and towards tightly constrained frameworks anchored on floating exchange rates and characterized by strict controls on the growth in money aggregates. These frameworks reflected—and were reinforced by—the theory and practice of 'financial programing' that underpinned IMF support for stabilization efforts across the continent. Financial programming embodied a diagnosis that located concerns about macroeconomic stabilization in a structural lack of fiscal control, in other words in problems of fiscal dominance. IMF programmes and associated monetary policy frameworks became increasingly rule-based and focused narrowly on the control of the asset side of central bank balance sheets. Quantitative targets on reserve money growth emerged as the intermediate target of monetary policy and these in turn were secured by tightly binding ceilings on net domestic assets (i.e. credit from the central bank to government), ceilings that were often enforced through crude but effective 'cash budgeting' fiscal rules. These structures effectively purged all vestiges of discretion from monetary frameworks.

As it turned out, prevailing global economic conditions were favourable to aggressive price stabilization, but nonetheless African central banks, working in concert with fiscal authorities, were remarkably successful in delivering on the core objective of price stability. Inflation tumbled across the continent so that since the early 2000s, median inflation is now firmly anchored in the mid-single-digit range.

But as inflation has been brought under greater control, central banks in Africa have begun to focus their attention on the other elements of their mandate and in particular on how the gains from the hard-won struggle to limit fiscal dominance can be used to allow monetary policy to play a more supportive role in macroeconomic policy making. Attention is therefore turning to questions of how policy instruments should be deployed to manage short-run volatility in domestic economic activity, in exchange rate movements, and in interest rate instruments themselves; of how institutional reforms can support greater transparency of central bank actions and improved communication of economic analysis and forecasting; and of how the channels of transmission of monetary policy can be better understood and modelled to support policy implementation.

The IMF has been a central player throughout this period of transition, initially as the external 'agency of restraint' supporting (and some would say driving) technocrats' attempts to address fiscal dominance through the 1990s and, latterly as the champion of the move to modernize monetary frameworks and to give operational substance to the model of the independent central bank operating under a regime of constrained discretion.

Much of the work in this book draws on the accumulated experience of the IMF as an institution and of some of their counterparts in African central banks. The result is a superb collection of papers that contribute to frontier research in applied monetary economics and combine this analytical rigour with a deep understanding of how the structural realities of African economies necessarily shape and inform this analysis, whether in understanding the role of food price shocks, or handling aid flows, or conducting monetary policy when domestic asset markets remain thin, or where information and data are scarce.

As Series Editors, we are delighted with the collection which we believe will be an invaluable resource for researchers and scholars but, more importantly, for practitioners and policymakers in central banks in Africa.

Christopher S. Adam and Paul Collier

November 2017

Series Preface

POLICIES FOR PROSPERITY

Since the mid-1990s the economic prospects for Africa have been transformed. The change has been uneven: some countries remain mired in conflict and economic stagnation. But for many macroeconomic stability has been achieved—even through the global economic crisis—and far-reaching policy reforms have been put in place. For these countries, growth prospects in the early 21st century are much brighter than at any time during the final quarter of the last century. But converting favourable prospects into sustained growth and decisive poverty reduction requires a degree of good luck, good policy formulation, resources, and a lot of good economic management. For policy improvements to be sustained they must be underpinned by more fundamental shifts in political power; sectional interests ruling through patronage must be defeated by the public interest. For the shift in power to be decisive, the achievements of individual reformers must be locked in through the development of institutions. The challenges are formidable: they range beyond the conventional agenda of macroeconomic management, infrastructure provision, and the improvement of the investment climate. For example, land policy, which has usually been left dormant, will need to be rethought in the face of high population growth rates and growing urbanization. Trade and industrial policies will need to be rethought so as to engage more effectively with changing global opportunities. The continent will need to develop adaptive policies in the face of rapid climate change.

Many of the successes of recent decades have been wrought by the progressive leadership of a new generation of policymakers. To build on these successes, this same generation needs both the support of, and restraint by, an informed and engaged society. This is the fundamental philosophy of this series: informed societies are strong societies. If citizens are to hold governments to account, they require information, debate and dispassionate analysis on the challenges and choices confronting countries and their people. This is especially relevant in the realm of economic policy where path-dependency is powerful and the consequences of choices are far-reaching and long-lasting.

In many industrialized economies there is a long tradition of informed debate and analysis sustained in large measure by high-quality financial journalism. In Africa, by contrast, while a dynamic and often fearless free press is now quite widely established, it still lacks a tradition of solid, durable, and independent writing on economic policy. As a result local debate is too often ill-informed or is perceived to be driven by the agendas, and cheque-books, of sectional interests and international organizations.

There is now considerable academic research on the issues that matter for Africa and it could potentially inform Africa's debates. But to date it has been disconnected from them. Increasingly, academics write only for other academics rather than to inform the public. With this series of books we seek to build bridges between the evidence from solid research and contemporary policy debates.

Each book aims to bring together the best international and domestic scholars with policymakers working on economic policy issues across the continent. Throughout, our contributors are required to write with clarity, avoiding academic jargon, but equally avoiding advocacy. Focusing on the key issues that matter for a society, each chapter aims to leave readers better able to draw their own conclusions about important choices.

Christopher S. Adam
Paul Collier
Series Editors
Oxford, July 2014

Preface

This book represents our close collaboration over many years on the topic of monetary policy in sub-Saharan Africa (SSA). It began when we were both in the African Department of the IMF in 2006, and continued through many years at the IMF's research department.

The topic was massively understudied. Without a doubt, the major economic questions in SSA involve health and education, infrastructure, financial development, the effectiveness of the state, and more broadly, the promotion of institutions conducive to development. Even within macroeconomics narrowly construed, fiscal policy drives more volatility than monetary policy, causes more crises, and is more closely linked to these broader issues. But while monetary policy deserves only a small fraction of total attention, it receives much less than that. Almost all economists working on low-income countries naturally focus on 'development economics', which has little room for monetary policy. And almost no monetary economists work on low-income countries, where the data are poor, the share in world GDP low, and the investment required to understand the policy issues and regimes is large. Meanwhile, central bankers and academics from the region face capacity challenges.

Our work received a huge boost when we joined forces with the UK's Department of International Development (DFID), which starting in 2012 financed a research project with the IMF on the macroeconomics of low-income countries, with an important component on monetary policy. Like us, DFID was eager to generate research that was actually used by policymakers in low-income countries. We were thus able to combine academic-style research with applications of this research directly in central banks and with IMF country teams. We also participated in the writing of two major IMF policy papers on monetary policy regimes in low-income countries. This book is largely the fruit of all these efforts.

Our background in advanced-country and emerging markets macroeconomics has shaped our overall analytic approach. One upshot of this experience was a growing dissatisfaction with the usefulness of the quantity-based models that in those days formed the basis of IMF 'financial programming', at least for the purpose of analysing monetary policy in a floating exchange rate context. Another was an appreciation, learned from Douglas Laxton, about the merits of small models as the core of an inflation forecasting and policy analysis system in inflation-targeting (IT) central banks.

One implication of this background is that we tend to see monetary policy issues in low-income countries in SSA as differing in degree, but not fundamentally in kind, from those of more developed countries. There is no sharp analytic divide with Peru and Mexico on one side and Uganda and Mozambique on the other. We thus in general have attempted to start with approaches that have been fruitful in emerging markets and then capture the most important differences in low-income countries.

We have worked closely with many colleagues on these topics over the years. We would like to single out Michael Atingi Ego, Deputy Director of the IMF's

African Department and formerly Executive Director of Research at the Bank of Uganda. For over ten years, and to our great intellectual benefit, we have been discussing the questions at the heart of this book with Michael. And we have worked hand in hand with him when collaborating with colleagues in the African Department of the IMF and in African Central Banks.

We would like to thank many colleagues at the IMF and in academia for their advice, cooperation, and friendship in this endeavor, especially: Chris Adam, Rahul Anand, Olivier Blanchard, Mirek Benes, Ed Buffie, Romain Houssa, Yaroslav Hul, Darryl King, Douglas Laxton, Andy Levin, Nils Maehle, Stephen O'Connell, Maxwell Opoku-Afari, Jonathan Ostry, Catherine Pattillo, Adam Remo, Filiz Unsal, David Vavra, and Felipe Zanna. We would also like to thank our colleagues at various central banks in SSA, including Thomas Kigabo, Adam Mugume, Esman Nyamongo, Governor Benno Ndulu, Former Governor Njunguna Ndung'u, and Deputy Governor Louis Kasekende. Our work has benefitted from excellent research assistance over the years, including from Enrico Berkes, Will Clark, Pranav Gupta, and more recently Xi Zhang and Jun Ge, and excellent administrative assistance from Biva Joshi and Stephanie Fallas.

Contents

Contents

PART III. APPLIED MODELS FOR POLICY ANALYSIS AND FORECASTING IN SSA: SELECTED CASE STUDIES

List of Illustrations

List of Tables

List of Contributors

EDITORS

Andrew Berg is Deputy Director of the IMF's Institute for Capacity Development. He first joined the IMF in 1993, most recently in the Research Department as chief of the development macroeconomic division and before that in the African Department, including as chief of the regional studies division and mission chief to Malawi, and in the Department of Strategy Policy and Review. He has also worked at the US Treasury and as an associate of Jeffrey Sachs. He has a PhD in Economics from MIT and an undergraduate degree from Harvard. He has published articles on, among other things, growth accelerations, the macroeconomics of aid, predicting currency crises, inequality, and the implications of public investment for debt sustainability, in addition to monetary policy.

Rafael Portillo is Deputy Chief of the Economic Modelling Division in the Research Department of the IMF. He has also worked in the Western Hemisphere, Monetary and Capital Markets and African Departments. He took leave from the IMF in 2016–17 to work at the Joint Vienna Institute. His work has focused on macroeconomic modelling and monetary policy issues, through surveillance, research, and technical assistance. Mr Portillo has co-authored several IMF policy papers, working papers, and academic publications. He received his PhD in Economics in 2006 from the University of Michigan and also holds degrees from the Université Paris I (Panthéon-Sorbonne) and the Université Paris IX (Dauphine).

AUTHORS

Christopher Adam is Professor of Development Economics, Head of the Department of International Development, and Research Associate at the Centre for the Study of African Economies at the University of Oxford. He is currently the Lead Academic for Tanzania for the International Growth Centre (IGC) and a Visiting Scholar at the IMF. He is a Fellow of the European Development Network (EUDN). He holds a DPhil in Economics from Nuffield College, Oxford and is an associate editor of the *Journal of Development Economics* and the *Oxford Review of Economic Policy*.

Ali Alichi is a Senior Economist on the United States desk in the IMF's Western Hemisphere Department. He previously held positions in different departments in the IMF, including most recently in Research, and Asia and Pacific Departments. His research covers a broad range of topics, including monetary policy, fiscal policy, exchange rate dynamics, sovereign debt, income polarization, and economic modelling. Mr Alichi holds a PhD in Economics from Boston University.

Michal Andrle is a senior economist at the IMF's research department, where he works mainly on development and policy analysis with multi-country models. Before joining the IMF in 2010, he was a member of the New Area Wide Model team at the European Central Bank's research department. While at the Czech National Bank, he was instrumental in the development and implementation of the core forecasting and policy analysis DSGE model 'g3', which is still actively used as a core policy model. He also gained five years of experience at the Financial Policy Department of the Czech Ministry of Finance.

Alfredo Baldini is the IMF Resident Representative in Zambia. At the IMF since 2000, he worked at the IMF's Institute, the Fiscal Affairs and African Departments. Before joining the IMF, he served on the Council of Economic Advisers of the Ministry of Finance of Italy. He held teaching and research positions at various universities: Bocconi University in Milan, London School of Economics, New School for Social Research in New York and DELTA in Paris. He holds an MSc and PhD in Economics from the University of London, UK and a degree in Economics from Bocconi University, Italy.

Jaromir Benes is a senior economist at the IMF.

Enrico Berkes is a PhD candidate at Northwestern University. He worked as a Research Officer at the IMF Research Department between 2010 and 2012. His current research focuses on growth and innovation. He holds an MSc ETH in Mathematics from the Swiss Federal Institute of Technology of Zurich and an MA in International Economics from the Graduate Institute of Geneva.

Martin Brownbridge has served as the Economic Advisor to the Governor of the Bank of Uganda (BOU) since 2009, where he has helped the BOU to introduce its inflation targeting monetary policy framework, establish a Financial Stability Department, and implement the Basel III reforms. He has a PhD from the University of Manchester and has also worked in Belize, Ghana, the Gambia, and Tajikistan providing technical assistance on macroeconomics, monetary policy, fiscal policy, and financial regulation. He has published papers on bank regulation, bank resolution, fiscal policy, and monetary policy.

Luisa Charry is a Senior Economist at the African Department of the International Monetary Fund, contributing with technical assistance and policy papers on the modernization of monetary policy frameworks in developing countries. Previous to joining the IMF, Luisa worked at the Central Bank of Colombia (Banco de la República) for over ten years, where she was a member of the forecasting team focusing on model-based medium term macroeconomic forecasts. She was also a senior economist at Citigroup and Head of Equity Research in Valores Bancolombia.

Mai C. Dao is an economist at the IMF.

Pranav Gupta is an Economist in the Strategy, Policy and Review (SPR) department of IMF. He has wide-ranging experience in economic modelling and forecasting for emerging and developing countries. He has been part of IMF official missions to India, Mongolia, Rwanda, Sri Lanka, and Tanzania, where he assisted the Central Banks develop advanced macroeconomic forecasting models. Currently he is involved in the development and review of IMF policies and facilities for low-income countries and is doing research in areas of debt and macro-structural reforms. Prior to SPR, he was in the Research Department of IMF.

Louis Kasekende is Deputy Governor at the Bank of Uganda, a post he held during 1999–2002 and from 2009 to date. He was the Chief Economist of the African Development Bank (2006–09), where he played a leading role in the AfDB's efforts to help African economies withstand the impact of the global economic crisis. Prior to that, he served as Alternate Executive Director and later as Executive Director for the World Bank Africa Group 1. He currently chairs the Board of the Africa Economic Research Consortium and is on the boards of the African Export Import Bank and the International Economics Association. He holds a PhD in Econometrics from the University of Manchester.

Douglas Laxton is the Division Chief of the Economic Modelling Division (EMD) in the Research Department of the IMF. He has worked with many central banks over the years developing Forecasting and Policy Analysis Systems to support Inflation-Forecast Targeting frameworks. Mr Laxton has published many papers on a large range of topics, including building multi-country models to support the Fund's surveillance activities. More recently, he has been working on models with strong macro-financial linkages designed to support macro prudential policies. Prior to joining the IMF, Mr Laxton held numerous positions in the Research Department at the Bank of Canada (1981–93).

Bin Grace Li is a Senior Economist in the Research Department at the International Monetary Fund. Her research is in the areas of Macro-Finance, Development Economics, and International Finance. Previously she was desk economist for the US and Canada covering economic issues of monetary policy and external sector. She was also an Adjunct Assistant Professor at Johns Hopkins University's Paul H. Nitze School of Advanced International Studies (SAIS) teaching Development and Growth in 2009–10. She has published in peer-reviewed international journals on banking, development, commodity, and fiscal policy. She holds a PhD in Economics from the University of Chicago.

Giovanni Melina is an economist in the Research Department of the IMF. Before joining the Fund, he worked as an Associate Professor of Macroeconomics at City University London. He obtained a PhD in Economics from Birkbeck, University of London. He has made scientific contributions in the areas of Macroeconomics and Monetary and Fiscal Policy. His research focuses on understanding the sources and propagation of macroeconomic shocks, on the design of monetary and fiscal stabilization policies, and the link between macroeconomic policy and growth in developing countries.

Marshall Mills has worked at the International Monetary Fund since 2005, where he has been mission chief for Madagascar, Seychelles, and Togo in the African Department. He also worked on capital flows, trade, and programme conditionality in the Strategy, Policy and Review Department. Previously, he was the economist assigned to follow monetary policy in Ghana. Before the IMF, he worked at the US Treasury, including as Office Director for the Middle East; at the OECD; and at the US Office of Management and Budget. Mr Mills holds degrees from the University of North Carolina, Princeton University, and France's Ecole nationale d'administration.

Tokhir Mirzoev is the IMF's Resident Representative for Pakistan.

Peter Montiel is the Farleigh S. Dickinson Jr. '41 Professor of Economics at Williams College in Williamstown, Massachusetts. Professor Montiel has worked at the IMF and the World Bank; he has also served as a consultant for the Asian Development Bank and the InterAmerican Development Bank, as well as for several central banks. His research is on macroeconomic issues in developing countries. He has written several books, of which the most recent is the fourth edition of *Development Macroeconomics*, co-authored with Pierre-Richard Agenor of Manchester University and published by Princeton University Press, as well as a number of papers in professional journals.

R. Armando Morales is the IMF Resident Representative in Kenya since September 2014. Before moving to Nairobi, he worked for the IMF in different capacities, including as a mission chief for Financial Sector Assessment Programmes and technical assistance missions on monetary and financial issues for Latin American and African countries. Before joining the IMF, he worked in his home country Peru, including at the central bank; as a professor at Universidad del Pacífico; and chief economist at several think-tanks. He completed graduate studies at Northeastern University, Boston and at the Institute of World Economics in Kiel, Germany.

Stephen O'Connell is Gil and Frank Mustin Professor of Economics at Swarthmore College. Steve served as Chief Economist of the United States Agency for International Development (USAID) in 2014 and 2015. He co-ordinated the African Economic Research Consortium's two-volume study *The Political Economy of Economic Growth in Africa, 1960–2000*, and was a Visiting Scholar at the IMF in 2013. Steve has worked closely with African central banks, the Centre for Study of African Economies, the International Growth Centre, and multilateral organizations on issues of macroeconomic policy in low-income Africa.

Catherine Pattillo is an Assistant Director in the Fiscal Affairs Department at the IMF. She was formerly Assistant Director in the Strategy, Policy and Review Department and formerly Chief of the Low-Income Countries Strategy Unit in the same department. Prior to that, she was a mission chief in the Western Hemisphere Department, and worked in the African and Research Departments. She earned a BA from Harvard University and PhD in economics from Yale University. Before joining the IMF, she was a fellow at Oxford University, Centre for the Study of African Economies and St Antony's College. Her research interests and published articles are in the areas of growth, investment, debt, monetary frameworks and policies, exchange rates, aid, currency crises, macroeconomic policies and economic development, gender, income distribution and labour markets, and firm performance in Africa.

Richard Peck is a doctoral student in Economics at Northwestern University. He has worked for Innovations for Poverty Action and the Federal Reserve Bank of New York. He holds a BA in Economics and Mathematics from Swarthmore College.

Vimal Thakoor is an economist at the International Monetary Fund.

Filiz Unsal is an economist at the International Monetary Fund, where she has worked at the Strategy, Policy and Review (SPR), Research, and Asia and Pacific Departments. Ms Unsal has also worked for the World Bank's Financial Sector Advisory Center (FINSAC). She received her PhD in Economics in 2009, and MSc in Economics and Finance in 2006 from the University of York. Ms Unsal's research interests include monetary and financial stability policies. She has published in several academic journals, including the *International Journal of Central Banking*, the *IMF Economic Review*, and *Journal of Asian Economics*, and has written several policy papers.

David Vavra is currently Managing Partner of OGResearch, a Prague-based macroeconomic consultancy specializing in macroeconomic modelling and forecasting. Prior to that David had worked for the International Monetary Fund and the Czech National Bank. He has advised dozens of central banks and national authorities, including in Russia, Turkey, Ukraine, and Serbia, on monetary policy issues, helping the authorities to move to flexible exchange rate regimes and implement inflation targeting frameworks. David is also an expert in macroeconomic modelling and forecasting. He has contributed to the forecasting and decision-making support systems in many central banks in Europe, Latin America, and Africa.

Jan Vlcek is an experienced macroeconomist with a research background. He works at the Czech National Bank as an advisor to the Board. Prior to his current position, he worked as a TA advisor at the IMF focusing on issues of macro-financial linkages and frictions. He contributed to the work of the MAG and LEI groups assessing effects of increasing capital requirements. He has also been working as an external expert for the IMF. He has largely benefited from his experiences with monetary policy implementation and forecasting at several central banks, including those of developing and low-income countries. His publications cover monetary policy, macro-financial linkages, macroeconomic forecasting, and modelling. He holds a PhD in Economics.

Hans Weisfeld is a deputy division chief in the IMF's Strategy, Policy, and Review Department. He has recently helped develop further the methods used at the IMF to assess low-income countries' vulnerability to macroeconomic and financial crises. In recent years, he has also helped prepare the IMF's Reports on Macroeconomic Developments and Prospects in Low-Income Developing Countries. Mr Weisfeld holds a doctorate in economics from the Free University of Berlin and previously worked in the IMF's European and African Departments.

Luis-Felipe Zanna is a senior economist at the IMF Institute for Capacity Development. Before joining the Fund, he worked as an economist in the US Federal Reserve Board. He has a PhD in Economics from the University of Pennsylvania and undergraduate and Master's degrees from Universidad de Los Andes (Colombia). He has published articles on monetary and exchange rate policy rules in developing countries, including on macroeconomic stability and learnability issues and on managing aid and natural resource windfalls. His current research agenda is in the areas of monetary and fiscal policy in developing countries, focusing on model-based frameworks for policymaking.

1

Monetary Policy in Sub-Saharan Africa

Andrew Berg and Rafael Portillo

1 INTRODUCTION

Central banks (CBs) in sub-Saharan Africa (SSA) have made great progress over the past two decades in stabilizing inflation, to single digits on average, in the context of greater central bank independence, support from fiscal-based stabilization efforts, and more sustained and stable growth. They have done so by relying on monetary policy arrangements centred, at least de jure, on money targets, often with some form of a de facto exchange rate peg.

In about half of SSA countries, a hard peg provides a nominal anchor. In those countries that are the main focus of this book, however, the exchange rate is now at least partly flexible. Especially in these countries, policymakers are beginning to ask more of monetary policy than the achievement of some basic degree of stabilization, and existing regimes have lacked clear and effective policy frameworks. This has affected central banks' ability to steer financial conditions, respond appropriately to shocks, and avoid policy misalignments. Fully aware of these limitations, many central banks are therefore in the process of modernizing their monetary policy frameworks.

In this chapter we provide an overview of the issues facing monetary policymakers as they modernize. For the most part, we draw on the rest of the chapters in this book, as well as on recent efforts at the IMF to develop a view on some of these issues—efforts in which we were involved.[1]

Our focus is on SSA countries excluding South Africa. Monetary policy challenges in the latter country warrant a separate treatment; fortunately, in general its challenges are those of many commodity-dependent emerging market economies, about which there is a voluminous literature. For the most part we concentrate on countries with some degree of exchange rate flexibility, though we also briefly discuss the main challenges facing central banks in countries with hard pegs.[2]

This chapter, and indeed the entire book, represents an effort to bridge the economic and political realities of monetary policymaking in SSA with the lessons from the broader monetary policy literature and experience. Part of the foundation

---

[1] See IMF (2015a). We also draw extensively on Berg et al. (2015) and Adam et al. (forthcoming).
[2] We do not cover the important topic of the role of central banks in promoting financial stability. See Adam et al. (forthcoming).

of this bridge is built in Section 2, which takes a historical perspective, describing the evolution of the macroeconomic environment and monetary policy landscape over the past three decades. Section 3 first proposes a set of benchmark principles for effective monetary policy regimes. It then discusses some critical features of the SSA economic environment that have shaped existing regimes and which any application of these principles to SSA must confront. Section 4 reviews the monetary policy landscape in countries with flexible exchange rates, while Section 5 considers the modernization agenda. Section 6 briefly considers hard pegs, particularly the CFA zone, while Section 7 discusses a strategy for using models to study monetary policy issues in SSA. Section 8 concludes.

2 A BRIEF HISTORY OF MONETARY POLICY IN SSA

2.1 From Independence to the 1980s: The Breakdown of Overly Ambitious Monetary Policy Regimes

Central banks in Africa began to emerge in their modern form in the 1950s and 60s as the countries regained their independence from European colonial powers.[3] Pre-independence monetary arrangements were tightly managed by a set of currency boards, mainly anchored to sterling, the French franc, and the South African Rand. In the post-colonial era, the Rand Monetary Area and the CFA franc zone structures remained intact, even as their members attained political independence, and both continue to operate today with almost the same institutional structures they inherited at independence.

In the face of growing opposition amongst emergent nationalist movements, the currency board arrangements with the British Pound were dismantled and gave way to a set of independent central bank institutions. Established at a time where the dominant intellectual climate in economics favoured strong and centralized development planning, the role of these fledgling central banks institutions was very different from today. Along with other visible manifestations of the state, such as a national army, an airline, and a seat at the UN, a national currency and a national central bank, independent from colonial legacy, were seen as a subsidiary tool of national development.

Their distinctive character began to emerge particularly after the collapse of the Bretton Woods system of fixed exchange rates in the early 1970s. Central banks found themselves administering heavily managed exchanged rates, often in situations of severe rationing, so that parallel markets in foreign exchange were widespread; setting administered interest rates, typically far below market-clearing values; directing the allocation of domestic credit between sectors, in many cases through a state-dominated and highly oligopolistic banking system whose operations were often limited to mobilizing private savings for on-lending to government

---

[3] This section draws heavily on Berg et al. (2015) and Adam et al. (forthcoming), which contain more comprehensive references.

and SOEs at highly repressed rates; and—crucially—providing direct monetary financing of the budget deficit.

By the early 1980s it was clear that many central banks were being asked to do too much and were failing to deliver on most if not all of these multiple objectives, including the core monetary objective of providing an effective nominal anchor for prices. Many countries across Africa faced difficult external circumstances, including low prices for primary export commodities and external and domestic conflict. However, the highly distorted macroeconomic and monetary policy regimes also exerted a serious drag on economic growth and welfare. High and variable inflation became pervasive. Perhaps even more destructive to the broader economy were the flourishing parallel foreign exchange markets that badly distorted incentives for investment and encouraged widespread rent-seeking across the continent.

Central to this failure was the pressure on central banks to finance fiscal deficits from their own balance sheets. With under-developed domestic asset markets and tight controls on capital flows, and widespread financial repression, the demand for money was relatively inelastic. This presented governments with the scope to mobilize substantial seigniorage revenues, an attractive option where traditional tax revenue mobilization capacities were limited. But as controls weakened, and the velocity of circulation rose, inflation began to rise sharply and fiscal balances worsened.

2.2 1990s: Fiscal-Based Stabilization Efforts

From the mid-1980s to the late 1990s countries began reform programmes, often with exchange rate unifications and movement toward more market-determined, flexible exchange rates, and dismantling of exchange and trade controls (Figure 1.1). As in other developing regions, the number of countries with de facto managed or floating exchange rates in SSA increased by about 50 per cent between 1980 and 1990 (Figure 1.2).[4]

The initial conditions of these programmes (heavily managed or even de facto pegged exchange rates, pervasive capital controls, and fiscally driven monetary policy) explain the appeal of a monetary policy framework anchored on the control of money-financing of the fiscal deficit. The logic of the 'monetary approach to the balance of payments' applies.[5] Typical IMF-Reserve money programming in Africa combined a diagnosis of the stabilization problem that located the fundamental macroeconomic weakness in a lack of fiscal control within an operational framework that targeted domestic credit from the central bank to government. Embedded within broader reform programs aimed at the liberalization of domestic prices, interest rates, and the exchange rate, and supported by substantial donor assistance and official debt relief, reserve money programmes of this kind played

---

[4] Developing countries include countries classified as emerging markets and developing countries according to the IMF world economy outlook (WEO).

[5] See, for example, IMF (1977).

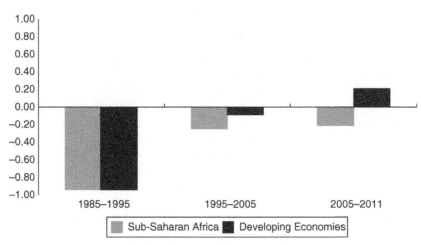

Figure 1.1. Capital Account Openness (Chinn-Ito) Index[a] (Period Averages)

[a] Excluding countries fixed exchange rate regimes. A higher number indicates a more open capital account.

Source: http://web.pdx.edu/~ito/Chinn-Ito_website.htm

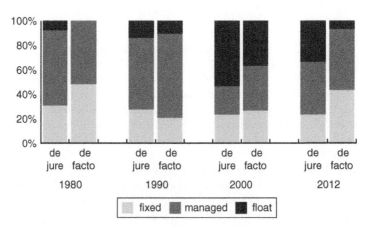

Figure 1.2. Exchange Rate Classification (Sub-Saharan Africa[a])

[a] excludes CFA Zone countries

Source: AREAER Database, IMF.

a major role throughout the 1990s and early 2000s in restoring macroeconomic stability across the continent.

Other key elements of the two-decade transition were sharp reductions in central bank financing of government and financial liberalizations that eliminated interest-rate controls and introduced competition into the banking sector. With the assistance of IMF-supported programmes, substantial debt relief, and a favourable external environment, domestic credit to government declined from an average of 13 per cent in 1985–95 to 8 per cent in 1995–2005, and has remained broadly at that level to date. The re-establishment of fiscal control provided support for money-based disinflation programs to bring down inflation to single digits (or near single) in the context of higher economic growth and higher international reserves by the late 1990s, in line with the experience in other developing countries (Table 1.1).

Liberalization of direct controls over the commercial banking system helped alleviate the prolonged financial repression (Adam and O'Connell, 2005).[6] Real interest rates turned positive in 1995–2005, averaging 5 per cent as compared with about -11 per cent in the previous decade. Interest rate spreads, around 11 per cent, have remained high but are comparable to other developing countries (Table 1.2). Bank deposits and private credit as a share of GDP steadily increased during the last three decades (Table 1.2). These developments also coincide with greater use of open market operations by central banks in the region, all of which have increased the role of market signals and the importance of managing expectations in the implementation of monetary policy.

By the early 2000s, then, countries such as Ghana, Nigeria, Uganda, Kenya, Zambia, and Tanzania were beginning to enjoy sustained growth with low and stable inflation.[7] Macroeconomic stability was increasingly accompanied by the deepening and development of domestic asset markets and, in some cases, by moves to liberalize the capital account in order to encourage greater private capital inflows, including into sovereign debt.

3 CHALLENGES FOR MONETARY POLICY IN SSA·

The story so far is one of success. However, it is incomplete. The reduced role for the exchange rate as nominal anchor and increasingly developed financial markets revealed weaknesses with existing policy frameworks. In particular, the money targeting regimes did not provide effective frameworks for formulating and implementing policy. At the same time, ambitions grew for monetary policy to not just contribute less volatility but to play a greater countercyclical role. More generally, effective monetary policy, including smoother functioning of interbank markets and the provision of clearer interest rate signals, became part of the broader financial development agenda.

Before assessing the current state of affairs, it is useful—and more transparent—to present a benchmark for effective policy regimes. In the decades prior to the global financial crisis there was a revolution in the practice and thinking of monetary policy, which started in small advanced economies and then spread to other countries. The IMF (2015a) recently summarized these lessons into seven principles. First, central banks should have a clear mandate, set in the law, and the operational independence to pursue it. Second, price stability should be the

---

[6] For countries in SSA with available data (and excluding pegs), the financial reform index reported by Giuliano et al. (2010) more than doubled on average in the decade between 1985–90 and 1995–2000 (the countries are Ghana, Kenya, Madagascar, Mozambique, Nigeria, South Africa, Tanzania, and Uganda).

[7] See for example Kessy et al. (2016).

Table 1.1. Inflation in SSA: 1985–95, 1995–2005, 2005–12

	1985–95			1995–2005			2005–12		
	Inflation	Growth	International Reserves	Inflation	Growth	International Reserves	Inflation	Growth	International Reserves
Mean	28.7	2.5	6.8	14.9	4.4	9.0	10.1	5.8	14.0
Median	16.5	3.5	4.6	13.3	4.2	8.8	9.2	5.5	12.7
Standard Deviation	18.8	4.5	3.0	10.6	4.3	3.1	5.1	2.6	2.8
Mean (Developing countries)	27.9	1.3	7.3	17.1	4.4	12.4	8.0	5.5	15.8

Note: Excluding countries with exchange rate pegs according to 2013 AREAER.

Source: World Economic Outlook Database. Annual data (y/y growth) is used to calculate inflation and GDP growth. International Reserves are in percentage of GDP.

Table 1.2. Bank-Deposits, Private Credit, and Spreads: SSA (Mean, in per cent)

	1985–95	1995–2005	2005–10	
	SSA	SSA	SSA	Developing Economies
Bank deposits to GDP	16.8	23.2	29.3	37.5
Private credit to GDP	11.7	14.8	20.5	28.9
Interest rate spreads	11.8	14.0	11.3	9.9

Note: Excluding countries with exchange rate pegs.

Source: International Monetary Fund.

primary objective of monetary policy, at least over the medium term. Third, central banks should have a numerical medium-term inflation objective to operationalize the price stability mandate and guide policy actions. Fourth, central banks should nonetheless take into account the implications for output and financial stability when making policy decisions. Fifth, central banks should have an effective operational framework, generally centred on the control of short-term interest rates. Sixth, delivering on price stability requires a forward-looking strategy that maps objectives into policy decisions. And finally, a central element of the monetary policy framework is clear communications, to help explain policy decisions and outcomes and provide guidance about the future.[8]

Two questions immediately arise when thinking about the application of these principles to monetary policy in SSA. First, have they been made obsolete by the lessons from the global financial crisis? And second, can they really be imported effectively to SSA countries with such different economies and monetary policy challenges from the countries where they were developed over the past twenty or so years?

The global financial crisis has, if anything, strengthened the value of these principles along certain important dimensions. For example, inflation-targeting (IT) emerging market countries performed better during the financial crisis than non-IT countries, including in responding more quickly to the global downturn and avoiding deflationary inflation expectations.[9] The prospect of deflation in advanced economies has underscored the importance of medium-term numerical inflation targets to help anchor expectations. In addition, the crisis served to reinforce the importance of central bank communications, in particular the use of forward guidance as a monetary policy tool.

The crisis did, however, starkly underscore the limitations of price stability as the sole focus of central bank actions, and the importance of financial stability. Much of the broader post-crisis policy discussion has focused on how to incorporate tools for macro-prudential and how to integrate them with traditional monetary policy tools in service of financial stability.[10] The implications of this debate, especially for Africa and low-income countries more generally, have yet to be fully fleshed out.[11] However, we see the new focus on financial stability and macro-prudential tools as important refinements to pre-crisis arrangements, rather than a complete overhaul. Modernizing policy frameworks along the lines described earlier should remain the priority for SSA central banks, even as they pay greater attention to financial stability issues.

One notable change relative to the pre-crisis consensus has been greater experimentation with new instruments in advanced economies, mainly quantitative easing. We see little scope for the use of these tools in SSA CBs, given the

---

[8] Inflation targeting clearly embodies these principles, as it was the historical development of this regime that helped clarify these desirable properties of monetary policy. In policy debates in Africa, however, as elsewhere, the term 'inflation targeting' has at times been a source of controversy. Some have interpreted it as implying a strict and exclusive concern with inflation, deeming it inappropriate for low-income countries. Others feel that central banks can only adopt 'inflation targeting' after a long sequence of reforms. The focus on principles is an attempt to move the debate forward.

[9] See De Carvalho Filho (2011).

[10] See IMF (2013) and IMF (2015b), among many others.

[11] See IMF (2014) and Adam et al. (forthcoming).

lower likelihood of monetary policy being constrained by the zero lower bound on interest rates. This does not imply that SSA CBs limit themselves to a single instrument. CBs in the region, and other developing counties, do (and will continue to) rely on a variety of instruments. These include reserve requirements and sterilized foreign exchange interventions, which should be thought of as a separate tool from short-term interest rates, and used for different purposes. We discuss this issue in more detail in Sections 4 and 5.[12]

The question of the applicability of these principles to SSA economies is a more central one for our purposes. Serious thinking about monetary policy in SSA implies a reasonably accurate view of how these economies work, and in particular about the effects of monetary policy. The range of uncertainties among economists and policymakers is huge. Does monetary policy even matter for output or inflation, for example? Underlying these questions are even deeper ones about whether standard macroeconomics really applies to economies with such different economic structures.

This standard macroeconomics was developed first on the basis of decades or even centuries of experience of fairly stable institutions and consistent data series, and thousands of research papers, in countries such as the United States and the United Kingdom, and then more recently a still relatively large volume of research and experience in emerging markets. And even in these countries, a strong consensus is hard to achieve. Every major recession in advanced countries is accompanied by a torrent of discussion within the economics profession about how the basic models of economics are broken, and about the most basic facts of monetary policy. See, for example, the vigorous recent debate between prominent US economists about whether higher interest rates will raise or lower inflation, or whether inflation responds to output gaps any more, if it ever did.[13]

Low-income economies are certainly different. In a typical SSA country, the bulk of the population works in smallholder agriculture, the formal sector amounts to perhaps 10 per cent of GDP, and there is little in the way of manufacturing exports. So the research agenda is huge and the literature sparse. Subsequent chapters in this book look at some of these key differences and their empirical implications, and adapt modelling frameworks that have been successful in emerging markets to capture the key features of low-income countries and analyse their implications for monetary policy. Here we summarize some of the key points.

3.1 The Monetary Transmission Mechanism

Perhaps the most critical question is about the transmission mechanism of monetary policy. An extremely weak or unreliable transmission of monetary policy to the economy might limit the scope for monetary policy to serve as a

---

[12] On the topic of reserve requirements, see the discussion in Federico et al. (2014).

[13] On the argument that higher interest rates can help raise inflation expectations when the economy is at the zero lower bound, see Schmitt-Grohe and Uribe (2010). On the slope of the Phillips curve, see Blanchard, Cerutti and Summers (2015) and references therein.

key policy tool for macroeconomic stabilization.[14] Or, perhaps transmission is much stronger from the exchange rate or monetary aggregates to inflation and output than is the case for interest rates, which might have implications for the design of a monetary policy framework.

There are many reasons to think that the transmission mechanism in low-income countries may be different and, in particular, relatively weak. The overall magnitude of the effects on aggregate demand and inflation from monetary policy decisions is likely to depend on the extent of financial deepening. African countries have shallow financial markets, so that changes in financial conditions brought about by monetary policy may directly affect a smaller share of the population. Furthermore, the nature of the policy itself decisively shapes the nature of transmission, and the opacity of existing frameworks may be undermining the effectiveness of policy. Where exchange rates are heavily managed or the capital account closed, transmission through exchange rates is also likely to be attenuated.

Some policymakers and researchers conclude from this assessment that the transmission mechanism is weak or even non-existent. Mishra and Montiel (2013) argue that the impulse responses to monetary policy shocks derived from structural VARs, the tool of choice for identifying the effects of monetary policy shocks, are typically weak and statistically insignificant in low-income countries.

In our view, this evidence may result from difficulties in applying standard empirical approaches to LICs rather than a lack of underlying transmission. Chapter 6 shows that typical features of LIC data, including short sample lengths, measurement error, and frequent policy regime changes can greatly reduce the power of VARs to uncover the monetary transmission mechanism.

In addition, the policy regime itself strongly shapes transmission, rather than or in addition to deeper structural factors. Monetary policy relies on a clear understanding by financial market participants of central bank actions, both current and likely future (the expectations channel). Such a clear understanding is likely not to emerge under existing arrangements in SSA: the combination of money target misses, noisy short-term interest rates, and incipient communications make it difficult to assess policymakers' intentions (more on this in Section 4). Under these conditions, the analysis in Chapter 9 reveals that monetary policy decisions have a smaller impact on longer-term rates, inflation, and output, compared to interest-rate-based frameworks, even when policy intentions are the same, and even when the underlying economic structure is supportive of monetary policy effectiveness. The corollary is that we should expect a strengthening in the monetary transmission as the policy framework becomes clearer.

Arguably, the strongest evidence that monetary policy 'works' in developed countries comes not from VARs but from the history of the Volker disinflation and the Great Depression. Armed with the experience of these episodes, decades of careful research have gone into producing empirical work that yields the 'right' signs. Even in the US, with its uniquely long, stable data series and policy regimes, economists experimented for many years before arriving at acceptable results, e.g. solving the 'price puzzle', that inflation seemed to rise after a monetary policy shock, and the 'liquidity puzzle', that interest rates tended to rise in response to an

---

[14] See Mishra, Montiel and Spilimbergo (2012), for example.

increase in the money supply.[15] Inspired by this perspective, Chapter 5 looks at
the effects of a dramatic tightening in monetary policy in the East African
Community in 2011. It finds a well-functioning transmission mechanism, especially in those countries where the stance of monetary policy was communicated
clearly, consistent with the previous argument. It also finds that the depth of
financial markets is a less clear indicator of the strength of transmission than the
clarity of the regime.

It may still be that transmission in LIC is generally weaker and more uncertain
than in other countries. This in turn can suggest caution in trying to fine-tune
monetary policy. However, this point can easily be overemphasized. First, deep
uncertainty about the transmission mechanism is not unique to low-income
countries but rather is a general characteristic, perhaps especially of countries
implementing new policy frameworks, often in the face of rapid structural change
or financial crises. And second, this does not in general justify inaction. Indeed,
weak transmission may explain the much larger policy movements that are often
observed in SSA countries.

Stepping back, the idea that policy action requires a precise and reliable
quantitative understanding of transmission represents an excessively idealized
view of the monetary policymaking process. There is a critical element of
'tâtonnement' for all countries, including low-income countries: assess the state
of the economy and the outlook; adjust policy if it seems too tight or too loose; and
repeat. For this process only some confidence about the sign of the effect of
monetary is critical. And finally, even a weak transmission mechanism leaves
monetary policy to play the role of nominal anchor, and doing so in a way that
responds effectively to shocks and avoids generating its own argues for the
application of the principles discussed above.

3.2 Supply Shocks and Macroeconomic Volatility

The economies of low-income countries are dominated by supply shocks (Chapters
4 and 11). Indeed, it is difficult to identify a Phillips curve-type relationship in the
data because of the dominance of supply shocks, which tend to generate a negative
correlation between the output gap and inflation in these countries, see Figure 1.3.
These supply shocks critically shape the role of monetary policy.

The so-called 'divine coincidence' of monetary policy is that, in the face of
shocks to aggregate demand, the stabilization of inflation also serves to stabilize
output.[16] Supply shocks, in contrast, push inflation up at the same time as they
reduce output, presenting a trade-off between output and inflation stabilization.
Fortunately, the principles articulated above can help manage this trade-off.
Indeed, the difficulties of managing this trade-off, notably in small open
commodity-dependent countries such as New Zealand and Canada, were some
of the main driving forces behind the evolution in monetary policymaking that is

---

[15] On these points see Summers (1991), Sims (1992) and Leeper and Gordon (1992).
[16] See Blanchard and Gali (2007).

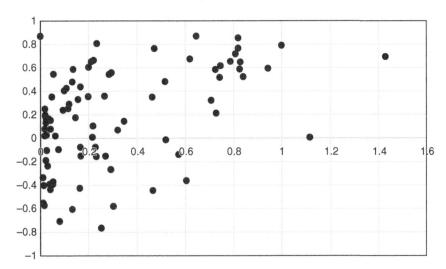

Figure 1.3. Correlation (at Business Cycle Frequency) between Inflation and the Output Gap, Against Income per Capita[a]

[a] Income per capita (2012) is normalized by income per capital for the US

Source: IMF, World Bank Development Indicators, Haver, OECD.

captured in the principles, most notably the emphasis on price stability over the medium-term.[17]

Many of these supply shocks call for adjustments to the real exchange rate. Developing countries with more flexible exchange rate regimes, including in Africa, tend to do a better job of shielding their economies from the effects of these shocks, thanks to the shock-absorbing role of the exchange rate.[18] The challenge under floating regimes is to prevent the fluctuations in nominal exchange rates from spilling over into inflation, especially when a large nominal depreciation is required. In this regard, floats in SSA have a mixed record, with higher average inflation relative to pegs. Of course, a floating regime is not in itself a monetary policy regime, and so countries wishing to reap the benefits of greater exchange rate flexibility must develop well-formulated monetary policy frameworks to keep inflation anchored.

Shocks to international food and fuel prices pose an additional set of challenges. In the African context, food makes up a large share of the consumer basket, so that the direct impact of food price shock is larger. In addition, SSA countries are net food importers on average, and many are net oil importers, so that the inflationary impact from higher international prices could be compounded by the real and nominal depreciation required for external adjustment.[19] These shocks have

---

[17] This point is argued forcefully in Bernanke et al. (1998).

[18] See Broda (2004) and Edwards and Levi-Yeyati (2005) for evidence on the effect of terms of trade shocks in developing countries across exchange rate regimes, and Hoffmaister et al. (1998) and Ahmad and Pentecost (2010) for similar analyses for sub-Saharan African countries.

[19] See Adam (2011).

therefore been a source of inflationary pressures, especially during 2007–08 and 2010–11. One complication, however, is that the direct effect of these shocks often masks underlying monetary policy misalignments, which then amplifies the overall inflationary effect. This was the case in Kenya during 2011 (Chapter 15).

Domestic supply shocks are an even larger source of inflation volatility. This is because the agricultural sector is heavily exposed to weather-related shocks. One implication is that inflation is inevitably more volatile in low-income countries— SSA countries included—with the larger volatility reflecting supply-side changes to relative food prices (see Chapter 11). Much of this volatility is unlikely to disappear even as countries modernize their policy frameworks.

Capital flows are an additional source of external shocks. SSA countries are less integrated with global capital markets, which, all else being equal, suggests less exposure to shocks stemming from the capital account.[20] However, the experience of Zambia during the global financial crisis, which is discussed in Chapter 17, shows SSA countries are not immune to capital flow reversals, and that the latter can have a large impact on domestic financial systems and the economy. In addition, SSA countries are becoming more integrated, as can be attested in the growing number of countries that have tapped international bond markets, many for the first time, in recent years.[21] Greater exposure to these shocks is thus to be expected in the future.

3.3 Fiscal Policy as a Source of Volatility and Pressures on Monetary Policy

Fiscal dominance—where the need to finance the government deficit through money printing determines the rate of inflation—remains a fundamental challenge to monetary policy in only a few countries in SSA, after the progress described in Section 2 above. In a much larger group of countries, however, fiscal policy can greatly complicate the conduct of monetary policy. Central banks in Africa must contend with highly volatile and pro-cyclical fiscal policy. Sometimes the source of fiscal volatility is a high dependence on revenues from the commodity sector, and the lack of binding fiscal rules to ensure inter-temporal smoothing. In other cases fiscal pro-cyclicality stems from the political cycle. Certain features of African economies, for example the large share of the population that lives on their current income, amplify the effect of these shocks on aggregate demand.[22]

Even if fiscal dominance is a (not-so-) distant memory, the volatility and pro-cyclicality of fiscal policy creates other forms of fiscal pressures on monetary policy. One stems from the cost of monetary operations.[23] This is a source of contention with the government, particularly in cases where the financial system is in a situation of structural liquidity surplus, for example due to sizeable interventions

---

[20] Measures of de facto financial openness, for example based on the sum of international assets and liabilities in per cent of GDP, also show SSA countries lagging. See Lane and Milesi Ferretti (2007).

[21] See IMF (2013b).

[22] See Chapter 12.

[23] Chapter 2 provides a discussion of these issues in the case of Uganda.

in FX markets, and a legacy of past quasi-fiscal operations have left the central bank with low or negative net worth. In this case sterilization operations, which are necessary to maintain an appropriate policy stance, can sharply reduce central bank profits (seigniorage). In principle, this can be resolved simply by recapitalizing the central bank, for example through the transfer of government bonds. But concerns that the Treasury will use the opportunity to look into the CB's operating expenses, or the mistaken belief that the central bank should not make losses, can often result in a monetary policy stance that is more accommodative than optimal.

Another type of pressure occurs when the central bank does not tighten policy as aggressively as it would like to, out of concern for the effect of that policy on fiscal solvency. Pressures of this type are likely to materialize in regimes, such as IT, in which the central bank takes direct responsibility for short-term interest rates. Avoiding this type of pressure may be one possible reason why many central banks in SSA have yet to formally adopt interest-rate-based frameworks, and why those that do often implement changes to the policy stance without changing the (highly visible) official policy rate.

3.4 Management of External Revenues and the Coordination of Fiscal Policy and Central Bank Operations

Central banks in SSA play an important role in managing external government revenues, such as aid and commodity windfalls. As the government's banker, the central bank helps manage the associated foreign exchange, and in its monetary policy-making function it manages the domestic money creation that results from these foreign exchange transactions. In principle, there is a benchmark of separation: foreign exchange from aid or commodity windfalls is sold into the market or to a fiscal entity (such as a sovereign wealth fund), while monetary policy is set through a policy interest rate, and any domestic money supply implications of the foreign exchange transactions are automatically sterilized. In practice, however, the central bank management of foreign exchange frequently becomes entangled with monetary policy.

To take one important example, Berg et al. (2007) document how, during aid surge episodes in several African countries with managed floats (Ghana, Mozambique, Tanzania, Uganda), concerns about real appreciation resulted in large accumulations of reserves. This policy response may have helped contain the appreciation pressures. But it also resulted in a peculiar situation in which the authorities tried to use the aid twice: once to increase government spending with the domestic currency counterpart to the aid inflows, and once to increase the stock of reserves with the dollars. The private sector was crowded out as a result, mainly through higher interest rates (when the accumulation was sterilized) and in some cases also through the inflation tax (when otherwise).[24]

The underlying general point is that central bank active management of foreign exchange reserves is a sort of quasi-fiscal policy that is closely related to other

---

[24] See Chapter 12, Adam et al. (2009), and Buffie et al. (2008, 2010) on the pros on cons of various policy responses in this context.

aspects of fiscal policy. This raises the issue of whether greater coordination of reserve policy with fiscal policy could help improve macroeconomic outcomes. It is difficult to see how this coordination can take place without affecting central bank independence, however. We return to the closely related issue of exchange rate management in Sections 4 and 5.

4 THE CURRENT MONETARY POLICY LANDSCAPE IN COUNTRIES WITH SOME EXCHANGE RATE FLEXIBILITY

Many policy changes have been institutionalized in SSA through reforms cementing central bank independence and the adoption of new central bank charters. The majority of the central banks in the region have de jure (legislated) independence,[25] and their de facto independence has been on average (0.26) very close to the developing countries' average (0.25), using the measure in Lucotte (2009).[26] Moreover, 70 per cent of SSA countries had accepted Article VIII of the IMF's Articles of Agreement by the late 1990s (more than 90 per cent as of 2012), committing to refrain from imposing restrictions on payments and transfers for current account transactions and to refrain from discriminatory currency arrangements or multiple currency practices.

The de jure policy regime in place in most countries is best characterized as a hybrid regime (IMF, 2008, 2015a). An overview of the objectives and targets of monetary policy in the region reveals a set of managed floaters with a variety of conventional-looking objectives (price and exchange rate stability), but with money aggregates still present as both operational and intermediate targets (Table 1.3).

With this brief overview, we now dig somewhat deeper to look at salient issues with the current state of monetary policy regimes in SSA, using the above principles as an organizing device.

4.1 Legal Frameworks and Operational Independence

The stabilization efforts post-1980s were supported by the adoption of new legal charters in many central banks in SSA. Assessments of central bank independence, however, show many SSA countries lagging behind richer countries. Ghana provides a case in point. A new Act adopted in 2002 established price stability as the central bank's primary objective, granted operational independence, and created a monetary policy committee. The Act did not, however, prohibit the CB from lending to the government, nor did it provide MPC members with sufficient tenure protection.

---

[25] Central Bank Legislation Database, International Monetary Fund, 2012.

[26] Indices of central bank independence combine assessments of tenure protection of central bank's senior management, operational independence, clearly legally defined objectives for monetary policy, and limits to central bank lending to the government. The construction of the indices is based on the methodology outlined in Cukierman (1992) for de facto independence and Cukierman et al. (1992) for de jure independence.

Table 1.3. De Jure Monetary Policy Frameworks in Sub-Saharan Africa

Regimes	Policy Objectives	Intermediate	Operational Target	Main Instruments
Pegs (23)	Stability of the exchange rate regime (23) Price stability (23) Economic growth (12)	Private sector credit (1)	Exchange rate (23)	Open market operations Foreign exchange sales
Money targeting (18)	Price stability (all countries) External competitiveness (5) Exchange rate smoothing (12) Economic growth (9)	Monetary aggregates (16)	Reserve money (18)	Open market operations (17) Foreign exchange sales (18)
Inflation targeting (3)	Price stability (all countries) External competitiveness (1) Exchange rate smoothing (1)		Interest rates (3)	Open market operations (3) Foreign exchange sales (3)

Source: Regional Economic Outlook 2008; International Monetary Fund.

These two issues have come into focus during the recent period of high inflation in that country.

Adherence to existing legal frameworks has also been uneven. Though measures of de facto independence are more difficult to estimate, there is plenty of anecdotal evidence. In Zimbabwe the adoption of a new charter granting greater independence to the CB preceded the complete loss of monetary autonomy and the rise in inflation—and subsequent hyperinflation—in that country. Even in countries with more stable inflation, deviations from legal limits to direct central bank financing are common, which attests to the pressures that central banks continue to face.

4.2 Price Stability, the Medium-Term Inflation Target, and the Pursuit of Other Objectives

SSA CBs have bought into the idea that price stability is the primary goal of monetary policy, at least de jure. In many countries, however, the primacy of price stability remains to be established. Many CBs continue to pursue other objectives, for example supporting growth, financial deepening, or external competitiveness. This multiplicity of objectives and lack of clear hierarchy among them typically results in erratic policies, although to a smaller degree than in the past: the monetary stance is loosened, for example to support financial deepening, only to be tightened later once inflationary pressures appear.

This state of affairs is most visible in the central role that the exchange rate plays in policy frameworks of many SSA countries, including those with de jure exchange rate flexibility. Though some attention to the exchange rate is inevitable given its importance for inflation dynamics, in some countries exchange rate stability often takes precedence over price stability (Figure 1.4). The exchange rate serves as the de facto anchor, at least temporarily, and operations aimed at influencing the exchange rate end up determining the stance of policy, for example through the use of unsterilized interventions in the FX market. This risks removing the buffering role of the exchange rate and creating exchange rate misalignments, while the disconnect between the de jure and the de facto frameworks undermines the credibility, transparency, and effectiveness of monetary policy.[27]

There are several related factors that account for the policy confusion. First, with the exception of IT countries, most central banks in the region lack an explicit, medium-term, inflation objective that can discipline policy and operationalize the pursuit of price stability.[28] In its absence, policy is more likely to be driven by political pressures, recent events, or the pressing issue of the day. Second, even if the primacy of price stability is recognized, central banks typically lack a strategy for mapping objectives into policy decisions or for taking other objectives into account in a way that does not undermine price stability. Third, operational

---

[27] IMF (2016) notes some movement back from de facto floats to de facto intermediate regimes, particularly in the face of supply shocks in commodity-dependent countries. It also observes relatively problematic macro performance in these countries, on the whole.

[28] To the extent there is an inflation objective, it is more akin to a short-term inflation forecast, which is revised to account for short-term pressures and does not guide policy in a meaningful way.

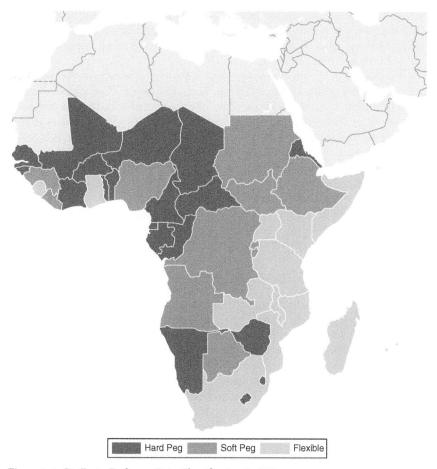

Figure 1.4. De Facto Exchange Rate Classification in SSA

Note: Hard peg includes no separate legal tender, currency board, and conventional pegged arrangement; soft peg includes stabilized arrangement, crawling peg, crawl-like arrangement, pegged exchange rate within horizontal bands, and other managed arrangement; flexible includes floating and free floating.

Sources: AREAER and IMF staff analysis.

frameworks are not in line with international best practice, which obscures the actual stance of policy and facilitates deviations from policy intentions. We next discuss the last two points in more detail.

4.3 Operational Frameworks in SSA CBs

Reserve money targeting (RMT) remains the de jure operational framework of choice in SSA, in contrast with the now standard practice of setting operational targets on (and controlling) very short-term interest rates adopted by most advanced and emerging market central banks.[29] This reflects in part the legacy of IMF-supported programmes, which emphasize targets on central bank balance sheet items as part of their conditionality, and which played an important role in the stabilization of inflation in SSA.

As discussed in Chapter 8, money targeting is implemented very flexibly, with frequent economically significant misses of money targets. These misses mainly seem to represent accommodation of money demand shocks, though some may involve policy shifts. Flexible implementation of money targeting is also evident in the process of adjustment after misses. In 'textbook' money targeting, where a constant growth rate of money serves as the 'nominal anchor', deviations from targets would be undone in subsequent quarters as the actual stock would be brought back to the predetermined target path. This does not seem to be what happens, however. Rather, the new targets themselves tend to accommodate, at least in part, deviations from previous targets. There is no sign that actual money growth itself moves so as to reduce earlier deviations from target. There is also little sign that inflation responds to these misses, at least in countries with inflation below the low teens.[30]

More recently, many CBs have introduced policy rates to signal the stance of policy, but deviations between policy and actual rates are common, and tensions between money targets and interest rate policy are inevitable. RMT can lead to highly volatile short-term interest rates, as the authorities respond partially and unpredictably to money demand shocks.[31] In addition, tensions between money targets and desired interest rate outcomes frequently lead to complex regulations and interventions in short-term financial markets and a multiplicity of short-term interest rates. All this discourages financial market development (Table 1.4).[32]

In addition, RMT makes the stance of policy noisy and difficult to interpret, both by financial market participants and the central bank itself; this topic is discussed in Chapter 9. Not all money demand shocks are accommodated, so that interest rates are a volatile and imperfect indicator of the current and expected stance of policy. Greater de facto flexibility vis-à-vis money targets reduces this volatility but at costs of greater discretion and opacity about the true operational framework. Of course, not all deviations from target represent accommodation of money demand, but it is very hard to tell in any particular situation. The effectiveness of the operational framework is hampered as a result.

An additional layer of complexity is brought about by recurrent interventions in FX markets, which are the main tool for managing the exchange rate in most SSA countries. There is often insufficient coordination between interventions in FX markets and other operations. As a result, interventions influence the stance of policy in unintended and undesired ways.

---

[29] Targets on reserve money are part of a broader monetary programming exercise in which targets are also set for broad money, which is considered an intermediate target of policy. With a few exceptions, however (e.g., Tanzania), targets on broad money play a smaller role in policy discussions in practice.

[30] Because of this de facto flexibility, we see little impact of the introduction of electronic payments systems such M-Pesa for monetary policy implementation. The much more important implications for financial inclusion and regulation are outside the scope of this book.

[31] Berg et al. (2013) (the working paper version of Chapter 5) describe the implications of strict money targeting for interest rate volatility in Uganda.

[32] See IMF (2015a).

Table 1.4. Characteristics of Deviations from Reserve Money Targets for Selected SSA Countries

Country	Share of observations with absolute deviations bigger than 1% (in per cent)	2.5th percentile (in per cent of the target)	87.5th percentile (in per cent of the target)
Kenya	94.9	−6.8	5.7
Tanzania	71.7	−4.9	4.1
Mozambique	94.1	−7.6	5.9
Rwanda	40.0	−1.7	1.1

Source: IMF Staff Calculations.

Given all this flexibility, the difficulty in inferring the stance of policy from the money targets or target misses, and the failure of money targeting itself to provide a nominal anchor, how are we to understand these policy regimes? The answer seems to be that these countries tend to practice an opaque version of 'inflation targeting lite', in which decisions about the setting and achievement of the money targets themselves depend on progress relative to inflation, output, exchange rate, and in many cases other objectives.[33]

One of the effects of the opacity of these regimes, in addition to poor transmission of monetary policy, is that they break the important separation between policy design and policy implementation. In most CBs outside SSA, the former is typically determined by a monetary policy-making committee, following input from the staff of the forecasting, research, or economics teams, whereas the latter is done by the trading desk. Under RMT, it is typically the operations staff who decide whether to hit or miss targets partly for technical reasons, for example not to avoid disrupting money markets. And yet the decision to miss targets has implications for the stance of policy, even if there is no consultation with the monetary policy committee. This creates confusion about the division of labour and governance structure within CBs.

Some of this opacity may be desired by central banks aiming to avoid public responsibility for policy decisions ('We are not setting interest rates so high; it is the markets. We are just following our monetary programme.') In some particular instances this may be a second-best response to political pressures, whereby technocrats can hide behind the obscurity of the regime to conduct policy. However, international experience, and also that of a handful of countries in SSA that have made the most progress with regime reform, such as Uganda (Chapter 2), is that this is very much second best; the effectiveness and independence of policy is best served by adherence to the above principles, even in SSA.

---

[33] See Stone and Bhundia (2004). Chapter 8 argues that there is little case that monetary aggregates play a special direct role in the transmission of monetary policy. It explores a role for money aggregates in the face of weak real data and uninformative financial markets. Our subsequent thinking, partly captured in Chapter 9 and Chapter 16, as well as in this chapter, is less sanguine about this interpretation and puts more weight on the negative effects of money aggregate targeting on the information content of financial markets. Chapter 14 discusses the influence of our experience working with central banks in this evolution in our thinking.

4.4 Forward-Looking Strategy and Communications

As central banks in other regions have increasingly focused on the medium-term inflation outlook, a forward-looking strategy that guides policy decisions and communications has become the defining feature of policy. To a large extent, such a strategy is missing in many SSA CBs. This is not surprising, given the lack of numerical medium-term inflation objectives and the limitations of the operational framework. A policy framework aimed at stabilizing expected inflation is valuable for several reasons. Such a framework can lead to pre-emptive action that is less costly than falling 'behind the curve', as discussed in Chapter 19. Of course, it is difficult to have confidence in a particular inflation forecast, given all the uncertainties. Even so, aiming to stabilize the inflation forecast is a way of organizing many complex considerations into a simple narrative. The forward-looking policy process involves developing and communicating an understanding about why the economy is where it is now, in terms of shocks and imbalances, and then projecting how policy should react and how these will unwind.

In the case of SSA, the lack of clear strategy is most visible when thinking about how to respond to large external supply shocks, for example the international food and fuel commodity price surge of 2007–08. As discussed above, policy has long settled on the adage that central banks should accommodate first-round effects but prevent spillovers from these shocks into broader wage and price setting (second-round effects). However, it is far from clear what the above policy advice implies for money targets. Should these be missed, and if so, in which direction? And how is the missing of money targets meant to influence wage and price dynamics in response to these shocks?[34]

In practice, the framework itself becomes a handicap for articulating a clear policy response. For instance, in Zambia, concerns with money targets in the aftermath of the global financial crisis resulted in excessively tight monetary policy at a time when domestic banking systems were under stress. These policies were later reversed, but it can be argued that the policy framework amplified the initial impact of the crisis.[35] The case of Zambia is discussed in more detail in Chapter 17.

An additional and related factor is insufficient internal analytical and forecasting capacity in many central banks, which limits the staff's ability to provide senior management with an assessment of the state of the economy, sound macroeconomic forecasts, and policy recommendations. Most SSA CBs have yet to develop in-house modern macro models that are standard in most advanced economies and emerging market CBs, though the issue of which models to use for these countries is an open question, as we discuss in Section 7. The absence of models adds to the lack of a clear quantitative view within central banks on how monetary policy is transmitted to the economy.

Communication policy is yet another area of modern monetary policy in which SSA central banks have much catching up to do. This is reflected in the low score

---

[34] These issues are treated in Chapters 8 and 9.

[35] Zambia had also experienced unintended changes in its policy stance during 2005–06, again related to the monetary framework, as increases in money demand that were not accommodated resulted in higher interest rates and exchange rate overshooting.

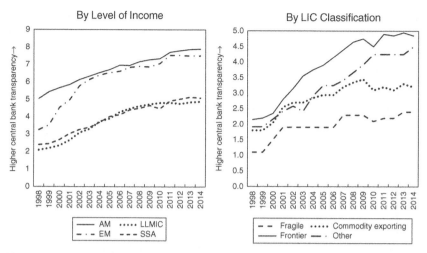

Figure 1.5. Measure of Central Bank Transparency

Note: The de jure transparency index was developed by Dincer and Eichengreen (2014). It ranges from 0–15, and is the sum of scores to questions ranging from political, economic, procedural, policy, and operational transparency.

Sources: Dincer and Eichengreen (2014) and IMF (2014d).

most African CBs have in measures of central bank transparency (Figure 1.5).[36] For example, very few CBs publish a medium-term inflation outlook or provide a forward-looking assessment as a basis for their policy decisions. Again, the lack of a clear communication strategy goes hand in hand with the lack of clear monetary policy frameworks. Perhaps not surprisingly, CBs that have adopted inflation targeting regimes, such as Ghana, have made important progress in clarifying their policy announcements.[37]

5 MODERNIZING MONETARY POLICY IN SUB-SAHARAN AFRICA

SSA central banks are well aware of the limitations of their existing frameworks and are looking to improve along the various dimensions we have discussed. Ghana was an earlier adopter of IT, though the experience there has been mixed. Uganda was next in line; that country's experience with IT is discussed in Chapter 2. Several other central banks, including Kenya, have explicitly discussed the possibility of adopting IT, even if they have yet to formally commit. Many other countries, while not explicitly considering the move to IT, are working to

---

[36] See Dincer and Eichengreen (2014).
[37] On Ghana, see MPC Press Release May 2016: https://www.bog.gov.gh/index.php?option=com_content&view=article&id=2557:mpc-press-release-may-2016&catid=47:press-releases&Itemid=120.

improve their operational framework by giving more prominence to policy interest rates, and by improving the design and use of open market operations and standing facilities. And many central banks are investing in their internal capacity, for example through technical assistance programs developed jointly with the IMF.[38] SSA CBs are also increasingly exchanging views on these and other topics, through peer-to-peer events and regional fora.

Although there is no one-size-fits-all approach to monetary policy modernization, central banks can learn from the experience of many countries outside SSA, as well as from early movers within the region. One key lesson is that progress requires sufficient operational independence and a sufficiently clear central bank mandate for price stability, even if adherence to these two principles is always work in progress. Building and maintaining political commitment is therefore critical. The central bank has a leading role to play in building the necessary consensus for reform.

Another lesson is that central banks can make progress in a number of areas simultaneously. Progress can be self-reinforcing: the development of analytical capacity is more likely to impact policymaking if it is consistent with the way policy is designed and implemented, which requires clarity about the strategy and the operational framework. The adoption of an explicit numerical objective can provide an impetus to investing in analytical capacity and the communication strategy; while an effective operational framework can make central banks more comfortable about explicitly committing to an inflation objective. These synergies call for a comprehensive approach to reform.

A related issue is whether to explicitly adopt a new regime, namely 'IT', and if so whether to do so at a specific stage of the modernization process. What the international evidence corroborates, and the above discussion implies, is that countries do not need to satisfy a strict number of preconditions before they can adopt IT.[39] If anything, the opposite is true. A clear framework is more conducive to reform. This should not be surprising in view of the observation above that current RMT frameworks already amount to an obscure form of IT 'lite.'

Central banks are naturally conservative institutions, and some may be concerned with their ability to deliver on their inflation objectives, in which case both reforms and the adoption of new regimes may be gradual. And the evidence does suggest that the announcement of IT per se does not generally yield immediate benefits, for example in terms of better-anchored inflation expectations or a lower sacrifice ratio, i.e., the cost of reducing inflation in terms of output.[40] However, there is substantial evidence from emerging markets that the benefits of IT accrue over time, as banks learn by doing and gradually gain credibility and as observers come to understand the regime, all this despite initial errors in the achievement of the inflation target.[41]

---

[38] See IMF (2015a). Countries that are investing in their analytical capacity include Ghana, Kenya, Mauritius, Mozambique, Rwanda, and Uganda.

[39] See Batini and Laxton (2007).

[40] See Ball (2011) for a critical review of the literature on this topic. See also Goncalves and Salles (2008) and Goncalves and Carvalho (2009).

[41] The case of the Czech Republic is informative in this regard. See Jonas and Mishkin (2003).

A critical aspect of modernizing monetary policy frameworks relates to the questions of *how* to apply forward-looking monetary policy effectively in the SSA context, along the lines of the principles briefly articulated in Section 3. Here, we briefly review two of the issues, corresponding to some of the most important challenges discussed in Section 3.[42]

5.1 Responding to supply shocks

Adherence to the above principles of monetary policy, particularly the emphasis on a clearly communicated forward-looking strategy to achieve the inflation objective over the medium term, should help smooth the adjustment to supply shocks. It is sometimes argued that core inflation—typically defined as infla- tion in the consumer price index, but excluding some key goods that are particularly subject to transitory supply shocks, notably food and fuel—may better reflect the sort of underlying pressures to which policy should respond. However, in SSA countries, food prices are such a large part of the CPI that explicitly targeting core inflation may not serve to anchor the public's overall inflationary expectations.[43] There is an important commonality between em- phasizing current core and expected headline inflation: in both cases, there is less need to respond to transitory supply shocks, as long as expectations are well-anchored. However, not all non-core shocks are temporary (for example food prices can also respond to aggregate demand), so the explicit targeting of future headline is perhaps more robust, as well as keeping the focus on the index most people know.

It is a sort of a central bank (and IMF) folk theorem (with essentially no mention in the academic literature) that policymakers should let the 'first- round' effect of shocks pass through and react only to 'second-round' effects. As Chapter 10 describes, this policy can be difficult to implement in practice, when examined closely. It is difficult because even the first-round or impact effect of a shock (i) depends on the particular shock and the structure of the economy, including the country's integration with international capital markets; and (ii) even for a given shock is a property of the entire system, depending among other things on the monetary policy reaction function. Thus, the first round depends on how policy reacts to the second round.

Even with the best monetary policy framework, the prevalence of supply shocks speaks to the limits to monetary policy. Monetary policy should not be asked to influence relative prices, for example of food relative to non-food, which can experience significant and persistent movements (Chapter 11). And given nominal rigidities and the desire to minimize output fluctuations, there are limits to the extent to which monetary policy can eliminate the temporary

---

[42] A third and obvious issue are the various pressures stemming from fiscal policy. We do not discuss these issues further here to keep the discussion brief, though some of the implications for monetary policy are discussed in Chapter 12.

[43] When the relative price of food is trending, targeting core is particularly problematic as it would imply that the overall CPI could drift away from the target. Chapter 15 provides a brief discussion of these issues.

inflationary effects of supply shocks and, given the prevalence of these shocks, the volatility of inflation itself.

5.2 The Role of the Exchange Rate

One perhaps particularly thorny question for many SSA CBs with flexible exchange rates relates to the role of exchange rate management and FX interventions.

The international experience shows that countries that modernize their monetary policy frameworks also move towards more exchange rate flexibility. Indeed, that has already been the case in SSA. The de facto anchoring role of the exchange rate is diminished in favour of a more explicit focus on price stability. Foreign exchange interventions do not disappear, however, as can be seen in their widespread use in many emerging market CBs with explicit inflation targeting regimes. These countries are attempting to influence the real exchange rate and external financial conditions facing their country, while maintaining their inflation objectives. Given these trends, it is very likely that some degree of exchange rate management will endure in SSA.

There has been growing interest in understanding how FX interventions fit in EM's monetary policy frameworks, an issue we tackle in Chapter 13.[44] The focus is on sterilized interventions, which ensure that the central bank retains control of short-term interest rates as the monetary policy instrument used for domestic stabilization. For sterilized interventions to serve as a separate instrument, they must operate through a different channel, in this case the portfolio balance channel.

Interventions in IT countries and others that adhere to the principles articulated above are guided by a different concept of exchange rate stability. Rather than stabilizing the exchange rate so that it serves as a nominal anchor, the objective is to respond to large and costly deviations of the exchange rate from its medium-term equilibrium value, for example because of risk-on risk-off episodes (associated with sizeable capital flows) or other temporary factors unrelated to fundamentals. Given the uncertainty associated with the assessment of these deviations, central banks tend to lean against the wind, that is to intervene when the exchange rate is appreciating or depreciating more rapidly than usual, but without targeting a specific level.

The possible benefits of an active FX intervention policy will have to be weighed against the costs. In practice, it is not easy to identify exchange rate misalignments; over-stabilization would reduce the exchange rate's shock absorbing role. Frequent interventions can undermine the clarity and coherence of the regime and raise doubts about the primacy of the inflation objective, which can be especially dangerous when central banks are building credibility. Finding the right role for the exchange rate will continue to be an unsettled and evolving issue in many SSA countries. However, improving monetary policy itself along the lines discussed above requires, and in turn should encourage, exchange rate flexibility and more coherence between exchange rate intervention and the monetary policy regime.

---

[44] See also Ostry et al. (2012).

6 HARD PEGS AND CURRENCY UNIONS IN SSA

A sizable share of SSA economies are members of the CFA franc zone (CEMAC and UEMOA, 16 countries in total), with their currency pegged to the euro, while others are members of the Common Monetary Area (Namibia, Swaziland, Lesotho) and have their currencies pegged to the South African Rand.[45] Other African countries are not part of monetary unions but have hard pegs, e.g., Cape Verde. We briefly review the main issues for these central banks, with a focus on the CFA zone.

Hard pegs to strong currencies offer countries a strong nominal anchor, which typically results in low inflation. The CFA zone is no exception, as countries in that region have lower average inflation than their SSA peers.[46] In this sense, CBs in countries with hard pegs are importing the credibility of the monetary institutions they are pegging to (the ECB, in this case).

The cost is twofold. First, central banks lose much control over monetary policy. In the case of the CFA zone the two central banks may retain some monetary control due to limited capital mobility in that region. Even then, however, maintaining the peg, among other things by preserving a sufficient level of international reserves, still takes precedence over all other considerations. Other policies are therefore necessary to achieve macro stability (fiscal, or even macro-prudential).

Second, under a hard peg, adjustments to the equilibrium real exchange rate can only come about through changes in the price level, which implies that variations in inflation are to a large extent necessary for external adjustment and beyond the control of the monetary authorities (see Chapter 20 for a discussion of inflation dynamics in the CEMAC region). In addition, not all real exchange rate adjustments are equal. Achieving large real depreciations is very costly and difficult, given the need for prolonged deflation, and in most cases countries are forced to abandon or adjust their peg. The CFA zone was confronted with such a scenario in January 1994 when, after a prolonged period of real exchange over-valuation, the CFA franc was devalued by 50 per cent, the first and, so far, only nominal adjustment to parity since 1948. The resulting devaluation of the CFA franc is still remembered to this day. Preventing overvaluation of the currency is therefore of the utmost importance, which puts additional onus on a stable fiscal policy.

While the CMA and CFA franc zone pre-date independence, the idea of common regional currencies (and even a continental currency) has long been a goal of various regional groupings, including the Africa Union.[47] Of these, the putative East African Monetary Union (consisting of Kenya, Uganda, Tanzania, Rwanda, Burundi, and, possibly, South Sudan) is at the most advanced stage.

---

[45] It is important to note that neither the CMA nor the CFA are entirely conventional hard peg arrangements, since in both cases the hegemon (the Reserve Bank of South Africa in the former instance and the French Treasury—not the ECB—in the latter) provides support to the small member states.

[46] See IMF, AFR Regional Economic Outlooks, for example IMF (2008).

[47] A common currency for Africa was a stated objective of the Organization of African Unity when it was founded in 1963 and was endorsed at the founding of the successor body, the African Union, in 2002 (see Masson and Pattillo, 2005).

The enabling legislation—the equivalent of Europe's Maastricht Treaty—was ratified in December 2013, with the currency union scheduled for 2024. Unlike the CFA or CMA arrangements, the ambition of EAMU is to create a monetary union among a community of equals with a common currency that is guaranteed by neither a regional nor an international hegemon. As with the Eurozone, the plan is that the common currency will float so that the nominal anchor will be provided by the credibility and commitment of the supranational central bank's monetary policy. It remains to be seen if this monetary union will be realized.

7 A MODELLING STRATEGY FOR ANALYSING MONETARY POLICY ISSUES IN SSA

Thus far in this chapter, we have made a number of empirical, analytic, and policy claims without reference to an explicit analytic framework. This can be useful, but there is great need for models to undertake policy analysis in SSA CBs. In our view, these models must meet two criteria. First, they must reflect modern thinking on monetary policy, drawing on both state-of-the-art macro theory and current practice in central banks in advanced and emerging markets. Second, they must be tailored to address key low-income-country specific issues. Despite the importance of the topic, there has been very little work in the academic and policy literature tailored to low-income countries.

As can be seen in many of the chapters of this book, our general approach has been to exploit the large literature based on fairly standard New Keynesian economic models, appropriately modified to capture key issues and features for SSA countries. This immediately presents one fundamental prior consideration, which is whether models based on nominal rigidities are useful ways to think about monetary policy in SSA low-income countries. It might be argued, for example, that these countries are dominated by flex-price informal markets and few explicit indexation mechanisms. Gali (2015) cites two broad lines of evidence in support of this sort of model as applied to advanced economies: micro data-based analysis such as Bils and Klenow (2004) that demonstrate price rigidities, and VAR evidence that monetary policy affects output, such as Christiano, Eichenbaum, and Evans (1999). Unfortunately, such micro evidence has not been analysed in low-income countries, as far as we know, presumably largely because the data are hard or impossible to find. And as discussed in Section 3 above and in Chapter 6, VAR-based evidence on the impact of monetary policies is even less reliable than elsewhere.

However, we believe that this (the assumption of nominal rigidities) is the right place to start for several reasons. First, the broader evidence on transmission, discussed in Section 3 above, is consistent with the basic features of these sorts of models. Second, major nominal experiments such as the monetary policy tightening episode examined in Chapter 5, and the devaluation of the CFA franc in 1994, had evident real effects. The large CFA step devaluation mentioned earlier—an understudied episode from this perspective—led to an almost-equivalent and highly persistent movement in the real exchange rate, with clear real effects.[48] For developing countries more broadly, the nature of the nominal exchange rate regime matters for the real effects of supply shocks, again consistent with this sort of framework.[49] In terms of underlying mechanisms, even less research has been done. But a number of drivers of nominal rigidities seem plausible in SSA: information-based lags in price adjustment, as in Mankiw and Reis (2002), seem if anything more plausible in the relatively information-scarce SSA environment. Public wage and price setting are also relatively important, including with a likely direct influence on private formal-sector wages.[50]

In the rest of this book, we draw on two sorts of models. The first type, which for the most part are covered in the chapters in Part II of the book, are structural models that are designed to better understand the mechanisms and policy trade-offs facing SSA countries. The models are structural in that they are fully derived from micro-foundations and are best focused on particular policy issues. One of the most significant sets of differences between SSA countries and the canonical model is the nature of the policy framework, and in this context of the monetary policy reaction function. As we have already discussed, many countries have targeted money; Chapter 8 attempts to understand this practice as a reaction to fragmented financial markets and poor high-frequency information on output. Chapter 9 analyses the implications of typical SSA money-targeting operational frameworks for the transmission of monetary policy. Chapter 13 makes the case that managed floats are best understood in a model with two reaction functions, a Taylor-type rule for the domestic interest rate and another for the exchange rate, with sterilized interventions as the instrument.

A second major distinction in SSA economies relates to the supply shocks discussed above. Chapter 10 comes to grips with the meaning of 'first-round' effects of commodity price shocks, while Chapter 11 looks at the implications of subsistence for inflation and monetary policy. Finally, the fiscal/monetary inter-actions in the case of public sector windfalls are explored in a dynamic stochastic general equilibrium (DSGE) model in Chapter 12.

As mentioned earlier, many authors have emphasized lack of financial depth as a distinctive feature of developing countries for monetary policy.[51] Chapter 17 develops a DSGE model with a banking sector to analyse the impact of the global financial crisis on Zambia. It finds that monetary policy added unnecessarily to macroeconomic volatility, for reasons related to the money targeting framework. It also argues, however, that even well-designed and implemented policies may not be able to do much to resist the volatility associated with the sorts of shocks encountered by Zambia during the crisis.

Finally, a lack of credibility is a common feature of central banks in SSA, a feature they share with many countries without a long history of successful monetary policy. Chapter 19 presents a model of endogenous policy credibility to study the optimal path of disinflation and the attainment of an inflation target,

---

[48] See Hernandez-Cata et al. (1998).

[49] See Broda (2004) and other references in n. 18.

[50] Chapter 11 discusses the evidence on the (relative lack of) nominal rigidities in the food sector and implications for monetary policy.

[51] See Mishra, Montiel, and Spilimbergo (2012).

and applies it to Ghana. It finds that the output inflation trade-off is more severe at earlier stages of credibility, and policy needs to be geared toward achieving its target, at the expense of output.

The second sort of model is a small semi-structural New-Keynesian model for applied monetary policy analysis and forecasting in central banks. The model is semi-structural in that the model is not fully derived from first principles (micro-foundations), even though each equation has a structural interpretation. The analyses presented in Part III focus on a workhorse model, emphasizing the interaction of the output gap, the exchange rate, and inflation (a Phillips curve), the implications of the stance of monetary policy and the level of the exchange rate for output (an IS curve), a monetary policy reaction function, and an exchange rate determination equation based on some form of purchasing power parity.[52]

This is an entirely standard model. Many features of SSA economies, such as a strong exchange rate effect on prices, or a weak transmission mechanism due to lack of financial depth and a fragmented banking system, can be handled through the calibration of the model parameters. Other features require more significant modifications. In Part III of the book we examine explicit treatment of food and fuel prices (Chapter 15), additional arguments in the reaction function (money targets in Chapter 16, exchange rate objectives in Chapter 18), and limited capital mobility. In many cases, the richer models analysed above can inform the use of these simpler models in more operational setting, such as the analysis of capital account and banking system risk shocks (Chapter 17).

Central banks in the region are gradually making use of these types of models. This is part of a broader effort to develop in-house forecasting and policy analysis systems (FPAS), drawing on best practices that have emerged from the experience of central banks in other regions.[53] For the most part, the focus has been on simple models that focus exclusively on monetary policy.

8 CONCLUSION

Central banks in SSA have come a long way. They played a critical role, though perhaps subordinate to fiscal policy, in stabilizing macroeconomies and thereby helping set the stage for the growth resurgence that much of the continent has enjoyed since roughly the mid-1990s. The challenges, however, seem to be getting tougher. Perhaps foremost is the difficult global economic environment: will SSA countries be able to keep growth going in the face of shocks related to uncertain growth prospects in China and the developed world, swings in commodity prices, volatile global capital flows, and other aftershocks from the global financial crisis? Are monetary policy institutions strong enough? Have central banks achieved effective enough monetary policy frameworks to adjust to these shocks, keep expectations anchored, and resist political pressures? Much progress has been

---

[52] See Laxton, Rose, and Scott (2009) and Berg, Karam and Laxton (2006), for example.

[53] These efforts have benefitted from support by the IMF and the UK Department for International Development (DFID). More information can be found at: https://www.imf.org/external/np/res/dfidimf/topic1.htm.

made and much more is underway. Will pressures expose weaknesses that spur further reforms or rather derail them?

Many of these challenges lie in the domain of fiscal policy and more broadly still in the resilience of a broad range of institutions both public and private. Most of the shocks are 'real', not nominal: real commodity prices, resource output, FDI flows, foreign demand, and fiscal policy. However, in our view the agenda for monetary policy that we have outlined here can play a critical supporting role.

Central banks can work to implement clear forward-looking policy regimes that respond coherently to the full range of shocks. This will help avoid macroeconomic and financial crises, allow the exchange rate flexibility to avoid persistent misalignments due to commodity price shocks, and keep inflation expectations anchored while avoiding unnecessary swings in interest rates, inflation, exchange rates, and output. All this can keep bad times from exploding into vicious circles of macroeconomic disarray and allow policymakers time to address the full range of challenges. The lessons of the global financial crisis for monetary policy regimes themselves are still being digested. But in our view all of this broader reform is better built on the solid foundations we have discussed here.

REFERENCES

Adam, C. (2011). On the Macroeconomic Management of Food Price Shocks in Low-Income Countries. *Journal of African Economies,* 20, 63–9.

Adam, C. and O'Connell, S. (2005). Monetary Policy and Aid Management in Sub Saharan Africa, mimeo. Oxford: University of Oxford; Swarthmore, PA: Swarthmore College.

Adam, C., Berg, A., Portillo R., and Unsal, F. (forthcoming). Monetary Policy and Central Banking in Sub-Saharan Africa. In P. Conti-Brown and R. Lastra (Eds.), *Research Handbook on Central Banking.* New York: Edward Elgar Publishing.

Adam, C., O'Connell, S., Buffie, E., and Pattillo, C. (2009). Monetary Policy Rules for Managing Aid Surges in Africa. *Review of Development Economics,* 13(3), 464–90.

Ahmad, A. and Pentecost, E. (2010). *Terms of Trade Shocks and Economic Performance Under Different Exchange Rate Regimes.* Loughborough University Working Paper 2010–08.

Ball, L. (2011). The Performance of Alternative Monetary Regimes. In B. Friedman and M. Woodford (Eds.), *Handbook of Monetary Economics,* 3B, New York: North Holland Elsevier.

Batini, N. and Laxton, D. (2007). Under What Conditions Can Inflation Targeting be Adopted? The Experience of Emerging Markets. *Central Banking, Analysis, and Economic Policies Book Series,* 11, 467–506.

Berg, A., Karam, P. D., and Laxton, D. (2006). *A Practical Model-Based Approach to Monetary Policy Analysis-Overview.* IMF Working Paper 06/80. Washington, DC: International Monetary Fund.

Berg, A., J. Vlcek, L. Charry, and Portillo, R. (2013). *The Monetary Transmission Mechanism in the Tropics: A Narrative Approach.* IMF Working Paper 13/197. Washington, DC: International Monetary Fund.

Berg, A., O'Connell, S., Pattillo, C., Portillo, R., and Unsal, F. (2015). Monetary Policy Issues in Sub-Saharan Africa. In C. Monga and J. Y. Lin (Eds.), *The Oxford Handbook of Africa and Economics: Policies and Practices.* Oxford University Press.

Berg, A., Aiyar, S., Hussain, M., Roache, S., Mirzoev, T., and Mahone, A. (2007). *The Macroeconomics of Scaling Up Aid: Lessons from Recent Experience.* IMF Occasional Paper 253. Washington, DC: International Monetary Fund.

Bernanke, B., Laubach, T., Mishkin, F., and Posen, A. (1998). *Inflation Targeting: Lessons from the International Experience*. Princeton: Princeton University Press.

Bils, M. and Klenow, P. (2004) Some Evidence on the Importance of Sticky Prices. *Journal of Political Economy*, 112(5), 947–84.

Blanchard, O. and Gali, J. (2007). Real Wage Rigidities and the New Keynesian Model. *Journal of Money, Credit, and Banking*, 39(1), 35–66.

Blanchard, O., Cerutti, E., and Summers, L. (2015). *Inflation and Activity—Two Explorations and their Monetary Policy Implications*. IMF Working Paper 15/230. Washington, DC: International Monetary Fund.

Broda, C. (2004). Terms of Trade and Exchange Rate Regimes in Developing Countries. *Journal of International Economics*, 63, 31–58.

Buffie, E., Adam, C., O'Connell, S., and Pattillo, C. (2008). Riding the Wave: Monetary Responses to Aid Surges in Low-Income Countries. *European Economic Review*, 52(8), 1378–95.

Buffie, E., O.Connell, S., and Adam, C. (2010). Fiscal Inertia, Donor Credibility, and the Monetary Management of Aid Surges. *Journal of Development Economics*, 93(2), 287–98.

Christiano, L., Eichenbaum, M., and Evans, M. (1999). Monetary Policy Shocks: What Have We Learned and To What End? In M. Woodford and J. Taylor (Eds.), *Handbook of Macroeconomics*, 1A. North Holland Elsevier.

Cukierman, A. (1992). *Central Bank Strategy, Credibility, and Independence—Theory and Evidence*. Cambridge, MA: MIT Press.

Cukierman, A., Webb S., and Neyapti, B. (1992). Measuring the Independence of Central Banks and its Effect on Policy Outcomes. *The World Bank Economic Review*, 6, 353–98.

de Carvalho Filho I. E. (2011). 28 Months Later: How Inflation Targeters Outperformed Their Peers in the Great Recession. *The B.E. Journal of Macroeconomics*, 11(1), 1–46. De Gruyter.

Dincer, N. and Eichengreen, B. (2014). Central Bank Transparency and Independence: Updates and New Measures. *International Journal of Central Banking*, 38(3), 189–253.

Edwards, S., and Levi-Yeyati, E. (2005). Flexible Exchange Rates as Shock Absorbers. *European Economic Review*, 48(9), 2079–105.

Federico, P., Vegh, C., and Vuletin, G. (2014). *Reserve Requirement Policy over the Business Cycle*. NBER Working Paper 20612.

Gali, J. (2015). *Monetary Policy, Inflation and the Business Cycle*, 2nd edn. Princeton University Press.

Giuliano, P., Mishra, P., and Spilimbergo, A. (2010). Democracy and reforms: Evidence from a new dataset. *American Economic Journal*, 5(4), 179–204.

Goncalves, C. and Carvalho, A. (2009). Inflation Targeting Matters: Evidence from OECD Economies' Sacrifice Ratios. *Journal of Money, Credit, and Banking*, 41(1), 233–43.

Goncalves, C. and Salles, J. (2008). Inflation Targeting in Emerging Economies: What Do the Data Say? *Journal of Development Economics*, 85(1–2), 312–18.

Hernandez-Cata, E., François, C., Masson, P., Bouvier., Peroz, P., Desruelle, D., and Vamvakidis, A. (1998). *The West African Economic and Monetary Union*. IMF Occasional Paper 170. Washington, DC: International Monetary Fund.

Hoffmaister, A., Roldos, J., and Wickham, P. (1998). Macroeconomic Fluctuations in Sub-Saharan Africa. *IMF Staff Papers*, 45(1), 132–60.

International Monetary Fund. (1977). *The Monetary Approach to the Balance of Payments*.

International Monetary Fund. (2008). Monetary and Exchange Rate Policies in Sub-Saharan Africa. *Regional Economic Outlook, Sub-Saharan Africa*. Washington, DC: International Monetary Fund.

International Monetary Fund. (2013a). *The Interaction of Monetary and Macro-Prudential Policies*. IMF Policy Paper. Washington, DC: International Monetary Fund.

International Monetary Fund. (2013b). Issuing International Sovereign Bonds: Opportunities and Challenges for Sub-Saharan Africa. *Regional Economic Outlook, Sub-Saharan Africa*. Washington, DC: International Monetary Fund.

International Monetary Fund. (2014). *Staff Guidance Note on Macro-Prudential Policy—Considerations for Low Income Countries*. IMF Policy Papers. Washington, DC: International Monetary Fund.

International Monetary Fund. (2015a). *Evolving Monetary Policy Frameworks in Low-Income and other Developing Countries*. IMF Policy Papers. Washington, DC: International Monetary Fund.

International Monetary Fund. (2015b). *Monetary Policy and Financial Stability*. IMF Policy Papers. Washington, DC: International Monetary Fund.

International Monetary Fund. (2015c). *West African Economic and Monetary Union: Common Policies of Member Countries*. IMF Country Report 15/100. Washington, DC: International Monetary Fund.

International Monetary Fund. (2016). Exchange Rate Regimes in Sub-Saharan Africa: Experiences and Lessons. *Regional Economic Outlook, Sub-Saharan Africa*. Washington, DC: International Monetary Fund.

Jonas, J. and Mishkin, F. (2003). Inflation Targeting in Transition Economies: Experience and Prospects. In B. Bernanke and M. Woodford (Eds.), *The Inflation Targeting Debate*. Chicago: NBER The University of Chicago Press.

Kessy, P., O'Connell, S., and Nyella, J. (2016). Monetary Policy in Tanzania: Accomplishments and the Road Ahead. In C. Adam, P. Collier, and B. Ndulu (Eds.), *Tanzania: The Path to Prosperity*. Oxford: Oxford University Press.

Lane, P. and Milesi-Ferretti, G. (2007). The External Wealth of Nations Mark II: Revised and Extended Estimates of Foreign Assets and Liabilities, 1970–2004. *Journal of International Economics*, 73(2), 223–50.

Laxton, D., Rose, D., and Scott, A. (2009). *Developing a Structured Forecasting and Policy Analysis System to Support Inflation-Forecast Targeting (IFT)*. IMF Working Paper 10/65. Washington, DC: International Monetary Fund.

Leeper, E. M., and D. B. Gordon (1992). In Search of the Liquidity Effect. *Journal of Monetary Economics*, 29(3), 341–69.

Lucotte, Y. (2009). *The Influence of Central Bank Independence on Budget Deficits in Developing Countries: New Evidence from Panel Data Analysis*. Laboratory of Economics in Orleans, University of Orleans.

Mankiw, N. G., and Reis, R. (2002) Sticky information versus sticky prices: A proposal to replace the new Keynesian Phillips curve. *Quarterly Journal of Economics*, 117(4), 1295–1328.

Masson, P. and Pattillo, C. (2005). *The Monetary Geography of Africa*. Washington, DC: The Brookings Institution.

Mishra, P. and Montiel, P. (2013). How Effective is Monetary Transmission in Developing Countries: A Survey of the Empirical Evidence. *Economic Systems*, 37(2), 187–216. Elsevier.

Mishra, P., Montiel, P., and Spilimbergo, A. (2012). Monetary Transmission in Low-Income Countries: Effectiveness and Policy Implications. *IMF Economic Review*, 60, 270–302.

Ostry, J.D., Ghosh, A.R., and Chamon, M. (2012). *Two Targets, Two Instruments: Monetary and Exchange Rate Policies in Emerging Market Economies*. IMF Staff Discussion Note SDN/12/01. Washington, DC: International Monetary Fund.

Schmitt-Grohe, S. and Uribe, M. (2010). *Liquidity Traps: An Interest-Rate-Based Exit Strategy.* NBER Working Paper 16514.

Sims, C. A. (1992). Interpreting the Macroeconomic Time Series Facts: The Effects of Monetary Policy. *European Economic Review* 36(5), 975–1000.

Stone, R. and Bhundia, A. (2004). *A New Taxonomy of Monetary Regimes.* IMF Working Paper 04/191. Washington, DC: International Monetary Fund.

Summers, L. H. (1991). The Scientific Illusion in Empirical Macroeconomics. *The Scandinavian Journal of Economics*, 129–48.

2

Inflation Targeting in Uganda

What Lessons Can We Learn from Five Years of Experience?

Martin Brownbridge and Louis Kasekende

1 INTRODUCTION

The Bank of Uganda (BOU) introduced its inflation targeting (IT) monetary policy framework in July 2011, replacing a monetary targeting (MT) framework which had been in operation for two decades. This chapter reviews Uganda's experience with IT, examines the pertinent lessons that have been learned so far, and discusses the technical and institutional challenges of implementing the framework.

The chapter is organized as follows. Section 2 discusses the reasons why the BOU replaced its MT framework with IT. It discusses what the BOU regarded as the essential prerequisites for the introduction of IT and also outlines the main features of the IT framework and the differences with MT. Section 3 examines how the introduction of IT has required fundamental changes in relationship between fiscal policy and monetary policy and the challenges that these changes have entailed. Section 4 discusses the formation of monetary policy in the IT framework, including the challenges of forecasting inflation and estimating the output gap. Section 5 discusses the implementation of monetary policy, in particular the evolving methods the BOU has used to achieve its operating target of aligning interbank interest rates with the policy interest rate. Exchange rate policy and how this has impacted on monetary policy is discussed in section 6. The BOU's communications strategy is examined in section 7. Section 8 evaluates the outcomes in terms of the performance of the IT framework, including assessing the evidence for the strength of the monetary transmission mechanism and the extent to which the BOU's primary policy target has been achieved. Section 9 offers some conclusions and lessons from Uganda's experience with IT.

2 MOTIVES FOR THE INTRODUCTION, AND SALIENT FEATURES, OF IT IN UGANDA

The BOU's primary motive for introducing an IT framework was the recognition that the monetary targeting framework, which had been used by the BOU since the early 1990s, was becoming obsolete. In particular, its efficacy was being undermined because the development of the financial sector and its increasing integration with the regional and global economy was making both the money demand function and the money multiplier more unstable and unpredictable. Between 1999/2000 and 2010/11, the velocity of circulation of domestic currency broad money (M2) declined, from 9.4 to 5.5, and the rate of decline was erratic (see Table 2.1). The annual change in the velocity in this period varied between positive 1 per cent and negative 14 per cent, which made setting intermediate monetary targets on the basis of a forecast of velocity difficult and, therefore increased the probability that errors in forecasts of demand for money would lead to sub-optimal monetary targets. The broad money multiplier was also quite volatile in the last three years of this period, when it rose from 2.2 in 2007/08 to 2.6 in 2010/11 (Table 2.1). An unstable money multiplier complicates the task of achieving broad money targets through control of base (reserve) money. Because an IT framework uses a policy interest rate rather than the monetary base as the operating target, autonomous shifts in the velocity of money or the money multiplier do not automatically alter the stance of monetary policy.

The IT framework offered two further advantages over MT. First, it provided a mechanism for clearly signalling the stance of monetary policy to the public, through the public announcement of a policy interest rate. Second, it offered the BOU much greater scope for short-term fine tuning of monetary policy, through adjustments to the policy interest rate, in response to macroeconomic shocks.

Before deciding to replace its MT framework with IT, the BOU considered whether Uganda was ready to implement the latter. At around the turn of the millennium, when several emerging market economies were adopting IT frameworks, it was believed that the successful adoption of IT was dependent upon a number of demanding institutional and technical preconditions being met; for example deep and efficient financial markets to facilitate the transmission of monetary policy and sophisticated technical capacities in the central bank to forecast inflation and simulate the impact of policy changes on target variables (e.g. IMF, 2004; Masson et al., 1997). Subsequent research, much of it conducted by the IMF Research Department, suggested that the actual preconditions for a successful introduction of IT could be more narrowly defined. Freedman and Otker-Robe (2010) identified three essential preconditions: i) the central bank's primary policy objective must be the control of inflation; ii) there must be no fiscal dominance; and iii) the central bank must have instrument independence. These are essentially institutional preconditions, which the BOU believed could be met

Table 2.1. Velocity of Broad Money (M2) and M2 money multiplier, 1999/2000 to 2010/11

	1999/ 2000	2000/ 2001	2001/ 2002	2002/ 2003	2003/ 2004	2004/ 2005	2005/ 2006	2006/ 2007	2007/ 2008	2008/ 2009	2009/ 2010	2010/ 2011
M2 velocity	9.4	9.1	8.3	7.7	7.7	7.8	7.6	7.5	7.1	6.8	6.4	5.5
change in velocity		−2%	−10%	−7%	0%	1%	−3%	−2%	−6%	−4%	−5%	−14%
M2 money multiplier	2.2	2.2	2.1	2.4	2.2	2.2	2.3	2.2	2.2	2.4	2.5	2.6

Source: BOU.

Table 2.2. Key Features of the Monetary Targeting and IT Frameworks in Uganda

	MT framework	IT framework
Primary policy objective	Inflation	Inflation
Secondary policy objective		Output
Instruments	Primary securities auctions	Secondary market operations
Operating target	Reserve money	Short-term interest rate
Intermediate target	Broad money	Inflation forecast
Frequency of adjustments to policy stance	Usually annually	Initially monthly, now bi-monthly
Communications	Minimal	Integral

in Uganda. Controlling inflation, with a publicly announced target for core or underlying inflation, had been the BOU's primary objective of monetary policy since the 1990s. The 1995 Constitution of Uganda conferred operational independence on the central bank.[1] The issue of fiscal dominance was not regarded as a serious threat to the success of an IT framework, given the Government's good track record of fiscal discipline since the early 1990s, but this issue is complex, and is examined in more detail in Section 3. Freedman and Otker-Robe also argued that the adoption of IT stimulates the central bank to improve its technical capacities and implement reforms to develop financial markets.

Table 2.2 delineates the main features of the IT framework in Uganda and compares them with the MT framework which it replaced. The primary policy objective, controlling core inflation, was unchanged with the introduction of IT, as was the numerical target: 5 per cent for annual core inflation, although with the introduction of IT the BOU explicitly stated that its objective is to achieve the 5 per cent target on average over the medium term.[2] With the introduction of IT, the BOU added a secondary objective, stabilizing real output as close as possible to estimated potential output. Under the MT framework, real output had been viewed as being mainly exogenous to demand management policies, and instead determined on the supply side of the economy. Developments in the economy during the 2000s, not least the impact of the global financial crisis, suggested that the demand side shocks could also affect real output, although supply-side shocks were clearly still an important source of output volatility.

The operating target of monetary policy in the IT framework is a short-term money market interest rate: the seven-day interbank interest rate. In the MT framework, reserve money was the operating target. The MT framework utilized

---

[1] Article 162 of the 1995 Constitution states that: 'In performing its functions the Bank of Uganda shall conform to the Constitution but shall not be subject to the direction or control of any person or authority'.

[2] Core inflation excludes the prices of food crops and utilities, fuel, and energy which together comprise 17.6 per cent of the overall (headline) consumer price basket. The BOU targets core inflation, rather than headline inflation, because the prices of food crops and energy, fuel, and utilities are subject to supply-side shocks to a greater extent than other components of the consumer price index, and are thereby much less influenced by monetary policy, and also because they (especially food crop prices) are more volatile. The standard deviation of food crop inflation was more than double that of core inflation between 2006 and 2015.

an explicit intermediate target, broad money. An intermediate target does not play such a critical role in the IT framework, because it is much less rules-based than monetary targeting, although the inflation forecast can be viewed as an intermediate target in the IT framework. A key difference between the MT and IT frameworks is that while in the former, monetary policy is determined by current conditions, notably an estimate of current demand for a monetary aggregate, the latter is forward-looking in that monetary policy is determined by a forecast of future inflation, based on the premise that there are lags between a change in the policy interest rate and its full impact on inflation.

Communications with the public play an integral role in the IT framework, because of the importance of the central bank being able to influence inflationary expectations and convince the public of the credibility of monetary policy. As such, the BOU radically overhauled its communications policy to support IT, with the centrepiece being the press briefing given by the Governor after each Monetary Policy Committee meeting, at which the interest rate decision is announced and explained in a Monetary Policy Statement.

3 THE SEPARATION OF FISCAL AND MONETARY POLICY AND THE ISSUE OF FISCAL DOMINANCE

The condition of no fiscal dominance was interpreted by the BOU as entailing two conditions. First, that the central bank is not forced to finance the government's domestic borrowing requirement, and second, that government borrowing is sustainable, so that the market will not take the view that eventually the government debt will have to be monetized (à la Sargent and Wallace, 1981).

The second condition is clearly applicable to Uganda. Although public debt has risen since 2009, it is still relatively low and far below the thresholds at which it would be considered to be unsustainable, as shown in Table 2.3. As such, the likelihood that a government default would force the BOU to refinance public debt looks remote.

However, the fact that public debt is sustainable is not sufficient by itself to prevent central bank financing of the government's domestic borrowing requirement: there needs to be both political commitment and institutional safeguards to

Table 2.3. Gross Nominal Public Debt, Per cent of GDP: 2009–16

Year	External	Domestic	Total
2009	10.3	6.1	16.5
2010	13	6.7	19.7
2011	16	7.9	23.9
2012	13.5	8.9	22.4
2013	15.4	10	25.4
2014	15.8	11.5	27.3
2015	18.1	12.5	30.7
2016	20.7	13.6	34.3

Source: BOU.

prevent this from happening. Unfortunately, the institutional arrangements for fiscal and monetary policy under the MT framework, while adequate for that framework, could not meet the requirements of an IT framework.

Under the operational arrangement in place during the MT period, fiscal and monetary policy was intertwined. The government was subject to ceilings on its net domestic financing (under the IMF-supported programmes), but it did not explicitly issue securities to fund its domestic financing requirement, nor aim to avoid any borrowing from the central bank. Instead, the BOU issued government securities, through primary auctions, to mop up the liquidity needed to meet its reserve money targets. This meant that the distribution of the government's domestic financing requirement, between the central bank and market participants, was determined passively as the outcome of the interaction of the needs of the reserve money programme and the magnitude of domestic financing. It also meant that it was impossible to distinguish where fiscal policy, in terms of the government's financing needs, ended and where monetary policy began. As a consequence, monetary and fiscal policy both lacked transparency.

This was not a satisfactory arrangement for an IT framework. Two changes were needed to support the implementation of IT: to clearly separate the domestic financing of the budget from monetary policy and to avoid government borrowing from the central bank. The first reform has been accomplished. Since the start of the 2012/13 fiscal year, the primary issues of government securities (which take place in three out of every four weeks) are only used for mobilizing finance for the budget. The Ministry of Finance, Planning and Economic Development (MFPED) determines the size of these issues based on the domestic financing requirements of the budget, and the annual amount of net issues of securities is announced in the budget.[3] Monetary policy is now conducted on the secondary market, through conducting repurchase or reverse repurchase operations and, more occasionally, through secondary market sales of the BOU's own holdings of government securities.[4] As a consequence, it is now possible for the market to distinguish clearly between fiscal and monetary policy operations. Separating monetary and fiscal policy operations in this manner has been a crucial reform in the implementation of the IT framework.

The issue of government borrowing from the BOU is more complex. Up until the time of the global financial crisis, the government had, in most fiscal years, saved money with the BOU (net financing from the BOU was negative). This was a passive outcome of the needs of the macroeconomic programme. Between 1995/96 and 2008/09, the government saved money with the BOU at an annual average rate of 1.1 per cent of GDP, while overall net domestic financing (which includes financing from the BOU) averaged negative 0.3 per cent of GDP. However, since the global financial crisis, the government's domestic borrowing requirement has risen—between 2009/10 and 2015/16, net domestic financing averaged 2.0 per cent of GDP—and it is no longer axiomatic that it will make savings with the BOU.

---

[3] Under the monetary targeting framework, in which primary securities issues were used only for monetary policy, the BOU alone determined the amount issued.

[4] These were issued to recapitalize the BOU, beginning in May 2013.

Table 2.4. Government Net Financing from the Bank of Uganda: Shs Billions, 2011/12–2015/16

	2011/2012	2012/2013	2013/2014	2014/2015	2015/2016
Billions of Shillings	323	−2	−293	149	466
Per cent of Money Base	11.2	−0.1	−8.8	4	10.3

The computation of net financing excludes transactions to and from dedicated accounts, such as the oil revenue and donor project accounts as well as transactions related to monetary policy operations. Net financing as a per cent of base money is calculated using base money at the start of the relevant financial year.

Source: BOU.

Since the introduction of IT, the actual record of government financing from the BOU has been mixed, as shown in Table 2.4. For the purposes of monetary policy, the most pertinent measure of net financing for the budget is the change in the net government position with the BOU, excluding the project accounts and other dedicated accounts such as oil revenue accounts, which hold funds raised from specific sources, such as donor project funds, and are earmarked for specific expenditures.[5] The BOU financed the government budget in three of the first five financial years of the implementation of the IT framework, and in two of these financial years the financing was more than 10 per cent of base money at the start of the year.

Government borrowing from the central bank is potentially problematic for monetary policy for two reasons. The first is that it entails the creation of money. Under the IT framework the BOU has to use its secondary market instruments to implement its monetary policy, but if government borrowing is large and sustained, this leads to the creation of 'structural liquidity' which may require a different set of sterilization instruments and may be costly for the central bank, as discussed in Section 5. Second, central bank financing of the budget can undermine the BOU's credibility to fight inflation.

Although the MFPED is committed in principle to avoid borrowing from the BOU, there are no practical institutional mechanisms which can prevent it. There are constraints on government borrowing from the central bank in both the BOU Act and the Public Financial Management Act, but neither act precisely defines government borrowing and there are differences of opinion within government as to whether borrowing should be defined in terms of a stock or a flow of resources through time; it is the latter which is most relevant for macroeconomic management. Government has introduced a Single Treasury Account System (STA) for its accounts in the central bank which might eventually provide a mechanism for curbing borrowing from the central bank. Ideally a floor should be placed on the balance in the STA and the MFPED should then manage its cash flows to ensure that this floor is not breached. Parliament, through the Parliamentary Committee on the Economy and Budget, should also play a more assertive role in monitoring the government borrowing from the BOU and holding it to account for deviations from budget plans.

---

[5] This is the definition of temporary advances from the central bank to the government which is used to compute the indicative target on this variable in the Policy Support Instrument programme which Uganda has with the IMF. The indicative target was introduced in 2015.

4 FORMULATING MONETARY POLICY

The policy interest rate—the Central Bank Rate (CBR)—is set on a bi-monthly basis by the BOU's Monetary Policy Committee (MPC).[6] The BOU sets the rate based on two key considerations: a 12-month forecast of core inflation, plus an assessment of the risks to the forecast, and an estimate of the output gap. The inflation forecast takes priority because controlling core inflation is the BOU's primary target. The technical challenges of formulating monetary policy are threefold. The first is making accurate inflation forecasts, the second is to estimate the output gap, and the third is to determine, if outturns are forecast to deviate from targets, how large a change in the policy interest rate is needed to achieve the targeted outturns.

Medium-term forecasts of inflation require a good understanding of the determinants of inflation, the capacity to project changes, over the medium term, in the exogenous drivers of inflation, and a robust forecasting model. When the IT framework was first introduced, an inflation forecast derived from a VAR model was used by the MPC. However, although a VAR model, which projects past trends forward, is useful for short-term forecasts, it is much less so for medium-term forecasts. This is partly because inflation is quite volatile in Uganda, with quite large cyclical swings from troughs to peaks over periods of from seven to twenty months. Consequently, current levels of inflation are a poor guide to future inflation beyond a few months' time. A large part of the volatility in core inflation is caused by the impact on domestic prices of volatility in the exchange rate (discussed in Section 6). Econometric estimates of the long-run pass-through of the exchange rate to inflation in Uganda are around 0.5 (Bwire, Anjugo, and Opolot, 2013; Apaa Okello and Brownbridge, 2013). For the purposes of forecasting inflation this presents a problem: one of the major variables driving inflation is very volatile and is itself very difficult to forecast.

In 2014 the Research Department of the BOU replaced the VAR model with a semi-structural quarterly projection model (QPM). The QPM, which is a dynamic stochastic general equilibrium model, incorporates forecasts of determinants of inflation such as the exchange rate, the fiscal deficit, and the output gap. It is embossed in a forecasting and policy analysis system (FPAS) that includes near term forecasting, data management, and other elements to shape the discussion, formulation, and communication of the policy stance.[7] However, the effectiveness of this approach faces two challenges. The first is to make robust forecasts of variables such as the exchange rate. The second is to calibrate the model to accurately reflect the causal factors in the inflation process, including the relative magnitude and timing of these factors in driving inflation.

---

[6] Initially the CBR was set on a monthly basis, at the start of every month, but the BOU switched to a bi-monthly basis, in the middle of the relevant month, at the start of the 2014/15 fiscal year. The change was motivation by the fact that the inflation volatility which characterized 2011 and 2012 had been reduced and, as such, inflation forecasts did not vary much from month to month, hence a monthly change in the CBR was not necessary to ensure that the monetary policy stance was aligned with medium-term forecasts; see Mutebile-Tumusiime (2014).

[7] The model was developed with technical assistance from the IMF's Research Department.

Table 2.5. Core Inflation Forecasts and Outturns

Date at which forecast was made	Forecast (per cent)	Outturn (per cent)	Date to which forecast applies
Oct 13	7–8	2.4	Oct 14
Nov 13	6.5–7.5	2.3	Nov 14
Jan 14	6.5–7.5	2.7	Late 2014
Mar 14	5.5–6.5	3.7	Mar 15
Apr 14	6–7	4.6	Apr 15
May 14	3–7	4.8	May 14
Jun 14	5–6	4.9	Jun 15
Aug 14	5.5–6.5	5.5	Aug 15
Oct 14	5	6.3	Oct 15
Dec 14	5	7.5	Dec 15
Feb 15	4–6	6.7	Feb 16
Apr 15	7–9	6.9	Jun 16
Jun 15	8–10	6.9	Jun 16
Jul 15	8–10	5.7	Jul 16

Source: Forecasts are from the BOU's Monetary Policy Statements; outturn data are from UBOS.

Table 2.5 provides details of the BOU's core inflation forecasts and the outturns. In most cases the forecasts were 12-month forecasts, but occasionally the forecast period was slightly less or more than 12 months. The forecasts were included in the Monetary Policy Statements issued immediately after the MPC meetings. The outturn data are taken from the 2005/06 base year CPI series, because this was the series in use at the time when the forecasts were made. However, the 2005/06 base year series was discontinued in November 2015 and replaced with a 2009/10 base year series, hence the outturn data from December 2015 onwards are based on the latter series. Two points can be made about the core inflation forecasts. First, it has been difficult to forecast the turning points in the inflation cycle; for example, the BOU had not expected the upward swing of the inflation cycle in 2015–16 to peak until mid-2016, yet the actual peak occurred at the end of 2015. Second, the forecasts have underestimated the volatility of inflation, especially with respect to the downward swings of the cycle, when core inflation turned out to be lower than forecast (e.g. in October and November 2014). On average, the published forecasts shown in Table 2.5 were higher than the outturns by 1.4 percentage points.[8]

Incorporating the output gap into the setting of the CBR is very problematic for several reasons. The first is the difficulty of making robust estimates of potential output. The BOU has estimated potential output by fitting a trend, using a Hodrick-Prescott filter, through the quarterly real GDP data. However, this method does not capture potential structural breaks in the time series data. Furthermore, because of the recent rebasing of GDP estimates by the Uganda Bureau of Statistics (UBOS), a fully consistent time series for GDP only extends back to 2008/09, which obviously undermines the efficacy of estimates of potential output derived from an H-P filter. In addition, there are often substantial revisions

---

[8] Where the forecast was a range, we have used the mid-point of the range to calculate the deviation of outturn from forecast.

made to the quarterly estimates in subsequent quarters. Consequently, neither the estimates of actual quarterly output, nor the estimates of potential output, are very reliable. In December 2010, for example, six months before the BOU introduced the IT framework, the BOU had concluded that, although aggregate demand was increasing, the economy was still operating with a negative output gap, based on the annual GDP estimates for 2009/10, whereas subsequent revisions to the national accounts data showed that real GDP in 2010/11 was substantially above potential. The BOU also prepares its own composite indicator of economic activity on a monthly basis. This can provide indications on whether growth in real activity is accelerating or slowing down, but by itself it provides no information on whether there is a positive or a negative output gap.

In setting monetary policy, the BOU aims to follow the Taylor Principle,[9] whereby the real interest rate is raised whenever inflation is forecast to rise above the policy target and vice versa.[10] The risks to the inflation outlook are also taken into account. The factors driving forecast inflation also affect the policy response. The BOU reacts less aggressively to supply-side shocks to prices which are expected to be reversed; in such cases the BOU's main concern is to prevent spill overs from the supply shocks which might prove more persistent; for example increases in school fees arising from food price shocks. When large changes in the CBR are warranted, as with the sharp rise in the inflation forecast between February and June 2015 shown in Table 2.5, the BOU spreads the required interest rate change out over several months to avoid too much disruption to financial markets.

5 IMPLEMENTING MONETARY POLICY

The key task of implementing monetary policy is to align a short-term risk-free interest rate with the CBR so that it sets a benchmark for other interest rates in the economy. Interbank lending in Uganda mostly entails overnight and seven-day loans. In Uganda the seven-day interbank rate serves as the operating target for monetary policy.

Implementation of monetary policy takes place through regular interventions in the money market, through an offer to the commercial banks for either a repo (which removes liquidity) or a reverse repo. The repos/reverse repos are transacted at the CBR, with the BOU accepting all offers from the banks which are consistent with the CBR (i.e. the BOU fixes the price of liquidity and allows the market to determine the quantity). In effect, if there is too much liquidity in the market, the BOU offers to pay the banks the CBR on their surplus reserves.

Until May 2012, the BOU had auctioned a fixed quantity of repos or reverse repos, allowing the market to determine the interest rate, although a ceiling was

---

[9] See Taylor (1993).

[10] Goncalves (2015) estimated an interest rate reaction function for three East African central banks in a small econometric model to assess whether they followed the Taylor principle. He found that interest rates in Uganda were consistent with the Taylor principle.

imposed on the rate for the reverse repo and a floor on that for the repo, with the ceilings and floors linked to the CBR. The switch to the current modalities has brought two advantages. First, it has ensured that the repo/reverse repo rate matches the CBR at every issue and second, it obviates the need for the BOU to make precise liquidity forecasts before issuing a repo or reverse repo. All that the BOU needs to know to prevent the seven-day interbank rate from deviating from the CBR is whether the banking system in aggregate will have surplus or deficit liquidity.

5.1 Challenges for the Implementation of Monetary Policy

Monetary policy implementation has faced a challenge from structural liquidity. Structural liquidity refers to long-term liquidity, rather than simply temporary fluctuations of liquidity. It is also an approximation of how much liquidity the BOU needs to remove from the banking system to align interbank interest rates with the CBR. The sources of structural liquidity are factors which lead to the creation of reserve money in excess of its demand (by the banks and the public), which are mainly the accumulation of foreign exchange reserves by the BOU and government borrowing from the BOU.

Figure 2.1 provides estimates of structural liquidity, in the 21 months from January 2015 to the beginning of October 2016. These estimates are derived by adding together the deviation of actual excess bank reserves over the average level of excess reserves for the whole period,[11] plus the volume of liquidity which has been mopped up or injected by the BOU through the issuance of repos or reverse repos and the net sales of the BOU's recapitalization securities on the secondary market. As can be seen in Figure 2.1, structural liquidity was always positive in this period, but it rose very sharply in the final quarter of the 2015/16 financial year, mainly because of the government borrowing from the BOU, shown in Table 2.4. A stagnation of demand for reserve money during 2016 has also contributed to the build-up of structural liquidity.

The problems emanating from structural liquidity are twofold. First, when the volume of structural liquidity is very large, it exceeds the amount of recapitalization securities which the BOU holds to mop up liquidity for longer than very short periods. As a consequence, the BOU has to use short-term repos with maturities of seven days or less to mop up liquidity which will remain in the banking system for much longer than seven days. Consequently, large volumes of repos mature each week, injecting liquidity back into the system, which can weaken the BOU's control over liquidity conditions. Second, mopping up large volumes of liquidity is expensive for the BOU, as it must pay the interest costs of the securities it issues, or forgo the interest income.

---

[11] Banks always hold some reserves in excess of their minimum statutory level of required reserves, as a buffer against shocks. Excess bank reserves averaged Shs 119 billion over the period January 2015 to October 2016, which is 10 per cent of the banking system's required reserves.

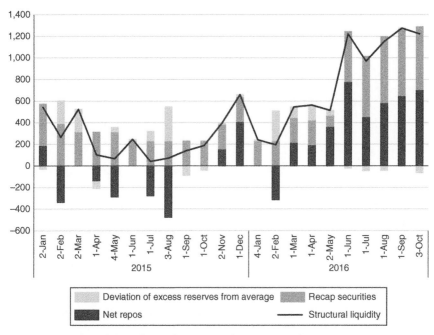

Figure 2.1. Structural Liquidity and Issuance of Monetary Policy Instruments to Mop it up, Shilling Billions: Jan 2015–October 2016

Where the bars depicting net repos show a negative number, as at 2 Feb 2015, the BOU had injected liquidity with reverse repos.

Source: BOU.

6 EXCHANGE RATE POLICY AND MONETARY POLICY

Since the 1990s Uganda has maintained a floating exchange rate, primarily motivated by the conviction that exchange rate flexibility helps to stabilize the real economy in the face of external shocks. However, the nominal exchange rate has often been very volatile in Uganda, as can be seen in Figure 2.2, driven by both current account and capital account shocks. The latter include fluctuations in short-term flows of portfolio capital which are invested in the domestic money and securities markets. The BOU is not indifferent to exchange rate volatility, for several reasons. Volatility causes disruption to economic agents needing to transact in foreign exchange. There have also been extended periods when the real effective exchange rate has been overvalued, thereby undermining external competitiveness and long-run economic growth.[12] Given that the current account of the balance of payments has widened in recent years, from 6.8 per cent of GDP in 2008/09 to 9.7 per cent of GDP in 2015/16, the BOU has been concerned to avoid

---

[12] Many cross-country empirical studies have identified a robust correlation between the level of the real exchange rate and economic growth in developing countries over the long term, with a more depreciated real exchange rate supporting higher long-term growth and/or accelerations in the growth rate (e.g. Elbadawi, Kaltani, and Soto, 2012; Johnson, Ostry, and Subramanian, 2007).

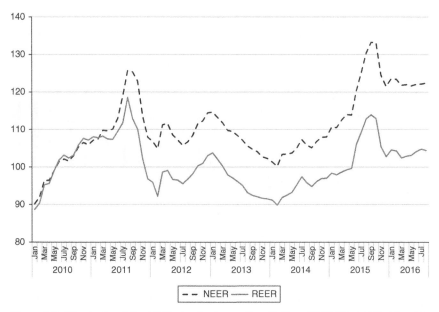

Figure 2.2. Nominal and Real Effective Exchange Rate Indices (2009/10 = 100), Monthly Averages, January 2010–August 2016
Source: BOU.

a deterioration of competitiveness. Nominal exchange rate movements are also a major determinant of inflation, as discussed in Section 4.

The volatility of the exchange rate poses dilemmas for the central bank. It is too important for the economy to simply ignore. On the other hand, including the exchange rate among the targets for monetary policy (i.e. including the exchange rate among the variables in the reaction function for the policy interest rate) would compromise the BOU's ability to deliver on its target for inflation and possibly also generate more volatility in output and inflation rates (Eichengreen, 2002). Instead the BOU has attempted to manage the volatility of the exchange rate, when necessary, through sterilized intervention, defined as intervention which leaves the target interest rate (the seven-day interbank rate) unchanged. The intervention takes place through BOU sales or purchases of foreign exchange to the interbank foreign exchange market (IFEM) while sterilization is implemented using the money market interventions described in Section 5. Sterilized intervention is effective in influencing the exchange rate in Uganda because capital mobility is far from perfect, given the small size of domestic financial markets. BOU interventions can be large relative to daily flows in the interbank foreign exchange market. In effect, the BOU has two instruments to address two targets, as discussed by Ostry et al. (2012) and in Chapter 13.

Sterilized intervention is motivated by two objectives. The first is to dampen short-term exchange rate volatility; i.e. sharp daily movements in the exchange rate, especially when the BOU believes that such movements are not driven solely by economic fundamentals. These interventions are usually quite successful in stemming rapid appreciation or depreciation but there have been infrequent occasions, when the exchange rate has been under very strong pressure to depreciate rapidly, when the BOU has not fully sterilized foreign exchange sales, thereby tightening liquidity; this was because the foreign exchange sales alone were not sufficient to stem the depreciating pressures. Obviously, in such circumstances, achieving the operating target (the seven-day bank rate) is temporarily subordinated to the need to restore stability to the exchange rate.

The second motive for intervention is to avert sustained real appreciation beyond what is estimated to be the long-term equilibrium real effective exchange rate. This is more problematic because, if the appreciation pressure is strong, it often requires repeated interventions, the sterilization of which contributes to the accumulation of structural liquidity and hence creates potential problems for the implementation of monetary policy, as discussed in Section 5. The BOU intervened in 2013 to stem real appreciation, but the build-up of structural liquidity constrained the scope for doing this.

The BOU has also purchased foreign exchange from the IFEM for purposes of accumulating foreign reserves. Given that it sells far more foreign exchange to the government (for external debt servicing, government imports, etc.) than it purchases from the government (e.g. from donor budget support inflows), if the BOU did not purchase foreign exchange from the IFEM, its foreign reserves would be steadily depleted. These purchases are not intended to influence the exchange rate or send any signal to the market about the BOU's desires with respect to the exchange rate. Hence the BOU has carried out these purchases on a regular, predictable basis, buying a small amount each working day through an auction process, with the exact amount purchased each day dependent on the offers received from banks. These purchases are also sterilized, directly through the BOU's money market interventions and indirectly by government debt issuance.[13]

7 COMMUNICATIONS

The BOU radically revamped its communications strategy to support the introduction of the IT framework. The main objectives of the communications strategy are to enhance the signal of the policy stance and to influence inflationary expectations. In particular, it aims to make the public aware of the policy interest rate decision and the reasons which underlie it, especially the core inflation forecast.

The key component of the communications strategy is the press briefing which follows the MPC and at which the Governor reads out a monetary policy statement (MPS) and answers questions from journalists. The MPS is uploaded to

---

[13] If the government fully funds its domestic borrowing requirement by issuing securities to the market, it must accumulate a surplus in domestic currency with the central bank to offset its net foreign currency purchases from the central bank. Hence in principle, the foreign currency which is purchased by the BOU, over and above that which is used to accumulate foreign reserves, and which is sold to government, should not need to be sterilized. However, there may be timing differences between the purchase of foreign currency by the BOU and government debt issuance which necessitate temporary sterilization by the BOU.

the BOU's website. The BOU also posts a monthly monetary policy report on the website, which includes material from the reports presented to the MPC. Finally, the BOU uses speeches by the Governor and Deputy Governor to address monetary policy issues and to explain how the IT framework works; these are also posted on the website. In drafting the MPS and the monetary policy reports, the BOU aims to be transparent and to avoid painting an unwarrantedly optimistic picture of future prospects. For example, the inflation forecast presented to the MPC is included in the MPS.

The communications strategy has been successful in strengthening the coverage of the BOU's monetary policy in both the local and foreign media. All of the serious local newspapers and electronic media carry reports of the press briefing, often with quotes from the Governor. The local TV and radio stations also cover the press briefing and sometimes supplement this with interviews with BOU officials. Specialist international media, such as Reuters and Bloomberg, and more occasionally MSBC Africa, also carry reports on the interest rate decision. Some of the large international banks which operate in Africa, such as Standard Bank, provide to their clients regular market analysis on Uganda which makes reference to the MPS and other communications from the BOU. Hence it is possible to draw two conclusions which are positive for monetary policy. First, there is much greater awareness among the general public in Uganda of what the BOU is doing, because of the widespread media coverage. Nevertheless, the quality of macroeconomic analysis, even in the serious local media, is not very high. Second, among economic and financial sector specialists in the media and private sector, there is a greater understanding of the reasoning behind the BOU's monetary policy actions; for example, where the BOU believes the main threats to inflation reside.

8 HOW EFFECTIVE HAS MONETARY POLICY BEEN IN THE IT FRAMEWORK?

In this section we review the evidence on the effectiveness of the IT framework in Uganda in terms of the capacity of monetary policy to achieve its targets. This is essentially a discussion about the monetary policy transmission mechanism: i.e., do changes in the policy interest rate bring about the desired changes in macroeconomic variables, particularly inflation? The monetary policy transmission mechanism entails two stages. The first is an interest rate transmission, whereby a change in the policy interest rate affects market interest rates in the economy. The second stage entails changes in market interest rates affecting private sector behaviour and hence macroeconomic variables. We start by examining the interest rate transmission mechanism.

8.1 How Strong is the Interest Rate Transmission Mechanism?

The link between the CBR and the seven-day interbank rate is the first stage in the interest rate transmission mechanism. Between April 2012 and August 2016, the monthly average seven-day interbank rate was close to the CBR, deviating in absolute terms on average by only 52 basis points over this period.[14] The months in which there were larger deviations of the average seven-day interbank rate from the CBR were mostly those in which the exchange rate was under strong pressure such that the BOU restricted liquidity to the banking system because of fears that this might fuel further depreciation, as was the case for some months in 2015.

The second stage in the interest rate transmission mechanism involves changes in the seven-day interbank rate affecting longer-term interest rates, notably time deposit rates and bank lending rates. Average time deposit rates, which are heavily influenced by a few wholesale depositors, have been slightly more volatile than seven-day interbank rates, but they have tracked the CBR quite closely (Figure 2.3). Between April 2012 and August 2016, the average absolute deviation between the average monthly time deposit rate and the CBR was 115 basis points.

The BOU's influence over bank lending rates is less than over deposit rates. Estimates by staff of the Research Department indicate that the bank lending rate

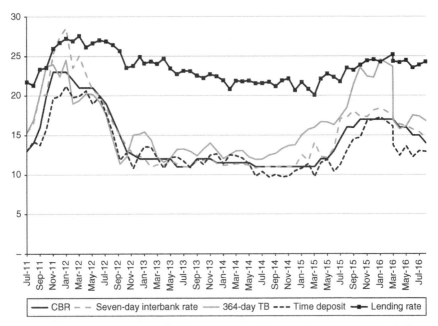

Figure 2.3. CBR, Seven-Day Interbank Rate, 364-Day TB Rate, Average 7–12 Month Time Deposit Rate and Average Lending Rate; July 2011–August 2016
Source: BOU.

---

[14] We have excluded the first nine months of the IT period (July 2011–March 2012) because in this period the BOU intentionally aimed to keep the seven-day interbank rate close to the top of the band around the CBR, which at that time was four percentage points above the CBR, because inflation was very high. This was done by issuing sufficient repos to push the weighted average repo rate close to the top of the band around the CBR. After March 2012, the BOU adjusted its intervention policy so that the weighted average repo rate was closer to the CBR itself.

responds to a 100 basis point change in the CBR by slightly less than 50 basis points (Sande and Apaa Okello, 2013). Abuka et al. (2015) find that a 100 basis points rise in the seven-day interbank rate is associated with a rise of between 33 and 49 basis points in the bank lending rate. There has also been an asymmetry in the speed of adjustment of the lending rate to the CBR. As can be seen in Figure 2.3, when the CBR was raised sharply in 2011, the bank lending rate also increased over roughly the same period, but when the CBR was reduced in 2012, the reduction in bank lending rates was drawn out over a much longer period of time.

8.2 Do Changes in Market Rates Affect Macroeconomic Variables?

Changes in market interest rates can affect macroeconomic variables through various channels—volumes of bank credit to the private sector, savings decisions by consumers, exchange rates, and private sector expectations of inflation and other variables. In practice, it is difficult to isolate and estimate the impact of these different channels. However, a few studies have been completed which examine the empirical evidence for the transmission mechanism since the introduction of the IT framework, which we briefly review below.[15]

Opolot (2013) uses balance sheet data from commercial banks to estimate the response of credit aggregates to changes in Treasury Bill interest rates, as a proxy for the stance of monetary policy, during the period 2000–2012 which straddles both the MT and IT frameworks in Uganda. He finds that a rise in interest rates reduces bank lending, although the impact is quite weak. He also finds that high levels of liquidity in banks dampen the bank lending channel. Abuka et al. (2015) use microeconomic data from the Credit Reference Bureau database to investigate how changes in bank lending rates affected volumes of loans disbursed by banks over the period from 2010 to 2014. They find that a rise in the banking lending rate reduces the probability that a bank will grant a loan to a borrower and the volume of credit granted to borrowers. They also find that the degree to which lending rates affect credit aggregates in individual banks depends on the strength of those banks' capital and liquidity positions; higher capital ratios weaken the bank lending channel but higher liquidity ratios strengthen it. They find that the quantitative impact of a given change in lending rates in Uganda is only about half that estimated for advanced economies. Hence, there is evidence of a functioning bank lending channel in Uganda, albeit one which is weaker than that in advanced economies. This finding is consistent with theories of credit market imperfections which suggest that imperfect information about the quality of borrowers causes banks to ration credit rather than allowing the interest rate to clear the credit market.

Berg et al. (Chapter 5) employ a narrative or event study approach to evaluate the efficacy of the monetary policy transmission mechanism in East African countries, focusing on the monetary tightening triggered by the steep rise in inflation in these countries in 2011. They found evidence of an effective transmission mechanism in

---

[15] Empirical studies which cover the period before the introduction of the IT framework in Uganda include Mugume (2011), Montiel (2013), and Davoodi et al. (2013). The first two of these studies finds a weak monetary policy transmission mechanism, while that of Davoodi et al. finds evidence of a more substantial channel.

Uganda, which they attributed to the clarity and transparency of the monetary policy regime. In the episode that they studied, a policy-induced rise in interest rates led to an appreciation of the exchange rate, a fall in inflation, and a decline in output growth.

8.3 Inflation Outcomes under the IT Framework

Figure 2.4 depicts annual core inflation from July 2006 to September 2016. Unfortunately, there is no single consumer price series which spans this period. Instead there is a 2005/06 base year series which began in July 2006 and was discontinued in November 2015, and a second series, with a 2009/10 base year, which began in July 2011. IT was introduced when inflation was climbing very rapidly, as a result of a combination of rising global and regional food prices, steep nominal exchange rate depreciation (which had begun in early 2010, as shown in Figure 2.2), and very strong credit growth. After introducing IT in July 2011, the BOU raised the CBR by 10 percentage points to 23 per cent by October 2011 (Figure 2.3), with the results noted by Berg et al. in Chapter 5. Core inflation peaked in October–November and then fell back sharply, so that by September 2012 it was back to around 5 per cent.

Table 2.6 compares core inflation outcomes under both the MT and IT frameworks. We have excluded the period of high inflation from February 2011 to June 2012 from the analysis, because this period spanned both frameworks. Furthermore, given the lags in the monetary transmission mechanism, an inflation outcome which occurred during the first few months of the operation of the IT framework cannot fairly be attributed to that framework, and certainly not to it alone.

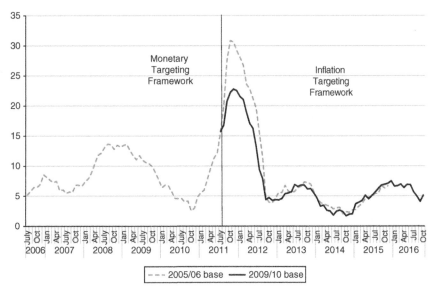

Figure 2.4. Annual Core Inflation Rates: July 2006–October 2016 (two series)

Source: UBOS.

Table 2.6. Average Annual Core Inflation and Standard Deviations of Core Inflation Rates under Monetary Targeting and Inflation Targeting Frameworks

	Monetary Targeting	Inflation Targeting
	July 2006–January 2011	July 2012–October 2016
Annual Average core inflation (per cent)	8.2	5.1
Standard deviation (percentage points)	3.1	1.8

Source: BOU and UBOS.

Two notes of caution are warranted in comparing inflation outcomes under the two frameworks. First, we have had to use different CPI series for each framework, the 2005/06 series for the MT framework and the 2009/10 series for the IT framework, because the latter series does not cover any of the period in which the MT framework was operated by the BOU and the former covers only part of the period in which the BOU has been implementing the IT framework. Second, inflation outcomes are not purely the result of monetary policy but also reflect exogenous shocks which are not identical to both the periods of the MT and IT frameworks.

Table 2.6 shows that, since inflation was brought under control in mid-2012 (a period of 52 months), core inflation has averaged 5.1 per cent, very close to the BOU's policy target of 5 per cent over the medium term. Core inflation rates were higher under the MT framework, averaging 8.2 per cent in the 55 months from July 2006 to January 2011, although part of the higher average inflation can be attributed to the global food price shocks and the impact of the global financial crisis on the exchange rate in 2008 and 2009. Core inflation has also been less volatile, with a lower standard deviation, since the IT framework was introduced.

9 CONCLUSIONS

After more than five years of implementing IT in Uganda, what lessons can be learned from this experience? In this conclusion we ask three questions. How feasible is IT in a low-income economy? What are the basic prerequisites for the adoption of IT? What are the most important elements for the success of IT?

There are undoubtedly challenges to implementing an IT framework in a low-income economy; these include shallow financial markets, which impede the monetary policy transmission mechanism, volatile exchange rates, supply price shocks which make inflation more volatile and difficult to forecast, and a lack of reliable and timely data, especially on the real sector of the economy. Nevertheless, an IT framework can offer a central bank traction over the medium-term evolution of inflation, which is at least as effective, if not much more so, than the alternative of a MT framework. The evidence reviewed in the previous section suggests that the use of a policy interest rate as the operating target of monetary policy drives a functioning monetary policy transmission mechanism, through both the interest rate transmission from the policy rate to market interest rates and the subsequent impact on bank lending and nominal exchange rates, together with the public announcement of the policy interest rate as a signal of the monetary policy stance.

Uganda's experience bears out the findings of Freedman and Otker-Robe (2010), that the essential preconditions for the adoption of IT are that the central bank must have operational independence to set monetary policy and that controlling core inflation must be the unambiguous primary target of monetary policy. Each of these factors has been important, both in shaping the BOU's monetary policy and in establishing its credibility as a central bank with a strong commitment to control inflation, a commitment which has been noted in some of the commentaries by market participants, such as international banks. The absence of fiscal dominance is also important, but this is difficult to define precisely in practice. Ideally it should preclude borrowing by the government from the central bank except in small quantities and on a purely temporary basis, with effective institution mechanisms to enforce this. The latter are lacking in Uganda and BOU financing of the budget has not been negligible or purely temporary, as discussed in Section 3. This highlights the importance of a fourth precondition for the adoption of IT; the central bank must have sufficient instruments at its disposal, usually marketable government securities, to conduct monetary policy through open market operations. If government does borrow from the central bank, this implies that the latter will require a larger volume of instruments, ceteris paribus, with which to manage the liquidity created by government borrowing.

What are the elements which have contributed to the successful adoption of IT in Uganda? We would argue that a key factor is that the BOU has constructed the IT framework around a set of basic principles which have guided the development of operational procedures and the setting of policy. As a result monetary policy has clear, coherent, and transparent objectives which have contributed to better understanding of it by market participants and the public, and which in turn has an important influence on the effectiveness of monetary policy. These principles are discussed below.

First, the primary determinant of monetary policy is the inflation forecast, together with an assessment of risks to the forecasts. As such, the BOU has implemented monetary policy on a forward-looking basis, putting faith in its inflation forecasts, which is necessary given the lags in the transmission mechanism. Although it has proved difficult to make accurate inflation forecasts, given the volatility of inflation, the forecasts nevertheless provide the monetary policy committee with clear guidelines for setting the policy interest rate, based on the Taylor principle. The BOU has been prepared to raise the policy interest rates when inflation is forecast to rise, even if, at the time of the decision, actual inflation, as opposed to forecast inflation, was still close to target. This was probably important in curbing the rise in inflation in the second half of 2015, driven by a steep depreciation of the exchange rate. The BOU has also been prepared to implement quite aggressive changes in the monetary policy stance when inflation is forecast to rise, which is necessary because the monetary policy transmission mechanism is weaker than in advanced economies and hence larger changes in the policy instruments are needed to bring about a given change in the target variables.

Second, the BOU has disentangled monetary policy from fiscal policy, by clearly separating monetary operations carried out on the secondary market from the issuance of securities to finance of budget which are conducted in the primary auctions. This is important for two reasons. It has ensured that the BOU has full control over its monetary policy operations, and it has enhanced the transparency of monetary policy.

Third, the BOU has focussed the implementation of monetary policy, through the regular interventions in the money market, on the objection of aligning the seven-day interbank rate with the policy interest rate (i.e. achieving the operating target of monetary policy) rather than any other objective. It has not pursued multiple operating targets, such as trying to target both interest rates and monetary aggregates at the same time. Since introducing the IT framework, the BOU has been flexible in experimenting with different approaches to determine the most effective methods for achieving this objective, such as different strategies for issuing repos, but the operating target has not changed.

Finally, the BOU has prioritized its communications strategy, putting emphasis on explaining to the public the reasons for monetary policy decisions and making public its medium-term inflation forecasts. Communications is viewed as an essential complement to monetary policy decisions and actions, because of the important role which public understanding of monetary policy plays in enhancing its effectiveness in an IT framework.

REFERENCES

Abuka, C., Alinda, R. K., Minoiu, C., Peydro, J. L., and Presbitero, A. F. (2015). *Monetary Policy in a Developing Country: Loan Applications and Real Effects.* Working Paper 15/270. Washington, DC: International Monetary Fund.

Apaa Okello, J. and Brownbridge, M. (2013). *Exchange rate pass through and its implications for monetary policy in Uganda.* Working Paper 10/2013. Bank of Uganda.

Bwire, T., Anjugo, F. L., and Opolot, J. (2013). *A Re-estimation of exchange rate pass-through to domestic prices in Uganda: Evidence from a Structural Vector Auto-Regression (SVAR).* Working Paper 05/2013. Bank of Uganda.

Davoodi, H. R., Dixit, S., and Pinter, G. (2013). *Monetary Transmission Mechanism in the East African Community: An Empirical Investigation.* Working Paper 13/39. Washington, DC: International Monetary Fund.

Eichengreen, B. (2002). *Can emerging markets float? Should they inflation target?* Working Paper 36. Central Bank of Brazil.

Elbadawi, I., Kaltani, L., and Soto, R. (2012). Aid, Real Exchange Rate Misalignment and Economic Growth in Sub-Saharan Africa. *World Development,* 40(4), 681–700.

Freedman, C. and Otker-Robe, I. (2010). *Important Elements for Inflation Targeting for Emerging Economies.* Working Paper 10/113. Washington, DC: International Monetary Fund.

Goncalves, C. E. (2015). *Taylor visits Africa.* Working Paper 15/258. Washington, DC: International Monetary Fund.

International Monetary Fund. (2004). *Monetary Policy Implementation at Different Stages of Market Development.* Washington, DC: International Monetary Fund.

Johnson, S., Ostry, J. D., and Subramanian A. (2007). *The Prospects for Sustained Growth in Africa: Benchmarking the Constraints.* Working Paper 52/07. Washington, DC: International Monetary Fund.

Masson, P. R., Savastano, M. A., and Sharma, S. (1997). *The Scope for Inflation Targeting in Developing Countries.* Working Paper 97/130. Washington, DC: International Monetary Fund.

Montiel, P. (2013). *The monetary transmission mechanism in Uganda.* International Growth Centre.

Mugume, A. (2011). *Monetary Transmission Mechanisms in Uganda.* Working Paper 01/2011, Bank of Uganda.

Mutebile-Tumusiime, E. (2014, June 27). Remarks by the Governor at the Uganda Bankers' Association Informal Dinner, Kampala.

Opolot, J. (2013). *Bank Lending Channel of the Monetary Policy Transmission Mechanism in Uganda: Evidence from Panel Data Analysis.* Working Paper 01/2013. Bank of Uganda.

Ostry, J., Ghosh, A. R., and Chamon, M. (2012). *Two Targets, Two Instruments: Monetary and Exchange Rate Policies in Emerging Market Economies.* Staff Discussion Note 12/01. Washington, DC: International Monetary Fund.

Sande, D. and Apaa-Okello, J. (2013). *Interest Rate Pass Through in Uganda.* Working Paper 02/2013. Bank of Uganda.

Sargent, T. J. and Wallace, N. (1981). Some Unpleasant Monetarist Arithmetic. *Federal Reserve Bank of Minneapolis Quarterly Reviews*, 5(3), 1–17.

Taylor, J. B. (1993, December). Discretion versus policy rules in practice. *Carnegie-Rochester Conference Series on Public Policy*, 39, 195–214. Elsevier.

Part I
Empirical Evidence

3

Introduction to Part I

Andrew Berg and Rafael Portillo

Our understanding of monetary policy in LICs, as with any economic subject, must be fundamentally empirical. Theory is unlikely to give an unambiguous answer to any important policy question; at most it can help shape how we look at the data. This empirics-first approach captures much of the flavour of the macro profession. For example, Gali (2008) justifies writing a book on the application of the New Keynesian model to monetary policy by emphasizing two empirical results: studies using microeconomic data demonstrating nominal price rigidities, such as Bils and Klenow (2004), and VAR results demonstrating that monetary policy shocks have real effects, e.g., Christiano, Eichenbaum, and Evans (1999).

When we began to work on the topic of this book many years ago, two broad considerations shaped our approach. First, we felt that, at least in the policy circles we were in, there was something of an imbalance in favour of empirics without theory. There was a large number of VAR and regression-based papers, e.g. attempting to estimate money demand in low-income countries, and little attempt to give economic structure to the empirical analysis and hence little in the way of usable results.[1]

And second, analysts of low-income countries inevitably live in a data-poor environment. There is simply relatively little reliable macroeconomic data. For example, only thirteen of the forty-five SSA countries in the IMF databases have any quarterly GDP data and only five have data on both nominal and real GDP (Botswana, Mauritius, Rwanda, Seychelles, and South Africa). Excluding South Africa, which has consistent nominal and real quarterly GDP data back to 1980, the median span of quarterly data is less than nine years (Li et al., 2016).

And for the data we do have, measurement error is likely to be unusually large. Absent a direct line to the true data, it is hard to get a clear sense of measurement error. But several indications are telling. Re-basing of GDP resulted in estimates that GDP was higher than previously thought by almost 90 per cent (Nigeria, 2014), 60 per cent (Ghana, 2010), and 30 per cent (Kenya, 2015). That these revisions were so large reflects rapid structural change and the fact that the surveys that provide the basis for the construction of GDP (household and labour market surveys, agricultural and population censuses) are often incomplete and outdated

---

[1] See for example the papers referenced in Mishra and Montiel (2012). On SSA, examples include Davoodi, Dixit, and Pinter (2013) and Nsabimana and Ocran (2015).

(African Development Bank, 2013). Another perspective comes from the analysis of revisions to GDP estimates even well after the year in question. Ley and Misch (2014) examine the deviation between final estimates of annual real GDP in year t (made in year t+5) and those made by IMF staff in the spring of year t+1, as a proxy for real-time measurement error. They find that the variation of this deviation is about twice as large in LICs as in OECD countries (in both cases excluding resource-rich countries).

Finally, even these relatively short and unreliable time series may overstate the availability of usable data, because frequent regime shifts make it hard to make inferences. For example, when countries such as Uganda, Ghana, and Kenya switch monetary policy regimes, empirical relationships shift.

This empirical Part of the book takes three very different looks at the data. The first, in Chapter 4, sets the basic stage for the rest of the analyses in the book with a purely empirical and descriptive look at the key economic features of countries in the region. This chapter identifies some of the fundamental characteristics of SSA economies, both in terms of their structure and in terms of the basic macroeconomic data. The weaknesses of the data mentioned above, notably the lack of sufficient quarterly data, limit the exercise relative to similar ones conducted for advanced and emerging economies. Nonetheless, some important and striking patterns emerge. Many of its main conclusions, such as the size of the agricultural sector, the importance of supply shocks, and the lack of correlation between the current account deficit and fluctuations in consumption, are the basic stylized facts that motivate much of the rest of the book. For example, Chapter 10 examines the interactions of limited capital mobility and food price shocks, Chapter 11 takes up the importance of food prices, supply shocks, and poverty—and the proximity of so many consumers to subsistence—while Chapter 17 emphasizes the importance of the bank-led financial system.

Turning to the empirics of monetary policy specifically, Chapter 6 resulted from discussions we had with some of our collaborators, notably Peter Montiel, about the implications of the available empirical evidence on monetary transmission in LICs. He and his co-authors have argued that the particular characteristics of LICs, such as the small size of the financial sector, limit the role for monetary policy, pointing to VAR estimates with insignificant coefficients on interest rates, for example.[2]

We, in some contrast, have generally felt that too much time and energy was being spent on estimates of money demand and on VARS attempting to estimate the effects of monetary policy shocks. In part, our impatience resulted from a view that some of the questions in that literature were not really critical to efforts to improve policy regimes. Our reading of the experience of emerging markets engaged in regime transition was that a precise handle on the transmission mechanism was not available prior to implementation of new regimes. In part, this is because the regime transition itself inevitably changes transmission. In addition, we felt that little of clear policy relevance hangs on the question of whether the coefficient on say the interest rate in the IS curve is 0.2 or 0.4.

---

[2] See Mishra, Montiel, and Spilimbergo (2013), and Mishra and Montiel (2012).

We also doubted whether the assumptions implicit in the methodology were valid. With frequent regime shifts and hence short data series, measurement error, and perhaps above all the challenge to identifying monetary policy shocks in regimes in which the central bank targets a mix of interest rates, money aggregates, and the exchange rate, what should we reasonably expect from these VAR methods applied to our questions of interest?

Chapter 6, jointly written with Peter, attempts to give a precise answer to this question in a particular setting. We know the nature of the world (in the form of the data coming from a fairly simple DSGE model of the sort used in several other chapters in this book). We can then in effect hand these data to an econometrician and ask them to implement standard VAR-based estimations, and see whether they can reliably recover the true nature of the data-generating process. Our reading of the exercise is that, under reasonable-for-SSA-LIC assumptions—about say the length of time series and the degree of measurement error—they cannot.

Where does that leave us, empirically? The conclusion to Chapter 6 discusses some possible ways forward with macro time-series analysis. We are sceptical that confident identification of monetary policy will ever be possible in small open economies that pay attention both to interest rates and the exchange rate, at least with the contemporaneous restrictions that characterize most of the literature. We have some hope that identification through sign restrictions may be fruitful, though we place more stock on relying on easily identified shocks, such as to the terms of trade, and examining their interaction with prior known features of the regime, such as the existence of a hard peg or a float. Analyses based on micro data, such as Abuka et al. (2015), are clearly useful where the data can be found.

An emphasis on case studies represents another sort of methodological approach. Even for advanced countries, one can question, as in Summers (1991), how much of our basic understanding of monetary policy really results from econometrics per se. Privately if not in print, many economists may agree that the experience of major events—for example the sharp and deep recession that accompanied the Volker disinflation—strongly shapes the way we think about macroeconomics and specifically how econometricians know when to stop running regressions and declare victory.

Chapter 5 takes a close look at another such major event, a moment in 2011 when four countries in the East African Community acted dramatically—some raising interest rates by hundreds of basis points—to tighten monetary policy in the face of high inflation. There are limits to this exercise. First, we cannot fully isolate the exogenous component of the policy shock. And we only have the one incident and the four countries to look at. On the other hand, we can take a relatively rich look at the interplay of external and domestic factors in the build-up of inflation, the tightening episode, and the aftermath, in each of the four cases.

The magnitude of the tightening event, and the variation across the four countries in terms of underling economic structure and monetary policy regime, allow us to draw some important conclusions. First, in at least some of the four countries, after a large policy-induced rise in the short-term interest rate, lending and other interest rates rose, the exchange rate tended to appreciate, output tended to fall, and inflation declined. And second, the cross-country variation in transmission seems to depend sharply on the policy regime in place.

In later Parts of the book, we will exploit the empirical understanding gained in this Part I to address specific policy questions. For example, the calibrations of the models in Chapters 15 and 18 benefit from the close narrative analysis of Chapter 5. More generally, the case studies in Chapters 15–19 combine elements of a narrative approach with the calibration of small structural models. But first, what are the basic stylized facts we should have in mind when thinking about monetary policy in Africa?

REFERENCES

Abuka, C., Alinda, R. K., Minoiu, C., Peydro, J. L., and Presbitero, A. F. (2015). *Monetary Policy in a Developing Country: Loan Applications and Real Effects.* IMF Working Paper No. 15/270.

African Development Bank. (2013). *Situational Analysis of the Reliability of Economics Statistics in Africa: Special Focus on GDP Measurement.*

Bils, M. and Klenow, P. (2004). Some Evidence on the Importance of Sticky Prices. *Journal of Political Economy,* 112(5), 947–84.

Christiano, L., Eichenbaum, M., and Evans, M. (1999). Monetary Policy Shocks: What Have We Learned and to What End? In M. Woodford and J. Taylor (Eds.), *Handbook of Macroeconomics,* 1(A). North Holland: Elsevier.

Davoodi, H. R., Dixit, S., and Pinter, G. (2013). *Monetary Transmission Mechanism in the East African Community: An Empirical Investigation.* IMF Working Paper 13/39. Washington, DC: International Monetary Fund.

Gali, J. (2008). *Monetary Policy, Inflation and the Business Cycle.* Princeton University Press.

Ley, E. and Misch, F. (2014, January). Output data revisions in Low-Income Countries. Conference presentation at the IMF-DFID Conference on Macroeconomic Challenges Facing Low-Income Countries: New Perspectives, Washington, DC.

Li, G., O'Connell, S., Adam, C., Berg, A., and Montiel, P. (2016). *VAR meets DSGE: Uncovering the Monetary Transmission Mechanism in Low-Income Countries.* IMF WP/16/90. Washington, DC: International Monetary Fund.

Mishra, P. and Montiel, P. (2012). Monetary transmission in low-income countries: effectiveness and policy implications. *IMF Economic Review,* 60, 270–302.

Mishra, P., Montiel, P., and Spilimbergo, A. (2013). How Effective is Monetary Transmission in Developing Countries: A Survey of the Empirical Evidence. *Economic Systems,* 37(2), 187–216.

Nsabimana, A. and Ocran, M. K. (2015). Money demand stability and inflation prediction in the EAC countries: Burundi, Kenya, Rwanda, Tanzania, and Uganda. *Studies in Economics and Econometrics,* 39, 71–98.

Summers, L. H. (1991). The Scientific Illusion in Empirical Macroeconomics. *The Scandinavian Journal of Economics,* 93(2), 129–48.

4

Economic Fluctuations in Sub-Saharan Africa

Giovanni Melina and Rafael Portillo

1 INTRODUCTION

In this chapter we provide (i) an overview of some of the structural features of the economies of sub-Saharan Africa (SSA) and (ii) a systematic characterization of economic fluctuations in the region. For both sets of issues we compare the evidence for SSA with data from advanced, emerging, and other low-income countries. We believe such an approach helps place the discussion of SSA in the right context, and provides a first step toward the more structural analysis that is undertaken in subsequent chapters of this book. Unlike the rest of the book, however, the focus here is mainly on real, as opposed to monetary, factors.

In terms of economic structure, there are fundamental differences between the economies of rich and poor countries. These range from the share of agriculture in the economy, and the related weight of food expenditure in consumption, to the development of the financial system and access to international capital markets, and to the structure of production and the level of productivity and physical and human capital. These differences are even more pronounced in SSA relative to other low- and lower-middle-income countries.

Regarding economic fluctuations, we analyse the data for SSA by looking at the variance and comovement of key macro variables, previously filtered to remove longer-term fluctuations (trends). This type of analysis has a long-standing tradition in modern macro, starting with the pioneering work of Prescott (1986), and has been used extensively in the real business cycle theory and so to some extent in the New Keynesian literature. While the macroeconomic literature has produced some papers on stylized facts concerning business cycle regularities in some emerging market economies (EMs) (see Agénor et al., 2000; Ahmed and Loungani, 2000; Rand and Tarp, 2002, among others), to our knowledge there is no such systematic analysis for SSA, nor one that compares the features of macroeconomic fluctuations of this group of countries and the rest of the world. The purpose of this chapter is to fill this gap, though with the caveat that the poor quality of macroeconomic statistics in Africa may bias this analysis in possibly unknown ways.

Our findings can be summarized as follows. First, African economies stand out by their macroeconomic volatility, reflected in the volatility of output and other macro variables. Second, inflation and output tend to be negatively correlated in SSA. Third, unlike advanced economies and EMs, trade balances and current accounts are acyclical. Fourth, the volatility of consumption and investment relative to GDP is larger than in other countries. Fifth, the cyclicality of consumption and investment is smaller than in advanced economies and EMs. Sixth, there is little comovement between consumption and investment. Seventh, consumption and investment are strongly positively correlated with imports.

Our review of structural features and other stylized facts provide some clues as to the features that may be behind these findings. To start with, the greater volatility in SSA is indicative of large shocks, and equally important, of lack of mechanisms for dampening the effects of these shocks, such as greater economic diversification, financial sector development, or access to international capital markets. As to what those shocks may be, we see three main suspects: supply-side, policy, and external.

The importance of supply-side shocks can be inferred from the correlation of inflation and output and from the size and characteristics of the agricultural sector. Policy volatility can be inferred from the standard deviation of government consumption and government spending more generally. The possible role of external shocks can be inferred in part from the volatility of terms of trade and other balance of payments (BOP) shocks, though the correlation between the former and output is not strong, and perhaps also from the volatility of the real exchange rate. Relatedly, the acyclicality of the trade balance is consistent with the limited access to international capital markets mentioned above, which also lends support to the view that shocks to the balance of payments, mainly stemming from the current account side, are behind the comovement between consumption/investment and imports.

A notable feature for SSA is the lack of strong comovement between consumption, investment, and GDP. In this sense, it could be argued that SSA economies do not have a clear business cycle, i.e., a common factor driving the dynamics of key macro variables. The above-mentioned shocks could also help make sense of this finding if they affect specific sectors rather than the economy as a whole. In addition, the lack of strong comovement suggests that shocks coming from the financial sector play less of a role in these economies.[1]

Finally, our findings in this chapter have important implications for monetary policy, even if the latter is not the topic of this chapter. The real nature of shocks in the region points to the limits of monetary policy-based macro stabilization in SSA. As a corollary, our findings strengthen the need to focus monetary policy on the pursuit of price stability over the medium term. In addition, many of the structural features presented here need to be incorporated in the models used for monetary policy analysis, in order to make those models relevant for SSA. This is the approach pursued in Parts II and III of the book.

The remainder of the chapter is structured as follows. Section 2 presents the data. Section 3 provides an overview of SSA economies. Section 4 discusses the empirical methodology for measuring economic fluctuations. Section 5

---

[1] Christiano et al. (2014) argue that shocks to the financial sector are necessary to replicate business cycle features in advanced economies, a key element of which is comovement.

summarizes the empirical evidence. Section 6 discusses the results. Finally, Section 7 concludes.

2 DATA

We present summary statistics separately for SSA and for the rest of the world. As our comparison is meant to emphasize the role of economic development, we divide the latter group into three categories: high-income countries, HIC; upper-middle-income countries, UMIC; and lower-middle-income and low-income countries, LLMIC.[2] In addition, given that for many SSA countries, natural resources are—or are projected to become—a major source of national income, we distinguish between resource-abundant and non-resource-abundant economies, using the classification employed in IMF (2012).[3] For each statistic we present the median value, though in some cases we also present box plots to give a sense of the distribution within each group.

Details on data sources and country coverage are provided in Tables 4A.1 and 4A.2 (Appendix 4A). We mainly rely on the publicly available databases of the IMF (International Financial Statistics and World Economic Outlook), the OECD (National Accounts), and the World Bank (World Development Indicators). We focus on annual data covering the period 1960–2007, to avoid contaminating our general conclusions from the peculiarities of the Great Recession (though with some exceptions). In terms of country coverage, we exclude 'small states', given their unique economic characteristics (see IMF, 2014b). We also exclude countries with less than thirty years of uninterrupted data series. Data availability leads to the number of countries in each group reported in Table 4.1, with 109 countries in total. The SSA groups cover thirty-one countries, which is representative of the region (forty-five countries, excluding South Africa). We exclude the latter given the size of its economy, level of income, and EM status.

Table 4.1. Number of Countries Covered in Each Group

Sub-Saharan Africa	
Resource-abundant	13
Non-resource-abundant	18
Non-sub-Saharan Africa	
HIC	34
UMIC	24
LLMIC	20

[2] We follow the World Bank/IMF classification, which has four groups: low-income: GDP per capita of US$1,005 or less; lower-middle-income: US $1,006–$3,975; upper-middle-income: US$3, 976–US$12,275; and high-income: US$12,276 or more. The reason for combining lower-middle-income and low-income countries into a single group representative of poor countries is to have a sufficient number of countries with enough data availability in each group.

[3] A country is classified as resource-abundant if its resource revenue or resource exports are at least 20 per cent of total fiscal revenue or exports, respectively, in 2006–10.

3 AN OVERVIEW OF SSA ECONOMIES

An entire book would not suffice to document the many economic dimensions that set SSA countries apart.[4] Our overview is therefore highly selective, with an emphasis on the issues that matter for monetary policy.

3.1 Income and Growth

As seen in Table 4.2, the level of income per capita in the median SSA countries is well below high- and middle-income countries, and even below other LLMICs. Overall, there is little variation within SSA, with only two countries (Botswana and Namibia) having income levels that are comparable to those in the middle-income group. As is well known in the growth literature, such a large income gap reflects large differences in human and physical capital accumulation, and the level of total factor productivity (Hall and Jones, 1999).

A related observation is that these economies have failed to converge to their higher income peers. Table 4.3 reports the median annual real per-capita output growth (and inflation rates) for the five country groups. SSA economies have grown on average, at a lower rate than countries in the other groups and have therefore become relatively poorer. Even in the more recent 1995–2007 period, in which SSA economies performed much better than previously, growth was still lower than in the other groups (Table 4.3).

Lack of convergence notwithstanding, there is a growing consensus that economic prospects have improved markedly in the region over the last two decades, albeit with variations across countries. Growth has increased, lifting a significant share of the population out of poverty (McKay, 2013). Associated with higher growth there has been an increase in measures of political stability and democracy, improved governance and macroeconomic policies (as can be inferred from the improved inflation performance seen in Table 4.3 and discussed in more detail

Table 4.2. Income per Capita (Median Values)

Country groups	GDP per Capita	GNI per Capita
	US$	
Sub-Saharan Africa		
Res.-abt	577.41	575.82
Non-res.-abt	300.56	334.15
Non-sub-Saharan Africa		
HIC	19350.19	18401.56
UMIC	2867.01	2772.19
LLMIC	929.75	894.11

Note: Res.-abt and non-res.-abt refer to resource-abundant and non-resource-abundant countries, respectively.

Source: Authors' calculations based on OECD and World Bank data.

[4] A useful overview can be found in Monga and Lin (2015).

Table 4.3. Median Real Output Growth and Inflation Rates

Country groups	Real output (%)		Inflation—GDP Deflator (%)		Inflation—CPI (%)	
	Full sample	1995–2007	Full sample	1995–2007	Full sample	1995–2007
Sub-Saharan Africa						
Resource	0.57	1.58	7.23	8.41	6.82	6.13
Non-Resource	0.37	0.74	9.02	6.55	8.62	7.67
Non-sub-Saharan Africa						
HIC	2.58	2.15	5.48	2.78	5.13	2.19
UMIC	2.26	2.68	8.79	7.38	11.26	8.64
LLMIC	1.43	2.25	9.02	7.03	8.93	6.94

Source: Authors' calculations based on IMF, OECD, and World Bank data.

in Chapter 1), an improved business environment, and the widespread adoption of new technologies (Radelet, 2010). A benign external environment also played a role, for example through high commodity prices favouring resource-abundant countries. It is interesting to observe, however, that growth has continued in the very recent period, even as external financial conditions have tightened, though this time limited to non-resource-rich countries (IMF, 2016).

3.2 The Structure of SSA Economies: the Supply Side

An important feature that sets SSA countries apart is the sectoral structure of their economy. Table 4.4 shows the shares of agriculture, services, and industry for the median country in each group, over the entire sample period. SSA countries have a much larger (smaller) share of agriculture (services) than their HIC and UMIC peers. Non-resource-abundant countries in SSA also have lower industry shares than HIC, UMICs, and other LLMICs. This evidence is consistent with the 'structural transformation' view, which argues that poor countries, i.e., countries with lower overall productivity, allocate a large share of their factors of production to the agricultural sector to satisfy their basic subsistence needs. As productivity grows, demand for non-subsistence goods and services increases, and resources shift out of agriculture and into other sectors.[5]

The share of employment allocated to agriculture is even larger than the share of agriculture in GDP, which is indicative of low levels of productivity and capital in that sector (see Mcmillan and Harttgen, 2015; Collier and Dercon, 2014, among others). One implication for monetary policy is that supply-side shocks stemming from the agricultural sector are the dominant source of inflation volatility, while also playing an important role in output volatility. In addition, it can be argued that the degree of economy-wide price stickiness is lower in SSA, as prices of agricultural products adjust rapidly to changes in supply and demand.

---

[5] See Kongsamut et al. (2001) for a model-based exposition of the structural transformation hypothesis.

Table 4.4. GDP by Sectors (Median Values)

Country groups	Agriculture	Industry	Service	Total natural resources rents
			% of GDP	
Sub-Saharan Africa				
Res.-abt	30.27	28.89	43.04	14.37
Non-res.-abt	36.82	18.83	43.02	7.95
Non-sub-Saharan Africa				
HIC	2.90	30.00	67.20	0.66
UMIC	10.65	32.29	54.32	4.75
LLMIC	23.61	29.18	47.58	2.45

Note: Res.-abt and non-res.-abt refer to resource-abundant and non-resource-abundant countries, respectively.

Source: Authors' calculations based on OECD and World Bank data.

The mechanisms and the evidence are discussed extensively in Chapter 11; some of the stylized facts presented below are supportive of this view.

Finally, consistent with our classification, resource-abundant countries in SSA have a higher share of natural resource rents in per cent of GDP, though non-resource-rich SSA countries also receive sizable rents from that sector. The rent variable is defined as earnings from producing natural resources minus their cost of production. A related point is that exports from SSA countries consist mainly of commodities (either agricultural or mining products), with manufacturing playing a smaller role (IMF, 2015). It follows that these rents, which are highly sensitive to international commodity prices, are an important source of volatility in these economies.

3.3 The Structure of SSA Economies: the Demand Side

Table 4.5 shows the components of aggregate demand as percentages of GDP. SSA countries are similar to other low-income countries, and differ from the rest, in terms of the relatively higher share of private consumption and the lower shares of government consumption and investment. These differences appear striking at first, as neo-classical growth theory would suggest higher investment shares in poorer countries, all else equal. One possible rationalization is again structural transformation: proximity to subsistence limits the ability to set resources aside for the future, and can result in a higher consumption share at the expense of lower investment (Kraay and Raddatz, 2007). Similarly, the lower share of government consumption can be explained by the lower demand for 'public' goods in an environment of relative near-subsistence (Mourmouras and Rangazas, 2008).

With regards to trade, Table 4.5 shows that both groups of SSA countries have sizable trade deficits on average, in the order of 7 per cent of GDP. This differs markedly from high- and middle-income countries, which feature small trade surpluses, but coincides with the experience of other low-income countries. These deficits are widespread across SSA countries and have continued in the more recent period, as can be seen in the box plots in Figure 4.1. As will be shown below, this can be explained by the reliance on remittances and foreign aid in these

Table 4.5. Demand Components in Per cent of GDP (Median Values)

Country groups	Private consumption	Government consumption	Investment	Exports	Imports
			% of GDP		
Sub-Saharan Africa					
Resource-abundant	70.21	11.84	18.71	23.75	32.11
Non-resource-abundant	79.90	14.75	15.40	23.10	30.94
Non-sub-Saharan Africa					
HIC	57.00	18.17	22.57	30.10	29.48
UMIC	66.01	13.73	22.80	27.07	26.66
LLMIC	72.43	11.16	21.65	23.67	29.08

Source: Authors' calculations based on OECD and World Bank data.

countries. Given the capacity to fund imports through non-debt-creating flows (or with debt set in concessional terms), it is not surprising that SSA countries also feature lower export shares. Unlike trade deficits, SSA countries vary considerably when looking at measures of openness, though without a clear pattern, as shown in Figure 4.1.

3.4 Financial Sector Development

Table 4.6 shows various indicators of financial sector development. Despite considerable improvement over the last two decades, credit to the private sector in per cent of GDP—the most commonly used measure of financial sector development—is about 30 percentage points below the median value for UMICs, and about 20 per cent lower than other LLMICs. The region also lags in two measures of access: ATMs and bank branches per 1000 adults. Lack of access to finance is pervasive for African households and firms; for example only 20 per cent of firms have access to a bank loan or a line of credit, compared with 95 per cent in advanced countries and 58 per cent in other developing countries (Dabla-Norris et al., 2015).

Economists have long argued that financial development is good for growth (Levine, 2005), though the global financial crisis has raised the question of whether there can be too much finance (Berkes et al., 2015). Shallow financial markets also have implications for macroeconomic volatility. Wang et al. (2016) argue that better access to credit markets implies that non-financial aggregate shocks have less impact on individual firms' investment decisions, with the latter being driven instead by idiosyncratic prospects. Similarly, households are also able to smooth their consumption if they have access to financial markets, the lack of which will make consumption more volatile. A related point is that incipient financial development also complicates the task of monetary policymakers by reducing the aggregate sensitivity to interest rate movements.

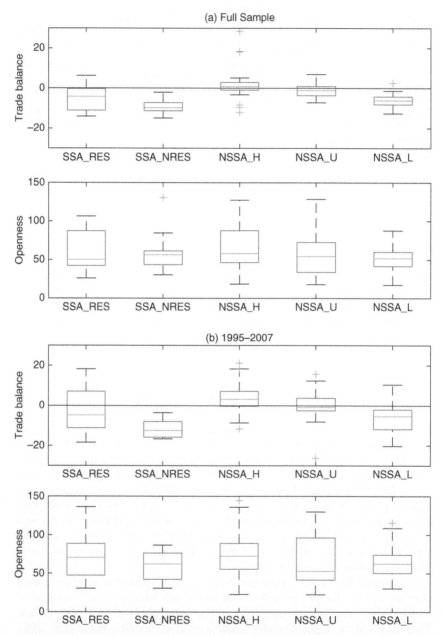

Figure 4.1. Box Plots of the Trade Balance and Openness to International Trade (% of GDP), (a) Full Sample; (b) 1995–2007

Notes: The trade balance is computed as exports/GDP minus imports/GDP. Openness is computed as exports/GDP plus imports/GDP. RES and NRES refer to resource-abundant and non-resource-abundant, respectively. H, U, and L refer to HIC, UMIC, and LLMIC, respectively.

Source: Authors' calculations based on IMF, OECD, and World Bank data.

Table 4.6. Financial Sector Development (Median Values)

Country groups	Domestic credit to private sector	ATMs	Commercial bank branches
	% of GDP	Per 1 Million Adults	
Sub-Saharan Africa			
Res.-abt	18.08	6.86	4.68
Non-res.-abt	19.69	5.52	4.61
Non-sub-Saharan Africa			
HIC	110.96	74.29	20.14
UMIC	51.96	54.22	14.57
LLMIC	42.87	19.71	12.16

Note: Res.-abt and non-res.-abt refer to resource-abundant and non-resource-abundant countries, respectively.

Source: Authors' calculations based on OECD and World Bank data.

Table 4.7. Balance of Payment Indicators (Median Values)

Country groups	CA balance	Trade balance	Personal remittances	FDI net inflows	Net ODA	Volatility of TOT
	% of GDP					SD
Sub-Saharan Africa						
Res.-abt	−4.91	−4.31	0.79	2.61	8.64	38.59
Non-res.-abt	−6.12	−11.71	1.22	2.01	10.93	59.72
Non-sub-Saharan Africa						
HIC	0.56	0.94	0.34	1.91	0.30	19.15
UMIC	−1.86	−0.35	1.14	2.09	0.60	21.96
LLMIC	−2.01	−6.33	5.49	1.08	4.05	45.36

Source: Authors' calculations based on OECD and World Bank data.

3.5 The Balance of Payments, Capital Account Openness, and External Shocks

Table 4.7 shows selected components of the balance of payments across the five groups. Both SSA groups display a much larger share of aid flows (official development assistance or ODA) than HICs, UMICs, and even other LLMICs. Remittance flows appear relatively small, but this is a byproduct of using the entire sample period. Efforts to correctly measure remittance flows are more recent; focusing on the post-1995 period reveals much higher remittance shares in SSA, comparable to other LLMICs. The amount of FDI received by SSA countries is similar to other groups, with resource-rich countries receiving a slightly larger share. FDI in the former group has also been on the rise in recent years, reflecting in part greater involvement of Chinese companies in mining projects in Africa. The evidence suggests, however, that SSA countries have not been succesful at attracting large FDI flows despite their low capital base (and therefore high potential returns to investment).

We do not show portfolio and other investment flows for the sake of brevity. Our choice also reflects the limited integration in international capital markets in some

Table 4.8. De Jure Capital Account Openness (Median Values)

Country groups	Capital account overall restrictions index
Sub-Saharan Africa	
Res.-abt	0.23
Non-res.-abt	0.70
Non-sub-Saharan Africa	
HIC	0.09
UMIC	0.54
LLMIC	0.61

Note: Res.-abt and non-res.-abt refer to resource-abundant and non-resource-abundant countries, respectively.

Source: Authors' calculations based on dataset used in Fernandez et al., 2016.

SSA countries, due in part to restrictions on capital account transactions. Table 4.8 shows the index of de jure capital account openness compiled by Schindler (2009) and extended in Fernandez et al. (2016). The index ranges from zero to one, with a higher value indicating greater restrictions. Non-resource-abundant countries in SSA have the highest degree of capital account restrictions, though other LLMICs are not too far behind. It is interesting to note that resource-abundant countries have the second lowest degree of de jure restrictions, perhaps reflecting efforts to attract external funding for mining projects.

The cross-country comparisons mask an increase in access to international capital markets in some SSA countries in recent years (IMF, 2014a). As of 2014, ten countries other than South Africa had issued sovereign bonds in international jurisdictions. In some cases the sovereign bond has facilitated additional bond issuances by the corporate sector, for example in Nigeria. The volume of bonds outstanding is tiny, however (0.02 per cent of the total stock), which points to limited appetite by foreign investors for SSA financial assets.

Finally, SSA countries also feature low levels of sovereign external assets and liabilities, in this case external debt and international reserves in per cent of GDP (see Table 4.9 for 2015 numbers). The lower level of debt reflects, inter alia, the considerable debt relief received by many countries in the context of the HIPC/MDRI initiative, efforts to limit excessive debt accumulation in IMF-supported programmes, and the limited appetite for LIC debt mentioned above. Differences in the level of reserves are also consistent with different motives for reserve accumulation: self-insurance against large capital flow reversals in the case of UMICs, and EMs more generally, versus shocks to the current account in the case of SSA and LLMICs.

This brief overview of the BOP helps identify what are likely to be the main sources of external shocks in SSA, which fall largely on the current account side. The commodity intensity of exports, and the volatility of international commodity prices, makes SSA countries highly vulnerable to exogenous changes in the terms of trade. This is confirmed in Table 4.7, which shows the volatility of the commodities terms of trade measure created by Spatafora and Tytell (2009) (HP-filtered, see discussion below).[6] Both groups of SSA countries face terms of

---

[6] This terms of trade index uses price data on 46 commodities; for each country it weighs price fluctuations by the share of commodity exports and imports in GDP.

Table 4.9. Sovereign Assets and Liabilities (Median Values)

Country groups	Total reserves	External debt stocks
	% of GDP	
Sub-Saharan Africa		
Res.-abt	13.2	25.9
Non-res.-abt	11.9	32.8
Non-sub-Saharan Africa		
HIC	11.7	131.5
UMIC	20.1	38.6
LLMIC	18.1	30.7

Source: Authors' calculations based on OECD and World Bank data.

trade that are more volatile than in HICs and UMICs. Aid flows are also quite volatile and thus constitute an additional source of external shocks (Bulir and Hamann, 2008). Remittances on the other hand seem to play a countercyclical, and hence volatility-reducing, role (Chami et al., 2008). Given limited access to international capital markets, shocks to capital flows are not as relevant in SSA as in EMs, although these have played a role in some countries more recently, as discussed for example in Chapters 5 and 17. At the same time, limited integration also reduces the ability of residents to smooth the effects of domestic and external shocks, so that the overall effect on volatility is somewhat unclear.

4 ASSESSING THE STYLIZED FACTS OF ECONOMIC FLUCTUATIONS: METHODOLOGICAL ISSUES

Producing statistics on the fluctuations of non-stationary macroeconomic variables requires the removal of trends. In the business cycle literature on both advanced economies and EMs there is no agreement on which is the most appropriate detrending methodology. A common procedure is the use of statistical filters, though even then there is no consensus on which filter to use, or on the choice of parameters for any given filter (more on this below). Yet another approach is to simply focus on growth rates and their fluctuations (e.g., Pritchett, 2000). The choice of technique is often part of a broader debate on whether economic fluctuations are the results of shocks to economic trends (or growth rates) (see Pritchett, 2000; Aguiar and Gopinath, 2007, among others), or whether they reflect temporary deviations around a more-or-less deterministic path (see Garcia-Cicco et al., 2010, among many others).

This methodological uncertainty applies to SSA countries. We do not take a stand on this debate. Instead, we search for stylized facts that are robust to the statistical procedure. Though we do not always show the results for the sake of brevity, we employ three popular detrending techniques: (i) the HP filter of Hodrick and Prescott (1997) with the conventional smoothing parameter $\lambda = 100$ for annual data; (ii) the Band-Pass (BP) filter recommended by Christiano and Fitzgerald (2003) identifying cyclical components with periods between two and

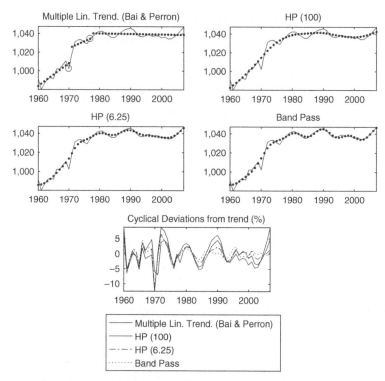

Figure 4.2. Kenya's Log-Real-Per-Capita GDP: Smooth and Piecewise Linear Trends (HP and Band Pass refer to the Hodrick-Prescott and the Band-Pass filters, respectively; the circles represent trend break dates identified by the Bai and Perron (2003) test)

Source: Authors' calculations based on World Bank data.

eight years; and finally (iii) the first-difference (FD) filter. In addition, in our applications, it turns out that smooth filters such as the HP and BP produce cyclical deviations with a strong comovement with deviations resulting from an application of piecewise linear trends exploiting break dates identified by a popular statistical test such as that of Bai and Perron (2003) (see, e.g. the case of Kenya's log-real-per-capita GDP in Figure 4.2).[7]

5 BUSINESS CYCLE DYNAMICS

5.1 Output Volatility

Table 4.10 reports standard deviations and autocorrelation coefficients of detrended log-real-per-capita GDP. As regards output volatility, results change

[7] Note that, for robustness, in Figure 4.2 we report also HP-filtered data with the correction more recently made by Ravn and Uhlig (2002), who suggest a $\lambda = 6.25$.

Table 4.10. Real Output—Median Volatility and Persistence

Country groups	Real output			
	Standard deviation (%)		Autocorrelation	
	Full sample	1995–2007	Full sample	1995–2007
Sub-Saharan Africa				
Resource-abundant				
HP	5.50	3.35	0.55	0.51
BP	2.94	1.82	−0.08	−0.07
FD	5.74	3.09	0.29	0.10
Non-resource-abundant				
HP	4.00	3.53	0.35	0.51
BP	2.91	2.04	−0.04	0.04
FD	4.93	4.28	−0.06	0.30
Non-sub-Saharan Africa				
High-income				
HP	2.59	1.65	0.60	0.63
BP	1.44	0.83	0.12	0.18
FD	2.72	1.35	0.32	0.29
Upper-middle income				
HP	4.59	3.34	0.60	0.67
BP	2.63	1.94	0.12	0.19
FD	4.59	2.96	0.29	0.29
Low and lower-middle income				
HP ($\lambda=100$)	3.36	2.19	0.62	0.64
BP	1.98	1.21	0.10	0.10
FD	3.67	2.12	0.32	0.25

Note: HP and BP refers to the cyclical components of real-per-capita output using the Hodrick-Prescott and the Band-Pass filters, respectively; FD refers to first differences of the logs of real-per-capita output and the price levels.

Source: Authors' calculations based on IMF, OECD, and World Bank data.

considerably across filters but the qualitative conclusions remain unaltered. In SSA, both the cyclical components of real GDP (HP and BP) and its rate of growth are more volatile than in the other country groups. The difference becomes even sharper when looking at resource-abundant countries: in this group, output is two times more volatile than in advanced economies and about 1.5 times more volatile than in non-SSA LLMIC. Across the board, volatility has decreased over the more recent sample (1995–2007), including in SSA, but the latter region still displays more volatility than the rest. The serial correlation of output varies considerably across filters but is generally weaker in SSA.

5.2 Volatility and Cyclicality of GDP Components

Getting more granular, in the spirit of the seminal work by Stock and Watson (1999) on the US, we compute the standard deviations of key macroeconomic variables relative to that of real output, and the dynamic correlations of real output with leads and lags of the same variables. This exercise allows us to assess how volatile macroeconomic aggregates are relative to GDP, whether they lead, lag or move approximately coincidentally with aggregate cycle, and perhaps most importantly whether there are significant differences across country groups. Results are reported in Tables 4.11 and 4.12.

SSA has the highest median relative volatility of private consumption: up to 1.5 times more volatile than output in resource-abundant SSA, even if UMICs and other LLMICs also have consumption to output volatility ratios greater than one. Moreover, this aspect of economic fluctuations in SSA has not abated in the more recent period. A similar comparison emerges when looking at investment. Though it is well known that the latter variable is more volatile than GDP, SSA stands out again by the magnitude of its investment fluctuations. Both consumption and investment are procyclical everywhere but the degree of procyclicality is much lower in SSA. We return to this weaker comovement below.

Government consumption is also more volatile in SSA than in HICs and UMICs, though comparable to other LLMICs. The higher policy volatility implied by this comparison is corroborated in Table 4.12, which shows the volatility of government spending and revenues. In the case of resource-rich countries, fiscal policy has also become more volatile in the recent period. Government consumption (spending) displays relatively weak cyclicality everywhere, with the exception of UMICs, while government revenues are procyclical everywhere (less so in resource-rich African countries).

The picture for exports and imports is more mixed. Real exports in resource-rich SSA countries are less volatile and more procyclical than in the other groups. This is consistent with: (i) mining production being less responsive to short-term developments and determined instead by longer-term factors, and (ii) lower degree of diversification in these economies. Exports in non-resource-rich SSA are volatile and mildly procyclical, comparable in this regard to other LLMICs. Imports are as volatile in SSA as elsewhere, though the degree of cyclicality is somewhat less than in HICs and UMICs. The trade balance is only slightly more volatile in SSA, though the latter stands out by the degree of trade acyclicality compared with the countercylical balances in HICs and UMICs. The differences in this correlation between SSA and the rest are quite stark, see Figure 4.3. A similar comparison emerges for the current account (see Table 4.12).

The volatility of SSA economies extends to their real effective exchange rates, as can be seen in Table 4.12. This is consistent with the greater volatility in the terms of trade, which is reproduced in the same table, this time relative to GDP volatility. Both the real effective exchange rate and the terms of trade are approximately acyclical across all groups, although the latter variable has been somewhat more procyclical in resource-rich countries in the more recent period.

Finally, we compute the correlation with a measure of global output across all groups (see Table 4.12). A striking finding is that SSA economies are much less synchronized with global output, with the lack of comovement persisting in the more recent period. We interpret this finding as reflecting a more limited global integration of SSA economies.

Table 4.11. Standard Deviations of Key Macroeconomic Variables relative to that of Real Output and Correlations of Real Output with Leads and Lags of the Same Variables (Detrending Method: HP100)

Variable	Resource SD	Resource corr $i=-1$	Resource corr $i=0$	Resource corr $i=1$	Non-Resource SD	Non-Resource corr $i=-1$	Non-Resource corr $i=0$	Non-Resource corr $i=1$	HIC SD	HIC corr $i=-1$	HIC corr $i=0$	HIC corr $i=1$	UMIC SD	UMIC corr $i=-1$	UMIC corr $i=0$	UMIC corr $i=1$	LLMIC SD	LLMIC corr $i=-1$	LLMIC corr $i=0$	LLMIC corr $i=1$
	Sub-Saharan Africa								Non-sub-Saharan Africa											
Private consumption	1.24	0.41	0.47	0.18	1.48	0.32	0.67	0.19	1.02	0.47	0.70	0.40	1.17	0.38	0.74	0.44	1.10	0.22	0.64	0.20
	1.62	*0.30*	*0.39*	*0.17*	*1.54*	*0.40*	*0.54*	*0.31*	*1.10*	*0.54*	*0.70*	*0.42*	*1.27*	*0.39*	*0.75*	*0.42*	*1.37*	*0.45*	*0.59*	*0.27*
Government consumption	2.62	0.18	0.22	0.11	3.35	0.19	0.34	0.08	1.40	0.28	0.21	-0.10	1.97	0.45	0.47	0.22	2.98	0.23	0.43	0.21
	4.65	*0.32*	*0.20*	*-0.23*	*3.26*	*0.25*	*0.21*	*0.05*	*1.32*	*0.32*	*0.18*	*-0.07*	*1.84*	*0.64*	*0.51*	*0.37*	*3.30*	*0.05*	*0.21*	*0.10*
Investment	4.41	0.21	0.34	0.25	5.28	0.09	0.33	0.28	3.90	0.43	0.80	0.45	3.56	0.39	0.74	0.41	4.75	0.32	0.64	0.43
	4.87	*-0.09*	*0.03*	*0.19*	*6.31*	*0.06*	*0.39*	*0.27*	*3.30*	*0.45*	*0.85*	*0.57*	*3.49*	*0.48*	*0.79*	*0.54*	*4.84*	*0.35*	*0.61*	*0.39*
Exports	2.58	0.16	0.52	0.43	3.63	0.02	0.34	0.26	2.87	0.14	0.41	0.19	3.09	0.17	0.31	0.19	3.80	0.22	0.31	0.29
	3.81	*-0.03*	*0.45*	*0.15*	*4.60*	*0.03*	*0.19*	*0.27*	*3.45*	*0.20*	*0.62*	*0.54*	*3.19*	*0.18*	*0.12*	*0.25*	*3.22*	*0.18*	*0.46*	*0.31*
Imports	3.01	0.18	0.34	0.24	3.15	0.15	0.37	0.29	3.23	0.29	0.51	0.27	3.02	0.36	0.55	0.38	3.80	0.21	0.37	0.33
	4.19	*0.17*	*0.24*	*0.27*	*4.01*	*0.15*	*0.31*	*0.35*	*3.70*	*0.41*	*0.69*	*0.45*	*2.73*	*0.33*	*0.70*	*0.52*	*4.03*	*0.34*	*0.60*	*0.29*
Trade balance	0.89	0.01	0.02	0.08	0.81	-0.06	-0.05	0.02	0.64	-0.22	-0.34	-0.05	0.74	-0.21	-0.35	-0.12	0.81	-0.06	-0.09	-0.08
	1.57	*0.00*	*0.06*	*-0.13*	*0.85*	*-0.10*	*-0.16*	*-0.11*	*0.70*	*-0.13*	*-0.20*	*-0.05*	*0.77*	*-0.38*	*-0.55*	*-0.22*	*0.98*	*-0.34*	*-0.24*	*-0.13*

Notes: For each variable, the cross-sectional median within the country group is reported; the first line refers to the full sample, while the second line (in italic) refers to the more recent subsample (1995–2007). SD refers to the standard deviation of each macroeconomic variable relative to that of real output, while corr (y_t, x_{t+i}) denotes the correlation between real output (y_t) and leads and lags of each variable x_{t+i}.

Source: Authors' calculations based on IMF, OECD, and World Bank data.

Table 4.12. Standard Deviations of Key Macroeconomic Variables relative to that of Real Output and Correlations of Real Output with Leads and Lags of the Same Variables (Detrending Method: HP100)

	Sub-Saharan Africa								Non-sub-Saharan Africa											
	Resource				Non-Resource				HIC				UMIC				LLMIC			
		corr (y_t, x_{t+i})				corr (y_t, x_{t+i})				corr (y_t, x_{t+i})				corr (y_t, x_{t+i})				corr (y_t, x_{t+i})		
	SD	$i=-1$	$i=0$	$i=1$	SD	$i=-1$	$i=0$	$i=1$	SD	$i=-1$	$i=0$	$i=1$	SD	$i=-1$	$i=0$	$i=1$	SD	$i=-1$	$i=0$	$i=1$
Total govt. expenditures	3.58	0.15	0.24	0.01	3.51	0.23	0.32	0.10	2.49	0.12	−0.04	−0.04	2.44	0.24	0.51	0.27	3.21	0.31	0.29	0.21
	4.25	*−0.01*	*0.00*	*−0.05*	*3.28*	*−0.09*	*0.27*	*−0.05*	*1.69*	*0.16*	*−0.03*	*−0.15*	*2.32*	*0.32*	*0.55*	*0.30*	*3.47*	*0.42*	*0.48*	*0.14*
Total govt. revenues	3.03	0.19	0.35	0.18	4.00	0.23	0.58	0.17	2.60	0.35	0.42	0.22	—	0.36	0.57	0.42	3.48	0.20	0.38	0.35
	3.51	—	—	—	*4.42*	—	—	—	*2.13*	—	—	—	*2.13*	—	—	—	—	—	—	—
Current account balance	0.74	0.19	0.23	0.05	1.04	0.18	0.50	0.05	2.29	0.34	0.64	0.45	2.19	0.37	0.56	0.46	3.71	0.33	0.43	0.28
	1.21	*−0.11*	*−0.11*	*0.01*	*0.84*	*−0.09*	*−0.09*	*0.01*	*0.67*	*−0.29*	*−0.33*	*−0.09*	*0.81*	*−0.39*	*−0.44*	*−0.13*	*0.92*	*−0.09*	*−0.14*	*−0.13*
Real eff. exchange rate	3.20	−0.03	0.01	−0.06	3.24	−0.11	−0.20	−0.03	2.36	−0.23	−0.21	−0.20	0.73	−0.38	−0.61	−0.39	1.02	−0.26	−0.30	−0.02
	2.32	*0.11*	*0.05*	*−0.16*	*2.79*	*0.17*	*−0.08*	*−0.18*	*2.39*	*0.11*	*0.05*	*−0.19*	*2.95*	*0.25*	*0.28*	*0.21*	*3.34*	*0.15*	*0.13*	*−0.04*
Terms of trade	5.42	0.23	0.24	−0.09	7.91	0.10	0.15	0.01	5.69	−0.31	−0.43	−0.40	2.35	0.26	0.15	0.11	2.84	0.33	0.25	0.22
	6.36	*0.01*	*0.11*	*0.19*	*9.03*	*−0.07*	*−0.05*	*−0.03*	*5.74*	*−0.06*	*−0.01*	*0.12*	*4.23*	*0.07*	*0.04*	*0.01*	*5.57*	*0.08*	*0.00*	*−0.01*
Global output	0.22	0.14	0.19	0.16	0.30	0.12	0.09	0.18	0.47	0.16	0.48	0.37	0.28	0.02	0.11	0.01	0.35	0.17	0.07	−0.03
	0.24	*0.23*	*0.21*	*0.14*	*0.24*	*0.24*	*0.26*	*0.17*	*0.48*	*0.06*	*0.41*	*0.39*	*0.27*	*0.34*	*0.46*	*0.09*	*0.36*	*−0.01*	*0.40*	*0.18*

Notes: For each variable, the cross-sectional median within the country group is reported; the first line refers to the full sample, while the second line (in italic) refers to the more recent subsample (1995–2007). SD refers to the standard deviation of each macroeconomic variable relative to that of real output, while *corr* (y_t, x_{t+i}) denotes the correlation between real output (y_t) and leads and lags of each variable x_{t+i}.

Source: Authors' calculations based on IMF, OECD, and World Bank data.

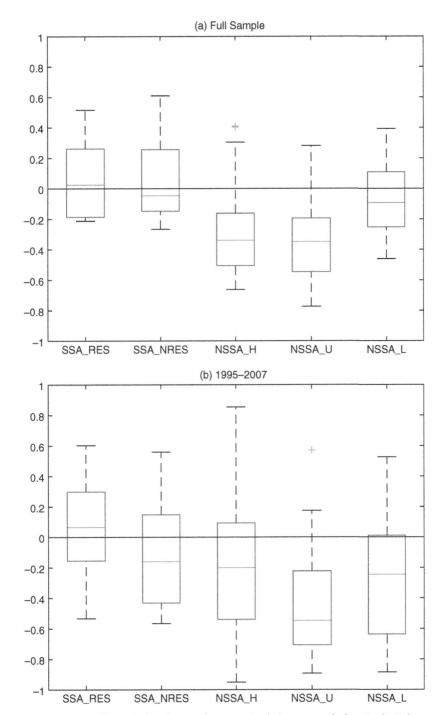

Figure 4.3. Box Plots of Correlations between Real Output and the Trade Balance. Detrending Method: HP(100), (a) Full Sample; (b) 1995–2007

The trade balance is computed as exports/GDP minus imports/GDP. RES and NRES refer to resource-abundant and non-resource-abundant, respectively. H, U, and L refer to HIC, UMIC, and LLMIC, respectively.

Source: Authors' calculations based on IMF, OECD, and World Bank data.

Table 4.13. Correlations of Key Macroeconomic Variables (Detrending Method: HP100)

	Private Cons	Investment	Government Cons	Exports	Imports	Current Account
			Sub-Saharan Africa: Resource			
Private Cons	1					
Investment	0.11	1				
Government Cons	−0.07	0.11	1			
Exports	0.03	0.26	−0.05	1		
Imports	0.49	0.66	0.03	0.48	1	
Current Account	−0.38	−0.41	−0.20	0.27	−0.42	1
			Sub-Saharan Africa: Non-Resource			
Private Cons	1					
Investment	−0.16	1				
Government Cons	0.1	0.42	1			
Exports	−0.09	0.31	0.24	1		
Imports	0.36	0.63	0.18	0.56	1	
Current Account	−0.22	−0.51	−0.31	0.16	−0.27	1
			Non-sub-Saharan Africa: HIC			
Private Cons	1					
Investment	0.62	1				
Government Cons	0.22	0.06	1			
Exports	0.04	0.04	−0.25	1		
Imports	0.49	0.57	0.08	0.64	1	
Current Account	−0.57	−0.46	−0.35	0.27	−0.45	1
			Non-sub-Saharan Africa: UMIC			
Private Cons	1					
Investment	0.31	1				
Government Cons	0.18	0.36	1			
Exports	−0.2	0.05	−0.24	1		
Imports	0.42	0.80	0.22	0.61	1	
Current Account	−0.53	−0.66	−0.41	0.33	−0.57	1
			Non-sub-Saharan Africa: LLMIC			
Private Cons	1					
Investment	0.18	1				
Government Cons	0.04	0.28	1			
Exports	−0.00	0.23	−0.01	1		
Imports	0.50	0.63	0.05	0.64	1	
Current Account	−0.33	−0.57	−0.24	0.01	−0.48	1

Notes: For each variable, the cross-sectional median within the country group is reported

Source: Authors' calculations based on IMF, OECD, and World Bank data.

5.3 Comovement Across GDP Components

We now study the degree of correlation across GDP components (see Table 4.13). These correlation statistics complement the analysis of cyclicality; they can reveal whether fluctuations are driven by a common factor or, on the contrary, whether they are driven by component-specific shocks.

Unlike HICs and MICs, SSA countries stand out by the lack of comovement between consumption and investment. This comovement is typically considered one of the defining characteristics of business cycles, at least in advanced economies; its absence in the case of SSA is puzzling. As in other regions, both consumption and investment are positively (negatively) correlated with imports (the current account). Finally, the correlation between private and government consumption is generally weaker in SSA; while the correlation between investment and government consumption is weak in resource-rich SSA and strong in non-resource-rich.

5.4 Inflation and its Relation with Output Fluctuations

We turn next to inflation. Table 4.14 includes two inflation measures across our five groups: inflation based on variations in the consumer price index and in the GDP deflator. Overall, inflation in SSA countries is more volatile than in their peers. GDP deflator-based inflation is especially volatile, consistent with the volatile terms of trade discussed earlier.[8] Inflation persistence (measured by the autocorrelation of the variable) is highest in HIC and smaller anywhere else; it falls as we move from the richest to the poorest group, and it is smallest in non-resource-abundant SSA economies. As was the case for output, inflation volatility has declined across the board in the more recent subsample.

But how does inflation relate with output fluctuations? The answer to this question depends heavily on the income group. In Figure 4.4, we report box-plots of correlations between the cyclical deviations of output and inflation. An interesting pattern that stands out from the figure is that while output correlates positively with inflation in HIC, the correlation falls—and turns negative—as we move to poorer country groups. In particular, in virtually all SSA countries this correlation is systematically negative. Although such a finding does not imply that aggregate demand shocks are not at play in SSA or LLMIC, it may be an indication of a dominance of aggregate supply shocks.[9]

---

[8] The difference between the GDP deflator and the consumer price index partly reflects movements in (some of the components of) the terms of trade.
[9] This fact is also explored extensively in Chapter 11.

Table 4.14. Inflation—Median Volatility and Persistence

Country groups	Inflation—GDP Deflator				Inflation—CPI			
	Standard deviation (%)		Autocorrelation		Standard deviation (%)		Autocorrelation	
	Full sample	1995–2007	Full sample	1995–2007	Full sample	1995–2007	Full sample	1995–2007
Sub-Saharan Africa								
Resource-abundant								
HP	8.14	6.14	0.03	0.04	5.94	3.14	0.14	−0.01
BP	7.05	5.03	−0.21	0.00	5.12	3.01	−0.16	0.00
FD	9.33	6.38	0.26	0.12	7.15	3.52	0.48	0.14
Non-resource-abundant								
HP	7.73	7.81	0.01	−0.13	6.83	4.80	0.08	0.16
BP	7.11	6.45	−0.22	−0.26	5.77	4.57	−0.18	−0.02
FD	9.42	7.75	0.35	−0.01	8.54	6.13	0.32	0.27
Non-sub-Saharan Africa								
High-income								
HP	2.43	1.07	0.31	0.19	2.25	0.82	0.46	0.36
BP	1.99	1.08	−0.03	0.06	1.54	0.68	0.11	0.23
FD	4.50	1.45	0.79	0.40	4.01	0.86	0.84	0.40
Upper-middle-income								
HP	6.63	4.05	0.05	0.15	5.24	3.78	0.33	0.42
BP	6.00	4.25	−0.11	0.08	3.52	2.55	0.06	0.12
FD	9.72	6.04	0.41	0.28	8.48	5.62	0.65	0.65
Low and lower-middle-income								
HP	5.33	4.33	0.06	0.05	4.91	3.13	0.22	0.14
BP	4.50	4.26	−0.15	−0.21	4.30	2.49	−0.01	−0.03
FD	6.57	3.62	0.42	0.17	7.56	3.43	0.59	0.36

Note: HP and BP refers to the cyclical components of the GDP-deflator and CPI inflation rate using the Hodrick-Prescott and the Band-Pass filters, respectively; FD refers to first differences of the logs of the price levels, i.e. the inflation rate itself.

Source: Authors' calculations based on IMF, OECD, and World Bank data.

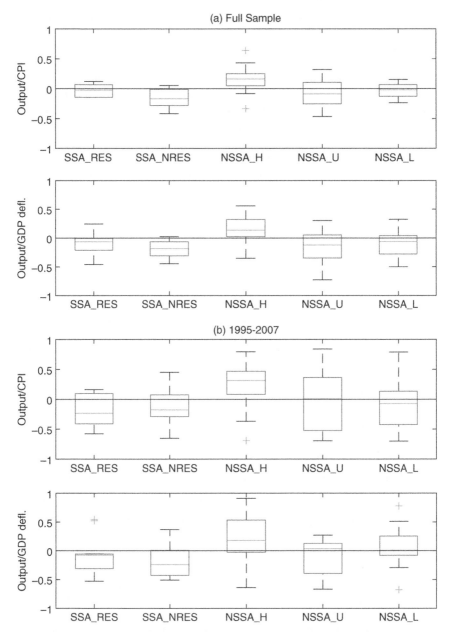

Figure 4.4. Box Plots of Correlations between Real Output and Inflation Rate (CPI and GDP deflator based). Detrending Method: HP(100), (a) Full Sample; (b) 1995–2007

Notes: RES and NRES refer to resource-abundant and non-resource-abundant, respectively. H, U, and L refer to HIC, UMIC, and LLMIC, respectively.

Source: Authors' calculations based on OECD and World Bank data.

5.5 Is Volatility Related to Growth and Inflation Performances?

We conclude our data comparison by returning to Table 4.3, which also reports the inflation rates for the median country in the five country groups. SSA countries have experienced inflation rates that are comparable in magnitude to UMICs and other LLMICs in the rest of the world. While in the rest of the world, inflation has dropped significantly in the recent subsample, in SSA the drop was more modest. In the case of resource-rich countries, deflator-based inflation increased during the more recent sample, though this is mainly a reflection of large improvements in the terms of trade in those countries. The big picture from these statistics is that the significant drop in output and inflation volatility observed in SSA and poorer economies has gone in tandem with improved output growth and inflation performances.

6 DISCUSSION

We can summarize the above evidence as follows:

- African economies stand out by their macroeconomic volatility, which is reflected in the volatility of output and other macro variables.
- Inflation and output tend to be negatively correlated in SSA countries.
- Unlike advanced economies and EMs, trade balances and current accounts are acyclical in SSA.
- The volatility of consumption and investment relative to GDP is larger than in other countries.
- The cyclicality of consumption and investment is smaller than in advanced economies and EMs.
- There is little comovement between consumption and investment.
- Consumption and investment are strongly positively correlated with imports.

In this section we provide a tentative interpretation of the above evidence, drawing in part on the recent academic literature on business cycles.

The greater volatility in SSA is indicative of large shocks, and of lack of mechanisms for dampening the effects of these shocks. Two mechanisms come to mind: economic diversification or financial sector development. At the same time, the macroeconomic volatility is somewhat shorter-lived. One possible interpretation is that these economies adjust relatively rapidly to shocks, for example because real rigidities may be less pronounced. Another possible interpretation is that the shocks that drive output tend to have temporary effects, e.g., supply shocks stemming from weather-related disruptions. A third interpretation is that measurement error is white noise, which all else equal would tend to reduce output persistence.

The acyclicality of the trade balance and the current account is consistent with limited access to international capital markets, or more generally with the presence of externally imposed borrowing constraints on these economies. To the extent that access to international capital markets helps dampen the effects of domestic and external shocks, limited access can also help understand why SSA economies are so volatile. Moreover, movements in the external borrowing constraint can also be a source of external shocks, as argued for the case of Zambia in Chapter 17.

One possible interpretation for the lack of strong comovement between consumption and investment is that these economies do not have a standard business cycle, in the sense of a common factor driving the dynamics of most macro variables. The lack of comovement can instead reflect the predominance of sector-specific shocks, i.e., shocks that affect consumption and investment separately. These shocks could be domestic or external in nature. Another possibility is that variable-specific measurement error is more pervasive in these economies, which would tend to reduce comovement, all else equal. The measurement error hypothesis begs the question, however, of why there is comovement between consumption/investment and imports.

6.1 Which Shocks are Likely to be the Main Drivers of Economic Fluctuations in SSA?

Our analysis of the data has identified three possibly-relevant sources of shocks in SSA: supply-side, policy, and external. The likely importance of supply-side shocks can be inferred from the correlation of inflation and output and from the size and characteristics of the agricultural sector. The role of policy volatility can be inferred from the standard deviation of government consumption and government spending more generally. The possible role of external shocks can be inferred in part from the volatility of terms of trade and other BOP shocks, though the correlation between the former and output is not as strong in SSA as our priors would have predicted. The large volatility of the real exchange rate is another possible indication of the magnitude of external shocks. Not all external variables seem relevant for economic fluctuations in Africa, as can be seen for example in the weak correlation between SSA country growth and global growth.[10] These shocks tend to affect specific sectors, which would also help explain the lack of comovement.

We see less evidence that shocks are coming from the financial sector. Models where developments in the financial system are an important source of economic fluctuations typically generate comovement by simultaneously relaxing borrowing constraints for households and firms (see Christiano et al., 2014 and Benes et al., 2014). If access to finance is limited, however, then there is less scope for

---

[10] There is some debate in the literature as to whether external shocks are an important source of fluctuations in low–income countries. For example, Easterly et al. (1993) show that an important part of the variation in growth rates across countries can be explained by terms of trade, whereas Raddatz (2007) argues instead that external shocks (terms of trade, aid, global growth, and various types of disasters) explain only a small fraction of the volatility of output in LICs.

comovement through this channel. A related point is that lack of financial sector development would limit the opportunities for smoothing sector-specific shocks and could therefore result in more volatile and less-synchronized spending decisions.

The volatility of consumption relative to output has been used as a litmus test for assessing the relevance of various shocks in the open economy real business cycle framework. Aguiar and Gopinath (2007) argue that a ratio greater than one indicates that shocks to trend output are the dominant source of volatility in EMs, hence their expression that 'the cycle is the trend'. Although it may be the case that trend shocks are also dominant in SSA, and developing countries more generally, as argued for example in Pritchett (2000), the mechanism put forward in Aguiar and Gopinath (2007) requires access to international capital markets and must go hand-in-hand with a countercyclical trade balance. This is not consistent with evidence for SSA.[11]

An alternative hypothesis has been put forward by Garcia-Cicco et al. (2010). These authors look at macro data (in first differences) for Argentina and Mexico going back to 1900. The economic fluctuations in those countries share some similarities with our SSA sample, in that consumption is more volatile than output, and the trade balance is acyclical vis-à-vis output but comoves negatively with both consumption and investment. They argue that this is consistent with limited availability of (and volatility in) external financing, as shocks to external financing create movements in consumption and investment that are also reflected in movements in the trade balance.[12] We suspect such a mechanism could also be at play in SSA countries. We leave a formal evaluation of these hypotheses for future work.

7 CONCLUSION

In this chapter we have provided an overview of economic fluctuations in SSA and the structure of these economies. The focus has been on real and not monetary factors, even if the discussion has important implications for the design and analysis of monetary policy in the region. Many of the themes discussed here are picked up again in subsequent chapters of the book, including in the structure of the models used for monetary policy analysis in Parts II and III.

---

[11] Aguiar and Gopinath (2007) argue that productivity follows an autoregressive process in first differences, which implies higher/lower output today signals even higher/lower output in the future. When confronted with a postive shock, the rational response is for consumption to increase by more than output, which, all else equal, requires an increase in external indebtedness, and therefore a countercyclical trade balance. The mechanism is basically an open economy version of the permanent income hypothesis.

[12] Garcia-Cicco et al. (2010) also pay close attention to the autocorrelation function of the ratio of the trade balance to output, a statistic we do not analyse here.

APPENDIX 4A: DATA SOURCES AND COUNTRY COVERAGE

Table 4A.1. Data Sources

Variables	Sources
GDP per capita	World Bank, World Development Indicators, and OECD National Accounts
Gross capital formation	World Bank, World Development Indicators, and OECD National Accounts
Government consumption expenditure	World Bank, World Development Indicators, and OECD National Accounts
Exports of goods and services	World Bank, World Development Indicators, and OECD National Accounts
Imports of goods and services	World Bank, World Development Indicators, and OECD National Accounts
Household final cons. expend.	World Bank, World Development Indicators, and OECD National Accounts
GDP deflator	World Bank, World Development Indicators, and OECD National Accounts
Inflation, GDP deflator	World Bank, World Development Indicators, and OECD National Accounts
Inflation, consumer prices	IMF, International Financial Statistics
Consumer price index	IMF, International Financial Statistics
Real effective exchange rate index	IMF, International Financial Statistics
GDP (current US$)	World Bank, World Development Indicators, and OECD National Accounts
Current account (US$)	IMF, International Financial Statistics
Total government expenditure	IMF, International Financial Statistics, and IMF World Economic Outlook
Total government revenue	IMF, International Financial Statistics, and IMF World Economic Outlook
World GDP (constant 2005 US$)	World Bank, World Development Indicators, and OECD National Accounts
Terms of trade index (2005=100)	Estimates based on 46 commodities by Spatafora and Tytell (2009)

Table 4A.2. Country Coverage

Sub-Saharan Africa	Resource-abundant	Botswana; Cameroon; Chad; Democratic Republic of the Congo; Republic of Congo; Cote d'Ivoire; Liberia; Mali; Mauritania; Niger; Nigeria; Sudan; Zambia
	Non-resource-abundant	Benin; Burkina Faso; Burundi; Central African Republic; Ethiopia; Gambia; Ghana; Kenya; Lesotho; Madagascar; Malawi; Republic of Rwanda; Senegal; Sierra Leone; Somalia; Tanzania; Togo; Zimbabwe

(*continued*)

Table 4A.2. Continued

Non-sub-Saharan Africa	HIC	Australia; Austria; Belgium; Canada; Republic of Chile; Denmark; Finland; France; Germany; Greece; Hong Kong; Ireland; Israel; Italy; Japan; Korea; Kuwait; Latvia; Netherlands; New Zealand; Norway; Oman; Poland; Portugal; Puerto Rico; Saudi Arabia; Singapore; Spain; Sweden; Switzerland; United Arab Emirates; United Kingdom; United States of America; Uruguay
	UMIC	Algeria; Argentina; Brazil; China; Colombia; Costa Rica; Cuba; Dominican Republic; Ecuador; Hungary; Iran; Iraq; Jamaica; Jordan; Libya; Malaysia; Mexico; Panama; Peru; South Africa; Thailand; Tunisia; Turkey; Venezuela
	LLMIC	Bangladesh; Bolivia; Egypt; El Salvador; Georgia; Guatemala; Haiti; Honduras; India; Indonesia; Morocco; Myanmar; Nepal; Nicaragua; Pakistan; Papua New Guinea; Paraguay; Philippines; Sri Lanka; Syria

REFERENCES

Agénor, P.-R., McDermott, C. J., and Prasad, E. S. (2000). Macroeconomic fluctuations in developing countries: Some stylized facts. *The World Bank Economic Review*, 14(2): 251–85.

Aguiar, M. and Gopinath, G. (2007). Emerging market business cycles: The cycle is the trend. *Journal of Political Economy*, 115: 69–102.

Ahmed, S. and Loungani, P. N. (2000). Business Cycles in Emerging Market Economies. *Money Affairs*, 0(1):87–111, https://ideas.repec.org/a/cml/moneya/vxiiiy2000i1p87-111.html.

Bai, J. and Perron, P. (2003). Computation and analysis of multiple structural change models. *Journal of Applied Econometrics*, 18(1): 1–22, http://dx.doi.org/10.1002/jae.659.

Benes, J., Kumhof, M., and Laxton, D. (2014). *Financial crises in DSGE models: Selected applications of mapmod*. IMF Working Paper 14/56, International Monetary Fund.

Berkes, E., Panizza, U., and Arkand, J.-L. (2015). Too much finance? *Journal of Economic Growth*, 20(2): 105–48.

Bulir, A. and Hamann, J. (2008). Volatility of development aid: From the frying pan into the fire? *World Development*, 36: 2048–66.

Chami, R., Barajas, A., Cosimano, T., Fullenkamp, C., Gapen, M., and Montiel, P. (2008). *Macroeconomic consequences of remittances*. IMF Occasional Paper 259, International Monetary Fund.

Christiano, L. J. and Fitzgerald, T.J. (2003). The band pass filter. *International Economic Review*, 44(2): 435–65.

Christiano, L., Motto, R., and Rostagno, M. (2014). Risk shocks. *American Economic Review*, 104(1): 27–65.

Collier, P. and Dercon, S. (2014). African agriculture in 50 years: Smallholders in a rapidly changing world? *World Development*, 63: 92–101.

Dabla-Norris, E., Ji, Y., Townsend, R. M., and Filiz Unsal, D. (2015). Distinguishing constraints on financial inclusion and their impact on GDP, TFP, and inequality, http://www.nber.org/papers/w20821.pdf.

Easterly, W., Kremer, M., Pritchett, L. and Summers, L. (1993) Good policy or good luck? Country growth performance and temporary shocks. *Journal of Monetary Economics*, 32(3): 459–83.

Fernandez, A., Klein, M. W., Rebucci, A., Schindler, M., and Uribe, M. (2016). Capital control measures: A new data set. *IMF Economic Review*, 64: 548–74.

Garcia-Cicco, J., Pancrazi, R., and Uribe, M. (2010). Real business cycles in emerging countries? *American Economic Review*, 100(5): 2510–31.

Hall, R. and Jones, C. (1999). Why do some countries produce so much more output per worker than others? *Quarterly Journal of Economics*, 114(1): 83–116.

Hodrick, R. J. and Prescott, E. C. (1997). Postwar U.S. business cycles: An empirical investigation. *Journal of Money, Credit and Banking*, 29(1): 1–16.

IMF (2012). *Macroeconomic policy frameworks for resource-rich developing countries*. International Monetary Fund.

IMF (2014a). *Regional Economic Outlook, Sub-Saharan Africa*, volume Spring. International Monetary Fund.

IMF (2014b). *Staff guidance note on the Fund's engagement with small states*. IMF Policy Paper.

IMF (2015). *Regional Economic Outlook, Sub-Saharan Africa*, volume Fall. International Monetary Fund.

IMF (2016). *Regional Economic Outlook, Sub-Saharan Africa*, volume Fall. International Monetary Fund.

Kongsamut, P., Rebelo, S., and Xie, D. (2001). Beyond balanced growth. *Review of Economic Studies*, 68(4): 869–82.

Kraay, A. and Raddatz, C. (2007). Poverty traps, aid and growth. *Journal of Development Economics*, 82(2): 315–47.

Levine, R. (2005). Finance and growth: Theory and evidence. Vol. 1, Part A of *Handbook of Economic Growth*. Elsevier, pp. 865–934.

McKay, A. (2013). Growth and poverty reduction in africa in the last two decades: Evidence from an AERC growth-poverty project and beyond. *Journal of African Economies*, 22: 49–76.

Mcmillan, M. and Harttgen, K. (2015). Africa's quiet revolution. Vol. II, *The Oxford Handbook of Africa and Economics*. Oxford University Press, pp. 39–61.

Monga, C. and Lin, J. Y. (2015). *The Oxford Handbook of Africa and Economics*. Oxford University Press.

Mourmouras, A. and Rangazas, P. (2008). *Fiscal policy and economic development*. IMF Working Paper 08/155, International Monetary Fund.

Prescott, E. C. (1986). Theory ahead of business cycle measurement. *Quarterly Review, Federal Reserve Bank of Minneapolis*, 10(4): 9–22.

Pritchett, L. (2000). Understanding patterns of economic growth: Searching for hills among plateaus, mountains, and plains. *World Bank Review*, 14(2): 221–50.

Raddatz, C. (2007). Are external shocks responsible for the instability of output in low-income countries? *Journal of Development Economics*, 84: 155–87.

Radelet, S. (2010). *Emerging Africa: How 17 Countries Are Leading the Way*. Center for Global Development.

Rand, J. and Tarp, F. (2002). Business cycles in developing countries: Are they different? *World Development*, 30(12): 2071–88, http://ideas.repec.org/a/eee/wdevel/v30y2002i12p2071-2088.html.

Ravn, M. O. and Uhlig, H. (2002). On adjusting the Hodrick-Prescott filter for the frequency of observations. *The Review of Economics and Statistics*, 84(2): 371–5, http://ideas.repec.org/a/tpr/restat/v84y2002i2p371-375.html.

Schindler, M. (2009). Measuring financial integration: A new data set. *IMF Staff Papers*, 56: 222–38.

Spatafora, N. and Tytell, I. (2009). *Commodity terms of trade: The history of booms and busts.* IMF Working Papers 09/205, International Monetary Fund, https://ideas.repec.org/p/imf/imfwpa/09-205.html.

Stock, J. H. and Watson, M. W. (1999). Chapter 1 Business cycle fluctuations in US macroeconomic time series, Vol. 1, Part A of *Handbook of Macroeconomics*. Elsevier, pp. 3–64.

Wang, P., Wen, Y., and Xu, Z. (2016). *Financial development and long-run volatility trends.* Working Paper 2013-003B, Federal Reserve Bank of St Louis.

5

The Monetary Transmission Mechanism

Lessons from a Dramatic Event

Andrew Berg, Jan Vlcek, Luisa Charry, and Rafael Portillo

1 INTRODUCTION

In this chapter, we attempt to learn about the transmission mechanism by looking closely at a set of related cases in which policymakers in four countries (Kenya, Uganda, Tanzania, and Rwanda—hereafter the EAC4) suddenly and unexpectedly tightened monetary policy to varying degrees. Methodologically, we take inspiration from Summers (1991: 130), who suggests that 'Skillful exploitation of natural experiments that provide identifying variation in important variables represents the best hope for increasing our empirical understanding of macroeconomic fluctuations. While lacking the scientific pretension of an explicit probability model, careful historical discussions of events surrounding particular monetary changes, such as those provided by Friedman and Schwartz (1963), persuade precisely because they succeed in identifying relevant natural experiments, and describing their consequences'.

We thus apply a version of what Romer and Romer (1989) call the 'narrative approach' to identifying the effects of monetary policy: 'The central element of this approach is the identification of monetary shocks through non-statistical procedures . . . The method involves using the historical record . . . to identify episodes when there were large shifts in monetary policy or in the behavior of monetary policy that were not driven by developments on the real side of the economy'.[1] To the best of our knowledge, this is the first attempt to apply a case-study methodology to monetary policy transmission in low-income countries.

Some of the same features of the monetary policy environment in low-income countries that make the VAR-based analyses discussed in Chapter 6 extremely challenging also greatly complicate our approach here. In part because of the rapid evolution of monetary policy regimes, we are not able to identify several independent and comparable tightening events, so that we cannot conduct statistical analyses. And it is hard to argue, as do Romer and Romer (1989), that the tightening episodes are unrelated to recent economic developments,

---

[1] Romer and Romer (1989: 1).

notably supply shocks.[2] Thus, more along the lines of the seminal work of Friedman Schwartz (1963), which preceded and motivated the R&R approach but did not rely on explicit statistical inference, we rely on a close reading of the narrative and the data to 'provide identifying variation', in the language of Summers (1991), with regard to the macroeconomic effects of a tightening in monetary policy.

On the positive side, we are able to draw on variations across the four countries studied—notably in terms of economic structure and policy regime—to shed light on the influences of these factors on monetary policy transmission. Two ideas emphasized in the recent literature are salient. Mishra et al. (2012) argue that structural features of the LIC environment, notably underdeveloped and monopolistic financial systems and inflexible exchange rates, are likely to make transmission weak and unreliable, because policy rates do not transmit to lending rates in underdeveloped and monopolistic banking systems, and in any event these rates do not matter that much to the real economy. In addition, as we have stressed in this book, policy regimes themselves will influence the transmission mechanism.

Our narrative centres on a significant tightening of monetary policy that took place—to varying degrees and in different ways—in October 2011 in the EAC4. In 2010–11 there was a major commodity price shock, and inflation took off in the EAC4, echoing the events of 2007–08. Throughout 2010 and most of 2011, monetary policies remained fairly loose in Kenya, Uganda, and Tanzania, with only cautious and ineffective efforts to tighten, perhaps encouraged by the experience of gradually moderating inflation without policy tightening during the earlier episode in 2009. The commodity price shocks turned out to be much more persistent this time, and they combined with vigorous economic activity, a negative balance of payments shock, and accommodative policy to further accelerate inflation and de-anchor expectations, weakening the exchange rate in an inflationary spiral.

Some of the countries began to respond, to varying degrees. In July 2011, Uganda announced a new inflation targeting (IT) 'lite' policy regime, and in August began a still-somewhat gradual tightening of policy. Kenya enacted fitful, partial, and ineffective tightening measures, but did clarify its regime in September 2011. In Rwanda, by contrast, tighter monetary policy and a stable exchange rate throughout the period kept inflation from taking off.

Finally, the governors of the four central banks agreed at an unusual October 2011 meeting that policy needed to be tightened significantly in order to bring inflation under control, even at a cost to output, and they acted immediately.[3] This tightening and surrounding events are our topic here. While the tightening took place in response to economic events, this does not make it entirely endogenous and thus does not invalidate our narrative approach to identifying the monetary transmission mechanism. Throughout 2011, concerns about the adequacy of the

---

[2] The exogeneity of Romer and Romer's policy events is challenged in Shapiro (1994) and Dotsey and Reid (1992). See the discussion in Christiano et al. (1999).

[3] See the communique from the 12 October 2011 meeting at http://www.bot.go.tz/Adverts/PressRelease/2011-Oct-13-PressRelease.pdf.

policy stance were increasingly widespread. However, it was unclear when a tightening might come or how strong it would be. Indeed, the narrative suggests that some observers were becoming concerned that it might not come at all. Thus, when it came, it was at least partly unexpected—*unusual,* in the language of Friedman and Schwartz (1963). We can thus ask, what did this large monetary policy tightening shock do?

We find some evidence consistent with a clear transmission mechanism. In some of the four countries, after a large policy-induced rise in the short-term interest rate, lending and other interest rates rose, the exchange rate tended to appreciate, output tended to fall, and inflation declined.

The variation in experiences among the four cases is informative. Most importantly, the cross-country variation in transmission seems to depend sharply on the policy regime in place. In particular, we find the clearest transmission in Uganda, where the IT-lite regime itself was simpler and more transparent, and in Kenya, particularly once the authorities explicitly signalled the monetary policy stance with a short-term interest rate and described their intentions in terms of their inflation objective. In regimes where the stance of monetary policy was harder to assess, such as Tanzania, which conducted monetary policy under a de jure monetary targeting regime, and Rwanda, which had a de facto exchange rate peg, the transmission of monetary policy to lending rates is less evident. Nonetheless, in Tanzania, the exchange rate seemed to respond strongly to adjustments of the monetary policy stance.

We see mixed signs of the importance of financial development. All four countries, like other LICs, have relatively small, concentrated, and bank-dependent financial systems, but to varying degrees. In particular, Kenya's large financial sector makes it an outlier, and it also had perhaps the most complete and unambiguous transmission. However, Uganda, which also clearly demonstrated the main elements of monetary policy transmission, has a relatively small financial sector compared to those of the other three countries.

While the shock was not entirely expected, it was not isolated from outside influences, particularly shocks to global risk appetite and commodity prices, which directly affected exchange rates and prices of traded goods. A close reading of the timing and some statistical evidence suggests that such shocks do not explain most of the exchange rate and price movements around the time of the tightening event, such that the residual unexplained component is consistent with our emphasis on the role of monetary policy itself. Moreover, Uganda's somewhat earlier policy tightening—starting after its regime change in July—matches an earlier if also somewhat more gradual turnaround in its exchange rate and inflation.

The chapter proceeds as follows. We first briefly present the stylized facts of the countries under study, including structural features of the economy, the financial system, prices, and the policy regimes. We then proceed to the event study, identifying the policy shock and tracing out the effects of these shocks on the main macroeconomic variables: interest rates, credit aggregates, the exchange rate, output, and inflation. We then analyse more closely the role of important exogenous shocks to capital flows commodity prices that complicate interpretation of the events. Finally, we draw some tentative lessons.

2 THE ENVIRONMENT FOR MONETARY POLICY

2.1 Structure of the Economy and the Financial Sector

The four countries of interest here are in many ways typical of SSA LICs, making their experiences of general interest. Moreover, they share a recent macroeconomic history that is sufficiently stable that the recent monetary policy contraction is a salient event. They are among SSA's many 'success stories' since the mid-1990s, with the achievement of macroeconomic and political stability and rapid economic growth (Table 5.1). Their economic structure is also broadly characteristic of SSA LICs: low-trade shares, mostly commodity exports, high though falling aid dependence, service sector-led growth, and large agricultural sectors and rural populations. The terms of trade have been fairly stable or rising in recent years.[4]

Inflation in the EAC4 is volatile and highly correlated across countries, mostly explained by the high share of food items in the overall CPI. The weight of food prices in the CPI is highest in Tanzania (47 per cent), followed by Kenya (36 per cent), Rwanda (35 per cent), and Uganda (27 per cent).[5] Domestic food crops yields in the region are highly dependent on weather patterns, which are characterized by a bimodal annual rainfall cycle. The existence of trade barriers to protect the domestic agricultural production has increased the sensitivity of the domestic food supply to unfavourable weather conditions.

Financial systems also share the characteristics that have been associated with weak transmission, though with important cross-country variation. Financial development has been rapid in recent years, but these countries still generally have small and concentrated private-bank-dominated financial systems, a large informal financial sector, shallow capital markets (except Kenya), short yield curves (except Kenya and more recently Uganda), and substantial dollarization (Table 5.2). In all four countries, commercial banks maintain substantial excess reserve deposits at the central bank. Additionally, the four economies exhibit different degrees of financial openness, with Uganda and Kenya being the more financially integrated of the four and Rwanda and Tanzania the least. Looking across the four countries, Kenya stands out for its relatively developed financial sector, with a larger and less concentrated banking system.

As in most SSA countries with managed floats, all four (except Uganda after July 2011) conducted monetary policy under a de jure monetary aggregate targeting framework, in principle adjusting the money supply to achieve intermediate targets in terms of broad money growth. However, these three regimes were much more flexible, and complex, in practice (Appendix 5A: Table 5A.1).

The broader experience with such de jure money targeting regimes is that target misses are frequent, and at least in relatively low-inflation environments, such deviations are not associated with misses of inflation objectives. Rather, central banks tend to make judgements on an ongoing basis as to whether targets should

---

[4] Berg et al. (2013) present much more background information and references.
[5] The Tanzania CPI survey includes rural households, unlike the surveys in Kenya, Uganda, and Rwanda.

Table 5.1. Basic Economic Indicators, 2011

Country	Population (Millions)	Real GDP Per Capita (USD, PPP)	Average Real GDP Growth (Per cent, 2001–11)	Public Debt/ GDP (Per cent, 2011)
Kenya	42	476	4.2	43.0
Uganda	35	374	7.3	23.6
Tanzania	46	460	6.9	27.8
Rwanda	11	360	7.9	23.1

Sources: IMF and the World Bank.

Table 5.2. Financial Sector Indicators, 2011

Groups	Credit to the Private Sector (Per cent of GDP)	Bank Credit to the Private Sector (Per cent of GDP)	Five-Bank Asset Concentration (Per cent)[a]	Stocks Traded, Total Value (Per cent of GDP)	Dollarization[b]	Chinn-Ito Financial Openness Index[c]
Kenya	38.1	33.6	60.5	2.6	10.8	1.1
Uganda	17.9	13.8	73.6	0.1	21.8	2.5
Tanzania	17.8	15.8	67.6	0.1	20.3	−1.2
Rwanda	16.9	13.2	100.0	n.a.	20.0	−0.9
Average EAC4	22.7	19.1	75.4	0.9	18.2	0.4
Low-Income Countries	19.6	18.8	80.0	4.9	12.8	−0.4
Emerging Economies	60.9	49.1	69.6	26.6	4.0	0.3
Advanced Economies	145.3	133.7	84.8	70.2	0.5	2.2

[a] Assets of five largest banks as a share of total commercial banking assets.
[b] Foreign currency deposits as a share of total deposits in the banking system.
[c] Index values are for 2010. The index takes a maximum value of 2.5 for the most financially open economies and a minimum of −1.9 for the least financially open. See Chinn and Ito (2008).

Sources: IMF estimates and the World Bank.

be achieved, and if not, how they should be revised for the next quarter, depending on outcomes in money and exchange rate markets and a broader sense of whether inflation and output (and other) objectives are being achieved. This is for various reasons, not least because to adhere to the targets would generate excessive volatility of short-term interest rates in the face of money demand shocks. This makes the stance of policy hard to grasp and in particular very hard to infer from monetary aggregates themselves.[6]

Tanzania and especially Rwanda adhered most closely to their de jure money targeting regime, though even here, economically meaningful deviations were

---

[6] See Chapters 1, 8, and 9, and Adam et al. (2010) for discussions of this issue, and Chapter 16 for Kenya specifically.

frequent.[7] Kenya had over time paid less and less attention to monetary aggregates, culminating in September 2011 with a clear announcement of a move to use the short-term interest rate as its main policy instrument, with the objective of achieving its inflation objectives (Chapter 15). Uganda too had undergone an important evolution in this regard, moving in October 2009 from quite strict to flexible money targeting with substantial attention to interest rates as the operating target, to an explicit inflation targeting 'lite' regime in July 2011 with use of short-term interest rates in pursuit of its inflation objectives.

The different degree of attention to monetary aggregates in practice has corresponded to varying degrees of interbank interest rate volatility. This is clearest in Tanzania and least in Uganda and Kenya, consistent with their de facto use of interest rates as operating targets and indicators of the stance of policy.

In these hybrid regimes, it is often difficult to know how to interpret any particular interest rate. Sometimes 'policy rates' are not market-clearing, present no arbitrage opportunities with other short-term interest rates, and contain no signal of policy intention. But this can change suddenly as the details of central bank operations change. Pressures from fiscal authorities can encourage these central banks to create deviations between 'policy rates' and some market rates, particularly those at which the Treasury finances its activities, sometimes creating further opacity with respect to interest rates.

In assessing the stance of policy, we in general refer to the interbank rate as an indicator of the market short-term interest rate, with due reference to 'policy rates', exchange rate interventions, and money aggregates as appropriate. Other instruments, such as changes in reserve requirements, may have some independent signalling import but also are likely to work at least in part through their influence on interbank rates.

3 THE EVENT STUDY

We define a shock as an episode in which a central bank undertakes overt and unusual—large and substantially unexpected—actions to exert a contractionary influence on the economy in order to reduce inflation. The tightening we consider here took place mainly in October 2011 around the time of a meeting of EAC Central Bank governors at which it was stated that inflation was getting out of control and that monetary policy needed to be tightened. This meeting and the resulting sharp policy actions represent the distinct monetary policy shock that allows us to trace the transmission mechanism. We now take a closer look at the tightening episode.

---

[7] As discussed in Chapter 8, deviations that occur roughly once per year correspond in magnitude, by back-of-the-envelope calculations, to interest rate deviation of 5 percentage points in Rwanda and 20 percentage points in Tanzania. Rwanda's close control of the nominal exchange rate created some tensions with the money targets in practice.

3.1 The Run-Up

Through mid-2011, international prices of food and energy shot up by more than 30 per cent and 40 per cent, respectively (Figure 5.1, Panel 1). Meanwhile, economic activity in the EAC4 was generally recovering from the earlier effects of the global financial crisis (Panel 2). Direct evidence suggests that the monetary policy stance was mostly accommodative, with nominal rates fairly flat and real interest rates mostly negative in all three countries (Panels 3 and 4). Partly reflecting this policy stance, but also at times owing to pressures on the capital account from swings in global risk aversion, nominal real exchange rates were generally weakening (Panels 5 and 6).[8]

By 2011 Q3, these factors were reflected in headline inflation in Kenya, Uganda, and Tanzania that surpassed the common inflation target of 5 per cent (Panel 7).[9] Even though most of the increase in headline inflation during this period is explained by the acceleration in food and fuel inflation, core inflation also increased substantially in all countries, almost doubling during the course of a year, and in all cases considerably overshooting the common inflation target (Panel 8).[10]

Consistent with the negative real interest rates, the monetary policy authorities were generally 'behind the curve' in responding to the building inflationary pressures.[11] Moreover, policy responses were generally poorly signalled both in terms of the statements of the authorities and in that different instruments, such as different short-term interest rates, gave different signals.

As inflation in Kenya continued to increase and the nominal exchange rate depreciated by about 10 per cent in the period from March until September 2011, the Central Bank of Kenya (CBK) responded fitfully and opaquely. For example, a March increase of the Central Bank Rate (CBR) by 25 basis points to 6 per cent, reversing a lowering of 25 basis points in January 2011, was accompanied by mixed signals as to the intent of the CBK, and had no discernible effect on lending rates or the exchange rate.[12] In August 2011, the central bank resorted to stronger moves, including restricting access to the discount facility and restricting liquidity provision through open market operations, still keeping the CBR unchanged. These moves resulted in a brief intra-month 2,200 basis point spike in interbank

---

[8] Rwanda was an exception to these generalizations, with output below potential (though rising), a stable nominal exchange rate, and positive real interest rates. Section 5 examines the role of exogenous external shocks more closely to disentangle them from that of policy.

[9] Output gaps are estimated with a Hodrick-Prescott filter on the four-quarter cumulative real GDP in Uganda and Tanzania and Non-Agricultural GDP in Kenya and Rwanda. The estimation sample includes data up to 2012 Q3 to correct for end-of-sample bias. Real interest rates are calculated using the twelve-month backward-moving average CPI-based inflation rate. The real exchange rates are CPI-based bilateral rates with the US dollar.

[10] For details on the construction of these series, see Berg et al. (2013).

[11] In part, this may have reflected the experience of the earlier episode of external price shocks in 2007/08, when temporarily rising inflation was followed by the commodity price and external demand collapse of the global financial crisis, obviating the need for a monetary policy response in that case, as discussed in Berg et al. (2013).

[12] In March 2011, the CBK suggested somewhat contradictorily that 'this tightening will provide a solution to inflationary pressure and will stabilize the exchange rate while still protecting economic activity' (Central Bank of Kenya, 2011a). In July, they still considered this action sufficient to mitigate soaring inflation (Central Bank of Kenya, 2011b).

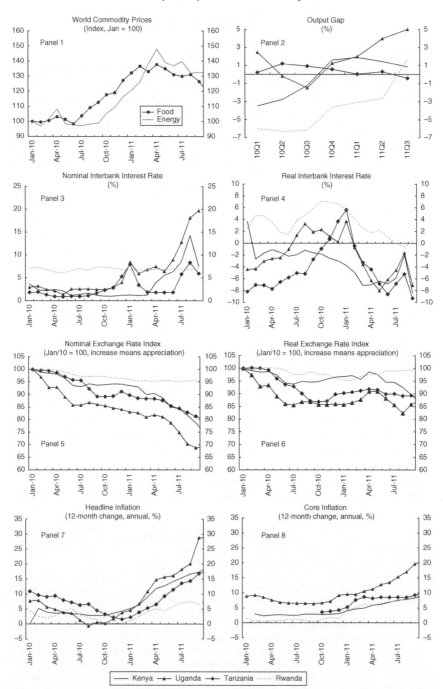

Figure 5.1. The Run-Up

Sources: IMF estimates, Haver, national authorities. See footnote 9 for detailed calculation.

rates, which had little apparent effect on treasury bill rates and none on lending rates or the exchange rate, which continued to depreciate.

In September, the CBK clarified its operating regime, emphasizing that it would use the CBR as its main policy instrument with the objective of achieving its inflation objectives. However, while the central bank raised the CBR from 6.25 per cent to 7 per cent, at the same time, and in contradiction, it provided liquidity to the interbank market at 5.75 per cent. Meanwhile, policy statements from the CBK were ambiguous and lacked a clear announcement of policy tightening.[13]

Tanzania began acting as early as 2010 Q4, by some measures. A sharp contraction in the real growth rate of money in late 2010 caused a jump in the interbank rate, with a hint of pass-through to T-bill rates, but this proved short-lived even as the growth rate of money continued to slow. As real money growth reached nearly zero in mid-2011, interbank (but not T-bill) rates again spiked. There was no discernible effect of these actions on lending rates, the exchange rate, or credit.

Uganda, in contrast, began effective tightening earlier. Interbank rates increased by some 500 basis points during the first half of 2011, though with little apparent effect; for example, lending rates remained unchanged. The BOU tightened much more consistently and coherently after the July 2011 announcement of a new 'IT-lite' regime and the introduction of the CBR to signal the policy stance.[14] The central bank raised the CBR in two steps, from 13 per cent in July to 16 per cent in September. In this case, the lending rate increased by 340 basis points from July until September 2011, and the exchange rate began to stabilize, with the real exchange rate appreciating in September. We return to the effects of these measures in the next section.

Rwanda presents a contrasting picture: through 2010–11, output was below trend, the real exchange rate and real interest rates were stable (and the latter positive). This may have reflected a tighter monetary policy stance, as well as the de facto crawling peg exchange rate regime. It is hard to infer much about the stance of policy during this period; for example, real reserve money growth varied sharply in a way that seems unrelated to short-term interest rates and the exchange rate or for that matter inflation and the output gap.

4 THE EVENT AND ITS AFTERMATH

As 2011 unfolded, inflation accelerated on the strength of higher food and oil inflation, strong demand, weakening exchange rates, and still-negative interest rates (Rwanda was the exception). The EAC4 came to the realization by their October meeting that action was needed to stabilize the situation.

---

[13] At an extraordinary meeting on 14 September 2011, the CBK announced that 'The high overall inflation environment is mainly a consequence of high food prices and high fuel and energy prices ... The CBK will pursue the inflation objective through a continuation of the gradual tightening of monetary conditions' (Central Bank of Kenya, 2011c).

[14] With the introduction of the IT-lite framework also came the release of a monetary policy statement signed by the governor and providing forward guidance to market participants.

On 5 October, the CBK increased the CBR by 400 basis points and on 1 November by a further 550 basis points to 16.5 per cent. During this period, it also increased the cash reserve requirement by 75 basis points to 5.25 per cent, and adjusted the discount window rate by more than 20 per cent, 'as decisive and immediate action is required from the monetary policy side to stem these inflationary expectations'.[15] In addition, the Ministry of Finance lowered the foreign exchange exposure limit for commercial banks to 10 per cent of core capital from 20 per cent.[16]

The Bank of Uganda (BUG) followed up early substantial tightening, and the introduction of its new regime in July, by raising its policy interest rate by 400 basis points in October and a further 300 basis points in November, to 23 per cent, and stepped up its intervention in the foreign exchange market to contain the depreciating pressures on the Shilling, stating that 'the upside risks to inflation have increased, it is necessary to tighten monetary policy further ... [this] should be seen as a clear signal of the BOU's determination to bring inflation under control. However, should the upside risk to inflation continue in the months ahead, then monetary policy will be tightened further'.[17]

In Tanzania, the central bank increased its policy rate by 200 basis points in October and a further 202 basis points in November to 11.00 per cent, and on 26 October augmented the minimum reserve requirements on government deposits held by banks from 20 per cent to 30 per cent, reduced commercial banks' limit on foreign currency net open positions from 20 per cent to 10 per cent of core capital, tightened capital controls, and increased sales of foreign exchange in the interbank market.[18] This shift was more decisive than earlier efforts, perhaps partly because this time the authorities put more emphasis on the policy rate, as well as on the quantitative actions.

Finally, the National Bank of Rwanda took a variety of much more moderate tightening measures, consistent with the much lower degree of disequilibrium throughout 2011. Again, it is hard to point to any specific measurable action with respect to money aggregates, but the central bank's policy rate was increased by 50 basis points to 6.5 per cent, as 'the Central Bank finds it appropriate to review its policy rate in order to keep the monetary aggregates at optimal levels to limit inflation pressures while continuing to support economic growth'.[19]

Having identified the policy-tightening event and the variations across the four countries, we now turn to an assessment of the various channels of transmission of monetary policy across our group of countries. The variety of instruments and (time-varying) differences in regimes can make it difficult to characterize in a simple way the stance of policy itself. We generally use the interbank rate as the best single measure of the policy shock itself. As a measure of the short-term market rate in all four countries, it captures aggregates of the effects of policy rates and quantitative policies (quantitative interventions, reserve requirements) and

---

[15] Central Bank of Kenya (2011d).

[16] In October 2011, the CBK clarified its communications by stating that 'this upward adjustment of the CBR was expected to provide a signal to banks that interest rates should rise and therefore reduce the expansion in credit to the private sector' (Central Bank of Kenya, 2011d).

[17] Bank of Uganda (2011b).   [18] IMF (2011c).   [19] National Bank of Rwanda (2011).

distils the divergent effects of potentially inconsistent actions taken with various not-necessarily-market-clearing 'policy rates'.

4.1 The Interest Rate Channel

In Uganda and Kenya, the pass-through from policy rates to interbank rates was fast and complete (Figure 5.2, Panels 1 and 2) (and to T-bill rates, shown in the working paper). Tanzania's battery of measures also transmitted quickly to money market rates.

The relevance of the policy regime is evident in the transmission to banking rates (Panel 3). Lending rates, in particular, responded swiftly—though partially—to the monetary policy contraction in Kenya and Uganda. Uganda's lending rates began to respond somewhat earlier, corresponding to the August/September tightening. There is little sign of transmission to lending rates in Tanzania and Rwanda. The lack of response of lending rates in Tanzania and Rwanda, despite the increases in the interbank rates in these two countries, is reminiscent of the non-response of lending rates to Kenya's August spike in interbank rates.

Even in Kenya and Uganda, the pass-through from short-term market to lending rates was partial. This may reflect lack of competition or other structural weaknesses in the financial system, as argued in Mishra et al. (2012). However, lending rates are longer-term rates, so partial pass-through to (at least somewhat temporary) tightening is also consistent with fully functioning markets, by which we mean arbitrage across returns of different assets, and an expectation that the period of high short rates will be somewhat shorter than the tenor of the loans.[20] Moreover, standard data in these countries (such as we use here) report average, not marginal lending rates. Finally, as we have already argued above, the pass-through of policy rates to short-term market and lending rates will depend on the clarity of the regime and in particular the ability of market participants to infer that the increase reflects policy intent and will not be quickly reversed.[21] It may be that there was still some uncertainty about whether the authorities in Kenya and Uganda would stay the course.

4.2 The Bank Lending Channel

The data indicate the existence of the credit channel in Kenya, Uganda, and Tanzania. In these three countries growth in credit to the private sector peaked soon after the policy contraction started and decelerated substantially as the

---

[20] The average maturity of loans in the cleaned loan-level Uganda dataset of Abuka et al. (2015) is 1.5 years. Moreover, it is a characteristic of fully credible regimes that very long rates do not move much with short rates, because inflation expectations are well anchored (Gurkaynak et al., 2007). See also Bulir and Vlcek (2015).

[21] While not necessarily relevant in this episode of dramatic tightening, this point is closely related to the argument, e.g., in Woodford (2001), that the substantial smoothing seen in advanced-country monetary policy reaction functions implies a large pass-through to lending rates. A lesser degree of smoothing thus implies lower pass-through.

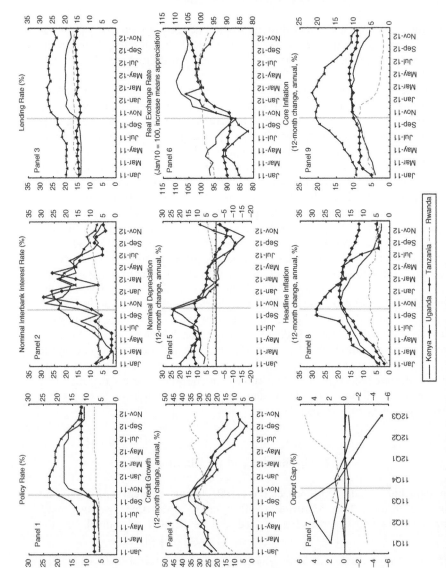

Figure 5.2. The Monetary Policy Contraction and its Aftermath

Source: IMF and authors' calculations.

monetary authorities stepped up the pace of tightening. Accordingly, during the 2011 Q3 to 2012 Q3 period, credit to the private sector growth in Kenya, Uganda, and Tanzania decelerated. Again, Uganda's contraction began a month or two before the others. There are also signs of credit rationing in the case of Tanzania: even though lending rates did not respond to the tightening, there was a meaningful impact on the quantity of credit extended to the economy. In Rwanda, there is little sign of slower credit growth, perhaps reflecting the much less significant tightening.

Abuka et al. (2015) provide important supportive evidence for the bank lending channel in the case of Uganda. A unique dataset of loan-level data spanning the period in question allows them to control for demand effects through region-industry dummies and aggregate variables such as GDP, directly. This allows them to interpret the effects of the policy shock as causal for credit supply and as not due to demand effects. They find that higher short-term market interest rates are associated with an increase in banks' lending rates and reductions in loan volume at the extensive and intensive margins. The strength of this bank lending channel is significant, albeit about half of that observed in advanced economies studied with similar data and techniques.[22]

4.3 The Exchange Rate Channel

In Kenya, Uganda, and Tanzania, the increase in short-term interest rates was associated with a contemporaneous appreciation of the currency. Notably, this took place during the decisive tightening phase in 2011 Q4, but not earlier when policy was more cautious and less clearly signalled. Uganda is again a partial exception insofar as the exchange rate stabilization began two months earlier, corresponding to its earlier tightening phase.

4.4 Output

The tightening episode is associated with a contraction of output in Uganda and to a lesser extent in Tanzania (Panel 7). The absence of a visible decline in the output gap in Kenya is notable. Of course, factors other than monetary policy such as fiscal policy and foreign demand also influence the output gap, and it is difficult to measure the output gap in the context of frequent supply shocks.[23]

The Abuka et al. (2015) analysis based on loan-level data provides supportive analysis of the effects of this particular monetary policy shock on output in Uganda. By identifying differential loan supply effects in districts with varying

[22] They also identify a bank balance sheet channel in which balance sheet conditions of banks influence these effects, with for example poorly capitalized banks transmitting the interest rate changes more strongly.

[23] In Uganda, the output gap increased from 2010 Q3 to 2011 Q3 despite positive real interest rates for the first half of that period. Fiscal policy was expansionary during the first part of this period, with a fiscal impulse (the change in the primary balance adjusted for the cyclical position, estimated at 1 per cent of GDP for the 2010 Q3–2011 Q2 period (IMF, 2011b)).

banking sector conditions, and measuring real effects through night-time light output measured from satellites, they can plausibly identify the real effects of monetary policy acting through the bank balance sheet channel. They find that output does indeed contract more in those districts where banks have balance sheets, suggesting a strong balance sheet channel for the monetary contraction.

4.5 Inflation

Finally, the inflation rate came down sharply with the monetary contraction. Headline inflation began turning around rather quickly, within a month or two, presumably reflecting the rapid pass-through of exchange rate movements. The turnaround was sharpest in Uganda and Kenya but was apparent in Tanzania as well. Again, Rwanda shows a much more gradual pattern, reflecting the fact that inflation was never far from target. Core inflation followed, albeit much more gradually (Panel 9).

5 ON THE ROLE OF GLOBAL RISK APPETITE AND SUPPLY SHOCKS

The backdrop against which the coordinated October 2011 tightening took place was challenging in that the countries faced both a negative balance of payments shock and a negative supply shock in the context of accommodative policies and growing imbalances. We now discuss the direct role of these two factors, concluding that, while they were important, they cannot provide an alternative explanation of the events we have documented.

First, can shifts in capital flows and global risk aversion explain the exchange rate dynamics during the run-up and following the coordinated tightening? The year 2011 was one of increased global risk aversion, with the rising political tensions in the Middle East associated with the Arab Spring, the sovereign debt crisis in Europe, and the downgrading of the credit rating of major industrial economies. This surely contributed to exchange rate pressures on the EAC4, but cannot plausibly explain the timing and magnitude of the real depreciations observed. The currencies of Kenya, Uganda, and Tanzania started to weaken in 2010, well in advance of the episode, standing during 2010 and 2011 amongst the most depreciated currencies in the emerging and frontier markets world (excluding fixed exchange rate regimes, Figure 5.3).

Taking a closer look, swings in global risk appetite can partly explain the sharp depreciation during the July–September period and perhaps some of the appreciation that followed the monetary policy tightening. However, the timing of the turnaround indicates a strong independent role for the monetary policy contraction. Global risk appetite, as proxied by the VIX Index, deteriorated markedly in August and September as the credit ratings of the United States, Japan, and Italy were downgraded and Europe's debt crisis intensified (Figure 5.4). Tensions in international capital markets eased by late September.

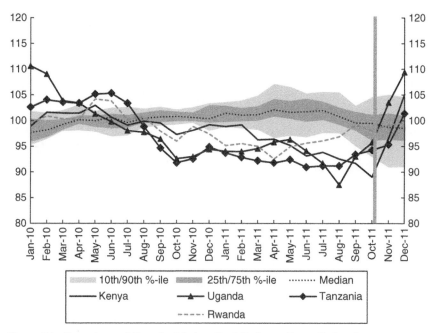

Figure 5.3. Emerging and Frontier Markets Real Exchange Rates (Index, Jan. 2010 = 100, increase means appreciation[24])

Sources: IMF and authors' computation.

However, the currencies of Kenya and Tanzania reached their lowest levels weeks later.[25] The Kenyan shilling strengthened immediately on the second day of the policy-tightening announcement, after staying near low levels despite improved global sentiment. The Tanzanian shilling, on the other hand, continued to weaken even after the announcement of the coordinated policy, interrupting its slide only after a further battery of measures was announced in the week commencing 24 October.

A second alternative narrative emphasizes the role of the increase in global commodity prices in the region's inflationary dynamics. On this view, the inflationary pressures were not a reflection of vigorous economic activity and loose monetary policy but a result of the higher food and fuel prices. Two points are worth noting here. First, as shown earlier, core inflation (mainly excluding food and energy prices) also increased substantially through 2011, almost doubling and overshooting the target, before beginning to come back down. Second, movements in food and fuel inflation are themselves influenced by the monetary

---

[24] REER is downloaded from IMF database. The median and percentiles are calculated from REER of Brazil, Chile, Colombia, Czech Republic, Estonia, Ghana, Hungary, India, Indonesia, Israel, Korea, Mauritius, Mexico, Pakistan, Peru, Philippines, Poland, Romania, Serbia, Slovenia, South Africa, Sri Lanka, Thailand, and Turkey.

[25] Uganda stabilized somewhat earlier, in August, in this case coinciding more closely with the levelling off of the VIX but also with the earlier beginning of the monetary policy tightening phase, which also peaked in October.

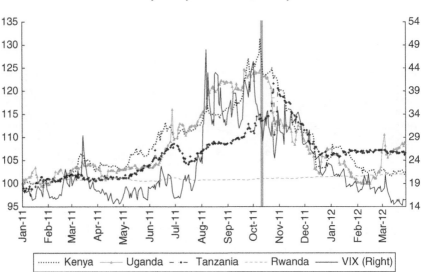

Figure 5.4. VIX (Index) and EAC4 Exchange Rates
Source: Bloomberg.

policy stance. Monetary policy influences the domestic price of imported food and fuel through the exchange rate. For locally produced (and not fully traded) food, monetary policy can work through aggregate demand. Thus, disentangling the contribution of monetary policy from that of supply shocks cannot solely be based on separating food/fuel and core inflation. Chapter 15 discusses these issues and applies a simple structural model to events in Kenya during 2011 to find that monetary policy accounts for much of the inflation dynamics, including the behaviour of domestic food prices.

We can provide a more quantitative if less nuanced characterization of the role of global risk appetite and global commodity prices by seeing how much of the month-to-month variation in the exchange rates in the EAC4 can be associated statistically with movements in the VIX and global interest rates. This is a simple regression to interpret: we assume that any policy actions that are correlated with these global shocks are reactions to these events; any residual policy reactions can thus be left in the error term. This assumption gives maximum weight to these global shocks. It permits us to use OLS to regress nominal exchange rate level on the VIX, the US interest rate, and several lags, country by country. We interpret the residual as the candidate variation to be explained by other factors, such as monetary policy.

The regression explains a fair amount of the variance of the exchange rate (from 56 per cent in Uganda to 46 per cent in Rwanda, presumably low owing to its quasi-managed regime). Most of this is due to the importance of the lagged exchange rate itself, though the exogenous variables are highly significant. In Figure 5.5, we plot the predicted value of the exchange rate based only on the exogenous shocks and associated endogenous dynamics (the 'counterfactual', which we interpret as reflecting the dynamics of the exchange rate in the absence

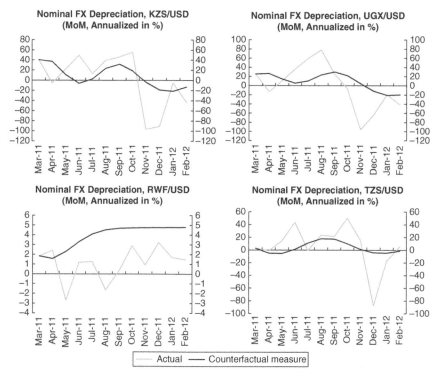

Figure 5.5. Nominal Exchange Rate Depreciation, MoM Annualized in Per cent
Source: Authors' computation.

of unexpected monetary policy decisions).[26] As Figure 5.5 shows, in all but Rwanda the exogenous factors go in the right direction in explaining the depreciations in Q3 and subsequent appreciations, but much less than observed and with not quite the right timing. The peak depreciation of the predicted exchange rate in all countries occurs around September, but the actually (much weaker) bottom occurs in October in Tanzania and Kenya and in August in Uganda, more consistent with the timing of the monetary policy shock.

The results for headline inflation paint a similar story. Inflation peaks coincide or follow with a one-month lag in the nominal exchange rate depreciation and they cannot be explained by the counterfactual (Figure 5.6).

To summarize this section, the swings in global risk aversion and the food and fuel supply shock during 2011 did play an important role during the episode under study, they are only part of the story, both in terms of magnitude and timing, and do not overturn the conclusion that monetary policy seems to have played a decisive role.

---

[26] That is, we create a 'counterfactual' based on the predictions of the estimated model given the exogenous variables, rather than using actual lagged values of the endogenous variable.

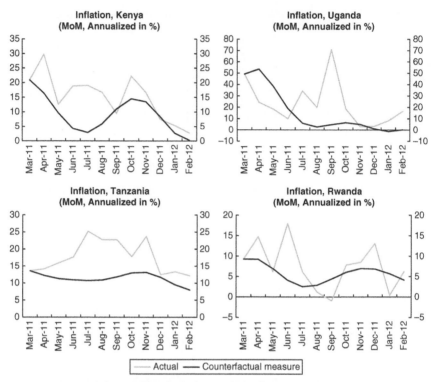

Figure 5.6. CPI Inflation, MoM Annualized in Per cent

Source: Authors' computation.

6 SUMMARY AND INTERPRETATIONS

We have identified a moment when three of the EAC4 broke from previous behaviour and executed more-or-less clearly signalled monetary policy contractions with the explicit intent of reducing inflation. We find clear evidence of most elements of the standard transmission mechanism in most of the countries.

The transmission was clearest in Kenya and Uganda, where market and lending rates followed the policy rate with little lag, the exchange rate appreciated sharply on the policy announcement, credit growth (and, at least in Uganda, the output gap) began to decline immediately. Both headline and core inflation also began to decline almost immediately. Transmission was less clear in Tanzania, where the effects on some interest rates, activity, the exchange rate, and inflation were still broadly evident, but lending rates failed to respond and the effects on output were barely evident. Rwanda presents a control along several dimensions: initial imbalances were much smaller, the tightening much less significant, and the various components of transmission much more muted or invisible.

Based on and summarizing the preceding narrative, we can now evaluate the two hypotheses discussed in the instruction to explain the variation in cross-country experience. In the episode under study, we find substantial explanatory power in the idea that the nature of the policy regime conditions transmission.

In the cases of clearest transmission, Kenya and Uganda, the regimes in October 2011 most resembled inflation targeting in that the authorities prioritized inflation, emphasized the role of the policy rate, allowed the exchange rate a large degree of flexibility, and broadly avoided multiple objectives. Earlier tightening efforts by Kenya, e.g. in August 2011, were more incoherent in terms of the consistency across different instruments and communications and did not translate into lending rates or the exchange rates. Uganda's earlier tightening efforts were more coherent and stronger following its July 2011 move to 'IT lite' in July, and indeed had some effect on lending rates, credit, the exchange rate, and inflation about two months before Kenya and Tanzania.

In Tanzania the money targeting regime led to highly volatile short-term interest rates, a variety of instruments were used in not always consistent ways, and overall there was less clear signalling of the policy stance.

Rwanda's regime was the most complex, with a quasi-pegged exchange rate, direct influence on private sector credit, monetary aggregate targets, and a policy rate. The emphasis on the exchange rate left little room for monetary policy itself to act, and insofar as it could, the regime did not provide a clear signal. In the event, there was apparently less tightening, and less need to tighten.

The second hypothesis is that transmission worked better in countries with greater financial depth and more open capital accounts. We find mixed support for this story in this episode. It remains plausibly the case that countries with more liquid and deeper financial markets will observe stronger transmission from policy rates to the macroeconomy.[27] However, in this particular case measures of financial depth do not seem determinative for the clarity of transmission. A glance back at Table 5.2 reminds us that Kenya is the clear outlier for all measures of financial depth, with the other three countries remarkably similar. And yet, as we have argued, the evidence for transmission looks fairly strong, and similar, for Uganda and Kenya, in contrast to Tanzania and Rwanda.

On the other hand, the narrative is consistent with the view that the lower degree of financial openness in Tanzania and Rwanda (Table 5.2) may have contributed to obscuring or impairing transmission in these two countries. The exchange rate did seem to respond in Tanzania, but less dramatically than in Kenya and Uganda.

Finally, it is often asserted that the high levels of excess reserves usually observed in SSA countries prevent the operation of the monetary transmission mechanism, for example because tightening policy may amount to 'pushing on a string', as banks respond to a contraction by withdrawing excess reserves.[28] In the episode we examine here, excess reserves did not seem to impair the transmission mechanism. As Figure 5.7 shows, there are indeed substantial reserves in excess of required levels in all four countries, with large variations across time and countries but with no evident influence on transmission. While in Kenya, excess reserves fell during 2011, they remained above 6 per cent of required reserves even in October, and they rose in Uganda and varied around 20 per cent of required

---

[27] Mishra et al. (2016) find evidence to this effect in a large sample of developing countries.
[28] Saxegaard (2006).

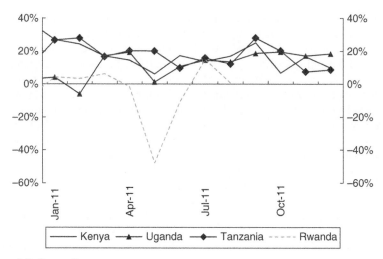

Figure 5.7. Excess Reserves
Source: IMF and authors' computation.

reserves during the peak of the tightening phase, higher than they had been since 2007.[29]

7 CONCLUSIONS

The identification of monetary policy transmission is difficult under any circumstances, and especially so in countries with poor data, obscure and time-varying policy regimes, and frequent supply shocks. As emphasized by Summers (1991) among others, the analysis of dramatic events such as the Great Depression and the Volker disinflation in the United States has played a critical role in forming professional opinion and framing the discussion in advanced countries. However, such analyses are scarce in developing countries.

We have taken advantage of a dramatic tightening of monetary policy in four countries in East Africa in October 2011 to trace through the effects of this tightening on interest rates, credit, the exchange rate, output, and inflation. We find clear evidence of a working transmission mechanism in two of the countries: after a large policy-induced rise in the short-term interest rate in Kenya and Uganda, lending rates rose, the exchange rate appreciated, output growth tended to fall, and inflation declined. The other two countries represent a contrast to varying degrees. In Tanzania, some but not all market rates and the exchange rate seem to respond to adjustments of the monetary policy stance, and we see some

[29] This evidence suggests that these 'excess' reserves may be an equilibrium phenomenon reflecting factors such as risk aversion on the part of banks and structural deficiencies in the functioning of the interbank market. Addressing these deficiencies that create excess liquidity is likely important for the promotion of financial development but, judging from this episode, it does not appear necessary for the transmission of monetary policy.

signs of the effects of policy in output (possibly through credit rationing); in Rwanda, the initial disequilibrium was much smaller, any tightening much less evident, and the effects obscure.

These case studies provide many illustrations of the role that the policy framework itself plays in governing the strength of transmission. Most importantly, Kenya and Uganda by October had clarified their inflation objective and the centrality of the policy rate as the main signal. In this context, they were able to clearly articulate that they were raising rates to bring inflation down. Earlier efforts in Kenya in August, before this clarification, were ineffective. Tanzania represents an intermediate case, in which a continued focus on money targeting and some inconsistency across policy instruments coexisted with a somewhat less clear transmission.

The proliferation of policy instruments was common across all four countries. This put a premium on coherence and communication in signalling the policy stance. The difficulty in interpreting the different measures of policy may impact not only our ability as researchers to discern events but the capacity of interest rates to clear markets and signal policy. From a methodological point of view, this active use of a wide set of instruments under differing policy regimes with multiple objectives, along with the suggested quasi-contemporaneous nature of the transmission mechanism, suggest that extra care should be applied when using standard statistical procedures, such as VARs, to measure the effects of policy, especially when those studies are conducted for country groups.

In contrast, we found some role for financial openness, but little for financial depth or the degree of excess reserves in explaining the cross-country patterns of transmission in these particular cases. We should not overemphasize or over-generalize this result. It remains plausible that countries with less developed financial markets and less open capital accounts will observe weaker transmission. However, this does not seem to have been a determinative feature here.

Clearly, in general, shocks other than those to monetary policy are the main drivers of macroeconomic outcomes in countries such as those we examine here, as various chapters of this book (Chapters 4, 11, 15, 17, 18, and 20) make clear. And here as elsewhere, monetary policy was not made in a vacuum, and identification of shocks and their effects is challenging. It is always a great leap of faith to suppose that a residual in an estimated monetary policy reaction represents such a shock and not a misspecification (e.g. an omitted variable or a nonlinearity) in the reaction function. In our cases, we have used the historical narrative to attempt to argue that much of the shock was a surprise, and we have tried to exclude simple alternative hypotheses about the drivers of some of the key variables. But ultimately the results cannot be definitive.

Much remains unknown about the transmission mechanism in these countries. The role of supply shocks, food prices, the banking system and limited financial participation, fiscal policy, limited capital account openness, and many other features deserve further exploration. Nonetheless, the results are consistent with the view that getting monetary policy broadly right may nonetheless be an important contributor to macroeconomic stability and thus eventually financial development and growth. They should be encouraging for the central banks considering moving toward forward-looking monetary policy frameworks such as inflation targeting. The transmission mechanism appears to be working, but it functions best when signals are clear and the regime simple and coherent. This point is shown analytically in Chapter 9 of this book.

APPENDIX 5A

Table 5A.1. Policy Regimes as of 2011

Country	Exchange Rate Arrangement[a]	Monetary Policy Framework[b]
National Bank of **Kenya** (NBK)	**Free float** Limited foreign exchange intervention, open capital account	**Flexible money targeting** De jure money targets. Central Bank Rate (CBR), announced monthly, important policy signal. In September 2011 the CBK clarified operating procedures and emphasized the CBR as the reference rate.
Bank of **Uganda** (BOU)	**Float** Occasional f/x intervention to 'maintain stability in the foreign exchange market' and build up reserves. Open capital account.	**Inflation targeting lite (as of July 2011)** Moved from flexible money targeting in July 2011. Interest rate operating target, set monthly. A corridor around the CBR is also defined, with its width frequently adjusted.
Bank of **Tanzania** (BOT)	**Float** Substantial f/x intervention. In 2012, the Tanzania shilling traded in a 2 per cent range against the dollar. Widespread capital account controls yield a de facto fairly closed capital account.	**Money targeting** The BOT's Monetary Policy Committee (MPC) sets—and Parliament approves— an operational target on reserve money and intermediate targets on the growth in M2 and M3. Economically meaningful deviations are common. The bank also indicates the stance of policy through movements in the Bank Rate.
National Bank of **Rwanda** (NBR)	**Crawling-peg-like arrangement** Regular f/x intervention. Restrictions to capital account transactions are not prevalent, but the absence of capital inflows is consistent with the view that the capital account is de facto closed.	**Flexible money targeting** Reserve money as operational target and a floor on net foreign assets as an intermediate target. The relatively closed capital account likely allows a certain degree of independence between exchange rate management and monetary policy. The MPC also sets the Key Repo Rate (KRR), which guides liquidity operations. Some direct controls on credit.

[a] According to IMF (2012).
[b] According to Chapter 15 (Kenya), Chapter 18 (Rwanda), Bank of Uganda (2011a) and Chapter 2 (Uganda), and IMF (2015) (for Tanzania).

REFERENCES

Abuka, C., Alinda, R., Minoiu, C., Peydro, J., and Presbitero, A. (2015). *Monetary Policy in a Developing Country: Loan Applications and Real Effects.* IMF Working Paper 15/270. Washington, DC: International Monetary Fund.

Adam, C., Maturu, B., Ndung'u, N., and O'Connell, S. (2010). Building a Monetary Regime for the 21st Century. In C. Adam, P. Collier, and N. Ndung'u (Eds.), *Kenya: Policies for Prosperity.* Oxford: Oxford University Press.

Bank of Uganda. (2011a, July). *Monetary Policy Statements.*

Bank of Uganda. (2011b, October). *Monetary Policy Statements.*

Berg, A., Vlcek, J., Charry, L., and Portillo, R. (2013). *The Monetary Transmission Mechanism in the Tropics: A Narrative Approach.* IMF Working Paper 13/197. Washington, DC: International Monetary Fund.

Bulir, A. and Vlcek, J. (2015). *Monetary Transmission: Are Emerging Market and Low Income Countries Different.* IMF Working Paper 15/239. Washington, DC: International Monetary Fund.

Central Bank of Kenya. (2011a, March). Monetary Policy Committee Meeting [Press release].

Central Bank of Kenya. (2011b, March). Monetary Policy Committee Meeting [Press release].

Central Bank of Kenya. (2011c, September). Monetary Policy Committee Meeting [Press release].

Central Bank of Kenya. (2011d, October). Monetary Policy Committee Meeting [Press release].

Chinn, M. and Ito, H. (2008). A New Measure of Financial Openness. *Journal of Comparative Policy Analysis,* 10(3), 309–22.

Christiano, L. J., Eichenbaum M., and Evans, C. L. (1999). Monetary Policy Shocks: What Have We Learned and to What End? *Handbook of Macroeconomics* (Vol. 1, pp. 65–148). Elsevier.

Dotsey, M. and Reid, M. (1992, July–August). Oil shocks, monetary policy, and economic activity. *Federal Reserve Bank of Richmond Economic Review,* 78, 14–27.

Friedman, M. and Schwartz, A. (1963). *A Monetary History of the United States.* Princeton: Princeton University Press.

Gurkaynak, R., Levin, A., Mardar, A., and Swanson, E. (2007). Inflation Targeting and the Anchoring of Inflation Expectations in the Western Hemisphere. *Economic Review.* San Francisco: Federal Reserve Bank of San Francisco.

International Monetary Fund. (2012). *Annual Report on Exchange Arrangements and Exchange Restrictions.* Washington, DC: International Monetary Fund.

International Monetary Fund. (2015). *Evolving Monetary Policy Frameworks in Low-Income and Other Developing Countries.* Washington, DC: International Monetary Fund.

Mishra, P., Montiel, P., and Spilimbergo, A. (2012). Monetary Transmission in Low-Income Countries: Effectiveness and Policy Implications. *IMF Economic Review,* 60, 270–302.

Montiel, P., Adam, C., Mbowe, W., and O'Connell, S. (2012). *Financial Architecture and the Monetary Transmission Mechanism in Tanzania.* Working Paper. International Growth Center.

National Bank of Rwanda. (2011). The BNR Key Repo Rate Increased From 6% to 6.5%.

Romer, C. and Romer, D. (1989). Does Monetary Policy Matter? A New Test in the Spirit of Friedman and Friedman. In *NBER Macroecononomics Annual,* 4, 121–84. National Bureau of Economic Research.

Saxegaard, M. (2006). *Excess Liquidity and Efectiveness of Monetary Policy: Evidence from Sub-Saharan Africa.* IMF Working Paper 06/115. Washington, DC: International Monetary Fund.

Shapiro, M. D. (1994). Federal Reserve Policy: Cause and Effect. In N. G. Mankiw (Ed.), *Monetary Policy.* NBER Working Paper 4342. Chicago: University of Chicago Press.

Summers, L. (1991). The Scientific Illusion in Empirical Macroeconomics. *Scandinavian Journal of Economics,* 93(2), 129–48.

Woodford, M. (2001, August 30–September 1). Monetary Policy in the Information Economy. Proceedings from the Federal Reserve Bank of Kansas City Annual Symposium Conference: *Economic Policy for the Information Economy,* 1, 297–370. Jackson Hole, Wyoming.

6

Identifying the Monetary Transmission Mechanism in Sub-Saharan Africa

Bin Grace Li, Christopher Adam, Andrew Berg,
Peter Montiel, and Stephen O'Connell

1 INTRODUCTION

Central banks and researchers in low-income countries often use structural vector auto-regression (SVAR) models estimated on aggregate macroeconomic data to develop a reliable understanding of the monetary transmission mechanism (MTM) linking a central bank's policy instruments and the outcomes it is seeking to influence—typically, aggregate demand and inflation.[1] The task of generating robust estimates of the speed, direction, and relative strength of the MTM is demanding in all economies, but particularly so in countries such as those of sub-Saharan Africa where financial markets are thin, the economy is undergoing rapid structural change, and policy regimes are seeking to adjust to this structural change. This task is made even harder by the relatively poor quality of macroeconomic data in many low-income countries.

Most studies of the monetary transmission mechanism in LICs, the majority of which tend to rely on conventional SVAR or models, would appear to confirm the extent of this challenge. Mishra, Montiel, and Spilimbergo (2012) and Mishra and Montiel (2013) survey a large literature on the effectiveness of the monetary transmission mechanism (MTM) in low-income countries. They find that standard empirical methods, in the form of vector auto-regressions (VARs) applied to macroeconomic data, imply that MTMs are *weaker* and *less reliable* in low-income countries than in high-income and emerging economies. By *weaker*, they mean that monetary policy instruments tend to have small estimated effects on aggregate demand. By *less reliable*, they mean that these estimated impacts are not precisely estimated, leaving considerable statistical uncertainty about the true MTM. Mishra et al. (2012) suggest two broad possible explanations for these findings:

- **Facts on the ground.** Formal financial markets are small and poorly arbitraged in these countries, and many low-income countries (LICs) maintain

---

[1] This chapter is based on Li et al. (2016).

fixed or heavily managed exchange rates; as a consequence, the link between the short-term interest rates that central banks can control and the variables that matter for aggregate demand (e.g., longer-term interest rates, the exchange rate) may be weak or absent. Even the bank lending channel may tend to be weak when the formal financial sector is small, financial frictions are severe, and the banking industry is characterized by imperfect competition.

- **Limitations of the method.** The MTM is not in fact weak, but the data-intensive, atheoretic methods typically used to evaluate the MTM empirically are not capable of measuring its strength accurately in the research environment characteristic of LICs. If this explanation is correct, then it is the VAR evidence in LICs that is weak and unreliable, not the MTM itself.

Our aim is to discriminate between the 'facts on the ground' and 'limitations of the method' interpretations of the missing MTM, focusing on the extent to which the characteristics of a LIC research environment are hostile to VAR-based approaches to identification. The stakes here seem high. If the 'facts on the ground' explanation is correct, the empirical literature suggests challenges to successful monetary policies in low-income countries. Along with other features of the LIC environment, such as frequent large supply shocks, weak and uncertain transmission may make it more difficult for policymakers to keep inflation within narrow bounds and to stabilize activity in the face of demand shocks. On the other hand, if the missing MTM mainly reflects methodological limitations, then the results of the VAR-based literature should be suitably discounted and researchers evaluating the strength and reliability of the MTM should seek to compliment VAR-based analyses with approaches that are more robust to the peculiar weaknesses of these methods in LIC-like environments. For example, the use of bank-level or even loan-level data to investigate the strength of the bank lending channel is an obvious candidate (e.g., Mbowe, 2012; Abuka et al., 2015).

In this chapter we attempt to assess the 'limitations of the method' interpretation of the missing MTM, focusing on whether specific characteristics of a LIC research environment are particularly hostile to VAR-based approaches to identification. Specifically, if a strong MTM is present, can standard VAR methods uncover it in a LIC-like research environment? We address this question by applying VAR-based methods to a world in which a strong MTM exists but the research environment has some of the features that are characteristic of LICs. A list of these features might include, for example, poorly understood economic structure and non-transparent central banks; short data samples due to missing data or recent major structural changes or policy reforms; large measurement errors; and a high volatility of macroeconomic shocks (especially the prevalence of large temporary supply shocks). Here, we focus on the former set of structural concerns, rather than issues of data and measurement. These are dealt with in detail in Li et al. (2016).

To implement this programme we set up a Monte Carlo experiment to assess the statistical properties of the kind of SVAR models typically deployed on low-income country data. Underlying the data-generating process is a small dynamic stochastic general equilibrium (DSGE) model of a small open economy that embodies a well-defined MTM with an interest-rate channel and an exchange-rate channel. We use the solution to this DSGE to generate multiple independent runs of data, and then within each of these runs, mimic the process of an empirical researcher using SVAR-based methods to infer the nature of the MTM. In particular, we examine the properties of the impulse response functions (IRFs) that she would produce. We compare her median estimated IRFs to the true one, study the spread of estimated IRFs across simulations, and examine the power of conventional significance tests against the hypothesis of a zero response.

Section 2 introduces our DSGE model in four macroeconomic variables, the GDP gap, the inflation rate, the real exchange rate, and the nominal interest rate, while in Section 3 we discuss the relationship between DSGEs and structural VARs that can be identified using restrictions on the contemporaneous inter-actions between the variables. Section 4 begins by documenting the empirical success of the VAR-based approach when the researcher has chosen a valid identification scheme and is operating in a favourable research environment (as may be found in a mature open economy such as Canada, for example). Section 5 quantifies the effects on inference of various sorts of weak transmission, some of which are plausibly related to the structure of LIC economies and others to the characteristics of monetary policy regimes themselves.

Section 6 offers a cautionary detour. It is well-understood that correct identi-fication is critical. When the environment in which the central bank operates and its mode of operation are poorly understood—as is perhaps particularly the case in most LICs, both because of the opacity of the regimes and the scarcity of research—identification is especially challenging, and estimates of the MTM can go badly wrong. Section 7 drills deeper into misidentification by analysing the implication of non-transparent central bank policy frameworks, in such as the hybrid money targeting regimes, which characterize many LICs. We conclude that misidentification related to hybrid monetary policy reaction functions is a plaus-ible and difficult challenge. Section 8 concludes with a summary of findings and with a discussion of possible extensions and policy implications.

2 DSGES AS A DATA-GENERATING PROCESS

The MTM is about the ability of monetary policy to exert a temporary effect on aggregate demand.[2] To focus on these effects we ignore stochastic trends in the data, implicitly assuming that these can be estimated with reasonable statistical confidence so that the stationary part of the data is cleanly isolated. Our DSGE models will therefore generate a stationary vector $x_t = [\tilde{y}_t, \pi_t, \tilde{e}_t, i_t]'$ of quarterly values for the GDP gap ($\tilde{y}_t$, defined as the gap between actual GDP and unob-servable potential GDP), the inflation rate (π_t), the real exchange rate ($\tilde{e}_t$, with an increase being a real appreciation), and the annualized nominal interest rate (i_t). In this chapter we treat the model-generated GDP gap as observable, although in Li et al. (2016) we introduce an underlying trend in GDP to examine how

---

[2] Weak and unreliable transmission in the short run is, of course, perfectly consistent with monetary policy providing an effective long-run anchor for inflation.

difficulties in inferring the GDP gap from observed measures of output affect inference.

The four endogenous variables in the model will in turn be functions of a vector $\epsilon_t = [\epsilon_t^y, \epsilon_t^\pi, \epsilon_t^e, \epsilon_t^i]'$ of structural shocks that are not directly observable by the researcher. The objects of interest to the researcher are the responses of x_{t+j} to a one-time unit-value shock to monetary policy ($\Delta\epsilon_t^i = 1$). To estimate these, the researcher starts by estimating a reduced-form VAR of the form

$$x_t = A(L)x_{t-1} + u_t, \tag{1}$$

where $A(L)$ contains enough lags to render the reduced-form innovations u_t approximately white noise. In the absence of measurement error or inappropriate truncation, this produces consistent estimates of the lag parameters in $A(L)$ and the covariance matrix Ω of the reduced-form innovations.[3] The researcher then imposes enough restrictions on the reduced form to identify the structural shocks to monetary policy. In our case, these take the form of zero restrictions on elements of the square and invertible matrix B in

$$u_t = B\epsilon_t. \tag{2}$$

Conditional on identification, the impulse responses (IRs) can then be calculated as nonlinear functions of the estimated lag parameters and reduced-form shock covariances. The researcher computes these estimated IRs and, in a final step, bootstraps their standard errors and calculates t ratios for each impulse-response step. When a 'true' MTM is present in the data-generating process, the researcher should see impulse responses that are appropriately signed and shaped, of roughly correct magnitude, and of reasonable statistical significance. We loop over multiple simulated datasets in order to study the population distribution of estimated impulse responses, the associated t-ratios, and the power of the t-ratio test in a wide variety of specific environments.

2.1 The DSGE Model

The model we employ for our experiments is a canonical New Keynesian open-economy model that combines an IS curve, a New Keynesian Phillips curve, an interest-parity condition, and a Taylor Rule for monetary policy (e.g., Berg, Karam, and Laxton, 2006). There is no empirical consensus on the appropriate parameterization of such a model for LICs, but in choosing parameters we can draw on recent research that develops partly calibrated and partly estimated DSGEs for low-income countries in Africa. We rely particularly on Chapter 8, which develops DSGEs with similar four-equation structure for Kenya, Tanzania, and Uganda. Our basic model, complete with parameters, is:

IS equation:

$$\tilde{y}_t = 0.5 \cdot E_t[\tilde{y}_{t+1}] + 0.5 \cdot \tilde{y}_{t-1} - 0.2 \cdot [0.5 \cdot (i_t - E_t[\pi_{t+1}] - \bar{r}) + 0.5 \cdot \tilde{e}_t] + \epsilon_t^y, \tag{3}$$

---

[3] The VAR representation of the DSGE solution may be infinite-order; discussed on page 116.

New Keynesian Phillips curve:

$$\pi_t = 0.5 \cdot E_t[\pi_{t+1}] + 0.5 \cdot \pi_{t-1} + 0.15 \cdot \tilde{y}_t - 0.15 \cdot \tilde{e}_t + \epsilon_t^\pi, \tag{4}$$

Uncovered interest parity equation:

$$\tilde{e}_t = 0.5 \cdot E_t[\tilde{e}_{t+1}] + 0.5 \cdot \tilde{e}_{t-1} + (1/4) \cdot [i_t - E_t[\pi_{t+1}] - \bar{r}^*] + \epsilon_t^e, \tag{5}$$

Taylor-type rule for monetary policy:

$$i_t = 0.5 \cdot (\bar{r} + 1.4 \cdot E_t[\pi_{t+1}] + 0.5 \cdot E_t[\tilde{y}_{t+1}]) + 0.5 \cdot i_{t-1} + \epsilon_t^i, \tag{6}$$

Structural shocks:

$$\epsilon_t \sim i.i.d \ \ N(0, I_4) \tag{7}$$

Here E_t denotes an expectation conditional on information available at time t. As explained below, we allow information sets to vary across equations, reflecting differences in the information available to agents. Note also that equation (7) departs from the bulk of the DSGE literature by assuming *i.i.d.* shocks, in preference to the standard AR(1) structure: our version allows for distributed lag responses similar to those in the literature, but these are governed completely by the lags within the behavioural equations. By eliminating purely exogenous dynamics, we substantially simplify the task of solving the DSGE and representing its solution as a structural VAR, although in principle the VAR could be conditioned on strongly exogenous variables such as world oil prices.

The model we are employing was of course not developed for LICs, and in characterizing the MTM it makes no effort to capture the financial architecture or other 'facts on the ground' that may differentiate LICs from the advanced countries for which these models were developed. For most of the analysis, monetary policy follows a Taylor-style rule, even though many LICs use the monetary base and other measures rather than a policy interest rate as the main operational instrument. In Section 7 we briefly consider the case where the authorities' true reaction function gives weight to deviations in money aggregates from target, but where this reaction function may not be correctly identified by the econometrician. We also omit a banking sector from the model, even though the nature of the credit channel may differ in LICs as compared to more advanced countries. Finally, we simplify by assuming that the structural shocks are mutually uncorrelated. These simplifications reflect our focus on aspects of the research environment that are largely model-independent. Our Monte Carlo approach can of course be applied to *any* structural model, a topic to which we return in the concluding section.

Our data-generating process will not be the DSGE model itself, but rather its solution in terms of the endogenous state variables and the shock vector ϵ_t. This introduces a set of technical issues that are well understood in the DSGE and VAR literatures but that appear here in combination. First, for VAR-based methods to have a chance of uncovering the features of the MTM, the solution to the DSGE must be representable, at least approximately, as a finite-order VAR in observable variables. As discussed in detail in Li et al. (2016) some of our model solutions have *exact* representations as finite-order VARs, while others are well approximated by VARs with short lags (we use four-quarterly lags). Second, the monetary policy shocks must be identifiable through the imposition of conventional structural-VAR restrictions on this representation. We focus on short-run restrictions, because these remain the dominant approach to identification in the applied literature reviewed by Mishra et al. (2012). As discussed below, such restrictions work by limiting the contemporaneous interactions between the variables in the VAR.

3 MOTIVATING CEE-RECURSIVE STRUCTURE

The restrictions we impose at the estimation stage are typically motivated in the structural VAR literature by appealing to a structural simultaneous equations model of the form

$$B_0 x_t = B(L)x_{t-1} + \epsilon_t. \tag{8}$$

The shocks ϵ_t are *i.i.d.* and mutually uncorrelated variables that can be normalized without loss of generality to have unit variances ($E[\epsilon_t \epsilon_t'] = I$).[4] As long as B_0 is invertible, equation (8) implies the reduced-form VAR representation in equation (1), with $A(L) = B_0^{-1}B(L)$. The relationship between the structural and reduced-form innovations is then given by equation (2), with $B = B_0^{-1}$.

Within the class of short-run restrictions, the most common are those that impose a recursive structure on B_0. Cholesky decompositions assume that the model is fully recursive, so that B_0 is lower triangular. As Christiano, Eichenbaum, and Evans (1999) have shown, however, if the focus is on the impulse responses just to monetary policy shocks, these can be recovered from the reduced form VAR under the considerably weaker condition that the system be contemporaneously block-lower-triangular, with the interest rate occupying its own diagonal block. We refer to any system that can be ordered into two or more block-recursive segments, with the interest rate occupying its own diagonal block, as 'CEE-recursive'. When a structural VAR model is CEE-recursive, the impulse responses to monetary policy shocks can be recovered from the reduced-form VAR even if the remaining impulse responses cannot.[5]

A glance at equations (3)–(7) confirms that the solution to our DSGE will not exhibit the block-recursiveness property under full information. Instead, it will tend to be highly simultaneous. This is in part because monetary policy is assumed to affect all endogenous variables contemporaneously, so the interest rate does not occupy its own diagonal block. However, it also reflects the role of expectation variables, since any endogenous variable that is in the information set of a particular class of agents will contemporaneously affect all of the endogenous variables that are influenced by the forecasts or 'now-casts' formulated by those

---

[4] A one-unit shock to ϵ_t^j is then equivalent to one standard deviation of the structural shock to monetary policy.

[5] For the same reason, the ordering of variables within each of the recursively prior and posterior blocks is irrelevant to obtaining the responses to interest-rate shocks (Christiano, Eichenbaum, and Evans, 1999).

agents. Since all of the equations in our model contain such expectation variables, under full information *all* of the model's endogenous variables would tend to appear in every equation.

We therefore have to impose additional restrictions on our DSGE in order to produce a data-generating process that is identifiable via short-run restrictions. We retain the simultaneity of the structural model and obtain exclusion restrictions through assumptions about the information sets available to the private sector and the central bank. For most of the chapter, we place the interest rate first in the CEE block-recursive ordering so that it affects all other variables contemporaneously. What this means is that the private sector has full information, but the central bank can only observe the endogenous variables with a lag.

This structure can be rationalized as follows: the central bank (strictly its monetary policy committee) sets the systematic part of the policy interest rate at the beginning of the period, before any shocks arrive. Shocks then hit the system and are observed by the private sector and the monetary policy committee. The private sector can react immediately, but the central bank cannot do so until the beginning of the next period (i.e. the next MPC meeting). The central bank is, therefore, setting the systematic part of its policy on the basis of $t-1$ information, while the private sector is behaving on the basis of time-t information. We suggest this structure may have greater plausibility in a LIC context, where the central bank has less access to timely information on the state of the economy, than in higher-income countries. To denote the informational advantage of the private sector, we refer to this block-recursive identification strategy as 'CEE-PS'.

For robustness, we also examine an alternative strategy in which the informational advantage accrues to the central bank. It sets the interest rate with full information, but the interest rate does not affect the model's other endogenous variables contemporaneously, not because of a behavioural lag, but because the private sector does not observe the shock to monetary policy contemporaneously, so it reacts to its *forecast* of the time-t interest rate based on information dated at time $t-1$. This structure, which corresponds to a block-recursive structure in which the interest rate block comes last, follows Christiano, Eichenbaum, and Evans (2005) and reflects the common practice in the advanced-country VAR literature of attributing an information advantage to the central bank. We refer to this identification strategy as 'CEE-CB'.

These identification strategies still fall foul of the serious challenge to recursively identified VARs in an open-economy context posed by Kim and Roubini (2000). As they point out, the interest rate cannot occupy its own diagonal block unless the central bank does not respond contemporaneously to the current exchange rate (in our preferred CEE-PS formulation) or if the exchange rate does not respond to the current interest rate (in the CEE-CB formulation). Absent either of these two conditions, the interest rate and exchange rate are simultaneously determined regardless of the recursive structure of the remainder of the model. This is addressed within the structural VAR literature by appealing to non-recursive short-run restrictions, sometimes in combination with theoretically motivated long-run restrictions (e.g., that monetary policy has no long-run impact on real variables).

4 STRONG VAR PERFORMANCE UNDER BASELINE CONDITIONS

Figure 6.1 sets the stage for the subsequent discussion. Here we report the performance of a validly identified CEE-recursive VAR using forty years of quarterly data. The experiment assumes equal variances for the four structural shocks, and the information structure is CEE-PS. The researcher estimates the VAR with four lags.[6] To focus on parameters of interest we report only the impulse response functions for the monetary policy shock. Since the components of Figures 6.1a and 6.1b will appear throughout the chapter, we begin by describing their content.

The researcher is trying to uncover the true, model-based impulse responses, which appear as the bold lines identified by dots in Figure 6.1a. As shown in the figure, these IRFs display the conventional hump-shaped responses of the real exchange rate, inflation, and output to a monetary contraction. On impact, a 100 basis point increase in the interest rate leads to a 1 percentage point contraction in inflation and a reduction in the output gap by around 0.7 per cent of GDP, values that are broadly in line with Christiano et al. (2005). To examine whether VAR methods can uncover these responses, we generate 1,000 data samples from our model, based on independent simulations of the DSGE solution, each generated by 40 quarters of independent draws on the shock vector ϵ_t. For each data sample, a researcher estimates a VAR and constructs IRs by imposing the CEE-PS identifying restrictions. The empirical performance of these IRs is summarized by the three dashed lines in Figure 6.1a. These lines show the fifth, fiftieth, and ninety-fifth percentiles of the population distribution of simulated point estimates for the impulse responses (with percentiles computed separately for each impulse-response step).

For each of the 1,000 simulations, the researcher computes the VAR coefficients and standard errors using conventional Bayesian estimation methods. The figure shows the probability of rejecting the null hypothesis of a zero impulse-response coefficient at each step. We assume that the researcher treats the t ratios as asymptotically normal and applies the relatively undemanding hurdle of 10 per cent significance.

Figures 6.1a and 6.1b establish that with appropriate identification and in the presence of ample and high-quality data, the VAR methodology does very well at uncovering strong monetary transmission when it is present. The estimated impulse responses for output and inflation show only a trivial degree of small-sample attenuation at the median, and for the first few quarters fully 90 per cent or more of the point estimates lie on the correct side of zero.

The researcher's own inference will of course frequently be less confident than suggested by Figure 6.1b, because the researcher has only one data sample. Figure 6.1c reflects this by showing the full distribution of t ratios across

---

[6] In the CEE-CB case, the DSGE solution is an exact VAR(1). The true lag length may be infinite in the CEE-PS case, and it would be straightforward to embed a data-driven choice of appropriate lag length. Our baseline VAR(4) estimates differ only trivially, however, from estimates generated by VARs with eight or twelve lags (results available on request). These lag comparisons suggest that any loss of efficiency from suboptimal choice of lag length is not large.

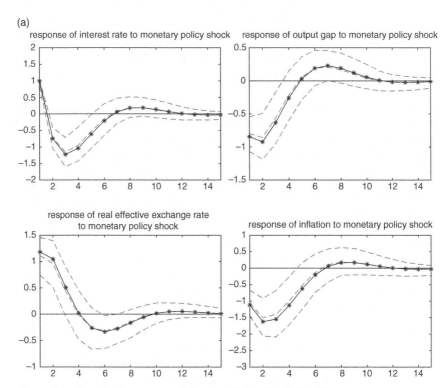

(a)

Figure 6.1.a Impulse Responses to Monetary Policy Shock: Baseline

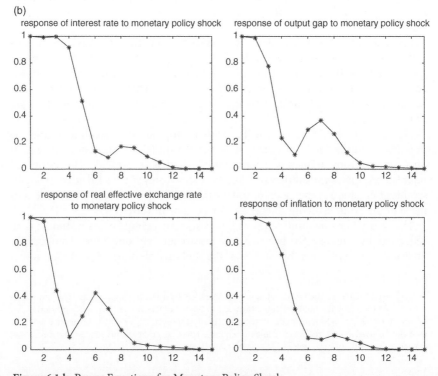

(b)

Figure 6.1.b Power Functions for Monetary Policy Shock

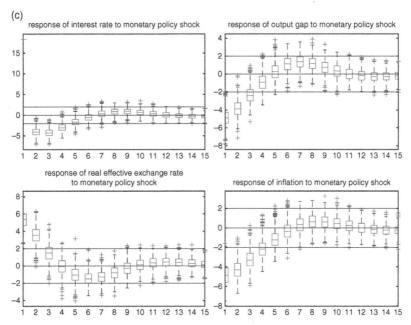

Figure 6.1.c T-stat for Monetary Policy Shocks

the 1,000 runs. The structure of the exercise suggests that the width of boot-strapped confidence intervals for the IR coefficients will not be far from that implied by the population distribution of impulse responses, and the comparison of Figures 6.1a and 6.1c bears this out. When one end of the population distribution of IRs is close to zero in Figure 6.1a, roughly half of the *t* statistics reported in Figure 6.1c fail to reject the null.[7]

5 LOW POWER TO DETECT WEAK TRANSMISSION

Unfortunately, the power of the SVAR method to reject the null of no transmission deteriorates significantly when true transmission is present, but weak. In this section we illustrate this property under several alternative sources of weak transmission. Figure 6.2 shows the results of the alternative CEE-CB experiment, where the central bank has the information advantage and the model solution places the interest rate last. To keep the presentation of results manageable we reproduce, on the top row, the impulse response plots for output and inflation only and the corresponding power plots on the bottom row of the figure. The model parameters are identical in the two cases, but there is a substantial

---

[7] The inference plots are very consistent with this effect. This suggests that the bootstrapped standard errors calculated by the researcher on each run of data tend to closely approximate the spread of the population distribution.

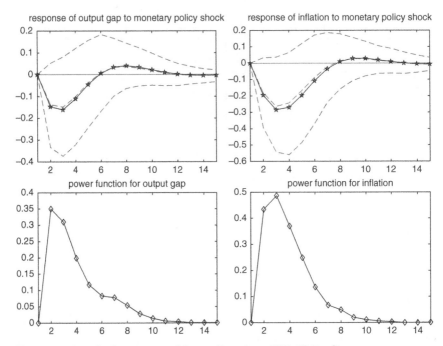

Figure 6.2. Impulse Responses and Power Functions: CEE-CB Baseline

difference in the true impulse responses, with the MTM being much weaker in this case (compare the top row of Figure 6.2 with Figure 6.1a, noting the difference in the vertical scales). The difference is driven by the effect of lags in diluting the impact of a monetary policy change in the CEE-CB case. The SVAR results are somewhat weaker in this case: though the median estimated IRF continues to track the true IRs generated by the model very closely, the fifth and ninety-fifth percentiles of the estimated IRFs are now more widely dispersed relative to the median, and there is a correspondingly substantial loss of power. The deterioration in the inference environment relative to Figures 6.1a and 6.1b reflects the unfavourable effect on inference of smaller true effect sizes.

The weaker MTM just described arose from an alternative information structure, with unchanged model parameters. To explore further the implications for inference of a weak MTM, we now consider the impact on VAR-based inference of small true effects driven by model parameters, rather than by the information environment. To do so, we return to the CEE-PS information structure as the baseline. Even within a tightly parameterized DSGE, there are many parameters that may differ substantially between LIC and higher-income applications. The private-sector block incorporates both an interest-rate channel that operates though the IS curve and an exchange-rate channel that branches off from the interest parity condition to the IS and Phillips curves, while the monetary policy rule incorporates feedback from both inflation and the GDP gap along with a parameter that governs the degree of interest-rate smoothing. Based on Mishra et al. (2012) and Mishra and Montiel (2013), we focus here on two simple experiments. In Figure 6.3, we scale down the transmission elasticities in the IS

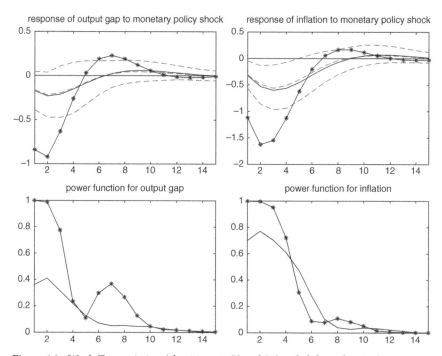

Figure 6.3. Weak Transmission (elasticities in IS and PC scaled down by 75%)

and Phillips curves by a uniform 75 per cent relative to the baseline model, and in Figure 6.4 we leave the transmission elasticities untouched but reduce the lag parameter in the monetary policy rule by 75 per cent.

Figure 6.3 shows the impact of uniformly low interest-rate and exchange-rate elasticities in the private-sector block. The (new) true IRs in this case are shown by the heavy solid line. As before, the dashed lines show the fifth, fiftieth, and ninety-fifth percentiles of the population distribution of simulated point estimates. For reference, the true IRs with the original model parameters are retained in the figure in the form of the heavy line with dots. As expected, the change in the parameters weakens the effect of monetary policy on aggregate demand, which shows up in the form of smaller impacts on the GDP gap and the inflation rate. The true MTM is particularly weakened with respect to its effects on real activity. Notably, however, the estimated impulse responses continue to show very strong fidelity at the median, with the median IRs corresponding very closely to the true ones. Comparing Figures 6.3 and 6.1a, there is also no discernible impact on the spread of estimated impulse responses. To a first approximation, therefore, the impact of weak transmission elasticities operates exclusively through the impact of small true effect sizes on the power of t-ratio tests against the null hypothesis of no effect. That impact is substantial, however, with the scope for confident inference cut roughly in half (bottom row of Figure 6.3).[8]

---

[8] The exchange-rate channel is quantitatively important in our model. In simulations not reported here, we show that if only the interest-rate elasticity differs between LIC and non-LIC

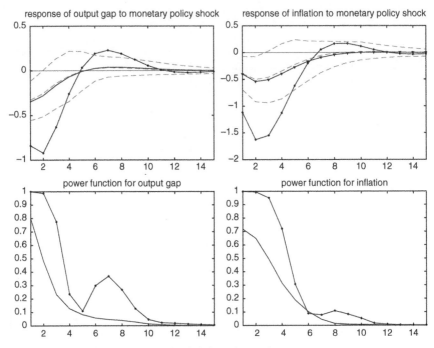

Figure 6.4. Smoothing Parameter (scaled down by 75%)

Finally, in New Keynesian models such as (3)–(6), the strength of transmission depends not only on spending elasticities, but also on a transmission channel that may differ sharply between LICs and higher-income countries. Mishra, Montiel, and Spilimbergo (2012) find that the correlation between short-term interest rates and lending rates tends to become progressively weaker at lower levels of development. While equations (3)–(6) do not directly incorporate a lending channel, the IS curve and interest-parity condition can be solved forward to express the levels of the current GDP gap and real exchange rate gap as functions of current and expected future short-term interest rates. As emphasized by Woodford (2001), monetary policy shocks affect the 'tilt' of the spending and real exchange rate gaps via the short-term interest rate, but they alter the equilibrium *level* of these variables only to the degree that they change current long-term rates. The pass-through of short rates to long rates is in turn governed both by the parameters of the private sector block and, very importantly, by the degree of interest-rate smoothing implemented by the central bank.[9] To investigate the role of the latter, in Figure 6.4, we leave the transmission elasticities unchanged and reduce

applications, and not the exchange rate elasticity, the deterioration in the inference about the MTM is mild.

[9] Our simple model does not incorporate a separate bank lending channel, which would introduce an additional potential source of weak transmission related to imperfect competition and/or high intermediation costs in the banking sector of low-income economies (Mishra et al. 2012, 2013).

the smoothing parameter in the monetary policy rule by 75 per cent. Monetary policy shocks now pass through much more weakly into long rates and spending.

These results underscore the leverage of interest-rate smoothing in the New Keynesian model. The true impulse responses (shown by the solid line in bold) decline slightly more sharply than when the transmission elasticities are reduced by the same proportion, but the overall shapes are virtually identical. Consistent with our previous results, there is minimal evidence of bias in the impulse responses: the very weak true IRs are faithfully reproduced by the median estimated IRs. Not surprisingly, there is now much less scope to reject the null hypothesis of zero monetary policy effects.

Overall, Figures 6.1 to 6.4 are consistent with a 'facts on the ground' interpretation of the 'missing MTM' puzzle. Given a valid block-recursive identification scheme and sufficient data, structural VARs identified through short-run restrictions do well at uncovering the true MTM—whether it is strong or weak—in the strict sense that the median estimated IRs track very closely those generated by the true MTM. At the same time, however, we have found that the population dispersion in estimated IRs is not substantially affected by the strength of the underlying 'true' MTM. Therefore, the weaker the true MTM, the harder it is for the data to reject the null of no response—i.e., the weaker the power of tests of the null hypothesis that the MTM is entirely missing. Even where a (plausibly weak) MTM exists, the researcher armed with only one dataset, even a pristine one that is 40 years long, may well conclude that it is missing.

6 IDENTIFICATION THROUGH BEHAVIOURAL LAGS AND INFORMATION SETS

Up to this point, we have maintained the assumption of correct identification. The perils of incorrect SVAR identification are of course neither surprising nor LIC-specific. However, there tends to be no consensus on the nature of behavioural lags and information sets in the LIC environment. Thus, identification of monetary policy shocks is likely to prove far more difficult in the LIC environment than in the more familiar environment of high-income countries.

In this section, we examine the case in which the researcher places the interest rate too late in the recursive structure of the model. If our CEE-PS ordering has any special plausibility in low-income applications, this error might be a natural one for a researcher trained in the advanced-country literature. The researcher in Figure 6.5 assumes a CEE-CB information structure when the true structure is in fact CEE-PS. The solid line with dots in bold represents the true CEE-PS impulse responses (reproduced directly from Figure 6.1) while the dashed lines once again represent the fifth, fiftieth, and ninety-fifth percentiles of the estimated IRFs when the data are generated by CEE-PS but the researcher mistakenly imposes CEE-CB identification.

The result of this error is sufficient to produce impulse responses that are 'weak and unreliable' in the extreme: they are essentially zero, both economically and statistically. At the median, they closely approximate the relatively weak shapes of

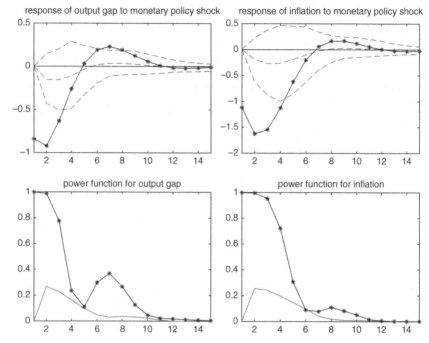

Figure 6.5. CEE-PS Wrong Identification

the impulse responses that would have been generated by a CEE-CB structure, even though the true responses are the much stronger ones generated by CEE-PS. However, the dispersion of the estimated IRFs is dramatically wider than was observed when CEE-CB was in fact the correct identification (compare Figure 6.5 with Figure 6.2). Not surprisingly, statistical tests based on bootstrapped standard errors for the estimated IRs will have essentially no power to reject the null of zero monetary policy effects in this case (Figure 6.5), even though the true effects are in fact extremely powerful.

7 CENTRAL BANK TRANSPARENCY

Central banks in LICs tend in general to be far less transparent than those in high-income countries, making the nature of the monetary policy rule less evident.[10] To examine the pitfalls posed for estimation of the MTM by misspecification of the monetary policy rule, we consider a case where the authorities optimally update their policy interest rate on the basis of the growth of money aggregates relative to target, but where this additional information on money growth is not exploited by the researcher. This setting is described in Chapter 8, where money

---

[10] See Chapter 8 for a discussion.

aggregates, which are essentially observed in real time, are systematically related to expected output and inflation through the private sector's demand for money. Ex ante, there is therefore an exact equivalence between any given interest rate rule and a corresponding money target. This equivalence does not hold when the economy is subject to shocks, including to money demand, so that the authorities' optimal policy rule entails giving weight to both deviations of the interest rate from target and money from its target. How much weight is placed on money in the policy rule will depend on the volatility of money demand shocks relative to real shocks and on the interest elasticity of the demand money. When money demand is highly volatile and the interest elasticity is high, the optimal weight placed on money should be low, and vice versa.

To operationalize this idea, we augment our baseline model by introducing the nominal money target into the Taylor rule defined in equation (6), recalling that the inflation and nominal money growth targets are both zero. First, consider a pure money-targeting rule, in which the authorities allow interest rates to move so as to achieve the desired growth rate of money, assumed to be 0 for simplicity. We can start with a conventional money demand equation for the change in money, Δm_t:

$$\Delta m_t - \pi_t = \Delta y_t - \theta \Delta i_t + \Delta \epsilon_t^d. \tag{9}$$

The associated interest rate that sets money growth to the target, i_t^M, is then:

$$i_t^M = \frac{1}{\theta}(\pi_t + \Delta y_t + \Delta \epsilon_t^d) - i_{t-1}. \tag{10}$$

Following Chapter 16, we can define a hybrid rule as follows:

$$\lambda(i_t - i_t^T) + (1 - \lambda)(i_t - i_t^M) = \epsilon_t^i, \tag{11}$$

where $i_t{}^T$ is the interest rate target defined in equation (6) (excluding the monetary policy shock in that equation, which is now explicit in equation (11)). The parameter λ defines the weight placed on the interest rate rule. When $\lambda = 1$, the result is a standard Taylor-type rule as we discuss before; when $\lambda = 0$, policy is defined in terms of a target (0 in this case) for the growth rate of money, and the interest rate is a residual in that it follows from the authorities' efforts to hit their money target. In many 'money targeting' countries, it is plausible to think that λ lies somewhere in the middle.[11]

Solving equation (11) for the interest rate yields a hybrid rule:

$$i_t = \lambda i_t^T + (1 - \lambda)i_t^M + \epsilon_t^i \tag{12}$$

Replacing i_t^T with equation (6)and i_t^M with equation (10), we recover an implicit interest rate rule of the form:

$$i_t = \psi_0 + \psi_i i_{t-1} + \psi_{y,t-1} y_{t-1} + \psi_{y,t} y_t + \psi_{\pi,t} \pi_t + + \psi_\pi E_t[\pi_{t+1}] + \psi_y E_t[\tilde{y}_{t+1}] + \epsilon_t^m, \tag{13}$$

---

[11] See Chapter 16 on money targeting in practice and Chapter 8 on reaction functions of this sort.

where, critically, ϵ_t^m is a composite of the money supply and money demand shocks, and the appearance of y_t and π_t implies that all shocks that matter for these variables, notably contemporaneous aggregate demand and supply shocks, also affect the interest rate contemporaneously.

With the true model now defined by equations (3)–(5) and (7) and (9) plus (6), (10), and (12) (or (13)), the researcher armed with the four-variable vector of data $x_t = [i_t, \tilde{e}_t, y_t, \pi_t]'$, will only correctly identify the monetary policy shock if $\lambda = 1$. For any $\lambda < 1$, however, where money growth provides the central bank with information on the evolution of inflation and the output gap, the researcher is unable to decompose the composite error term in (13) so as to cleanly identify the monetary policy shock.

Figure 6.6 shows the outcome of applying our standard four-variable VAR with the same recursive identification to data produced by a model with hybrid monetary policy, where $\lambda = 0.95$, i.e. where in the model the authorities place only a small weight on money deviations from target. As the figure shows, even this seemingly minor deviation strongly attenuates the median estimated impulse responses and greatly reduces power relative to the baseline.[12]

In both the case of the alternative information structure (implying a different recursive ordering) and the case of hybrid policy rules involving money, the nature of the impulse response functions might lead the researcher to re-think their estimation strategy (rather than conclude that transmission is weak, for example). In the first case, experimenting with alternative recursive orderings would help. In the second case, however, it would not. Even with the full five-variable vector, neither recursive identification strategy can isolate the monetary policy shock in its own block.

Imposing more structural identification schemes such as SVARs might help in the hybrid rule case.[13] However, this solution is far from trivial. First, our conventional specification of money demand is very limited. In the DSGE tradition, money demand may also depend on expected inflation and other variables.[14] In this situation, no contemporaneous zero restrictions in the money demand equation are available to identify the SVAR. More generally, getting SVAR zero restrictions right would require being precise about the details of a quite complex policy framework. If our money-targeting example is indicative, there is not likely to be a one-size-fits-all solution to the proper identification of monetary shocks in more complex settings.

Taken together, the results in this and the last sections suggest that incorrect identification of monetary policy shocks is itself a prime suspect in the case of the missing MTM.

---

[12] It need not be the case that this misspecification strongly attenuates the impulse responses towards zero. Depending on the relative frequency of the different structural shocks and the value of λ (and other parameter values), different outcomes are possible. For example with $\lambda = 0.5$, and all structural shocks having equal variances as we have been assuming, the estimated impulse responses are not attenuated towards zero but rather are the opposite of the true ones.

[13] For example Boughton and Tavlas (1991) used instrumental variables to estimate money demand and money supply shocks via a two-step least squares method. See also Sims and Zha (2006).

[14] Nelson (2002) argues forcefully that money demand depends on the long interest rate, which would bring all shocks that matter for future interest rates into the money demand equation.

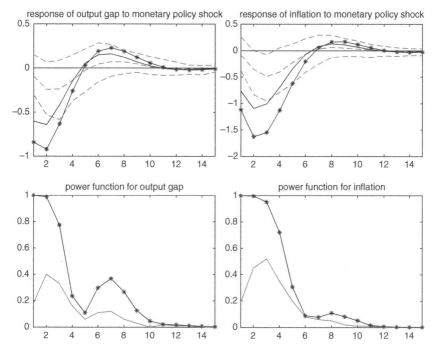

Figure 6.6. CEE-PS Money Target Model ($\lambda = 0.95$)

8 CONCLUSIONS

In an effort to come to grips with the 'missing MTM' in the empirical literature on LICs, we have reversed the standard dialogue between DSGEs and VARs. In the standard dialogue, VAR-based impulse responses provide an empirical standard against which DSGEs or other theory-based models can be evaluated. We have instead used DSGEs as a data-generating process, in order to ask a question about the validity of VAR-based impulse responses. If a strong MTM is present in the data, can standard VAR methods uncover it?

No parametric method will do very well if it mis-specifies the data-generating process. This is the basis of Sims' critique of structural econometric modelling, and as long as the data are generated by a stable but unknown data-generating process, this critique favours the use of as few structural restrictions as possible to identify the MTM. VARs identified via short-run restrictions are very widely used in the literature on LICs, and perhaps even more intensively there than elsewhere, given the relative dearth of structural modelling in these countries. Within this class, we have focused on CEE-recursive VARs, which impose just enough recursive structure to identify the monetary policy impulse responses, while leaving the other responses potentially unidentified. Our off-the-shelf DSGE will not generate a solution with this property, but we have demonstrated that an otherwise-canonical DSGE is capable of doing so under mixed-information assumptions of the type often seen in the structural VAR literature.

When the VAR researcher imposes a valid identification scheme and has access to ample and high-quality data, the virtues of the VAR approach come through strongly. The LIC environment nonetheless poses a set of well-defined challenges to a strategy that 'lets the data speak': we investigate the effects on statistical power of weak transmission arising from various sources as well as inappropriate identification of monetary policy shocks due to incorrect assumptions about behavioural lags and information asymmetries or to opaque monetary policy rules.

We find that a weaker—but otherwise standard—MTM would be hard for a typical VAR to detect, even with forty years of pristine data and proper identification. Point estimates of the impulse responses to monetary shocks are at most only mildly attenuated when the MTM is unusually weak. However, the power of the VARs to reject the null that the MTM is 'missing' is very low. Among the potential sources of weak transmission, we have emphasized three: lags in private sector responses, small interest rate and exchange rate elasticities in the goods markets, possibly caused by the small size of the formal financial system and the structure of external trade in LICs, and a limited degree of interest-rate smoothing that reduces the signalling power of a given interest rate change. Some of these features would presumably be highly persistent features of the economies. Those that depend on the policy regime, notably low smoothing, could change quickly.

We also find that, unsurprisingly, improper identification can easily produce estimates suggesting a weak MTM, even when a strong MTM is present. Because the identification challenge is likely more severe in the LIC context than in the better-understood context of high-income countries, deficiencies in identification strategy are another prime suspect in the 'case of the missing MTM'. Such challenges can arise from poorly understood behavioural and information lags, and/or from opaque central bank policy rules. In some cases, econometric due diligence may rescue matters, as experimentation with alternative block-recursive orderings would do in one of the examples of the previous section. The possibility that more serious mis-specifications are obscuring the MTM, however, requires a willingness to re-think the SVAR identification strategy and, in some cases, to explore different approaches to identification.

There is a paucity of information on which to base standard block-recursive identification of monetary policy shocks in the LIC context, and the role of exchange rates and perhaps money aggregates as well as interest rates, complicates the identification challenge and renders exclusion restrictions particularly difficult to justify. Unless a strong case for a specific set of short-run restrictions can be made in specific applications, other approaches to identification may prove more fruitful. A natural extension of the approach of this chapter would be to acknowledge the reality that agents in the economy (central bank and private sector alike) can observe both the exchange rate and the interest rate in real time. When these two variables form a simultaneous block, the monetary policy shock will not be identifiable by imposing a block-recursive structure.[15] Another approach to

---

[15] Kim and Roubini (2000) identify the monetary policy shock by imposing a non-recursive set of behavioral and information restrictions on the B_0 matrix. From a DSGE perspective, however, their key exclusion restriction (that countries do not react directly to foreign interest rates) may be hard to

identification of monetary policy shocks makes use of long-run restrictions, as in Mishra, Montiel, Pedroni, and Spilimbergo (2014).

Altogether, all these VAR based methods seem worth pursuing. Further country-specific analyses that carefully tailor the approach to the particular country-specific institutional framework for monetary policy may permit progress. Even in the US, with its unusually long, stable data series and policy regimes, economists experimented for many years before reliably generating acceptable results, only eventually solving the 'liquidity puzzle' that interest rates tended to rise in response to an increase in the money supply and the 'price puzzle' that inflation seemed to rise after a shock that tightened monetary policy.[16]

However, this chapter does suggest that the challenges to achieving similar success in LICs will be severe. Moreover, in Li et al. (2016) we note a further set of LIC-specific challenges, using the same analytic framework. Three are particularly important. First, the relevant time series data for LICs are very rarely longer than ten years, rather than the forty assumed here, especially considering breaks associated with monetary policy regime shifts. Second, measurement error seems to be much larger in LICs than in middle-income and advanced economies. And finally, the prevalence of supply shocks in LICs complicates the estimation of the output gap. Each of these problems sharply reduces the power of VAR-based methods to uncover even a strong and properly identified MTM, and together they are devastating. Other empirical methods may thus be helpful. The case study approach adopted in Chapter 5 examines the implications of a large monetary policy shock identified through a narrative approach. Abuka et al. (2015) use loan-level data to assess the bank-lending channel in Uganda. Perhaps more radically, the imposition of more economic structure and use of Bayesian techniques is a natural way to make use of available data while accepting its scarcity.

It seems clear, despite the possible ways forward, that uncertainty about the MTM is likely to continue to face LIC central banks. Moreover, while we have shown that inappropriate identification can lead to downward biased coefficients, while various features of the data environment can produce low t-statistics and substantial variation in estimates of the MTM, we have also shown that weak transmission is also a possible reason for poor VAR results.

What broader implications follow from these conclusions? One view is that, in the face of this uncertainty, monetary policy should be passive. In particular, frameworks that do not require confident knowledge of the MTM may be more appropriate, notably fixed exchange rate regimes.

Chapter 1 and indeed the rest of this book present another perspective that recognizes that this uncertainty is hardly unique to LICs and that learning-by-doing is a necessary counterpart to the reform of monetary policy regimes. However, clearly further empirical work is a critical component of this learning process. We hope that the results of this chapter will help to guide the agenda.

---

justify. See the discussion in Faust and Rogers (2003). Sims and Zha (2006) motivate similar restrictions in a DSGE context, though in a closed-economy context.

[16] On these points, see Sims (1992), and Leeper and Gordon (1992).

REFERENCES

Abuka, C., Alinda, R. K., Minoiu, C., Peydro, J. L., and Presbitero, A. F. (2015). *Monetary Policy in a Developing Country: Loan Applications and Real Effects.* IMF Working Paper 15/270. Washington, DC: International Monetary Fund.

Berg, A., Karam, P. D., Laxton, D. (2006). *A Practical Model-Based Approach to Monetary Policy Analysis.* IMF Working Paper WP/06/80. Washington, DC: International Monetary Fund.

Boughton, J. M. and Tavlas, G. S. (1991). *What Have We Learned about Estimating the Demand for Money? A Multicountry Evaluation of Some New Approaches.* IMF Working Papers 91/16. Washington, DC: International Monetary Fund.

Christiano, L., Eichenbaum, J. M., and Evans, C. L. (1999). Monetary Policy Shocks: What Have We Learned? In J. B. Taylor and M. Woodford (Eds.), *Handbook of Macroeconomics,* 1A. Amsterdam: North Holland.

Christiano, L., Eichenbaum, M., and Evans, C. L. (2005, February). Nominal Rigidities and the Dynamic Effects of a Shock to Monetary Policy. *Journal of Political Economy,* 113(1), 1–45.

Faust, J. and Rogers, J. (2003, October). Monetary Policy's Role in Exchange Rate Behavior. *Journal of Monetary Economics,* 50(7).

Kim, S. and Roubini, N. (2000). Exchange Rate Anomalies in the Industrial Countries: A Solution with a Structural VAR Approach. *Journal of Monetary Economics,* 45, 561–86.

Leeper, E. M. and Gordon, D. B. (1992). In Search of the Liquidity Effect. *Journal of Monetary Economics,* 29(3), 341–69.

Li, B. G., O'Connell, S., Adam, C., Berg, A., and Montiel, P. (2016). *VAR meets DSGE: Uncovering the Monetary Transmission Mechanism in Low-Income Countries.* IMF Working Paper 16/90. Washington, DC: International Monetary Fund.

Mbowe, W. (2012, August 3). *The Bank Lending Channel of Monetary Policy Transmission: Dynamic Bank-Level Panel Data Analysis on Tanzania.* Bank of Tanzania.

Mishra, P. and Montiel, P. (2013). How Effective is Monetary Transmission in Developing Countries: A Survey of the Empirical Evidence. *Economic Systems,* 37(2), 187–216. Elsevier.

Mishra, P., Montiel, P., and Spilimbergo, A. (2012). Monetary Transmission in Low-Income Countries: Effectiveness and Policy Implications. *IMF Economic Review,* 60, 270–302.

Mishra, P., Montiel, P., Pedroni, P., and Spilimbergo, A. (2014). Monetary Policy and Bank Lending Rates in Low-Income Countries: Heterogeneous Panel Estimates. *Journal of Development Economics,* 111, 117–31.

Nelson, E. (2002, May). Direct Effects of Base Money on Aggregate Demand: Theory and Evidence. *Journal of Monetary Economics,* 49(4), 687–708.

Sims, C. (1992). Interpreting the Macroeconomic Time Series Facts: The Effects of Monetary Policy. *European Economic Review* 36(5), 975–1000.

Sims, C. and Zha, T. (2006). Does Monetary Policy Generate Recessions? *Macroeconomic Dynamics,* 10: 231–47.

Woodford, M. (2001, August 30–September 1). Monetary Policy in the Information Economy. Proceedings from the Federal Reserve Bank of Kansas City Annual Symposium Conference: *Economic Policy for the Information Economy,* 1, 297–370. Jackson Hole, Wyoming.

Part II

Analytical Issues Relevant for Monetary Policy Analysis in Sub-Saharan Africa

7

Introduction to Part II

Andrew Berg and Rafael Portillo

The chapters in Part II reflect our efforts over the last few years to use simple dynamic general equilibrium models to analyse monetary policy issues facing sub-Saharan African (SSA) countries. A few words on the genesis of this research agenda will help clarify, we hope, both the approach and the choice of topics. Our journey started when we were at the 'policy wing' of the IMF's African department and then continued at the development macroeconomics division of the research department.[1] These divisions can be thought of as providing support to IMF country teams, and indeed many teams would approach us with thorny policy issues they were facing, either in the context of fund surveillance, or programme design and review. When faced with specific requests, our task would be to offer general policy recommendations, drawing on the policy and academic literature.

Policy thinking typically centred around four broad areas: (i) how to analyse policy under existing monetary frameworks in SSA, (ii) how to think about supply shocks and the adequate policy response, (iii) how to think about exchange rate management via interventions in the foreign exchange (FX) market, in countries with some degree of exchange rate flexibility, and (iv) how to support the authorities in their move to modernize their policy frameworks and what kind of analytical approaches are best suited to these countries. The chapters in Part II mainly cover issues (i)–(iii), while issue (iv) is discussed extensively in Part III.[2]

As we thought about these policy issues, we concluded that the analysis would benefit enormously from greater use of dynamic stochastic general equilibrium (DSGE) models, especially of the New Keynesian variety, though suitably adjusted to incorporate structural features of low-income countries (LICs).[3] These sorts of models dominate monetary policy analysis in the advanced-country context,

---

[1] In one case (Andrew Berg), the research agenda goes back a bit further, mainly his time at the strategy and policy review department of the IMF. This wandering through several departments is typical in the career of IMF economists, as the institution tends to value 'fungibility' and general expertise.

[2] Issue (iv) also reflects another function provided by these divisions, especially the development macroeconomics division of the research department, which is to directly engage with various central banks in SSA on these issues through technical assistance and capacity development projects.

[3] For a discussion of the standard closed and open economy New Keynesian Models, see Clarida, Gali, and Gertler (1999) and Gali and Monacelli (2005), respectively. On their application to low-income countries, see Berg et al. (2014).

despite having important detractors. In the LIC policy world their use has been much scarcer, and this scarcity puts their deficiencies in perspective. Indeed, we found and continue to find other approaches wanting. Financial programming, for example, which is the traditional approach used in IMF policy work, emphasizes linkages across sectors in the economy, including monetary, fiscal, and balance of payment accounts.[4] In order to perform quantitative policy analysis, however, the framework is complemented with simple behavioural relations, which tend to be primarily focused on monetary stocks and flows and are not suited for meaningful discussions about monetary policy.

Yet another approach is to use simple ad-hoc models, of the type presented in Agenor and Montiel (2008). These can be useful, but in our opinion they often do not sufficiently emphasize the dynamic nature of macro-fluctuations and the importance of expectations in the analysis of monetary policy. Moreover, lack of micro-foundations makes it more rather than less difficult, as is often assumed, to clarify how LICs differ from emerging markets and advanced countries. It also makes it difficult to place the LICs policy debate within the context of the burgeoning academic and policy literature on monetary policy, which over the last twenty years has relied almost exclusively on the New Keynesian framework. Although the latter—at least in its canonical form—misses some of the relevant mechanisms for thinking about policy in LICs, it provides many useful insights for thinking about monetary policy. Our approach has therefore been to build on the latter approach, and to extend or revise these models as needed.

A related observation is that there is a continuity of themes, and in some cases somewhat similar model structures, between Part II and Part III. What distinguishes the two is that the focus in Part II is mainly on qualitative insights rather than quantitative results, and if there are quantitative results, as in Chapter 11, they tend to focus on a narrow dimension of the data. The chapters here are thus meant to provide general guidance, rather than the country-specific policy prescriptions found in Part III. This distinction is also reflected in the approach to modelling. The models in Part II are fully micro-founded, and they tend to be stylized. This is because they are meant to help illustrate how introducing a particular LIC feature into an otherwise standard model may (or may not) influence the policy prescriptions or the effects of policy typically found in the literature. In our view, this type of comparative analysis is most useful if carried out in micro-founded models, as the effort of deriving mechanisms from first principles helps sharpen the discussion.

As previously mentioned, the chapters in Part II introduce a variety of LIC-specific features into otherwise standard New Keynesian models. Some are relatively well known, such as limited influence by LICs over their terms of trade, limited access to international capital markets, and exposure to volatile sources of external funding. Some are related to the broad policy framework, for example the central role of FX interventions, or the issue of coordination with fiscal policy. Other features have not featured prominently in macro models used in LICs, at least until recently. These include pervasive information incompleteness faced by both the public and the private sectors, proximity to subsistence and its

---

[4] See Polak (2005), among others.

implications for the supply side of the economy, limited participation in domestic financial markets and its implications for the effects of various domestic and external shocks, and portfolio balance effects as the channel through which sterilized FX interventions affect the real economy. A summary of the policy issue and the relevant modelling assumptions in each chapter is provided below.

1 INCOMPLETE INFORMATION AND THE ANALYSIS OF EXISTING MONETARY POLICY ARRANGEMENTS IN SSA

As discussed extensively in Chapter 1, many SSA countries with some degree of exchange rate flexibility have money targeting frameworks, which are also reflected in the design of IMF-supported programmes in the region, i.e., in the conditionality related to monetary policy. In practice there is considerable flexibility, and money target misses are common, partly because central banks wish to avoid either excessive interest rate volatility or large misalignments in the level of short-term rates. Such flexibility, however, complicates the analysis of monetary policy, including under fund programmes. As has become clear from our many interactions with IMF country teams over the years, the latter often struggle to reconcile the broader discussion of the adequate monetary policy stance with the programme conditionality. The two chapters summarized below reflect an attempt to provide guidance on this issue.

Chapter 8 reflects relatively early efforts on our part to engage constructively with prevalent practices by deriving the conditions under which paying some attention to money targets (with flexibility vis-à-vis target misses) could make sense from a policy perspective. In the context of a simple New Keynesian model, we show that some adherence to money targets can emerge endogenously when the central bank wishes to implement a Taylor-type rule, a standard monetary policy prescription, but cannot perfectly observe the state of the economy or the relevant interest rate for private sector decisions. The latter is a short cut for the idea that financial markets are insufficiently developed to be able to easily infer the relevant risk-free interest rate from market outcomes. The degree of money target adherence, which we denote λ, emerges endogenously as part of a signal extraction problem faced by the central bank. We derive an analytical solution for the optimal degree of target adherence, which we denote λ^*, and show that it depends on structural parameters of the model, including the deviation (noisiness) between observed and relevant interest rates, and the volatility of indicators of the state of the economy and various real shocks. Our approach also yields a simple rule for the design of money targets: these should be thought of as optimal forecasts of future money demand, consistent with the desired stance of policy, i.e., the interest rate level implied by the Taylor rule.

The previous discussion could be interpreted as implying that the current state of affairs with regards to monetary policy in SSA is optimal. As we continued to engage with countries attempting to use these sorts of frameworks, we came increasingly to emphasize that their flexibility reflects some costly disarray in the implementation of monetary policy, with lack of clarity about what the operational target is or should be, and lack of instruments or frameworks for controlling short-term financial conditions. Chapter 9 looks at such 'policy implementation errors,' and analyses their implications for the effectiveness of policy in the same model, except this time it is the private sector that faces information incompleteness. Agents in the economy have to infer the intended stance of policy solely from money market developments, a reasonable assumption given the typical absence of clear communication by central banks in LICs. In such an environment we show that the effectiveness of policy decisions can be greatly reduced when implementation errors are pervasive. As a result, it may appear as though monetary policy has weak effects on output and inflation, and indeed this is what many empirical studies seem to find, in the case of Africa. Chapters 5 and 6 argued that these results could reflect limitations in the use of empirical tools for assessing the monetary transmission mechanism. Here it is shown that they could also reflect policy shortcomings, which are easier to fix than the deeper structural issues that are often put forward in the literature.[5] A policy corollary from this analysis is that de facto flexibility with regards to money targets is no substitute for clear and transparent frameworks for policy design and policy implementation, with the latter centred around the explicit control of short-term interest rates.

From an analytical perspective, the lesson we draw from Chapters 8 and 9 is that the explicit modelling of information incompleteness can be useful for studying monetary policy issues in LICs, especially given the data shortcomings and the overall policy opacity.

2 SUPPLY-SIDE SHOCKS AND THE STRUCTURE OF THE ECONOMY

Understanding how supply shocks propagate through the economy, and whether monetary policy should respond to the resulting inflationary pressures, is one of the fundamental questions in monetary policy. Not surprisingly, interest in the topic tends to spike when there are large supply-side disturbances, for example as during the oil shocks of the 1970s, and more recently during the 2007–08 international food and fuel commodity crisis. As economists working on Africa during the latter period, we were thus confronted with this difficult policy question.

Standard policy advice, including at the IMF, calls for central banks to respond only to 'second-round' effects—spillovers from food prices to wages and core inflation—and to accommodate first-round effects. The latter term is rather vague, but is meant to describe the inherent inflationary pressure from the shock, which stems from the need for relative prices to adjust. Relative to other regions, SSA stands out, however, by the perceived prevalence and magnitude of supply shocks, and in the case of shocks to food prices, the effect is amplified by the large weight of food in the CPI. Does the standard advice still apply under these conditions?

---

[5] See Mishra, Montiel, and Spilimbergo (2012).

Chapter 10 attempts to provide a formal definition of first-round effects, in the context of a stylized New Keynesian open economy model, and examines whether international food price shocks are more inflationary in countries with a larger food share in consumption, denoted a_F. This issue was of great concern in Africa during 2007–08, as large increases in international food prices coincided with a marked increase in inflation in many countries in the region.

The analysis in the chapter reveals that much depends on the country's access to international capital markets. If a country has ample access, then a_F is indeed the key parameter determining the magnitude of first-round effects. However, if a country has limited access to capital markets, then the key parameter is the country's trade deficit in agricultural products ($a_F - \kappa_F$ in the model), rather than a_F. The reason is that under limited international capital mobility, it is the income effect from the shock that determines the magnitude of the relative price adjustment, and this effect is proportional to the trade balance.[6] As $a_F - \kappa_F$ is on average small in SSA countries, and it can be argued that access to international capital markets is rather limited, the chapter makes the provocative claim that inflationary pressures from international food price shocks are small in SSA, at least on average.

Although the stylized nature of the model cautions against taking this result too literally, the analysis suggests that other factors may have accounted for the inflationary pressures observed back in 2008, most notably the stance of monetary and fiscal policy. This issue is taken up again in Chapter 15 in the case of Kenya. The results in the chapter also hint at the complexities involved in formally deriving 'first-round' effects, as it shows that they depend on equilibrium changes in nominal exchange rates, which themselves depend on the specific monetary policy response that keeps core inflation stabilized. Such complexity limits the applicability of the 'first-round' concept for policy analysis. The vagueness mentioned above is, to some extent, inevitable.

Chapter 11 studies how the structure of African economies affects the properties of inflation and the monetary policy response. It does so by introducing subsistence requirements in food consumption in a simple New Keynesian model with two sectors, food and non-food, and with shocks to food productivity (supply shocks) and to aggregate demand. Subsistence requirements are used in growth models to generate structural transformation: they imply that, as overall productivity in the economy increases, the share of food in consumption (and the share of factors of production allocated to agriculture) decreases endogenously. Here, instead, subsistence requirements are used to analyse how the properties of inflation change, also endogenously, across levels of income. The chapter shows that greater proximity to subsistence (lower levels of development) makes inflation predominantly supply-driven and more volatile, for purely structural reasons, as the share of food in consumption is larger and there is more limited economy-wide ability to adjust to supply shocks. In spite of this greater exposure to supply shocks, the standard policy prescription remains: stabilizing core (non-food) inflation is optimal from a welfare perspective. Moreover, the model analysis

---

[6] Under ample access to international capital markets, it is the substitution effect that drives the magnitude of the relative price change. Substitution effects are proportional to a_F.

reveals that stabilizing overall inflation, instead of core, is costlier in poor countries, as monetary policy needs to generate large output volatility to stabilize an inherently volatile inflation.

3 THE MACROECONOMIC IMPLICATIONS OF RESERVE ACCUMULATION AND FX INTERVENTION POLICIES

The discussion so far implicitly assumes that monetary policy is about the choice of one policy instrument, the short-term interest rate (or the monetary base). In SSA countries, and developing countries more generally, things are more complex. A key missing element, in countries with some degree of exchange rate management, is FX interventions, both to achieve a desired level of reserves, and to limit exchange rate volatility or protect competitiveness. Until recently there was no standard framework for thinking about interventions and whether, and if so how, they should be coordinated with interest rate policy or the broader macro policy stance.[7] This is reflected in the sometimes erratic policy responses of central banks, as well as in the analysis of IMF country teams, who often struggle when assessing what the effect of those interventions may be, and whether interventions are desirable or compatible with the broader macro framework. The chapters below develop models that fill this gap.

Chapter 12 focuses on FX interventions in the context of surges in aid flows, an important issue in many SSA countries, especially in the early 2000s. Governments receiving aid disbursements would initially deposit the FX at the central bank. As they drew down on these deposits to spend on local goods and services, liquidity would be created. Against this backdrop, central banks felt they were confronted with a policy trilemma: if they sold the aid-related FX to sterilize the liquidity, the real exchange rate would appreciate; if instead they sold government bonds or issued their own sterilization instruments, interest rates would increase; and if they did not sterilize, inflation would rise. Looking at various countries in SSA, Berg et al. (2007) found that many central banks ended up keeping the aid proceeds as reserves, with the experience of Uganda (which is also summarized in the chapter) providing a case in point. It was the challenge of thinking about this policy choice that led to the analysis in the chapter.

Using a small open economy model that includes a specification of the government sector and a rule for FX interventions, Chapter 12 shows that the policy trilemma is more than just an issue of liquidity management by the central bank. The underlying issue is that the real effects of the aid are very different depending on whether the FX proceeds are accumulated as reserves or not. Reserve accumulation implies that the public sector is using the aid twice, once as higher government spending and once as reserves. If access to international capital markets is limited, then the private sector ends up being crowded out, either through higher interest rates (if the reserve accumulation is sterilized) or through

---

[7] This is much broader than the issue of whether interventions should be sterilized or not.

the inflation tax (if it is not). The core policy issue is the need for coordination between the response of the fiscal authorities and those of the central bank: either the aid is used, in which case higher government spending should be associated with higher FX proceeds being made available to the economy, or it is not used, in which case higher public savings can help support higher FX reserves.

What the above analysis makes clear is that FX intervention policies have real effects that are different from the 'traditional' effects of monetary policy, stemming from the control of short-term nominal variables. The last chapter in Part II explores this issue in more detail. It extends a standard open economy New Keynesian model to include a rule for sterilized FX interventions operating alongside interest rate policy, and portfolio effects of FX intervention policies. The portfolio effects stem from the wedges or premia on the expected returns of different assets and liabilities which depend on the relative supply of the financial assets themselves. By affecting the relative holdings of central bank paper in the financial system, sterilized interventions influence nominal and real exchanges and therefore can also influence output and inflation.

The existence of multiple instruments (interventions and interest rates) and channels of transmission increases the range of policies, for example the possible co-existence of an interest-rate-based inflation targeting regime with a managed float. Chapter 13 shows that there can be benefits to these hybrid regimes, for example when the economy is hit with temporary shocks to foreign interest rates or risk premia: relying on FX interventions helps insulate domestic interest rates, and the economy, from these external shocks. In other words, the use of FX interventions can increase monetary policy autonomy with regards to external developments. Not all FX rules are equal, however. 'Leaning against the wind' rules, which attempt to reduce the pace of appreciation/depreciation, without targeting a specific level for the exchange rate, are preferable to rules that do target an exchange rate level, as the former are more robust to weak portfolio balance effects and are less likely to result in the depletion of reserves. More generally, the latter raise the risk of pursuing multiple, inconsistent objectives, and can lead to runs on the currency and macro instability.

This concludes the summary of the chapters in Part II. We hope it has shown that the analysis of monetary policy issues in LICs, and SSA in particular, can benefit tremendously from building dynamic stochastic general equilibrium models that capture important features of these economies, including complex policy environments, and by using them in a sensible manner, i.e., not mechanically but rather to build intuition about the channels involved. Many issues remain to be analysed, for example on the use of macro-prudential tools in LICs, or the distributional effects of macro policies, just to name two broad policy areas.[8] Studying these issues in meaningful ways will also require further development of these models along the relevant dimensions, for example by carefully modelling the financial sector, as done to some extent in Chapter 17, and by introducing greater heterogeneity among households and firms. This is left for future work.

---

[8] A recent contribution on the model-based analysis of macro-prudential policy in low-income countries is Unsal and Rubio (2017).

REFERENCES

Agenor, P. and Montiel, P. (2008). *Development Macroeconomics*. Princeton, NJ: Princeton University Press.

Berg, A., Yang, S. C., and Zanna, L. F. (2014). Modeling African Economies: A DSGE Approach. In C. Monga and J. Y. Lin (Eds.), *Oxford Handbook of Africa and Economics: Context and Concepts*. Oxford: Oxford University Press.

Berg, A., Aiyar S., Hussain M., Roache S., Mirzoev T., and Mahone, A. (2007). *The Macroeconomics of Scaling Up Aid: Lessons from Recent Experience*. IMF Occasional Paper 253. Washington, DC: International Monetary Fund.

Clarida, R., Gali, J., and Gertler, M. (1999). The Science of Monetary Policy: A New Keynesian Perspective. *Journal of Economic Literature*, 37(4), 1661–1707.

Gali, J. and Monacelli, T. (2005). Monetary Policy and Exchange Rate Volatility in a Small Open Economy Model. *Review of Economic Studies*, 72, 707–34.

Mishra, P., Montiel, P., and Spilimbergo, A. (2012). Monetary transmission in low-income countries: effectiveness and policy implications. *IMF Economic Review*, 60, 270–302.

Polak, J. J. (2005). The IMF monetary model at forty. In J. Boughton (ed.), *Selected Essays of Jacques J. Polak, 1994–2004* (pp. 209–26). New York and London: Sharpe.

Unsal, F. and Rubio, M. (2017). *Macroprudential Policy, Incomplete Information and Inequality: The case of Low-Income and Developing Countries*. IMF Working Paper 17/59. Washington, DC: International Monetary Fund.

8

On the Role of Money Targets in the Monetary Policy Framework in SSA

Insights from a New Keynesian Model with Incomplete Information

Andrew Berg, Rafael Portillo, and Filiz Unsal

1 INTRODUCTION

This chapter introduces a theme to which we return in several of the chapters of the book—the role of money targets. This theme grows out of the fact that, as discussed in Chapter 1, countries in sub-Saharan Africa continue to describe their monetary policy in terms of quarterly or even monthly targets on monetary aggregates, typically narrow money. Relatedly, the analysis of monetary policy in most central banks in the region remains closely related to the quantity theory MV=PQ, with money targets set so as to be consistent with a desired path for prices (P) given real output (Q) and under some assumption about the trajectory of velocity (V). This state of affairs contrasts with the monetary policy consensus observed elsewhere: an increasing number of countries have adopted an explicit inflation targeting strategy, using interest rates as their operational target, and with very little role for monetary aggregates. Why do SSA central banks continue to target money?

One special case is worth mentioning, because it may be at the root of the IMF's own persistent adherence to a money-targeting framework in the way it conducts 'financial programming'.[1] Where the need to finance a fiscal deficit dictates central bank behaviour, the use of aggregates can be useful. In these circumstances of 'fiscal dominance', the borrowing requirements of the government can map into money growth, which along with an estimate of velocity can determine a consistent inflation rate.

However, we see little case for the argument that monetary aggregates play a special direct role in the transmission of monetary policy. The New Keynesian modelling approach—the workhorse model for studying monetary policy questions—does not assign money a special role in controlling inflation (e.g. Clarida et al., 1999).

---

[1] See Polak (2005), among others.

Monetary policy is instead formalized as a rule for steering short-term interest rates. Unlike interest rates, monetary aggregates do not enter the transmission mechanism.[2] Considering further that the relation between money and prices (and output) is often volatile and unstable, a policy message from these models suggests disregarding monetary aggregates altogether in the analysis of monetary policy.[3]

It is occasionally argued that in low-income countries money aggregates directly drive output or inflation, such that they would belong directly as an argument in the IS curve (which determines output) or perhaps directly in the Phillips curve (which determines inflation). A priori, it is possible that monetary aggregates exert a 'real balance' effect, whereby as elements of wealth they drive consumption and hence output. However, this is likely to be quantitatively unimportant and dwarfed by other wealth effects.

One view (discussed briefly in Chapter 3) is that financial systems are too small for interest rates to matter much for demand and hence inflation, so that money aggregates may be a better measure of the stance of policy. However, it is important to understand that if the financial system is too small for interest rates to matter much, then this same small size implies that money aggregates would also be unimportant, at least those aggregates that can be controlled by the central bank. All quantitative operations of the central bank work through their effects on the balance sheets of the banks. The central bank can only affect the other component of the money base—cash in circulation—to the extent that these central-bank-induced changes reserves have a knock-on effect on demand for cash. But this knock-on effect would work mainly through interest rates. Thus the small-banking-system argument applies to both quantity-based and interest-rate-based measures of the stance of policy.

In this chapter, we show that a potential role for money targets emerges naturally in a simple New Keynesian framework in which the central bank wishes to implement an interest-rate-based policy rule but must contend with lack of timely or reliable information about the state of the economy and the degree of tightness in financial conditions. With regards to the state of the economy, the only information available to the central bank comes from money market developments, i.e., the combination of monetary aggregates and interest rates. As for financial conditions, we allow for the possibility that the observed interest rate may be a noisy measure of the interest rate relevant for private sector decisions. Here we have in mind the idea that financial markets are sufficiently undeveloped that it is not easy to infer a risk-free interest rate from the market. For example, in many SSA countries there are substantial counterparty risks and non-arm's-length transactions in the interbank market, such that even the reported short-term rates there are volatile or perhaps not market-clearing. Meanwhile, even short-term government securities markets may be illiquid.

As we will show, this perspective can rationalize a regime in which central banks set money targets ex ante, and then pay some attention to them but

---

[2] Although these models feature long-run neutrality of money, this does not imply any causality running between money and prices.

[3] See Woodford (2008) for a detailed discussion.

decide—frequently—to under- or overshoot them. This flexibility of money targeting regimes in practice is a critical feature that is generally overlooked in textbooks and other academic treatments. Money targets are set, typically at the beginning of the year for the next four quarters, with the targets often revised every six months, sometimes substantially. This is already a far cry from the traditional call, e.g. in Friedman (1960), to set and stick to a fixed growth rate of the money stock. Moreover, not only is the medium-term growth rate of money not targeted, but the quarterly or six-monthly targets are frequently missed by substantial amounts.

2 MONEY TARGETING IN PRACTICE

The view that money targets represent an adaptation to incomplete information has a basis in the flexible way money targeting regimes actually work in practice. IMF (2015) focuses on a sample of four SSA developing countries with de jure targeting regimes involving reserve money targets: Kenya, Mozambique, Rwanda, and Tanzania. This sample ranges from countries with CBs following their targets relatively strictly (Tanzania and Rwanda) to a country with a de facto interest rate-based operational framework (Kenya). The main finding is that money target misses are frequent and significant in an economic sense. As Table 8.1—taken from IMF (2015)—shows, misses of 1 per cent of the target are common; misses that range from 2 per cent of the target (Rwanda) to 7 per cent of the target (Mozambique) are observed about 25 per cent of the time.

These deviations are economically significant. To see this, it is useful to consider the counterfactual of how much interest rates would have had to move had the monetary authorities chosen to push the money stock so as to eliminate the deviations, all else held equal. For this back-of-the-envelope calculation, it is enough to have an estimate of the interest elasticity of money demand, that is, of how much money demand shifts for a given change in the interest rate.[4] A reasonable estimate for that number is 0.2, implying that a 1 percentage point increase in interest rates reduces money demand by 0.2 per cent.[5] With this assumption, eliminating even the very common 1 per cent deviations of money from target reported in column 1 of Table 8.1 would have caused interest rate

---

[4] This is "back-of-the-envelope" in part because the calculation takes as given real output and inflation, asking only about how a different money stock would call for a different interest rate to equilibrate money demand. In general equilibrium, the different interest rate would presumably move output and inflation and thereby change money demand through this channel as well. However, these effects are likely to emerge with a lag. And of course their explicit consideration would only underscore that the deviation is significant economically.

[5] Chapter 16 calibrates the elasticity of 0.56 in the case of Kenya. However, most estimates for developing countries in the literature actually seem to be much smaller (see Kumar and Rao, 2012; Sriram, 2001; and Sichei and Kamau, 2012), though this is hard to establish because estimated coefficients are often imprecisely estimated, and most of the attention is on broader money aggregates and often on long-term elasticities. It is plausible that short-term elasticities and those on base money are lower than for these broader aggregates. In this case, the interest rate movements associated with a given change in money would be larger.

Monetary Policy in Sub-Saharan Africa

Table 8.1. Characteristics of Deviations from Reserve Money Targets

Country	Share of observations with absolute deviations bigger than 1% (in per cent)	12.5th percentile (in per cent of the target)	87.5th percentile (in per cent of the target)
Kenya	94.9	−6.8	5.7
Tanzania	71.7	−4.9	4.1
Mozambique	94.1	−7.6	5.9
Rwanda	40	−1.7	1.1

Source: IMF Staff Calculations.

movements in the order of 5 percentage points. The roughly annual deviations observed in column 2 would have required interest rate adjustments ranging from 7 percentage points in Rwanda to 36 percentage points in Mozambique.[6]

These deviations presumably happen for a variety of reasons, including to change policy and to accommodate unexpected money demand shocks. IMF (2015) also shows, though, that on average, these deviations are not indicative of loose monetary conditions. On the contrary, positive deviations from money targets are if anything associated with higher-than-average interest rates and generally exhibit a weak and ambiguous relationship with subsequent inflation. This is consistent with the view that they may often reflect accommodation of money demand shocks.[7]

The money targeting frameworks in practice do not provide a 'nominal anchor'. In 'textbook' money targeting, where a constant growth rate of money serves as the nominal anchor, deviations from targets would be undone in subsequent quarters as the actual stock would be brought back to the predetermined target path. This does not seem to be what happens, however. In the sample mentioned above, rather, the new targets themselves tend to accommodate, at least partly, to deviations from previous targets. There is no sign that actual money growth itself moves so as to reduce earlier deviations from target.

3 A MONETARY REACTION FUNCTION WITH MONEY

To summarize the above discussion in terms of a simple equation, we can represent the central bank's policy choice with a simple relation:

$$\lambda(\Delta M_t - \Delta M_{t|t-1}^T) - (1 - \lambda)(R_t - R_t^T) = 0, \tag{1}$$

---

[6] This calculation does not assume that the only reason for the money deviations from target is to account for money demand shocks. Whatever the reason for the deviation, the idea is that to move money stocks back to target would have required an adjustment in money demand, and (holding output and other factors constant) would have required interest rate movements that can be backed out from the money demand equation.

[7] IMF (2008) and IMF (2015) show in a large sample that money target misses are not correlated with subsequent inflation deviations from target, at least for countries with inflation below mid-double-digits.

where ΔM_t denotes actual money growth at time t, $\Delta M^T_{t|t-1}$ is the previously set money target, R_t is the actual short-term interest rate, R^T_t denotes some objective for the interest rate, and λ is the degree of target adherence. The relation makes clear that large deviations of interest rates from some possibly implicit target R^T_t are undesirable, which is why in practice money targets are often missed, i.e., $\lambda<1$. Therefore, a more complete view of money targeting is that it involves: (i) the derivation of the money target $\Delta M^T_{t|t-1}$, (ii) the derivation of an interest rate objective R^T_t, and (iii) the degree of target adherence λ. In this chapter we provide a framework for thinking about the joint determination of these three elements.

The interest rate rule has obvious implications for R^T_t, which emerges as the time $(t-1)$ forecast of time t interest rates. More interestingly, it also has implications for the design of the money target $\Delta M^T_{t|t-1}$, which should be understood as the forecast of money demand under said interest rate rule. By construction, money and interest rate targets are perfectly consistent, in that they both embody the same policy intentions, at least ex ante.

The degree of target adherence λ reflects the central bank's optimal use of developments in the money market when revising its estimate of the target variable, in this case the current, unobserved levels of the output gap and the private sector's expected inflation. Specifically, λ can be thought of as the solution to a signal extraction problem faced by the central bank, similar to the problem in Svensson and Woodford (2003, 2004). The signal extraction problem is not trivial, because the money market outcome also depends on the monetary policy response, and the Kalman filter must be revised to account for this circularity.[8] We provide a simple step-by-step derivation of the model solution to explain how we resolve this issue.

In our setup, the more informative is the money market about shocks to aggregate demand, the greater the degree of target adherence (the higher the λ). The same occurs when the interest elasticity of overall demand, and the interest elasticity of money demand, are large. A higher interest elasticity of demand amplifies the effects of aggregate demand shocks, and greater adherence to money targets can then help deliver the appropriate policy tightening. A higher interest elasticity of money demand makes shocks to money demand less costly, from a policy perspective, while also calling for greater money-target adherence to generate the appropriate policy tightening.

When we introduce noise in the observed short-term interest rates we find, not surprisingly, that the central bank places less weight on interest rate stabilization. We also extend the model to introduce a noisy measure of economic activity, and show that the optimal adherence to money targets could be reduced, though much depends on the relative volatilities of the shocks and measurement errors.

We believe the assumptions that lead to our results are not extreme. Information gaps in LICs are pervasive. Key variables like output and inflation are observed imperfectly and with substantial lags. For example, quarterly GDP is

---

[8] In the context of an optimal monetary policy problem, Svensson and Woodford (2004) refer to this circularity as the failure of the separation principle between signal extraction and (the choice of optimal) monetary policy.

unavailable in many countries and there are often no economy-wide wage data at all. Output gaps in particular are hard to assess on the basis of standard indicators of economic activity: measures of capacity utilization are scarce, agricultural supply shocks dominate, and informal markets are pervasive. In addition, the noisiness of interest rate data may also be an issue. Even key markets such as interbank and government bond markets are often thin and opaque. Contract enforcement may be poor. Meanwhile, a large fraction of the population does not even participate in formal financial markets. In these circumstances, a readily observed interest rate such as the interbank money market rate may bear only a loose connection to the (latent or shadow) interest rate relevant to private sector decisions.

Monetary aggregates, on the other hand, are measured accurately and with little lag. And these aggregates are systematically related to key variables such as output and the relevant interest rate through money demand. The relation is subject to money demand shocks, but with sufficient information gaps, money targets may nonetheless be worth attention.

Our work is closely related to the seminal work of Poole (1970) on the choice of policy instrument, and the work of Friedman (1975) on the use of intermediate targets.[9] Analytically, our main innovation is to embed the target choice question in a fully articulated inter-temporal model, whose information structure rationalizes the notion that adherence to operational targets depends on imperfect information. Thus, we model jointly the choice of the monetary policy committee and the decision about what to do between meetings, as Walsh (2003) describes the problem in Poole (1970).

Our work is also closely related to more recent work, starting with Svensson and Woodford (2003, 2004), on the optimal use of indicator variables in forward-looking models. In particular, Coenen, Levin, and Wieland (2005) and Lippi and Neri (2007) quantify the relevance of money as an indicator variable in the euro area. These papers simultaneously solve for optimal monetary policy and the optimal use of indicator variables—such as, but not limited to, money—in the conduct of policy. Our analysis is considerably simpler: we focus on simple Taylor-type rules, which allows us to derive the model solution analytically. The type of incompleteness of information these authors focus on is also different from ours. We believe our information structure, based on Aoki (2003), is ideally suited to analyse money-targeting issues that are common in low-income countries, such as the ex ante choice of targets and how to interpret ex post target misses.

Though we believe our results could help rationalize some role for money targets, we strongly caution the reader against taking these results too literally, given the many simplifying assumptions we have made. In addition, our approach requires that central banks think systematically about the right level of short-term interest rate, even when they set money targets. If this is not the case, then the informational content of money target deviations is likely to be greatly reduced.

---

[9] See Friedman (1990) for a thorough discussion.

4 THE MODEL

4.1 The Non-Policy Block of the Economy

We present a simple New Keynesian model along the lines of Clarida, Gali, and Gertler (1999). Quarterly output (y_t) is the sum of two components: potential output (y_t^*) and the output gap $(\tilde{y}_t)$:

$$y_t = y_t^* + \tilde{y}_t \tag{2}$$

Potential output follows a random walk with drift:

$$y_t^* = g + y_{t-1}^* + \epsilon_t^{\Delta y^*}, \tag{3}$$

while the output gap is determined by a forward-looking IS curve:

$$\tilde{y}_t = E[\tilde{y}_{t+1}|FI_t] - \sigma[R_t - E[\pi_{t+1}|FI_t] - r_t^n]. \tag{4}$$

R denotes the relevant short-term interest rate, π is the inflation rate, σ is the inter-temporal elasticity of substitution, and r_t^n is the natural or equilibrium real interest rate. $E[x_z|W_j]$ denotes expectations of variable x at time z on the basis of information set W at time j. For the private sector we assume expectations are formed on the basis of information set FI_t, which stands for full information (see details below).

Movements in the natural rate r_t^n capture changes in aggregate demand. We assume the rate fluctuates over time and follows an AR(1) process:

$$r_t^n = (1 - \rho)\bar{r}^n + \rho r_{t-1}^n + \epsilon_t^r. \tag{5}$$

Inflation is determined by a forward-looking Phillips curve:

$$\pi_t = \kappa \tilde{y}_t + (1 - \beta)\bar{\pi} + \beta E[\pi_{t+1}|FI_t], \tag{6}$$

in which κ denotes the elasticity of inflation to movements in the output gap, and $\bar{\pi}$ is the inflation target.[10] The non-policy block of the model is complete with the specification of real money demand:

$$m_t = y_t - \eta R_t - v_t, \tag{7}$$

where the term v_t follows a random walk with drift:

$$v_t = \Delta \bar{v} + v_{t-1} + \epsilon_t^{\Delta v}. \tag{8}$$

---

[10] The term $(1 - \beta)\,\bar{\pi}$ can be obtained using the Calvo sticky price framework, under the assumption that firms that do not get to optimally readjust their prices follow an indexation scheme in which prices adjust by the inflation target (see Yun, 1996). This indexation assumption ensures there is no long-run tradeoff between inflation and output.

Finally, nominal money growth is the sum of real money growth and inflation:

$$\Delta M_t = \Delta m_t + \pi_t. \tag{9}$$

4.2 Monetary Policy

We assume the central bank sets a target for the short-term interest rate following the prescriptions of a forward-looking Taylor rule:

$$R_t^T = \bar{r}^n + \bar{\pi} + \phi_\pi(E[\pi_{t+1}|LI_t] - \bar{\pi}) + \phi_y E[\tilde{y}_t|LI_t]. \tag{10}$$

Parameters ϕ_π and ϕ_y capture the central bank's systematic response to deviations in expected inflation from its target and the output gap, respectively. We assume, however, that the central bank does not have the same information set as the private sector ($LI_t \neq FI_t$). LI_t stands for limited information. Note that the central bank does not observe the output gap directly, and must infer its value on the basis of LI_t.

For now, we will assume the central bank is able to hits its interest rate target perfectly, i.e., $R_t = R_t^T$. We will revise this assumption later.

4.3 Information Sets

Both the private sector and the central bank know the structure of the economy (the equations and the parameters), but differ in their information sets. At time t, the private sector observes all variables and shocks up to time t directly:

$$FI_t = R_t, \Delta M_t, \tilde{y}_t, \pi_t, y_t, m_t, y_t^*, \epsilon_t^{\Delta y^*}, r_t^n, \epsilon_t^r, v_t, \epsilon_t^{\Delta v}, FI_{t-1}.$$

The central bank observes all variables and shocks up to time t-1, but does not observe private sector variables at time t, with the exception of interest rates and monetary aggregates:

$$LI_t = R_t, \Delta M_t, FI_{t-1}.$$

Given that the central bank's information set is limited it must engage in a signal extraction problem, which we discuss below. By definition we have $FI_{t-1} \subseteq LI_t \subseteq FI_t$.

4.4 Model Solution and Signal Extraction

We now characterize the model's equilibrium. The derivation of the equilibrium is complicated by the fact that private sector decisions depend on monetary policy, but monetary policy faces a signal extraction problem. The signal extraction problem itself depends on variables that react contemporaneously to monetary policy, such as ΔM_t and R_t, which complicates the filtering problem.

4.4.1 Solution under Complete Information

We start by deriving the model solution under complete information (CI), i.e., $LI_t = FI_t$, which we will use when solving for the incomplete information case. In this case the model solution is the standard rational expectations equilibrium:

$$\tilde{y}_t = \Phi_{\tilde{y}} \tilde{r}_t^n + \Omega_{\tilde{y}}^{CI} \epsilon_t^{\Delta y^*} + \Theta_{\tilde{y}}^{CI} \epsilon_t^{\Delta v}$$

$$\tilde{\pi}_t = \pi_t - \bar{\pi} = \Phi_{\pi} \tilde{r}_t^n + \Omega_{\pi}^{CI} \epsilon_t^{\Delta y^*} + \Theta_{\pi}^{CI} \epsilon_t^{\Delta v}$$

$$\tilde{R}_t = R_t - \bar{r}^n - \bar{\pi} = \Phi_R \tilde{r}_t^n + \Omega_R^{CI} \epsilon_t^{\Delta y^*} + \Theta_R^{CI} \epsilon_t^{\Delta v}$$

$$\Delta y_t = g + \Phi_{\Delta y} \Delta \tilde{r}_t^n + \Omega_{\Delta y}^{CI} \epsilon_t^{\Delta y^*} + \Theta_{\Delta y}^{CI} \epsilon_t^{\Delta v}$$

$$\Delta \tilde{M}_t = \Delta M_t - g + \bar{\pi} - \Delta \bar{v} = \Phi_{\Delta M} \Delta \tilde{r}_t^n + \Omega_{\Delta M}^{CI} \epsilon_t^{\Delta y^*} + \Theta_{\Delta M}^{CI} \epsilon_t^{\Delta v},$$

where $\tilde{r}_t^n = r_t^n - \bar{r}^n$ and:

$$\Phi_{\tilde{y}} = \Lambda(1 - \beta\rho) \quad \Phi_{\pi} = \Lambda\kappa \quad \Phi_R = \Lambda((1 - \beta\rho)\phi_y + \kappa\phi_{\pi}\rho) \quad \Phi_{\Delta y} = \Lambda(1 - \beta\rho)$$

$$\Phi_{\Delta M} = \Lambda((1 - \beta\rho)(1 - \eta\phi_y) + \kappa(1 - \eta\phi_{\pi}\rho)) \quad \Lambda = \frac{\sigma}{(1 - \beta\rho)(1 - \rho + \sigma\phi_y) + \sigma\kappa(\phi_{\pi} - 1)\rho}$$

and

$$\Omega_{\tilde{y}}^{CI} = \Omega_{\pi}^{CI} = \Omega_R^{CI} = 0, \ \Omega_{\Delta y}^{CI} = \Omega_{\Delta M}^{CI} = 1,$$

$$\Theta_{\tilde{y}}^{CI} = \Theta_{\pi}^{CI} = \Theta_R^{CI} = \Theta_{\Delta y}^{CI} = 0, \ \Theta_{\Delta M}^{CI} = -1.$$

Under CI, there is a clear separation between the effects of shocks to aggregate demand (movements in r_t^n) and the effects of shocks to potential output ($\epsilon_t^{\Delta y^*}$) and velocity ($\epsilon_t^{\Delta v}$). Inflation, the output gap, and the stance of policy are only influenced by shocks to aggregate demand. Output growth is affected by shocks to aggregate demand and shocks to potential output, while money growth is affected by all shocks.

4.4.2 Solution under Incomplete Information

To solve the model under incomplete information (II), we start by rearranging equations (4) and (6) as follows:

$$\tilde{y}_t = \underbrace{-\sigma \tilde{R}_t}_{a} + \underbrace{E[\tilde{y}_{t+1} + \sigma \tilde{\pi}_{t+1} | FI_t]}_{b} + \sigma \tilde{r}_t^n, \tag{11}$$

$$\tilde{\pi}_t = \underbrace{-\sigma\kappa\tilde{R}_t}_{c} + \underbrace{E[\kappa\tilde{y}_{t+1} + (\sigma\kappa + \beta)\tilde{\pi}_{t+1}|FI_t]}_{d} + \sigma\kappa\tilde{r}_t^n. \tag{12}$$

As the above equations make clear, the level of output and inflation today depend on: (i) the current stance of monetary policy $\tilde{R}_t$ (terms a and c), (ii) expectations of future endogenous macro variables (terms b and d), and (iii) current levels of the exogenous variable $\tilde{r}_t^n$. Our assumptions about the information set of the central bank allow us to solve for terms b and d first, before solving for terms a and c, which is where the signal extraction comes in.

4.5 Private Sector Expectations

Terms b and d depend on the private sector's expectations of future exogenous variables ($\tilde{r}^n, \epsilon^{\Delta y^*}, \epsilon^{\Delta v}$) and the future behaviour of policy, given by equation (9):

$$E[R_{t+J}|FI_t] = \tilde{r}^n + \bar{\pi} + \phi_\pi(E[E[\pi_{t+J+1}|LI_{t+J}]|FI_t] - \bar{\pi}) + \phi_y E[E[\tilde{y}_{t+J}|LI_{t+J}]|FI_t],$$

$$J = 1, 2, \ldots$$

The private sector knows that the central bank's information set is limited, which affects the setting of current interest rates. Going forward, however, the central bank will have access to an updated information set which will include all variables observed at time t. Therefore, from the perspective of time t:

$$E[E[\pi_{t+J+1}|LI_{t+J}]|FI_t] = E[\pi_{t+J+1}|FI_t], E[E[\tilde{y}_{t+J}|LI_{t+J}]|FI_t] = E[\tilde{y}_{t+J}|FI_t], \text{ and}$$

$$[R_{t+J}|FI_t] = \tilde{r}^n + \bar{\pi} + \phi_\pi(E[\pi_{t+J+1}|FI_t] - \bar{\pi}) + \phi_y E[\tilde{y}_{t+J}|FI_t].$$

Since $FI_{t-1} \subseteq LI_t$, the private sector's expectations of the central bank's estimates of future target variables are the same as the private sector's expectations of those variables. In other words, the signal extraction problem does not affect the private sector's expectations of future monetary policy setting. This implies that expectations of future variables under II are the same as the expectations under CI:

$$E[\tilde{y}_{t+1}|FI_t] = \Phi_{\tilde{y}} E[\tilde{r}_{t+1}^n|FI_t] = \Phi_{\tilde{y}}\rho\tilde{r}_t^n$$

$$E[\tilde{\pi}_{t+1}|FI_t] = \Phi_\pi E[\tilde{r}_{t+1}^n|FI_t] = \Phi_\pi\rho\tilde{r}_t^n. \tag{13}$$

Equations (10) and (11) can now be restated as:

$$\tilde{y}_t = -\sigma\tilde{R}_t + ((\Phi_{\tilde{y}} + \sigma\Phi_\pi)\rho + \sigma)\tilde{r}_t^n = -\sigma\tilde{R}_t + \iota\tilde{r}_t^n, \text{ and} \tag{14}$$

$$\tilde{\pi}_t = -\sigma\kappa\tilde{R}_t + ((\kappa\Phi_{\tilde{y}} + (\sigma\kappa + \beta)\Phi_\pi)\rho + \sigma\kappa)\tilde{r}_t^n = -\sigma\kappa\tilde{R}_t + \varphi\tilde{r}_t^n, \tag{15}$$

where, after some algebra, $\iota = \Phi_{\tilde{y}} + \sigma\Phi_R$ and $\varphi = \Phi_\pi + \kappa\sigma\Phi_R$.

4.6 Central Bank Estimates of Endogenous Variables

Applying the expectations operator $E[*|LI_t]$ to both sides of equation (13), and introducing in the interest rate rule together with equation (11), yields:

$$\tilde{R}_t = \Phi_R E[\tilde{r}_t^n | LI_t].$$

In other words, targeting a linear combination of the estimates of the current output gap and expected inflation is equivalent to targeting the estimate of $\tilde{r}_t^n$. This simplifies the signal extraction problem, as it can be applied to a variable $(\tilde{r}_t^n)$ that is exogenous.

Replacing the above equation into (11) and (12) helps us understand how the II case deviates from the CI case:

$$\tilde{y}_t = \Phi_{\tilde{y}} \tilde{r}_t^n - \sigma \Phi_R [E[\tilde{r}_t^n | LI_t] - \tilde{r}_t^n], \tag{16}$$

$$\tilde{\pi}_t = \Phi_{\pi} \tilde{r}_t^n - \kappa \sigma \Phi_R [E[\tilde{r}_t^n | LI_t] - \tilde{r}_t^n]. \tag{17}$$

Output and inflation deviate from the standard solution only to the extent that the central bank's estimate of $\tilde{r}_t^n$ deviates from its actual level. An overly optimistic (pessimistic) assessment of aggregate demand pressures $(E[\tilde{r}_t^n | LI_t] < \tilde{r}_t^n)$ results in output and inflation being higher (lower) than under CI.

4.7 The Signal Extraction Problem

For the purposes of the signal extraction problem, we add and subtract the expected level of interest rates, on the basis of time $t - 1$ information, from the policy rule:

$$\tilde{R}_t = \underbrace{E[\tilde{R}_t^T | FI_{t-1}]}_{e} + \underbrace{\Phi_R(E[\tilde{r}_t^n | LI_t] - E[\tilde{r}_t^n | FI_{t-1}])}_{f}. \tag{18}$$

Term e can be thought of as the forecast made at time $t - 1$ of the interest rate at time t. Term f is the revision to the policy stance made on the basis of new, but limited, time t information, in this case the developments in the money market (the joint movement of ΔM_t and R_t).

Using the law of iterated projections, term f can be recast as:

$$f = \Phi_R \, E[\tilde{r}_t^n | (\Delta \tilde{M}_t - E[\Delta \tilde{M}_t | FI_{t-1}], \ \tilde{R}_t - E[\tilde{R}_t | FI_{t-1}])]$$

where $\Delta \tilde{M}_t = \Delta M_t - g - \bar{\pi} + \Delta \bar{v}$. The stance of policy is revised only to the extent that money market developments deviate from their time $t-1$ forecast, which implies policy revisions depend on the information set: $(\Delta \tilde{M}_t - E[\Delta \tilde{M}_t | FI_{t-1}],$ $\tilde{R}_t - E[\tilde{R}_t | FI_{t-1}])$.

The signal extraction problem therefore requires that we subtract the time $t - 1$ forecast from all endogenous variables, which we will denote with a hat (^).

Combining equations (14) and (15) with money demand equations (7–9), we obtain:

$$\Delta \hat{M}_t = \Delta \tilde{M}_t - E[\Delta \tilde{M}_t | FI_{t-1}] = -(\sigma(1+\kappa)+\eta)\hat{R}_t + (\iota+\varphi)\epsilon_t^r + \epsilon_t^{\Delta y^*} - \epsilon_t^{\Delta v},$$

which implies there is a linear combination of money growth and interest rate innovations that depends on exogenous shocks only:

$$\Delta \hat{M}_t + (\sigma(1+\kappa)+\eta)\hat{R}_t = (\iota+\varphi)\epsilon_t^r + \epsilon_t^{\Delta y^*} - \epsilon_t^{\Delta v}. \tag{19}$$

Using the first iteration of the Kalman filter, the optimal estimate $E[\epsilon_t^r | (\Delta \hat{M}_t, \hat{R}_t)]$ is the following:

$$E[\epsilon_t^r | (\Delta \hat{M}_t, \hat{R}_t)] = K(\Delta \hat{M}_t + (\sigma(1+\kappa)+\eta)\hat{R}_t),$$

where K is the initial Kalman gain:

$$K = \frac{(\iota+\varphi)\sigma_{\epsilon^r}^2}{(\iota+\varphi)^2\sigma_{\epsilon^r}^2 + \sigma_{\epsilon^{\Delta y}}^2 + \sigma_{\epsilon^{\Delta v}}^2},$$

where $(\sigma_{\epsilon^r}^2, \sigma_{\epsilon^{\Delta y}}^2, \sigma_{\epsilon^{\Delta v}}^2)$ denote the variances of shocks to the natural rate of interest, potential output, and velocity, respectively. Given the estimate $E[\epsilon_t^r | (\Delta \hat{M}_t, \hat{R}_t)]$, revisions to the stance of policy are given by:

$$\hat{R}_t = \Phi_R \, E[\epsilon_t^r | (\Delta \hat{M}_t, \hat{R}_t)] = \Phi_R K(\Delta \hat{M}_t + (\sigma(1+\kappa)+\eta)\hat{R}_t),$$

which implies the following policy relation between interest rates and monetary aggregates:

$$R_t - E[R_t^T | FI_{t-1}] = \frac{\Phi_R K}{1 - \Phi_R K(\sigma(1+\kappa)+\eta)}(\Delta M_t - E[\Delta M_t | FI_{t-1}]). \tag{20}$$

Finally, introducing the solution of the signal extraction problem into eq. (18) yields:

$$E[\tilde{r}_t^n | LI_t] = E[\tilde{r}_t^n | FI_{t-1}] + E[\epsilon_t^r | (\Delta \hat{M}_t, \hat{R}_t)] = \rho \tilde{r}_{t-1}^n + K\left((\iota+\varphi)\epsilon_t^r + \epsilon_t^{\Delta y^*} - \epsilon_t^{\Delta v}\right), \tag{21}$$

which allows us to provide a complete solution for the model under II, using equations (2), (3), (7), (8), (9), (16), (17), and (21):

$$\tilde{y}_t = \Phi_{\tilde{y}}\tilde{r}_t^n + \Gamma_{\tilde{y}}^{II}\epsilon_t^r + \Omega_{\tilde{y}}^{II}\epsilon_t^{\Delta y^*} + \Theta_{\tilde{y}}^{II}\epsilon_t^{\Delta v}$$

$$\tilde{\pi}_t = \Phi_{\pi}\tilde{r}_t^n + \Gamma_{\pi}^{II}\epsilon_t^r + \Omega_{\pi}^{II}\epsilon_t^{\Delta y^*} + \Theta_{\pi}^{II}\epsilon_t^{\Delta v}$$

$$\tilde{R}_t = \Phi_R\tilde{r}_t^n + \Gamma_R^{II}\epsilon_t^r + \Omega_R^{II}\epsilon_t^{\Delta y^*} + \Theta_R^{II}\epsilon_t^{\Delta v}$$

$$\Delta y_t = g + \Phi_{\Delta y}\Delta\tilde{r}_t^n + \Gamma_{\Delta y}^{II}\Delta\epsilon_t^r + \Omega_{\Delta y}^{II}\epsilon_t^{\Delta y^*} + \Theta_{\Delta y}^{II}\epsilon_t^{\Delta v} + A_{\Delta y}^{II}\epsilon_{t-1}^{\Delta y^*} + B_{\Delta Y}^{II}\epsilon_{t-1}^{\Delta v}$$

$$\Delta\tilde{M}_t = \Phi_{\Delta M}\Delta\tilde{r}_t^n + \Gamma_{\Delta M}^{II}\Delta\epsilon_t^r + \Omega_{\Delta M}^{II}\epsilon_t^{\Delta y^*} + \Theta_{\Delta M}\epsilon_t^{\Delta v} + A_{\Delta M}^{II}\epsilon_{t-1}^{\Delta y^*} + B_{\Delta M}^{II}\epsilon_{t-1}^{\Delta v},$$

where

$$\Gamma^{II}_{\tilde{y}} = \sigma\varrho, \quad \Gamma^{II}_{\pi} = \kappa\sigma\varrho, \quad \Gamma^{II}_{R} = -\varrho, \quad \Gamma^{II}_{\Delta Y} = \Gamma^{II}_{\tilde{y}}, \quad \Gamma^{II}_{\Delta M} = (\sigma(1+\kappa)+\eta)\varrho,$$

$$\varrho = (1 - K(\iota+\varphi))\Phi_R,$$

$$\Omega^{II}_{\tilde{y}} = -\sigma\Phi_R K, \quad \Omega^{II}_{\pi} = -\kappa\sigma\Phi_R K, \quad \Omega^{II}_{R} = \Phi_R K, \quad \Omega^{II}_{\Delta y} = 1 - \sigma\Phi_R K, \quad \Omega^{II}_{\Delta M} = \Omega^{II}_{\Delta y},$$

$$\Theta^{II}_{\tilde{y}} = \sigma\Phi_R K, \quad \Theta^{II}_{\pi} = \kappa\sigma\Phi_R K, \quad \Theta^{II}_{R} = -\Phi_R K, \quad \Theta^{II}_{\Delta y} = \sigma\Phi_R K, \quad \Theta^{II}_{\Delta M} = -1 + \sigma\Phi_R K,$$

$$A^{II}_{\Delta y} = A^{II}_{\Delta M} = \sigma\Phi_R K, \qquad\qquad \text{and} \qquad\qquad B^{II}_{\Delta Y} = B^{II}_{\Delta M} = -\sigma\Phi_R K.$$

Shocks to the natural rate of interest affect the economy through the standard channel, captured by the term Φ_z, as well as through the policy errors induced by the signal extraction problem. The latter effect is captured by the term Γ^{II}_z. Similarly, the aggregate demand side of the model ($\tilde{y}_t$, $\tilde{\pi}_t$, $\tilde{R}_t$) is now affected by shocks to potential output $\epsilon^{\Delta y^*}_t$ and shocks to velocity $\epsilon^{\Delta v}_t$, and also through policy errors. The effect of those shocks on the policy stance also has implications for output and nominal money growth in equilibrium, i.e., $\Omega^{II}_{\Delta y} \neq \Omega^{CI}_{\Delta y}$, $\Omega^{II}_{\Delta M} \neq \Omega^{CI}_{\Delta M}$, $\Theta^{II}_{\Delta y} \neq \Theta^{CI}_{\Delta y}$, $\Theta^{II}_{\Delta M} \neq \Theta^{CI}_{\Delta M}$. These additional effects coming from policy errors have only one-off effects on growth rates, which explains the appearance of terms $A^{II}_{\Delta y}\epsilon^{\Delta y^*}_{t-1} + B^{II}_{\Delta Y}\epsilon^{\Delta v}_{t-1}$ and $A^{II}_{\Delta M}\epsilon^{\Delta y^*}_{t-1} + B^{II}_{\Delta M}\epsilon^{\Delta v}_{t-1}$.

This concludes the presentation of the model and its solution.

5 A ROLE FOR MONEY TARGETS IN THE MONETARY POLICY FRAMEWORK

As we have just shown, a natural role for money targets emerges from the central bank's efforts to implement its desired policy stance under incomplete information, which we show by rewriting eq. (20):

$$(1 - \lambda^*)(R_t - R^T_{t|t-1}) = \lambda^*(\Delta M_t - \Delta M^T_{t|t-1}), \tag{22}$$

where:

$$R^T_{t|t-1} = \bar{r}^n + \bar{\pi} + \phi_\pi(E[\pi_{t+1}|FI_{t-1}] - \bar{\pi}) + \phi_y E[\tilde{y}_t|FI_{t-1}] \tag{23}$$

$$\Delta M^T_{t|t-1} = \underbrace{E[\Delta y_t|FI_{t-1}] + E[\pi_t|FI_{t-1}] - E[\Delta v_t|FI_{t-1}]}_{q} - \underbrace{\eta(R^T_{t|t-1} - R_{t-1})}_{l} \tag{24}$$

$$\lambda^* = \frac{\Phi_R K}{1 - \Phi_R K(\sigma(1+\kappa) + \eta - 1)}. \tag{25}$$

The role of money targets in the policy framework is captured by the money target term $\Delta M^T_{t|t-1}$ and the degree of target adherence λ^*. We discuss these in turn.

The previously announced money target $\Delta M^T_{t|t-1}$ is the forecast of money demand on the basis of $(t-1)$ information, under the assumption that the central bank wishes to follow the interest rate rule in (10). Specifically, the money target combines: (i) a forecast of money demand terms to be accommodated, term q, and (ii) intended changes in financial conditions in response to developments in the economy, term l, and which can be thought of as the policy content of the money target. The relative importance of these two terms depends on the interest elasticity of money demand η: a higher η raises the policy content of the money target. Large movements in velocity Δv_t, on the other hand, reduce its policy content.

The term λ^* captures the optimal degree of adherence to $\Delta M^T_{t|t-1}$, again under the assumption that the central bank wishes to implement the interest rate rule in (10) under incomplete information. λ^* is related to the size of the Kalman gain K: the more informative are the developments in the money market, the more the central bank will adhere to its previously set money targets (higher λ^*). To assess how the model parameters affect the optimal adherence to money targets, we first construct λ^* using an illustrative calibration (provided in Table 8.2) and then vary one parameter at a time.[11] Note that under this baseline calibration $\lambda^* = 0.3226$. This implies a non-negligible role for money targets in monetary policy: interest rates should increase by 48 basis points when ΔM_t deviates from its target by 100 basis points.

The sensitivity analysis of λ^* with regards to key parameters and shock volatilities is shown in Figure 8.1. An increase in the volatility of shocks to money demand ($\sigma^2_{\epsilon\Delta v}$) reduces the informational content of money market developments and therefore calls for less adherence to money targets (lower λ^*). The same happens when movements in output are increasingly driven by shocks to potential output (an increase in $\sigma^2_{\epsilon\Delta y}$, not shown).

Table 8.2. Parameters and Standard Deviations

Parameter	Value	Definition
σ	0.25	Inter-temporal elasticity of substitution
β	0.99	Discount factor
η	0.3	Interest rate elasticity of money demand
κ	0.34	Sensitivity of inflation to output
ϕ_π	1.5	Taylor rule coefficient
ϕ_y	0.5	Taylor rule coefficient
ρ	0.7	Persistence of equilibrium real interest rates
$\sigma^2_{\epsilon^r}$	1	Volatility of shocks to equilibrium real interest rates
$\sigma^2_{\epsilon\Delta y}$	1	Volatility of shocks to potential output
$\sigma^2_{\epsilon\Delta v}$	1	Volatility of shocks to velocity

[11] We do not provide a calibration for parameters $g, \Delta \bar{v}, \bar{\pi}, \bar{r}^n$, as these do not affect the derivation of λ^*.

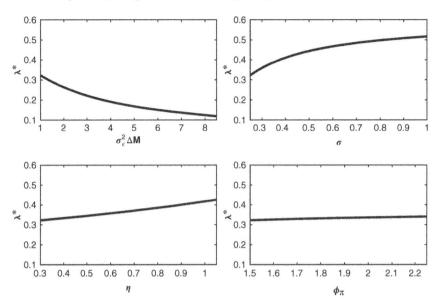

Figure 8.1. Sensitivity Analysis for λ^*

A higher inter-temporal elasticity of substitution (σ) has two opposing effects on λ^*. On the one hand a higher σ amplifies the effects of ϵ_t^r on the money market. This implies that, for any money market movement, the estimate of ϵ_t^r is now *lower*, which reduces K and therefore the degree of adherence to money targets. On the other hand, a higher σ amplifies the effects of shocks to the natural rate of interest rate on the economy, and therefore calls for a stronger policy response (higher Φ_R). This makes policymakers more responsive to money market developments. The second effect dominates, which implies λ^* increases (adherence to money targets increases) with σ.

A higher interest rate elasticity of money demand also raises λ^*. This is because, for a given level of adherence, interest rates become less sensitive to changes in money demand, including from shocks ϵ_t^r. Greater adherence therefore helps deliver the right amount of interest rate movement by compensating for this smaller effect. Finally, a more hawkish central bank (higher ϕ_π) would respond more aggressively to money market developments, which also implies greater adherence, though the overall effect is small.

5.1 Introducing a Noisy Measure of the Relevant Interest Rate

We now extend the model by assuming that the observed short-term interest rate—the one under the possible direct control of the central bank—is a noisy measure of the nominal interest rate that matters for private sector decisions:

$$R_t^{obs} = R_t + \epsilon_t^{R^{obs}}.$$

We add R_t^{obs} to the information set FI_t, and replace R_t with R_t^{obs} in LI_t. We can think of this relation as a useful shortcut to model some of the shortcomings of financial markets in low-income countries. Key markets such as the interbank and government bond markets are thin and opaque. Contract enforcement may be poor; and a large fraction of the population does not even participate in financial markets. In these circumstances, a readily observed interest rate such as the money market rate may bear only a loose connection to the (latent or shadow) interest rate relevant for private sector decisions.

To derive the implications for the optimal adherence to money targets, we add the term $(\sigma(1+\kappa)+\eta)\epsilon_t^{R^{obs}}$ to both sides of eq. (19), which yields:

$$\Delta\hat{M}_t + (\sigma(1+\kappa)+\eta)\hat{R}_t^{obs} = (\iota+\varphi)\epsilon_t^r + \epsilon_t^{\Delta y^*} - \epsilon_t^{\Delta v} + (\sigma(1+\kappa)+\eta)\epsilon_t^{R^{obs}}. \quad (26)$$

There is still a linear combination of money growth and observed interest rate innovations that depends on exogenous shocks only, which now includes the interest rate noise term $(\sigma(1+\kappa)+\eta)\epsilon_t^{R^{obs}}$. The estimate of shock ϵ_t^r is now given by:

$$E[\epsilon_t^r|(\Delta\hat{M}_t, \hat{R}_t^{obs})] = K_{\epsilon^r}(\Delta\hat{M}_t + (\sigma(1+\kappa)+\eta)\hat{R}_t^{obs}),$$

$$K_{\epsilon^r} = \frac{(\iota+\varphi)\sigma_{\epsilon^r}^2}{(\iota+\varphi)^2\sigma_{\epsilon^r}^2 + \sigma_{\epsilon^{\Delta y}}^2 + \sigma_{\epsilon^{\Delta v}}^2 + (\sigma(1+\kappa)+\eta)^2\sigma_{\epsilon^{R^{obs}}}^2},$$

where $\sigma_{\epsilon^{R^{obs}}}^2$ is the volatility of the interest rate noise. In addition, the central bank also constructs a measure of the noise $\epsilon_t^{R^*}$ on the basis of money market developments, which is given by:

$$E[\epsilon_t^{R^*}|(\Delta\hat{M}_t, \hat{R}_t^{obs})] = K_{\epsilon^{R^{obs}}}(\Delta\hat{M}_t + (\sigma(1+\kappa)+\eta)\hat{R}_t^{obs}),$$

$$K_{\epsilon^{R^{obs}}} = \frac{(\sigma(1+\kappa)+\eta)\sigma_{\epsilon^{R^{obs}}}^2}{(\iota+\varphi)^2\sigma_{\epsilon^r}^2 + \sigma_{\epsilon^{\Delta y}}^2 + \sigma_{\epsilon^{\Delta v}}^2 + (\sigma(1+\kappa)+\eta)^2\sigma_{\epsilon^{R^{obs}}}^2}.$$

The central bank then sets a level for R_t^{obs} on the basis of these two estimates:

$$\hat{R}_t^{obs} = \hat{R}_t + \epsilon_t^{R^*}$$

$$\hat{R}_t^{obs} = \Phi_R E[\epsilon_t^r|(\Delta\hat{M}_t, \hat{R}_t^{obs})] + E[\epsilon_t^{R^*}|(\Delta\hat{M}_t, \hat{R}_t^{obs})]$$

$$\hat{R}_t^{obs} = \Phi_R K_{\epsilon^r}(\Delta\hat{M}_t + (\sigma(1+\kappa)+\eta)\hat{R}_t^{obs}) + K_{\epsilon^{R^{obs}}}(\Delta\hat{M}_t + (\sigma(1+\kappa)+\eta)\hat{R}_t^{obs}),$$

which implies the following value for λ^*:

$$\lambda^* = \frac{\Phi_R K_{\epsilon^r} + K_{\epsilon^{R^{obs}}}}{1 - (\Phi_R K_{\epsilon^r} + K_{\epsilon^{R^{obs}}})(\sigma(1+\kappa)+\eta-1)}. \quad (27)$$

When the volatility of the interest rate noise increases ($\sigma^2_{\epsilon^{Robs}} \uparrow$), the informational content of money market development vis-à-vis ϵ^r_t decreases ($K_{\epsilon^r} \downarrow$), which pushes for less adherence to money targets. At the same time, however, the estimate of the interest rate noise increases ($K_{\epsilon^{Robs}} \uparrow$), which reduces the importance of interest-rate stabilization. The latter effect dominates, and greater adherence to money targets emerges as a result (higher λ^*). Moreover, as $\sigma^2_{\epsilon^{Robs}} \to \infty, \lambda^* \to 1$. For illustrative purposes, if we set $\sigma^2_{\epsilon^{Robs}} = 1$, the optimal level of λ^* decreases relative to the baseline ($\lambda^* = 0.4089$): short-term interest rates should now increase by 69 basis points following a money target deviation of 100 basis points.

5.2 Introducing a Noisy Measure of Economic Activity

We conclude our analysis of the model with the introduction of an additional variable in the central bank's information set LI_t.[12] The central bank can observe a noisy measure y^{obs}_t of output y_t :

$$y^{obs}_t = y_t + \epsilon^{y^{obs}}_t.$$

Subtracting (t-1) forecasts and combining with equations (1), (2), and (11), we obtain a linear combination of output and interest rates that depends on exogenous shocks only, similar to equation (19):

$$\hat{y}^{obs}_t + \sigma\hat{R}_t = \iota\epsilon^r_t + \epsilon^{y^{obs}}_t + \epsilon^{\Delta y^*}_t. \tag{28}$$

We now have two indicators of exogenous shocks: money market developments $(\Delta\hat{M}_t + (\sigma(1+\kappa)+\eta)\hat{R}^{obs}_t)$ and observed output/interest rate movements $(\hat{y}^{obs}_t + \sigma\hat{R}_t)$. Applying the Kalman filter in this case yields the following revisions to the policy stance:

$$\hat{R}_t = \Phi_R E[\epsilon^r_t | (\Delta\hat{M}_t, \hat{R}_t, \hat{y}_t)] = \Phi_R K_M(\Delta\hat{M}_t + (\sigma(1+\kappa)+\eta)\hat{R}_t) + \Phi_R K_y(\hat{y}_t + \sigma\hat{R}_t),$$

$$\begin{bmatrix} K_M \\ K_y \end{bmatrix} = \begin{bmatrix} (\iota+\varphi)\sigma^2_{\epsilon^r} \\ \iota\sigma^2_{\epsilon^r} \end{bmatrix} \begin{bmatrix} (\iota+\varphi)^2\sigma^2_{\epsilon^r} + \sigma^2_{\epsilon\Delta y} + \sigma^2_{\epsilon\Delta v} & (\iota+\varphi)\iota\sigma^2_{\epsilon^r} + \sigma^2_{\epsilon\Delta y} \\ (\iota+\varphi)\iota\sigma^2_{\epsilon^r} + \sigma^2_{\epsilon\Delta y} & \iota^2\sigma^2_{\epsilon^r} + \sigma^2_{\epsilon\Delta y} + \sigma^2_{\epsilon^{yobs}} \end{bmatrix}^{-1},$$

where $\sigma^2_{\epsilon^{yobs}}$ is the volatility of the measurement error. Finally, rearranging terms yields an extended version of eq. (22):

$$(1 - \overset{*}{\lambda}_M - \overset{*}{\lambda}_y)(R_t - R^T_{t|t-1}) = \overset{*}{\lambda}_M(\Delta M_t - \Delta M^T_{t|t-1}) + \overset{*}{\lambda}_y(y^{obs}_t - E[y_t|FI_{t-1}]),$$

where:

$$\overset{*}{\lambda}_M = \frac{\Phi_R K_M}{1 - \Phi_R(K_M(\sigma(1+\kappa)+\eta-1) - K_y(1-\sigma))}$$

---

[12] We set $\sigma^2_{\epsilon^{Robs}} = 0$ and return to the baseline case for the sake of simplicity.

$$\lambda_y^* = \frac{\Phi_R K_y}{1 - \Phi_R(K_M(\sigma(1 + \kappa) + \eta - 1) - K_y(1 - \sigma))}.$$

In this case monetary policy also responds to the measure of economic activity. The more informative is this variable (higher K_y), the smaller the degree of money target adherence (lower λ_M^*) and the larger the policy response to output movements (higher λ_y^*) .

The informational content of y_t^{obs} relative to $\Delta \hat{M}_t$ is hampered by two issues, however. First, movements in nominal money growth also reflect movements in (in this case, unobserved) inflation. The loading of money growth on shocks ϵ_t^r is therefore larger ($\iota + \varphi$) than the loading of measures of real activity (given by ι), which all else equal raises the informational content of ΔM_t relative to y_t^{obs}. In addition, measures of economic activity also reflect shocks to potential in addition to measurement error $\epsilon_t^{\Delta y^*}$, which reduce their informational content regarding aggregate demand. For illustrative purposes, setting $\sigma^2_{\epsilon^{yobs}} = 0.2$ results in $\lambda_M^* = 0.2949$ and $\lambda_y^* = 0.0395$, in which case a deviation in money targets of 100 basis points generates a 44 basis point increase in interest rates. This is very similar to the baseline. Numerical simulations (not shown) suggest the adherence to money targets decreases considerably only if both $\sigma^2_{\epsilon^{\Delta y}}$ and $\sigma^2_{\epsilon^{yobs}}$ are low (relative to $\sigma^2_{\epsilon^r}$ and $\sigma^2_{\epsilon^{\Delta v}}$).

6 CONCLUSION

We have shown how a standard New Keynesian model can be extended to provide a potentially important role for monetary aggregates in the conduct of monetary policy. We believe our results point to interesting, qualitative, conclusions, but we caution against taking them too literally.

One notable absence in our analysis is the exchange rate. Almost all LICs that target money also conduct a managed-floating exchange rate regime. And the exchange rate is, like money aggregates, observable at high frequency. Our closed economy model was silent on these issues. We leave this for future work.

We believe our work can be helpful for central banks that are transitioning toward interest rate-based frameworks, and inflation targeting more broadly, while nonetheless feeling reluctant about abandoning their money targets altogether. Our analysis shows how to combine a money targeting approach with a clear view on the level of interest rates, and can therefore be helpful for central banks that use elements of both.

Our analysis also can be used to document the costs of excessive adherence to monetary aggregates. Hitting money targets too obsessively would generate unnecessary volatility.[13] This point speaks to a finale rationale sometimes offered in support of money targeting: unlike for example inflation forecasts, money aggregates are directly observable and thus arguably can serve as useful intermediate

---

[13] This issue is discussed at more length in Berg et al. (2010).

targets for regimes with limited credibility. In the framework we have presented here, hitting targets for credibility's sake (that is, just because they have been preannounced) is costly. While it may be possible to rationalize this as the price required to demonstrate credibility, we are of the view that it is not ultimately credibility-enhancing to make otherwise bad policy choices just for credibility's sake. Rather, credibility is earned over time by carrying out good, time-consistent, policy. However, this topic may deserve further work.

Importantly, we have abstracted from important considerations that may make such a hybrid approach difficult. The flexibility of money targeting documented and rationalized here permits a degree of responsiveness to macroeconomic conditions and to various shocks, including to money demand. The cost, however, is the complexity and tendency to opacity, including a lack of separation between policy and operations that often characterize such regimes. Deviations from targets may sometimes reflect money demand shocks or operational consider-ations, but at other times they may reflect shifts in policy (appropriate or not). And it is very difficult to tell which is which in practice. We return to this point in the next chapter.

REFERENCES

Aoki, K. (2003). On the Optimal Monetary Policy Response to Noisy Indicators. *Journal of Monetary Economics*, 50, 501–23.

Berg, A., Unsal, F., and Portillo, R. (2010). *On the Optimal Adherence to Money Targets in a New-Keynesian Framework*. IMF Working Paper 10/134. Washington, DC: International Monetary Fund.

Clarida, R., Gali, J., and Gertler, M. (1999). The Science of Monetary Policy: A New Keynesian Perspective. *Journal of Economic Literature*, 37, 1661–1707.

Coenen, G., Levin, A., and Wieland, V. (2005). Data Uncertainty and the Role of Money as an Information Variable for Monetary Policy, *European Economic Review*, 49, 975–1006.

Friedman, B. (1975). Targets, Instruments, and Indicators of Monetary Policy. *Journal of Monetary Economics*, 1, 443–73.

Friedman, B. (1990). Targets and Instruments of Monetary Policy. In B. M. Friedman and F. H. Hahn (Eds.), *Handbook of Monetary Economics*. New York, NY: Elsevier North Holland, pp. 1186–1230.

Friedman, M. (1960). *A Program for Monetary Stability*. New York: Fordham University Press.

IMF (2008, April). Monetary and Exchange Rate Policies in Sub-Saharan Africa. *Regional Economic Outlook, Sub-Saharan Africa*, 2, 24–44. Washington, DC: International Monetary Fund.

IMF (2015). *Evolving Monetary Policy Frameworks in Low-Income and Other Developing Countries*. Washington, DC: International Monetary Fund.

Kumar, S. and Rao, B. B. (2012). Error-correction Based Panel Estimates of the Demand for Money of Selected Asian Countries with the Extreme Bounds Analysis. *Economic Modelling*, 29(4), 1181–8.

Lippi, F. and Neri, S. (2007). Information Variables for Monetary Policy in an Estimated Structural Model of the Euro Area. *Journal of Monetary Economics*, 54, 1256–70.

Polak, J. J. (2005). The IMF monetary model at forty. In J. Boughton (Ed.), *Selected Essays of Jacques J. Polak, 1994-2004*. New York and London: Sharpe, pp. 209–26.

Poole, W. (1970). Optimal Choice of Monetary Policy Instruments in a Simple Stochastic Macro Model. *Quarterly Journal of Economics*, 84, 197–216.

Sichei, M. and Kamau, A. W. (2012). Demand for Money: Implications for the Conduct of Monetary Policy in Kenya. *International Journal of Economics and Finance*, 4(8), 72–82.

Sriram, S. (2001). A Survey of Recent Empirical Money Demand Studies. *IMF Staff Papers*, 47(3), 334–65.

Svensson, L. E. O. and Woodford, M. (2003). Variables for Optimal Policy. *Journal of Monetary Economics*, (50), 691–720.

Svensson, L. E. O. and Woodford, M. (2004). Indicator Variables for Optimal Policy Under Asymmetric Information. *Journal of Economic Dynamics and Control*, 28, 661–90.

Walsh, C. (2003). *Monetary Theory and Policy*. Cambridge, MA: The MIT Press.

Woodford, M. (2008, December). How Important is Money in the Conduct of Monetary Policy? *Journal of Money, Credit and Banking*, 40(8), 1561–98.

Yun, T. (1996). Nominal price rigidity, money supply endogeneity, and business cycles. *Journal of Monetary Economics*, 37(2–3), 345–70.

9

Implementation Errors and Incomplete Information

Implications for the Effects of Monetary Policy in Low-Income Countries

Rafael Portillo, Filiz Unsal, Stephen O'Connell, and Catherine Pattillo

1 INTRODUCTION

As discussed in Chapter 6, recent empirical work has failed to find much evidence of a monetary transmission mechanism in low-income countries, including in Africa. Some researchers have concluded that structural features of these economies, e.g., shallow financial markets, limit the ability of monetary policy to deliver on price and macro stability, and that other policies may be better suited to this task.

In this chapter we show that limited effects of monetary policy can reflect shortcomings of existing policy frameworks in these countries rather than (or in addition to) structural features. We focus on two issues that are pervasive, as emphasized in Chapter 1. First, central banks often lack effective frameworks for implementing policy, so that short-term interest rates display considerable volatility. Second, clear communication is often lacking, as attested by indices of policy transparency, which makes it difficult for market participants to understand policymakers' intentions.

We introduce these features in an otherwise standard New Keynesian model. We model implementation errors as insufficient accommodation of shocks to money demand, which creates a noisy wedge between actual interest rates and the level intended by policymakers. The latter is not directly observed by the representative agent (incomplete information) and must be inferred from movements in interest rates and money.

Under these conditions we show that exogenous and persistent changes in the stance of monetary policy can have weak effects on the economy. This is the case even though the underlying transmission mechanism is strong, as reflected in the effects of the same policy under complete information. We believe our finding is important: if policy shortcomings are the source of weak transmission, then the solution is to improve on existing frameworks rather than give up on monetary policy altogether.[1]

2 THE MODEL

The economy is described by a New Keynesian model, consisting as in other similar models in this book (e.g. Chapter 15) of a forward-looking IS equation and an expectations-augmented Phillips curve:

$$y_t = E_{t-1}y_{t+1} - \sigma E_{t-1}[R_t - \pi_{t+1}] \tag{1}$$

$$\pi_t = \kappa E_{t-1}y_t + \beta E_{t-1}\pi_{t+1}, \tag{2}$$

where y_t is output, π_t is the inflation rate, and R_t is the short-term interest rate. Output and inflation rate are determined on the basis of (*t-1*) information, i.e., they are predetermined. The economy also features a demand for real money balances (m_t) similar to those found in other chapters (e.g., Chapter 8):

$$m_t = \gamma y_t - \eta R_t + u_t, \tag{3}$$

where u_t is an unexpected change in money demand. It is composed of two shocks: $u_t = u_{1,t} + u_{2,t}$. The role of these two shocks will become clear later. Nominal balances (M_t) can be written as:

$$M_t = m_t + P_t, \tag{4}$$

where P_t is the nominal price level.

3 THE CENTRAL BANK

3.1 Policy Intentions

Monetary policy is guided by a Taylor rule:

$$R_t^T = \phi_y y_t + \phi_\pi \pi_t + z_t \tag{5}$$

$$z_t = \rho z_{t-1} + \epsilon_t. \tag{6}$$

---

[1] This is consistent with the results of Chapter 5, which finds that a large joint policy tightening observed in East Africa in 2011 had stronger effects in those countries where the tightening was clearly communicated.

Formal analysis of incomplete information regarding central bank intentions goes back to Dotsey (1987); a recent partial equilibrium discussion is provided by Bindseil (2004) for the case of the ECB.

We refer to z_t as the stance of policy, subject to shocks ϵ_t and with persistence ρ. Policy intentions can also be represented as a money rule by combining (3), (4), and (5):

$$M_t^T = (\gamma - \eta\phi_y)y_t - \eta\phi_\pi\pi_t + P_t - \eta z_t + u_t. \qquad (7)$$

3.2 Policy Implementation

The central bank implements policy by setting M_t. The objective is $M_t = M_t^T$, so that $R_t = R_t^T$. However, the central bank makes implementation errors: it accommodates $u_{1,t}$ but not $u_{2,t}$. Monetary aggregates therefore follow:

$$M_t = (\gamma - \eta\phi_y)y_t - \eta\phi_\pi\pi_t + P_t - \eta z_t + u_{1,t}. \qquad (8)$$

As a result, actual interest rates differ from the intended policy stance ($R_t \neq R_t^T$):

$$R_t = \phi_y y_t + \phi_\pi\pi_t + z_t + \frac{1}{\eta}u_{2,t}.$$

4 COMPLETE VERSUS INCOMPLETE INFORMATION

The representative agent knows all the parameters of the model, including the specification of the interest rate rule and money demand, and the volatilities of the shocks.

Under complete information, the representative agent observes all variables $(y_{t-1}, R_{t-1}, \pi_{t-1}, m_{t-1}, M_{t-1}, P_{t-1},)$, policy intentions (R_{t-1}^T, M_{t-1}^T), and shocks $(u_{1,t-1}, u_{2,t-1}, z_{t-1})$ up to time $t-1$. Under incomplete information, the representative agent observes the macro variables but does not observe the shocks nor the policy intentions. The agent observes two linear combinations of the three shocks, however. First is the difference between interest rates and the endogenous monetary policy response:

$$resR_{t-1} = R_{t-1} - \phi_y y_{t-1} - \phi_\pi\pi_{t-1} = z_{t-1} + \frac{1}{\eta}u_{2,t-1}. \qquad (9)$$

Second is the difference between money and the level implied by the endogenous determinants of the money rule in (7):

$$resM_{t-1} = M_{t-1} - (\gamma - \eta\phi_y)y_{t-1} + \eta\phi_\pi\pi_{t-1} - P_{t-1} = -\eta z_{t-1} + u_{1,t-1}. \qquad (10)$$

The agent faces a signal extraction problem: to infer the stance of policy, z_{t-1}, on the basis of two noisy signals ($resR_{t-1}$ and $resM_{t-1}$).[2]

---

[2] The representative agent also observes the difference between M and the endogenous determinants of money demand: $resM_{t-1}^* = M_{t-1} - \gamma y gap_{t-1} + \eta R_{t-1} - P_{t-1} = u_{1,t-1} + u_{2,t-1}$. But this does not provide an additional source of information, as $resM_{t-1}^* = resM_{t-1} + \eta \, resR_{t-1}$.

4.1 The Model Solution under Complete and Incomplete Information

Under complete information, it is straightforward to show that:

$$y_t = \Psi_y E[z_t|FI_{t-1}] + \tau_y E[u_{1,t}|FI_{t-1}] + a_y E[u_{2,t}|FI_{t-1}], \qquad (11)$$

$$\pi_t = \Psi_\pi E[z_t|FI_{t-1}] + \tau_\pi E[u_{1,t}|FI_{t-1}] + a_\pi E[u_{2,t}|FI_{t-1}], \qquad (12)$$

where $FI_{t-1} = (z_{t-1}, u_{1,t-1}, u_{2t-1})$, and:

$$\Psi_y = -\Lambda_z(1 - \beta\rho) \quad \Psi_\pi = -\Lambda_z\kappa \quad \Lambda_z = \frac{\sigma}{(1 - \beta\rho)(1 - \rho + \sigma\phi_y) + \sigma\kappa(\phi_\pi - \rho)}$$

$$\tau_y = 0 \qquad\qquad\qquad \tau_\pi = 0$$

$$a_y = -\Lambda_u \qquad\qquad a_\pi = -\Lambda_u\kappa \quad \Lambda_u = \frac{\sigma}{\eta(1 + \sigma\phi_y + \sigma\kappa\phi_\pi)}.$$

When a shock to monetary policy hits at time t, starting from $z_{t-1} = 0$, the immediate effect on output and inflation is zero since $E[z_t|FI_{t-1}] = 0$. The effect from t+1 onwards is given by $y_{t+j} = \Psi_y\rho^j z_t$ and $\pi_t = \Psi_\pi\rho^j z_t$, for $j = 1, 2. \dots$

Regarding money demand, accommodated shocks ($u_{1,t}$) have zero effects. In principle, unaccommodated shocks could affect the economy. However, since output and inflation are predetermined and shocks to money demand are *i.i.d.*, it follows that $E[u_{2,t+j}|FI_{t+j-1}] = 0$ for $j = 0, 1, 2. \dots$ As a result errors in policy implementation have no effects.

Under incomplete information, the solution is similar:

$$y_t = \Psi_y E[z_t|LI_{t-1}] + \tau_y E[u_{1,t}|LI_{t-1}] + a_y E[u_{2,t}|LI_{t-1}], \qquad (13)$$

$$\pi_t = \Psi_\pi E[z_t|LI_{t-1}] + \tau_\pi E[u_{1,t}|LI_{t-1}] + a_\pi E[u_{2,t}|LI_{t-1}], \qquad (14)$$

where $LI_{t-1} = (resR_{t-1}, resM_{t-1})$. The estimates are derived using the Kalman filter (see Hamilton, 1994: ch. 13). Just as in the case of full information, $E[u_{2,t+j}|FI_{t+j-1}] = 0$ for $j = 0, 1, 2. \dots$ Errors in policy implementation still have no direct effects, though they now affect the estimation of $E[z_t|LI_{t-1}]$. For the Kalman filter problem at time t the state equation is given by (6)

$$z_t = \rho z_{t-1} + \epsilon_t,$$

and the observation equations are given by:

$$LI_t = \begin{bmatrix} resR_t \\ resM_t \end{bmatrix} = \underbrace{\begin{bmatrix} 1 \\ -\eta \end{bmatrix}}_{H} z_t + \underbrace{\begin{bmatrix} 0 & 1/\eta \\ \eta & 0 \end{bmatrix}}_{Q} \begin{bmatrix} u_{1,t} \\ u_{2,t} \end{bmatrix}. \qquad (15)$$

Under incomplete information, when a shock to monetary policy hits at time t, starting from $z_{t-1} = u_{1,t-1} = u_{2,t-1} = 0$, the immediate effect on output and inflation is also zero since $E[z_t|LI_{t-1}] = 0$. The effect from t+1 onwards is given by $ygap_{t+j} = \Psi_y\rho^j E[z_t|LI_{t+j-1}]$ and $\pi_t = \Psi_\pi\rho^j E[z_t|LI_{t+j-1}]$, for $j = 1, 2. \dots$ Unlike in the case of full information, the estimate of z_t changes over time, as the persistence of the effect of z_t on LI_{t+j} leads the private sector to reassess its initial estimate.

5 SIMULATIONS

We focus on a policy loosening of 1 per cent, i.e., $\epsilon_t = -1$, and compare the responses of output and inflation under complete and incomplete information. We use a standard calibration, summarized in Table 9.1. The Kalman filtering also requires that we calibrate the standard deviations of the shocks. Under this calibration, z_t is slightly more volatile than $u_{2,t}(\sigma_z^2 = 3.33)$, which implies that policy loosening (z_t) and errors in policy implementation ($u_{2,t}$) each account for about half of the deviation between interest rates and what is implied by the systematic part of the Taylor rule.

Figure 9.1 shows the impulse responses. Under complete information, a 1 per cent decrease in the policy rate at time t raises inflation by 0.46 per cent and output by 0.42 per cent in period $t+1$, and with both output and inflation displaying the same persistence than the policy shock. Under incomplete information, the impact is much lower and takes longer to have an impact: inflation and output peak in period $t+2$ at 0.13 and 0.12 per cent, respectively.

The stark difference between the two cases reflects the difficulty of inferring policy intentions when implementation errors are common. Under these circumstances policy actions have little effect on the economy. The representative agent eventually realizes the extent of policy accommodation, but by then the stance of policy has been largely corrected.

Relative volatility matters. If $\sigma_{u_1}^2 = \sigma_{u_2}^2 = \sigma_e^2 = 1$, the effects on inflation and output peak at 0.22 and 0.21, respectively. Also, both shocks to money demand are needed for the result to hold. If $u_2 = 0$, z can be inferred from $resR$; if $u_1 = 0$, z can be inferred from $resM$. Greater persistence of z (a higher ρ) also increases the effects of policy, as the signal extraction improves over time.

Table 9.1. Parameters and Standard Deviations

Parameter	Value	Definition
σ	1	Inter-temporal elasticity of substitution
β	0.99	Discount factor
η	0.5	Interest rate elasticity of money demand
γ	1	Income elasticity of money demand
κ	0.34	Sensitivity of inflation to output
ϕ_π	1.5	Taylor rule coefficient
ϕ_y	0.5	Taylor rule coefficient
ρ	0.7	Persistence of monetary policy shock
σ_e^2	1	Volatility of monetary policy shock
$\sigma_{u_1}^2$	3	Volatility of accommodated money demand shocks
$\sigma_{u_2}^2$	3	Volatility of unaccommodated money demand shocks

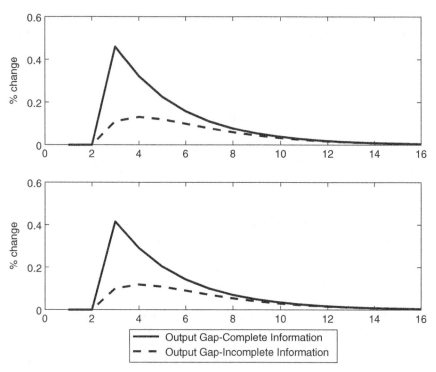

Figure 9.1. Impulse Response Functions Under Complete and Incomplete Information

6 CONCLUSION

We have shown that the combination of errors in policy implementation and incomplete information regarding policy intentions can greatly reduce the effects of policy on output and inflation. We believe our model can help understand the limited evidence of the monetary transmission mechanism in developing countries.

Our focus has been on shocks, consistent with the empirical literature. However, the issues here also apply to the endogenous component of policy. This can be the case if agents have less information about the state of the economy than the central banks.[3]

REFERENCES

Bindseil, U. (2004). *Monetary Policy Implementation*. Oxford: Oxford University Press.

Dotsey, M. (1987). Monetary Policy, Secrecy, and Federal Funds Rate Behavior. *Journal of Monetary Economics*, 20, 463–74.

Hamilton, J. (1994). *Time Series Analysis*. Princeton: Princeton University Press.

Melosi, L. (2012). *Signalling Effects of Monetary Policy*. Working Paper 2012–05. Chicago: Federal Reserve Bank of Chicago.

[3] See Melosi (2012).

10

On the First-Round Effects of International Food Price Shocks

Rafael Portillo and Luis-Felipe Zanna

1 INTRODUCTION

In this chapter[1] we use a stylized open-economy model to define, analytically, first-round effects on inflation stemming from international food price shocks. This is an important issue for African countries, which have faced large swings in international food prices in recent years. Policy advice usually calls for the central bank to respond *only* to 'second-round' effects—spillovers from food prices to wage and core inflation—and accommodate, instead, 'first-round' effects.[2] What is meant by first-round effects is not always clear. It is often assumed that first-round effects capture the direct impact of food price shocks on the consumer price index (CPI) and, therefore, depend on the weight of food in this index, but in the absence of a clear analytical framework it is difficult to provide a more formal definition.

Implicit in the standard policy advice is the idea that an increase in commodity prices requires an adjustment in relative prices and macroeconomic aggregates. Since an increase in headline (CPI) inflation can help implement this necessary adjustment, this advice is implemented in practice by using core inflation, which excludes temporary food price movements, as the nominal anchor of monetary policy. In addition, the choice of this anchor is not innocuous.[3] Core inflation embodies the distortions resulting from nominal price rigidities; as a result, stabilizing core rather than headline inflation is desirable from a welfare perspective. This justifies the policy advice of responding only to 'second-round' effects.[4]

---

[1] This chapter is a revised short version of Portillo and Zanna (2015).

[2] To our knowledge, this advice has its origins in policy decisions taken by the Bundesbank in the 1970s, which in the face of shocks to the international price of oil raised its one-year-ahead inflation objective to accommodate the inflation caused by the shock (see Bernanke et al., 1999). The standard advice likely became more clearly articulated with the adoption of inflation-targeting regimes, as these helped focus the policy discussion on better understanding the sources of inflation and tailoring the policy response accordingly. From an academic perspective, although not explicitly stated, the advice can be traced back to the seminal work of Robert Gordon (1975).

[3] See Woodford (2003), among others.   [4] See Aoki (2001).

The literature has focused on whether to target core or headline inflation in the presence of supply shocks, e.g., Bodenstein et al. (2008), but there has been little work on understanding first-round effects per se and how they depend on the structure of the economy. Is it always the case that first-round effects depend positively on the share of food in consumption, so that countries with higher food shares should experience larger increases in inflation? Or are there other, possibly mitigating, factors? Given that these are international shocks, what role does the country's access (or lack of access) to international capital markets play in shaping these effects?

In this chapter, we study the determinants of first-round effects in a tractable New Keynesian small open-economy model, which itself is a simplified version of the model in Portillo and Zanna (2015). The model has three goods: a sticky-price non-traded good, a flexible-price food, and a flexible-price generic traded good. It also features a domestic endowment of food and various specifications of the country's access to international financial markets—complete markets, financial autarky, and incomplete markets. Our definition of first-round effects is the following: increases in headline inflation that, holding core inflation perfectly stabilized, help implement the required relative-price and macroeconomic adjustment. The 'hold core inflation' part requires a certain monetary policy response, which highlights the fact that the concept of first-round effects, strictly speaking, cannot be fully separated from monetary policy.

Under this definition, inflation is given by (minus) changes in the relative price of non-traded goods. Moreover, in our simple model the relative price of non-traded goods co moves one for one with the real wage. The larger the required decline in real wages (the relative price of non-traded goods), the larger the first-round effects. Our model-based definition of first-round effects captures the inherent inflationary pressures associated with commodity price shocks while also being consistent with the new-Keynesian literature for modern monetary policy analysis.

In Portillo and Zanna (2015) we show that first-round effects rarely correspond to the *direct* effects of food price shocks on headline inflation, by which we mean the weight of (traded) food in the CPI. Policymakers usually (mis)interpret these direct effects as first-round effects. Here we emphasize one aspect of their findings, which is that first-round inflationary effects crucially depend on a country's international asset market structure.

In our simple model, the inflationary effect *is* proportional to the food share in the CPI only in the case of complete markets (CM), i.e., in an environment consistent with perfect international risk-sharing.[5] In this case, the real effects of international food shocks depend solely on the *inter-temporal substitution* effects they trigger, which depend on the share of food in the CPI. The larger the food share, the larger the increase in the relative price of the domestic consumption basket, and the larger the incentive to temporarily reduce aggregate consumption when hit by an increase in international food prices. The decline in consumption determines the magnitude of the decrease in the relative price of non-traded goods and therefore the magnitude of first-round effects.

---

[5] Most New Keynesian small open economy models follow the seminal work by Gali and Monacelli (2005), which assumes complete markets.

As developing countries have large food shares, CM then predict large first-round effects.

Under financial autarky (FA), i.e., an environment in which countries cannot borrow from or lend to the rest of the world, the inflationary impact is instead proportional to the country's net food balance—the difference between the country's food endowment and its food consumption—rather than the food share in the CPI. The key mechanism stems from the impact of the shock on the country's external income (*income* effects). If the country is self-sufficient in food, there are no balance-of-payment pressures from increases in international food prices, no pressures for the relative price of non-traded goods to change, and hence no inflationary pressures. If the relative price of non-traded goods were to fall, the country would demand less traded goods overall and an incipient current account surplus would arise. This incipient surplus would appreciate the nominal exchange rate—and reduce the relative price of non-traded goods—up to the point where the balance of payment clears again. This striking result stems from the inability to run a current account surplus (or deficit) in response to the shock. As food balances in developing countries are, on average, small—about one or two percentage points of GDP—FA then predicts tiny increases in inflation (or even deflation if the country is a net food exporter).

Finally, under incomplete markets (IM), an environment where agents can borrow internationally but face portfolio adjustment costs and risk sharing is limited, the country can in principle run current account surpluses or deficits in response to the shock. In this case, first-round effects depend on both the share of food in consumption and on the country's overall food balance, and the solution is a weighted combination of the previously discussed two asset market specifications. The size of portfolio adjustment costs determines the relative importance of each specification in the model solution: larger costs push the equilibrium toward the financial autarky case. While the weight of food in the CPI still captures the *substitution* effects associated with the shock, the food balance now captures its *wealth* effects; the more persistent the shock is, the larger the wealth effects and therefore the more important the country's food balance becomes in conditioning the inflationary response.

To assess the quantitative implications of our results we perform a simple numerical exercise along the lines of Portillo and Zanna (2015). In particular, we calibrate our simple model to a generic/median sub-Saharan African country. Consistent with the analytical results, alternative specifications yield very different inflationary pressures. Under CM a 1 per cent increase in international food prices can result in an increase in first-round inflation of as much as 0.50 of a percentage point. Under FA, the median increase in inflation is close to 0.01 per cent, which is tiny. Under IM, the median increase in inflation falls somewhere in-between (0.12 per cent). In addition, while the inflationary effect varies, in both the FA case and the IM case a nominal appreciation offsets either a large part or most of the direct effect of the shock. The wide range of estimates, both across asset market specifications and relative to the food share, underscores the challenges of quantifying first-round effects, including for policy purposes.

The remainder of this chapter is organized as follows. Section 2 presents the model. Section 3 provides an analytical solution, while section 4 presents a graphic representation of the solution and a simple numerical assessment. Section 5 concludes.

2 THE MODEL

2.1 The Representative Consumer

The representative consumer chooses a stream of consumption baskets c_t, labour efforts n_t, and holdings of nominal assets to maximize lifetime utility:

$$E_0 \sum_{t=0}^{\infty} \beta^t \left[\log(c_t) - \iota \frac{n_t^{1+\psi}}{1+\psi} \right],$$

where $\beta \in (0, 1)$ is the subjective discount factor, ι measures the importance of disutility from labour in overall utility, $\psi > 0$ is the inverse of the Frisch elasticity of labour supply, and E_0 denotes the expectations operator. Expectations are rational.

The representative consumer is also subject to the budget constraint:

$$P_t c_t + B_t + \phi_1 E_t \{Q_{t+1} D_{t+1}\} + \phi_2 S_t [B_t^* + \mathcal{H}(B_t^*)]$$
$$= W_t n_t + \Omega_{N,t} + P_{F,t} y_F + P_{T,t} y_T - T_t + R_{t-1} B_{t-1} + \phi_1 D_t + \phi_2 S_t R^* B_{t-1}^*.$$

$$(1)$$

P_t is the consumer price index (CPI), W_t is the nominal wage and $\Omega_{N,t}$ are profits from the non-traded sector. We assume the agent is endowed with two types of traded goods: food y_F and a generic traded-good y_T, valued at prices $P_{F,t}$ and $P_{T,t}$, respectively. T_t are government taxes and B_t denotes holdings of a non-contingent nominal domestic bond that pays gross interest R_t at time $t + 1$. The bond is not traded internationally.

We consider several international asset market structures: complete markets (CM) and incomplete markets (IM), and financial autarky (FA). The combination of the parameters ϕ_1 and ϕ_2, in equation (1), captures these various options: the pair $\{\phi_1 = 0, \phi_2 = 0\}$ implies FA; $\{\phi_1 = 1, \phi_2 = 0\}$ captures CM; and $\{\phi_1 = 0, \phi_2 = 1\}$ reflects IM.[6]

Under CM, $D_{t,t+1}$ denotes time-t holdings of contingent claims, which pay one unit of currency if a specific state of nature is realized (in period $t + 1$) and nothing otherwise, and $Q_{t,t+1}$ is the one-period stochastic discount factor for that state of nature. With IM, B_t^* refers to a non-contingent bond, denominated in foreign currency (S_t is the nominal exchange rate), which pays a free-risk gross interest R^* and is subject to portfolio adjustment costs $\mathcal{H}(B_t^*)$, as in Schmitt-Grohé and Uribe (2003):

$$\mathcal{H}(B_t^*) = \frac{\nu}{2} (B_t^*)^2.$$

These costs ensure the stationarity of the country's net foreign asset position (B_t^*) and allow us to model various degrees of international capital mobility depending on the value of ν.

---

[6] Once $\phi_1 = 1$, the value of ϕ_2 does not matter: access to a complete set of contingent assets makes incomplete (non–contingent) assets redundant.

Inter-temporal utility maximization leads to the following first-order conditions:

$$\frac{1}{c_t} = \beta E_t \left[\left(\frac{R_t}{\pi_{t+1}} \right) \frac{1}{c_{t+1}} \right], \tag{2}$$

and

$$\iota n_t^\psi c_t = w_t, \tag{3}$$

where $\pi_t \equiv \frac{P_t}{P_{t-1}}$ is the gross inflation rate and $w_t \equiv \frac{W_t}{P_t}$ is the real wage. These conditions—representing, respectively, the Euler equation related to domestic bonds B_t and the equation that equalizes the marginal rate of substitution between labour and consumption to the real wage—hold regardless of the international asset market structure. With CM ($\phi_1 = 1$), the maximization problem results in a state-specific Euler equation related to the state-contingent bonds $D_{t,t+1}$:

$$\frac{1}{c_t} = \left(\frac{\beta}{Q_{t+1}\pi_{t+1}} \right) \frac{1}{c_{t+1}}, \tag{4}$$

which holds across all states of nature; while for IM ($\phi_1 = 0$ and $\phi_2 = 1$) the maximization problem yields a different Euler equation related to the non-contingent bond B_t^*:

$$\frac{1}{c_t} = \beta R^* E_t \left[\left(\frac{s_{t+1}}{s_t} \right) \left(\frac{1}{1 + v b_t^*} \right) \frac{1}{c_{t+1}} \right], \tag{5}$$

where $s_t \equiv \frac{S_t P^*}{P_t}$ is the CPI-based real exchange rate and $b_t^* \equiv \frac{B_t^*}{P^*}$ with P^* denoting the foreign CPI which, for simplicity, is assumed to be constant and equal to one. Depending on the international market structure, corresponding transversality conditions hold.

2.2 The Consumption Basket and Prices

The consumption basket is the following:

$$c_t = (c_{N,t})^{\alpha_N} (c_{F,t})^{\alpha_F} (c_{T,t})^{1-\alpha_N-\alpha_F}.$$

The triplet $(c_{N,t}, c_{F,t}, c_{T,t})$ denotes consumption of non-traded goods, food, and the generic traded good, respectively; and α_N (α_F) is the share of non-traded goods (food) in consumption. Cost minimization leads to the following demand functions:

$$c_{N,t} = \alpha_N \left(\frac{P_{N,t}}{P_t} \right)^{-1} c_t = \alpha_N \frac{c_t}{p_{N,t}}, \tag{6}$$

$$c_{F,t} = \alpha_F \left(\frac{P_{F,t}}{P_t} \right)^{-1} c_t = \alpha_F \frac{c_t}{p_{F,t}}, \tag{7}$$

and

$$c_{T,t} = (1 - a_N - a_F)\left(\frac{P_{T,t}}{P_t}\right)^{-1} c_t = (1 - a_N - a_F)\frac{c_t}{p_{T,t}}. \tag{8}$$

$P_{i,t}$ is the price of good i with $i = N, F, T$. The triplet $(p_{N,t}, p_{F,t}, p_{T,t})$ denotes the price of each good relative to the CPI, which is given by:

$$P_t = (P_{N,t})^{a_N}(P_{F,t})^{a_F}(P_{T,t})^{1-a_N-a_F}. \tag{9}$$

In our baseline specification, we assume the domestic prices of food and the generic traded good are given by the law of one price:

$$P_{F,t} = S_t P_{F,t}^* \quad \text{and} \quad P_{T,t} = S_t P^*, \tag{10}$$

where $P_{F,t}^*$ is the international nominal price of food. This assumption implies the following domestic relative prices:

$$p_{F,t} = s_t p_{F,t}^*, \quad \text{and} \quad p_{T,t} = s_t. \tag{11}$$

Lower case $p_{F,t}^* \equiv \frac{P_{F,t}^*}{P^*}$ is the international relative price of food, which we assume is exogenous and time-varying.

Using equations (9)–(11), it is possible to write CPI (gross) inflation as:

$$\pi_t = (p_{N,t-1}\pi_{N,t})^{a_N}(s_{t-1}p_{F,t-1}^*\pi_{F,t})^{a_F}(s_{t-1}\pi_{T,t})^{1-a_N-a_F}, \tag{12}$$

where $\pi_{i,t}$ denotes (gross) inflation of good i with $i = N, F, T$, satisfying the following:

$$\pi_{N,t} = \left(\frac{p_{N,t}}{p_{N,t-1}}\right)\pi_t, \quad \pi_{F,t} = \left(\frac{s_t}{s_{t-1}}\right)\left(\frac{p_{F,t}^*}{p_{F,t-1}^*}\right)\pi_t, \quad \text{and} \quad \pi_{T,t} = \left(\frac{s_t}{s_{t-1}}\right)\pi_t. \tag{13}$$

2.3 The Non-Traded Sector

The non-traded sector is composed of a continuum of monopolistic competitors, each providing a variety $y_{N,t}(i)$, with $i \in [0, 1]$, and facing the following Dixit-Stiglitz aggregate demand for variety i:

$$y_{N,t}(i) = \left(\frac{P_{N,t}(i)}{P_{N,t}}\right)^{-\epsilon} y_{N,t},$$

where ϵ is elasticity of substitution between varieties, $P_{N,t}(i)$ is the price charged by firm i and $P_{N,t}$ is the price index for the entire sector: $P_{N,t} = [P_{N,t}(i)^{1-\epsilon}]^{\frac{1}{1-\epsilon}}$. Production of non-traded varieties is given by $y_{N,t}(i) = n_t(i)$.

Firms set prices for their varieties to maximize their profits. As in Calvo (1983), firms are not allowed to change their prices unless they receive a random signal. The probability that a given price can be re-optimized in any particular period is constant and equal to $(1 - \theta)$. If firm i gets the random signal at time t, it chooses a reset price $\bar{P}_{N,t}(i)$ to maximize its discounted stream of expected profits:

$$Max\, E_t \sum_{j=0}^{\infty} (\beta\theta)^j \lambda_{t+j} \left[\left(\frac{\bar{P}_{N,t}(i)}{P_{N,t+j}} \right)^{-\epsilon} y_{N,t+j} \left(\bar{P}_{N,t}(i) - W_{t+j}(1 - \delta) \right) \right],$$

where λ_{t+j} is the stochastic discount factor, and δ is an employment subsidy. Profit maximization results in the following reset price:

$$\bar{P}_{N,t} = \frac{\epsilon}{\epsilon - 1}(1 - \delta) \frac{E_t \sum_{j=0}^{\infty} (\beta\theta)^j \lambda_{t+j} \left[\left(\frac{1}{P_{N,t+j}} \right)^{-\epsilon} y_{N,t+j} W_{t+j} \right]}{E_t \sum_{j=0}^{\infty} (\beta\theta)^j \lambda_{t+j} \left[\left(\frac{1}{P_{N,t+j}} \right)^{-\epsilon} y_{N,t+j} \right]}. \tag{14}$$

The aggregate price index in the non-traded sector $P_{N,t}$ is the weighted sum of those prices $\bar{P}_{N,t}$ that were reset (with mass $1 - \theta$) and those prices that were not reset that can be approximated by yesterday's price index $P_{N,t-1}$ (with mass θ):

$$P_{N,t} = [(1 - \theta)\bar{P}_{N,t}^{1-\epsilon} + \theta P_{N,t-1}^{1-\epsilon}]^{\frac{1}{1-\epsilon}}.$$

2.4 Monetary Policy: Identifying First-Round Effects

There is an interesting parallel between a) the standard policy advice of allowing for the direct first-round effects on headline inflation but not for the second-round effects, and b) the selection of core inflation, instead of headline, as the nominal anchor and target that guides policy decisions of central banks that practice inflation targeting.[7] In the end, by targeting core inflation—excluding flexible and volatile prices, such as those associated with food and energy—the monetary authority implements, to a great extent, the standard advice of allowing for first-round effects while reacting to second-round effects.

We invoke this parallel to identify the first-round effects. Our approach consists of focusing on the flexible-price equilibrium that arises in a new-Keynesian model where the central bank perfectly stabilizes core inflation—i.e., sticky-price non-traded goods inflation.[8] By doing this, we abstract from nominal price-rigidity issues and, therefore, from second-round effects.[9] As we will elaborate below, this means that the inflation dynamics will be determined by the (negative) changes in the relative price of non-traded goods, which are associated with the first-round effects.

---

[7] See International Monetary Fund (2011), among others. The policy objective of responding only to second-round effects is to avoid persistent effects on inflation. The first-round or direct effects—which also include the effects associated with the use of oil as an intermediate production input—capture changes in relative prices in the economy and therefore their impact on headline inflation should be short-lived. In contrast, the second-round effects involve increases in prices that are more persistent, including those that result from pressures to preserve real wage levels. For issues related to the selection of core inflation as the appropriate target see, for instance, Aoki (2001), among others, in the context of the New Keynesian literature.

[8] This approach is not uncommon in the New Keynesian literature. Woodford (2011), for instance, proposes to identify the size of the government expenditure multiplier 'when monetary policy is unchanged', by assuming that the monetary authority is endowed with a technology that keeps the *real* interest rate constant.

[9] The exchange rate is assumed to be flexible.

Given our strategy, we can further simplify the equilibrium conditions that drive the dynamics of the economy. We focus then on a symmetric equilibrium where $P_{N,t-1}(i) = P_{N,t-1} = P_{N,0}$ for all $i \in [0, 1]$ and

$$y_{N,t} = n_t. \tag{15}$$

We assume that, using its perfectly-stabilizing-inflation technology, the central bank sets core inflation equal to one—i.e., $\pi_{N,t} = 1$, for $t = 1, 2, \ldots, \infty$. This implies that $P_{N,t} = P_{N,t+1} = \ldots = P_{N,0}$ and that the reset price $\bar{P}_{N,t}$ must also equal $P_{N,0}$ in equation (14). For simplicity, but without loss of generality, we assume the employment subsidy corrects the monopolistic distortion—i.e., $\delta = 1/\epsilon$. Then the Calvo pricing equation (14) holds if:[10]

$$p_{N,t} = w_t, \tag{16}$$

which reflects labour demand decisions and implies zero profits ($\Omega_{N,t} = 0$).

To complete the specification of policies in this model, we assume the government follows a passive fiscal policy by setting taxes (T_t) to satisfy its budget constraint at all times ($B_t = R_{t-1}B_{t-1} + \delta w_t n_t - T_t$). For simplicity we assume it does not have access to foreign bonds/claims.

2.5 Market Clearing Conditions and Model Closure

The market clearing condition in the non-traded sector can be expressed as

$$c_{N,t} = y_{N,t} = n_t. \tag{17}$$

While combining the labour supply equation (3) with the labour demand equation (16) yields the market clearing condition of the labour market

$$\iota n_t^{\psi} c_t = w_t = p_{N,t}. \tag{18}$$

We close the model using the various asset structures described earlier: financial autarky (FA), complete markets (CM) and incomplete markets (IM).

Under FA ($\phi_1 = 0$ and $\phi_2 = 0$), the representative agent cannot buy or sell financial assets to foreigners. Total demand for traded goods must therefore equal the value of domestic endowments:

$$s_t p_{F,t}^* c_{F,t} + s_t c_{T,t} = s_t p_{F,t}^* y_F + s_t y_T. \tag{19}$$

---

[10] To see this, use $\bar{P}_{N,t} = P_{N,0}$ and set $\delta = 1/\epsilon$ in equation (14) and divide both sides of this equation by $P_{N,0}$ to obtain

$$1 = \frac{E_t \sum_{j=0}^{\infty} (\beta\theta)^j \lambda_{t+j} \left[y_{N,t+j} \frac{w_{t+j}}{P_{N,t+j}} \right]}{E_t \sum_{j=0}^{\infty} (\beta\theta)^j \lambda_{t+j} [y_{N,t+j}]},$$

which holds if:

$$\frac{w_{t+j}}{p_{N,t+j}} = 1 \text{ for } j = 0, 1, \ldots.$$

Under CM ($\phi_1 = 1$ and $\phi_2 = 0$), we can combine equation (4) with a similar condition for foreign consumers and derive the following equilibrium condition:[11]

$$c_t = \varphi s_t c^*, \tag{20}$$

where c^* is foreign consumption, which is assumed to be constant, and φ denotes initial conditions. Under complete markets, c_t will deviate from φc_t^* only if the domestic basket becomes more or less expensive than the foreign one, i.e., only if the real exchange rate appreciates or depreciates.

Under IM ($\phi_1 = 0$ and $\phi_2 = 1$), the country's balance of payment now includes the accumulation of foreign assets, interest income from abroad, and portfolio adjustment costs:

$$s_t p_{F,t}^* c_{F,t} + s_t c_{T,t} + s_t[b_t^* + \mathcal{H}(b_t^*)] = s_t p_{F,t}^* y_F + s_t y_T + s_t R^* b_{t-1}^*. \tag{21}$$

2.6 Definition of the First-Round Effects Equilibrium and the Steady State

We now provide a definition of the first-round effects equilibrium for the case of FA.

Definition 1 *Given $\{y_T, y_F\}$ and the stochastic process $\{p_{F,t}^*\}_{t=0}^{\infty}$, a first-round effects equilibrium under financial autarky is a set of stochastic processes $\{c_t, c_{N,t}, c_{F,t}, c_{T,t}, n_t, y_{N,t}, R_t, p_{N,t}, p_{T,t}, p_{F,t}, w_t, s_t, \pi_t, \pi_{N,t}, \pi_{F,t}, \pi_{T,t}\}_{t=0}^{\infty}$ satisfying (i) the optimal conditions (2) and (6)–(8); (ii) the definitions (11)–(13); (iii) the central bank's policy that perfectly stabilizes core inflation as $\pi_{N,t} = 1$; (iv) the market clearing conditions (17) and (18); and (v) the closing condition (19).*

Similar definitions could be provided for CM or IM. For the case of CM, the equilibrium definition would also consider the stochastic process $\{Q_{t+1}\}_{t=0}^{\infty}$ and the Euler equation (4), while it would replace the closing condition (19) by (20). On the other hand, the equilibrium definition under IM would include the stochastic process $\{b_t^*\}_{t=0}^{\infty}$ and the Euler equation (5), and it would replace the closing condition (19) by (21).

The steady state is the same across all international asset structure specifications. We impose the condition $\beta R^* = 1$, which in the case of IM imposes $b^* = 0$. More generally, we set aggregate consumption, relative prices, and gross inflation to 1:

$$c = s = p_N = p_F^* = w = \pi = 1.$$

Steady-state values of (c_N, c_F, c_T) are given by $(a_N, a_F, 1 - a_N - a_F)$, respectively. Variables y_N and n also equal a_N, which requires $\iota = a_N^{-\psi}$. Finally, we set $y_F = \kappa_F$, which imposes $y_T = 1 - a_N - \kappa_F$.

---

[11] See Backus and Smith (1993).

3 ANALYTICAL SOLUTION

3.1 The Log-linear Version of the Model

We log-linearize the equations of the model around the non-stochastic steady state and present the equations that describe the dynamics of the economy, depending on the international asset market structure.

3.1.1 Financial Autarky (FA)

Under FA, the equations of the first-round effects equilibrium in Definition 1 can be reduced, after some algebra, to a system of two equations:

$$\hat{c}_t = \hat{p}_{N,t}, \tag{22}$$

and

$$\hat{c}_t = -\frac{a_N}{1 - a_N}\hat{p}_{N,t} - \frac{a_F - \kappa_F}{1 - a_N}\hat{p}_{F,t}^*, \tag{23}$$

where a hat indicates per cent deviations from steady state. Equation (22) describes internal balance: the relation between aggregate consumption ($\hat{c}_t$) and the relative price of non-traded goods ($\hat{p}_{N,t}$) that ensures equilibrium in the non-traded goods sector and the labour market. The relation is straightforward: an increase in $\hat{p}_{N,t}$ results in a decrease in the demand for non-traded goods and an increase in the supply of labour; an increase in overall consumption is therefore required to increase non-traded demand and reduce labour supply, through the Frisch labour supply curve (3). Equation (23) describes external balance—the clearing of the balance of payments (BOP). In this case, an increase in $\hat{p}_{N,t}$ results in an increase in traded goods demand; a decrease in $\hat{c}_t$ is then required to clear the BOP. $\hat{p}_{F,t}^*$ operates as an exogenous shifter of the external balance curve.

3.1.2 Complete Markets (CM)

Under CM, internal balance remains the same as in (22). We derive an alternative external balance condition, by combining the log-linear versions of equations (9) and (20):

$$\hat{c}_t = -\frac{a_N}{1 - a_N}\hat{p}_{N,t} - \frac{a_F}{1 - a_N}\hat{p}_{F,t}^*. \tag{24}$$

Note that, unlike equation (23), this alternative condition does not reflect the need to clear the BOP. Instead, it describes how changes in relative prices affect the representative agent's demand for current consumption, through their effect on the risk sharing condition (20). Because of this, external balance under CM does not depend on the economy's endowment of food. This will have important consequences for the inflationary effect of food shocks.

3.1.3 Incomplete Markets (IM)

Finally, under IM, the solution of the model can be reduced to a system of three equations. First, the internal balance equation, which is the same as (22). The second equation—which is derived from combining equations (7), (8), (9), (11), and (21)—is the relation between $\hat{p}_{N,t}$, $\hat{c}_t$ and $\hat{b}_t^*$ that clears the BOP:[12]

$$\hat{c}_t = -\frac{a_N}{1 - a_N}\hat{p}_{N,t} - \frac{a_F - \kappa_F}{1 - a_N}\hat{p}_{F,t}^* - \frac{1}{1 - a_N}\hat{b}_t^* + \frac{R^*}{1 - a_N}\hat{b}_{t-1}^*. \tag{25}$$

Unlike FA, accumulation or decumulation of foreign assets now allow the representative agent to consume more or less traded goods than the value of this endowment.

The third equation is the relation between present and future values of $(\hat{c}_t, \hat{p}_{N,t}, \hat{p}_F^*)$ and $\hat{b}_t^*$ implied by combining the Euler equation (5) with equation (9):

$$\hat{c}_t = E_t\hat{c}_{t+1} - \frac{a_N}{1 - a_N}(\hat{p}_{N,t} - E_t\hat{p}_{N,t+1}) - \frac{a_F}{1 - a_N}(\hat{p}_{F,t}^* - E_t\hat{p}_{F,t+1}^*) + v\hat{b}_t^*. \tag{26}$$

Consumption now depends on future values of domestic and foreign relative prices, while the portfolio adjustment cost encourages agents to increase consumption when they accumulate net foreign assets (as these lower their net return).

Because of the forward-looking nature of the Euler equation, the solution of the model is no longer static. To characterize expectations of future variables, we need to specify stochastic processes for international relative prices:

$$\hat{p}_{F,t}^* = \rho_{p_F^*}\hat{p}_{F,t-1}^* + \epsilon_{p_F^*,t}, \tag{27}$$

where $\rho_{p_F^*} \in (0, 1)$ captures the persistence of the process and $\epsilon_{p_F^*,t}$ is an *i.i.d.* shock.

3.1.4 The Link between Inflation, Relative Prices, and First-Round Effects

Under the assumption that the monetary authority always stabilizes core inflation—i.e., $\hat{\pi}_{N,t} = 0$—equation (13) implies that headline inflation is given by (minus) changes in the relative price of non-traded goods:

$$\Delta\hat{p}_{N,t} = \hat{p}_{N,t} - \hat{p}_{N,t-1} = \hat{\pi}_{N,t} - \hat{\pi}_t \quad \leftrightarrow \quad \hat{\pi}_t = -\Delta\hat{p}_{N,t}. \tag{28}$$

As a result, first-round effects from international food price shocks will be determined by the impact of these shocks on the relative price of non-traded goods. To motivate and provide some preliminary insights of our analysis, it is helpful to use this expression and the *direct* effect of the commodity price shock on inflation—the effect $a_F\Delta\hat{p}_{F,t}^*$ holding all domestic nominal prices constant, except the nominal price of food, which in policy circles is often (mis)interpreted as the first-round effect—to obtain:

---

[12] Here $\hat{b}_t^*$ indicates deviations of b_t^* from its steady-state value (0) in per cent of steady state consumption.

$$\hat{\pi}_t - a_F\Delta\hat{p}^*_{F,t} = -(\Delta\hat{p}_{N,t} + a_F\Delta\hat{p}^*_{F,t}).$$

From this it is clear that, unless the change in the relative price of non-traded goods $\Delta\hat{p}_{N,t}$ fully offsets the direct effect $a_F\Delta\hat{p}^*_{F,t}$, the first-round effect may not necessarily coincide with this direct effect, in which the share of food on the CPI a_F plays such a crucial role. For instance, if the relative price of non-traded goods falls by less than the direct effect of the shock $(\Delta\hat{p}_{N,t} > -a_F\Delta\hat{p}^*_{F,t})$ then inflation also increases by less than the direct effect.

Of further interest is that, given the assumption of full tradability of the food basket and the choice of the nominal anchor, differences between actual inflation and the direct effect must come from changes in the nominal exchange rate $\Delta\hat{S}_t$. To see this, use equations (9), (10), and $\pi_{N,t} = 1$ to derive:

$$\hat{\pi}_t = (1-a_N)\Delta\hat{S}_t + a_F\Delta\hat{p}^*_{F,t} \leftrightarrow \Delta\hat{S}_t = \frac{1}{1-a_N}(\hat{\pi}_t - a_F\Delta\hat{p}^*_{F,t}) = -\frac{1}{1-a_N}(\Delta\hat{p}_{N,t} + a_F\Delta\hat{p}^*_{F,t}).$$

In the case of $\Delta\hat{p}^*_{F,t} = 0$, any resulting increase in inflation would come from a nominal depreciation.

What determines $\Delta\hat{p}_{N,t}$, and therefore the first-round effects, in our model? The answer depends on the international asset market structure, as we proceed to explain.

3.2 Solving for the First-round Effects

We now provide analytical solutions for the impact of food shocks on inflation, under FA, CM, and IM.

Under **financial autarky (FA)**, there exists a unique rational expectations equilibrium for inflation, which is given by: $\hat{\pi}^{FA}_t = (a_F - \kappa_F)\Delta\hat{p}^*_{F,t}$ and where the first-round effects depend on the net food balance $a_F - \kappa_F$.

Under FA, the impact of international food prices on inflation is given by the net food balance $a_F - \kappa_F$. This result derives from the role of the balance of payment BOP) in the adjustment process. To see why, assume that the increase in food prices initially results in a decline of the relative price of non-traded goods (i.e., initially $\Delta\hat{p}_{N,t} = -a_F\Delta\hat{p}^*_{F,t}$), and consider three cases: zero initial food balance $(a_F = \kappa_F)$, food deficit $(a_F > \kappa_F)$, and food surplus $(a_F < \kappa_F)$. If the country has a zero initial food balance, the higher food bill is exactly offset by the higher value of the food endowment. In this case, the initial drop in $\hat{p}_{N,t}$ would result in an incipient trade surplus, as consumers would switch away from traded goods (in general) and toward non-traded goods. The excess net supply of traded goods would then require a nominal appreciation, undoing the original decrease in $\Delta\hat{p}_{N,t}$ and helping rebalance trade. The BOP would clear only when the nominal appreciation has completely offset the direct effect of the food price increase: $\Delta\hat{S}_t = -\frac{a_F}{(1-a_N)}\Delta\hat{p}^*_{F,t}$, which implies inflation would not change $(\hat{\pi}^{FA}_t = \Delta\hat{p}_{N,t} = 0)$.[13] If the country is a net food importer, then $\hat{p}_{N,t}$

---

[13] In this case, the CPI-based real exchange rate appreciates by the same magnitude as the nominal exchange rate: $\Delta\hat{s}_t = \Delta\hat{S}_t$. Note that while inflation does not change, the increase in international food

must decline—and inflation increase—to help re-establish external balance. However, the required adjustment depends on the initial BOP pressure—again, holding expenditure on traded goods constant at first—which itself depends on the starting net food balance. If the country is a net food exporter, then $\hat{p}_{N,t}$ must increase and inflation must decrease!

Under **complete markets (CM)**, there exists a unique rational expectations equilibrium for inflation, which is given by $\hat{\pi}_t^{CM} = a_F \Delta \hat{p}_{F,t}^*$, and where the first-round effects depend on the share of food in the consumption basket a_F.

The results under CM contrast sharply with those for FA. Under CM, changes in international food prices have an effect on inflation only to the extent they affect the relative price of the domestic basket, and the representative consumer's demand for current consumption. This channel depends on the share of food in the consumption basket a_F, and in this sense it may capture the policy concerns about inflationary pressures in developing economies that typically feature high shares of food.

Since FA and CM can be probably seen as two extreme market structures, we consider next the case of incomplete markets.

Under **incomplete markets (IM)**, there exists a unique rational expectations equilibrium for inflation, which is given by:

$$\hat{\pi}_t^{IM} = [\omega_{p_F^*} a_F + (1 - \omega_{p_F^*})(a_F - \kappa_F)]\Delta \hat{p}_{F,t}^* - (\mathfrak{a} - R^*)\Delta \hat{b}_t^*, \qquad (29)$$

where

$$\mathfrak{a} = \frac{1}{2}\left\{1 + R^* + v(1 - a_N) - \sqrt{[1 + R^* + v(1 - a_N)]^2 - 4R^*}\right\} \in (-1, 1).$$

The first-round effects depend on $\omega_{p_F^*} a_F + (1 - \omega_{p_F^*})(a_F - \kappa_F)$, where

$$\omega_{p_F^*} = \frac{1 - \rho_{p_F^*}}{1 - \rho_{p_F^*} + R^* + v(1 - a_N) - \mathfrak{a}} \in [0, 1).^{14}$$

The IM solution shows that the first-round pass-through parameter $\omega_{p_F^*} a_F + (1 - \omega_{p_F^*})(a_F - \kappa_F)$ is a convex combination of the first-round effects for CM and FA, with the weight $\omega_{p_F^*}$ pushing toward the CM case. Note, however, that although the IM solution nests as a specific case the FA solution, it does not nest the CM solution—i.e., $\omega_{p_F^*} \in [0, 1)$—since one cannot replicate equilibrium allocations of CM under IM. Moreover, the combination of the two solutions reflects two separate channels that are present when markets are incomplete. The first channel captures the inter-temporal substitution effects associated with food shocks. This channel is proportional to the CM solution because it is the only channel present in that specification. The second channel captures the income or

---

prices has real effects, namely on the composition of trade. The real appreciation increases consumption of the generic traded good and a 'generic' trade deficit opens up, and the opposite occurs for food. Overall trade remains balanced, however.

[14] For the derivation of this result see the Appendix in Portillo and Zanna (2015).

wealth effect of the shocks. Similarly, this channel is proportional to the FA solution because it is the only driving channel in that FA specification. And, in contrast to the previous two solutions, when markets are incomplete the country's net foreign asset position affects equilibrium inflation, since $a - R^* \neq 0$.

Summarizing, our analysis reveals that first-round effects are not necessarily related to the share of food in the CPI a_F, except for CM. Of course, if the food endowment was equal to zero ($\kappa_F = 0$), then the first-round effects would be depend on this share even under FA or IM. But in general they will differ, depending on the asset market structure.

4 A SIMPLE NUMERICAL ASSESSMENT

We now quantify the first-round effects of shocks to $\hat{p}_{F,t}^*$ for the different asset market structures using our simple model. Throughout these simulations we keep all parameters of the model constant, with the exception of the food endowment κ_F. We draw on evidence from the universe of developing countries to provide values to some of the parameters. In particular, we pick $a_F = 0.5$, since the average share of food in the CPI in sub-Saharan African countries is 48.5 per cent.[15] In a group of three African countries (Kenya, Ghana, Uganda) the share of non-traded goods and services (housing, health, education, recreation, transportation, and communication) is 33 per cent on average, therefore we choose $a_N = 0.3$.[16] We infer ψ from Goldberg (2016), who estimates a wage elasticity in the day labour market in rural Malawi of $0.15 - 0.17$. We set $\psi = 5$, which implies a Frisch elasticity of 0.2. The choice of 0.99 for the inter-temporal discount rate β is standard in the literature. Moreover, following the empirical estimates by Akitoby and Stratmann (2008), we set $v = 0.1875$. Their estimate provides a lower bound on the value of v in low-income countries, which is likely to be much higher as many of these countries do not even have access to international capital markets (and would therefore be excluded from their sample of countries). Finally, we pick $\rho_{p_F^*}$ using data on an international food price index compiled at the IMF, deflated by the US CPI.[17] We extract the business cycle component using a band pass filter, and find that the sample autocorrelation is 0.87.[18]

The inflationary impact of a 1 per cent increase in $\Delta \hat{p}_F^*$ is represented in Figure 10.1. The figure plots the impact on inflation against the country's net food deficit ($a_F - \kappa_F$). The straight black line represents the inflationary impact under financial autarky ($a_F - \kappa_F$), the dashed-dotted line represents the infla-tionary impact under complete markets a_F, as well as the direct effect, and the straight grey line represents the impact under incomplete markets $\omega_{p_F^*} a_F + (1 - \omega_{p_F^*})(a_F - \kappa_F)$.

[15] See IMF (2011).

[16] On Uganda, see 'Consumer Price Index April 2001', available at www.ubos.org. On Ghana see 'Time Series P1', available at www.statsghana.gov.gh. On Kenya see 'CPI December 2008', available at https://www.knbs.or.ke/download/december-2008/.

[17] The data are available at http://www.imf.org/external/np/res/commod/index.aspx.

[18] See Baxter and King (1999).

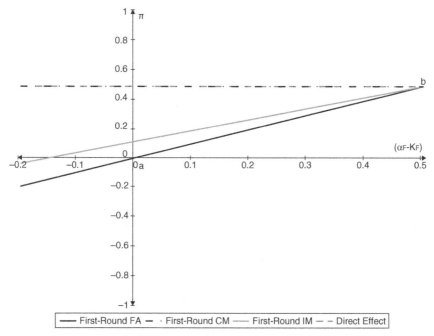

Figure 10.1. First–Round Effects: Financial Autarky (FA), Complete (CM) and Incomplete Markets (IM)

As previously discussed, the inflationary impact under CM does not depend on κ_F and it is equal to the direct effect ($a_F = 0.5$). On the other hand, the impact under FA ranges from -0.2 per cent, when the country's endowment of food is 70 per cent (the highest possible value for κ_F), to 0.5 per cent when $\kappa_F = 0$, i.e., a situation where the country does not produce any food (point b in the figure). The IM solution is closer to the FA solution: under the current parameterization, the weight on the CM case $\omega_{p_F^*}$ is less than one-fourth ($\omega_{p_F^*} = 0.23$). By construction the IM solution matches both FA and CM at point b.

While the FA and IM solutions provide a range of possible first-round effects, we need to discipline the choice of κ_F to provide a quantitative estimate. We therefore draw on trade data from a sample of twenty-eight sub-Saharan countries, for the period 2000–06. The median food balance in this sample was a deficit of 0.9 per cent of GDP, with the highest food deficit being 10.12 per cent and the highest food surplus being 14.12 per cent.[19] In our model this implies a median food endowment $\kappa_F = 0.481$, with a range of (0.389, 0.641). In this case, the median inflationary effect predicted under FA is 0.009 per cent, with a range of

---

[19] Data are available on http://wits.worldbank.org. We define food trade as consisting of the following categories: live animals except fish, meat and preparations, dairy products and eggs, fish/ shellfish, cereals/cereal preparation, vegetables and fruit, sugar/sugar/honey, coffee/tea/cocoa/spices, animal feed, miscellaneous food products, beverages, tobacco/manufactures, oil seeds/oil fruits, crude animal/vegetable matters, animal/vegetable oil/fat/wax.

$(-0.1412, 0.1012)$. Under incomplete markets, the median is 0.12 per cent, with a range of $(0.0060, 0.2067)$.

5 CONCLUSIONS

In this chapter, we develop a tractable small open economy model to study the first-round effects of international food price shocks in developing countries. We show that first-round effects—changes in headline inflation that, holding core inflation constant, help implement relative price adjustments—depend crucially on the asset market structure. Under complete markets (CM), these effects are proportional to the share of food in the CPI; under financial autarky (FA), they are instead proportional to the country's food balance. In developing countries the former are large and the latter are small, which implies large variations in first-round effects across asset market structures. Incomplete markets (IM) yield a combination of these two extremes. Our results cast some doubt on the view that international food price shocks are inherently inflationary in developing countries, as it can be argued that these countries are closer to FA than they are to CM. As we further discuss in Portillo and Zanna (2015), incomplete food tradability does not significantly affect these results.

Our model-based exercise helps provide a clear definition of the concept of first-round effects that is consistent with the New Keynesian literature on monetary policy. Stating such definition is considerably more challenging in the absence of a clear analytical framework. Although the inflationary effect of international food price shocks is ultimately an empirical question, there are limits to what the data can reveal about first-round effects. This is because it is in practice very difficult to empirically disentangle first- and second-round effects and the monetary policy response. In fact, we are not aware of any robust empirical work that has disentangled and estimated these effects.[20] In this regard, our approach might help inform and complement future work based on purely empirical approaches.

REFERENCES

Akitoby, B., and T. Stratmann (2008). Fiscal Policy and Financial Markets. *Economic Journal*, 118(533), 1971–85.

Aoki, K. (2001). Optimal Monetary Policy Responses to Relative-Price Changes. *Journal of Monetary Economics*, 48(1), 55–80.

Backus, D., and G. Smith (1993). Consumption and real exchange rates in dynamic economies with non-traded goods. *Journal of International Economics*, 35(3–4), 297–316.

Baxter, M., and R. King (1999). Measuring Business Cycles: Approximate Band-Pass Filters For Economic Time Series. *The Review of Economics and Statistics*, 81(4), 575–93.

---

[20] There are some papers that, without disentangling these effects, have tried to relate the overall inflationary impact of commodity price shocks to a broad range of structural characteristics and policy frameworks, across countries. See for instance, Gelos and Ustyugova (2012).

Bernanke, B., T. Laubach, F. Mishkin, and A. Posen (1999). *Inflation Targeting: Lessons from the International Experience*, Princeton: Princeton University Press.

Bodenstein, M., C. Erceg, and L. Guerrieri (2008). Optimal Monetary Policy with Distinct Core and Headline Inflation Rates. *Journal of Monetary Economics*, 55, 18–33.

Calvo, G. (1983). Staggered Prices in a Utility-Maximizing Framework. *Journal of Monetary Economics*, 12, 983–98.

Gali, J., and T. Monacelli (2005). Monetary Policy and Exchange Rate Volatility in a Small Open Economy. *Review of Economic Studies*, 72(3), 707–34.

Gelos, G. and Y. Ustyugova (2012). *Inflation Responses to Commodity Price Shocks–How and Why Do Countries Differ?* IMF Working Paper 12/225.

Goldberg, J. (2016). 'Kwacha Gonna Do? Experimental Evidence about Labor Supply in Rural Malawi'. *American Economic Journal: Applied Economics*, 1, 129–49.

Gordon, R. (1975). Alternative Responses of Policy to External Supply Shocks. *Brookings Papers on Economic Activity*, 1975(1), 183–206.

International Monetary Fund (2011). *Managing Global Growth Risks and Commodity Price Shocks—Vulnerabilities and Policy Challenges for Low-Income Countries*. IMF Policy Paper 092111.

Ogaki, M., J., Ostry, and C., Reinhart (1996). *Saving Behavior in Low- and Middle-Income Countries*. IMF Staff Papers, 43(1), 38–71.

Portillo, R., and L.-F. Zanna (2015). *On the First-Round Effects of International Food Price Shocks: The Role of the Asset Market Structure*. IMF Working Paper 15/33.

Schmitt-Grohé, S., and M. Uribe (2003). Closing Small Open Economy Models. *Journal of International Economics*, 61, 163–85.

Woodford, M. (2003). *Interest and Prices: Foundations of a Theory of Monetary Policy*, Princeton: Princeton University Press.

Woodford, M. (2011). Simple Analytics of the Government Expenditure Multiplier. *American Economic Journal: Macroeconomics*, 3, 1–35.

11

Implications of Food Subsistence for Monetary Policy and Inflation

Rafael Portillo, Luis-Felipe Zanna, Stephen O'Connell,
and Richard Peck

1 INTRODUCTION

Central banks in low-income countries (LICs) have been adopting elements of inflation targeting since the mid-1990s, including an elevated focus on price stability and a commitment to transparency in the conduct of policy (Chapter 1).[1] In concert with a move to market-determined exchange rates and interest rates, these developments have narrowed the gap between the monetary policy frameworks in use among LICs and those employed by emerging-market and high-income economies.

This convergence at the level of policy frameworks coexists with sharp differences in the structure of the economy by income level. In this chapter we focus on the disproportionate size of the food-producing sector in many low-income countries. We trace this phenomenon to subsistence requirements in food consumption, a time-honoured source of what Chenery and Syrquin (1975) called the *structural transformation*. As we document, a large agricultural sector can help account for some striking differences between business cycle patterns in LICs and in richer countries, including the greater volatility of inflation and the real economy in LICs, the larger share of relative food prices in inflation volatility, and the negative business-cycle correlation in LICs between inflation and economy-wide output. The question we then address is: what are the implications of a large food sector for the conduct of monetary policy?

In this chapter, we summarize the results of Portillo et al. (2016), who use a two-sector version of the New Keynesian model to study monetary policy at different stages of development. The subsistence requirement in food gives rise to Engel's Law, which drives a demand-side version of the structural transformation as long as food is imperfectly tradable (we assume a closed economy).

---

[1] This chapter summarizes our existing research. Figure 11.2 is new, but the model, simulations, and analytical propositions are drawn from Portillo et al. (2016), the material of which is reprinted here with permission from Oxford Economic Papers. See that paper and its online appendix for more detail.

Consumer budgets and sectoral employment levels shift away from the food sector as aggregate productivity rises, and the non-food sector—comprised of manufacturing and services—correspondingly expands. Key demand parameters also change as development proceeds, because proximity to subsistence reduces the income and price elasticities of demand in the food sector (while increasing them in the non-food sector), reduces the inter-temporal elasticity of substitution, and diminishes the effects of changes in food prices on household consumption. These features amplify the impact of food-sector productivity shocks on the relative price of food and therefore on inflation, at earlier stages of development. But the structural transformation also alters the relative importance of sticky prices, a core preoccupation of monetary policy. Consistent with item-level evidence on price flexibility, we model the food sector as a flex-price sector and the non-food sector as subject to sticky prices. A key corollary to the structural transformation is then an increase in the prevalence of sticky prices in the economy.

The New Keynesian literature suggests that if sticky prices are the only distortion in the economy, monetary policy should focus on keeping these prices stable. In a two-sector setting without subsistence, this means that the central bank should target non-food inflation rather than overall (headline) inflation, as shown by Aoki (2001). We show that this result continues to hold in the presence of a subsistence requirement in food. We also show, however, that despite the increased prevalence of sticky prices as income rises, the welfare stakes in choosing the appropriate inflation target are higher in poor countries than in rich countries. A policy of targeting headline inflation, in particular, leads to greater welfare losses in countries at lower levels of development.

These results follow from the impact of the subsistence requirement on the structure of the economy and (therefore) on the objective function of the monetary authority. In the presence of supply shocks, a policy of stabilizing headline inflation requires larger adjustments in non-food inflation and non-food production in poor countries. Output volatility increases considerably as a result, which is welfare-reducing. This effect is not solely due to the larger share of food in poor economies; it also depends on the limited economy-wide substitutability that prevails in the presence of subsistence. The central bank's welfare-based loss function, in turn, places weight on the variances of non-food inflation, the aggregate output gap, and the gap of the relative price of food. Yet as we show, a policy that stabilizes only the first of these components succeeds in perfectly stabilizing the other two—thereby keeping both aggregate output and the relative price of food around their efficient levels, as in the Aoki (2001) model without subsistence.

A modified version of the 'divine coincidence' of Blanchard and Gali (2007) therefore holds in our model with subsistence: stabilizing the appropriate concept of inflation is sufficient to stabilize the real economy. At face value this result seems at odds with Anand, Prasad, and Zhang (APZ, 2015), who find that headline inflation performs better than core inflation within a class of Taylor-type interest-rate rules applied to similar low-income economies. The resolution of this puzzle turns on the distinction between instrument rules, which govern the settings of variables the central bank directly controls like the short-term interest rate, and targeting rules, which govern (through unspecified means) one or more of the economic outcomes the central bank may care about (Svensson, 2003). This distinction proves crucial because our analysis of targeting rules reveals that a version of the divine coincidence is very close to holding under the conditions studied by APZ. The APZ model incorporates not only subsistence but also limited asset-market participation and segmented labour markets, two distortions that in combination invalidate the strict Aoki result, as we show using a version of their model.[2] But the optimal weight on food inflation in the APZ model—within the class of targeting rules that fully stabilize some measure of inflation—remains close to zero for a low-income country, and therefore far below its weight in the CPI. Core inflation is therefore close to being the single appropriate objective of monetary policy, even when these additional distortions are present. A headline-targeting instrument rule *can* outperform a core-targeting instrument rule in this setting, but only when conditions are such that a moderately aggressive response to headline inflation ends stabilizing core inflation more successfully than the same moderately aggressive response to core inflation. We discuss the intuition behind this result and argue against drawing definitive conclusions on policy objectives from the analysis of simple instrument rules.

2 RELATED LITERATURE

Engel's Law is sufficient to drive the structural transformation in our model. To keep the analysis simple, we eliminate alternative drivers, including sectoral differences in factor intensity. We also follow the bulk of the structural transformation literature in assuming a closed economy (Herrendorf et al., 2014), an assumption that is not as restrictive as it first appears. Evidence from Gilbert (2011), for example, suggests that domestic grain markets in LICs (particularly for rice) are not strongly integrated with world markets. FAO et al. (2011) attribute this to a combination of restrictive trade policies and high transport and transaction costs. Gollin and Rogerson (2010, 2014) document the high costs of overland trade in Africa and argue that these costs can explain why the vast majority of the food consumed in many African countries does not enter international trade. If food is non-traded, then of course domestic demand plays a major role in determining its relative price regardless of whether or not non-food is traded. Our treatment of differential price flexibility in the food and non-food sectors draws on a recent micro-empirical literature (cited below).

---

[2] While limited financial participation is a prominent feature of LIC economies, the assumption of segmented labour markets—implying complete labour immobility at business-cycle frequencies—is at odds with the informal and fluid nature of LIC labour markets (Fox, 2015) and with our reading of the evidence on structural transformation in LICs (Gollin et al., 2013 and IMF, 2012). We therefore allow for full labour mobility for the bulk of our analysis.

3 STYLIZED FACTS ABOUT DEVELOPED AND DEVELOPING COUNTRIES

Figure 11.1 documents a set of key characteristics of developed and developing countries. The data cover part or all of the period 1995–2011 and comprise twenty-eight OECD countries, twenty-three sub-Saharan African countries, and fifteen non-OECD countries (the latter mostly emerging market countries).[3]

3.1 The Share of Food in the Consumer Price Index Falls as Income Rises

The upper-left panel in Figure 11.1 plots the weight of food in the consumer price index against average income per capita in PPP dollars over the period 2001–10.[4] Income per capita for the US has been normalized to one. The relationship appears to be convex: the food share increases by more as income per capita decreases. This is captured by the good least-squares fit of the food shares to the log of GDP (the grey dashed line). We also show the relation between income per capita and the share of food implied by the model (the black dashed line), which we derive below.

3.2 Food Prices are More Flexible than Non-Food Prices

In Table A.1 of the online appendix to Portillo et al. (2016), we summarize a substantial micro-empirical literature that follows the Bils and Klenow (2004) approach of tracking item-level changes in the prices used to compute the monthly consumer price index. For each country we report the average frequency of price changes for food products, raw food products (where reported), and all products. These data show that food prices change more frequently than average, and that unprocessed food prices change with markedly higher frequency than overall food prices. The difference in flexibility between food prices and overall prices is most pronounced in LICs, probably because a greater share of the food category is unprocessed in these countries. Our assumptions about price flexibility are therefore highly appropriate for LICs.[5]

3.3 Inflation Volatility Falls as Income Rises

The upper-right panel in Figure 11.1 shows the standard deviation of headline inflation (quarter-on-quarter) against income per capita. The focus here is on

---

[3] The data for some countries, especially LICs, start in 2000.

[4] GDP data are from the World Bank. Price indices are from the IMF. Food weights in the CPI come from several sources: OECD Stat Extracts for OECD countries and Haver Analytics for non-OECD non-African countries. Food weights for African countries come from central bank websites, a list of which is available upon request.

[5] However, our model will understate the change in relative price stickiness as structural transformation occurs, because we do not model the shift towards more highly processed foods as income rises.

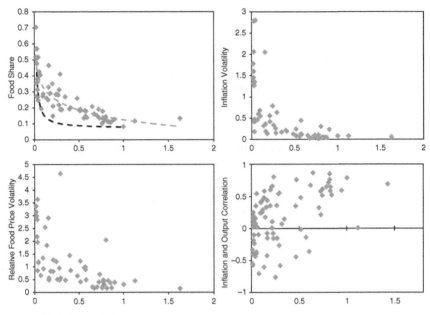

Figure 11.1. Stylized Facts

business-cycle frequency, so we use a band-pass filter that retains frequencies between six and thirty-two quarters.[6] There is a decidedly negative relationship with real GDP per capita: countries with lower income per capita have inflation rates that are considerably more volatile. The bottom-left panel shows that there is also a negative relationship between the volatility of changes in the relative price of food (in relation to the CPI) and income per capita.

3.4 The Correlation Between Headline Inflation and Output Increases with Income

The bottom-right panel in Figure 11.1 plots the correlation between headline inflation and output against income per capita at a business-cycle frequency. It reveals that there is a positive relationship between this variable and income per capita, starting from a negative value representing most of the LICs.

We now present a model consistent with these features.[7]

---

[6] Lower-frequency movements in inflation are usually interpreted as changes in the explicit or implicit inflation target of the country, the choice of which is beyond the scope of this chapter. We also drop higher-frequency movements in order to remove any noise or leftover seasonality.

[7] For a complete presentation of the model, see Portillo et al. (2016) and the accompanying online appendix.

4 THE MODEL

4.1 Consumers and Producers

The representative consumer chooses a consumption aggregate c_t^*, labour effort n_t and holdings of a nominal bond to maximize lifetime utility, which is given by:

$$E_0 \sum_{t=0}^{\infty} \beta^t \left[\ln(c_t^*) - \frac{(n_t)^{1+\psi}}{1+\psi} \right].$$

The composition of c_t^* is:

$$c_t^* = Z(c_{F,t} - \bar{c}_F)^{\alpha_F} c_{N,t}^{1-\alpha_F}. \tag{1}$$

The pair $(c_{F,t},\ c_{N,t})$ denotes consumption of food and non-food, with the parameter $\bar{c}_F$ indicating the subsistence level of food consumption, a threshold below which food consumption cannot decline. Z is a scaling parameter that takes the value $(\alpha_F)^{-\alpha_F}(1-\alpha_F)^{-(1-\alpha_F)}$ to simplify notation. In Figure 11.2, the Cobb-Douglas consumption aggregator generates indifference curves for food and non-food consumption that are homothetic starting from the displaced origin point $(\bar{c}_F, 0)$.

The food sector features perfect competition and flexible prices. Food production is given by:

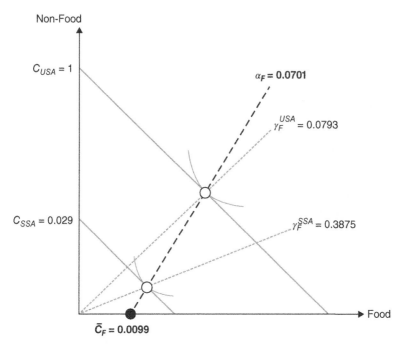

Figure 11.2. Calibration

$$y_{F,t} = A_{F,t}(An_{F,t})^{\alpha}K_F^{1-\alpha}, \tag{2}$$

where K_F is the equilibrium level of capital in the sector given an economy-wide level of labour augmenting productivity A, $n_{F,t}$ is the demand for labour in the food sector, α is the labour share, and $A_{F,t}$ is a productivity shock in agriculture. Our short-run analysis takes place around long-run equilibria (steady states) that correspond to different values for A.

The non-food sector is composed of a continuum of monopolistic competitors, each providing a variety $y_{N,t}(i)$, with $i \in [0, 1]$. Varieties are combined by consumers into a Dixit-Stiglitz aggregate, $y_{N,t}$, giving rise to the sectoral price index

$$P_{N,t} = [\int P_{N,t}(i)^{1-\epsilon}di]^{\frac{1}{1-\epsilon}} \tag{3}$$

where ϵ is the elasticity of substitution between varieties. Production of non-food varieties is given by:

$$y_{N,t}(i) = [An_{N,t}(i)]^{\alpha} K_N^{1-\alpha}, \tag{4}$$

where K_N, again is the equilibrium level of capital corresponding to aggregate productivity A. We assume Calvo (1983) pricing in the non-food sector. Each period's aggregate price index for non-food items is therefore a weighted average of the previous period's prices, for firms unable to make any price adjustment, and the forward-looking price that maximizes the discounted stream of expected profits, for the fraction $(1 - \theta)$ of firms that are randomly given the opportunity to reset their prices.

Along with market-clearing conditions for food, non-food, and labour markets,[8] the model requires a description of the stochastic environment. Food-sector productivity shocks are crucial to our analysis, and we specify these using an autoregressive process of order 2:

$$\hat{A}_{F,t} = (1 + \rho_A)\hat{A}_{F,t-1} - (\rho_A + \varrho)\hat{A}_{F,t-2} + \epsilon_{A_F,t},$$

where a hat on top of a variable $(\hat{*})$ denotes a per cent deviation from steady state. This process differs from a persistent AR(1) in allowing food-productivity shocks to have a persistent effect on food inflation. To parameterize the AR(2), we rely on the observed behaviour of both international relative food prices and relative food prices in a sample of low-income countries in sub-Saharan Africa. Estimates of the persistence of relative food prices are reported in Table 11.1. These variables are well characterized by AR(2) processes with values of ρ_A between 0.5 and 1 and positive but small values of ϱ.

The model also features shocks to nominal aggregate demand, which we discuss below.

---

[8] For simplicity we assume the depreciation rate is zero, which implies there is no investment to keep track of in the model (including in the market clearing conditions).

Table 11.1. Relative Price of Food: Estimated AR(2)

Dependent Variable:	(1)	(2)
ln(Relative Price of Food)	Coef.	Std. Error
1st lag	1.631	(0.012)***
2nd lag	−0.736	(0.012)***
Constant	−0.001	(0.000)***

Notes: $R^2 = 0.975$. Estimates are based on quarterly data from 23 sub-Saharan African countries (1,319 time-country observations). The time series are the natural logarithm of the ratio of food prices to non-food prices, filtered with a band-pass filter to retain frequencies between six and thirty-two quarters. ***p<0.01, **p<0.05, *p<0.1

4.2 THE STRUCTURAL TRANSFORMATION

The structural transformation emerges across steady states that correspond to different values for economy-wide productivity, A. With mobile labour and capital and identical factor proportions in the two sectors, the steady-state relative price of food is 1 and the values of capital equate the marginal products of capital in each sector with the steady-state rental rate $1/\beta - 1$.

The presence of a subsistence threshold for food consumption $\bar{c}_F$ makes the relationship between aggregate consumption (output) and economy-wide productivity non-linear, with an elasticity that is below one but approaches one as labour productivity increases. When consumption is close to subsistence, income effects dominate substitution effects in the supply of labour and agents work more in order to satisfy their subsistence needs. As productivity and income increase, agents reduce their labour supply and enjoy more leisure at the cost of a smaller increase in total consumption.

We use γ_F to denote the share of expenditure and labour that is allocated to the food sector in a steady state. This key parameter is a function of the level of aggregate productivity, through the influence of the latter on aggregate consumption. When $\bar{c}_F > 0$, γ_F converges to a_F from above as steady-state consumption increases. Four new parameters depend on the value of γ_F and will play a role in the log-linearized version of the model:

$$\xi = \frac{\gamma_F}{1 - \gamma_F} \geq \frac{a_F}{1 - a_F}, \quad \phi = \xi(1 - a_F) - a_F \geq 0,$$

$$\delta = \frac{a_F}{\gamma_F} \leq 1, \text{ and } \sigma = \frac{1 - a_F}{1 - \gamma_F} \geq 1.$$

In the presence of subsistence, as steady-state consumption increases, ξ converges toward $a_F/(1 - a_F)$ from above, ϕ converges toward zero from above, and δ and σ converge toward one, the former from below and the latter from above.

4.3 LOG-LINEARIZATION

We focus here on how food subsistence modifies the standard three-equation New Keynesian model that emerges after log-linearization. The existence of a subsistence threshold is captured by $\gamma_F > a_F$ and the values of the related parameters (ξ, ϕ, δ, and σ), all of which are specific to the economy's level of aggregate productivity.

The forward-looking IS equation takes the form

$$\hat{y}_t = -\sigma^{-1} E_t(\hat{R}_t - \hat{\pi}_{t+1} + \phi \Delta \hat{p}_{F,t+1}) + E_t \hat{y}_{t+1}. \tag{5}$$

Subsistence introduces two modifications into this equation. First, the inter-temporal elasticity of substitution for output is given by σ^{-1}, which is less than one—the value that would be obtained if $\bar{c} = 0$—when $\gamma_F > a_F$ ($\bar{c}_F > 0$). This modification is related to the difference between the consumption aggregate that matters for private sector decisions (c_t^*) and measured consumption (c_t), with the former always smaller than the latter. The second difference concerns the presence of the expected change in relative food prices ($\Delta \hat{p}_{F,t+1}^*$). When $\gamma_F > a_F$, the inflation rate that matters for private sector decisions ($\hat{\pi}_t$) differs from the measured headline inflation rate ($\hat{\pi}_t$) by the quantity $\phi \Delta \hat{p}_{F,t}$. As the economy develops, this term disappears and changes in the expected relative price of food no longer exert a direct effect on inter-temporal decisions.

Second, inflation in the non-food sector is determined by the New Keynesian Phillips curve

$$\hat{\pi}_{N,t} = \beta E_t \hat{\pi}_{N,t+1} - \kappa \hat{\mu}_{N,t}, \tag{6}$$

where $\hat{\mu}_{N,t}$ denotes changes in markups in the non-food sector, and κ is defined as:

$$\kappa = \frac{(1 - \theta\beta)(1 - \theta)a}{\theta a + \epsilon(1 - a)}.$$

Overall inflation is given by:

$$\hat{\pi}_t = \hat{\pi}_{N,t} + \xi \Delta \hat{p}_{F,t}, \tag{7}$$

and the definition of aggregate GDP and the relation between aggregate employment and output can be expressed as:

$$\hat{y}_t = \gamma_F \hat{y}_{F,t} + (1 - \gamma_F)\hat{y}_{N,t} = a\hat{n}_t + \gamma_F \hat{A}_{F,t}. \tag{8}$$

For purposes of welfare-based analysis it is helpful to distinguish between movements in output that would hold if prices were flexible—the potential output component—and movements in output due to the presence of nominal rigidities—the output gap component $\tilde{y}_t$. The latter is directly related to inflationary pressures in the sticky-price sector:[9]

$$\hat{y}_t = \hat{y}_t^{flex} + \tilde{y}_t. \tag{9}$$

Written as a function of the aggregate output gap and the inflation rate of non-food prices, the IS curve and New Keynesian Phillips curve in this two-sector setting take the form

---

[9] For a thorough discussion of the flexible-price equilibrium and the gap representation of the model, see the online appendix to Portillo et al. (2016).

$$\tilde{y}_t = -\Theta E_t(\hat{R}_t - \hat{\pi}_{N,t+1} - \hat{r}_t^{flex}) + E_t\tilde{y}_{t+1}, \tag{10}$$

$$\hat{\pi}_{N,t} = \beta E_t\hat{\pi}_{N,t+1} + \kappa_y\tilde{y}_t, \tag{11}$$

where the coefficients Θ and κ_y are functions of the model parameters and where $(\sim)$ denotes a percentage difference relative to the short-run equilibrium under flexible prices.

Finally, we must define a monetary policy rule. For model simulations designed to generate business-cycle patterns at alternative levels of development, we describe monetary policy as the following rule:

$$\hat{R}_t = (\hat{r}_t^{flex} + \xi E_t\Delta\hat{p}_{F,t+1}^{flex}) + s\hat{\pi}_{N,t} + u_{MP,t}, \tag{12}$$

where

$$u_{MP,t} = \rho_{MP}u_{MP,t-1} + \epsilon_{MP,t}.$$

Here, $\hat{r}_t^{flex}$ is the natural rate of interest, the interest rate that would hold under flexible prices, and $\hat{p}_{F,t}^{flex}$ is what the relative price of food would be if non-food prices were flexible. When $u_{MP,t} = 0$, this rule ensures that core inflation is perfectly stabilized. Instead, a negative shock to $\epsilon_{MP,t}$ will generate a monetary policy loosening, which can be thought of as an expansionary shock to aggregate demand, and affects core (and headline) inflation. This policy specification therefore generates a simple dichotomy between supply and demand shocks.

For the welfare analysis, we will focus on targeting rules rather than instrument rules because our interest is in understanding the optimal target of monetary policy. In particular, we consider the welfare implications of policies that succeed in stabilizing a weighted sum of food and non-food inflation. These take the form

$$\hat{\pi}_t^\omega = \omega\hat{\pi}_{F,t} + (1-\omega)\hat{\pi}_{N,t} = 0, \text{with } \omega \in [0,1], \tag{13}$$

which embeds the specific cases of non-food-inflation targeting ($\omega = 0$), food-inflation targeting ($\omega = 1$), and (iii) headline-inflation targeting ($\omega = \gamma_F$).

4.4 CALIBRATION

The calibration is presented in Table 11.2. Most of our parameter choices are standard in the new-Keynesian literature; for details see Portillo et al. (2016). Figure 11.2 shows how we calibrate the structural transformation, the trajectory of which depends on the food-subsistence floor $\bar{c}_F$ and the marginal budget share devoted to food, a_F. Our aim is to encompass the disparate situations of high- and low-income economies—say, the US economy and the economy of a typical country in sub-Saharan Africa. In our model, the sole difference between high- and low-income economies is the level of aggregate productivity, which drives not only the level of aggregate consumption but also its distribution between food and non-food. Setting aggregate consumption per capita in the USA to 1, the median average consumption level in the set of sixteen low-income countries in

Table 11.2. Calibration

Parameter	Definition	Value
$\bar{c}_F$	Subsistence level of food consumption	0.0099
α_F	Non-subsistence food consumption share	0.0701
α	Labour income share	0.7
β	Discount factor	0.99
θ	Probability of not being able to reset price	0.75
s	Response coefficient to non-food inflation in the rule	1.5
ψ	Inverse of Frisch elasticity of labour supply	5
ϵ	Elasticity of substitution between different varieties	6
ρ_A	Parameter in the AR(2) process for food productivity shocks	0.631
ϱ	Parameter in the AR(2) process for food productivity shocks	0.105
σ_{A_f}	Standard deviation of food productivity shocks	0.6
ρ_{MP}	Persistence in the AR(1) process for monetary policy shocks	0.8
σ_{MP}	Standard deviation of monetary policy shocks	0.6

sub-Saharan Africa for which we have data is 0.029. In Figure 11.2, these numbers tie down the positions of the linear transformation curves for consumption in each location. To locate actual consumption we use the observed values of γ_F—the budget shares devoted to food in the USA and the median low-income African country—to pin down the slopes of the rays through the origin in Figure 11.2. A straight line drawn through the two intersection points between food shares and transformation curves then jointly determines both the marginal budget share devoted to food and the value of the subsistence floor.

The upper-left panel of Figure 11.1 shows the cross-country relationship between food share and income generated by our calibration. The model does a reasonably good job of replicating the relationship in the data, though it tends to under-predict the food share for middle-income countries.

4.5 IMPULSE RESPONSE ANALYSIS

4.5.1 An Exogenous Monetary Policy Loosening ($\epsilon_{MP,t} < 0$)

Figure 11.3 shows the effect of an exogenous monetary policy loosening, captured by a negative shock to $\epsilon_{MP,t}$. Food prices are flexible and therefore rise by more than non-food prices. The relative price of food rises by roughly 11 per cent more in the poor country, however, while the increase in non-food inflation is slightly smaller. Given the large size of its food sector, headline inflation increases by more than twice as much in the poor country. Overall output expands in both countries due to the presence of sticky non-food prices, and the food sector shrinks in response to demand-side substitution generated by the increased relative price of food. Sectoral impacts differ by income, with the non-food sector expanding by more and the food sector contracting by less in the low-income country.[10]

---

[10] Output in the food sector declines because it is priced out of the labour market as non-food output expands. This lack of sectoral comovement is typical of multisector New Keynesian models.

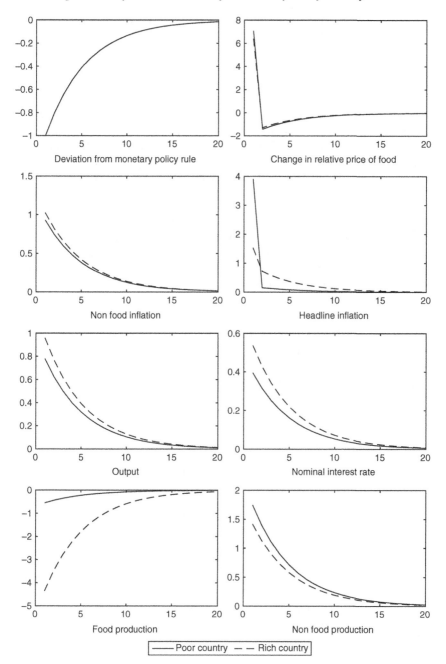

Figure 11.3. A Monetary Policy Shock, $\epsilon_{MP} < 0$

The overall expansion is larger in the rich country, however, because its sticky-price (non-food) sector is larger.

4.5.2 A Negative Shock to Food Production ($\epsilon_{A_F,t} < 0$)

Figure 11.4 shows the impact of a 1 per cent decline in productivity in the food sector $\epsilon_{A_F,t}$ Note that the productivity decline initially amplifies before correcting itself during the second year. Given the reduced substitutability in the economy—because of subsistence—the relative price of food increases by more in the poor country. For the same reason food production contracts by less in the poor country, at the cost of a larger contraction in the non-food sector. The specification of the monetary policy rule prevents non-food inflation from increasing in either location. But headline inflation increases by more in the poor country, reflecting its large food share. Note that inflation goes from positive to negative after one year, as the recovery in productivity during the second year creates deflationary pressure. Again, these effects are more pronounced in the poor country given the larger share of food in the consumer price index.

4.5.3 A Negative Shock to Food Production ($\epsilon_{A_F,t} < 0$) under Headline Inflation Targeting

If monetary policy targets headline inflation ($\hat{\pi}_t = 0$, Figure A.1 in the online appendix to Portillo et al., 2016), then the increase in the relative price of food described above must be compensated by a decrease in non-food inflation. In the presence of sticky prices, this can only come about through a demand-driven contraction in non-food production that exacerbates the contraction in overall output.

This effect is barely noticeable in a high-income country because the food sector is so small. Only a very small decrease in non-food inflation is needed, implying a tiny contraction of non-food output. The poor country, by contrast, requires a large decline in non-food prices to control headline inflation in the face of a food supply shock—which in turn means a sharp recession in the non-food sector. The effect on aggregate output is therefore larger.

The choice of inflation target is therefore more important for output in the poor country than in the rich country, even though price stickiness is more relevant in the latter case because it affects a larger share of goods. In Section 6 we show analytically that the welfare losses associated with targeting headline inflation are inversely related to development level.

4.6 SECOND-ORDER MOMENTS

In Portillo et al. (2016), we simulate the model and compare the model-generated second-order moments to those observed for the US and the median observation

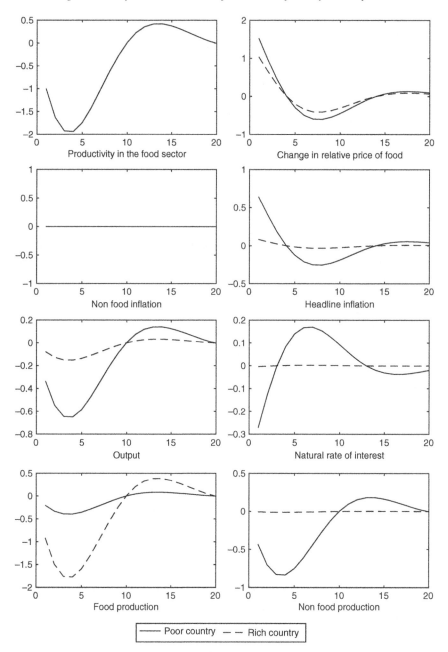

Figure 11.4. A Shock to Food Sector Productivity, $\epsilon_{A_F} < 0$

in our group of African countries. Our model replicates several stylized facts of inflation across levels of development. The relative price of food accounts for about 50 per cent of the volatility of inflation in LICs (79 per cent in the model), compared with 3 per cent in the US (16 per cent in the model). The model broadly

generates the right comovement between inflation and output: as shown in
Figure 11.1, LICs tend to have negative (or zero) inflation/output correlations,
while the correlation becomes increasingly positive at higher levels of development. The model generates inflation volatility in LICs that is about 160 per cent
higher than the volatility in the US economy, short of the roughly 300 per cent
difference observed in the data. We note, however, that the model, under-predicts
the volatility of changes in the relative price of food in LICs and over-predicts this
volatility in the US.

5 WELFARE ANALYSIS

5.1 Optimal Monetary Policy Under Subsistence

Despite the presence of food subsistence, optimal monetary policy requires complete
stabilization of sticky-price non-food inflation. Doing so is sufficient to stabilize both
aggregate output and the relative price of food around their efficient levels. To obtain
these analytical results, we derive a loss function in Portillo et al. (2016), using a
second-order approximation to the utility losses faced by the representative agent
due to deviations from the efficient equilibrium. The following proposition makes
this loss function explicit.

Proposition 1 Consider the model with food subsistence, described above, and
assume that $\alpha = 1$. The average welfare loss per period is given by the following
linear function:

$$\mathbb{L} = \frac{1}{2}\sigma\left[(1-\gamma_F)\frac{\epsilon}{\kappa}var(\hat{\pi}_{N,t}) + (\psi+\sigma)var(\tilde{y}_t) + \frac{\alpha_F}{1-\gamma_F}var(\tilde{p}_{F,t})\right], \quad (14)$$

where $\sigma = \frac{1-\alpha_F}{1-\gamma_F}$ and $\kappa = \frac{(1-\theta\beta)(1-\theta)}{\theta}$.

Thus the welfare loss can be expressed as the weighted sum of the variances of the
sticky-price non-food inflation ($\hat{\pi}_{N,t}$), the aggregate output gap ($\tilde{y}_t$), and the gap
of the relative price of food ($\tilde{p}_{F,t}$). Note that the weights are functions not only of
the preference parameters ($\alpha_F,\psi,\epsilon,\beta$) and the degree of price stickiness (θ), but also
of the share of expenditures allocated to food (γ_F) and the related parameter σ.
The latter parameters reflect subsistence and play an important role in determining the *relative* weights that the central bank gives to the variances of the aggregate
output gap and the gap of the relative price of food, relative to sticky-price non-
food inflation.

Online appendix Figure A.2 plots these relative weights for the loss function
(14)—i.e., $\frac{(\psi+\sigma)\kappa}{(1-\gamma_F)\epsilon}$ and $\frac{\alpha_F\kappa}{(1-\gamma_F)^2\epsilon}$—and shows that both relative weights are increasing in the degree of subsistence. The slope of the relative weight on the output gap is
much steeper than that on the relative price of food. In particular, holding everything
else constant, a poor country ($\gamma_F = 0.42$) should assign almost twice the weight a rich
country should to the objective of stabilizing the output gap ($\gamma_F = 0.08$).

Although stabilizing aggregate output and the relative price of food around
their efficient levels are appropriate goals for monetary policy, optimal policy is

still characterized as a strict inflation-targeting regime. More specifically, despite food subsistence, optimal monetary policy corresponds to the complete stabilization of a core inflation measure, as in Aoki (2001). The appropriate core measure in our model is sticky-price non-food inflation. The following corollary formalizes this result.

Corollary 1 The welfare loss (14) can be rewritten as

$$
\mathbb{L} = \frac{1}{2}\sigma \left\{ (1 - \gamma_F)\frac{\epsilon}{\kappa} var(\hat{\pi}_{N,t}) + \frac{1}{\kappa\kappa_y} \left[(\psi + \sigma) + \frac{\alpha_F}{1 - \gamma_F}\left(\frac{\psi + \sigma}{\sigma}\right)^2 \right] var(\hat{\pi}_{N,t} - \beta E_t \hat{\pi}_{N,t+1}) \right\},
$$
(15)

and therefore optimal monetary policy corresponds to strict targeting of sticky-price non-food inflation, as implemented by setting $\hat{\pi}_{N,t} = 0$ for every t.

Corollary 1 implies that *strict* targeting of sticky-price non-food inflation maximizes social welfare. This approach completely stabilizes aggregate output and the relative price of food around their efficient levels. The 'divine coincidence' of Blanchard and Gali (2007) therefore holds in our model: stabilizing (the appropriate concept of) inflation is equivalent to stabilizing the welfare-relevant output gap.

While food subsistence does not overturn the optimal policy result of strictly targeting core (sticky-price) inflation, it does raise the stakes for monetary stabilization policy. In particular, targeting headline inflation instead of core inflation is more costly in terms of welfare losses for countries that are closer to the subsistence threshold. Table 11.3 calculates the welfare losses for poor and rich countries of targeting headline versus core inflation, when the economies experience a negative shock to productivity in the food sector.[11] The table also shows the standard deviations of sticky-price non-food inflation ($\hat{\pi}_{N,t}$), the aggregate output gap ($\tilde{y}_t$), and the gap of the relative price of food ($\tilde{p}_{F,t}$) associated with these policies.

Table 11.3. Welfare Losses from Alternative Targeting Rules, Rich and Poor Countries

	Targeting Rules			
	Poor Country[a]		Rich Country[a]	
	Headline Inflation[b]	Non-Food Inflation[c]	Headline Inflation[b]	Non-Food Inflation[c]
$\sqrt{var(\hat{\pi}_{N,t})}$	0.374	0	0.079	0
$\sqrt{var(\tilde{y}_t)}$	0.103	0	0.028	0
$\sqrt{var(\tilde{p}_{F,t})}$	0.425	0	0.167	0
Welfare Loss	4.630	0	0.206	0

[a] For a poor country $\gamma_F = 0.42$, while for a rich country $\gamma_F = 0.08$.
[b] Headline inflation targeting: $\gamma_F \hat{\pi}_{F,t} + (1 - \gamma_F)\hat{\pi}_{N,t} = 0$.
[c] Core (non-food) inflation targeting: $\hat{\pi}_{N,t} = 0$.

---

[11] Similar results in terms of the ranking of policies can be found for Taylor rules that respond to non-food inflation versus Taylor rules that respond to headline inflation.

When both countries implement the optimal policy of targeting core inflation, standard deviations and welfare losses are equal to zero. Adopting headline inflation targeting increases the volatility of these economies and reduces welfare; and the welfare loss for the poor country is much greater than that of the rich country.[12] In a poor country that faces a negative productivity shock in the food sector (which increases the relative price of food), keeping broad measures of inflation stable implies engineering large decreases in non-food inflation. These decreases are bigger in poor countries than in rich countries, given the larger weight of food in the poor economy. And, because of sticky prices in the non-food sector, these drops are also accompanied by bigger contractions in non-food output and overall output in a poor country.

5.2 Subsistence is More Than a Higher Food Share

It is tempting to conclude that the importance of subsistence stems simply from generating a higher food share at lower levels of development. An argument could then be made that all that is necessary to analyse developing countries is the standard model without subsistence but with higher food share, i.e., $a_F = \gamma_F \approx large$. To show that this is not the case we compare the welfare costs of targeting various measures of inflation (according to equation (13)) in a poor economy with food subsistence ($a_F = 0.07$, $\gamma_F = 0.42$) to those costs in the same economy without subsistence ($a_F = \gamma_F = 0.42$).

Figure 11.5 shows the standard deviation of the output gap and the welfare loss as ω, which is the weight on food inflation in the measure of inflation that is targeted by the central bank, goes from zero (no weight on food inflation) to one (only food inflation is stabilized), for the two economies mentioned above.[13] For any positive weight on food inflation ($\omega > 0$), both the volatility of aggregate output and the welfare losses are bigger for the poor country with subsistence, and are increasing in that weight. The volatilities of non-food inflation and the gap of the relative price of food (not shown) are broadly similar, so most of the variations in welfare stem from the impact on output. But what accounts for the higher output volatility and higher welfare costs?

A poor economy with subsistence is an economy in which reallocation away from agriculture is hampered by the need to maintain a certain level of food consumption. The limited economy-wide factor reallocation implies that supply-side shocks have bigger aggregate effects. The corollary is that equilibrium relative food prices will be more volatile under subsistence. In this context, targeting the wrong price level is particularly costly because the associated real adjustment (shown in Figure A.2 in the online appendix to Portillo et al., 2016) increases with the level of relative food price volatility.

In addition to generating a more volatile output gap if policy is suboptimal, the economy with subsistence assigns a larger weight to output volatility in its loss function.

---

[12] This is consistent with the impulse response analysis of Figures 11.4 and A.1.

[13] Figure 11.5 is from Portillo et al. (2016) and uses a more persistent AR(2) for agricultural productivity (parameters $\rho_A = 0.8$ and $\varrho = 0.01$) than the one we estimated in Table 11.1.

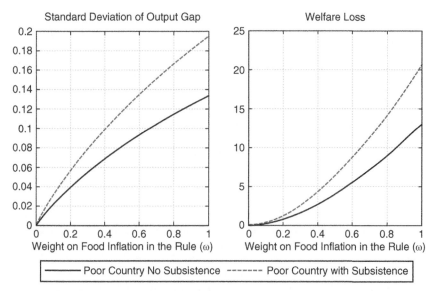

Figure 11.5. Standard Deviation of Output Gap and Welfare Loss, With and Without Subsistence

This can be seen by allowing the subsistence floor to approach zero in equation (14) so that subsistence concerns disappear. The coefficient on output volatility, $\frac{1}{2}\sigma(\psi+\sigma)$ with $\sigma \geq 1$, reduces to $\frac{1}{2}(\psi+1)$ when the subsistence floor is zero. In sum, this exercise reinforces our view that subsistence raises the stakes for monetary policy at earlier stages of development.

6 MODEL EXTENSION

The finding that subsistence does not overturn the divine coincidence result of Blanchard and Gali (2007) is at odds with recent findings by Anand and Prasad (2012) and Anand et al. (2015) (APZ).[14] These authors study a model that features limited asset market participation (LAMP) and segmented labour markets (SLM) in addition to subsistence, and they conclude that targeting headline inflation is superior to targeting core inflation from a welfare perspective. To reconcile our findings with theirs, we extend our model to include LAMP and SLM and reconsider the design of monetary policy through the lens of optimal targeting rules (the model is presented in more detail in the online appendix to Portillo et al., 2016). For simplicity we continue to assume here that the labour share (a) is 1.

We extend our model to include two types of agent. One type provides labour services exclusively to the non-food sector (urban agents, which make up a share λ^* of the population), and the second type provides labour exclusively to the food

---

[14] APZ features an open economy model with imported goods, whereas Anand and Prasad's specification is closer to ours as it assumes a closed-economy setting.

sector (rural agents, with share $(1 - \lambda^*)$). Because labour is immobile across the two sectors, wages in each sector are not necessarily equal. Furthermore, as in Anand and Prasad, rural agents do not have access to financial assets so interest rate movements do not affect their consumption.[15]

The interaction of subsistence, LAMP, and SLM dramatically changes the economy's response to food productivity shocks. Consider a negative shock to food productivity. First, SLM prevents the reallocation of labour across sectors, which amplifies the effects of the shock on sectoral production and leads to a larger increase in relative food prices. Second, food productivity shocks have large and opposing effects on the incomes of the two types of agent. Subsistence lowers the price elasticity in the food sector. The increase in relative food prices more than compensates for the decrease in food production, so the negative shock to food sector productivity has *positive* effects on real income for households that work in the food sector. Furthermore, rural agents respond to this income increase by consuming more leisure and decreasing their labour supply, which adds further to the contraction in food production. The opposite effects occur in the non-food sector, so that negative food productivity shock lowers the level of income of urban agents, and they increase their labour supply to compensate, contributing to an expansion in the non-food sector. If the economy is close to subsistence, the latter effect can dominate, to the extent that total output increases in response to a negative food supply shock. This is the case in our model, when calibrated to data from African countries.

To investigate how these features change the nature of optimal monetary policy, we derive the welfare-based loss function for this version of the model, focusing on the case in which $\lambda^* = (1 - \gamma_F)$.[16]

Proposition 2 Consider the model with food subsistence, limited asset market participation and segmented labour markets, and assume that $\alpha = 1$ and $\lambda^* = (1 - \gamma_F)$. We use a weighted sum of urban and rural agents' utility to derive the average welfare loss per period, given by the following function:

$$\mathbb{L} = \frac{1}{2}\sigma\left[(1 - \gamma_F)\frac{\epsilon}{\kappa}var(\hat{\pi}_{N,t}) + \frac{(\psi + \sigma)}{(1 - \gamma_F)}var(\tilde{\tilde{y}}_t)\right], \qquad (16)$$

where $\tilde{\tilde{y}}_t = \hat{y}_t - \hat{y}_t^{alt}$, where $\hat{y}_t^{alt} \neq \hat{y}_t^{flex}$.

As in the baseline model without LAMP and SLM, welfare depends on the volatility of core (and not headline) inflation, although it no longer depends on the volatility of the gap in relative food prices. Instead, it now depends on an alternative measure of the output gap $(\tilde{\tilde{y}}_t)$, which reflects the fact that the economy's response to food productivity shocks is inefficiently low (because of

---

[15] Although one type of agent has access to financial assets and the other type does not, the consumption of each type is given by their income. This is because, in a closed-economy setting such as ours, the net supply of assets is zero so that access to financial markets does not result in consumption smoothing or risk sharing unless there is heterogeneity within the set of agents with access to financial markets. This point is often overlooked in the discussion of models with limited asset market participation.

[16] This implies that the share of urban agents corresponds to the share of the non-food sector in the economy. This equality will arise endogenously if migration between sectors is allowed in the steady state.

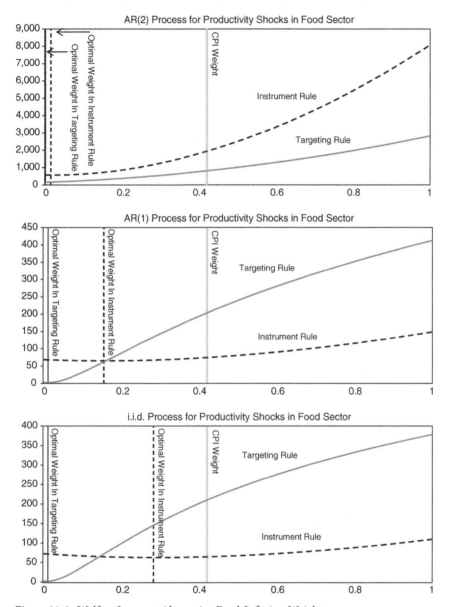

Figure 11.6. Welfare Losses at Alternative Food-Inflation Weights

the offsetting effect coming from non-food production) due to the interaction of the three features mentioned above (subsistence, LAMP, and SLM).[17]

Because of this new inefficiency, a trade-off between non-food inflation and output stabilization exists. The divine coincidence therefore breaks down: it is no longer optimal simply to stabilize non-food inflation. Specifically, when there is a negative food supply shock, optimal policy now calls for a policy tightening, so that the economy approaches the more efficient level of output. But this movement implies that a decline in non-food inflation is part of the efficient response. Including food prices in the measure of inflation that is targeted is an indirect way of approaching the optimal policy prescription, as it elicits the required policy tightening.

To assess whether this matters quantitatively, we evaluate targeting rules as in equation (13). These are shown in Figure 11.6, with each of the three panels showing results for a different degree of persistence in food productivity.[18] Although perfect core (non-food) inflation stabilization is no longer optimal because of the trade-off mentioned above, it is still very close to optimal. In all three cases considered, the optimal weight on food inflation (indicated by the black vertical line) is minimal, between zero and 2 per cent. This is much lower than the weight on food inflation in the CPI (at 0.42, as indicated by the dashed grey line), and it implies near-perfect core inflation stabilization.[19] Thus, (near-perfect) core inflation stabilization remains the main objective of policy even in the presence of these additional features.

How can we reconcile these findings with those of APZ? The apparent contradiction results from the authors' focus on optimal interest rate rules of the form:

$$\hat{R}_t = \rho_R \hat{R}_{t-1} + (1 - \rho_R)(\phi_\pi \hat{\pi}_t^\omega + \phi_y \hat{y}_t),$$

where $\hat{\pi}_t^\omega$ is given by the first equality in equation (13). Figure 11.6 also includes a welfare evaluation of their rule, for the case in which $\rho_R = 0.67, \phi_\pi = 1.5, \phi_y = 0.5$. Unlike targeting rules, the optimal weight in their rule (given by the dashed black line) depends to a large extent on the assumed persistence of the shock.[20] Under a persistent AR(2) process like the one used throughout this chapter, the optimal weight on food inflation is near zero. As the persistence decreases, however, the optimal weight on food inflation in their instrument rule increases, and begins to approach the weight in the CPI. With the persistence used in their paper (the middle panel), the optimal weight jumps to 15 per cent; with i.i.d. shocks it increases further to 29 per cent, broadly consistent with the findings in APZ.

---

[17] Additional derivations confirm that no two of these three features are enough to generate this result.

[18] Like Figure 11.5, Figure 11.6 uses the AR(2) employed by Portillo et al. (2016), with parameters $\rho_A = 0.8$ and $\varrho = 0.01$.

[19] This is not surprising, as New Keynesian models with Calvo prices tend to favour inflation stabilization over output.

[20] These calculations use the concept of unconditional welfare, which we have used throughout the chapter. Anand and Prasad (2012) and Anand et al. (2015), on the other hand, use the concept of conditional welfare. Results regarding the optimal weight, however, are very similar regardless of the welfare concept. Conditional welfare results are available upon request.

The APZ finding is therefore contingent on the use of a particular instrument rule in a particular stochastic setting. Headline inflation wins in their setting because when productivity shocks are sufficiently transitory, a central bank that responds to headline inflation in its interest-rate rule ends up stabilizing core inflation more effectively than if it had responded to core inflation. It is nonetheless core inflation that the central bank ultimately cares about, as revealed by our analysis of target rules.

This divergence between optimal instrument rules and optimal targeting rules is a well-known issue in the design of monetary policy. As emphasized by Svensson (2003) and Svensson and Woodford (2005), targeting rules are more closely related to the objectives of monetary policy and are therefore more robust to model parameters. The welfare properties of interest rate rules, in particular, depend on how nearly they approximate movements in the natural rate of interest. As discussed further in the online appendix to Portillo et al. (2016), a negative shock to food productivity increases the equilibrium real interest rate in an economy with subsistence, LAMP, and SLM—and by more, the less persistent the productivity shock. In this case, assigning greater weight to food inflation can help generate the desired increase in real interest rates, but for reasons that are not robust to the stochastic environment and are unrelated to the deeper policy objectives of the monetary authority.

7 CONCLUSION

This chapter demonstrates that proximity to a subsistence requirement for consumption has far-reaching implications for macroeconomic dynamics, but it does not alter the appropriate objective of monetary policy when sticky prices are confined to the non-food sector. Despite the food sector's outsized role in the economy, the optimal targeting rule calls for the stabilization of core inflation only, as in higher-income countries. But subsistence raises the stakes: the welfare costs of mis-specifying the goals of the monetary authority are higher for LICs.

Subsistence is just one of many dimensions that differentiate low-income countries from the rich-country contexts for which New Keynesian models were developed. Our findings are robust to the inclusion of limited asset-market participation and segmented labour markets, despite the fact that when these features are present, headline inflation may outperform core inflation within a Taylor-type instrument rule. The reason is that while these features invalidate the divine coincidence they do so only very narrowly. The monetary authority continues to care almost exclusively about core inflation. When food productivity shocks display the kind of persistence we observe in real food prices, even a tightly-specified Taylor rule favours the use of core inflation rather than headline.

It remains to be seen whether our results are robust to additional features of the low-income environment. These include activities like private and/or public food storage that may help account for the observed persistence of relative food prices—something we have built in from the outside via persistent productivity shocks—and open-economy considerations that would drive a wedge between food consumption and food output. We have also left aside some features of the structural transformation that may have implications for the conduct of monetary policy. These include the shrinkage of urban informal activity, which may alter the degree of wage and price flexibility in that sector, and the replacement of food staples with more processed varieties as development proceeds. Incorporating these structural features remains a crucial step in adapting the New Keynesian framework to the needs of low-income countries.

REFERENCES

Anand, R., and E. Prasad (2012). 'Core vs. Headline Inflation Targeting in Models with Incomplete Markets', Manuscript, Cornell University.

Anand, R., E. Prasad, and B. Zhang (2015). What Measure of Inflation Should a Developing Country Central Bank Target? *Journal of Monetary Economics*, (74), 102–16.

Aoki, K. (2001). Optimal Monetary Policy Responses to Relative-Price Changes. *Journal of Monetary Economics*, 48(1), 55–80.

Bils, M., and P. Klenow (2004). Some Evidence on the Importance of Sticky Prices. *Journal of Political Economy*, 112, 947–85.

Blanchard, O. and J. Gali (2007). Real Wage Rigidities and the New Keynesian Model. *Journal of Money, Credit, and Banking*, 39(1), 35–66.

Calvo, G. A. (1983). Staggered Prices in a Utility-Maximizing Framework. *Journal of Monetary Economics*, 12(3), 383–98.

Chenery, H. and M. Syrquin (1975). *Patterns of Development (1950–1970)* Oxford: Oxford University Press for the World Bank.

FAO et al. (2011). 'Price Volatility in Food and Agricultural Markets: Policy Responses,' (Policy Report including contributions by FAO, IFAD, IMF, OECD, UNCTAD, WFP, the World Bank, the WTO, IFPRI and the UN HLTF), http://documents.wfp.org/stellent/groups/public/documents/communications/wfp236530.pdf.

Fox, L. (2015). *Are African Households Heterogeneous Agents? Stylized Facts on Patterns of Consumption, Employment, Income and Earnings for Macroeconomic Modelers*, IMF Working Paper No. 15/102. Washington, DC.

Gilbert, C. (2011). Grains Price Pass-Through, in A. Prakash (Ed.) *Safeguarding Food Security in Volatile Global Markets*, Rome: Food and Agricultural Organization of the United Nations, 122–43.

Gollin, D., R. Jedwab, and D. Vollrath (2013). *Urbanization with and without Industrialization*, Working Papers 2013-290-26, Department of Economics, University of Houston.

Gollin, D., and R. Rogerson (2010). *Agriculture, Roads and Economic Development in Uganda*, National Bureau of Economic Research Working Paper No. 15863. Cambridge, MA.

Gollin, D. and R. Rogerson (2014). Productivity, Transport Costs, and Subsistence Agriculture. *Journal of Development Economics*, 107, 38–48.

Herrendorf, B., R. Rogerson, and A. Valentinyi (2014). Growth and Structural Transformation, in P. Aghion and S. Durlauf (Eds.). *Handbook of Economic Growth* Vol. 2, pp. 855–941.

IMF (2012). Structural Transformation in Sub-Saharan Africa, in *Regional Economic Outlook, Sub-Saharan Africa*, chapter 3. Washington, DC: International Monetary Fund.

Portillo, R., L. F. Zanna, S. O'Connell, and R. Peck (2016). Implications of food subsistence for monetary policy and inflation. *Oxford Economic Papers*, 68 (3), 782–810.

Svensson, L. E. O. (2003). What Is Wrong with Taylor Rules? Using Judgment in Monetary Policy through Targeting Rules. *Journal of Economic Literature*, 41(2), 426–77.

Svensson, L. E. O. and M. Woodford (2005). 'Implementing Optimal Policy through Inflation-Forecast Targeting,' in B. S. Bernanke and M. Woodford (Eds.), *The Inflation-Targeting Debate*. Chicago: University of Chicago Press for the National Bureau of Economic Research, pp. 19–91.

12

The Short-Run Macroeconomics of Aid Inflows

Understanding the Interaction of Fiscal and International Reserve Policy

Andrew Berg, Tokhir Mirzoev, Rafael Portillo, and Luis-Felipe Zanna

1 INTRODUCTION

African countries are exposed to a variety of external shocks, which can generate large swings in output, inflation, and the balance of payments. The impact on the domestic economy is typically mediated by the broad policy response to these shocks, though the role of different types of policy is often not fully understood. This is the case for example with (unexpected) changes in aid flows. Much of the discussion typically assumes that the effects of aid depend mainly on the fiscal response. To the extent aid is used to finance higher government spending, then it is assumed that it must also help finance a higher current account deficit net of aid, i.e., higher absorption. The appreciation of the real exchange rate plays an important role in this process: it helps reallocate private demand away from non-traded goods (which is what the government typically spends on) and toward traded goods (which helps absorb the additional aid).

Little attention is paid to how the reserve policy of the central bank may affect the impact of aid, an important issue when analysing the experience of African countries. In the case of Uganda, aid inflows and aid-financed government spending increased considerably during the first half of the 2000s, yet the current account deficit net of aid did not increase (Table 12.1). Instead, the additional aid ended up accumulated as reserves. In addition, the real exchange rate depreciated and the country experienced a considerable increase in real interest rates—a variable that is often ignored in the analysis of aid. As documented in Berg et al. (2007), other African countries with large aid surges also experienced a fiscal expansion, a large accumulation of reserves, and a real depreciation.

The above experience suggests that the distinction between the *spending* and the *absorption* of the aid can be an important factor in understanding its

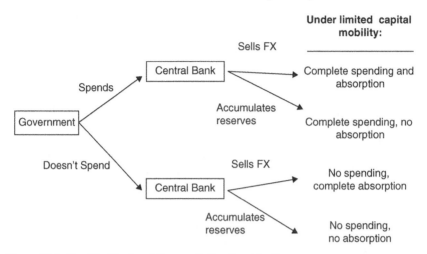

Figure 12.1. Possible Fiscal and Reserve Policy Combinations

macro effects.[1] While the former is determined by the fiscal policy response, the latter can be influenced by the reserve policy of the central bank. In the case of Uganda, aid was spent but not absorbed.

In practice, there is no institutional arrangement between the government and the central bank that ensures coordination of the two policy responses. In a canonical aid transaction, the foreign exchange (FX) from aid accrues to the government, which sells it to the central bank in exchange for a local currency deposit. The central bank in turn decides on its own whether to accumulate the FX as reserves, and whether such accumulation should be sterilized, as it was in Uganda. Depending on the policy mix, there can be several possible combinations of spending and absorption (Figure 12.1).

In this chapter we provide a framework for thinking about the macroeconomics of aid flows, centred on the fiscal/reserve policy interaction. Given the surprising depreciation of the real exchange rate and the simultaneous increase in real interest rates in Uganda, we study whether certain combinations of fiscal and reserve policy can account for this joint behaviour.

We present our analysis in the context of a tractable two-sector dynamic general equilibrium model with nominal rigidities. Our model conforms with the New Keynesian paradigm but emphasizes important features of low-income countries: little market power in export markets, limited international capital mobility, and consumers' limited participation in domestic financial markets. We also extend the policy set of the central bank to include two rules: the standard monetary policy rule and a separate rule determining the rate of reserve accumulation. Given the model's tractability, we can represent the short-run equilibrium using a graphic representation of external and internal balance.[2]

---

[1] The distinction between spending and absorption is reminiscent of the separation between the 'budgetary' and the 'transfer' problem in Keynes (1929).

[2] This is in the tradition of work by Salter (1959) and Swann (1960) on the 'dependent economy' model. See Dornbusch (1974).

With the help of our model we show that a policy combination that results in spending but not absorbing the aid can generate both an increase in real interest rates and, under certain conditions, a real exchange rate depreciation. The starting intuition for our results is that spending but not absorbing the aid is akin to a domestically financed fiscal expansion: public spending increases but the foreign exchange from the aid is not being used to increase the country's external financing. The increase in spending must therefore come at the expense of the private sector, which is crowded out. Another way of restating the same idea is that aid is being 'used' twice: once to increase government spending, and once to increase the stock of reserves. Note that this intuition also justifies the choice of a New Keynesian framework with non-Ricardian features—in this case limited participation in domestic financial markets—to study the short run macroeconomics of aid flows.

The results from the model can be summarized as follows:

- A policy mix that results in spending and absorbing the aid leads to an appreciation of the natural real exchange rate and little movement in the natural rate of interest, where 'natural' denotes the flexible-price equilibrium values. In contrast, a policy that results in spending without absorption moderates the appreciation of the natural real exchange rate and increases the natural rate of interest. The appreciation is moderated because there is no increase in external financing, while the rise in the natural rate of interest reflects the crowding out of the private sector.

- Once we introduce nominal rigidities in the non-traded sector, the increase in the natural rate of interest implies that spending but not absorbing the aid generates demand pressures, i.e., temporary increases in inflation and the aggregate output gap. This is a well-known result of the standard closed-economy New Keynesian model in which monetary policy is not optimal. Because our model is isomorphic to that setup (when the capital account is closed), the same result applies here.[3]

- Demand pressures are associated with a more depreciated real exchange rate relative to the flexible-price case. They result in an increase in aggregate labour demand and therefore generate an increase in real wages. This requires a more depreciated real exchange rate—relative to its 'natural' value—to guarantee external balance.[4]

For the real exchange rate to depreciate in absolute terms, demand-related pressures must dominate the 'natural' real appreciation. We use this distinction to clarify how various features of the model affect the results. Limited participation in domestic financial markets increases the likelihood of a real depreciation

---

[3] As discussed in Woodford (2003: chapter 4), this result stems from monetary policy—the interest rate rule—not responding directly to changes in the natural rate of interest. In Woodford's terms, there is no positive shift in the intercept term of the interest rate feedback rule.

[4] This result is reminiscent of the Mundell-Fleming model with limited capital mobility (see Agenor and Montiel, 2008: chapter 2). In that model, a domestically financed fiscal expansion requires a real depreciation if the increase in the demand for imports—as a result of the effects of the fiscal expansion on consumption—threatens external balance. In our model, the fiscal expansion results in an increase in real wages, and the pressures on external balance come mainly from the impact of higher wages on the supply of exports.

because it amplifies demand pressures. The same holds if monetary policy is loosened as a result of incomplete sterilization of reserves, whereas a more aggressive monetary policy (a higher coefficient on inflation in the Taylor rule) will have the opposite effect. On the other hand, the natural appreciation becomes smaller if the share of government spending on traded goods increases.

When we calibrate the model to Uganda, simulate a temporary aid increase, and assume aid is spent but not absorbed, the model generates a temporary real depreciation and an increase in the real interest rate. However, once the capital account is open, the mapping between reserve accumulation and absorption is considerably weakened. As a result, aid invariably leads to a real appreciation, unless the accumulation of reserves is not fully sterilized. While this is an important caveat, the assumption of limited capital mobility is broadly consistent with the behaviour of the capital account in Uganda following the aid surge.[5]

Our chapter is organized as follows. Section 2 briefly discusses the experience of Uganda. Section 3 presents the model, while Section 4 focuses on the short-run equilibrium when prices are flexible. Section 5 adds nominal rigidities, and discusses the calibration and simulated results. Section 6 concludes.

2 THE AID SURGE IN UGANDA

To provide some motivation and context for our approach, we briefly describe the experience of Uganda—summarized in Table 12.1. Starting in 2000, this country experienced a sustained increase in aid flows. Net aid, defined as the sum of gross aid flows and debt relief minus debt service and arrears clearance, increased by about 3 percentage points of GDP (on average) during 2000–04, with a subsequent fall below pre-surge levels after 2005. In present value terms, the surge represented 11 per cent of Uganda's GDP in 2000–01; by way of historical comparison, the transfer associated with the Franco-Prussian war indemnity—the largest transfer in history—represented 25 per cent of the French economy in 1870 (Devereux and Smith, 2007). Most of the increase took the form of budget support rather than project aid (Berg et al., 2007).

The surge to Uganda coincided with a sharp increase in overall aid to sub-Saharan Africa over the same period, up 42 per cent in real terms from 1999 to 2004 (IMF, 2008a). This increase reflected renewed donor enthusiasm for aid in the context of the UN Millennium Development Goals campaign, the end of a post-Cold War decline in aid, and the implementation of the highly indebted poor countries (HIPC) debt relief initiative. Uganda benefited from this trend because of its successful track record in the 1990s, pre-existing strong policy regime, and good relationships with major donors, all of which made it an attractive target for additional assistance.[6]

---

[5] In Berg et al. (2010), on which we draw the material for this chapter, we provide an extensive review of the related (i) aid and (ii) open economy New Keynesian literature.

[6] According to informal discussions with government officials, donors were so enthusiastic that in 2005 the Ugandan authorities deliberately turned down some grants for fear of the macroeconomic impact.

Table 12.1. Selected Macroeconomic Variables, Uganda, 1998–2004

	Average Pre-Aid Surge 1998–2000	Average Aid-Surge 2000–04	Difference
Fiscal Variables (in per cent of GDP)			
Net Aid	7.9	10.6	2.7
Expenditure (excluding external interest)	18.2	20.5	2.3
Balance of Payments (in per cent of GDP)			
Net Aid	7.7	10.8	3.1
Current account deficit net of aid	11.5	12.1	0.6
Capital account surplus net of aid	−3.6	−3.5	0.1
Reserve accumulation	−0.3	2.3	2.5
Central Bank Balance Sheet (in per cent of GDP)			
Reserve accumulation	−0.3	2.3	2.5
Changes in net domestic assets	0.7	−1.6	−2.3
Base money growth	0.4	0.7	0.3
Relative Prices			
Real effective exchange rate (depreciation)	9.1	6.3	
Terms of trade (worsening)	14.4	5.9	
91-day real Treasury-bill rate	5.6	8.4	2.8
Nominal Variables			
Nominal effective exchange rate (depreciation)	9.4	6.3	
Inflation	3.1	3.3	0.2
91-day Treasury-bill rate	8.2	11.6	3.4

Source: IMF Staff Reports, IFS, Bank of Uganda.

Following the aid surge, fiscal authorities responded by increasing public spending (net of interest payments on foreign debt) by an average of 2.3 percentage points of GDP over the same period, with the difference being used to improve the fiscal balance.[7] Most of the foreign exchange flow associated with the aid was accumulated as reserves by the central bank (2.3 per cent increase), with the difference financing a higher current account deficit before aid (of 0.6 per cent). Only a small fraction of the increase in reserves resulted in an increase in base money growth (0.3 per cent of GDP)—in other words almost all was sterilized.

The contrast between the fiscal and the reserve response reflected the de facto separation of policy objectives between the government and the central bank. The increase in government spending was consistent with the authorities' goal of providing public services and implementing investment projects, while also satisfying the donors demand that aid be used in the first place. On the other hand, the reserve policy response reflected the central bank's concern with 'external competitiveness'.

Against this backdrop, the real exchange rate depreciated considerably, most of it on account of a nominal depreciation. It is likely that some of the real

---

[7] The 3.1 per cent number for the increase in net aid in the third row of Table 12.1 is calculated using Uganda's balance of payments data. Instead, net aid derived from the fiscal accounts increased by 2.7 percentage points. The difference results from the channelling of some flows directly to the private sector.

depreciation reflected the worsening of the terms of trade, which started before the aid surge. However, back-of-the-envelope calculations in Berg et al. (2007) suggest the additional financing provided by the aid surge was much larger than the direct income effect of the terms of trade change. Finally, both nominal and (ex post) real Treasury-bill rates increased by about 200 basis points during the aid-surge period; while six-month and one-year rates increased by about 500 and 600 basis points, respectively.

We now proceed with the description and analysis of the model, before returning to simulations that capture some of these stylized facts.

3 THE MODEL

In this section we present our small open economy model, where the only source of uncertainty is a shock to foreign aid. The economy has two goods, a traded good (T) and a non-traded good (N), and consists of the following agents: i) households; ii) firms; iii) a central bank in charge of monetary policy and reserve accumulation; and iv) a fiscal authority.

3.1 Households

There is a continuum of households $[0, 1]$, all valuing consumption and hours worked. For any household j, consumption is given by a standard CES basket:

$$c_t^j = \left[\varphi^{\frac{1}{\chi}}(c_t^{jN})^{\frac{\chi-1}{\chi}} + (1 - \varphi)^{\frac{1}{\chi}}(c_t^{jT})^{\frac{\chi-1}{\chi}} \right]^{\frac{\chi}{\chi-1}}, \qquad (1)$$

which implies the consumer price index (CPI) $P_t = (\varphi(P_t^N)^{1-\chi} + (1 - \varphi)(P_t^T)^{1-\chi})^{\frac{1}{1-\chi}}$. P_t^T and P_t^N correspond to the prices of the goods, χ denotes the elasticity of substitution between traded and non-traded goods, and φ is the degree of home bias in consumption. Equation (1) implies the following demand functions for traded and non-traded goods:

$$c_t^{jN} = \varphi \left(\frac{P_t^N}{P_t} \right)^{-\chi} c_t^j = \varphi(p_t^N)^{-\chi} c_t^j; \quad \text{and} \quad c_t^{jT} = (1 - \varphi)(\frac{S_t P_t^{T*}}{P_t})^{-\chi} c_t^j. \qquad (2)$$

Households differ in their access to financial markets. A fraction p trade in asset markets, which allows them to smooth consumption in a forward-looking manner. These asset holders are indexed by the superscript 'a'. The remaining households—the fraction $(1 - p)$—have no assets and fully consume their current labour income. They are indexed by the superscript 'h.' We now describe the optimization problem faced by each type of agent.

Asset Holders The representative asset holder maximizes expected life time utility:

$$E_0 \sum_{t=0}^{\infty} \beta^t \left[\log(c_t^a) - \frac{\varkappa}{1 + \psi}(l_t^a)^{1+\psi} \right], \qquad (3)$$

where l_t^a is the amount of labour supplied and ψ is the inverse of the labour supply elasticity. His budget constraint, deflated by the domestic CPI, is given by:

$$c_t^a + b_t^{ac} + s_t b_t^{a*} = w_t l_t^a + i_{t-1}\frac{b_{t-1}^{ac}}{\pi_t} + s_t i^* b_{t-1}^{a*} - s_t Q(b_t^{a*}) + \Omega_t^{aN} - \tau, \quad (4)$$

where b_t^{ac} is the saver's real holdings of domestic bonds issued by the government, which pay a 'gross' nominal interest rate i_t; and b_t^{a*} denotes his holdings of foreign assets deflated by the foreign price index (P_t^*), which pay a gross nominal international interest rate i^* and are subject to portfolio adjustment costs $Q(b_t^{a*})$. The variable s_t is the CPI-based real exchange rate $(s_t = \frac{S_t P_t^*}{P_t})$, where S_t is the nominal exchange rate; π_t is gross domestic inflation $(\pi_t = \frac{P_t}{P_{t-1}})$; w_t is the real wage; Ω_t^{aN} denotes asset holders' profits from domestic firms in the non-traded sector; and τ is a real lump sum tax levied by the government.[8] Utility maximization results in the following first-order conditions:

$$\frac{1}{c_t^a} = \beta E_t\left[\left(\frac{1}{c_{t+1}^a}\right)\left(\frac{i_t}{\pi_{t+1}}\right)\right], \quad (5)$$

$$\frac{1}{c_t^a} = \beta E_t\left\{\left(\frac{1}{c_{t+1}^a}\right)\left(\frac{s_{t+1}}{s_t}\right)\left[\frac{i^*}{1 + Q'(b_t^{a*})}\right]\right\}, \quad (6)$$

$$\varkappa(l_t^a)^\psi = \frac{w_t}{c_t^a}. \quad (7)$$

Portfolio adjustment costs are given by $Q(b_t^{a*}) = \frac{v}{2}(b_t^{a*} - b^{a*})^2$, where b^{a*} is the steady state value of the foreign assets. These costs ensure stationarity of b_t^{a*} and allow us to model various degrees of international capital mobility.[9] When $v \gg 0$, a sterilized foreign exchange rate intervention will influence the exchange rate: *ceteris paribus*, by reducing b_t^a, a purchase of foreign exchange with domestic bonds will increase expected returns on foreign assets—net of adjustment costs—and cause a nominal depreciation.[10]

Non-Asset Holders Households that do not have access to asset markets maximize the same lifetime utility function as in (3) but subject to a static budget constraint:

$$c_t^h = w_t l_t^h - \tau^h. \quad (8)$$

The optimization programme for these consumers reduces to a single first-order condition:

$$\varkappa(l_t^h)^\psi = \frac{w_t}{c_t^h}. \quad (9)$$

---

[8] We assume foreign inflation π^* is constant and equal to one.

[9] See Schmitt-Grohe and Uribe (2003) for alternative methods to ensure stationarity of net foreign assets.

[10] Sterilized interventions affect the exchange rate because *private* foreign assets enter the portfolio adjustment cost function $Q(b_t^{a*})$.

Aggregation We define aggregate consumer-related variables as:

$$x_t = \mathfrak{p}x_t^a + (1 - \mathfrak{p})x_t^h \quad \text{for} \quad x_t = (c_t, c_t^N, c_t^T, l_t, b_t^*, b_t^c, \Omega_t^N).$$

3.2 Firms

Non-traded goods sector The non-traded good y_t^N is a composite good made from a continuum of varieties—indexed by $i \in [0, 1]$—satisfying $y_t^N = \left(\int_0^1 y_{it}^{N\frac{\theta-1}{\theta}} di\right)^{\frac{\theta}{\theta-1}}$, where θ is the elasticity of substitution between varieties. The demand for variety i is given by:

$$y_{it}^N = \left(\frac{P_{it}^N}{P_t^N}\right)^{-\theta} y_t^N, \tag{10}$$

with P_t^N defined as $P_t^N = (\int_0^1 P_{it}^{N1-\theta} di)^{\frac{1}{1-\theta}}$ The non-traded sector features monopolistic competition, with each firm producing a variety. Production by firm i is given by:

$$y_{it}^N = z^N (l_{it}^N)^\alpha, \tag{11}$$

where l_{it}^N is the amount of of labour employed, α is the labour share, and z^N is a productivity parameter. The monopolist also faces price adjustment costs that are similar to Rotemberg (1982): $F(p_t^N, y_t^N, \pi_{it}^N) = p_t^N \frac{\zeta}{2} (\pi_{it}^N - 1)^2$, where

$$\pi_{it}^N = \pi_t \frac{p_{it}^N}{p_{it-1}^N} \quad \text{and} \quad p_{it}^N = \frac{P_{it}^N}{P_t}. \tag{12}$$

The monopolist chooses p_{it}^N to maximize its real discounted flow of profits:

$$E_0 \sum_{t=0}^\infty J_t \left[p_{it}^N \left(\frac{p_{it}^N}{p_t^N}\right)^{-\theta} y_t^N (1 + \iota) - w_t^N \left(\frac{p_{it}^N}{p_t^N}\right)^{-\frac{\theta}{\alpha}} \left(\frac{y_t^N}{z^N}\right)^{\frac{1}{\alpha}} - F(p_t^N, y_t^N, \pi_{it}^N) - \iota p_t^N y_t^N \right],$$

where $J_t = \beta \frac{c_t^a}{c_{t+1}^a}$. Each firm receives a subsidy ι, which is financed with a tax common to the entire sector.[11] Focusing on a symmetric equilibrium, the first order condition is the following:

$$\pi_t^N (\pi_t^N - 1) = \beta E_t \left[\frac{c_t^a}{c_{t+1}^a} \pi_{t+1}^N (\pi_{t+1}^N - 1) \right] + \frac{1}{\zeta} \left[\frac{\theta}{(1+\iota)(\theta-1)} \left(\frac{w_t^N}{p_t^N}\right) \frac{(y_t^N)^{\frac{1-\alpha}{\alpha}}}{(z^N)^{\frac{1}{\alpha}}} - 1 \right]. \tag{13}$$

Traded goods sector The traded goods sector features perfect competition and flexible prices. We assume the law of one price holds: $P_t^T = S_t P_t^{T*}$, where P_t^{T*} is the foreign price of traded goods. Production by firm j is the following:

$$y_{it}^T = z^T (l_{it}^T)^\alpha. \tag{14}$$

---

[11] This ensures that distortions arising from monopolistic competition are zero at steady state.

The representative firm chooses l_{it}^T to maximize real profits: $E_0 \sum_{t=0}^{\infty} J_t [s_t z^T (l_{it}^T)^\alpha - w_t^T l_{it}^T]$, which leads to the following first-order condition:

$$\frac{w_t^T}{s_t} = \frac{(y_t^T)^{\frac{1-\alpha}{\alpha}}}{(z^T)^{\frac{1}{\alpha}}}. \tag{15}$$

3.3 The Government

The government spends on a basket of traded and non-traded goods:

$$g_t = min\left(\frac{g_t^N}{\varphi_g}, \frac{g_t^T}{1 - \varphi_g}\right),$$

which implies the following government price index, measured in real terms:

$$\frac{P_t^g}{P_t} = p_t^g = \left(\varphi_g p_t^N + (1 - \varphi_g)s_t\right) \tag{16}$$

and the following demand functions:[12]

$$g_t^N = \varphi_g g_t \quad \text{and} \quad g_t^T = (1 - \varphi_g)g_t. \tag{17}$$

The government budget constraint is given by:

$$p_t^g g_t = \tau - \frac{(i_{t-1} - 1)b_{t-1}^c}{\pi_t} + s_t A_t^* + \left(b_t - \frac{b_{t-1}}{\pi_t}\right) - \left(d_t - \frac{d_{t-1}}{\pi_t}\right). \tag{18}$$

The government finances spending with taxes τ, aid proceeds $s_t A_t^*$ (of which it is the direct recipient), changes in deposits held at the central bank $-\left(d_t - \frac{d_{t-1}}{\pi_t}\right)$, or domestic debt issuance $\left(b_t - \frac{b_{t-1}}{\pi_t}\right)$. It pays interest on government debt held by the private sector b_t^c, which is the difference between total debt and debt help by the central bank b_t^{cb}:

$$b_t = b_t^{cb} + b_t^c. \tag{19}$$

We assume foreign aid A_t^* follows the process:

$$A_t^* = A^* + \rho_A (A_{t-1}^* - A^*) + A^* \epsilon_t, \tag{20}$$

where A^* is the steady state level of aid and ϵ_t is an i.i.d. shock. Fiscal policy is determined by rules for deposits and gross debt. Deposits are determined as follows:

$$d_t = \rho_d d_{t-1} + (1 - \rho_d)d + (1 - \gamma)s_t(A_t^* - A^*), \tag{21}$$

where d is a deposit target. When aid increases, the government initially spends a fraction γ. In this regard, γ measures the degree of short-term *aid spending*. Aid-related deposits are drawn down at rate ρ_d. Debt accumulation follows a simple rule:

---

[12] We have assumed for simplicity that the government demand for traded and non-traded goods is not sensitive to changes in the real exchange rate.

$$b_t - b_{t-1} = -s\left(b_{t-1}^c - b^c\right), \tag{22}$$

where s is small but positive. This ensures that open market operations—which affect government interest payments—do not influence the steady state fiscal position.

3.4 The Central Bank

We initially assume the economy is cashless, which implies the central bank balance sheet does not contain any monetary liabilities. Changes in its balance sheet are given by:

$$b_t^{cb} - \frac{b_{t-1}^{cb}}{\pi_t} = \left(d_t - \frac{d_{t-1}}{\pi_t}\right) - s_t(R_t^* - R_{t-1}^*), \tag{23}$$

where R_t^* is the level of foreign reserves. Central bank policy is given by a Taylor rule:

$$i_t = \frac{1}{\beta}(\pi_t^N)^{\phi_\pi}, \tag{24}$$

which implicitly defines the inflation objective $\pi^N = 1$, and a reserve policy rule:

$$R_t^* = \rho_R R_{t-1}^* + (1 - \rho_R)R^* + (1 - \omega)(A_t^* - A^*), \tag{25}$$

where R^* is a long-run target.[13] The central bank initially accumulates a fraction $(1 - \omega)$ of the increase in aid as reserves, which will eventually be drawn down at rate ρ_R. When the capital account is closed, ω is a direct measure of short-term *aid absorption*.

3.5 Equilibrium Conditions

The labour market equilibrium (LL) is given by the following equation:

$$l_t^T + l_t^N = \mathfrak{p}l_t^a + (1 - \mathfrak{p})l_t^h. \tag{26}$$

Then there is the equilibrium in the non-traded goods market:

$$y_t^N = c_t^N + g_t^N + F(p_t^N, y_t^N, \pi_{it}^N). \tag{27}$$

The balance of payments (BOP) is derived by adding all budget constraints:

---

[13] As an extension, we introduce a role for money and consider money growth rate rules.

$$A_t^* = \underbrace{[c_t^T + g_t^T - y_t^T + \mathfrak{p}Q(b_t^{a*}) - (i_{t-1}^* - 1)b_{t-1}^*]}_{\text{current account deficit net of aid}} + \underbrace{(b_t^* - b_{t-1}^*)}_{\text{capital account surplus}}$$

$$+ \underbrace{(R_t^* - R_{t-1}^*)}_{\text{reserve accumulation}}.$$

(28)

Equation (28) summarizes the possible uses of aid: it can finance a higher current account deficit (net of aid), a capital account surplus, or an accumulation of reserves.

Finally, it is useful to introduce real GDP, which is defined as the sum of production in both sectors, valued at their normalized steady-state prices p^N and s:

$$y_t = p^N y_t^N + s y_t^T.$$

(29)

We define an equilibrium in this economy as follows:

Definition: *Given* $\{b_{-1}, b_{-1}^c, b_{-1}^*, R_{-1}^*, d_{-1}^g\}$ *the targets and policies* $\{b^c, b^{a*}, R^*, d^g, \pi^N, \tau, \iota,\}$ *and the stochastic process for aid* $\{A^*\}_{t=0}^{\infty}$, *a symmetric equilibrium is a set of stochastic process* $\{c_t^a, c_t^{aN}, c_t^{aT}, c_t^h, c_t^{hN}, c_t^{hT}, l_t^a, l_t^h, l_t^N, l_t^T, y_t^N, y_t^T, g_t, g_t^T, g_t^N, b_t, b_t^c, b_t^{ac}, b_t^{cb}, b_t^{a*}, b_t^*, R_t^*, d_t^g\}_{(t=0)}^{\infty}$ *and* $\{w_t, s_t, p_t^N, p_t^g, \pi_t, \pi_t^N, i_t\}_{t=0}^{\infty}$ *satisfying (i) the demand functions and price indices (2), (12), (16), and (17); (ii) the optimal conditions for consumers (5)–(7) and (8)–(9); (iii) the optimal conditions for firms (11), (13)–(15); (iv) the government rules and constraint (18)–(22); (v) the central bank rules and constraint (23)–(25); (vi) the aggregation and equilibrium market conditions for labour, non-traded goods and the BOP (26)–(28).*

This concludes the presentation of the model. We use a log-linearized version of the above equations (around the model's deterministic steady state) to generate impulse response functions to an increase in aid following various fiscal and central bank policy responses; the complete system of log-linear equations is presented in Berg et al. (2010). A hat ($\hat{x}$) indicates log-deviations from steady state, except for stocks, for which it indicates changes in per cent of steady state GDP.

3.6 Graphic Representation of the Model Solution

We show in Berg et al. (2010) that the equilibrium dynamics of the model can be simplified to a system of two equations and two variables, private consumption and the real exchange rate, $\hat{c}_t$ and $\hat{s}_t$, shown in Figure 12.2. Here we provide a non-technical description of the economics behind these two curves; for a full derivation see Berg et al. (2010).

The first equation captures *internal balance*: the equilibrium in the non-traded goods market and in the labour market in that sector. The relation between $\hat{c}_t$ and $\hat{s}_t$ is negative: an increase in aggregate private consumption ($\hat{c}_t \uparrow$) increases demand for non-traded goods and reduces the overall supply of labour (via the labour supply equation). A real appreciation ($\hat{s}_t \downarrow$) helps reduce demand and increases supply of non-traded goods (by reducing real product wages in the sector). The increase in government spending (in response to a positive aid shock)

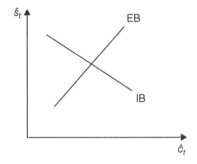

Figure 12.2. External and Internal Balance

shifts the internal balance curve to the left, with the magnitude of the shift given by the coefficient of short-term aid spending (γ) and the share of government spending spent on non-traded goods (φ_g).[14] In addition, deviations in non-traded firms' mark-ups $\hat{\mu}_t^N$, which stem from the presence of nominal rigidities, also shift the internal balance curve: a decrease in mark-ups $\hat{\mu}_t^N<0$ results in greater production of non-traded goods for any given real exchange rate, which implies the internal balance curve shifts right.

The second equation captures *external balance*: the combination of private consumption and the real exchange rate that helps clear the balance of payments and the labour market in the traded sector. The relation is positive. An increase in consumption ($\hat{c}_t \uparrow$) increases demand for traded goods and reduces overall labour supply; a real depreciation ($\hat{s}_t \uparrow$) helps reduce demand and increases supply for traded goods (by reducing real product wages in the sector). Increases in aid shift the external balance curve to the right, with the magnitude of the shift depending on whether international reserves increase (given by $(1 - \omega)$). Fiscal policy may also affect external balance if some of the government spending goes to traded goods ($\varphi_g<1$). Finally, note that increases in net foreign asset holding by the private sector also shift the external balance curve (in this case to the left).

4 FISCAL AND RESERVE POLICY INTERACTION UNDER FLEXIBLE PRICES, CLOSED CAPITAL ACCOUNT, AND $\varphi_g = 1$

To develop some intuition for our results below, we first focus on a simplified version of the model. In particular, we study the interaction of spending and reserve policy response to an increase in aid—the pair (γ,ω)—under: (i) flexible prices, $\zeta = 0$ and $\hat{\mu}_t^N = 0$, (ii) a closed capital account, $v_b = +\infty$, and (iii) no government spending on traded goods $\varphi_g = 1$. We relax these assumptions later. We will use a '$(*)^{n}$' superscript for equilibrium variables under flexible prices.

---

[14] Lagged government deposits and the stock of government debt also shift the internal balance curve as they affect the level of government spending.

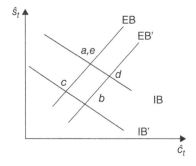

Figure 12.3. Alternative Spend and Absorb Scenarios

Note that, when $\varphi_g = 1$, the government's spending of the additional aid ($\gamma > 0$) affects internal balance only (the IB curve shifts to the left), while the central bank's sale of the aid-related FX ($\omega > 0$) affects external balance (the EB curve shifts downward). We look at four policy combinations (see Figure 12.3); point a refers to steady state.

4.1 Complete Spending and Absorption—Point b

If aid is spent and the central bank sells all the aid-related FX ($\gamma = 1$, $\omega = 1$), the short run equilibrium moves from point a to b. The real exchange rate appreciates and consumption increases slightly.[15]

Complete spending but no absorption—point c. If aid is spent but the central bank uses all of the FX to accumulate reserves ($\gamma = 1$, $\omega = 0$), there is a smaller real appreciation and private consumption is crowded out.

Complete absorption but no spending—point d. If the central bank sells the FX but government spending does not increase ($\gamma = 0$, $\omega = 1$), there is also a smaller real appreciation but with higher consumption.

No absorption and no spending—point e. Finally, if aid is not spent but the FX is accumulated as reserves ($\gamma = 0$, $\omega = 0$), there is no initial impact on the real exchange rate or consumption.

4.2 Reserves Policy, the Real Exchange Rate, and the Natural Rate of Interest

Much of the policy debate about the short-term response to aid takes spending as given and focuses on the central bank response; we will set ($\gamma = 1$) for the remainder of the chapter and analyse the role of ω.

---

[15] The increase in consumption happens because the private sector—being more intensive in the production of non-traded goods than in their consumption—benefits when relative demand for non-traded goods goes up.

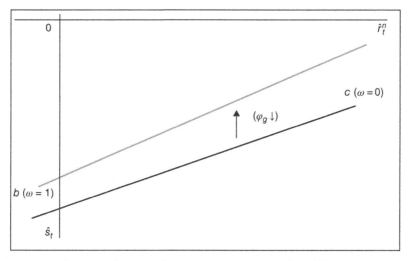

Figure 12.4. Alternative Reserve Policy Responses: Impact on $\hat{s}_t^n$ and $\hat{r}_t^n$

It is helpful to derive the implications of aid on the natural rate of interest, i.e., the real interest rate under flexible prices $\hat{r}_t^n$.[16] For a given increase in aid, Figure 12.4 displays the pair $(\hat{r}_t^n, \hat{s}_t^n)$, in the short term, as ω goes from one (complete absorption, shown as point b in the figure) to zero (no absorption, shown as point a). As reserve accumulation increases ($\omega \downarrow$), the size of the 'natural' real appreciation (represented on the y axis) is reduced while the natural rate of interest (represented on the x axis) increases—consistent with the crowding out of the private sector. We also show how the result changes when the share of spending on traded goods by the government increases ($\varphi_g \downarrow$). As $\varphi_g \downarrow$, the range of real exchange rate movements shifts up—there is less appreciation—while the range of real interest rates remains the same.

To summarize, the experiments presented here have shown that, when capital mobility is limited, the short-run impact of aid on the real exchange rate and other real variables depends crucially on the combination of fiscal and reserve policy responses, as well as the composition of spending. The differences become starker once we introduce nominal rigidities, which we discuss in the next section.

5 POLICY INTERACTIONS UNDER STICKY PRICES

We now analyse how nominal rigidities ($\zeta > 0$) affect the short-run effects of aid. It is no longer possible to fully characterize the short-run equilibrium with the system of external and internal balance, although we will use it to clarify the role of nominal rigidities. Instead, we simulate the model calibrated to the Ugandan economy.

---

[16] See Berg et al. (2010) for an analytical derivation of the natural rate of interest.

Table 12.2. Benchmark: Calibrated Parameters

Parameters		Parameters	
β	0.99	κ_A	0.078
ψ	2	κ_g	0.182
φ_g	0.8	κ_c	0.896
ζ	10	ρ_A	0.87
χ	0.85	ρ_R	0.9
α	0.7	v_b	10000000
φ	0.634	p	0.42
δ	0.75	ϕ_π	1.5

5.1 Calibration

The calibration is shown in Table 12.2. β is set so the equilibrium annual real interest rate is 4 per cent. The non-traded share of employment and GDP (δ), and the ratios of government spending and aid to GDP (κ_g and κ_A) are based on Uganda's national income and fiscal accounts prior to the aid surge.[17] We set $\varphi_g = 0.8$ based on data from the Bank of Uganda; the share of consumption in GDP (κ_c) and the share of non-traded goods in consumption (φ) follow from the country's resource constraints.[18] Our baseline maintains $v_b = +\infty$ (closed capital account).

The labour share α is calibrated to the employment compensation share in Uganda's 2002 input-output table, and χ is calibrated to the estimate of import demand elasticity for Uganda from Tokarick (2008). We do not have estimates of labour supply elasticity (ψ^{-1}); we set $\psi = 2$. We set $\zeta = 10$, which is consistent with firms changing prices every 3.5 quarters.

The share of asset holders p is set to 40 per cent, based on a comprehensive survey of financial access in Uganda.[19] The coefficient ρ_A is chosen so that the increase in aid has a half-life of about a year and half; the choice of ρ_R ensures reserve accumulation is persistent. Finally, Uganda, like many African countries, does not set operational targets on interest rates; we choose a Taylor rule for simplicity and our value for ϕ_π (1.5) is standard. We experiment with an alternative monetary policy rule below.

5.2 Simulation Results

We examine the dynamics of the model following a 50 per cent increase in A_t^* (about 3 percentage points of GDP), similar to what Uganda experienced during

---

[17] NIA data is available at http://www.ubos.org/. Fiscal accounts data was compiled from IMF staff reports, available at http://www.imf.org/external/country/UGA/index.htm.

[18] The Bank of Uganda compiles data on direct imports of goods and services by the general government financed with aid—both budget support and project aid. This statistic (16 per cent of total government spending in 1999) provides a lower bound on total government spending on traded goods. We thank Kenneth Egesa for providing us with these data.

[19] The survey, titled 'Financial Access Survey for Financial Sector Deepening' (Steadman Group, 2009) surveyed 3,000 Ugandans and covered access to both the formal and informal financial sectors. Information available at http://www.finscope.co.za/uganda.html.

the aid surge. Impulse response functions are computed under both sticky and flexible prices.[20]

5.2.1 Complete Spending and Absorption (Figure 12.5)

In this case, there is an equivalent increase in government spending and the current account deficit (net of aid).[21] The real exchange rate appreciates and the impact on real GDP is close to zero: the expansion of the non-traded sector is almost fully offset by the contraction in the traded sector. Real wages increase. There is a small increase in non-traded inflation (shown in annualized terms), which is consistent with a small decline in mark-ups. Headline inflation falls while nominal and real interest rates remain unchanged. Note that the simulation under sticky prices is very similar to its flexible price counterpart.

5.2.2 Complete Spending, Zero Absorption (Figure 12.6)

This case matches the policy response observed in Uganda (Table 12.1). Government spending increases but the current account deficit net of aid stays flat. The real exchange rate now displays a depreciation, there is a large decline in mark-ups, consistent with aggregate demand pressures, and inflation increases considerably. The monetary policy response results in a large increase in real interest rates, while output expands for two reasons: an increase in labour supply—related to the crowding out of consumption—and higher demand pressures. Note that the performance of the model with sticky prices is very different from the flexible-price version: we observe higher output and inflation, lower mark-ups, higher real wages, and a more depreciated real exchange rate.

5.3 Discussion

The simulations raise two related questions: why are there demand pressures when aid is spent but not absorbed, and how can these pressures generate a temporary real depreciation?

5.3.1 Why are There Demand Pressures When Aid is Spent but not Absorbed?

To understand this question, it is helpful to look at one-sector closed economy New Keynesian models. These models typically feature three equations: an IS curve that relates the output gap to the difference between the actual real interest rate and the natural rate of interest; a New Keynesian Phillips curve; and a monetary

---

[20] While the aid surge in Uganda lasted four years, our focus is mainly on the first year. Since most of the features in our model that can generate a real depreciation are related to the presence of nominal rigidities, and there are few real rigidities, we cannot generate a persistent real depreciation that lasts beyond the first few quarters.

[21] The log-linearized current account deficit net of aid (in per cent of GDP) is given by:
$$\hat{ca}_t = \kappa_A\left((1+\phi)\hat{s}_t + \hat{A}_t^* - \hat{y}_t\right) - \hat{R}_t^* - \hat{R}_{t-1}^*.$$

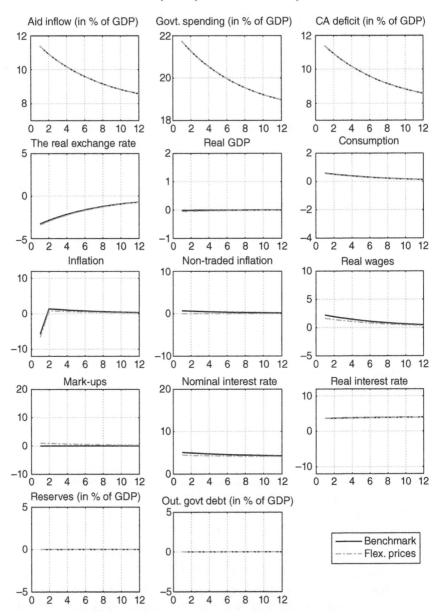

Figure 12.5. Spend and Absorb Scenario (Per cent Deviations from Steady State)

policy rule.[22] It is a well-known property of these models that real shocks affect inflation through their implication for $\hat{r}_t^n$. In particular, increases in $\hat{r}_t^n$ will generate a positive output gap, provided monetary policy is not optimal, i.e., $\phi_\pi \ll \infty$. When the capital account is closed, our model admits the same representation after some

---

[22] See Gali (2008).

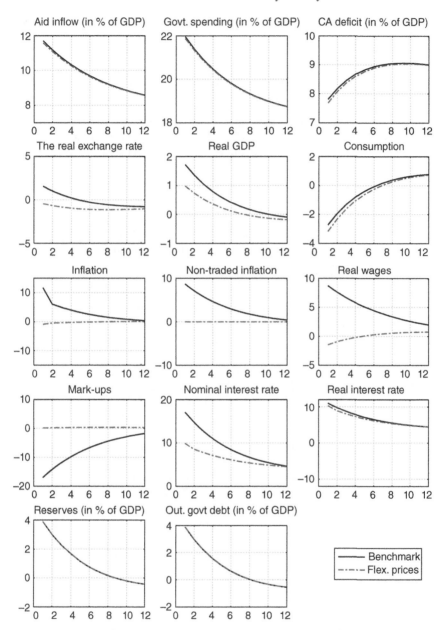

Figure 12.6. Spend, No Absorption Scenario (Per cent Deviations from Steady State)

additional derivation, i.e., it is isomorphous to the closed economy model.[23] So the same logic applies here: since spending but not absorbing the aid raises $\hat{r}_t^n$, it generates demand pressures. This is not the case when aid is both spent and absorbed, as can be seen in Figure 12.3. In that case the increase in aggregate

---

[23] This additional derivation is available upon request.

demand stemming from higher government spending is offset by an increase in the trade deficit (the current account deficit net of aid).

5.3.2 How Can Demand Pressures Generate a Temporary Real Depreciation?

Under sticky prices, the real exchange rate following an aid shock is the combination of the real exchange rate under flexible prices and an additional effect stemming from aggregate demand and the presence of nominal rigidities, which we denote $\hat{s}gap_t$:

$$\hat{s}_t = \hat{s}_t^n + \hat{s}gap_t. \tag{30}$$

We know that $\hat{s}_t^n < 0$ (the 'natural' real exchange rate appreciates somewhat) when aid is spent but not absorbed (see Figure 12.3)). For the actual real exchange rate $\hat{s}_t$ to depreciate when aid is spent but not absorbed, a necessary condition is that $\hat{s}gap_t^n > 0$, which is indeed the case.

To understand why this is the case, it is useful to recall that aggregate demand pressures shift the internal balance curve to the right, as these pressures generate a decrease in non-traded goods mark-ups and firms in that sector produce more goods (for a given real exchange rate). The shift in the internal balance curve stemming from lower mark-ups results, all else equal, in a relatively more depreciated real exchange rate (and a relatively higher level of private consumption). This is because, as non-traded firms increase their demand for labour, real wages increase. Since higher real wages tend to reduce the supply of traded goods— relative to the flexible price case—a more depreciated real exchange rate is necessary to re-establish external balance, by increasing product wages in the sector and switching expenditure away from traded goods.

Finally, for $\hat{s}_t > 0$ it must be the case that $\hat{s}gap_t > -\hat{s}_t^n$. This clarifies what makes a real depreciation more likely when aid is spent and not absorbed: factors that decrease the natural appreciation of the real exchange rate ($\hat{s}, n$) and factors that amplify demand pressures (and increase $\hat{s}gap_t$). Two features are worth mentioning here. First, in the model calibration for Uganda we have $\varphi_g < 1$, which reduces the natural appreciation. Second, we have rule-of-thumb consumers ($\mathfrak{p} < 1$) which, as we show below, tend to amplify the aggregate demand effects from a domestically financed fiscal expansion. The combination of these two features, together with the rest of the calibration, is sufficient to generate a small depreciation when aid increases.

5.4 Sensitivity Analysis

We now analyse how several features of the model affect the macro impact of aid and how these effects vary with the reserves policy response. We limit ourselves to three cases: (i) excluding rule-of-thumb consumers ($\mathfrak{p} = 1$), (ii) a perfectly open capital account, and (iii) incomplete sterilization of reserve accumulation.[24] The results from these alternative specifications are presented in Table 12.3.

---

[24] A more thorough sensitivity analysis is presented in Berg et al. (2010).

Table 12.3. Sensitivity Analysis

	Benchmark	Flex P. $\zeta = 0$	Asset holders $\mathfrak{p} = 1$	Open K. Acc. $v_b = 0.0125$	Inc. Sterilization $\mathfrak{f}=0.9$
No Res. Accumul. (Per cent dev. from SS)					
$\hat{s}$	−2.7	−2.8	−2.7	−2.0	−2.8
$\hat{y}$	0.0	0.0	0.0	0.2	−0.1
$\hat{\pi}$	−0.5	−1.1	−0.4	1.0	−0.5
$\hat{r}_t - E_t[\hat{\pi}_{t+1}]$	−0.3	−0.1	−0.3	0.8	−0.8
$\Delta\left(\frac{A}{Y}\right)$	3.0	–	–	3.0	–
$\Delta\left(\frac{CA\ n.o.a.}{Y}\right)$	3.0	–	–	2.4	–
$\Delta\left(\frac{Res}{Y}\right)$	0.0	–	–	0.0	–
$\Delta\left(\frac{KA}{Y}\right)$	0.0	–	–	0.6	–
Full Res. Accumul. (Per cent dev. from SS)					
$\hat{s}$	0.9	−0.7	−0.1	−1.5	6.6
$\hat{y}$	1.2	0.6	0.9	0.4	3.4
$\hat{\pi}$	7.0	−0.5	2.6	1.8	18.7
$\hat{r}_t - E_t[\hat{\pi}_{t+1}]$	5.5	4.7	2.5	1.1	14.7
$\Delta\left(\frac{A}{Y}\right)$	3.2	–	–	3.0	–
$\Delta\left(\frac{CA\ n.o.a.}{Y}\right)$	0.5	–	–	1.8	–
$\Delta\left(\frac{Res}{Y}\right)$	2.7	–	–	2.7	–
$\Delta\left(\frac{KA}{Y}\right)$	0.0	–	–	−1.5	–

5.4.1 Excluding Non-Asset Holders

When the share of non-asset holders falls from 60 per cent ($\mathfrak{p} = 0.4$) to zero ($\mathfrak{p} = 1$), the response of the economy varies depending on whether aid is absorbed or not. When aid is absorbed results are similar to the benchmark. When aid is not absorbed, demand pressures are now smaller and the real exchange rate no longer depreciates. This result confirms the fact that non-asset holders amplify demand pressures. A related point is that the increase in equilibrium real interest rates is larger when there are rule-of-thumb agents.

5.4.2 Opening the Capital Account

We now assume that the capital account is open with changes in private foreign asset holdings subject to small portfolio adjustment costs. We set $v_b = 0.0125$, which implies that, *ceteris paribus*, a decrease in private NFA by 5 per cent of annual GDP leads to an increase in annualized domestic interest rates of 100 basis points. In addition to $(\hat{s}_t, \hat{y}_t, \hat{\pi}_t, \hat{r}_t - \hat{\pi}_{t+1})$ we also study the impact on the BOP categories (see Table 12.3).

In this case, reserve accumulation has a smaller impact on real variables, including the current account deficit which is now determined in part by intertemporal considerations. When all aid-related foreign exchange is sold to the private sector, there is both a higher current account deficit net of aid and a capital account surplus. Since absorption is now smaller, real exchange rate pressures are smaller. When the central bank accumulates reserves, the private sector borrows from the rest of the world to maintain a broadly similar—although smaller— current account deficit, resulting in large capital inflows.

Relative to the previous discussion, the sterilized accumulation of reserves—during an aid-financed fiscal expansion—cannot generate a short-term real depreciation when the capital account is perfectly open. More generally, the (sterilized) reserve policy of the central bank has a limited impact on the macroeconomy. Note, however, that an *unsterilized* reserve accumulation will lead to a real depreciation, regardless of the degree of capital mobility. We discuss the role of sterilization next.

5.4.3 *Incomplete Reserve Sterilization*

As discussed in Berg et al. (2007), in contrast with Uganda, some of the countries that accumulated reserves during scaling-up episodes did not fully sterilize. To analyse this scenario, we introduce (real) money balances in the representative agent's utility function and in the central bank balance sheet (see Berg et al., 2010 for a derivation). Unlike in the cashless case, an increase in reserves need not lead to an increase in government bonds outstanding but can be financed instead with an increase in the money stock. Such lack of sterilization would result in a loosening of policy, which suggests the following variant of the Taylor rule:

$$\hat{r}_t = \phi_\pi \hat{\pi}_t^N - \frac{1-\mathfrak{f}}{\kappa_m \mathfrak{y}}(\hat{R}_t^* - \hat{R}_{t-1}^*), \tag{31}$$

where κ_m measures the ratio of reserve money to GDP, $\mathfrak{f}$ measures sterilization, and $\mathfrak{y}$ is the aggregate interest semi-elasticity of money demand. The impact of incomplete sterilization ($\mathfrak{f} < 1$) on the policy stance depends on κ_m and $\mathfrak{y}$. The parameter κ_m is calibrated to the share of reserve money in Uganda and the choice of $\mathfrak{y}$ is based on an OLS regression of nominal money balances on nominal interest rates and nominal output. We set $\mathfrak{f} = 0.9$.

When sterilization is incomplete, reserve accumulation results, not surprisingly, in a large depreciation of the real exchange rate, a large increase in output and a spike in inflation. In this case, the fiscal expansion is financed by the inflationary tax, which is expansionary in the short run.

6 CONCLUSION

We have focused on the macroeconomic implications of different responses to aid surges. In particular, and following recent episodes of aid surges in low-income countries, we emphasize the interaction of fiscal policy and reserve management. We find that this interaction matters for the short-run effects of aid.

When calibrated to Uganda, the model is able to capture some of the main features of the aid inflow episode, notably the response of the real exchange rate and the real interest rate.

Our analysis has focused on the short term. The interaction of reserve and fiscal policy also has implications for the medium-term effects of aid, since the (potentially) positive effects from higher aid-financed public investment can be offset by the crowding out of private investment induced by reserve accumulation.

The analysis is further complicated by Dutch Disease-type effects. We address these issues in Berg et al. (2010).

We believe our approach is applicable to issues besides aid. The macroeconomics of natural resource booms in low-income countries are closely related to those of aid surges.[25] More broadly, the fiscal monetary policy interactions involved here are of general importance in low-income countries. For example, a spend-and-absorb response resembles a domestically financed fiscal expansion, combined with a sterilized intervention (financed by the aid). An in-depth discussion of sterilized interventions is provided in Chapter 13.

REFERENCES

Agenor, P. and Montiel P. (2008). *Development Macroeconomics*. Princeton, NJ: Princeton University Press.

Berg, A., Gottschalk, J., Portillo, R., and Zanna L. (2010). *The Macroeconomics of Medium-Term Aid Scaling-Up Scenarios*. IMF Working Paper 10/160.

Berg, A., Mirzoev, T., Portillo, R., and Zanna L. (2010). *The Short-Run Macroeconomics of Aid Inflows: Understanding the Interaction of Fiscal and Reserve Policy*. IMF Working Paper 10/65.sh

Berg, A., Aiyar S., Hussain M., Roache S., Mirzoev T., and Mahone, A. (2007). *The Macroeconomics of Scaling Up Aid: Lessons from Recent Experience*. IMF Occasional Paper 253.

Dagher, J., Gottschalk, J., and Portillo, R. (2010). Oil Windfalls in a DSGE Model: The Case of Ghana. Draft Paper. IMF.

Devereux, M. and Smith, G. (2007). Transfer problem dynamics: Macroeconomics of the Franco-Prussian War Indemnity. *Journal of Monetary Economics*, 54, 2375–98.

Dornbusch, R. (1974). Real and Monetary Aspects of the Effects of Exchange Rate Changes, in Robert Z. Aliber (Ed.) *National Monetary Policies and the International Financial System*. Chicago, IL: University of Chicago Press.

Galí, J. (2008). *Monetary Policy, Inflation and the Business Cycle*. Princeton, NJ: Princeton University Press.

Keynes, J. M. (1929). The German Transfer Problem. *Economic Journal*, 39, 1–7.

Rotemberg, J. (1982). Monopolistic Price Adjustment and Aggregate Output. *Review of Economic Studies*, 49, 517–31.

Salter, W. E. G. (1959). Internal and External Balance: The Role of Price and Expenditure Effects. *Economic Record*, 35(71), 226–38.

Schmitt-Grohé, S. and Uribe, M. (2003). Closing Small Open Economy Models. *Journal of International Economics*, 61, 163–85.

Steadman Group (2009). Financial Access Survey for Financial Sector Deepening. Presentation available at http://www.finscope.co.za/uganda.html.

Swan, T. W. (1960). Economic Control in a Dependent Economy Model. *Economic Record*, 36(73), 51–66.

Tokarick, S. (2008). A Method For Calculating Export Supply and Import Demand Elasticities. Draft Paper, IMF.

Woodford, M. (2003). *Interest and Prices*. Princeton, NJ: Princeton University Press.

---

[25] See Dagher et al. (2010) for an application of a closely related model to the expected oil windfall in Ghana.

13

Modelling Sterilized Interventions and Balance Sheet Effects of Monetary Policy in a New Keynesian Framework

Jaromir Benes, Andrew Berg, Rafael Portillo, and David Vavra

1 INTRODUCTION

Monetary policy is defined by the objectives, targets, and instruments that both guide and characterize the behaviour of central banks.[1] Until recently, a typical summary of monetary policy would list price stability as the main policy objective, inflation (or the exchange rate or monetary aggregates in some cases) as the intermediate target, and short-term interest rate as the sole instrument. The above view was also reflected in the standard macroeconomic model, the New Keynesian framework, which typically models policy as a rule in which interest rates respond to deviations of inflation from its target.

Following the global financial crisis and the policy responses that have been implemented in advanced economies, it has become increasingly clear that such a simple characterization of monetary policy misses some of the main instruments and channels through which central banks have attempted to influence economic activity, especially when interest rates are stuck at the zero lower bound.[2] What is less clear, at least in the academic literature, is that monetary policy in emerging markets is also considerably richer than what is described in the simple New Keynesian framework, but for reasons that are unrelated to the zero lower bound and crisis episodes. The key missing element in policy analysis in emerging markets is the FX intervention policy of the central bank.

Foreign exchange (FX) interventions have always been an important component of central bank policy in emerging and developing economies. Beyond the

---

[1] Printed with permission of *Open Economies Review* (2015) 26(1), 81–108.
[2] See Curdia and Woodford (2011), and Gertler and Karadi (2011) for a model of the credit policy of the central bank.

accumulation of reserves to achieve a desired level, several surveys covering a large number of emerging markets (EM) document a wide recourse to interventions to limit exchange rate volatility or preserve competitiveness (BIS, 2005 and IMF, 2011, among others). This is clearly observed in the last few years, both pre- and post-crisis. EMs employed massive interventions to dampen currency appreciation during the period from 2007 to mid-2008 (Adler and Tovar, 2011). Later, when emerging currencies came under selling pressure, many central banks sold FX to control the speed of depreciation. In 2010—with a gradual return of capital inflows to emerging markets—central banks once again started accumulating FX reserves.[3] In addition, many of the emerging markets that intervene in their FX market also steer short-term interest rates to influence economic activity and communicate policy.

The main contribution of this chapter is the extension of a standard inflation targeting New Keynesian small open economy model to include FX interventions as an independent central bank instrument. Our framework adds to the standard New Keynesian model: (i) a rule for FX interventions operating alongside interest rate policy; (ii) balance sheets effects of intervention policies, and (iii) the possible coexistence of interest rate-based inflation targeting with a managed float or even a fixed exchange rate.

We focus on sterilized interventions, i.e., purchases of FX reserves that involve an offsetting operation, e.g., an issuance of central bank securities, such that the short-term interest rate is not affected (all else equal). For sterilized interventions to serve as a separate instrument of monetary policy, alongside interest rate policy, they must operate through a different channel. The independent channel through which interventions operate stems from the portfolio approach to exchange rate determination.

The intuition is the following. A sterilized intervention, in which the central bank issues a security to fund the purchase of FX reserves, increases the holdings of local currency-denominated assets by the domestic financial system. Holding net foreign liabilities constant, the increase in reserves requires an increase in the country's external borrowing (or a reduction in external assets), which in our model takes place through an increase in the foreign currency-denominated liabilities of the financial sector. As a result of the sterilized intervention, the financial system's exposure to exchange rate risk has therefore increased, which leads to an increase in the risk premia required for banks to hold domestic assets. Since the central bank controls short-term rates, the higher risk premia are manifest in a more depreciated nominal (and hence real) exchange rate. Note that this channel is different from the traditional interest rate channel of monetary policy, which depends crucially on the degree of nominal rigidities in the economy. The effectiveness of sterilized interventions depends instead on the degree to which they can influence risk premia.

---

[3] Even central banks in several developed countries (including Switzerland, Australia, and Israel, among others) embarked on regular interventions, as a part of their efforts to stabilize domestic financial conditions. See Reserve Bank of Australia (2008), Bank of Israel (2009), and Swiss National Bank (2008).

The existence of multiple instruments (interventions, interest rates) and channels increases the range of central bank policy, e.g., it allows for the combination of inflation targeting (IT) regimes with some degree of exchange rate management. The former can be implemented via interest rates and the latter via interventions. We use our expanded framework to study these hybrid regimes, relative to standard frameworks (pure IT, interest rate-based pegs), and focus on two external shocks: shocks to international financial conditions and shocks to the terms of trade. We also assess the implications of these regimes for welfare.

We find that there can be advantages to hybrid regimes, though much depends on the types of shocks, and the strength (and specific modelling) of the balance sheet effects. For instance, in the case of a shock to foreign interest rates, we illustrate the contrasting performance of exchange rate pegs maintained by interest rates and by interventions. In the former case, monetary policy has to follow foreign interest rates in order to keep the exchange rate unchanged, which has strong and negative implications for the rest of the economy. In the latter, FX interventions can potentially insulate the domestic interest rates from such pressures by acting instead on the interest rate wedge in the financial system. This insulating property makes hybrid regimes superior to the other regimes we consider, including pure forms of inflation targeting in which the authorities do not intervene.

In the case of shocks to the terms of trade, however, intervention policies can be counterproductive if they delay the necessary nominal and real exchange rate adjustment. Output will be more volatile as a result, and welfare will be lower. This is more likely to be the case with policies that target a nominal exchange rate level, as opposed to intervention policies that attempt to reduce exchange rate volatility ('leaning against the wind'). In addition, the costs of delaying adjustment increases as terms of trade shocks have more persistent effects. Much of the challenge of intervention policy is therefore to understand the nature of the (external) shocks facing the economy.

From a modelling perspective, an important insight from our analysis is that it matters a great deal whether sterilized interventions affect premia on all domestic assets (including the rates that matter for private sector decisions, such as lending rates) or only the premia of government/central bank debt. In the latter case, interventions will lose their effectiveness, e.g., in the case of a foreign interest rate shock, since they cannot insulate domestic lending conditions from external financial conditions.

The work presented in this chapter coincides with work by Ostry et al. (2012). These authors also argue that monetary policy in emerging markets is best characterized as having two targets (inflation and exchange rates) and two instruments (short-term interest rates and sterilized FX interventions), and that such regimes are preferable when deviations of exchange rates from medium-run values are costly.

The rest of the chapter is organized as follows. The next section describes the pitfalls of standard approaches to modelling exchange rate targeting by central banks. We then introduce our model. We illustrate and contrast various exchange rate/monetary policy regimes using model simulations, including by assessing performance from a welfare perspective, and discuss limits of intervention policy. The final section concludes.

2 EXCHANGE RATE TARGETING AND EXCHANGE RATE INTERVENTION: TWO UNRELATED LITERATURES

2.1 The Exchange Rate Targeting Literature

Much of the literature on the role of the exchange rate in monetary policy is concerned with investigating 'dirty' inflation targeting—a combination of inflation targeting with some degree of exchange rate targeting. The focus is typically on whether including the exchange rate in the interest rate rule helps achieve better macroeconomic outcomes (Taylor, 2001; Ravenna and Natalucci, 2002; and Roger et al., 2009).

While there is little theoretical support for targeting the exchange rate in developed economies, the situation is somewhat more complex for emerging markets. Several features of emerging markets have been analysed: financially vulnerable or dollarized economies (Moron and Winkelried, 2005; Batini et al., 2007), uncertainty about the policy transmission (Leitemo and Soderstrom, 2005), the role of policy credibility and expectations formation (Roger et al., 2009), or structural features such as high productivity growth or limited recourse to intertemporal substitution (Ravenna and Natalucci, 2002 and Roger et al., 2009).

Despite these complications the literature finds limited support for targeting the exchange rate, and emphasizes the significant risks involved. For instance, Roger et al. (2009) conclude that having the exchange rate in the interest rate rule may reduce the volatility of the exchange rate, the interest rate, and the trade balance, but at the cost of higher inflation and output volatility, especially if the economy is exposed to demand and cost-push shocks. They also note that any benefits tend to disappear with high degrees of exchange rate targeting.

Monetary policy is modelled in this literature as follows:

$$i = \bar{i} + a(\pi - \pi^T) + \delta\hat{y} + \chi\Upsilon, \tag{1}$$

where i denotes the nominal interest rate, $\bar{i}$ is the neutral or natural level of the former, π is the rate of inflation and $\hat{y}$ is the output gap in per cent of trend or potential output.[4] The superscript T denotes a target level for that variable. The term Υ specifies exchange rate targeting behavior. It can have a number of functional forms; Roger et al. (2009) cast it in real terms as:

$$\Upsilon = log(q) - \eta log(q_{-1}),$$

where q is the real exchange rate (the price of the foreign consumption basket relative to the domestic consumption basket). The real exchange rate is defined as $q = P^*S/P$, where S is the nominal exchange rate (the local currency price of foreign currency), and (P^*, P) denote the foreign and domestic price levels, respectively. The addition of Υ to the standard Taylor rule allows a response to

---

[4] Upper-case variables denote nominal variables in levels, while lower-case variables denote real variables or nominal rates such as inflation and interest rates. A 'hat' (*) denotes a log-deviation from the steady state.

real exchange rate 'misalignments' (when $\eta = 0$), as well as real exchange rate fluctuations (when $\eta = 1$).

Exchange rate targeting can also be cast in nominal terms:

$$\Upsilon = \eta log(S/S_{-1}) + (1 - \eta)log(S/S^T). \tag{2}$$

Less flexible exchange rate regimes are represented by a high χ and small η, as in Parrado (2004a) or Ravenna and Natalucci (2002).[5]

These approaches are unsatisfactory for several reasons:

- Sterilized interventions are the main instrument used by many emerging market central banks to affect the exchange rate. While some central banks may have explicit exchange rate objectives in mind when setting interest rates, that is not their main—or at least their only—instrument for influencing the exchange rate.

- In these models, including the exchange rate in the Taylor rule reduces the central bank autonomy in setting the interest rate. In the extreme case, fixing the exchange rate through the Taylor rule implies the interest rate becomes exogenous to domestic developments.[6] For instance, setting χ in (2) to infinity makes the Taylor rule collapse to $S = S^T$, and the interest rate is then determined through the uncovered interest rate parity (UIP) condition. By contrast, in practice many central banks manage exchange rates precisely to increase their autonomy and room for policy manoeuvring.

- It is clear that central banks resorting to exchange rate management hope to engage different transmission channels working through balance sheet effects and FX liquidity, and potentially also to target several objectives simultaneously (BIS, 2005). Yet in the standard models, the interest rates affect the economy, as usual, by influencing the nominal exchange rate (through UIP) and the consumption/investment behaviour of the private sector (through the Euler equation). There is no separate transmission channel involved in exchange rate targeting.

A few authors introduce a separate explicit rule for the exchange rate directly into their models. For instance, Parrado (2004b)—in his analysis of monetary policy in Singapore—suggests replacing the interest rate rule by a rule specified directly in terms of the exchange rate:

$$log(S) = \rho log(S_{-1}) - (1 - \rho)(\alpha(\pi - \pi^T) + \delta\hat{y}).$$

As with the previous specification, however, this approach leaves the interest rates to be determined by external developments via the UIP condition.

---

[5] A properly defined steady state requires perfect consistency between nominal targets. In the absence of a trend in the real exchange rate, so that the equilibrium real exchange rate is $\bar{q}$, π^T and S^T must satisfy the following identity: $log(S^T/S_{-1}^T) = log(\bar{q}/\bar{q}) + log((P/P_{-1})^T) - log((P^*/P_{-1}^*)^T) = \pi^T - \pi^{*T}$.

[6] The interest rate reflects domestic shocks only to the extent that the country's external risk premium responds endogenously to these shocks, e.g., by being sensitive to movements in the current account or in the country's net foreign asset position.

2.2 The FX Intervention Literature

The large literature on sterilized interventions mostly predates the New Keynesian models used to analyse inflation targeting in recent years. The portfolio-balance approach to exchange rate determination (Kouri, 1976; Henderson and Rogoff, 1982) embraced a potentially important role for sterilized intervention to affect the exchange rate, by allowing changes in the asset composition of portfolios to influence risk premia. This strand of work in open economy macroeconomics generally lost out to the assumption of perfect asset substitutability, going back to Dornbusch (1976).[7]

One reason why the portfolio balance approach fell out of favour was the difficulty in micro-founding the link between risk premia and the gross supply of public sector assets, from a general-equilibrium perspective. The strongest critique of sterilized foreign exchange interventions along this line is by Backus and Kehoe (1989): with the help of a general-equilibrium monetary model, they demonstrate that certain types of sterilized interventions—those that hold the time paths of fiscal and standard monetary policy constant—have no effect on private sector decisions (and hence on premia). Interventions that are associated with changes in fiscal and monetary policy do have real effects, but not because of the intervention itself.

However, Kumhof (2010) shows that it is theoretically possible to generate imperfect substitutability between various kinds of assets in a general equilibrium setting. He does so by introducing government spending shocks in a small open economy model. These shocks do not elicit a corresponding increase in taxes, ether now or in the future, so that a surprise nominal depreciation (inflation) is required to clear the government's budget constraint (via seignorage revenue). The exchange rate/inflation volatility that results from these shocks increases the risk to the private sector from holding local currency-denominated government debt. By changing the gross outstanding stock of such debt, sterilized interventions affect the private sector's exposure to exchange rate risk and therefore influence the interest rate premium required in equilibrium to clear asset markets. This mechanism is sufficient for sterilized interventions to affect the exchange rate.

There is a large empirical literature on whether sterilized interventions affect the exchange rate. A constant theme is the fundamental identification problems: the interventions presumably are motivated by events in the exchange rate market, confounding efforts to measure the effects of the interventions per se. Finding good instruments (variables correlated with the propensity to intervene but not with the exchange rate itself) is a serious challenge.

Event studies have in many cases found significant if often small effects. A more recent survey (Cavusoglu, 2010) concludes that interventions have a significant but short-lasting effect on exchange rates, with only a few studies looking at the effects on longer movements, and few clear results. For advanced economies, Fatum and Hutchison (2003) find that interventions do indeed affect the exchange rate in Germany and the US, while in the case of Japan, Fatum and Hutchison (2010) find that only sporadic and relatively infrequent interventions are effective. More recent studies have looked at emerging markets. Domac and Mendoza

---

[7] Blanchard et al. (2005) propose a revival of the portfolio approach, however.

(2004) (Mexico and Turkey), Guimaraes and Karacadag (2004) (Mexico), Gersl and Holub (2006) (Czech Republic), Egert (2007) (several central and Eastern European countries), and Kamil (2008) (Colombia) find some evidence that sterilized interventions affect the level of the exchange rate; Tuna (2011) (Turkey) find negative results. Adler and Tovar (2011) find some evidence that interventions can affect the pace of appreciation, particularly in countries that have a relatively closed capital account.

Beyond this evidence, we give some weight to the views of many practitioners, particularly in emerging markets and developing countries, that FX interventions can be effective (Neely, 2011; BIS, 2005; see also Canales-Kriljenko, 2003). Particularly for emerging and frontier markets, and a fortiori low-income countries that are just beginning to enter global capital markets, it seems plausible that assets are imperfect substitutes and that markets are relatively 'thin', in that changes in supplies can have substantial effects on relative prices. In what follows, we examine the implications of these assumptions.

3 THE MODEL

In this section we describe the model. Before proceeding to the optimization problem faced by various agents, it is helpful to provide a broad overview of the sectoral balance sheets, which are summarized in Table 13.1 below.

Table 13.1. Overview of Sectoral Balance Sheets

Central Bank	
F	O

Financial Sector	
O	B
L	

Households	
NS	L

The central bank keeps a stock of FX reserves, F, and issues its own securities, O, held by the financial sector. In addition, the commercial banks provide loans to households, L, and borrow from abroad, B. Borrowing by households is backed by the discounted sum of future expected net savings, NS.

All items are expressed in the domestic currency. F and B are denominated in foreign currency, while all the other assets are denominated in domestic currency. The economy is cashless and a net debtor, because the country's net foreign liabilities (the difference between gross foreign debt and gross foreign assets) are equal to the household debt L ($L = B - F$), which is positive.[8]

---

[8] We chose to use as simplistic balance sheets as allowed by the requirements of our analysis. In doing so, we disregarded many sometimes-important practical aspects, sacrificing realism.

3.1 Central Bank Behaviour

Every period, the central bank receives interest on its stock of reserves at an exogenously determined rate i^* (compounded over the period). It pays interest i (also compounded) on the stock of its own securities held by the financial sector (O_{-1}, issued last period) and transfers its cash-flow (CF^{CB}) to households:

$$CF^{CB} = \frac{S}{S_{-1}} F_{-1} \exp(i^*) - O_{-1} \exp(i) - F + O.$$

The central bank decides on the level of reserves and the interest rate it pays on its own securities. The central bank adjusts the stock of FX reserves as follows:

$$\log\left(\frac{F}{P}\right) = \rho_f \log\left(\frac{F}{P}\right)_{-1} + (1 - \rho_f)\left(\log\left(\frac{\bar{F}}{P}\right) - \omega\log\left(\frac{S}{S^T}\right) - \vartheta\log\left(\frac{S}{S_{-1}}\right)\right), \quad (3)$$

where $\left(\frac{\bar{F}}{P}\right)$ is the steady state real level of reserves.

If $\omega \to \infty$, the central bank can keep the exchange rate on its target level at all times by instantly adjusting the level of reserves; if $\omega = 0$, it will ignore exchange rate movements and keep FX reserves at some desired level. The last term $\vartheta log(\frac{S}{S_{-1}})$ captures exchange smoothing behaviour—so called 'leaning against the wind' interventions, while $\rho_f log(\frac{F}{P})_{-1}$ captures the degree of persistence in reserve movements.

For the sake of simplicity we ignore the lower bound on reserves. We implicitly assume the volume of reserves implied by rule (3) is always positive, or if it entails a negative number, we assume the country can receive external financing, e.g., from official sources like the IMF, for this purpose. We return to the lower bound on reserves in our discussion of the limits of interventions.

The interest rate paid on central bank securities follows an interest rate rule similar to (1):

$$i = \rho i_{-1} + (1 - \rho)\left(+ a(\pi - \pi^T) + \delta\hat{y} + \chi\Upsilon\right).$$

where Υ is defined as in (2).

For instance, our financial sector runs an unhedged short position in FX, which would not be allowed by prudential regulation. Our households are net borrowers, rather than savers. And we assume a central bank with a negative net domestic asset position, which is a necessary condition if the central bank holds a stock of foreign reserves but does not issue reserve money (in a cashless world). However, our exposition can be generalized. For instance, firms borrowing from the financial sector can be added to make households net savers. The financial sector can run separate balance sheets in FX and local currencies, thus assuming partial financial dollarization. And introducing reserve money can make the net domestic asset position of the central bank positive. For the purposes of our exposition these are unnecessary complications, though. What matters is that sterilized interventions affect the degree of exchange rate risk faced by the domestic financial system, which does not depend on whether the central bank's net domestic assets are positive or negative. In a separate appendix (available upon request), we show how reserve money can be added, but leave the analysis of interventions in the context of financial dollarization for future work.

Note that our treatment of central bank instruments is not symmetric: for the exchange rate we track movements in the central bank balance sheet, while for interest rates we do not.[9]

3.2 Financial Sector Behaviour

The behaviour of perfectly competitive financial sector firms (owned by households) is described by the following arbitrage relationships:

$$\exp(i) = \exp(i^*)\frac{S_{+1}}{S}\Omega_O\left(\frac{F}{P}\right), \Omega_O'(F/P) > 0 \tag{4}$$

$$\exp(j) = \exp(i). \tag{5}$$

Condition (4) postulates the uncovered interest parity (UIP) condition as an arbitrage between the interest rate on central bank bills and an exchange rate-adjusted foreign rate, augmented with a spread $\Omega_O(.)$ that is increasing in the stock of FX reserves (deflated by the price level P). As the rate i is defined by the Taylor rule, (4) defines the exchange rate expectations (for a given spread). Condition (5) implies loans and central bank securities are perfect substitutes.

The most important feature is that the UIP spread is *increasing* in the level of reserves (F), which is central to the FX intervention mechanism. As discussed in the introduction, the intuition is that a sterilized intervention increases the stock of local currency assets held by banks ($O + L$) and, all else equal, requires a corresponding increase in foreign borrowing B. This increase in banks' balance sheets raises their exposure to exchange rate risk (which is not modelled explicitly), since $O + L$ is denominated in local currency and B is denominated in foreign currency. In the face of this increased exposure, banks will demand a higher return for holding local currency denominated assets. Since $F = O$, it follows that an increase in reserves increases the premium on domestic assets.

This mechanism merits three remarks. First, the arbitrage conditions in (4, 5) are imposed rather than derived from micro-foundations. They are inspired by the results in Kumhof (2010) mentioned earlier.[10] Recent work on two-country

---

[9] We analyse the balance sheet operations required to implement interest rate policy in a separate appendix (available upon request). This asymmetry reflects central bank practices as well as some underlying economics. Exchange rate targets are analogous to targets on long-term interest rates, in that both imply setting prices for assets that yield capital gains or losses if prices change and hence that are more subject to speculative attacks than overnight rates (see Woodford, 2005 for the case of long rates). This implies that achieving these targets exactly, as represented by an infinite ω in (3) may strain central bank balance sheets and be difficult to achieve. We return to this point later. For current purposes, however, the implication is that many central banks conduct quantity-based operations aimed at achieving targets for the exchange rate without necessarily hitting the targets exactly. Similarly, recent efforts at 'quantitative easing' in developed countries aim to influence but not precisely target long interest rates.

[10] In the working paper version of this chapter, we studied whether such a relation could be derived from a simple portfolio allocation problem as well as a bank cost function that depended on banks' holdings of central bank securities and loans. Although these setups went some way toward generating

general equilibrium models go in a similar direction, though in setups that are different from ours. First, Canzoneri et al. (2013) show how a broadly similar relation can arise when foreign and domestic bonds are imperfect substitutes in each country's transaction's technology. Second, Gabaix and Maggiori (2014) introduce financiers which bear the risks resulting from international imbalances in the demand for financial assets, which then leads them to change their compensation for holding currency risk.

Second, the above argument suggests that the premium should depend on the total stock of domestic assets $(L + O)$, as opposed to only the stock of central bank securities (O). This shortcut is not an issue. As will be made clear below, households' financing needs determine the economy's stock of loans L, which implies that the central bank reserve's policy determines the overall size of the financial sector balance sheet: controlling O is equivalent to controlling $L + O$.[11]

A third and related issue is that the perfect substitutability of the two domestic assets has important consequences. As part of the model simulations we will explore an alternative specification in which loans and foreign assets are perfect substitutes, up to a constant risk premium. This implies replacing 5) with the following:

$$\exp(j) = \exp(i^*)\frac{S_{+1}}{S}\Omega_L.$$

Under this specification sterilized interventions will only affect the premia for central bank securities, but will not directly affect the pricing equation for loans. As a result, the premia between loans and central bank securities will vary as a result of the sterilized interventions:

$$\exp(j) = \exp(i)\frac{\Omega_L}{\Omega_O\left(\frac{L}{P}\right)}.$$

3.3 Households' Behaviour

The household's utility function is of the form $U = ln(c) - \psi(1 + \phi)^{-1}n^{1+\phi}$. Agents maximize the expected discounted sum of utility $E_t[\sum_{t=0}^{\infty}\beta^t U_t]$, over consumption (c), labour supply (n), and the nominal demand for loans (L), subject to the budget constraint:

$$Pc - L = -\exp(j_{-1})L_{-1} + Wn + CF^{CB} + \Pi - P\Psi(L/P),$$

$$\Psi'(L/P) > 0, \Psi''(L/P) > 0. \tag{6}$$

---

risk premia that were sensitive to holding of various assets, their functional forms differed considerably from the simple relations presented in the text.

[11] If the premium depends on the total stock of domestic assets, then the intervention rule in (3) can be specified in terms of $L + O$, and the model-based analysis would be the same.

W denotes nominal wages, while Π is the total amount of profits households receive from the firms and the financial sector. $\Psi(L/P)$ are quadratic adjustment costs, which provide a mechanism for determining the steady state values of real consumption and net foreign assets, similar to other mechanisms in the literature (see Schmitt-Grohe and Uribe, 2003).

First-order conditions are as follows:

$$\lambda P = \frac{1}{c},$$

$$\psi n^{\phi} = \frac{W}{P}\frac{1}{c} = \frac{w}{c},$$

$$\lambda\left(1 - \varrho\left(\frac{L}{P}\right)\right) = \beta e^{j}E[\lambda_{+1}],$$

where λ is the Lagrange multiplier associated with the budget constraint, and $\varrho(L/P) = \Psi'(L/P)$ introduces a credit-sensitive wedge between the interest and the discount factor in the Euler condition.

Consumption is an aggregate of non-traded goods c_n and imports c_m:

$$c = A c_n^{\omega_n} c_m^{1-\omega_n},$$

where ω_n is the weight on non-traded goods, and $A = \omega_n^{-\omega_n}(1 - \omega_n)^{-(1-\omega_n)}$.

Cost minimization results in the following demand functions:

$$c_n = \omega_n\left(\frac{P_n}{P}\right)^{-1}c = \omega_n p_n^{-1}c, \; c_m = \left(1 - \omega_n\right)\left(\frac{P_m}{P}\right)^{-1}c = (1 - \omega_n)p_m^{-1}c.$$

P_n and P_m denote prices for C_n and C_m, respectively, with $P = P_n^{\omega_n}P_m^{(1-\omega_n)}$. p_n and p_m denote relative prices (deflated by the CPI), with $p_n^{\omega_n}p_m^{(1-\omega_n)} = 1$. CPI inflation π is given by:

$$\pi = \omega_n(\log(P_n) - \log(P_{n-1})) + (1 - \omega_n)(\log(P_m) - \log(P_{m-1}))$$
$$= \omega_n\pi_n + (1 - \omega_n)\pi_m.$$

3.4 Non-Traded Producers

There is a continuum of firms in the non-traded sector, each having a monopoly on the production of a variety of the non-traded good and facing a demand curve with elasticity $\varpi = \mu/(1 - \mu)$. Firms hire labour to produce their good, with a production function that has decreasing returns to scale, and benefit from an employment subsidy ι. Cost minimization results in the following labour demand condition:

$$\gamma MC_n c_n = n_n W(1 - \iota) \leftrightarrow \gamma mc_n c_n = n_n w(1 - \iota_n)$$

where γ is labour share in the non-traded sector, MC_n (mc_n) denotes the representative firm's nominal (real) marginal cost, and n_n is the volume of labour employed in the sector. Firms face price adjustments à la Rotemberg (1982), modified to allow for indexation. Profit maximization results in the following Phillips curve:

$$\pi_n - \pi_{n-1} = \beta(\pi_{n+1} - \pi_n) + \xi_n \log\left(\frac{p_n^{flex}}{p_n}\right),$$

where p_n^{flex} is a notional flexible (relative) price level

$$p_n^{flex} = \mu mc_n.$$

Finally, equilibrium in the non-traded sector requires

$$c_n = A_n n_n^{\gamma}.$$

3.5 Exporters

Exporters are price takers, with the price of their product set in international markets, and have the same production function as non-traded firms. Profit maximization results in the following export supply curve:

$$P_x y_x = W n_x \leftrightarrow p_x y_x = w n_x,$$

where:

$$p_x = \frac{P_x}{P} = \frac{P_x^* S}{P} = \frac{P_x^* SP^*}{P^* P} = p_x^* q,$$

$$y_x = A_x n_x^{\gamma}.$$

3.6 Importers

Monopolistically competitive firms buy foreign goods and sell them in the domestic market, facing demand curves with elasticity ϖ. As with firms in the non-traded sector they also receive a subsidy ι for every unit of imports they acquire, and are also subject to nominal rigidities. Profit maximization leads to the following conditions:

$$p_m^{flex} = \mu mc_m,$$

$$mc_m = q(1 - \iota),$$

$$\pi_m - \pi_{m-1} = \beta(\pi_{m+1} - \pi_m) + \xi_m \log\left(\frac{p_m^{flex}}{p_m}\right).$$

3.7 Labour Market Equilibrium

Equilibrium in the labour market requires that demand for labour in the export and non-traded sectors equals labour supplied by households:

$$n = n_n + n_x.$$

3.8 Real GDP

We define real GDP as the weighted sum of non-traded consumption and exports, using steady state relative prices $(\bar{p}_n, \bar{p}_x)$:

$$y = \bar{p}_n c_n + \bar{p}_x y_x.$$

3.9 Balance of Payments

Combining the budget constraints of households and firms yields the country's balance of payments:

$$L = L_{-1} e^{(i^*_{-1} + \pi_s)} + (SP^* C_m - P_x Y_x),$$

where $\pi_S = log(S) - log(S_{-1})$. Deflating by the CPI and steady state output, we obtain a real measure of the balance of payments:

$$l = l_{-1} e^{(i^*_{-1} + \pi_s - \pi)} + \bar{y}^{-1}(q c_m - p_x y_x),$$

where $l = (L/P)/\bar{y}$ and $p_x = P_x/P$.

3.10 Rest of the World

We define a trade weighted measure of the real terms of trade $tot = p_x^{*1-\eta}/p_m^{*1-\eta-\overline{tb}}$, where $1 - \eta$ denotes the steady state share of exports in GDP and $\overline{tb}$ denotes the steady state trade surplus, also as a share of GDP. tot follows an autoregressive progress:

$$log(tot) = \rho_{tot} log(tot_{-1}) + \epsilon_{tot}.$$

Finally, foreign interest rates also follow an autoregressive process:

$$i^* = \rho_{i^*} i^*_{-1} + (1 - \rho_{i^*})\bar{i}^* + \epsilon_{i^*}.$$

4 STEADY STATE, LOG-LINEARIZATION, AND CALIBRATION

To characterize the steady state and log-linearized version of the model we first specify the functional forms of the premium (Ω_O) and the quadratic loan adjustment cost faced by consumers (Ψ). Ψ is given by $\Psi = \frac{1}{2}\varrho^*\left(\frac{L}{P} - \left(\frac{\bar{L}}{\bar{P}}\right)\right)^2$, which implies the following form for $\varrho\left(\frac{L}{P}\right)$:

$$\varrho\left(\frac{L}{P}\right) = \varrho^*\left(\frac{L}{P} - \left(\frac{\bar{L}}{\bar{P}}\right)\right) = \varrho^*\bar{y}\left(\frac{L}{P\bar{y}} \frac{1}{\bar{y}} - \left(\frac{\bar{L}}{P\bar{y}}\right)\right) = \varrho^*\bar{y}(l - \bar{l}).$$

l denotes the real value of loans (in units of consumption) relative to steady state output ($\bar{y}$, to be defined below). Ω_O has the following functional form:

$$\log(\Omega_O) = \Omega_O\left(\frac{F}{P} - \left(\frac{\bar{F}}{\bar{P}}\right)\right) = \Omega_O\bar{y}\left(\frac{F}{P\bar{y}} - \left(\frac{\bar{F}}{P\bar{y}}\right)\right) = \Omega_O\bar{y}(f - \bar{f}),$$

with f denoting the real value of FX reserves (in real terms) relative to steady state output.

4.1 Steady State

At steady state $\log(\Omega_O) = \Psi = \varrho = 0$. Subsidies are such that $\iota = (\mu - 1)/\mu$. With the exception of real wages, all relative prices and aggregate consumption are set to one:

$$\bar{c} = \bar{P}_m = \bar{P}_n = \bar{q} = \bar{P}_x^* = 1,$$

which implies $c_n = \omega_n$ and $c_m = 1 - \omega_n$. Given the net borrowing condition of the country ($\bar{l}>0$), exports must be greater than imports at steady state. From the balance of payments we obtain $y_x = 1 - \omega + \bar{l}(\beta^{-1} - 1)(1 - \bar{l}(\beta^{-1} - 1))^{-1} = 1 - \omega_n + \zeta$, which implies $\bar{y} = 1 + \zeta$. It follows that the share of non-traded goods in GDP (η) is given by $\eta = \omega_n/(1 + \zeta)$, while the trade balance ($\bar{tb}$, in per cent of GDP) is given by $\bar{tb} = \zeta/(1 + \zeta)$.

Real wages equal the labour share in production $\bar{w} = \gamma$, whereas employment is given by $\bar{n}_n = \omega_n, \bar{n}_x = 1 - \omega_n + \zeta, \bar{n} = 1 + \zeta$. The above steady state is made possible by the following choice of parameters: $\psi = \gamma(1 + \zeta)^{-\phi}$, $A_n = \omega_n^{1-\gamma}$, and $A_x = (1 - \omega_n + \zeta)^{1-\gamma}$. The inflation target π^T is zero, which implies: $\bar{i} = \bar{j} = \bar{i}^* = \beta^{-1}$. The starting value for S is $S^T = 1$. Depending on the specification of monetary policy, this starting value may constitute a steady state value for S, in the sense that the economy will converge back to S^T. Otherwise, S will drift.

Table 13.2. Calibration of the Model

Parameter	Value	Parameter	Value
ϕ	0.5	ξ, ξ_m	0.1,0.5
β	0.9975	ρ_i^*	0.8
ϱ^*	0.01	ρ_{tot} (temporary)	0.8
ω_n	0.5	ρ_{tot} (permanent)	0.9999
a	1.5	μ	1.2
δ	0	γ	0.7
ρ	0.7	ρ_f	0.7
Ω_0	0.1	π^T	0
$\bar{l}$	1	$\bar{f}$	1
$\bar{tb} \approx \zeta$	0.0025	η	0.4987

4.2 Calibration

The calibration of the model is presented in Table 13.2. We do not have a specific country in mind; instead our calibration is meant to capture a prototypical small open developing economy. The value of β implies real interest rates in annual terms are 1 per cent. The choice of ω_n implies exports constitute about 50 per cent of GDP. The value of the labour share γ and the inverse of the labour supply elasticity ϕ are broadly standard, as well as the parameters that describe nominal rigidities (ξ, ξ_m) and market power (μ). With the exception of the degree of exchange rate targeting (which we discuss in the next section), the parameters in the Taylor rule (ρ, a, δ) are also consistent with values in the literature. We discuss the calibration of the intervention rule in the next section.

At steady state, reserves add up to a quarter of annual GDP, or about 6 months of imports which is a simple metric often used to assess reserve adequacy, e.g., at the IMF. Loans by households are also equal to 25 per cent of GDP, which is at the lower end of the ratio of credit to GDP found in developing countries. The value of Ω_0 (0.1) implies an increase in reserve holdings of 1 per cent of GDP raises the risk premium by 10 basis points. We also explore the implications of much lower values of Ω_0 (0.01). Finally, the value of ϱ^* is very small: an increase in loans of 1 per cent of GDP drives a wedge between lending rates and the household's discount factor of one basis point. As already mentioned, this parameter only serves to ensure that consumption (and loans in real terms) eventually returns to its steady state value.

4.3 The Log-Linearized Model

The log-linearized version of the model is summarized in Box 13.1. All variables are presented in log-deviations from steady state, except for loans and reserves in real terms, which are presented as level deviations in per cent of steady state output ($\hat{x} = \frac{(x-\bar{x})}{\bar{y}}$, for $x = L/P, F/P$), and interest rates which are presented as level deviations ($\hat{z} = z - \bar{z}$, for $z = i = i^* = j$).

Box 13.1. The log-linearized model

The balance of payments, in real terms, relative to steady state output: $\hat{l} = \beta^{-1}\hat{l}_{-1}$
$+ \bar{l}\beta^{-1}(\hat{i}^{*}_{-1} + \hat{q} - \hat{q}_{-1}) + (1 - \eta - tb)(\hat{q} + \hat{c}_m) - (1 - \eta)(\hat{p}_x + \hat{y}_x)$

Demand for imports: $\hat{c}_m = -\hat{p}_m + \hat{c}$

Demand for non-traded goods: $\hat{c}_n = \frac{(1-\omega_n)}{\omega_n}\hat{p}_m + \hat{c}$

Euler equation: $\hat{c} = \hat{c}_{+1} - (\hat{j} - \hat{\pi}_{+1}) - (1 + \zeta)\varrho\hat{l}$

Labour supply: $\phi\gamma^{-1}\hat{y} = \hat{w} - \hat{c}$

Phillips curve for non-traded goods: $\hat{\pi}_n = \frac{1}{1+\beta}\hat{\pi}_{n-1} + \frac{\beta}{1+\beta}\hat{\pi}_{n+1} + \frac{\xi}{1+\beta}(\hat{w} + \frac{1-\gamma}{\gamma}\hat{c}_n + \frac{1-\omega_n}{\omega_n}\hat{p}_m)$

Phillips curve for imports: $\hat{\pi}_m = \frac{1}{1+\beta}\hat{\pi}_{m-1} + \frac{\beta}{1+\beta}\hat{\pi}_{m+1} + \frac{\xi_m}{1+\beta}(\hat{q} - \hat{p}_m)$

Inflation: $\hat{\pi} = \omega_n\hat{\pi}_m + (1 - \omega_n)\hat{\pi}_n$

Export supply curve: $\hat{y}_x = \frac{\gamma}{1-\gamma}(\hat{w} - \hat{p}_x)$

Relative price of imports: $\Delta\hat{p}_m = \hat{\pi}_m - \hat{\pi}$

Aggregate output: $\hat{y} = \eta\hat{c}_n + (1 - \eta)\hat{y}_x$

Uncovered interest parity with FX interventions: $\hat{i} = \hat{i}^{*} + \hat{q}_{+1} - \hat{q} + \hat{\pi}_{+1} + \Omega_0(1 + \zeta)\hat{f}$

Lending rates: $\hat{j} = \hat{i}$

Interest rate rule: $\hat{i} = \rho_{t-1} + (1 - \rho)(\alpha\hat{\pi} + \delta\hat{y} + \chi\hat{S})$

Intervention rule: $\hat{f} = \rho_f\hat{f}_{-1} - (1 - \rho_f)(\omega\hat{S} + \vartheta(\hat{S} - \hat{S}_{-1}))$

The real exchange rate: $\hat{q} = \hat{q}_{-1} + \hat{S} - \hat{S}_{-1} - \hat{\pi}$

The relative price of exports: $\hat{p}_x = (1 - \eta)^{-1}\hat{tot} + \hat{q}$

Terms of trade: $\hat{tot} = \rho_{tot}\hat{tot}_{-1} + \epsilon_{tot}$

Foreign interest rates: $\hat{i}^{*} = \rho_{i*}\hat{i}^{*}_{-1} + \epsilon_{i*}$

5 SIMULATIONS

5.1 A Shock to Foreign Interest Rates

We now simulate the model when it is hit with a foreign interest rate shock ($e_{i^*} = 1$, i.e., a 100-basis point increase in foreign rates). We compare the model's response under four monetary policy settings: (i) pure inflation targeting (IT)/flexible exchange rate regime, in which the authorities care solely about inflation and do not target the exchange rate nor intervene in the FX market; (ii) fixed exchange rate regime via interest rates; (iii) fixed exchange rate regime via interventions; and (iv) managed float, in which the authorities lean against the wind but do not target a specific exchange rate level. The pure IT case will serve as a benchmark. For all four regimes, the exchange rate objective in the interest rate rule (Υ) is set as in equation (2) with $\eta = 0$. The implications of each regime for the parameterization of the Taylor rule (1) and the intervention rule (3) are set out in Table 13.3.

The choice of regimes merits three remarks. First, we pay special attention to the two alternative ways of fixing the nominal exchange rate (interest rates and intervention) to help understand the mechanisms involved. It must be stressed that these are somewhat extreme cases; in practice, central banks that peg the exchange rate typically use a combination of interventions and interest rate policy. Second, in the case of the intervention–based peg and the managed float, the authorities continue to use interest rates to target inflation, i.e., they are relying on two policy instruments instead of one. Third, in the case of the managed float, there is some persistence in reserve accumulation (as ρ_f is set to 0.7).

Table 13.3. Implications of Each Regime for the Parameterization of the Taylor Rule and the Intervention Rule

Regime/parameter	χ	ω	ϑ
IT pure float	0	0	0
Fixed via interest rate	Inf	0	0
Fixed via interventions	0	Inf	0
Managed float	0	0	6

Figure 13.1 presents the results. The IT case shows the basic challenges such a shock presents to the authorities: a rise in foreign rates pushes the domestic currency to depreciate, inducing inflation through import prices, but at the same time supporting the export sector. Under 'pure' IT, monetary policy will respond by raising nominal rates, somewhat offsetting the impact of the shock on the exchange rate and putting downward pressures on domestic consumption. The trade balance improves, as exports increase and imports decline following the real exchange rate depreciation and the tightening of policy. Despite the increase in the trade balance, the country's net foreign liabilities worsen (not shown) because of the higher interest rate burden.

Under IT, the nominal exchange does not return to its initial level. The rising price level resulting from this shock leads the currency to settle at a more depreciated level. The same is true for the managed float specification, as the central intervenes to smooth the pace of adjustment but does not target the exchange rate level. By contrast, under both types of peg the exchange rate stays at its original level.

Fixing the exchange rate via interest rates leads to a decline in inflation, at the cost of a sharper economic decline than in the pure IT case. The reason is that domestic interest rates must match the foreign interest rate increase. The large policy tightening contracts consumption and results in the large decline in inflation. The trade balance improves by more than under IT on account of the much larger policy-induced squeeze in imports. This greater impact of the external shock on the real economy is a well-known weakness of fixed exchange rate regimes, going back to Friedman (1953).

The macroeconomic impact of the shock looks considerably different when the authorities fix the exchange rate through interventions. The offsetting effect on the UIP premium allows the nominal exchange rate to stay constant, while also insulating domestic interest rates. The economy contracts slightly: the temporary increase in foreign interest rates increases the debt repayment burden for households, as they are net foreign debtors, which slightly raises the effective interest rates faced by households (in the Euler equation). Inflation and policy rates decrease somewhat as a result. Despite these effects, the impact of the shock is almost zero. Note that, since the real exchange rate barely depreciates (not shown), there is little boost to exports (and hence output). The insulation of the economy comes at the cost of a large sale of reserves (10 per cent of its stock in real terms, which given the calibration is also equal to 10 per cent of the economy's quarterly GDP at steady state).

The managed float shows the advantages of active exchange rate management. Interventions allow interest rates to stay lower than in the pure float or the

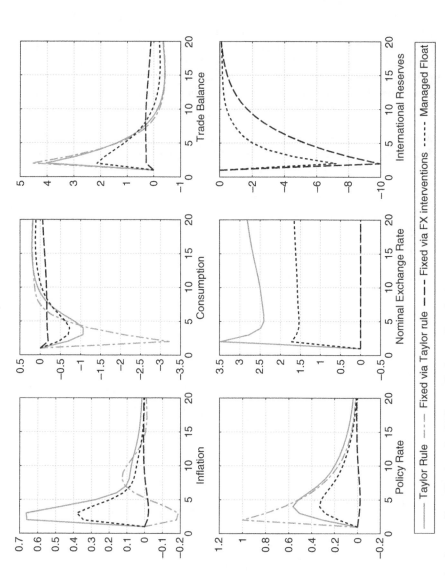

Figure 13.1. Foreign Interest Rate Shock under Different Exchange Rate Regimes

'Pure' IT (grey, solid line), fixed via interest rate rule (grey, dashed with dots), fixed via interventions (black, dashed), IT managed float (black, dotted). Units are percentage deviations from steady state.

interest-rate peg, thus reducing the impact on consumption. The managed float also allows for some exchange rate depreciation (at least temporarily), thus providing a short-term impulse to the export sector that is otherwise not available under fixed regimes. The decline in the stock of reserves is smaller and less persistent than under the intervention-based peg.

The simulations illustrate the costs of implementing a fixed exchange rate regime with interest rate policy alone. In the float case the rates increase *in order* to fight inflation pressures, while under the interest rate-based peg the rates increase *despite* a fall in inflation and in economic activity. Interventions, by contrast, give the policy rates room for manoeuvring in response to the (small) contraction of the economy. As a result, the economic impact is much smaller.

It is worth re-emphasizing that the channel through which interventions work is different from the traditional channel of monetary policy, which relies on nominal rigidities. This can be seen by simulating a version of the model in which nominal rigidities (in both the non-traded and import sector) are turned off, shown in Figure 13.2. The economy's response to the foreign interest rate

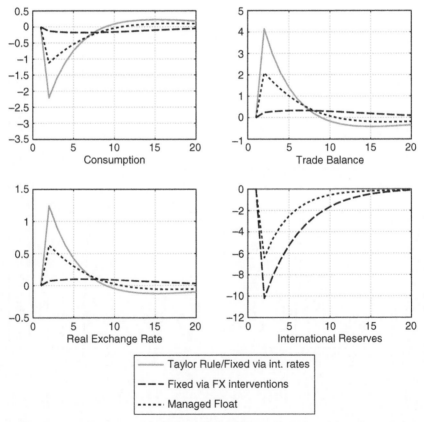

Figure 13.2. Foreign Interest Rate Shock under Different Exchange Rate Regimes, Flexible Prices

'Pure' IT and fixed via interest rates (grey, solid line), fixed via interventions (black, dashed), IT managed float (black, dotted). Units are percentage deviations from steady state.

shock is now identical under pure IT and under an interest rate-based peg, as the choice of nominal anchor has no real effects. Under both regimes, consumption declines as domestic real interest rates increase, and combined with the resulting real appreciation it leads to an improvement in the trade balance. Unlike these regimes, intervention policy does have real effects, as it influences interest rate premia and real decisions, and the choice of intervention policy matters. Moreover, the effects are broadly similar to the version of the model with nominal rigidities, which highlights the robustness of intervention policy to this particular mechanism.

The effect of interventions does depend on whether interventions affect premia on all domestic assets (central bank paper and loans) or only on the domestic asset whose gross supply is changing (central bank paper). To understand the importance of this assumption, we reintroduce nominal rigidities but replace the perfect substitutability between loans and central bank paper ($j = i$) with an alternative specification in which loans and foreign borrowing are perfect substitutes up to a constant premium ($j = i^* + \Delta \hat{S}_{+1} + log(\Omega_L)$), which implies ($j = i - log(\Omega_O(F/P)) + log(\Omega_L)$).[12] In this case, shown in Figure 13.3, the intervention-based peg delivers exactly the same result on consumption and other real variables as the interest rate-based peg. By selling reserves to maintain the peg, the central bank is increasing the premia on loans relative to central bank paper. Since the increase in the premia is proportional to the increase in foreign interest rates, lending rates (the only rates that matter for private sector decisions) increase by the same amount as foreign interest rates.

5.2 A Shock to the Terms of Trade

We now briefly discuss simulations of the model to a negative terms of trade shock ($e_{tot} = -1$, i.e., a worsening of 1 per cent), under the four policy regimes described above. We distinguish between a shock with temporary effects, in which the autoregressive coefficient for the terms of trade process (ρ_{tot}) is set to 0.8, and a shock with quasi-permanent effects ($\rho_{tot} = 0.999$). These simulations are shown in Figures 13.4 and 13.5, respectively.

Under IT a negative but temporary terms of trade shock triggers an immediate nominal and real depreciation, which helps offset the impact of the shock on exports. Output falls nonetheless. The shock lowers consumption because of the income effect, as overall demand for labour and hence wages decrease. The decline in consumption and the reallocation of labour from the exports sector to the non-traded sector generates a decline in inflation (despite the depreciation) which results in a decrease in the policy rate. Under a quasi-permanent shock, income effects are amplified, which reduces consumption further but also increases labour supply and helps support output. Nominal exchange rate flexibility allows for a rapid (larger) real appreciation, which helps offset the impact of the shock on exports but now results in an increase in inflation (and policy rates).

---

[12] We set $log(\Omega_L)$ to zero for the sake of simplicity.

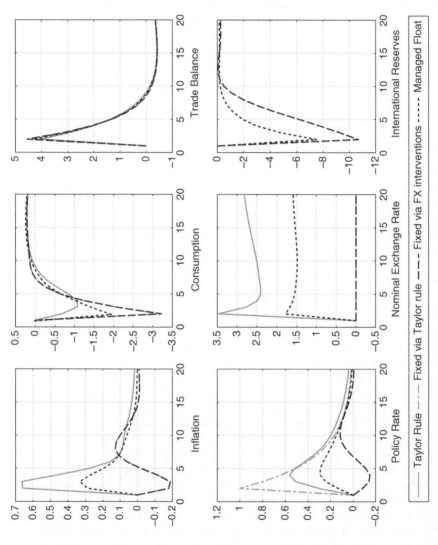

Figure 13.3. Foreign Interest Rate Shock under Different Exchange Rate Regimes, Alternative Specification

'Pure' IT (grey, solid line), fixed via interest rate rule (grey, dashed with dots), fixed via interventions (black, dashed), IT managed float (black, dotted). Units are percentage deviations from steady state.

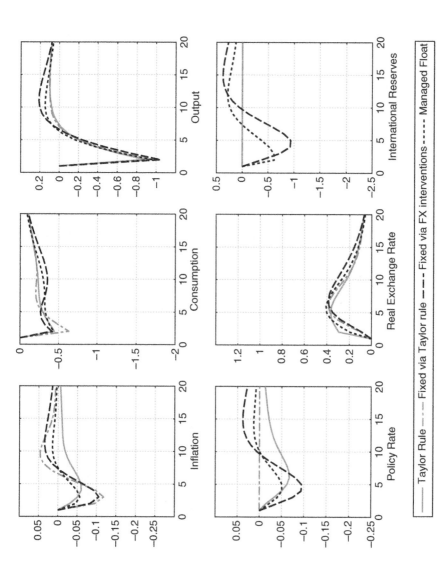

Figure 13.4. Temporary Terms of Trade Shock Under Different Exchange Rate Regimes

'Pure' IT (grey, solid line), fixed via interest rate rule (grey, dashed with dots), fixed via interventions (black, dashed), IT managed float (black, dotted). Units are percentage deviations from steady state.

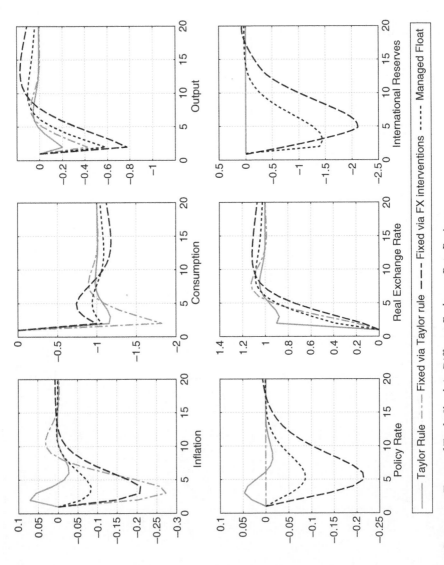

Figure 13.5. Quasi-Permanent Terms of Trade Shock in Different Exchange Rate Regimes

'Pure' IT (grey, solid line), fixed via interest rate rule (grey, dashed with dots), fixed via interventions (black, dashed), IT managed float (black, dotted). Units are percentage deviations from steady state.

Against this background, policies that target the nominal exchange rate reduce the immediate real depreciation and therefore amplify the effect of the shock on output, as the real depreciation must be achieved through a decrease in inflation. This is most visible when the shock is quasi-permanent. Intervention-based pegs delay the real appreciation the longest and hence have the largest decline in output. The reason for the longer delay is that interventions allow policymakers to reduce interest rates aggressively in response to the shock, which diminishes the decrease in inflation.

These simulations highlight the risk that intervention policies may amplify the effect of external shocks by limiting the exchange rate channel to play itself out.

5.3 Welfare Analysis

In this section we briefly summarize the macroeconomic volatility implied by the various rules in response to the two shocks we focus on. We also assess the various rules in response to these two shocks. To do so, we use: (i) the loss function implied by the preferences of the representative agent, and (ii) two ad-hoc loss functions.

As shown in Appendix 13A, a second-order approximation of the discounted sum of the representative agent's utility (denoted U) around its steady state value, using the model equations, results in the following relation: $\sum_{t=0}^{\infty}$

$$U - \bar{U} \approx -\frac{1+\phi}{\gamma} \sum_{t=0}^{\infty} \beta^t E_0[\hat{y}_t^2] + t.i.p.,$$

where *t.i.p.* stands for terms independent of policy. Up to a second-order approximation utility depends solely on the volatility of output, because of the implications of output volatility for employment volatility. It does not depend on consumption volatility because of our assumption of log utility. In addition, since we assume that price setting is symmetric across firms in each sector (non-traded and import sector), inflation volatility does not affect utility.

We also rely on two ad-hoc loss functions to complement the analysis. In the first one, $L_1 = -\sum_{t=0}^{\infty} \beta^t E_0[\hat{C}_t^2]$, so that consumption volatility is the sole objective of monetary policy. In the other function, $L_2 = -\sum_{t=0}^{\infty} \beta^t E_0[\hat{\pi}_t^2 + \hat{y}_t^2]$, which implies the central bank cares equally about inflation and output volatility.

These results are summarized in Table 13.4. Results are displayed in absolute value, so that the lower the number the smaller the welfare cost. For purposes of comparison, the welfare measures have been normalized with respect to the pure IT regime.

In the case of shocks to foreign interest rates, intervention-based pegs unambiguously dominate other regimes. This is not surprising; as Figure 13.1 indicates, this regime helps stabilize output, consumption, and inflation almost perfectly. In the case of terms of trade shocks, exchange rate flexibility flexibility/pure IT helps deliver smaller welfare costs, especially if welfare is evaluated in terms of output volatility (U) or output and inflation (L_2), but there is little difference across

Table 13.4. Summary of the Results

	IT pure float	Fixed via Taylor	Fixed via interventions	IT managed float
Foreign Interest Rate Shock				
U	1	0.55	0.03	0.36
L_1	1	3.93	0.08	0.48
L_2	1	0.50	0.02	0.36
Temporary ToT Shock				
U	1	1.13	1.53	1.13
L_1	1	1.22	1.30	1.20
L_2	1	1.15	1.54	1.12
Quasi-permanent ToT Shock				
U	1	4.26	24.08	9.61
L_1	1	1.02	1.01	1.00
L_2	1	6.74	23.12	8.69

regimes if welfare is evaluated in terms of consumption volatility (L_1). The more persistent the terms of trade shock, the larger the dominance of IT relative to the other regimes. In the case of a quasi-permanent shock, the intervention-based peg performs very poorly in terms of output and inflation volatility, but about the same as IT in terms of consumption volatility.

Our results suggest that interventions are best deployed in response to some shocks rather than others. We leave a formal investigation of the optimal intervention rule for further work.

5.4 Limits of Interventions

The previous section has shown that there can be advantages to using sterilized interventions as part of the monetary policy toolbox, especially as a way of insulating the economy against certain types of external shocks. The previous section has also shown that interventions can be counterproductive, however, from a welfare perspective, if they hamper exchange rate adjustment. Beyond the desirability of interventions, here we briefly discuss two broad sets of arguments that limit what can be achieved with intervention policy.

The first set of arguments is that, in practice, intervention policies are often abandoned if they lead to persistent reserve losses and countries run out of reserves. The opposite may also be true, i.e., that policies that result in persistent reserve accumulation may force the central bank to stop, e.g., out of concern with the quasi-fiscal implications (especially if there is a gap between the interest rate on reserves and the interest rate on government securities). Market perception that reserves policies may be reversed can often lead to speculative attacks, as is well known from the literature on balance of payment crises.[13] More generally, most intervening central banks prefer to keep their intervention tactics (i.e. the reaction function) hidden, if possible, to avoid facing such runs. This lack of

---

[13] See Krugman (1979).

transparency limits what can be achieved with these policies, since part of the effects of interventions we observed in our simulations stem from the predictability of the intervention rule. Such concerns are less acute for the interest rate rule, because the central bank is the ultimate market maker in the money market and because capital gains and losses are very limited for short-duration securities— unlike in the FX market.

While our analysis assumes the central bank always knows perfectly what kind of shock it deals with, in reality this perfect knowledge is difficult to achieve and markets often have a different opinion, leading them to probe the central bank's resolve. Our simulation of the terms of trade shock showed how a quasi-persistent shock to the terms of trade leads to much larger reserves losses than a temporary shock. If the central bank only intervenes to offset the effects of temporary shocks but markets believe it is mistaken in its assessment of the shock and will have to abandon its interventions in the near term, the threat of an attack increases.

The second set of arguments on why interventions may not be viable as a systematic policy instrument involves the so-called 'impossible trinity'.[14] This asserts that independent monetary policy cannot function with a fixed exchange rate and a free capital account, because the financial flows unleashed by any interest rate differential would make the peg short-lived. For instance, an attempt to keep interest rates lower (say, to stimulate the economy) than foreign rates adjusted for a risk premium would trigger an outflow, eventually bringing down the peg, as FX reserves run out.

Our analysis allows for the possibility that domestic and foreign assets are not perfect substitutes, even if the capital account is fully open, therefore allowing for a combination of exchange rate management and monetary policy autonomy. Although in principle this would seem to violate the impossible trinity, the additional degree of freedom ultimately depends on the sensitivity of risk premia to the intervention. To show the importance of this parameter, in Figure 13.6 we look at reserve losses when the economy is hit with a shock to the terms of trade, under both an intervention-based peg and a managed float. In the left quadrant, we show reserve losses under the benchmark calibration ($\Omega_0 = 0.101$); in the right quadrant we show the results when the elasticity of the premium is ten times smaller ($\Omega_0 = 0.101$). When the elasticity is much smaller, a 1 per cent shock to the terms of trade results in a 20 per cent loss of reserves under the intervention-based peg, as opposed to 2 per cent when the elasticity is higher. This simulation underscores the risks to pegging via interventions when interest premia are not very sensitive to balance sheet operations, as predicted by the impossible trinity.

An important corollary is that managed floating regimes can be more robust to uncertainty about the effectiveness of interventions. Because the rule is specified in terms of volumes of intervention, a low sensitivity of the premium to interventions implies that the intervention will not make much difference, but there is also little risk of running out of reserves.

[14] The literature on the impossible trinity is time-honoured and extensively large. See Obstfeld, Shambaugh, and Taylor (2004) for a historical perspective.

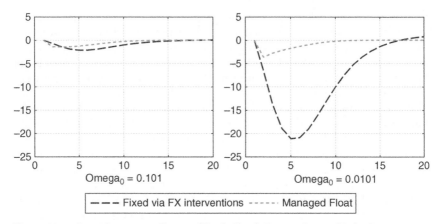

Figure 13.6. Quasi-Permanent Terms of Trade Shock, Reserve Losses Under Intervention–Based Exchange Rate Regimes

Strong sensitivity to interventions (left quadrant), weak sensitivity to interventions (right quadrant).

6 CONCLUSIONS

The modelling of regimes that combine IT with various degrees of exchange-rate management—and of the mechanisms that make such combinations possible—is an important issue for many central banks and institutions. Unlike for 'pure' IT, an analytical framework for these hybrid regimes has not yet been established, and standard analytical approaches appear unfit for the state of affairs in emerging and developing countries.

In general, the coexistence of IT with some kind of exchange rate management is a common phenomenon in many countries, at least informally. For instance, there are countries with a fixed or strongly managed exchange rate that are in transition towards a more flexible exchange rate regime and implement elements of inflation targeting by controlling short-term interest rates. Others attempt to control excessive exchange rate fluctuations by interventions of various forms (e.g., sterilization of inflows). Some even recognize two explicit intermediate targets in terms of the exchange rate and inflation bands.

By explicitly introducing balance sheet effects in a New Keynesian model with a simple banking sector, we have provided a framework for studying the effects of intervention policies as part of a broader monetary policy toolbox. Given the experience of many central banks, our focus has been on hybrid frameworks that use interventions to manage the exchange rate, while also maintaining control of short-term interest rates to keep inflation anchored. We have shown that intervention policies can help insulate the economy against certain types of shocks, though we have also shown that, in some cases, limiting exchange rate adjustment can also be counterproductive from a welfare perspective. This nuance raises the stakes for intervention policy, in that policy mistakes can be costly.

Two extensions of this work appear important for future research. First, more work can be done in mapping the intervention mechanism to micro-foundations, as well as the explicit modelling of the limits of interventions and the possibility of runs.

Second, the framework presented here could be extended to analyse other aspects of monetary/financial policy that have received considerable attention since the global financial crisis, such as macro-prudential policies and the need for coordination with intervention policy.

APPENDIX 13A: SECOND-ORDER APPROXIMATION TO UTILITY

Starting from the steady state (at period –1), taking a second-order approximation to the discounted sum of utility flows yields the following relation:

$$U = E_0 \left[\sum_{t=0}^{\infty} \beta^t U_t \right] \approx \bar{U} \sum_{t=0}^{\infty} \beta^t E_0 \left[\underbrace{\hat{c}_t - (1+s)\hat{y}_t}_{A_t} \right] - \frac{1+\phi}{\gamma} \sum_{t=0}^{\infty} \beta^t E_0 [\hat{y}_t^2].$$

Note that $\hat{c}_t - (1+s)\hat{y}_t = (1-\omega_n)\hat{c}_{m,t} - (1-\omega_n+s)\hat{y}_{x,t}$. Forward iterations of the balance of payments imply:

$$\sum_{t=0}^{\infty} \beta^t E_0[A_t] = (1+s) \sum_{t=0}^{\infty} \beta^t E_0[\hat{tot}_t - \bar{j}\beta\hat{i}_t^*] = t.i.p.,$$

where *t.i.p*: denotes terms independent of policy. The above relation implies the discounted sum of utility, up to a second-order approximation, is proportional to the discounted sum of squared variations in output:

$$U - \bar{U} \approx -\frac{1+\phi}{\gamma} \sum_{t=0}^{\infty} \beta^t E_0[\hat{y}_t^2] + t.i.p..$$

REFERENCES

Adler, G., and C. Tovar (2011). *Foreign Exchange Market Intervention: How Good a Defense Against Appreciation Winds?* IMF Working Paper 11/165. Washington DC: International Monetary Fund.

Backus, D. and P. Kehoe (1989). On the Denomination of Government Debt. *Journal of Monetary Economics,* 23, 359–76.

Bank of Israel (2009). Inflation Report January–March. Jerusalem: Bank of Israel.

Batini, N., P. Levine, and J. Pearlman (2007). Monetary Rules in Emerging Economies with Financial Market Imperfections, in J. Gali and M. J. Gertler (Eds.), *International Dimensions of Monetary Policy.* Chicago IL: University of Chicago Press.

BIS (2005). *Foreign Exchange Market Intervention in Emerging Markets: Motives, Techniques and Implications.* BIS Papers No. 24, Basel: Bank for International Settlements.

Blanchard, O., F. Giavazzi, and F. Sa (2005). International Investors, the U.S. Current Account, and the Dollar. *Brookings Papers on Economic Activity,* 36(1), 1–66.

Canales-Kriljenko, J. I. (2003). *Foreign exchange intervention in developing and transition economies: results of a survey.* IMF Working Paper 03/95. Washington DC: International Monetary Fund.

Canzoneri, M., R. Cumby, and B. Diba (2013). Addressing International Empirical Puzzles: the Liquidity of Bonds. *Open Economies Review,* 24(2), 197–215.

Cavusoglu, N. (2010). Exchange Rates and the Effectiveness of Actual and Oral Official Interventions: A Survey on Findings, Issues and Policy Implications. *Global Economy Journal*, 10(4).

Curdia, V. and M. Woodford (2011). The Central-Bank Balance Sheet as an Instrument of Monetary Policy. *Journal of Monetary Economics*, 58, 54–79.

Domac, I., and A. Mendoza (2004). *Is There Room for Foreign Exchange Interventions under an Inflation Targeting Framework? Evidence from Mexico and Turkey*. Policy Research Working Paper No. 3288. Washington DC: World Bank.

Dornbusch, R. (1976). Expectations and Exchange Rate Dynamics. *Journal of Political Economy*, 84(6), 1161–76.

Egert, B. (2007). Central bank interventions, communication and interest rate policy in emerging European economies. *Journal of Comparative Economics*, 35(2), 387–413.

Fatum, R. and M. M. Hutchison (2003). Is Sterilized Foreign Exchange Intervention Effective After All? An event study approach. *The Economic Journal*, 113(April), 390–411.

Fatum, R. and M. M. Hutchison (2010). Evaluating foreign exchange market intervention: Self-selection, counterfactuals and average treatment effects. *Journal of International Money and Finance*, 29(3), 570–84.

Friedman, M. (1953). The Case for Flexible Exchange Rates, in *Essays in Positive Economics*. Chicago, IL: University of Chicago Press.

Gabaix, X., and M. Maggiori (2014). *International Liquidity and Exchange Rate Dynamics*, NBER Working Papers 19854.

Gersl, A., and T. Holub (2006). Foreign Exchange Interventions Under Inflation Targeting: The Czech Experience. *Contemporary Economic Policy*, 24(4), 475–91.

Gertler, M., and P. Karadi (2011). A Model of Unconventional Monetary Policy. *Journal of Monetary Economics*, 58, 17–34.

Guimaraes, R., and C. Karacadag (2004). *The Empirics of Foreign Exchange Intervention in Emerging Markets: The Cases of Mexico and Turkey*. IMF Working Paper 04/123, Washington DC: International Monetary Fund.

Henderson, D., and K. Rogoff (1982). Negative Net Foreign Asset Positions and Stability in a World Portfolio Balance Model. *Journal of International Economics*, 13, 85–104.

IMF (2011). Foreign Exchange Market Intervention: How Good a Defense Against Appreciation Winds? *Regional Economic Outlook: Western Hemisphere*, Chapter 3. Washington DC: International Monetary Fund.

Kamil, H. (2008). *Is Central Bank Intervention Effective Under Inflation Targeting Regimes? The Case of Colombia*, IMF Working Paper 08/88. Washington DC: International Monetary Fund.

Kouri, P. (1976). *Capital Flows and the Dynamics of the Exchange Rate*, Seminar Paper 67. Stockholm: Institute for International Economic Studies.

Krugman, P. (1979). A Model of Balance-of-Payments Crises. *Journal of Money, Credit and Banking*, 11(3), 311–25.

Kumhof, M. (2010). On the Theory of Sterilized Foreign Exchange Intervention. *Journal of Economic Dynamics and Control*, 34(8), 1403–20.

Leitemo, K., and U. Soderstrom (2005). Simple Monetary Policy Rules and Exchange Rate Uncertainty. *Journal of International Money and Finance*, 24, 481–507.

Moron, E., and D. Winkelried (2005). Monetary Policy Rules for Financially Vulnerable Economies. *Journal of Development Economics*, 76, 25–51.

Neely, C. J. (2011). A Foreign Exchange Intervention in an Era of Restraint. *Federal Reserve Bank of St. Louis Review*, 93(5), 303–24.

Obstfeld, M., J. Shambaugh and A. Taylor (2004). *The Trilemma in History: Tradeoffs among Exchange Rates, Monetary Policies and Capital Mobility*. NBER Working Paper 10396. Cambridge: National Bureau of Economic Activity.

Ostry, J., A. Ghosh, and M. Chamon (2012). *Two Targets, Two Instruments: Monetary and Exchange Rate Policies in Emerging Market Economies.* Staff Discussion Notes No. 12/1. Washington DC: International Monetary Fund.

Parrado, E. (2004a). *Inflation Targeting and Exchange Rate Rules in an Open Economy.* IMF Working Paper 04/21. Washington DC: International Monetary Fund.

Parrado, E. (2004b). *Singapore's Unique Monetary Policy: How Does it Work?* IMF Working Paper 04/10. Washington DC: International Monetary Fund.

Ravenna F., and F. Natalucci (2002). *The Road to Adopting the Euro: Monetary Policy and Exchange Rate Regimes in EU Candidate Countries.* International Finance Discussion Papers 741. Washington DC: Board of Governors of the Federal Reserve System.

Reserve Bank of Australia (2008). Statement on Monetary Policy, November. Canberra: Reserve Bank of Australia.

Roger, S., J. Restrepo, and C. Garcia (2009). *Hybrid Inflation Targeting Regimes.* IMF Working Paper 09/324. Washington DC: International Monetary Fund.

Rotemberg, J. (1982). Monopolistic Price Adjustment and Aggregate Output. *Review of Economic Studies,* 49, 517–31.

Schmitt-Groh, S. and M. Uribe (2003). Closing Small Economy Models. *Journal of International Economics,* 61, 163–85.

Swiss National Bank (2008). *Quarterly Bulletin,* Fourth Quarter. Zurich: Swiss National Bank.

Taylor, J. (2001). The Role of the Exchange Rate in Monetary Policy Rules. *American Economic Review, Papers and Proceedings,* 91(2), 263–7.

Tuna, G. (2011). The effectiveness of Central Bank intervention: evidence from Turkey, *Applied Economics,* 43(14), 1801–15.

Woodford, M. (2005). Comment on 'Using a Long-Term Interest Rate as the Monetary Policy Instrument'. *Journal of Monetary Economics,* 52, 881–7.

Part III

Applied Models for Policy Analysis and Forecasting in SSA: Selected Case Studies

14

Introduction to Part III

Andrew Berg and Rafael Portillo

In Part III we present various applications of quantitative dynamic stochastic general equilibrium models to SSA countries. Unlike the previous chapters, which provided broad guidance, the emphasis here is on specific policy questions faced by the country under study—and by extension the IMF team—and on quantitative policy guidance for central banks. Each chapter mixes theory and data, along with close attention to the broader economic context.

The chapters in Part III resulted from the collaboration between economists from the IMF African and research departments, with both serving as co-authors. Our participation in Chapters 15–17 dates from our time at the development macroeconomics division (research), while Chapter 18 also stems from the division's work agenda. Chapter 19 predates those efforts and was produced by a different division in the research department (the modelling division), but it shares the same collaborative approach. The one exception is Chapter 20, which is single-authored: it was prepared when one of us (Rafael Portillo) was part of the IMF team working on the CEMAC region.

The efforts involved in deriving and applying these models, especially those in Chapters 15–17, have led to a more systematic collaboration between the IMF and central banks in SSA on the topic of analytical frameworks for policy analysis and forecasting.[1] As a result, and with the support of the IMF and external consultants, several central banks have been developing and using their own variant of these models to organize their internal discussion and forecasting systems.[2] This is an important part of the policy modernization efforts, as discussed in more detail in Chapter 1, and points to the synergies between research, IMF surveillance or programme work, and capacity development on the ground.

In terms of analytical approach, the models in Chapters 15, 16, 17, and 19 are semi-structural, by which we mean that they are not fully derived from first principles (micro-foundations), even though each equation has a structural interpretation, e.g., IS curve, Phillips curve, monetary policy rule, and even though the models resemble those in Part II. As these models are designed to confront the data, it is crucial that they generate plausible dynamics for the variables of interest

[1] Financial support by the UK's Department for International Development (DFID) has been pivotal in these efforts.
[2] This includes the central banks in Ghana, Kenya, Mozambique, Rwanda, Tanzania, and Uganda.

(inflation, output, etc.). This calls for relaxing some of the restrictions implied by theory, including across equations. What is lost in theoretical elegance is gained in the ability of the model to perform quantitative policy analysis, i.e., produce reasonable conditional forecasts. This does not mean that anything goes, however; we have tried as much as possible to be guided by the structure of the more explicitly micro-founded models presented in Part II. In our view, there are benefits from working on both types of models (fully micro-founded and applied/semi-structural).

1 APPLIED MODELS FOR POLICY ANALYSIS AND FORECASTING IN KENYA AND RWANDA

Kenya was one of the first country cases we worked on. It had come to our attention that the authorities at the Central Bank of Kenya (CBK) were interested in building a forecasting model, as part of their transition to a more forward-looking IT-style policy regime. We worked with IMF colleagues, notably R. Armando Morales, the co-author of Chapters 15 and 16, and at the time the senior economist responsible for following Kenya, as well as directly with the staff of the CBK, over several years to assist them in these efforts.

When we were first talking with the CBK, one of the CBK officials sceptically emphasized that farmers in Kenya cared a lot more about the rains than about interest rates, capturing the important points that agriculture and especially food drive the Kenyan economy, including inflation, and supply shocks provide the main action. Our rejoinder was that the CBK has a lot more influence over the interest rate than the rain, summarizing another set of important points: that even when supply shocks provide most of the volatility, it remains the unique and critical role of the central bank to provide a 'nominal anchor'. Monetary policy should never be the dominant driver of volatility, but through good policy it can limit volatility, avoid doing harm, and allow the flexible exchange rate to help buffer shocks.

Chapter 15 grew out of this initial set of concerns: how can we disentangle the role of, on the one hand, external and domestic supply shocks and, on the other, monetary policy and other domestic policies on inflation, and what lessons can we draw for the conduct of policy and the regime? Our period of analysis, from 2007 through 2012, was characterized by two major spikes in inflation, both driven at least in part by sharp increases in global food and commodity prices, as well as the swings in global financial market sentiment and global demand related to the global financial crisis. In this context it was difficult to assess whether the monetary policy stance was aggravating these inflationary pressures, partly because of the magnitude of the external shocks hitting the country but also because the monetary policy framework itself was somewhat opaque.[3]

---

[3] Chapter 5 takes a complementary narrative look at Kenya over the same period, comparing to Uganda, Rwanda (also discussed in Chapter 17), and Tanzania.

We chose to analyse this question through the application of a small semi-structural gap model, of the type advocated by Berg et al. (2006), augmented to address the dynamics of food and non-food inflation.[4] The core economics of the model are simple and involve the interaction of aggregate demand and supply, as influenced inter alia by monetary policy, in determining the deviations in output and inflation from trend. The extension raises a number of interesting complications, however. Most importantly, we pay substantial attention to the dynamics of food prices and the fact that the relative price of food seemed to be trending during this period, and also to the feedback between food price inflation and general inflation expectations. We chose to model monetary policy as a forward-looking Taylor rule. Clearly this is only a rough approximation, but it seemed like a useful benchmark through which to assess the policy stance.

One advantage of using this sort of model to analyse the data is that it is both simple enough and structural enough to be useful for regular forecasting and policy analysis in support of monetary policy decisions. Chapter 15 illustrates how to interpret the data in terms of the gaps between actual and equilibrium values, and how to decompose these gaps into the structural and policy drivers. The forward-looking Taylor provides a guide to the interest rate required to stabilize inflation. The whole apparatus facilitates communication, in that it tells an economic (as opposed to econometric) story about the direction of inflation, why the objectives may or may not have been met, and how policy is serving to steer towards the target.

When we used the model to interpret the Kenyan data, we found that excessively accommodating monetary policy had been fuelling the inflationary pressures in Kenya, in addition to the external supply shocks, and that a substantial policy tightening was required. The analysis in the chapter suggests a need to clarify the policy framework, a topic which is discussed in more detail in Chapter 5. It is worth noting that this is exactly what the central bank of Kenya did shortly after the first draft of the working paper that became this chapter (in the third quarter of 2011).

Chapter 16 returns us to a recurring obsession of this book, the role of money aggregates. As we discussed in Chapters 1 and 8, this obsession derives from the strong role that money targeting regimes have played, at least nominally, in many countries in SSA, itself partly related to the IMF's own long and persistent tradition of using quantity-based frameworks to analyse monetary policy.[5] From long experience working at the IMF on developing countries and emerging markets, we had come to have doubts about the practical utility of such quantity-based frameworks, but in our work with our IMF colleagues and member central banks, we felt the need to develop an applied framework that incorporates this approach.

Kenya provided a good case in point. Associated targets on narrow money were regularly set and announced as the guideposts for monetary policy. The simplest

---

[4] The structure of these models is similar to those in Chapters 8 and 9, though as mentioned above it breaks some of the restrictions implied by theory, mainly by allowing for ad-hoc backward-looking dynamics.

[5] See Polak (2005), among others.

approach might be simply to assume, following the traditional teachings of the IMF's 'financial programming' approach, that money targets are set three or six months ahead, and then monetary policy steered, e.g. through open market operations that control the quantity base money, so as to hit the targets.[6] However, as our experience elsewhere suggested would be the case, these targets in Kenya were frequently missed by large margins. And sometimes, this seemed like it may have been for good reason, for example because shifts in demand for money implied that hitting the target would have implied an unnecessary and harmful shift in the level of interest rates.

To capture money targeting as implemented in practice, Chapter 16 builds on the model in Chapter 15 by introducing some of the features we analysed in Chapter 8. These include: (i) a money demand equation, (ii) a rule specifying the setting of money targets, and (iii) a more general monetary policy setting that places some weight on hitting money targets and some weight on a more standard Taylor rule. On the latter we assess the actual weights placed on these two policy aspects and ask about the implications for macro dynamics of changing them.

We find that the CBK set money targets as if they were trying to forecast future money demand, and indeed they seem to have some ability to predict this money demand better than a very simple statistical model, implying that they use information about future liquidity shocks, e.g. due to fiscal operations.

However, we find no influence of the monetary aggregates on the stance of policy. Misses were large, and the subsequent adjustment came from shifting the target, not bringing the actual money stock back in line or from adjusting interest rates in response to target misses. Asking about the counterfactual, we see little role for greater adherence to the money targets, on the whole. The question is not simple. Echoing some of the results in Chapter 8, we find here too that greater adherence to money targets could have helped buffer demand shocks. Overall, though, more volatility would have resulted. This underscores an important general point we have made in Chapter 1, which is that money targeting is not a particularly useful solution to many of the particular challenges of monetary policy implementation in SSA, such as the dominant role of supply shocks.

We had hoped that the sort of framework developed in Chapter 16 would be useful in countries that, unlike Kenya, are interested in continuing to put some weight on monetary aggregates. We had and to some extent still continue to hope such frameworks will allow policymakers to disentangle money misses into shocks due to money demand (given adherence to an appropriate policy reaction function) and policy shocks (perhaps errors or deviations from conditionality under an IMF programme). And we and our IMF colleagues continue to work with a few such central banks along these lines. However, we are increasingly pessimistic about how fruitful this effort will be. The model and analysis in Chapter 16 is quite complex. Both in the chapter and in related operational work, we have found that the addition of one more structural equation

---

[6] 'Base money' is the money that is directly created by the central bank, and consists of deposits of commercial banks at the central banks as well as cash in circulation. 'Broad money' includes in addition checking and savings deposits at commercial banks.

(money demand) to a four-equation model increases the complexity involved in interpreting the data by much more than 25 per cent. As in Chapter 16, we have not found much use for this additional complexity in practice. Partly for this reason we have tended to encourage countries to simplify their frameworks and focus directly on interest rates, inflation, and the other elements of the analysis in Chapter 15.

Chapter 17 considers a country with an even more complex regime. Rwanda in practice has followed a hybrid approach. As in the stylized view of Kenya in Chapter 16, it puts some weight on money aggregates and also on an interest rate that responds to inflation, output, and other factors. At the time the chapter was written, the framework aimed at stabilization inflation, although the stabilization of the exchange rate was also central. Moreover, monetary policy operations were conducted in such a way that the 'policy rate'—the short-term interest rate assigned an explicit role as indicator of the stance of policy—often deviated from the short-term market rate. This deviation is a common feature of regimes in which multiple objectives and complex policy frameworks are hard for the central bank to reconcile.

In Chapter 17 the authors describe this hybrid regime, but then, to keep things tractable, focus their modelling efforts in particular on a simple way to capture the fact that the authorities directly manage the exchange rate. They do so by introducing an exchange rate target in the equation that describes exchange rate dynamics—the uncovered interest parity condition—and allowing the exchange rate to be driven both by expectations of future interest rate differentials/risk premia and by the exchange rate target. Although not modelled explicitly as such, the latter mechanism is meant to capture direct management of the exchange through exchange rate interventions, in the context of limited de facto capital mobility.[7] The authors argue that even with such a complex framework their simple model performs fairly well and can play a useful role in understanding and guiding policy.

The regime in Rwanda cannot be found in any textbook. And a model that captured it more fully, considering for example the role of money targets as well as the exchange rate in the objective function, might well be too opaque to be useful for regular policy analysis. However, Rwanda has had good success in coping with the food and fuel price shocks of 2008–12 (Chapter 5). This success may in part be due to other features of the overall policy regime, such as relatively flexible and countercyclical fiscal policy, but it reminds us that the mapping from policy regime to outcomes is not straightforward.

Readers steeped in the DSGE tradition may find the models in Chapters 15–17 too simple and ad-hoc. However, they are meant to be brought to the data and used, with a healthy dose of judgement, to inform policy decisions on a quarterly basis. This is in many ways a much more demanding task than building a model from first principles, estimating or calibrating it, and examining its properties in terms of impulse responses (for example). Sometimes, however, more complexity is required for the question at hand, as we see in the next three chapters.

---

[7] Chapter 13 provides a more formal treatment of this mechanism.

2 THE IMPACT OF THE GLOBAL FINANCIAL CRISIS
ON ZAMBIA AND THE POLICY RESPONSE

In Chapter 18 we began with a seemingly simple question: why are changes in policy rates often not followed by changes in lending and deposit rates? This is a commonly observed phenomenon, in SSA and elsewhere. It surfaced starkly in Zambia in 2008, when short-term rates fell by over 1,200 basis points, while the lending rate fell by about half that amount policymakers naturally wanted to know why. One set of views was that long rates are simply sticky or, for one reason or another, are not market-determined. We preferred to try to understand the situation explicitly in terms of economic forces.

This narrow question provided a window into a much broader question that forms the core of the chapter: how should we think about the impact of the global financial crisis on low-income countries, and in particular how should we model the most important channels. We explicitly modelled the banking system, because it is the banking system that translates short-term interbank or policy rates into lending and deposit rates, and more generally because we viewed it as a key source of transmission of the crisis. We viewed the crisis, for Zambia, in terms of three related shocks: a decline in the terms of trade, an increase in the country's external risk premium as part of a general 'flight to quality', and a decrease in the risk appetite of Zambian banks in the face of a general crisis-related increase in risk aversion.

Our preliminary hypothesis was that a standard 'financial accelerator' mechanism, a workhorse of macroeconomic models with banks, could help explain the trajectory of spreads. The idea is that the risk premium that banks demand on their loans relative to their cost of funds will depend on the stock of loans relative to the value of collateral, which is in part measured by stock market valuations or perhaps simply the value of output. In Zambia, according to this mechanism, the drastic decline in the price of Zambia's dominant export, copper, in 2007/08, which lowered asset prices and the value of collateral in Zambian firms, was responsible for raising the risk premium on loans.

A closer look at the data, through the lens of the DSGE model in Chapter 18, showed us the limits of this view for the episode in question. Simply put, the collapse in lending was much greater than the fall in asset prices, output, or other available measures of the value of collateral. So something besides an increase in the ratio of loans to collateral is needed to explain the rise in spreads.

We came to conclude that a shock to the risk aversion of the banks themselves was the best way to explain the data. In the face of the confusion and uncertainty of the global financial crisis, banks in Zambia switched preferences strongly towards investing in relatively safe government securities and deposits at the central bank, reducing as much as possible their exposure to firms. At the same time, foreign lenders attempted to reduce exposure to Zambia. The result was a sharp decline in lending, emergence of a large current account surplus, a rise in demand for liquid assets, and a rise in the spread between policy and lending rates.

Our use of a structural model allows us to ask about the role of the monetary policy regime. We find that some features of the regime may have led to a 'stop and go' policy that may have increased the real effects of the global financial crisis. The 'stop' was in increase in policy rates of some 400 basis points through mid-2009, which we attribute to a (backward-looking) concern about inflation, a desire to resist the large exchange rate depreciation associated with the negative terms of trade shock, and a concern about the large increase in 'liquidity' resulting from the risk-induced shift of banks from loans to high-powered money. A more forward-looking regime without the emphasis on monetary aggregates might have avoided this 'stop' and buffered the shocks a bit better. We should not overstate the magnitude of this effect, however: we assess that most of the effect of the crisis was due to real external shocks, and monetary policy could do relatively little to help. This again illustrates a general lesson, which is that we should not expect too much from monetary policy. It cannot affect trend relative prices (Chapter 15), and it cannot fully mitigate the effects of large real shocks.

3 ENDOGENOUS CREDIBILITY AND THE COST OF DISINFLATION IN GHANA

Chapter 19 brings into sharp relief some major weaknesses of all the models in the rest of this book, while providing an alternative. For good reason, we have relied entirely on so-called 'rational expectations' models, where the central bank has complete credibility. But this feature creates some major pitfalls in the application of these models.

Rational expectations, in which agents' expectations of future variables are also the model's own predictions, represent a simplification. Purely backward-looking models are simpler still, but they ignore the critical role that monetary policy regimes play in anchoring expectations. The lessons of the great inflation of the 1980s in advanced countries, and the resulting rational expectations revolution in macroeconomics, apply a fortiori to countries in SSA: people are reasonably quick to adapt their behaviour to the nature of the regime, and policies that attempt to systematically fool the public are not likely to be sustainable.

A dangerous feature of the rational expectations models we have been using so far is that any deviation of policy from that dictated by the policy rule in the model is assumed by agents in the model to be a one-off. This means that these models are not well-suited to answer one sort of question a central bank governor might ask: 'Suppose I lower policy relative to what we normally would do—what would happen?'. The problem is that the resulting boost to inflation is small and, in the model, not a problem, because agents assume that the deviation is certainly temporary and not symptomatic of a lack of willingness of the central bank to do what is necessary to achieve its objective. The perfect credibility of the central bank—the confidence that it will return to its policy rule and bring inflation back down—mitigates the inflationary consequences. Similarly, a decision to delay inflation stabilization because of an aversion to the policy tightening that would be called for by the announced regime would generally only have temporary and relatively minor effects.

In real life, though, the demand contraction required to reduce inflation back to target may be larger than the boom that generated that inflation, partly because the unexpected loosening may raise doubts about the goals of the central bank, requiring a larger contraction to convince the public that inflation will indeed be brought back to target.

In Chapter 19, the authors apply to Ghana a richer version of the standard framework we have seen several times, a version that introduces the notion that the credibility of the central bank depends on its inflation record. They apply this framework to discuss the question of the appropriate pace of disinflation from a position of imperfect credibility, arguing that appropriate front-loading of the required contraction will lower the total cost in terms of output.

The simpler models presented in earlier chapters remain the workhorse models in many central banks, particularly as they begin using policy-based policy analysis. And the assumption of perfect credibility remains a useful benchmark; the evidence suggests that credibility is generally gradually established as central banks implement inflation targeting regimes, and a central bank that behaves as it should under perfect credibility is in effect leading by example. However, the lessons of Chapter 19 need to be kept in mind. The analytic approach in this chapter has proven useful in other contexts (e.g. Israel in Argov et al., 2007, and India in Benes et al., 2017). And the chapter illustrates how more complex models can guide the use of simpler core models. In practice, the simpler models can be 'tuned' in an ad hoc fashion to capture the implications of weak credibility in particular cases.

4 THE ROLE OF EXTERNAL SHOCKS AND FISCAL POLICY IN THE DYNAMICS OF INFLATION IN THE CEMAC REGION

Chapter 20 takes us in another direction entirely. In almost the entire book, we have focused on countries with some degree of exchange rate flexibility, a natural approach given the scope this flexibility provides for monetary policy. However, about half the countries in SSA have a hard exchange rate peg, most of them as members of currency unions that have maintained a fixed parity with the French franc/euro (with a large step devaluation in 1994). Chapter 20 analyses the determinants of inflation in the six countries that make up the *Communauté Economique et Monetaire de l'Afrique Centrale* (CEMAC).

In principle and, in our experience in practice, countries with a peg but with some degree of closure of the capital account—which could come from legal restrictions or the imperfect substitutability of their assets for those of other countries—do face some choice with respect to the stance of monetary policy. However, the VAR-based empirical analysis in the chapter points to the importance of fiscal shocks, combined with a passive monetary policy, along with the usual supply shocks. Counterfactual analysis with a calibrated structural model that is consistent with this VAR evidence points to the merits of this passive monetary policy. A more aggressive anti-inflationary monetary policy may be feasible, but it would choke off the real exchange rate adjustment that helps adjust to shocks and thus likely increase output volatility.[8]

REFERENCES

Argov, E., Epstein, N., Karam, P., Laxton, D., and Rose, D. (2007). *Endogenous Monetary Policy Credibility in a Small Macro Model of Israel.* IMF Working Paper 07/207. Washington, DC: International Monetary Fund.

Benes, J., Clinton, K., Asish, G., Gupta, P., John, J., Kamenik, O., . . . Zhang, F. (2017). *Quarterly Projection Model for India: Key Elements and Properties.* IMF Working Paper 17/33. Washington, DC: International Monetary Fund.

Berg, A., Karam, P. D., and Laxton, D. (2006). *A Practical Model-Based Approach to Monetary Policy Analysis-Overview.* IMF Working Paper 06/80. Washington, DC: International Monetary Fund.

Polak, J. J. (2005). The IMF monetary model at forty. In J. Boughton (Ed.), *Selected Essays of Jacques J. Polak, 1994–2004.* New York and London: Sharpe, 209–26.

---

[8] Chapter 20 was written years before Chapter 6, which identified the challenges to VAR-based analysis in low-income countries. However, unlike almost all flexible-exchange-rate countries, CEMAC countries enjoy relatively long time series under a stable policy regime. Moreover, the chapter does not attempt to identify monetary policy shocks in the VAR, employing a DSGE model to help articulate the role of the monetary policy regime in propagating other, real, shocks.

15

On the Sources of Inflation in Kenya

A Model-Based Approach

Michal Andrle, Andrew Berg, R. Armando Morales,
Rafael Portillo, and Jan Vlcek

1 INTRODUCTION

Central banks in sub-Saharan Africa (SSA) have had a mixed inflation performance in recent years.[1] On the one hand, since the early 2000s many countries in SSA have succeeded in re-anchoring inflationary expectations, reducing median inflation in the region from 15 per cent in 2000 to 6 per cent in 2006. As described in Chapter 1, this has taken place in the context of fiscal-based stabilization efforts, in which many countries adopted policy regimes centred on targets for reserve and broad money. While de facto flexibility was and has always been the norm—money targets are frequently missed in either direction—the adoption of such targets was meant to signal that the central bank was 'holding the line', i.e., that stabilization efforts were on track and that fiscal pressures on monetary policy were contained.

On the other hand, more recently SSA has experienced large swings in inflation.[2] To a large extent, this reflects external factors. The region has been buffeted by large external shocks, starting with the first food and fuel crisis of 2007–08, spillovers from the global financial crisis in 2008–09, and the spike in commodity prices in 2010–11. However, an important question is the role that monetary policy may have played during these episodes, relative to the external factors. This is of particular importance to policymakers, as there is an acknowledgement that existing frameworks, with their emphasis on money targets and money target misses, have not provided a useful framework for thinking about external shocks and the role that policy may have played in amplifying them. In this chapter, we apply a model-based approach to answer this question, with an application to Kenya.

Central banks in advanced and emerging markets make use of a variety of models to study these types of questions. These models are typically New Keynesian, which embody the fairly general view that aggregate demand and monetary policy matter for output dynamics in the short run. At their core, they consist of a

---

[1] Printed with permission of *South African Journal of Economics* (2015), 83(4), 475–505.
[2] See *World Economic Outlook* Fall 2011, Chapter 3.

forward-looking IS equation, a hybrid Phillips curve, a monetary policy rule, and an uncovered interest parity equation.[3] An important feature of these models is the emphasis on gaps in output and the real exchange rate—deviations between observed values and trend or potential components—as drivers of inflation. Considerable effort therefore goes toward distinguishing gaps from trends.

Our emphasis in this chapter is on disentangling the role of external factors versus the contribution of monetary policy decisions (and other domestic factors) in the dynamics of food and non-food inflation. To that end, we extend the standard framework by introducing two separate Phillips curves, one for food and one for non-food. The disaggregation requires that special attention be paid to various relative food prices: both the domestic and the international relative price as well as the deviation between the two. It also calls for a careful treatment of trends in these relative prices, which we explicitly undertake here, for two reasons. First, trends in relative prices have implications for the consistency between sectoral inflation rates and the inflation target (toward which headline inflation eventually converges). Second, deviations between relative prices and their trend becomes an important source of inflationary pressures, both sectorally and in the aggregate, as these gaps enter the Phillips curves directly.

The Kenyan case is representative of the challenges SSA countries have faced in recent years. As Figure 15.1 indicates, Kenya experienced large swings in inflation,

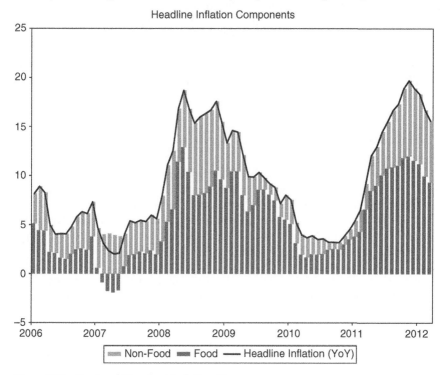

Figure 15.1. Food and Non-food Inflation, Kenya

---

[3] See Berg, Karam, and Laxton (2006) for an overview of the standard model.

first increasing to 16 per cent in mid-2008, falling back to under 4 per cent in mid-2010, only to increase again to almost 20 per cent at the end of 2011. While movements in international food prices account for some of these fluctuations, monetary policy may have also played a role, with short-term interest rates falling from 6 per cent in 2009 to about 1 per cent by early 2011.

We filter selected macroeconomic data from Kenya through the model, in order to recover a model-based decomposition of most series into gap and potential/trend components. The filtration exercise also serves to recover the sequence of macroeconomic shocks that, according to the structure of the model and our own view of recent history, account for business cycle dynamics over the last few years. This allows us to discuss the quantitative significance of various factors (international shocks, monetary policy) in explaining inflation developments. This process is iterative: as we have a prior opinion on the relative importance of various shocks, we repeat the filtration to adjust the calibration of the model until a consistent view of the economy emerges; this iteration also helps us adjust our own views in light of the empirical evidence.

Our results are the following. We find that imported food shocks have accounted for some of the inflation dynamics in Kenya, both in 2008 but also recently. Domestic food shocks (harvest shocks) were also relevant. However, we also find that accommodative monetary policy played an important role, both in 2007–08 and more recently. In 2007–08, the CB experienced 'good luck': domestic inflationary pressures were compensated by disinflationary forces associated with the global recession, without a need for tightening. The 2011 inflationary spike was different, in that such forces were not present.[4]

We also find that the difference between actual short-term interest rates and what would be predicted on the basis of an interest rate rule provides a useful measure of the stance of policy, even in a country such as Kenya, which at the time did not have a meaningful policy rate to signal the stance of policy and was a de jure money targeter. This policy measure helps identify episodes of policy loosening, which subsequently resulted in large increases in inflation. Using monetary policy statements, we argue that the excessive accommodation stemmed to a large extent from pursuing monetary objectives, namely credit growth.

There has been very little work in applying these types of models to study inflation in low-income countries.[5] It is sometimes argued that these models do not adequately capture the structure of these economies and the monetary transmission mechanism in place. Our results show otherwise, in that a careful application of these models can yield useful insights that are relevant for policy analysis.

The chapter is organized as follows. Section 2 introduces the model. Section 3 applies the model to Kenya. Section 4 discusses some possible reasons behind the monetary policy response in recent years and the validity of our model-based analysis for Kenya. Section 5 concludes.

---

[4] In the working paper version of this chapter, we undertake several forecasting exercises. Most notably, we perform an out-of-sample forecast to identify where the economy—and therefore policy—was likely headed given the inflationary pressures at the time, starting from where our data ends (third quarter 2011). Interestingly, our exercise indicated that short-term interest rates needed to increase, i.e., policy needed to be tightened to offset these inflationary pressures, which is exactly what the Central Bank of Kenya (CBK) implemented by the end of 2011. The coincidence between the latter response and the model's forecast validates the use of the model for policy analysis in LICs.

[5] Several chapters in this book represent exceptions.

2 THE MODEL

In this section we describe the model. In terms of general notation, for any given variable x a bar ($\bar{x}$) denotes that variable's trend or potential value. A *gap* term added to the variable ($xgap$) denotes deviation from trend or potential. A delta (Δ) in front of the variable indicates changes from one period to the next, except for inflation rates, which are denoted with a π. Finally, an asterisk $*$ denotes a foreign variable.

Before presenting the model it is useful to briefly mention its properties. The model is structural, in that each equation has economic interpretation, and general equilibrium, in that the model's equations jointly determine the dynamics of inflation, output, short-term interest rates, and the real exchange rate. It is also stochastic: the system of equations is subject to various shocks, the variance of which can help derive measures of uncertainty in the baseline forecast. Expectations of future variables matter for macroeconomic outcomes and are rational, in the sense that they depend on the model's own forecast. Despite these somewhat complex features, the core economics embedded in the model are simple: aggregate demand and supply shocks drive inflation but monetary policy provides the nominal anchor.

2.1 Price Indices and Relative Prices

We begin by defining price indices and various relative prices. First, the headline price index (p_t^{cpi}, all prices are in logs) is the weighted sum of food (p_t^f) and non-food prices (p_t^{nf}):

$$p_t^{cpi} = wp_t^f + (1 - w)p_t^{nf},$$

$$\pi_t^{cpi} = 4(p_t^{cpi} - p_{t-1}^{cpi}) = w\pi_t^f + (1 - w)\pi_t^{nf},$$

$$\pi_t^{4,cpi} = p_t^{cpi} - p_{t-4}^{cpi},$$

where w is the weight of food, π_t is the quarterly inflation rate (annualized) and π_t^4 is the year-on-year inflation rate.

The first relative price is the domestic price of food relative to non-food:

$$rlp_t = p_t^f - p_t^{nf}.$$

The second relative price is the domestic price of food relative to the international price of food measured in local currency:

$$dev_t = p_t^f - (p_t^{*f} + s_t),$$

where p_t^{*f} is the international price of food (in dollars) and s_t is the nominal exchange rate (shillings per dollars). dev_t measures the extent of the deviation between domestic and foreign food prices. As will be shown later, whether this deviation creates pressures for domestic food price inflation—in order to catch up with international prices—depends on whether the deviation reflects temporary or long-term factors.

The third relative price is the international price of food relative to the international CPI (p_t^{*cpi}):

$$rlp_t^* = p_t^{*f} - p_t^{*cpi}.$$

The fourth relative price is the real exchange rate, which is given by the international CPI (measured in domestic currency) minus the domestic CPI:

$$z_t = s_t + p_t^{*cpi} - p_t^{cpi}.$$

Note that, by construction, all four relative prices are related, as follows:

$$z_t = (1 - w)rlp_t - rlp_t^* - dev_t.$$

The above relation also holds for the gaps and trend components of these relative prices.

For reasons that will become clear later, we also define two alternative real exchange rate measures, a food and a non-food real exchange rate. Each of these relative prices can also be derived using z_t and rlp_t:

$$z_t^f = s_t + p_t^{*cpi} - p_t^f = z_t - (1 - w)rlp_t.$$

$$z_t^{nf} = s_t + p_t^{*cpi} - p_t^{nf} = z_t + wrlp_t.$$

2.2 Trends in Relative Prices

All relative prices are decomposed into gap and trend components:

$$x_t = xgap_t + \bar{x}_t, \quad for \quad x = rlp, rlp^*, dev, z, z^f, z^{nf}.$$

We only need to define stochastic processes for three relative price trends, as trends for the other relative prices will follow from the above relations. We assume first-order autoregressive processes in first (annualized) differences for the domestic relative price of food (rlp), the international relative price of food (rlp^*), and the real exchange rate (z):

$$\Delta\overline{rlp}_t = \theta_{rlp}\Delta\overline{rlp}_{t-1} + (1 - \theta_{rlp})\Delta\overline{rlp} + \epsilon_t^{\overline{rlp}}.$$

$$\Delta\overline{rlp^*}_t = \theta_{rlp^*}\Delta\overline{rlp^*}_{t-1} + (1 - \theta_{rlp^*})\Delta\overline{rlp^*} + \epsilon_t^{\overline{rlp^*}}.$$

$$\Delta\bar{z}_t = \theta_z\Delta\bar{z}_{t-1} + (1 - \theta_z)\Delta\bar{z} + \epsilon_t^{\bar{z}}.$$

The above specification merits two comments. First, the trend value of dev_t ($\overline{dev}_t$) will drift, as implied by the stochastic trends of rlp_t, rlp_t^*, and z_t. This drift implies the long-run value of domestic food prices is unrelated to the long-run value of international food prices: trend changes in international relative food prices $\overline{rlp^*}_t$ will simply result in an equal and offsetting increase in $\overline{dev}_t$, without any implication for trend changes in domestic relative food prices $\overline{rlp}_t$. This is a stronger assumption than lack of cointegration. While this disconnect may seem extreme, it only applies to long-run movements in relative prices and not to gap movements, which—as we will see—account for much of the dynamics in international food prices in the last few years. As will be shown below, it is also based on the observed trend movements in dev_t.

Second, the existence of relative price trends has implications for the inflation rates of certain price indices, even if the inflation rate for the headline index is (eventually) determined by the inflation objective. As the relative price of food is either growing or decaying along a stochastic trend (depending on the sign of $\overline{\Delta rlp}_t$), nominal food prices will tend to grow at a different rate than non-food prices. Specifically, for any time-varying inflation objective $\bar{\pi}_t$, implicit targets for food and non-food inflation must be as follows:

$$\bar{\pi}_t^f = \bar{\pi}_t + (1 - w)\overline{\Delta rlp}_t, \qquad \bar{\pi}_t^{nf} = \bar{\pi}_t - w\overline{\Delta rlp}_t.$$

In addition, the long-run (annualized) nominal rate of depreciation must be consistent with the process for trend real exchange rates and domestic and foreign inflation targets:

$$\Delta \bar{s}_t = \Delta \bar{z}_t + \bar{\pi}_t - \bar{\pi}^*.$$

2.3 Output and Real Interest Rates

Quarterly (non-agricultural) output is divided into its gap and potential components,

$$y_t = \bar{y}_t + ygap_t,$$

where potential output follows a random walk with time-varying drift g_t:

$$\Delta \bar{y}_t = g_t + \epsilon_t^{\bar{y}}, \qquad g_t = \tau_g \bar{g} + (1 - \tau_g)g_{t-1} + \epsilon_t^g.$$

Thus there can be both i.i.d. and persistent shocks to the growth rate, which allows for more flexibility in matching the data. The output gap is given by a hybrid IS curve. It depends on real monetary conditions (*rmc*) and foreign demand (*ygap**), as well as past and future output gaps:

$$ygap_t = \beta_1 ygap_{t-1} + \beta_2 E_t(ygap_{t+1}) - \beta_3 rmc_{t-1} + \beta_5 ygap_t^* + \epsilon_t^{ygap}.$$

Real monetary conditions are composed of the real interest rate gap (*rrgap*)—the difference between actual real interest rates $\left(rs_t - E_t(\pi_{t+1}^{cpi})\right)$ and neutral real interest rates ($\overline{rr}_t$)—and the real exchange rate gap:

$$rmc_t = (1 - \beta_4)rrgap_t + \beta_4(-zgap_t).$$

Note that neutral rates follow an AR(1) process:

$$\overline{rr}_t = \rho_{\overline{rr}} \overline{rr}_{t-1} + (1 - \rho_{\overline{rr}})\overline{rr} + \epsilon_t^{\overline{rr}}.$$

2.4 Phillips Curves

We introduce two Phillips curves: one for non-food prices and one for food prices. The non-food Phillips curve is of the form:

$$\pi_t^{nf} - \bar{\pi}_t^{nf} = \lambda_1\left(E_t(\pi_{t+1}^{nf}) - \bar{\pi}_t^{nf}\right) + (1 - \lambda_1 - \lambda_2)(\pi_{t-1}^{nf} - \bar{\pi}_t^{nf})$$
$$+ \lambda_2(\pi_{nf,t}^{imp} - \bar{\pi}_t^{imp}) + \lambda_3 rmc_t^{nf} + \epsilon_t^{\pi nf},$$

where

$$\pi_t^{imp} = \pi_t^{*cpi} + \Delta s_t, \qquad \bar{\pi}_t^{imp} = \bar{\pi}_t^{*cpi} + \Delta \bar{s}_t$$

and

$$rmc_t^{nf} = \lambda_4 ygap_t + (1 - \lambda_4)z^{nf}gap_t.$$

This specification allows temporary changes in imported inflation to have a direct effect on non-food inflation, as captured by the term $\lambda_2(\pi_{nf,t}^{imp} - \bar{\pi}_t^{imp})$. It also makes non-food inflation sensitive to expected future and lagged changes of itself, as well as changes in real marginal costs in the non-food sector (rmc_t^{nf}). These are given by a weighted sum of the domestic output gap and the real exchange rate gap in terms of non-food prices.[6]

The Phillips curve for food prices has a similar structure:

$$\pi_t^f - \bar{\pi}_t^f = b_1\left(E_t(\pi_{t+1}^f) - \bar{\pi}_t^f\right) + (1 - b_1 - b_2)(\pi_{t-1}^f - \bar{\pi}_t^f)$$
$$+ b_2(\pi^{imp} - \bar{\pi}_t^{imp}) + b_3 rmc_t^f + \epsilon_t^{\pi f},$$

where

$$rmc_t^f = (1 - b_4 - b_5)ygap_t + b_4 z^f gap_t - b_5 devgap_t.$$

In addition to a potentially different calibration, the main difference relative to non-food inflation is that real marginal costs also depend on temporary deviations between domestic and international food prices ($devgap_t$). This extra term implies that temporary increases in international food prices will be inflationary, as they open a gap relative to domestic food prices that will be closed (in part) by increases in domestic food prices.[7]

---

[6] In an appendix to the working paper version of this chapter, we show that the specification of the two Phillips curves in the model can be derived from micro-foundations. In the case of non-food inflation, the Phillips curve can be derived by assuming that the production of non-food requires a domestic input, e.g., labour, and imported goods. In this case, changes in the domestic cost of production are captured by changes in the output gap, while changes in the imported cost are represented by the real exchange rate gap. Note that, in two sector models, what is inflationary in each sector is not the real exchange rate gap per se but the cost of imported goods relative to prices in that sector, which is why $z^{nf}gap_t$ enters the equation and not $zgap_t$.

[7] In the separate appendix mentioned earlier, we show that this additional term can be micro-founded by assuming that the production of the domestic food basket also requires imported food, in addition to domestic labour and imported non-food items.

2.5 Exchange Rate (UIP)

We assume that uncovered interest parity (UIP) holds:

$$4(zgap_t - zgap_t^e) = -(rrgap_t - rrgap_t^*) + prem_t + \epsilon_t^s,$$

where $prem_t$ measures persistent movements in the risk premium associated with holding domestic currency, which follows an AR(1) process with coefficient ρ_{prem}, and ϵ_t^s measure one-time errors in exchange rate valuation. Real exchange rate expectations are allowed to deviate temporarily from rational expectations:

$$zgap_t^e = \phi E_t(zgap_{t+1}) + (1 - \phi)zgap_{t-1}.$$

2.6 Monetary policy rule

We assume that the central bank moves the interest rate in response to endogenous developments in the economy, as follows:

$$rs_t = \gamma_1 rs_{t-1} + (1 - \gamma_1)[\bar{rr}_t + \bar{\pi}_{t+1} + \gamma_2(\pi_{t+4}^{4,cpi} - \bar{\pi}_{t+4}^{cpi})$$
$$+ \gamma_3 ygap_t + \gamma_4 \Delta sgap_t] + \epsilon_t^{rs}.$$

The central bank also specifies a stochastic process for its inflation target:

$$\bar{\pi}_t = \rho_{\bar{\pi}}\bar{\pi}_{t-1} + (1 - \rho_{\bar{\pi}})\bar{\pi} + \epsilon_t^{\bar{\pi}}.$$

While this specification may appear surprising—why would the central bank subject its inflation target to persistent fluctuations?—it is meant to capture relatively low-frequency movements in inflation. These movements tend to reflect changes in the central bank's willingness to tolerate certain levels of inflation and have been proven to capture an important element of inflation dynamics in developed and emerging markets.[8]

2.7 Foreign Block

The dynamics of the model are complete with the foreign block, a set of six equations that describes the comovement of external variables:

$$ygap_t^* = \beta_1^* ygap_{t-1}^* + \beta_2^* ygap_{t+1}^* - \beta_3^* rrgap_{t-1}^* + \epsilon_t^{ygap^*},$$

$$\pi_t^{*cpi} = \lambda_1^* \pi_{t+1}^{*cpi} + (1 - \lambda_1^*)\pi_{t-1}^{*cpi} + \lambda_2^* ygap_t^* + \epsilon_t^{\pi^*},$$

$$rs_t^* = \gamma_1^* rs_{t-1}^* + (1 - \gamma_1^*)[\bar{rr}_t^* + \bar{\pi}^* + \gamma_2^*(\pi_{t+4}^{4,*cpi} - \bar{\pi}^{*cpi}) + \gamma_3^* ygap_t^*] + \epsilon_t^{RS^*},$$

$$rlpgap_t^* = \rho_{f^*} rlpgap_{t-1}^* + \epsilon_t^{rlp^*},$$

$$\bar{rr}_t^* = \rho_{rr^*}\bar{rr}_{t-1}^* + (1 - \rho_{rr^*})\bar{rr}^* + \epsilon_t^{rr^*},$$

---

[8] See Smets and Wouters (2007) and Ireland (2007), among others.

and the process for the trend in the international relative price of food described earlier. Note that international food inflation is given by $\pi_t^{*f} = \pi_t^{*cpi} + \Delta r l p_t^*$.

3 APPLYING THE MODEL TO KENYA

Having described the model, we now present various model-based exercises for Kenya. We begin by describing Kenya's recent experience. We then discuss the calibration and our dataset. We provide impulse response functions for selected shocks, and conclude with the filtration exercise, with an emphasis on two related issues: the decomposition of macro-variables into their trend and gap components, and the historical decomposition of recent business-cycle dynamics in Kenya by the relevant shocks.

3.1 Kenya: Inflation Developments and Monetary Policy 2007–11

Kenya has experienced large swings in inflation in recent years. Headline inflation accelerated from around 3 per cent at the beginning of 2007 to 16 per cent by mid-2008, and after having fully reversed by mid-2010, climbed again to almost 20 per cent by the end of 2011. Inflation dynamics were accounted for by both food and non-food (see Figure 15.1). Kenya is exposed to changes in imported food prices: 40 per cent of the total cereal consumption (of about 5 million metric tons, chiefly maize) is imported. This influence can be seen by comparing the Kenyan food price index (measured in dollars) with a price index of international food commodity prices (see Figure 15.2): the two series display considerable comovement, especially during the food crisis.[9] Policy challenges were compounded by domestic shocks and the downturn of the global economy in the period 2007–09.

Kenya's de jure monetary policy anchor has traditionally been reserve money targeting. It is difficult to characterize the CBK's de facto monetary policy framework, though there is considerable exchange rate flexibility. It maintained an inflation target of 5 $\pm$ 2 per cent. Its reserve money targets have often been missed and subsequently adjusted. From 2009 to 2011, reserve growth was consistently higher than targeted, explained by the CBK in terms of its objective of increasing financial intermediation (through higher broad money growth) and thus supporting economic activity.

The effectiveness, or at least transparency, of monetary policy was hampered by the operational framework in place. The CBK maintained a so-called 'policy rate', meant to signal the stance of policy (the Central Bank rate, or CBR). In practice, the rate was not relevant for the financial system: sizeable injections of liquidity resulted in a large decline in interbank rates, which fell to 1 per cent while the CBR stood at 6 per cent. The CBK employed repo and reverse repo operations to manage liquidity, with the rates associated with these operations delinked to the CBR and moving in line with the interbank rate.

---

[9] Cointegration between the two series is rejected. Regressing the Kenyan index on the international one (in first differences) generates a pass-through coefficient of 0.36.

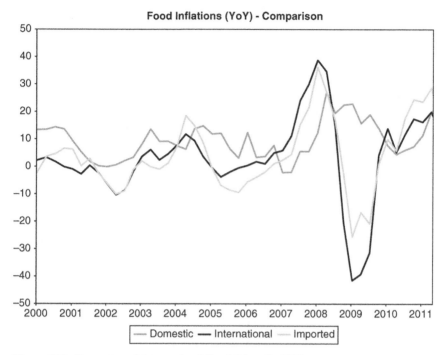

Figure 15.2. Domestic and International Food Prices (in US$)

Inflation started to accelerate significantly in 2011, reaching almost 19 per cent in November. The Shilling depreciated by 15 per cent in the six months to November 2011 as inflation expectations deteriorated. Facing this instability, the CBK modified its operational framework in September 2011, with a view to making the CBR useful as a signal of policy. It increased the CBR to 18 per cent by December 2011 from 6.25 in September. In addition, the CBR became the pivot rate for both repos and reverse repos; i.e., these operations would take place at the CBR rate plus or minus a margin. Since this reform and policy shift, inflation has been declining steadily, though it remains above the 5 per cent target, standing at 13 per cent as of April 2012.

In sum, Kenya fits the description of many SSA central banks in IMF (2008): it pursued an inflation objective in the context of a managed float, but with a variety of instruments and intermediate targets, including some—uneven—attention to monetary aggregates. In this chapter we choose to simplify by characterizing the stance of policy in terms of a single interest rate, the construction of which we describe below. We return to this issue in the Discussion section.

3.2 Calibration and Data

3.2.1 *Calibration*

We present the calibration in Tables 15.1–15.3. Our choice is guided by several principles. First, some of the parameters of the model (average growth rates of

Table 15.1. Calibration

Parameter	Description	Value	Source/Remarks
Relative Prices and their Trends			
w	Share of food in the CPI	0.36	Kenya National Bureau of Statistics
$\Delta\overline{rlp}$	Trend growth rate, relative price of food	6.5	Historical average
θ_{rlp}	Persistence, trend growth, relative price of food	0.8	System properties (S.P.)
$\Delta\bar{z}$	Trend growth rate, real exchange rate	−4	Historical average
θ_{rlp}	Persistence, trend growth, real growth rate	0.65	S.P.
Output and Real Interest Rates			
$\bar{g}$	Trend growth rate, non-agricultural GDP	4	Historical average
θ_g	Persistence, trend growth, GDP	0.5	S.P.
β_1	Backward-looking parameter, IS curve	0.6	Implies real economic activity
β_2	Forward-looking parameter, IS curve	0.1	is relatively backward looking
β_3	Output sensitivity to real monetary cond. (rmc)	0.15	Weak interest rate channel
β_4	Weight of real exchange rate in rmc	0.6	Strong exchange rate channel
β_5	Output sensitivity to foreign demand	0.15	Relatively large
$\rho_{\bar{rr}}$	Persistence, equilibrium real interest rate	0.75	S.P.
$\bar{rr}$	Equilibrium real interest rate	1	Historical average
Non-Food Phillips Curve			
λ_1	Forward-looking parameter	0.4	
λ_2	Exposure to imported food inflation	0.05	
λ_3	Sensitivity to real marginal cost (rmc)	0.2	
λ_4	Weight of output gap in rmc	0.5	
Food Phillips Curve			
b_1	Forward-looking parameter	0.5	
b_2	Exposure to imported food inflation	0.05	
b_3	Sensitivity to real marginal cost (rmc)	0.1	
b_4	Weight of food real exchange rate gap in rmc	0.1	
b_5	Weight of food deviation gap in rmc	0.7	

relative prices and output, long-run value of equilibrium real interest rates, average inflation target) reflect Kenyan averages or, in the case of the inflation target, the explicit objective of the central bank. These parameters are straightforward to calibrate.

Other parameters reflect our views about structural features of the Kenyan economy, relative to other economies. As there is an extensive literature applying these models to many advanced and emerging economies, these can serve as a starting point from which to build a Kenya-specific calibration.[10] In the IS curve, the relatively large backward-looking term and small forward-looking term reflect our view that expectations of future developments play a relatively small role in output dynamics. The small sensitivity of output to interest rates (given by $\beta_3(1 - \beta_4) = 0.06$) is consistent with the view that the interest rate channel is

---

[10] For example, a simpler but related version of this model was estimated for South Africa using Bayesian methods. See Harjes and Ricci (2006).

Table 15.2. Calibration (continued)

Parameter	Description	Value	Source/Remarks
Monetary Policy and Uncovered Interest Parity			
ρ_{prem}	AR parameter for country risk premium	0.75	S.P.
ϕ	Forward-looking term in UIP	0.85	...
γ_1	Interest rate smoothing in MP rule	0.8	...
γ_2	Long-run MP response to inflation	1.4	...
γ_3	Long-run MP response to output gap	0	...
γ_4	Long-run MP response to nominal depreciation	0.25	...
$\bar{\pi}$	Inflation target	5	...
$\rho_{\bar{\pi}}$	Persistence, inflation target	0.85	...
Rest of the World			
$\Delta\overline{rlp}^*$	Trend growth rate, intl. relative price of food	2	Historical average
θ_{rlp}^*	Persistence, trend growth, intl. relative price of food	0.5	S.P.
β_1^*	Backward-looking parameter, IS curve	0.5	...
β_2^*	Forward-looking parameter, IS curve	0.5	...
β_3^*	Output gap sensitivity to real interest rate gap	0.05	...
λ_1^*	Forward-looking parameter, Phillips curve	0.6	...
λ_2^*	Sensitivity to output gap, Phillips curve	0.06	
γ_1^*	Interest rate smoothing in MP rule	0.75	...
λ_2^*	Long-run MP response to inflation	1.7	...
λ_3^*	Long-run MP response to output gap	0.25	...
ρ_{pf}^*	Persistence, international food price gap	0.75	...
ρ_{rr}^*	Persistence, equilibrium real interest rate	0.5	...
$\overline{rr}^*$	Equilibrium real interest rate	2.5	Historical average

Table 15.3. Calibration (continued)

Parameter	Description	Value	Source/Remarks
Monetary Policy and Uncovered Interest Parity			
$\sigma_{\overline{rlp}}$	Volatility, dom. relative food price trend	2	S.P.
σ_z	Volatility, real exchange rate trend shocks	3	S.P.
$\sigma_{\bar{y}}$	Volatility, potential output growth shocks	1.5	S.P.
$\sigma_{\bar{g}}$	Volatility, potential output drift shocks	1	S.P.
σ_{ygap}	Volatility, output gap shocks	1	S.P.
$\sigma_{\bar{rr}}$	Volatility, equilibrium real interest rate shocks	0.7	S.P.
$\sigma_{\pi_{nf}}$	Volatility, dom. non-food shocks	1.5	S.P.
$\sigma_{\pi_{nf}}$	Volatility, dom. food shocks	2.5	S.P.
σ_s	Volatility, UIP shocks	3.5	S.P.
σ_{prem}	Volatility, risk premium shocks	3.5	S.P.
σ_{rs}	Volatility, monetary policy shocks	1.5	S.P.
$\sigma_{\bar{\pi}}$	Volatility, inflation targets	1	S.P.
σ_{ygap}^*	Volatility, US output gap shocks	0.3	S.P.
σ_{rs}^*	Volatility, US monetary policy shocks	0.3	S.P.
$\sigma_{\bar{rr}}^*$	Volatility, US equilibrium real interest rate shocks	0.08	S.P.
σ_{π}^*	Volatility, US CPI shocks	1.5	S.P.
$\sigma_{\overline{rlp}}^*$	Volatility, intl. relative food price trend shocks	0.35	S.P.
σ_{rlpgap}^*	Volatility, intl. relative food price gap shocks	0.3	S.P.

likely to be small in LICs, while the relative importance of the real exchange rate gap in *rmc* indicates the exchange rate channel is relatively stronger.

In the case of the two Phillips curves, non-food inflation is more sensitive to the output gap, with the sensitivity given by $\lambda_3\lambda_4 = 0.1$, than food inflation, with the sensitivity given by $b_3(1 - b_4 - b_5) = 0.02$. The same holds regarding sensitivity to the real exchange rate: it equals $\lambda_3(1 - \lambda_4) = 0.1$ in the non-food sector but only $b_3b_4 = 0.04$ in the food sector. This difference reflects our view that aggregate demand is crucial for understanding non-food inflation dynamics, and is less of a factor for food inflation. On the other hand, food inflation is quite sensitive to temporary gaps between international and domestic food prices (*devgap$_t$*): a 1 per cent widening of the gap—ignoring expectations of future values of *devgap*— results in an immediate 0.07 per cent increase in food prices. The effect is twice as large (0.13) once expectations about future gaps are incorporated into current prices. The calibration of the monetary policy rule is relatively dovish, with large smoothing of interest rates and a relatively small response to increases in expected inflation. The calibration also allows for some response to nominal exchange rate movements (an important issue in LICs) but no response to the output gap. The calibration for the rest of the world is taken from applications of similar gap models to the US economy.

Finally, the last set of parameters are calibrated in part based on the model's ability to deliver plausible interpretations of recent macro dynamics. The parameters that fall in this category are primarily the AR coefficients of most exogenous variables, as well as the variances of the shocks which are listed in Table 15.3. As is explained in Appendix 15B, the filtration exercise depends on the relative variance of the shocks, since there are more shocks than observables, so the choice of these as well as the AR coefficients help determine the model's account of Kenya's business cycle.[11] To pin down these parameter values, we start with an initial calibration, assess the model-based decomposition of the data, and iterate until the model-based story looks plausible.[12]

Several additional points are worth making about calibration. As mentioned above, the calibration is assessed in part on the plausibility of the model-based interpretation of recent events (our focus here). There are other dimensions which we do not discuss in this chapter which are equally important, such as the forecasting properties of the model, both in-sample and out-of-sample.[13]

---

[11] For example, we picked the variances of the shocks to potential or trend values to be such that they resulted in relatively smooth trends. Otherwise, the trends would absorb large part of the business cycle movements of variables such as output, relative prices, and interest rates.

[12] It is feasible to estimate the model through Bayesian methods (as for example in Berg et al., 2010, the working paper version of Chapter 8, for a similar model). However, for operational purposes the iterative process is preferable, at least at first. It helps the operator understand the mechanisms of the model and in particular the mapping between calibrations and the interpretation of history. It also allows the operator to embody views of the transmission mechanism derived from other sources, such as the judgement of policymakers. And it avoids the danger of 'overfitting', in particular of attempting to fit episodes when the operator knows (or should know) that there really were large unexpected and un-modeled events, e.g. fiscal shocks, movements in the risk premium from global events, or droughts or riots that temporarily drove food prices.

[13] In the working paper version of this chapter we find that the model makes reasonable forecasts, especially out-of-sample.

Second, we must acknowledge that considerable judgement is involved in this exercise as there is no unique way of calibrating the model, and therefore of interpreting the data. This is a general property of calibrated exercises. Third, there is a somewhat wide range of parameters which will yield broadly similar results, so it is not necessary to obsess over excessively precise calibration values. In addition, the range of possible parameter values is also limited by the fact that the model must have a unique rational expectations equilibrium. For example, the Taylor principle—the idea that real interest rates must increase in the event of a persistent surge in inflation—places a lower bound on γ_2^*. We will discuss the implications of an alternative calibration for the interpretations of recent events below.

3.2.2 Data

The data are described in Appendix 15A. The data are of mixed frequency, and go from the beginning of 2000 to 2011. Two series are worth discussing in some detail. The short-term interest rate used in the model—monthly series, averaged into quarters—differs from the CBK policy rate, since the latter did not reflect the true stance of monetary policy for reasons discussed in Part II (Figure 15.3 presents the various rates). Instead, we choose the rate that best captures the policy stance. From 2000:1 to 2009:1, and from 2011:5 to 2011:6, we use the repo rate as the central bank was mainly withdrawing liquidity from the money market.

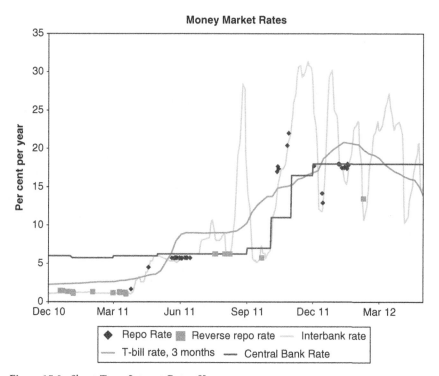

Figure 15.3. Short-Term Interest Rates, Kenya

From 2009:3 to 2011:4 we use the reverse repo rate since the central bank was mainly injecting liquidity. In 2009:2 we used the average of the two, as the central bank was engaging in both operations during that month.

The second series of interest is the CPI series and its components. There have been various changes in methodology in the construction of price indices in Kenya. Previous CPI inflation series suffered from upward biases, especially in food price inflation, in part reflecting the use of a chained arithmetic mean formula (the 'Carli' index). The Kenya National Bureau of Statistics switched to a geometric mean formula in 2009, for both food and non-food prices, and retroactively revised the aggregate CPI index (but not the sub-indexes) up to 2005. To construct a consistent series that would go back to the beginning of our sample, we estimated a bias coefficient from the period where the alternative indices (from the two methodologies) overlap and applied the correction to the older series.[14]

3.3 Impulse Response Analysis

We begin our assessment of the model by analysing how a 1 per cent temporary increase in international relative food prices ($\epsilon_t^{rlpgap\star} = 1$) affects Kenyan inflation. The purpose of this exercise is to highlight various aspects of the transmission mechanism.

Figure 15.4 plots impulse responses for international food price inflation as well as domestic food and CPI inflation (all presented on a year-on-year (YoY) basis) for two cases. Results are presented in deviations, i.e., movements in inflation rates above or below their long-run value. By construction, temporary changes to international relative food prices have very short-lived effects on international food inflation, since they result in one time increases in the food price *level*, which then declines over time. This is reflected in the large drop in YoY international food price inflation after four quarters. However, the effect on domestic inflation is longer-lived, since it takes longer for the increase to be (incompletely) passed on to domestic food prices.

In the first case (left quadrant), we assume that monetary policy does not respond and that the nominal exchange rate does not depreciate.[15] The increase in inflation can be thought of as the first-round effect of shocks to international food prices. In this case, the shock has a large effect on food inflation but no effect on non-food, so the impact on headline is given by the weight of food in the

---

[14] Our measure of output (non-agricultural GDP) was available at annual frequency; it was interpolated using the Chow-Lin procedure. We apply an HP filter with a very small λ ($\lambda = 0.8$), to remove some of the noise that resulted from the interpolation. This helps make the series slightly smoother and avoids forcing the model to provide a structural interpretation for every small jump in the series. An alternative, more cumbersome, approach would have been to explicitly model the noise in the series as part of the broader model.

[15] To generate this scenario, we simulate a subset of the model where the output gap is always set to zero and the nominal interest rate stays constant, in which case the nominal exchange rate—through uncovered interest parity—does not depreciate. As actual real interest rates are declining, this exercise implicitly assumes a decrease in equilibrium real interest rates to keep the output gap closed.

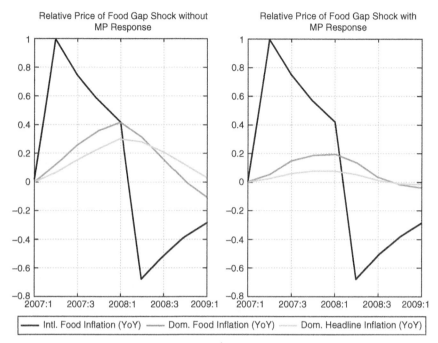

Figure 15.4. Impulse Response Functions, $\epsilon_t^{rlpgap\star} = 1$

CPI. In the second case (right quadrant), we allow for monetary policy to respond, in which case the central bank raises interest rates as inflation increases. This policy tightening leads to an incipient decline in the output gap, which, all else equal, creates pressures for both non-food and food inflation to decrease. In addition, the increases in interest rates results in a temporary appreciation of the currency, which also reduces inflation by reducing production costs in both sectors. The increase in inflation is therefore smaller.

Note that the direct effect of monetary policy can also be analysed with a monetary policy shock ($\epsilon_t^{RS} = 1$), shown in Figure 15.5. Consistent with the previous discussion, the shock results in an increase in the output gap, a decline in both components of inflation and a nominal and real depreciation.

We do not show impulse responses for all shocks, for the sake of brevity. A general result is that all non-trend shocks have an effect on inflation since they affect gap terms, and the monetary policy response will play a role in the propagation of the shock.[16] Shocks to trend components are not inflationary, with two exceptions. The first exception is a positive shock to the trend component of the domestic relative price of food ($\epsilon_t^{\overline{rlp}} = 1$), not shown. In this case, there would

---

[16] One such shock is the one that appears in the food Phillips curve. This shock can capture variations in food inflation due to temporary real factors, such as large variations in the weather that affect the production of food, or changes in food tariffs, subsidies or taxes. Understanding how these factors affect food inflation—and by how much—is an important area of research and merits further work.

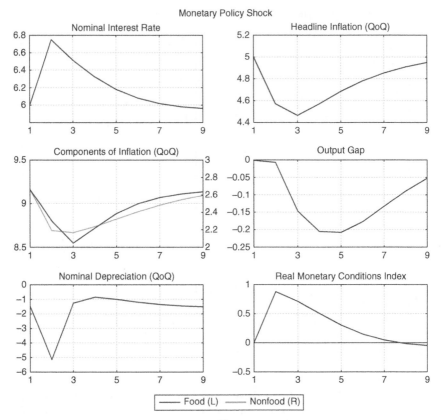

Figure 15.5. Impulse Response Functions, $\epsilon_t^{RS} = 1$

be an increase in the food inflation rate, a decrease in non-food inflation rate, but no change in the headline inflation rate (and no monetary policy response). The second exception concerns a shock to equilibrium real interest rates ($\epsilon_t^{\overline{rr}}$, not shown), which would have an impact on economic activity and inflation because of the slow adjustment in the monetary policy rule. Actual real interest rates would not keep up with equilibrium rates, thus opening a gap in real monetary conditions.

3.4 Filtering Kenyan Data through the Model

We now use the model to interpret the joint movement of macro variables in Kenya. To do so, we filter the data through the model using the Kalman smoother described in Appendix 15B. The Kalman filter and smoother are recursive algorithms used to estimate a sequence of unobserved state variables whose dynamics are described by a state space model—a vector autoregression of order one (VAR(1))—based on the observations of a sequence of other variables which are linearly related to them. In our case, the state variables are trend and gap components and the shocks—their dynamics are jointly described by the VAR(1) representation of the model solution—and the observables are the actual series.

The use of the Kalman smoother to estimate trends and gaps implies that the estimates at any point in time draw on information from the entire sample, e.g., the estimate of the output gap in 2005:Q1 depends on movements in inflation (and other observed variables) from both before and after 2005:Q1. This feature is convenient when trying to understand historical episodes, though it also implies that the economist doing the exercise can have a clearer picture of past macro developments than policymakers at the time.

We will focus primarily on two main outputs: a decomposition of most series into a trend (or potential) and a gap component, and a decomposition of the current value of any variable into the different shocks responsible for its dynamics.

3.4.1 Decomposition into Trends and Gaps

We begin the analysis by looking at the model's four main relative prices (z_t, rlp_t, rlp_t^*, dev_t), which are displayed in Figure 15.6. Kenya's real exchange rate (z_t) has appreciated over time (see upper left quadrant), which in the model is accounted for by a smooth trend appreciation. The real exchange rate also displays some

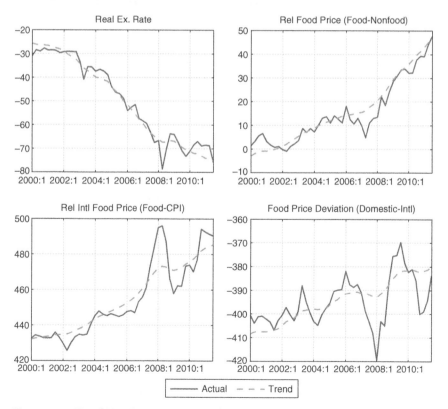

Figure 15.6. Trend/Gap Decomposition, Relative Prices

noticeable spikes, especially in 2008, accounted for by movements in the gap (the difference between the two series). The international relative price of food (rlp_t^*, bottom left quadrant) also displays a relatively smooth positive trend, with large movements in the gap. Of particular interest are the large increase in international food prices in 2007–08 and the more recent spike, which in our model are mainly accounted for by shocks to the international food price gap, although the trend also increased.

A different story emerges for the domestic relative price of food (rlp_t, upper right quadrant). The trend component also increases over time, though it slows down at the onset of the 2007–08 period before accelerating after that. The actual domestic relative price of food falls in early 2007, so that most of the increase in food inflation observed in 2008 can be interpreted as catching up relative to the trend. rlp_t falls below trend again in 2010, though the gap is smaller. The deviation between domestic and foreign food prices (dev_t, bottom right quadrant) oscillates widely, with the 2007–08 crisis—and the more recent spike—opening up large negative gaps. Given the role of dev_t in the food Phillips curve, we can foresee these gaps will be inflationary.

Figure 15.7 plots the time series for GDP. Output experienced fast growth during 2003–07, with a 6 per cent average growth and 7 per cent peak in 2007, before dropping to 2 per cent in 2008–09. Given our assumption about the volatility of shocks to potential, potential output displays a smooth path, although it accounts for most of the growth observed in 2003–06. Most of the acceleration

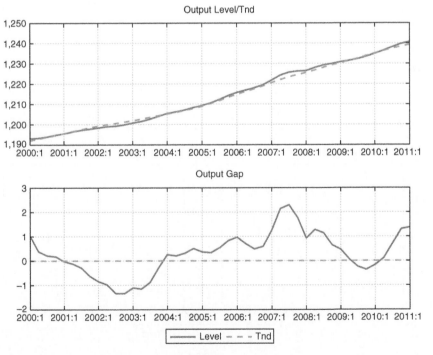

Figure 15.7. Trend/Gap Decomposition, GDP

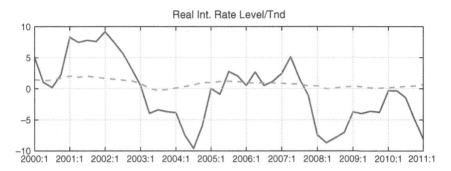

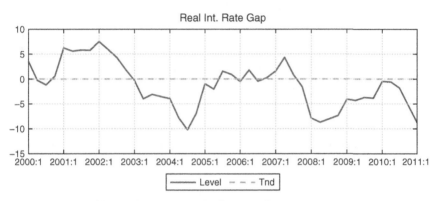

Figure 15.8. Trend/Gap Decomposition, Real Interest Rates

and deceleration of output around 2007 is explained by movements in the output gap, which peaks during that time but then contracts until it closes in mid-2009, in the midst of the global financial crisis. The gap opens up again from 2010 onwards.

Finally, the real interest rate (see Figure 15.8) displays large movements: largely positive from 2001 to early 2003, then largely negative until mid-2005 and again from mid-2007 until the end of the sample. Most of these movements are accounted for by movements in the real interest rate gap.

In sum, the trend/gap decomposition has identified various periods with sizeable gaps in output, relative prices, and real interest rates. As these gaps have inflationary effects, in the next subsection we account for some of them and for the resulting changes in inflation in terms of the model's shocks.

3.4.2 Decomposition into Shocks

With the help of the Kalman smoother, we decompose the dynamics of each series—both observed and unobserved—into the different estimated shocks and initial conditions (see Appendix 15B). Since we have eighteen different shocks, we regroup them into seven groups for convenience:

- Shocks that hit the output gap: ϵ_t^{ygap}, $\epsilon_t^{\overline{rr}}$.
- Shocks that hit sectoral inflation rates: $\epsilon_t^{\pi^f}$, $\epsilon_t^{\pi^{nf}}$, $\epsilon_t^{\overline{rlp}}$.

- Shocks that affect the international relative price of food: $\epsilon_t^{\overline{rlp}^*}$, $\epsilon_t^{rlpgap^*}$.
- Shocks related to monetary policy: ϵ_t^{RS}, ϵ_t^{π}.
- Shocks that directly affect the exchange rate: ϵ_t^S, ϵ_t^{prem}, $\epsilon_t^{\bar{z}}$.
- Shocks that originate in the rest of the world: $\epsilon_t^{ygap^*}$, $\epsilon_t^{\pi^*}$, $\epsilon_t^{RS^*}$, $\epsilon_t^{\overline{rr}^*}$.
- Other (initial conditions).[17]

The regrouping should not be interpreted too strictly, as some of the groups can overlap: some shocks to the exchange rate reflect changes in international market conditions and may be related to developments in the world economy. More generally, the model remains highly stylized and is likely to miss other transmission mechanisms which may be important in certain historical episodes. Estimated shocks may therefore comove as a result.

It is important to reiterate that shocks affect the model variables in a number of ways. In some cases, the effect is straightforward to understand. For example, shocks to the output gap will have a direct positive effect on that variable. In other cases, the interpretation is not simple. For example, shocks that persistently raise inflation would in principle have a positive impact on the output gap since, by raising expected inflation, they lower the real interest rate. However, this effect is more than offset by the fact that monetary policy endogenously responds to increases in inflation, which then tightens real monetary conditions and results in a real appreciation, both of which reduce the output gap. It is important for the model's user to understand the different channels through which shocks affects variables.

Finally, an important caveat to the shock-based analysis is the importance of own shocks, i.e., shocks that directly affect an observed variable (like temporary shocks to food and non-food inflation $\epsilon_t^{\pi^f}$ and $\epsilon_t^{\pi^{nf}}$). In general, these will soak up two types of movements in that variable. The first type of movement has an economic interpretation, e.g., negative shocks to the food harvest will result in an increase in food inflation, and will show up in $\epsilon_t^{\pi^f}$. The second type of movement captures any high frequency dynamics in that variable without a clear economic interpretation, and which is most likely due to the fact that the model is highly stylized. The latter type may result in an overstatement of the relative important of own shocks. We will therefore complement this analysis with alternative representations of the filtration exercise.

Figure 15.9 shows the shock decomposition for the output gap. Three main features emerge. First, an important share of output gap fluctuations is explained by developments in the international economy: the positive gap of the mid-2000s is driven in part by strong international output, with the deceleration of the economy in mid-2008 mainly due to the effects of the global financial crisis, and the recovery since mid-2010 supported by the relative improvement in the US economy. Second, output gap shocks account for much of the economic boom in 2007, associated in part with the increase in the fiscal deficit during that period.[18] Third, the Kenyan economy was supported by an accommodating monetary

---

[17] As previously discussed, shocks to potential output do not affect inflation and are therefore ignored in this analysis.

[18] Development expenditure increased by 60 per cent.

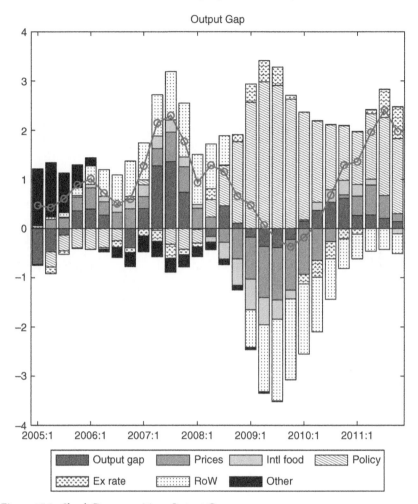

Figure 15.9. Shock Decomposition, Output Gap

policy ($\epsilon_t^{RS} < 0$, $\epsilon_t^{\pi} > 0$) from mid-2008 onwards, which helped offset some of the fallout from the global financial crisis. This monetary support became expansionary once the international economy recovered.

A related pattern emerges for non-food inflation (see Figure 15.10).[19] Shocks to non-food prices account for some of its movements. The benign international environment also helps account for some of the non-food movements, especially during the global financial crisis. But more importantly, non-food prices have been consistently buoyed by accommodating monetary policy, which resulted in the large acceleration in inflation observed in 2011.

---

[19] Inflation variables are de-meaned.

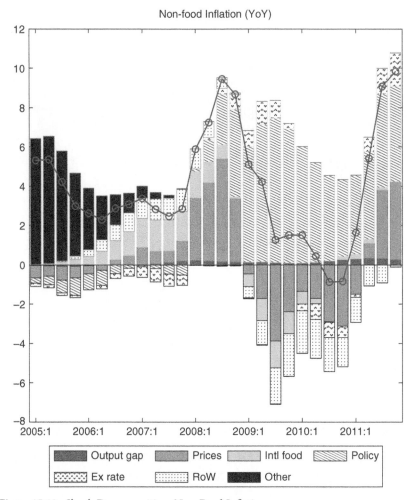

Figure 15.10. Shock Decomposition, Non-Food Inflation

The dynamics of food inflation (Figure 15.11) are somewhat different. Domestic food price shocks play an important role, reflecting the importance of shocks to the domestic food harvest such as the drought of 2008–09. More importantly, international food price shocks explain an important fraction of the upswing/downswing/upswing of food prices, while monetary conditions have again played a role. These two dynamics are then aggregated into headline inflation (Figure 15.12), with international conditions—including international food prices—but more importantly accommodating monetary policy being the two key factors.

We conclude this subsection with an analysis of nominal depreciation (Δs) relative to its long-run value—given by $\overline{\Delta s}$ —presented in Figure 15.13. The large depreciation observed in 2009 is accounted for by the shocks to monetary policy mentioned earlier, as well as shocks to the risk premium possibly associated with

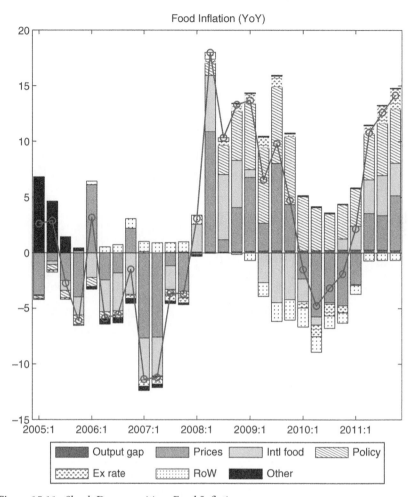

Figure 15.11. Shock Decomposition, Food Inflation

the worsening of the external environment during that time. The external improvement contributes to the nominal appreciation observed in early 2010. However, since then monetary policy and exchange rate shocks—the latter possibly associated with additional balance of payment pressures from the higher food and fuel import bill—resulted in the depreciation of the currency.

3.4.3 A Model-Based Interpretation of Monetary Policy

We now present an alternative representation of the model's results for the short-term interest rate (Figure 15.14). We compare observed interest rates with the path predicted by the model in the absence of the variable's own shock, which we refer to as 'KF Predicted'. We also present an alternative decomposition, based on the terms that enter the interest rate rule. Overall, the model-predicted interest

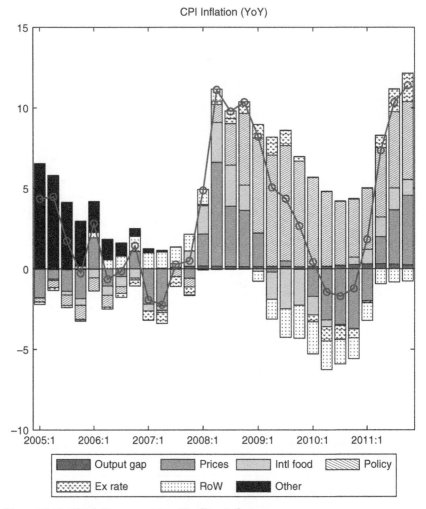

Figure 15.12. Shock Decomposition, Headline Inflation

rate tracks the actual interest rate relatively closely, which indicates the interest rate rule and the model more broadly (in its current calibration) do a reasonable job of accounting for interest rate dynamics.

However, since mid-2007, actual interest rates are consistently below those predicted by the model, with the difference due to the negative shocks to monetary policy described above. The gap is most prominent in 2008–09, where the model called for a policy tightening which did not take place. The gap opens up again starting in mid-2010 for similar reasons, though the widening is smaller. In sum, the application of the model to Kenya identifies a prolonged period of policy accommodation, which had important implications for inflation in 2008 and 2011.

In terms of the factors that describe the model's implied path for interest rates, we observe that most of the persistence in interest rates is due to the smoothing

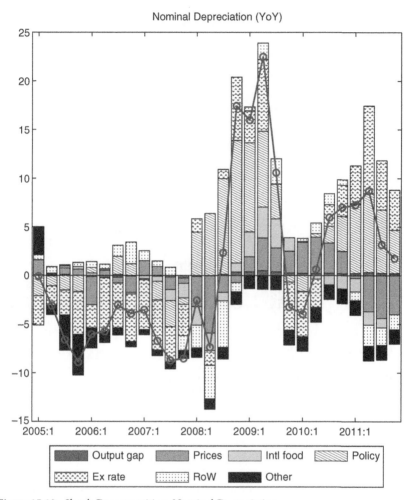

Figure 15.13. Shock Decomposition, Nominal Depreciation

factor in the policy rule. The increase in interest rates predicted by the model in 2008–09 and in 2011 is due to the increase in inflation observed during those periods, as well as the nominal depreciation in the first episode, whereas the decrease in rates in between is due to the decline in inflation.

3.5 Sensitivity Analysis

As previously mentioned, the model-based interpretation of the data depends crucially on the calibration of the model parameters, including the variances of the shocks. We now briefly discuss how alternative calibrations change the interpretation of recent history. In particular, we make the assumption that the variance of the monetary policy shock (σ_{rs}) and the variance of the shock to the inflation

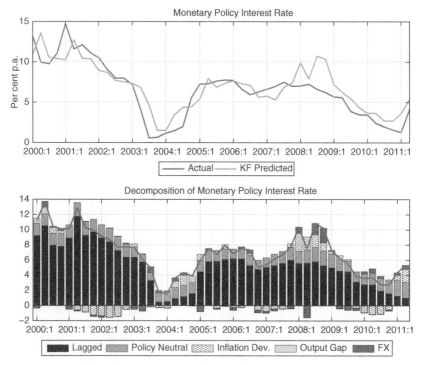

Figure 15.14. Central Bank Rate—Repo Rates

target ($\sigma_{\bar{\pi}}$) are almost zero. This is an extreme assumption, but it illustrates how to use the plausibility (or lack thereof) of the story that emerges from the filtration exercise to help inform the calibration. The comparison between the baseline and the alternative calibration are shown in Figure 15.15.

Imposing the absence of monetary policy shocks implies that the interest rate level observed in the data is perfectly accounted for by the interest rate rule. This has a number of implications. In the post-2008 period, the sustained decrease in interest rates coincides with an inflationary surge in 2010–11, and a corresponding increase in inflation expectations. Making the inflationary surge consistent with declining interest rates requires that some of the unobserved variables in the interest rate rule offset inflationary pressures. Given that the inflation target is forced to remain constant ($\sigma_{\bar{\pi}} = 0$), the equilibrium interest rate does the adjustment. The filtration therefore interprets 2008–11 as a period of large decline in equilibrium real interest rates (by as much as 1,000 basis points). In turn, this decline in equilibrium rates opens up a large gap in real monetary conditions and hence results in a largely negative output gap. It also results in positive shocks to aggregate demand to avoid too large a decrease in the output gap. In addition, a large negative output gap requires potential output (not shown) to be considerably higher. Finally, inflation is no longer accounted for by monetary policy shocks; instead, the bulk of the surge in inflation post-2010 is interpreted as supply-side shocks.

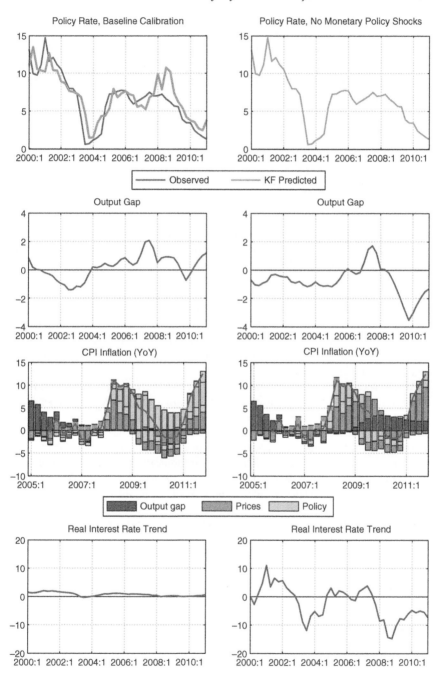

Figure 15.15. Sensitivity Analysis, Alternative Calibration

We can disregard this story as implausible. Among other things it requires that equilibrium/trend real interest rates make large swings, which is inconsistent with the idea that this variable should be relatively smooth. It also requires that the combination of low interest rates, increasing inflation and output acceleration post-2010 be unrelated. A more plausible story must therefore allow some role for monetary policy shocks.[20]

4 DISCUSSION

The use of the model for policy analysis has yielded various insights into the drivers of inflation in Kenya. One such insight is the role of excessively accommodating monetary policy in recent years. In this section we discuss some likely factors behind the policy stance during this period.

Monetary policy operates in an environment of considerable uncertainty and incomplete information. The central bank must rely on current and leading indicators that are noisy and may not reveal a clear picture until incipient inflationary pressures have built up, in which case it is too late to offset the impact on actual inflation given the lags in the transmission of monetary policy. Because of these information lags, central banks often find themselves responding to the inflationary effects of past shocks rather than responding to new developments. In the case of sub-Saharan Africa, these challenges are compounded by the scarcity of high frequency indicators.

An additional challenge for monetary policy is the management of multiple objectives, either explicit and implicit. While most if not all central banks place price stability as their primary objective, they also attempt to support economic growth and—at times—financial sector development and credit growth. While these objectives are sometimes consistent, they can also conflict with one another. In addition, because excessively tight or accommodating policies do not immediately show up in high inflation, it may take time before the central bank can realize the inconsistency. A related challenge is that the legacy of monetary aggregate targeting can at times lead to inconsistent views about the stance of policy if broad money growth appears consistent with previously set targets; even though interest rates may be too high or too low.

In the case of Kenya, the central bank loosened its policy in response to the global financial crisis of 2008–09, which had resulted in lower economic growth, contributed to a large decrease in inflation, and had negative implications for the growth of domestic credit. The policy loosening was maintained beyond this period, however, with rates continuously declining and reaching 1 per cent by the end of 2011.

---

[20] As an additional exercise, we also compared the baseline with an alternative calibration in which the sensitivity of aggregate demand to real monetary conditions (β_3) is divided by 10, and the volatility of shocks to potential output (output gap) is magnified (reduced). In this case, most of the variations in output are accounted for shocks to potential, which greatly reduces the role of aggregate demand (and monetary policy shocks) in accounting for inflation dynamics. We also find this alternative interpretation to be implausible for reasons similar to the one discussed above.

While very low interest rates should have acted as a signal that monetary policy was excessively accommodative, the central bank justified its stance in its December 2011 Monetary Policy Statement by emphasizing objectives for monetary and credit aggregates: 'The programmed growth in money supply . . . was considered adequate to support economic growth through expansion of credit to private sector . . . Generally, broad money supply, M3, remained within the set target. Credit to private sector increased, which was virtually on target' (Monetary Policy Statement, Dec. 2010, p. 3). It is worth noting that reserve money growth was also indicative of expansionary policies, as this variable was overshooting its target consistently through 2011.[21] Despite the overshooting of reserve money, as broad money and credit aggregates were in line with their targets, the perception was that monetary policy would have 'no effect on demand-driven inflation' (MPS, p. 3). This state of affairs may have been compounded by the sustained decline in inflation between late 2008 and mid-2010.

In hindsight, the targets for broad money and credit were based on an optimistically low assumption for broad money velocity and optimistic assumptions about the credit growth rates consistent with stable inflation. More generally, had the policy regime placed more emphasis on interest rates as indicating the stance of policy and less emphasis on credit growth and other quantitative targets, a clearer picture about the stance of policy may have emerged.

4.1 Is it Valid to Use Interest Rate Rules to Study Monetary Policy in Kenya?

From a methodological point of view, a related question to the above discussion is whether it is valid to apply a model with an interest rate rule to a de jure money targeter such as Kenya, in which, as the above discussion suggests, the stance of monetary policy has been influenced at times by objectives for monetary aggregates, and where policy rates did not provide clear guidance about the stance of policy. We provide several answers to this important question.

First, models are gross simplifications of reality and will inevitably miss many aspects that may be important. In our model we abstract from monetary and credit aggregates, and money targets, and focus exclusively on interest rates. Although these other aspects of policy are important, we believe that the right short-term interest rates provide a useful summary of variations in real financial conditions in Kenya, as emphasized in the previous section.

Second we believe that the Taylor principle is an essential component of monetary policy, regardless of the policy framework. Concerns with other objectives may mask this relation in the short run, but it must eventually hold if inflation expectations are to be anchored. This was the case for the CBK, which by the end of 2011 raised real interest rates by several hundred points to stabilize inflation,

---

[21] See Monetary Policy Statement by Central Bank of Kenya, December 2011.

a policy tightening similar in magnitude to the one prescribed by our model.[22] So modelling monetary policy as a rule in which the Taylor principle must eventually hold seems the correct approach to us.

Third, because of the relevance of the Taylor principle, deviations between the interest rate rule and the actual level of interest rates provide a useful measure of the stance of policy, which can then help in understanding the dynamics of inflation. This can be seen in our model simulations, in that the sustained deviation between interest rates and the level implied by the rule coincides with the increase in inflation observed in 2008 and 2011. This further validates the use of the policy rule as a way of thinking about monetary policy.

Fourth, it could be the case, however, that what the model identifies as shocks are actually systematic responses to achieve other objectives, e.g., hitting money targets. In this case, an important aspect of monetary policy would be left outside the model, which could invalidate the exercise. In Chapter 16, we study frameworks that include a systematic role for money targets and apply it to Kenya and find that this is not the case, i.e., that despite Kenya's de jure money targeting framework, there is no systematic relation between the monetary policy stance and money targets or money target deviations, even if there have been periods such as in 2010–11 when targets have mattered. We therefore conclude that monetary policy analysis in Kenya can be done, at least to a first approximation, in stylized models such as ours in which monetary policy is captured with an interest rate rule and which abstract from credit and money growth. We believe these insights may also apply to other countries with similar frameworks, but we leave such an analysis for future work.

5 CONCLUSION

In this chapter we have provided a framework for forecasting and policy analysis for low-income countries, with an application to Kenya. In particular, we have extended the standard framework to include an explicit role for food prices, by introducing two separate Phillips curves (one for food and one for non-food), and by paying special attention to the domestic and foreign relative food prices (both trend and gap component).

We have filtered key macroeconomic series from Kenya through the model to recover a model-based decomposition of most series into trend and gap components, and to discuss the quantitative significance of various factors (international shocks, monetary policy) in driving inflation. We find that, while imported food price shocks have accounted for some of the inflation dynamics in Kenya, both in 2008 but also recently, an accommodative monetary policy also played an important role. We believe the model's ability to provide a plausible interpretation of recent events in Kenya, validates the use of these types of models for policy analysis in low-income countries.

---

[22] We describe the policy tightening in more detail in Chapter 5.

APPENDIX 15A: DATA SERIES

	Data		
Variable	Data Used	Source	Remarks
s	Market rate, Shilling/Dollar	IMF IFS	
rs	Repo, reverse Repo rates	CBK	Repo rate (2000:1 2009:1,2011:5 2011:6), Reverse repo (2009:3 2011:4), Avg repo and reverse repo 2009M2
y	Non-Agricultural GDP	KNBS	Interpolated, smoothed with an HP filter ($\lambda = 0.8$)
p^{cpi}	CPI	KNBS, IMF staff	
p^f	Food Price Index	KNBS, IMF staff	
p^{nf}	Non-food Price Index	KNBS	
$p*^{cpi}$	US CPI	IMF IFS	
$rs*$	Fed Funds rate	IMF IFS	
$\overline{rr}*$	US equilibrium real interest rates	IMF modelling group	
$ygap*$	US Output Gap	IMF IFS	US GDP, HP filtered.
p^{*f}	International Food Commodity Index	FAO	

APPENDIX 15B: SOLVING AND USING THE MODEL

Solving and Simulating the Model

The actual model is a linear semi-structural forward-looking model, with model-consistent expectations, of the form $F(X_{t-1}, X_t, X_{t+1}, \epsilon_t | \theta) = 0$, where X_t denotes the vector of endogenous variables, ϵ_t are exogenous variables (shock innovations, of which there are k), and θ denotes the parameters of the model. The model is solved using a variant of the Blanchard and Kahn algorithm (see Blanchard and Kahn, 1982), implemented using the IRIS Toolbox for Matlab.[23]

Kalman Filter and Smoother

To estimate the model's structural shocks and unobserved variables, we proceed as follows. First, we present the solution of the model in state space representation:

$$X_t = TX_{t-1} + R\epsilon_t \qquad \epsilon_t \sim N(0, \Sigma_\epsilon), \qquad (1)$$

---

[23] See e.g. www.iris-toolbox.com or www.dynare.org.

where Σ_ϵ is the variance covariance matrix of the shock innovations.[24] Model variables X_t are linearly related to observed variables Y_t (inflation, output, exchange rates, etc.) via a measurement equation:

$$Y_t = ZX_t + H\eta_t \qquad\qquad \eta_t \sim N(0, \Sigma_\eta), \qquad\qquad (2)$$

where η_t indicates potential noise in the relation (and Σ_η denotes the noise covariance). Note that in the case of our model $\eta_t = 0$.

We then apply the Kalman filter to the data, using the system 1–2. The Kalman filter is a recursive algorithm used for updating estimates of the sequence of X_t and ϵ_t based on observations of Y_t. It can be summarized by the following sequence (see Hamilton, 1995: ch. 13):

$$\hat{X}_{t+1|t} = T\hat{X}_{t|t} = T\hat{X}_{t|t-1} + TP_{t|t-1}Z(Z'P_{t|t-1}Z + \Sigma_\eta)^{-1}(Y_t - ZX_{t|t-1}),$$

$$P_{t+1|t} = (T - K_t Z')P_{t|t-1}(T - K_t Z') + K_t\Sigma_\eta K'_t + \Sigma_\epsilon,$$

$$K_t = TP_{t|t-1}Z(Z'P_{t|t-1}Z + \Sigma_\eta)^{-1}, \quad \text{for} \quad t = 1, \ldots, T.$$

$P_{t+1|t}$ is mean square error of the estimate $\hat{X}_{t+1|t}$. The recursion is initiated with $\hat{X}_{1|0} = E(X_1)$ and $vec(P_{1|0}) = [I_{r^2} - (T \otimes T)]^{-1}vec(Q)$, where $Q = R'\Sigma_\epsilon R$.

The Kalman filter provides the best estimate of X_t using information up until time t. For many purposes, including for the filtration exercise presented in the text, it is useful to construct an estimate of X_t using the entire sample. This can be done using the Kalman smoother, another recursive algorithm which starts backwards from the last observation:

$$\hat{X}_{t|T} = \hat{X}_{t|t} + J_t[\hat{X}_{t+1|T} - \hat{X}_{t+1|t}],$$

$$J_t = P_{t|t}T'P_{t+1|t},$$

$$P_{t|T} = P_{t|t} + J_t(P_{t+1|T} - P_{t+1|t})J'_t, \quad \text{for} \quad t = T, T-1, \ldots, 1,$$

where:

$$P_{t|t} = P_{t|t-1} - P_{t|t-1}Z(Z'P_{t|t-1}Z + \Sigma_\eta)^{-1}Z'P_{t|t-1},$$

and $P_{t|T}$ is the mean square error of the smoothed estimate $\hat{X}_{t+1|T}$. A smoothed estimate of the structural shocks, $\hat{\epsilon}_{\tau|T}$, can also be derived as follows:

$$\hat{\epsilon}_{\tau|T} = R^{-1}(\hat{X}_{t|T} - T\hat{X}_{t-1|T})$$

When there are as many shocks as observed variables, and the observed variables are linearly independent, it is possible to recover the estimates of the unobserved variables without drawing on the covariance matrix of the shocks. For example, if $\eta_t = 0$, R is an identity matrix and Z is invertible, then the Kalman filter recursion reduces to:

$$\hat{X}_{t+1|t} = T\hat{X}_{t|t-1} + TZ^{-1}(Y_t - ZX_{t|t-1}),$$

---

[24] As there are many alternative space representations to represent the model solution, we can assume, without loss of generality, that X_t and ϵ_t have the same dimension, and that R is invertible.

which does not depend on Q. In general, however, there are more structural shocks—number of elements in ϵ_t and η_t—than observed macroeconomic variables (Y_t). In this case the estimate of $\hat{X}_{t+1|t}$ depends on the stochastic specification of the model, i.e. the covariance matrices of η, ϵ. In economic terms this implies that both the impulse response behavior of the model and the assumed variance of structural shocks will determine the plausibility of particular drivers of the economy. In this case the actual interpretation of the data will depend on both the deterministic (parameters) and stochastic parameterizations (variances). For example, the assumption that the volatility of shocks to potential output is large relative to the shocks to the output gap, combined with the assumption that the output gap is not very sensitive to real monetary conditions will result in a very small output gap, with the bulk of output movements accounted for by movements in potential. The assumption about variances is therefore key, as discussed in the text.

Shock decomposition Having estimates of exogenous shocks and initial conditions allows us to carry out a decomposition of the path of observed (and state) variables in terms of exogenous shocks. This can be done by solving (1)–(2) backwards, resulting in the following relation.

$$Y_t = Z\sum\nolimits_{\tau=0}^{t} T^{t-\tau} R\hat{\epsilon}_{\tau|T} + ZT^{\tau-t_0}X_{0|T} + H\hat{\eta}_{t|T}. \tag{3}$$

By construction, Y_t is the result of the sequence of shocks, recovered with the smoother $(T^{t-\tau}R\hat{\epsilon}_{\tau|T})$ and the lingering effect of initial conditions $(T^{\tau-t_0}X_{0|T})$. In the case of the estimated unobserved state variables $\hat{X}_{t|T}$, a similar decomposition yields:

$$\hat{X}_{t|T} = \sum\nolimits_{\tau=0}^{t} T^{t-\tau} R\hat{\epsilon}_{\tau|T} + T^{\tau-t_0}X_{0|T}. \tag{4}$$

Note that the contribution of shocks can be further disaggregated into the different elements of $\epsilon = (\epsilon_1, \dots, \epsilon_k)$, i.e., the different structural shocks:

$$Y_t = \underbrace{Z\sum\nolimits_{\tau=0}^{t} T^{t-\tau}RM_1\hat{\epsilon}_{\tau|T}}_{\text{Contribution of } \epsilon_1} + \underbrace{Z\sum\nolimits_{\tau=0}^{t} T^{t-\tau}RM_2\hat{\epsilon}_{\tau|T}}_{\text{Contribution of } \epsilon_2} + \dots + \underbrace{Z\sum\nolimits_{\tau=0}^{t} T^{t-\tau}RM_k\hat{\epsilon}_{\tau|T}}_{\text{Contribution of } \epsilon_k}$$

$$+ ZT^{\tau-t_0}X_{0|T} + H\eta_t, \tag{5}$$

where M_j is a matrix that has 1 in its jth row and zeros elsewhere. By construction, the contribution of each shock and the initial conditions add up to account all of the dynamics of any given variable at any point in time. Figures 15.9–15.13 in the main text show such a decomposition applied to both observed variables (inflation, exchange rates) and unobserved variables (the output gap).[25]

REFERENCES

Berg, A., P. D. Karam, and D. Laxton (2006). *A Practical Model-Based Approach to Monetary Policy Analysis-Overview*. IMF Working Paper 06/80.

Berg, A., R. Portillo, and F. Unsal (2010). *Optimal Adherence to Money Targets in Low-Income Countries*. IMF Working Paper 10/134.

Blanchard, O., and C. Kahn (1982). The Solution of Linear Difference Models under Rational Expectations. *Econometrica*, 48(5), 1305–13.

---

[25] Implementation of the Kalman filter and smoother is also readily available in the IRIS Toolbox for Matlab.

Calvo, G. A. (1983). Staggered prices in a utility-maximizing framework. *Journal of Monetary Economics*, 12(3), 383–98.

Central Bank of Kenya (2010). Monetary Policy Statement, December. Nairobi: Central Bank of Kenya.

Christiano, L. J., M. Eichenbaum, and C. L. Evans (2005). Nominal Rigidities and the Dynamic Effects of a Shock to Monetary Policy. *Journal of Political Economy*, 113(1), 1–45.

Hamilton, J. (1995). *Time Series Analysis*. Princeton, NJ: Princeton University Press.

Harjes, T. and L. Ricci (2010). *A Bayesian-Estimated Model of Inflation Targeting in South Africa*. IMF Staff Papers, 57(2), 407–26.

International Monetary Fund (2011). Target What You Can Hit: Commodity Price Swings and Monetary Policy. In *World Economic Outlook*, chapter 3. Washington, DC: IMF.

Ireland, P. (2007). Changes in the Federal Reserve's Inflation Target: Causes and Consequences. *Journal of Money, Credit and Banking*, 39(8), 1851–82.

Smets, F., and R. Wouters (2007). Shocks and Frictions in US Business Cycles: A Bayesian DSGE Approach. *American Economic Review*, 97(3), 586–606.

16

Do Money Targets Matter for Monetary Policy in Kenya?

Michal Andrle, Andrew Berg, Enrico Berkes,
R. Armando Morales, Rafael Portillo, and Jan Vlcek

1 INTRODUCTION

In the preceding chapter, we presented a semi-structural New Keynesian open economy model for low-income countries, and applied it to Kenya. We found that the model could help make sense of inflationary developments in Kenya in recent years. One notable feature was the treatment of monetary policy as an interest-rate-based rule, and the absence of monetary aggregates in the analysis. While a good first approximation to the country's de facto policy regime, this modelling choice was in stark contrast with the central role assigned to targets on monetary aggregates, and especially reserve money, in the de jure policy framework in Kenya, and more generally in sub-Saharan African countries (SSA) with managed exchange rates (Chapter 1). The purpose of this chapter is to fill this gap.

Here we extend our previous work to introduce a potential role for reserve-money targeting in the policy framework. We study three related issues: target design, potential link with interest rate policy, and interpretation of target misses. First, we introduce a general rule by which the authorities set targets for reserve money for the next quarter, which encompasses simple Friedman-type rules as well as money targets based on optimal forecasts of future money demand. The calibration of the rule captures the extent to which central banks engage in money demand forecasting when they set targets, which we show has important implications for the stabilization properties of monetary policy. Second, we allow for the possibility of a systematic relation between target misses, i.e., deviations of realized reserve money from its target, and the stance of policy, which in our framework is best captured by the deviation between short-term interest rates and the rate implied by a Taylor rule. We refer to this relation as target adherence, i.e., systematic but possibly incomplete efforts by the central bank to hit its targets. The resulting specification of monetary policy is quite general in that it combines both interest rates and money targeting rules, and therefore nests the policy rule in Chapter 15.[1]

---

[1] In this regard this chapter extends and applies the analysis of Chapter 8.

Third, we apply the extended model to Kenyan data from our previous work, adding data on reserve money and associated targets. The filtration of the data through the model helps us provide a novel interpretation of target misses in terms of structural shocks to the economy.

Our approach recognizes that, in practice, reserve money in a money-based framework is not a perfect analogue to interest rates in an inflation-targeting (IT) framework. The authorities set both money targets and interest rates with a view to achieve their final price stability objective. However, money targets are typically set several months in advance, so that adherence to the target is itself a policy choice. Perfect adherence is often impossible, given exogenous movements in the central bank balance sheet which are beyond the central bank's control. Given this de facto flexibility, the interpretation of target misses has in practice become an important element of monetary policy analysis in central banks with de jure money targeting regimes. Until now however this type of analysis suffered from lack of a comprehensive framework, which resulted in assessments based mainly on ad-hoc judgement.

In the case of Kenya, we find that money targets are set in a manner consistent with the forecasting of future money demand. Reserve money targets set by the Central Bank of Kenya (CBK) display two important empirical properties: they correct for past target misses and contain some information about (future) money growth. In our framework, such properties are consistent with money targets as forecasts of future money demand, which is a more sophisticated version of target-setting than simple money growth rules. The observation that target growth contains information about actual money growth reflects the efforts that central banks undertake to identify changes in the demand for liquidity in the near term, e.g., stemming from fiscal operations. The correction for past target misses implies the central bank of Kenya lets bygones be bygones. The correction is not complete, however, which suggests institutional or informational rigidities, likely stemming from the fact that targets are set every six months.

We do not find a systematic role for money targets in the conduct of monetary policy in Kenya, however. We call on three pieces of evidence. First, target misses are large and persistent, which suggests that hitting targets has not been a policy priority. When target misses have been corrected over time, it has been because of an adjustment of the target, as discussed above. Second, money growth dynamics are unrelated to past targets or target misses. Third and correspondingly, we fail to detect a systematic relation between the monetary policy stance and target misses. In our framework, target adherence implies that positive target misses (money above its target), all else equal, should elicit an increase in short-term interest rates relative to the Taylor rule benchmark, as the central bank attempts to withdraw liquidity to bring reserve money back in line with its target. This is not the case empirically. In some periods, the opposite is true: episodes of positive target misses are associated with accommodating monetary policy. In other periods, target misses are reversed or corrected without any corresponding change in the policy stance. Note that this lack of systematic relation does not imply that money targets have not mattered during certain episodes: as we argued in Chapter 15, efforts to hit broad money and credit targets during 2010 did contribute to an accommodating policy stance that resulted in a large increase in inflation in 2010–11. However, weak target adherence in Kenya implies that monetary policy analysis can, to a large extent, abstract from the analysis of money targets altogether, thus validating our earlier approach.

Money target misses in Kenya have been mainly driven by shocks to money demand. There have been periods when target misses have been driven in part by monetary policy shocks; as described above, this was the case in 2010. For the most part, however, misses have reflected unexpected changes in money demand, underscoring our assessment that money demand has been quite volatile. Shocks to aggregate demand and supply do not play an important role. These findings validate the weak target adherence observed in Kenya, as this shows that the CBK has been correct in not responding systematically to target misses.

Finally, we assess the implications of target design and adherence for the cyclical properties of the Kenyan economy. Greater adherence to pre-announced money targets in Kenya would imply high volatility of money market interest rates, favouring thus more accommodative rules. The same finding extends to both nominal and real exchange rates. The implication of greater money target adherence for output and inflation volatility depends on the shock, however. In the case of money demand shocks, the answer is unambiguous: target adherence results in considerably more volatile inflation and output, e.g., relative to an interest rate-based inflation targeting regime. In the case of cost push shocks, strict money targeting results in more volatile output but less volatile inflation, which implies that policy is tighter than under IT. The opposite holds in the case of demand shocks. We argue that the relative volatility of output and inflation under strict money targeting implied by our simulations is unlikely to be a desirable outcome for the authorities.

Our chapter is organized as follows: Section 2 surveys the policy landscape in sub-Saharan Africa, to lay a groundwork for the analysis. In Section 3 we introduce money targeting into a New Keynesian dynamic model for Kenya, motivate our modelling choices, and illustrate the main features of the model. Section 4 reviews monetary policy implementation in Kenya, and provides a model-based interpretation of money target misses. The last section summarizes the chapter's finding.

2 MONEY TARGETING FRAMEWORKS IN SUB-SAHARAN AFRICA

'Flexible money targeting' is a good characterization of the policy framework in most SSA countries with managed exchange rate regimes (Chapters 1 and 8). Most countries feature both reserve and broad money targets, which have a quarterly frequency. The former typically serves as operational targets while the latter serves as intermediate targets. These targets are set annually or semi-annually, often in the context of an IMF programme, using a monetary programming framework.[2] The framework is straightforward: starting with a forecast for

---

[2] This is often embedded in a more general and mutually consistent analysis of the economy (fiscal accounts, balance of payments) that relies on the IMF's Financial Programming approach, e.g., as described in Selassie et al. (2006).

GDP, an inflation objective, and estimates of money velocity and the money multiplier, the authorities construct an annual forecast for broad and base money. The annual forecast is then divided into quarters, in part by incorporating additional information about government flows and seasonal patterns. These quarterly forecasts then become the policy targets. Note that the emphasis is typically on the reserve money target, because it falls more squarely under the influence of the central bank. Central banks typically miss their reserve money targets in both directions, i.e., both overshooting and undershooting. Target misses have little consequence in terms of inflation, especially in countries that have succeeded in stabilizing inflation. Central banks allow these target misses because attempting to hit them would bring unnecessary volatility to the interest rate. Moreover, the assessment of the target miss is typically conditional on the state of the economy: they are considered unrelated to the 'true' stance of monetary policy if inflationary and aggregate demand pressures are contained, or if real interest rates are positive. The opposite assessment is made if inflation is increasing or if real interest rates are negative. In some cases, e.g., over some periods, central banks in some countries have hit their targets more systematically, or have made great efforts to do so, at the cost of sizeable interest rate volatility.

In this chapter we do not take a stand on why countries may want to target money in the first place. Rather, we take it as given and analyse some of the consequences. However, some discussion of the possible reasons may shed light on the applicability of the framework. One possible reason, explored for example in Chapter 8, has to do with imperfect information. Money aggregates may contain information about aggregate demand and interest rates that are not readily observable in real time. Even interest rates may not be market clearing in shallow financial system, such that it is hard to infer the true opportunity cost of future consumption from observable rates.[3] In this chapter, we make the simplifying assumption of full information. Another reason may be that the central bank has imperfect credibility, and adherence to pre-announced money targets may be a mechanism to build that credibility.[4]

Yet another possible reason why some SSA countries continue to target money is that the authorities are not prepared to pursue a forward-looking policy with the objective of stabilizing inflation and output. This may be due to a lack of operational independence. In this case, strict money targeting may provide a bulwark against fiscal dominance (Chapter 1). However, the cost may be excess volatility relative to a forward-looking IT-like policy. A related argument is that, if there is limited capacity to adjust policy as needed to stabilize inflation, there may be some advantages in having a passive money-targeting policy (like a constant-growth-rate rule). In such a regime, the Taylor principle—the notion that an increase in inflation eventually requires an increase in real interest rates for inflation to be stabilized—is likely to be satisfied due to the low short-term interest

---

[3] This is a refinement of Poole's original idea, as it emphasizes the role of money as an indicator variable, yet not fundamentally different from other indicator variables which may also be available to the central bank.

[4] See the discussion in Canzoneri (1985). Also, see Chapter 19 for a simple way of analysing the central bank credibility problem, though without monetary aggregates.

rate elasticity of money demand.[5] A similarly passive interest rate rule, on the other hand, would tend to lead to instability.

3 INTRODUCING MONEY TARGETING IN A NEW KEYNESIAN MODEL FOR KENYA

We modify the model in Chapter 15 to allow for monetary targeting. The modification consists of: (i) adding a money demand block (ii) introducing a rule for setting money targets, and (iii) modelling different degrees of adherence to these targets.

The model is a New Keynesian small open economy model featuring a set of nominal and real rigidities. There are four main equations in the model.[6] The IS curve links the output gap with foreign demand and real monetary conditions, including both real interest and exchange rate gaps. As the share of food prices in overall CPI is about 40 per cent in Kenya, there are two Phillips curves, for food and non-food prices, in the model. Real marginal costs are the main driving force of inflation. These are driven by domestic demand pressures, the real exchange rate, and import prices. The model also includes relative price trends anchoring relative food prices in the long run. We assume a version of the uncovered interest rate parity (UIP), which equalizes domestic and foreign interest rates, adjusted by the expected appreciation of the exchange rate and a country risk premium.

The model does not capture the money market operations that help implement the operational targets. The model is quarterly, reflecting the understanding that operational targets are revised only periodically. The operations that help achieve those targets, such as the setting of an overnight interest rate within a prescribed corridor or the management of required reserves, are not analysed here. However, liquidity management issues, e.g., the inability or unwillingness to implement the policy prescription that results from monetary policy analysis, can seriously affect the stance of policy and have undesired macroeconomic consequences.

3.1 Money Demand

We introduce a demand equation for money. We use an error-correction specification, which allows for both short-run and long-run dynamics:

$$\Delta m_t = \omega_y \Delta y_t - \omega_{rs} \Delta rs_t - \Delta v_t + \omega_m \hat{m}_{t-1} + \epsilon_t^{m_d} \tag{1}$$

$$\hat{m}_t = m_t - (\psi_{const} + \psi_y y_t - \psi_{rs} rs_t - v_t). \tag{2}$$

---

[5] This can be seen by equating money supply and money demand, and solving for the nominal interest rate. The latter variable would respond, at equilibrium, to movements in inflation, with a coefficient given by the inverse of the interest elasticity of money demand. The Taylor principle would be satisfied if the inflation coefficient is higher than one, or alternatively if the interest elasticity is less than one. See Davies et al. (2012) and Alvarez et al. (2001) for related discussions.

[6] The model is extensively described in Chapter 15. We provide a brief summary here.

Equation (1) states that changes in demand for real money balances Δm_t, where $m_t = M_t - P_t$, depend on the growth rates and the level of output y_t, the annualized nominal interest rate rs_t, velocity v_t, and the real money gap $\hat{m}_t$. We define the real money gap as the error-correction term, i.e., the deviation between real money balances and their long-run value.[7]

We distinguish two types of exogenous changes in money demand: liquidity shock $\epsilon_t^{m_d}$ and persistent changes in velocity v_t. Shocks to liquidity or velocity drive a wedge between movements in monetary aggregates and the stance of policy, which is best captured by the interest rate level. Liquidity shocks have temporary effects on the demand for money, with persistence determined by the error-correction specification of money demand. Velocity follows the following autoregressive process in first differences:

$$\Delta v_t = \rho_v \Delta v_{t-1} + (1 - \rho_v)\Delta \bar{v} + \epsilon_t^v. \tag{3}$$

The above specification implies shocks to velocity ϵ_t^v have persistent effects on the *growth rate* of money demand.

3.2 Monetary Policy

Monetary policy is described by a flexible policy rule that allows for pure forms of monetary and interest rate targeting as well as intermediate cases. As a specific case, it includes an interest rate rule in which the authorities respond to deviations of the inflation forecast from its target (the Taylor rule). It also allows policymakers to respond to deviations of money growth from its target. The rule is inspired by the analysis in Chapter 8. In this section we begin by presenting operational targets derived from the Taylor rule. We then discuss the modelling of money targets, before discussing how we combine both.

3.2.1 Interest Rate Rule

The interest rate rule reflects the preferences of the central bank for the stability of output and inflation around its target. This is the rule used in Chapter 15, and is the standard characterization of policy in IT or IT-lite central banks. The interest rate rule is the following:

$$rs_{R,t} = \gamma_1 rs_{R,t-1} + (1 - \gamma_1)[(\bar{rr}_t + \bar{\pi}_{t+1}) + \gamma_2\left(\pi_{t+i}^{4,cpi} - \bar{\pi}_{t+i}^{4,cpi}\right)$$
$$+ \gamma_3 ygap_t + \gamma_4 \Delta sgap_t]. \tag{4}$$

The term $(\bar{rr}_t + \bar{\pi}_{t+1}) = \bar{rs}_t$ stands for the neutral value of the policy rate, as determined by the neutral real rate and the inflation target.

Monetary policy reacts to deviations between projected year-on-year headline inflation and the inflation target, $(\pi_{t+i}^{4,cpi} - \bar{\pi}_{t+i}^{4,cpi})$. As part of a flexible inflation-targeting regime, the central bank may also consider the output gap, $ygap_t$, and the

---

[7] This money gap differs from another measure that is sometimes used, e.g., in Chapter 8, which is the difference between real money balances and the level that would hold if the economy was at potential and inflation was equal to target.

deviation between the nominal depreciation and its equilibrium value, $\Delta sgap_t$, as indicators of the cyclical position of the economy. The rule is forward-looking, in that policy is driven by the forecast of future inflation. As we will see below, this property of the rule can also extend to the (ex ante) choice of targets on money, depending on how these targets are set.

In its pure form, the interest rate rule exhibits no adherence to previously forecasted interest rate targets. Next period, as the economy gets hit by new structural shocks, a new path of interest rates is determined.[8] The new path is set to achieve the inflation target over the medium run. This is a crucial difference with targets on money growth, as shown below.

3.2.2 Money Growth Target

The rationale behind the setting of the money growth target can be of crucial importance for the stabilization properties of monetary policy. Here we specify the monetary aggregate to be targeted, the rule that determines the target and the timing of target announcements. We seek to mimic to the extent possible the way targets have been set in Kenya in the last decade, and more generally in many SSA countries.

In every quarter, e.g., $(t - 1)$, a reserve money target is announced for the quarter ahead, t. This is a slight simplification of current practices at the central bank of Kenya, which usually revisits its targets every six months.[9] Once a target is set it is not revised: the target for period t that was set in period $t - 1$ is not revised once quarter t (and the new information available then) arrives. We do, however, investigate the consequences of various degrees of target adherence. Note that we do not extend the analysis to the setting of broad money targets, for the sake of simplicity.

We first define the money growth target, $\overline{\Delta M}_t^*$, as the forecast of the growth in the demand for nominal money balances at t given the central bank's forecast of inflation and real money demand, and conditional on all available $(t - 1)$ information.[10] Specifically:

$$\overline{\Delta M}_t^* \equiv \overline{M}_t - M_{t-1} = M_{t|t-1} - M_{t-1} = \Delta m_{R,t|t-1} + \pi_{t|t-1}. \tag{5}$$

Here $M_{t|t-1}$, $\Delta m_{R,t|t-1}$ and $\pi_{t|t-1}$ denote expectations, at time $(t - 1)$, of nominal money balances, real money growth and inflation at time t. We assume that the

---

[8] Most countries resort to verbal indication of the future policy stance, without commitment. The Czech Republic, Israel, Norway, Sweden, and New Zealand, for instance, publish their interest rate paths. Note, however, that path dependence—committing to a previously announced interest rate path even if new developments call for a different policy stance—has been recently advocated in many advanced economies, in the presence of a binding zero lower bound on interest rates. See Woodford (2012), among many others.

[9] The current practice is difficult to implement in a recursive model such as ours. We can approximate this behaviour, however, by varying the persistence term in the setting of the target, shown below.

[10] This approximates the process involved in the IMF's Financial Programming approach, e.g., as described in Selassie et al. (2006).

forecast for real money demand is consistent with the interest rate implied by the interest rate rule in (4):

$$\Delta m_{R,t|t-1} = \omega_y \Delta y_{t|t-1} - \omega_{rs}(rs_{R,t|t-1} - rs_{t-1}) - \Delta v_{t|t-1} + \omega_m \hat{m}_{t-1} + \epsilon_{t|t-1}^{m_d}. \quad (6)$$

Part of the liquidity shock $\epsilon_t^{m_d}$ is anticipated by the central bank ($\epsilon_{t|t-1}^{m_d}$). This reflects additional information that the central bank may have about liquidity patterns (money demand), which is beyond the scope of the model. It can be due for instance to weather patterns, government financing needs, etc. In practical terms, this shock helps match the forecast of money demand implied by the model with the actual money target observed in the data. It will also result in money growth being correlated with the target, regardless of whether money targets are binding for monetary policy. $\epsilon_{t|t-1}^{m_d}$ should not be interpreted as reflecting a shock to the monetary policy stance.

The above specification implies that money targets do not respond to past target misses. As equation (5) indicates, the setting of $\overline{M}_t$ does not depend on past misses, i.e., bygones are bygones. This has implications for the rate at which targets grow, which we denote $\Delta \overline{M}_{T,t}$:

$$\Delta \overline{M}_{T,t}^* \equiv \overline{M}_t - \overline{M}_{t-1} = \Delta \overline{M}_t^* + (M_{t-1} - \overline{M}_{t-1}). \quad (7)$$

The corollary of eq. (5) is that the *growth rate* of money targets always accommodates past target misses $(M_{t-1} - \overline{M}_{t-1})$. Targets grow at a faster rate whenever reserve money is above the target, so that target levels catch up with the level of reserve money. The latter is a property of targets when interpreted as forecasts of future money demand.

If money targets follow rules (5, 6), there is perfect ex ante consistency between the money target and the interest rate rule. That is, the money target and expectations of next period's interest rates, given by rule (4), signal the same policy stance. As shown in Chapter 8, ex ante consistency is a desirable property of regimes with multiple targets because they greatly reduce the tension between these targets. Making money targets consistent with an interest rate rule is also desirable because the former inherit (in principle) the stabilizing property of the latter.

We nonetheless expand rules (5, 6, 7) to encompass a wider range of money-targeting rules, in order to examine policies that do not correspond to any interest rate rule of the form of (4). The general equation for money-target setting, specified in terms of their growth rate, is now the following:

$$\Delta \overline{M}_{T,t} = a[(1 - \rho_{\overline{M}})\Delta \overline{M}_{T,t-1} + \rho_{\overline{M}}\Delta \overline{M}_{T,t}^*] + (1 - a)\Delta \overline{M}. \quad (8)$$

$$\Delta \overline{M}_t = \Delta \overline{M}_{T,t} - (M_{t-1} - \overline{M}_{t-1}). \quad (9)$$

$\Delta \overline{M}_{T,t}^*$ is given by (7), i.e., the growth rate of money targets that is consistent with the optimal forecast of money demand under the interest rate rule. $\Delta \overline{M}$ denotes long-run money growth, which we assume equals the sum of potential output growth, the inflation objective, and the growth rate of velocity (in the long run). Parameters $\rho_{\overline{M}}$ and a move money targets away from the optimal money demand forecast $\Delta \overline{M}_t^*$. A $\rho_{\overline{M}} < 1$ makes money target setting sluggish (persistent), so that targets react gradually to an expected change in money demand. An $a < 1$ makes money targets less responsive to new information. In the limit, $a = 0$, money targets are set according to a Friedman rule.[11] This can be used to describe a passive central bank, which keeps the growth rate of targets unchanged regardless of any new developments. More generally, the pair $(\rho_{\overline{M}}, a)$ captures potential institutional rigidities in target setting. Realistically, institutional constraints and credibility issues—which we do not model explicitly—may prevent sharp revisions of targets.

The pair $(\rho_{\overline{M}}, a)$ has implications for how money targets react to past target misses. $\rho_{\overline{M}} < 1$ or $a < 1$ implies the accommodation described in (7) is less than complete. This incomplete accommodation is due to the same institutional constraints described above, especially the fact that targets are not set every one quarter in advance but every six months for the next two quarters. We will draw on the empirical evidence on money targets in Kenya to calibrate this rule.

The general specification in (8)–(9) implies that money targets may be ex ante inconsistent with the interest rate rule. $\rho_{\overline{M}} < 1$ or $a < 1$ implies the money target is not consistent with the interest rate implied by the rule in (4), even before time t comes along. If money targets matter for monetary policy, the ex ante tension between targets will have longer lasting effects on the stance of policy. We will analyse this case in the section below.

3.2.3 Intermediate Cases

Having described both targets, we now describe how to combine them in a general specification. We approximate intermediate policy frameworks, i.e., frameworks that pay attention to both interest rates and money, by assuming that the central bank sets the actual policy rate, rs_t, as a combination of the interest rate that would correspond to a Taylor rule, $rs_{R,t}$, and the interest rate implied by strict adherence to the money target, $rs_{MT,t}$:

$$rs_t = \gamma rs_{R,t} + (1 - \gamma)rs_{MT,t} + d_t, \tag{10}$$

$$d_t = \gamma_1 d_{t-1} + \epsilon_t^d, \tag{11}$$

where, d_t denotes a persistent shock to monetary policy. $rs_{MT,t}$ is obtained by inserting rule (8) in the money demand equation (2) and solving for the interest rate that would hold under that specification. Although this may appear counter-intuitive at first, this specification helps nest the two polar cases. Calibrating the parameter γ, we can model a pure Taylor rule that approximates inflation targeting ($\gamma = 1$), a pure money growth rule with full adherence to the money targets ($\gamma = 0$), or any combination of the two ($0 < \gamma < 1$).[12]

The Taylor rule emerges as a natural benchmark for assessing the stance of monetary policy in the general case. Combining the equation for money

---

[11] We use the term 'Friedman rule' to describe a constant money growth rule, without necessarily specifying the actual growth rate of money. This differs from the way the term 'Friedman rule' is often used in the macroeconomics literature, i.e., a rule that would set the nominal interest rate to zero, on average.

[12] In principle, any form of money growth target coupled with money demand can be rewritten as an interest rate rule and vice versa, see Razzak (2003). However, the equivalence between money based rule and interest rate rules does not constitute equivalence in the operational conduct of monetary policy; see Disyatat (2008) or Bindseil (2004).

demand (1), with the money demand that would hold under perfect adherence to the money target, we can provide an alternative presentation of the general rule in (10):

$$rs_t = rs_{R,t} + \underbrace{\frac{(1-\gamma)}{\gamma}\frac{1}{\omega_{rs}}(M_t - \overline{M}_t) + \tilde{d}_t,}_{\text{policy stance deviation}} \tag{12}$$

where $\tilde{d}_t = d_t/\gamma$. Note that in this specification, the interest rate prescribed by the Taylor rule and the money target play two distinct roles. The former serves as the policy prescription and helps anchor inflation expectations, while, depending on the value of γ, money target misses may help understand deviations in the policy stance.

A $\gamma < 1$ implies a systematic relation between the money target misses and the policy stance. Depending on how targets are set, this systematic relation can take various forms. To see this, we solve for $(M_t - \overline{M}_t)$, using eqs. (5)–(9):

$$(M_t - \overline{M}_t) = (1 - a\rho_{\overline{M}})(M_{t-1} - \overline{M}_{t-1}) + u_t,$$

where the innovation to the money target miss, u_t, is given by:

$$u_t = (1-a)(\Delta M_t - \Delta M) + a(1 - \rho_{\overline{M}})(\Delta M_t - \Delta \overline{M}_{T,t-1}) + a\rho_{\overline{M}}(\Delta M_t - \Delta \overline{M}_t^*).$$

When $a = 1$ and $\rho_{\overline{M}} = 1$ money target misses behave as forecast errors, i.e., $(M_t - \overline{M}_t) = (\Delta m_t - \Delta m_{t|t-1}) + (\pi_t - \pi_{t|t-1})$. These forecast errors are i.i.d.; in this case adherence to money targets introduces simple noise in interest rates.[13] When either $a < 1$ or $\rho_{\overline{M}} < 1$, money target misses follow an autoregressive process with persistence given by $(1 - a\rho_{\overline{M}})$. In addition, innovations to target misses (u_t) can also become persistent, e.g., if money growth deviates persistently from its long-run value. In this case, systematic target adherence implies persistent deviations in interest rates from the Taylor rule: episodes of policy accommodation or tightness would be explained by efforts by the central bank to hit its money targets. In sum, the specification of the target rule can have important implications for the properties of the policy stance.

Equation (12) can also be used to interpret policy in countries where the money target takes centre stage in policy discussions. The terms can be rearranged as follows:

$$M_t = \overline{M}_t + \frac{\gamma}{(1-\gamma)}\omega_{rs}(rs_t - rs_{R,t}) + \hat{d}_t,$$

where $\hat{d}_t = -\omega_{rs}/(1-\gamma)d_t$. In this version, deviations between the nominal growth rate of money and its target result from either monetary policy shocks ($\hat{d}_t$) or some concern with interest rate not straying too far from the rate implied by the Taylor rule ($rs_t - rs_{R,t}$). Even in this case, however, the stance of policy is best understood by the deviation between interest rates and the Taylor rule.

In summary, we have presented a general framework that nests various policy rules. The type of regime can be characterized by three parameter values: γ, a, and $\rho_{\overline{M}}$.

---

[13] The noise we are interested in is at the quarterly frequency.

Note that the policy specification in Chapter 15 amounts to $\gamma = 1$. We now discuss alternative calibrations for these parameters and their macro implications.

3.3 Key Features and Properties of the Model

This section describes the properties of the model under alternative specifications of the general rule. We have already extensively discussed the properties of the model under the interest rate rule, including its forecasting competence, and have also used it to provide an interpretation of Kenyan developments, in Chapter 15. Here, instead, we focus on the business cycle properties of the economy depending on the specification of policy and the relevant shock.[14] Table 16.1 compares

Table 16.1. Standard Deviations

	rs_t	π_t	$ygap_t$	$\Delta sgap_t$
Demand Shocks	Absolute Standard Deviations			
Friedman rule ($a = 0, \gamma = 0$)	4.8	0.3	0.8	7.5
Forward-looking rules ($a = 1, \rho_{\bar{M}} = 1$):	Relative to Friedman rule			
$\gamma = 0$	1.0	1.0	1.0	1.0
$\gamma = 0.25$	0.8	0.8	1.0	0.8
$\gamma = 0.5$	0.5	0.6	1.1	0.6
$\gamma = 0.75$	0.3	0.4	1.2	0.3
$\gamma = 1$	0.0	0.5	1.3	0.0
Supply Shocks	Absolute Standard Deviations			
Friedman rule ($a = 0, \gamma = 0$)	2.4	1.3	0.8	6.2
Forward-looking rules ($a = 1, \rho_{\bar{M}} = 1$):	Relative to Friedman rule			
$\gamma = 0$	1.1	1.3	0.7	0.8
$\gamma = 0.25$	0.9	1.3	0.7	0.7
$\gamma = 0.5$	0.7	1.3	0.7	0.5
$\gamma = 0.75$	0.5	1.4	0.6	0.4
$\gamma = 1$	0.4	1.4	0.6	0.3
Money Demand Shocks	Absolute Standard Deviations			
Friedman rule ($a = 0, \gamma = 0$)	1.0	0.3	0.2	1.9
Forward-looking rules ($a = 1, \rho_{\bar{M}} = 1$):	Relative to Friedman rule			
$\gamma = 0$	1.1	0.3	0.7	0.8
$\gamma = 0.25$	0.9	0.3	0.6	0.7
$\gamma = 0.5$	0.6	0.2	0.4	0.5
$\gamma = 0.75$	0.3	0.1	0.2	0.2
$\gamma = 1$	0.0	0.0	0.0	0.0

The table shows standard deviations for selected variables from simulations of the model under a subset of the shocks. Demand shocks denote shocks to the IS equation, supply shocks denote shocks to the Phillips curves for food and non-food inflation, and money demand shocks denote shocks to liquidity and velocity. Several specifications are presented: the Friedman rule ($a = 0, \gamma = 0$) and forward-looking policies with varying degrees of target adherence. Standard deviations under the Friedman rule are displayed in absolute terms, other results are presented relative to Friedman rule results.

[14] We do not assess the cyclical properties of the model against a central bank objective function, i.e., a weighted sum of key volatilities meant to reflect the preferences of the central bank. We could do so, although, because the model is not micro-founded, any objective function would be arbitrary.

Table 16.2. Calibration of the Money Block Parameters

Parameter	Description	Value	Source/Remarks
Money Demand			
ω_y	Elasticity to real output growth	1.00	Theory and VEC estimate
ω_{rs}	Elasticity to nom. interest rate changes	0.56	System Properties (S.P.) and VEC estimate
ω_m	Elasticity to real money gap	0.34	S.P. and VEC estimate
ψ_{const}	Money demand constant	1248.00	S.P. and VEC estimate
ψ_y	Elasticity to real output	1.00	Theory and VEC estimate
ψ_{rs}	Elasticity to nom. interest rates	0.02	S.P. and VEC estimate
Velocity			
ρ_v	Autoregressive parameter	0.25	S.P.
$\bar{v}$	Steady state growth	−0.5	Observed data
Hybrid Policy Rule			
γ	Weight on the Taylor rule implied rate	0.99	S.P.
Money Target			
a	Weight on expected money demand	0.7	Observed data
$\rho_{\bar{M}}$	Speed of money target adjustments	1	S.P.
Taylor Rule			
γ_1	Interest rate smoothing	0.80	S.P.
γ_2	MP sensitivity to inflation deviations	1.40	S.P.
γ_3	MP sensitivity to the output gap	0.00	S.P.
γ_4	MP sensitivity to nom. appreciation	0.25	S.P.

standard deviations of basic macroeconomic variables under different policy strategies—ranging from pure IT ($\gamma = 1$) to strict money forecast targeting ($\gamma = 0$), with no target persistence ($\rho_{\bar{M}} = 1$) and full use of information ($a = 1$). We look at three set of shocks: an aggregate demand shock, aggregate supply shocks, and money demand shocks. The analysis is conditional on the calibration from Chapter 15, including the relative volatilities of the shocks to aggregate demand and supply, to which we add the calibration of money demand and the volatility of shocks to liquidity and velocity (summarized in Tables 16.2 and 16.3, and discussed below).

Standard deviations in Table 16.1 are normalized with respect to the Friedman rule case ($\gamma = 0, a = 0$). The Friedman rule specification serves as a straightforward benchmark and should not be interpreted as a desirable, or even implementable, alternative to the existing regimes. The normalization is useful, however, in that it allows for two dimensions along which to assess money targeting: the degree of target adherence (varying γ) and the role of the targeting rule itself, which can be seen by comparing the most basic type (the Friedman rule, $a = 0$) with the most sophisticated (optimal money demand forecasting consistent with an interest rate rule, $a = 1, \rho_{\bar{M}} = 1$). Consistent with the discussion

Table 16.3. Calibration of Standard Deviations (STD) of Shocks

Shock	Description	STD	Source/Remarks
Money Demand			
ϵ^{md}	Liquidity shock	0.50	S.P.
$\epsilon^{md}_{t\|t-1}$	Expected money demand shock	1.00	S.P.
Velocity			
ϵ^{v}	Velocity shock	0.50	S.P.
Hybrid Policy Rule			
ϵ^{d}	MP shock	0.30	S.P.

in the previous section, the first comparison highlights the implications of the potential interest rate noise introduced by money targeting, while the latter measures the implications of persistent money-target driven movements in interest rates.

The results indicate that the more weight is placed on money targeting (lower γ), the larger is the variance of the nominal exchange rate and the interest rate. This is true across the three sets of shocks we analyse here, obviously in the case for money demand shocks, and also, surprisingly, in the case of aggregate demand shocks. For the latter, interest rates and exchange rates are a hundred times more volatile when money target adherence is complete ($\gamma = 0$) than when money targets play no role in policy ($\gamma = 1$). The higher nominal exchange rate volatility is a direct result of the higher variance of interest rates. This is because of the uncovered interest parity condition: holding future exchange rates constant, an unexpected increase in short-term interest rates feeds one-for-one into spot exchange rates. The closer the adherence to money targets, the larger (and immediate) the initial effect on interest rates is in response to shocks, to clear the money market, and therefore the larger the volatility of the exchange rate.[15] The type of money targeting rule (Friedman rule versus optimal money demand forecasting) does not seem to make much difference for the volatility of these two variables, which suggests most of the increased volatility comes from the effect on short-run volatility.

The impact of money demand shocks obviously depends on target adherence but also on the type of money targeting rule. The larger the target adherence, the larger the impact of money demand shocks on the economy. This is a well-known weakness of money targeting. More interestingly, the type of money targeting matters as well. Relative to the simple Friedman rule, target adherence based on optimal money demand forecasting reduces the costs of money target-related policy errors. This can be seen by looking at the ($\gamma = 0$) case: it delivers considerably lower inflation and output volatility than the Friedman rule, which is consistent with the discussion in the previous section.

---

[15] This outcome should not be confused with the higher variability of the exchange rate that typically results from inflation targeting and flexible exchange rate regimes. In fact, many countries conduct money growth targeting along with exchange rate interventions and smoothing, which would reduce the volatility of exchange rates.

In the case of real shocks, adherence to money targets has implications for the relative volatility of output and inflation. Under supply shocks, greater adherence to money targets helps reduce the volatility of inflation but at the cost of higher output volatility. The reason is the following: a supply shock that raises inflation also increases the demand for nominal balances. Greater target adherence implies this nominal money demand is not satisfied, which requires an increase in interest rates to clear the money market, and with the latter increase depending on the interest elasticity of money demand. The increase in interest rates helps offset the inflationary effect of the shock but at the expense of a contraction in output, which explains the change in relative volatilities. In the case of aggregate demand shocks, the opposite holds: adherence to money targets also results in a large increase in interest rates, which helps reduce the impact of the shock on aggregate demand but increases the volatility of inflation through its effects on exchange rate volatility. Note that these results do not depend on the type of money targeting.

The results in Table 16.1 highlight the benefits of moving towards more flexible money growth rules and IT-like regimes. First, the substantial increase in interest rate and exchange rate volatility, one hundredfold in some cases, is an enormous shortcoming of greater adherence to money targets. The stability and predictability of interest rates has become a policy objective in itself, as revealed by the experience of most central banks around the world, both for financial stability reasons and to help guide markets about future policy decisions.

Second, the properties of the economy under money targeting stem from the implications that these rules have for interest rates, via the structure of money demand. The latter is the only variable through which monetary policy affects the real economy, so that monetary policy is best specified as operating directly on this variable, and not indirectly via monetary aggregates. To see this link, let us focus on an extreme case (strict money targeting under the Friedman rule). Inserting the money target in the money demand equation (5), and solving for the interest rate we obtain the following:

$$
\begin{aligned}
rs_t = rs_{t-1} + \frac{1}{\omega_{rs}}(\pi_t - \bar{\pi}) + \frac{1}{\omega_{rs}}(\Delta y_t - \Delta y^*) - \frac{1}{\omega_{rs}}(\Delta v_t - \Delta v) \\
+ \frac{\omega_m}{\omega_{rs}}\hat{m}_{t-1} + \frac{1}{\omega_{rs}}\epsilon_t^{m_d} + d_t,
\end{aligned}
\tag{13}
$$

where we have relied on the identity $\Delta M = \bar{\pi} + \Delta y^* - \Delta v$ and have assumed $\omega_y = 1$. The performance of the Friedman rule relative to the case of no target adherence depends on how eq. (13) compares with eq. (4). The rule looks somewhat similar to the Taylor rule, except that it features even greater persistence in interest rates, and the coefficients on output and inflation depend on the short-term interest rate elasticity of money demand. As the latter coefficient is low, this rule will strongly react to output and inflation movements, regardless of their source. This elasticity is also likely to be time-varying, so that the policy link between interest rates and output and inflation may be quite unstable. In addition, the rule features changes in velocity and money demand as two direct sources of policy fluctuations, which adds to the overall volatility of the economy.

To the extent the authorities prefer the volatility of output and inflation delivered by money targeting, e.g., in the case of supply shocks, these outcomes are best achieved via an interest rate-based policy. As can be seen in eq. (13), these relative variances can be obtained with an interest rate rule that responds to inflation and output in an aggressive way. This will help deliver the desired outcome while also avoiding the policy volatility that results from target adherence, which in the above case is given by

$$-\frac{1}{\omega_{rs}}(\Delta v_t - \Delta v) + \frac{\omega_m}{\omega_{rs}}\hat{m}_{t-1} + \frac{1}{\omega_{rs}}\epsilon_t^{m_d}.$$

We now examine some of the impulse responses of the model. The response of the economy to a positive foreign demand shock is depicted in Figure 16.1. Under the Taylor rule, the increase in foreign demand raises the domestic output gap and creates a nominal depreciation, as foreign interest rates increase, all of which results in an increase in inflation and a gradual increase in domestic interest rates. Under partial adherence to money targets the increase in money demand creates upward pressures on the interest rate, which increases on impact by more than under no adherence. Depending on how money targets are set, the jump in the interest rate is either immediately corrected (under optimal money demand forecasting) or results in a persistently large increase in interest rates (when $\alpha < 1$). The interest rate spike also reduces the nominal depreciation and in the case of $\alpha < 1$ results in a nominal appreciation. The tighter policy stance results in

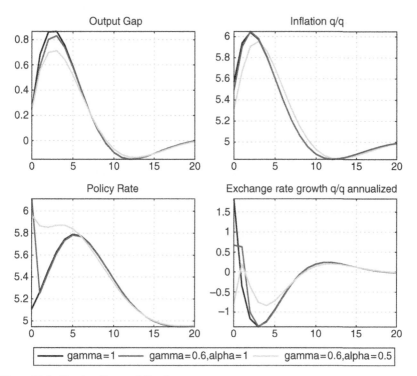

Figure 16.1. Foreign Demand Shock

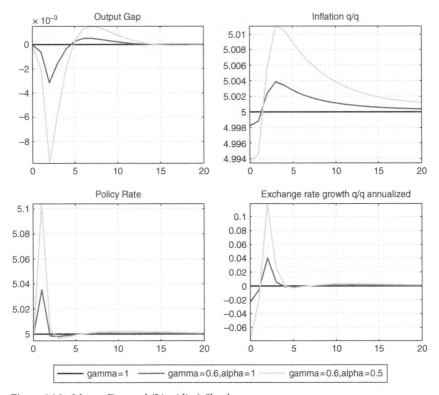

Figure 16.2. Money Demand (Liquidity) Shock

a smaller increase in output and inflation, again at the cost of large interest rate volatility.

Impulse responses of the model to shocks to liquidity and domestic demand are presented in Figures 16.2 and 16.3. When the authorities strictly adhere to money targets, liquidity shocks cause dramatic fluctuations in output and inflation, as opposed to no effects under an interest rate rule. Results for the domestic demand shock are similar to the foreign demand shock, though with larger relative volatility of macroeconomic variables, due to its faster propagation through the economy. In both cases, less responsive targeting rules ($\alpha < 1$) amplify the effects of the shocks on inflation.

4 EMPIRICAL APPLICATION—THE KENYAN ECONOMY

The model presented in the previous section is calibrated to the Kenyan economy. We use the model to analyse movements in reserve money and its target, and to decompose the actual data into structural shocks. First, we briefly review the monetary policy regime in Kenya.

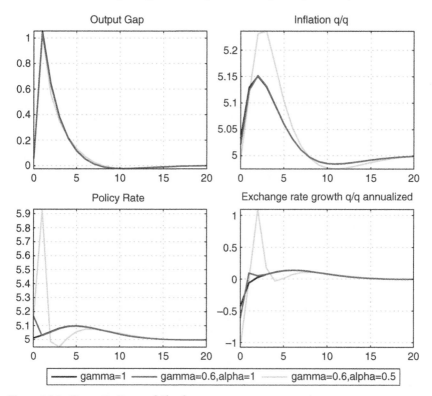

Figure 16.3. Domestic Demand Shock

4.1 The Monetary Policy Regime in Kenya—A Brief Review With a Focus on Money

The principal objective of the Central Bank of Kenya (CBK) is to achieve and maintain price stability and to sustain the value of the Shilling.[16] The CBK Act also requires the bank to support the growth objectives of the government and promote the health of the financial sector. The price stability objective is reflected in the inflation target set by the Ministry of Finance. Since December 2005, the target has been set to 5 per cent with a tolerance of ± 2 per cent for year-on-year overall inflation. Monetary policy is based on a modified monetary aggregate framework. Reserve money targets are declared as the de jure operational target, broad money (M3) is considered an intermediate target and the Central Bank Rate (CBR) is supposed to signal the monetary policy stance, see e.g. CBK (2011), Ndung'u (2012).

The stance of monetary policy has been frequently adjusted without revising the money target. The corollary is that money target misses have been frequent, as we will see below. In addition, although the CBK is also meant to signal the

---

[16] A more detailed discussion of the monetary policy stance is provided in Chapter 15.

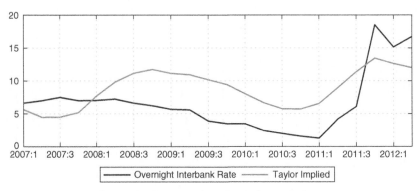

Figure 16.4. Overnight Interbank Rate and Taylor–Rule–Implied Rate

monetary policy stance via the Central Bank Rate (CBR), the level of which is announced by the Monetary Policy Committee every two months, it relevance has varied over time. Prior to 2011, changes of the CBR rarely affected money market rates, even though it served as the reference rate for overnight borrowing at the CBK's standing facility. Since November 2011, the CBR has served as the reference for the bank's liquidity operations, and in 2012 the CBR has been used primarily as a ceiling for repo auctions. The CBR has become increasingly effective in guiding interbank rates.

The stance of monetary policy in Kenya in recent years is well captured by deviations between the interest rate level and the interest rate implied by the Taylor rule in our model. The comparison is displayed in Figure 16.4 and extensively discussed in Chapter 15. This analysis identifies a prolonged period of monetary accommodation that lasted from early 2008 until late 2011. While the monetary accommodation did not result in high inflation in 2009 to mid-2010, as the economy was affected by spillovers from the global financial crisis, it did fuel inflationary pressures starting in mid-2010. The large policy tightening at the end of 2011 resulted in policy overshooting relative to the Taylor rule prescription, probably in order to build credibility. In the section below, we will study whether the inclusion of money targets in the analysis helps make sense of the policy stance during this period.

4.2 Money Demand in Kenya

Reserve and broad money in Kenya have experienced large swings in recent years.[17] Figure 16.5 displays year-on-year growth for real reserve and broad

---

[17] Reserve money comprises currency in circulation (currency outside banks and cash held by commercial banks in their tills) and deposits of both commercial banks and non-bank financial institutions held with the CBK. However, it excludes Government deposits. Aggregate M3 includes currency outside the banking system, demand deposits, time and saving deposits, certificates of deposits, deposit liabilities of non-bank financial institutions and residents' foreign currency deposits; see CBK (2012).

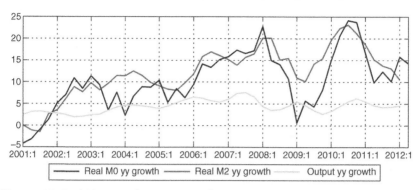

Figure 16.5. Real Money and Output Growth

money since 2001. There are two clear periods of rapid money growth, 2005:4–2008:2 and 2009:2–2011:1, with a marked slowdown during the global financial crisis. Both reserve and broad money comove quite strongly, although broad money grows faster on average. Note that real output growth, which is also displayed in Figure 16.5, also comoves somewhat with real money balances, with a correlation of about 0.5 with both measures. Despite the comovement, money relations are quite unstable. First money multipliers have been somewhat volatile and increasing, especially since 2008, see Figure 16.6. This is reflected in the decline in the cash to deposit ratio, due to increasing financial intermediation driven mainly by mobile-based banking initiatives (as the mobile phone-based payment system, M-pesa). In addition, deviations between real money and output growth imply that velocity has also been volatile and displayed large swings, as displayed in Figure 16.6.

The money demand function in (1) has been calibrated to the Kenyan economy. The calibration is presented in Table 16.2; it combines econometric estimates with prior judgements and restrictions imposed by the balanced growth path of the model. Consistent with the above discussion, shocks to liquidity and velocity are quite volatile. A corollary of this volatility is that the endogenous dynamics of the model cannot account for much of the variation in reserve money growth. This is reflected in Figure 16.7, which compares actual real reserve money growth (quarter on quarter) filtered through the model with the real money growth *predicted* by the model. The difference, which is accounted for by shocks to velocity and liquidity, is quite large, providing further evidence of the volatility of money demand.

4.3 Money Targets

Money targets and the actual path of reserve money move together over the medium term, but there are persistent target misses. Both variables are presented in Figure 16.8. Reserve money has been above its target for most of the period,

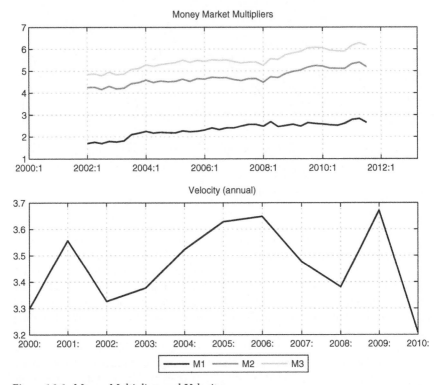

Figure 16.6. Money Multipliers and Velocity

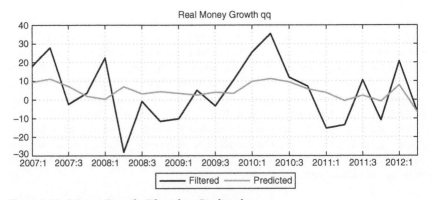

Figure 16.7. Money Growth: Filtered vs. Predicted

except during the global financial crisis, during which it fell below target. Target misses have fluctuated between plus and minus 10 per cent of the quarterly level of reserve money, and they also display persistence. Casual inspection of both series suggests that targets are revised to reduce or correct the target miss, i.e., money targets increase (decrease) when there is a positive (negative) target miss.

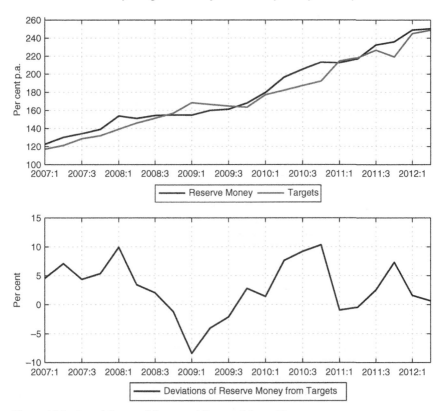

Figure 16.8. Actual Reserve Money and Reserve Money Targets

We run a vector error-correction estimation to assess the money/target relation and help calibrate the rule in (8).[18] We estimate the following system:

$$\begin{bmatrix} \Delta M_t \\ \Delta \overline{M}_{T,t} \end{bmatrix} = C + \Phi \begin{bmatrix} \Delta M_{t-1} \\ \Delta \overline{M}_{T,t-1} \end{bmatrix} + \Gamma [M_{t-1} - \overline{M}_{T,t-1}] + e_t,$$

where $e_t = [e_{M,t}, e_{\overline{M},t}]$. Results are presented in Table 16.4. The growth in money targets is driven mainly by two factors: correcting for previous target misses and innovations, with little role for lagged target growth. Regarding the former, the correction is less than complete: target misses result in an increase in the growth rate of the target that is less than one (0.67). Results in Table 16.4 have direct implications for the calibration of targeting rule (8), which can be rewritten as:

$$\Delta \overline{M}_{T,t} = (1 - a)\Delta \overline{M} + a(1 - \rho_{\overline{M}})\Delta \overline{M}_{T,t-1} + a\rho_{\overline{M}}[M_{t-1} - \overline{M}_{T,t-1}] + a\rho_{\overline{M}}\Delta \overline{M}_t.$$

The VECM results imply $a = 0.7$ and $\rho_{\overline{M}} = 1$. They also suggest that money targets are set using considerable information about future money demand: the R^2

---

[18] We ran an augmented Dickey-Fuller test on both series and failed to reject the null of a unit root. We also applied the Johanssen test and failed to reject cointegration between the two series. The estimate of the cointegrating vector using the Johansen procedure is [1 −0.99589].

Table 16.4. VECM estimates

	ΔM_t		$\Delta M_{T,t}$	
	Coeff.	t stat.	Coeff.	t stat.
Constant	0.015	2.99	0.010	1.82
ΔM_{t-1}	0.187	1.03	−0.131	0.64
$\Delta \bar{M}_{T,t-1>}$	0.034	0.30	−0.048	0.38
$M_{t-1} - \bar{M}_{T,t-1}$	0.054	0.44	0.667	4.81
R^2	0.063		0.395	
$Corr(e_{M,t}, e_{M,t})$	0.375			
Number of obs.	56			

from the regression is quite low, yet innovations to the money target are correlated with innovations to actual money growth. Finally, Table 16.4 indicates that the dynamics of money growth are completely unrelated, from a statistical perspective, to past target values.

4.4 Do Money Targets Matter for Monetary Policy in Kenya?

Various evidence on monetary aggregates suggest that target adherence $(1 - \gamma)$ has been very weak in Kenya. First, the large volatility of realized money growth suggests that money demand shocks have been for the most part accommodated. Second, the size and persistence of money target misses suggest target adherence has not been a policy priority. Third, the observation that money targets do not depend at all on past money target growth values or past target misses suggests that money targets have not steered money growth in any meaningful way, whereas the opposite is true: target misses steer the growth rate of target growth. Finally, while the positive correlation between target innovations and money growth innovations is in principle consistent with money targets affecting money growth, it is equally consistent with money targets providing a reasonable forecast of future money growth, but without implying any causation.

The relation between interest rates and money target misses is also suggestive of weak target adherence. Unlike other countries in the region in which money targets play a more central role in policy, interest rates do not display the type of quarterly noise, i.e., one-off movements, that would be expected under money targeting.[19] More importantly, money target misses do not help understand changes in the policy stance, unlike what is suggested by (12). To recap, equation (12) implies that positive target misses (money above its target) should result in increases in interest rates above the Taylor rule, and vice versa, all else equal. To see whether this relation holds in the date, the policy stance $(rs_t - rs_{R,t})$ and the target miss $(M_t - \bar{M}_t)$ are displayed in Figure 16.9. The episode of persistent policy accommodation observed between 2008 and 2011 coincides with money target misses oscillating from negative (money falling below its target) during the global financial crisis to positive during 2009:3 to 2011:1. During the latter period,

---

[19] This is the case in Tanzania, and in Uganda before 2009. See Chapter 5 for a discussion.

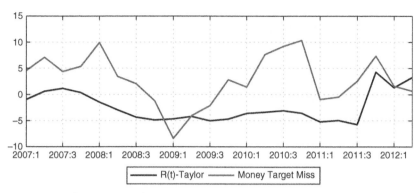

Figure 16.9. Policy Stance and Target Misses

episodes of positive target misses are associated with interest rates being below the Taylor-implied rate. Although in principle the empirical evidence could still be consistent with eq. (12), with the difference between the two variables in Figure 16.9 explained by offsetting movements in the monetary policy shock, the more likely explanation is that money targets have not played a systematic role in monetary policymaking.

The calibration of the model is consistent with this empirical evidence. We set $\gamma = 0.99$, which suggests a very small, almost negligible, role for money targets in the policy framework. Since quarterly money target misses are annualized, the above specification implies a 1 per cent increase in the money target miss results in an increase in interest rates of seven basis points. This compares with a 1 percentage point increase in expected inflation, which results in an immediate increase in interest rates of forty-three basis points and a long-run increase of 170 basis points. Note that this calibration is specific to Kenya, and it may vary considerably in other countries in which money targets play a larger role.

We have also assessed the possibility that target adherence was non-negligible but time-varying, but the evidence is inconclusive. The CBK sets its money targets six months ahead. Assuming that these targets are conditioned on the same information set, it could be conjectured that the optimal forecast for money one quarter ahead is more precise than the forecast two quarters ahead, and therefore that the central bank adheres more closely to its one-quarter ahead target than its two-quarter ahead target. If so, adherence would be time-varying, it could also mean that the effective target (two-quarters ahead) has in fact changed. Figure 16.10 plots a distribution of deviations of money from its target in the first and the second period. Although the second period misses are on average larger, one cannot make a conclusive statement due to the small sample size and the presence of outliers.[20] We therefore maintained the assumption of constant (but very low) target adherence.

---

[20] Figure 16.10 presents histograms of the first period after the declaration of target and the second period. The mean, standard deviation, and kurtosis are indicated. Note, that the kurtosis of a Gaussian distribution is three.

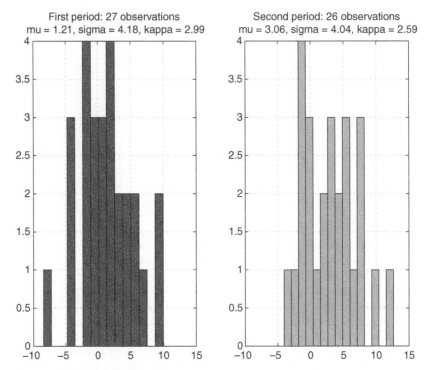

Figure 16.10. Reserve Money Deviations from Target

4.5 A Macroeconomic Decomposition of Money Targets and Monetary Policy in Kenya

The previous analysis has been based on a partial equilibrium context. We now use the model to make sense of developments in monetary aggregates and targets in the context of a comprehensive assessment of the state of the economy and of the monetary policy stance. Even if, as foreshadowed in the discussion of the previous section, we find that money aggregates do not shed much additional light on macroeconomic developments or monetary policy, the approach we present here may be useful in other contexts, in which monetary policy is more money aggregate-based. In particular, we will see how we can systematically and coherently analyse the setting of money targets, the causes of misses, and the implications for monetary policy. Of course the results we get depend on the other elements of the model, such as the volatility of supply and demand shocks. But this is a feature of the world, not of this particular approach, and we believe that the model can help put the various pieces together explicitly.

As part of the filtration of Kenyan macro data through the model, we recover a model-based decomposition of all the relevant variables into the different shocks: demand shocks, supply or inflation shocks, etc. A similar analysis was done in Chapter 15 for other macro variables such as sectoral inflation and the output gap; here the emphasis is on money target misses. We are particularly interested in whether money target misses reflect shocks to monetary policy or shocks to money demand (both liquidity and velocity). This is the standard problem facing policymakers in countries with money targets, yet the analysis of target misses has, until now, suffered from lack of a comprehensive framework. In practice this has resulted in assessments made purely on judgement and on an ad-hoc basis: if inflation is high then target misses are typically considered as driven by monetary policy, otherwise target misses are interpreted as reflecting money demand shocks with little implications for inflation.

The issue of the sources of target misses is related but different from the issue of whether money targets matter for the stance of policy. Mechanically, the two issues are related because the decomposition of target misses into shock depends on the calibration for γ. In the extreme case that $\gamma = 0$, the only possible explanation for target misses is a monetary policy shock, see eq. (3.2.3). If γ is instead closer to one, as in our calibration, then target misses will be accounted for by monetary policy shocks insofar as these shocks result in changes in the demand for nominal money balances, via their effects on short-term interest rates. In the latter specification, the transmission of the shock to monetary aggregates is less direct, but is more likely to reflect the way monetary policy shocks are transmitted into the economy. Beyond this mechanical relation, the analysis of target misses can provide a crosscheck on the assessment of monetary policy, even when target adherence is low as in Kenya. If targets reflect monetary policy shocks to some extent, then they can provide additional confirmation that the policy stance is tight or loose. Such cross check can be valuable in data-poor environments, as is the case in many LICs.

The model interpretation of actual data suggests that money target misses were mainly driven by shocks to money demand. The decomposition is shown in Figure 16.11. Each bar in the figure denotes the contribution of the particular shock to the target miss. Regarding monetary policy shocks, 2010 provides an interesting exception in that monetary policy shocks did contribute to target misses in that year. The CBK was aware of the misses, yet the frequent overshooting was not considered a threat for inflation as intermediate objectives—broad money, credit growth, and NDA—were close to their targets.[21] The observed overshooting was also consistent with the accommodative monetary policy pursued by the CBK during that period, as reflected in the analysis of interest rates shown in Figure 16.4. There are, however, other periods in which positive monetary policy shocks are associated with negative target misses. This was the case during the global financial crisis and in 2011. Business cycle shocks, such as demand and supply shocks, have played a small role in driving target misses, although they have contributed to lower frequency movements.

5 CONCLUSIONS

This chapter presented a strategy for incorporating money-targeting into the framework in Chapter 15 and assessed its relevance for Kenya, a de jure money targeter.

---

[21] See e.g. Monetary Policy Statement, June 2011, Central Bank of Kenya.

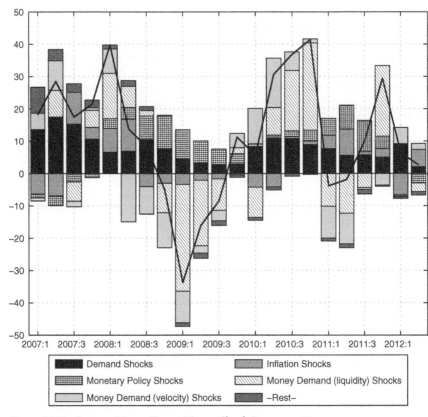

Legend:
- Demand Shocks
- Inflation Shocks
- Monetary Policy Shocks
- Money Demand (liquidity) Shocks
- Money Demand (velocity) Shocks
- –Rest–

Figure 16.11. Reserve Money Target Misses, Shock Decomposition

We use a dynamic economic model to investigate mixed operational targets and thus monetary policy regimes with different degree of adherence to money targets. We use the model to interpret target misses.

We find that, while money targets are set in a forward-looking manner, they do not play a systematic role in Kenyan monetary policy. We characterize the setting of money targets primarily as a money demand forecasting exercise, based on the empirical evidence. We also find that the dynamics of interest rates and monetary aggregates are not systematically related to money targets or money target misses, which we interpret as evidence that money target adherence has been very weak. Also, using the model to provide a historical interpretation of Kenyan data, we find that money target misses were mainly driven by shocks to money demand. The analysis suggests that policy shocks contributed to the misses in 2010.

Our results suggest that stronger adherence to pre-announced money growth targets leads to increased volatility of macroeconomic variables, particularly money market rates. Sticking to pre-announced money growth targets creates imbalances in money markets facing frequent shocks and implies potential for interest rate volatility and uncertainty, even when the policy rule is rather forward-looking. The instability of money demand and money multipliers contributes to the infeasibility of strong adherence to money targets, but is far from being the sole reason for our results. Notably, supply and demand shocks push money demand in ways that tend to result in undesirable macroeconomic volatility when policy is too focused on the attainment of money targets. Our finding validates the weak target adherence observed in Kenya.

Given the setup of our model and also many of our results, it is perhaps hard to understand why a central bank would in fact use money targets. In the case of Kenya, we argue that in fact they do not use them very much. Other countries may be different, however. Either they use money targets for reasons not modelled here, such as to achieve credibility or because incomplete financial markets make it difficult to observe the interest rate. For these central banks, the model presented in the chapter may be a useful practical tool. As shown in the case of Kenya, it is able to provide a better view on factors affecting the business cycle, and it helps identify structural shocks behind target misses. It also provides a platform to assess the macroeconomic implications of potential policy changes aimed at higher target flexibility.

There are several caveats to our analysis. Our analysis deals with low-income countries without fiscal dominance. Second, our dynamic model does not account for issues of limited credibility and imperfect, heterogeneous information. In case of incomplete information in the model, the role of money as an indicator variable would be enhanced. However, the main result regarding the costs of strong adherence to pre-announced targets should remain untouched.

REFERENCES

Alvarez, F., R. Lucas, and W. Weber (2001). Recent advances in monetary policy rules. *American Economic Review*, 91(2).

Bindseil, U. (2004). *Monetary Policy Implementation—Theory, Past and Present*. New York: Oxford University Press.

Canzoneri, R. (1985). Monetary policy games and the role of private information. *American Economic Review*, 75(5).

CBK (2011). Monetary policy statement. Technical Report December, Central Bank of Kenya.

CBK (2012). Monetary policy statement. Technical Report June, Central Bank of Kenya.

Davies, C., M. Gillman, and M. Kejak (2012). *Deriving the Taylor principle when the central bank supplies money*. Working paper, Central European University.

Disyatat, P. (2008). *Monetary policy implementation: Misconceptions and their consequences*. Working Paper December, No. 269, Bank for International Settlements.

Ndung'u, N. (2012). *International conference on monetary policy frameworks in developing countries: Practice and challenges—Kenya's experience*. Technical Report July 20, Central Bank of Kenya (Kigali, Rwanda).

Razzak, W. A. (2003). Is the Taylor rule really different from the McCallum rule? *Contemporary Economic Policy*, 21(4), 445–57.

Selassie, A.A., B. Clements, S. Tareq, J.K. Martijn, and G. Di Bella (2006). *Designing monetary and fiscal policy in low-income countries*. Occasional Paper 250, International Monetary Fund.

Woodford, M. (2012). *Methods of Policy Accommodation at the Interest-Rate Lower Bound, in The Changing Policy Landscape*, Federal Reserve Bank of Kansas City.

17

Monetary Policy in Low-Income Countries in the Face of the Global Crisis

A Structural Analysis

Alfredo Baldini, Jaromir Benes, Andrew Berg,
Mai C. Dao, and Rafael Portillo

1 INTRODUCTION

Understanding the impact of the global financial crisis in low-income countries (LICs) is an important task for national authorities and international organizations.[1] Beyond its intrinsic importance, the crisis provides a relatively clean 'experiment': it can be interpreted as an exogenous event for most LICs, while its magnitude facilitates tracing its effects. As such, it provides insights about the structure of these economies and their exposure to external factors. It also allows central banks to assess—and learn from—past decisions.

In this chapter we develop a quantitative model—adapted to the specific characteristics of LICs—to analyse the impact of the financial crisis on Zambia, and the role that monetary policy played in the transmission of the crisis. We compare the predictions of the model to a dataset of Zambian macroeconomic and financial variables.

Zambia is in many ways a representative low-income country. It is dependent on commodity exports (copper). It is financially underdeveloped, with foreign-owned banks playing the central role, along with the exchange rate, in the transmission of monetary policy. Its monetary policy framework is also fairly representative. The Bank of Zambia targets monetary aggregates under a floating exchange rate regime. As in other LICs, fiscal developments can pose a challenge for monetary policy through their effect on aggregate demand and the allocation of credit.

The design of our model explicitly incorporates these features. We model banks' various assets and liabilities and their respective interest rates, and assume that the private sector is unable to obtain financing beyond the banking system. We allow for the possibility that shocks to the banking system may be reflected in binding credit constraints in addition to higher interest rates. We also model fiscal

---

[1] Printed with permission of *Pacific Economic Review* (2015), 20(1), 149–92.

developments and their implications for the transmission of external shocks. Our model is otherwise standard, i.e., it conforms to the typical structure of DSGEs.[2]

From Zambia's perspective—and that of low-income countries in general—we view the global financial crisis in terms of three related shocks. The first was a large deterioration in Zambia's terms of trade, associated with the collapse in copper prices during 2008 and 2009. The second was an increase in the country's external risk premium, as foreign investors' demand for Zambian assets decreased. The third shock was a decrease in Zambian banks' risk appetite in response to the crisis, which we define as a shift away from (risky) lending toward safe assets. Specifically, banks increased lending rates (relative to interest rates on safer assets), reduced their overall lending to the domestic private sector, and increased their demand for liquidity and government bonds. We view these shocks as reflecting a single underlying event—the global financial crisis—though we do not undertake here to model this relationship.

The combination of these shocks led to a large nominal and real depreciation, a reversal in current account dynamics—from large deficits to balance—a decline in domestic demand, and a temporary decrease in inflationary pressures. On the fiscal front, government revenues declined and debt issuance increased. In the banking sector, the reallocation of assets away from loans to the private sector and toward government securities and liquidity, together with a steep slowdown in the growth of broad money, contributed to a decrease in the money multiplier (or alternatively, an increase in measures of banks' liquidity).

In this context, the actual response of monetary policy can be characterized as 'stop and go'. The T-bill rate (the preferred instrument for open market operations in Zambia) initially increased by 400 basis points between mid-2008 and mid-2009. As the crisis worsened, the policy stance was later reversed, allowing T-bill rates to fall by more than 1,000 basis points in the second half of 2009, and liquidity increased substantially.

We reproduce the crisis in our model by picking a combination of the aforementioned shocks that help match the exact path of key external variables (the terms of trade, the nominal exchange rate, and the current account).[3] We then compare the model's output with data on ten macroeconomic and financial variables, conditional on the 'stop and go' policy pattern, i.e., on a sequence of monetary policy shocks that replicates the large swings in T-bill rates.

Our main results are the following. First, we find that the model broadly reproduces the path of most variables, with the notable exception of GDP. This relative success suggests that DSGE models can contribute to the quantitative analysis of macroeconomic developments and policy in Zambia and low-income countries

---

[2] By typical structure we mean that profit and utility maximization by agents in the model result in equations that are standard in DSGEs: New Keynesian Phillips curves for prices and wages—with both forward- and backward-looking elements—a Euler equation for consumption, various factor demand functions by firms and interest parity conditions between domestic and foreign assets. In addition the economy is subject to a resource constraint (the balance of payments).

[3] We simulate our model using IRIS, a Matlab-based package developed by one of our co-authors (Benes). This package can be freely downloaded from https://github.com/IRIS-Solutions-Team/IRIS-Toolbox/wiki/IRIS-Macroeconomic-Modeling-Toolbox.

more generally, although more work is needed to understand the behaviour of GDP and the macro-financial-balance of payment linkages in these countries.

Second, we find that all three real shocks—terms of trade, external risk premium, and change in banks' appetite for risk—are necessary to help match the data. The first two shocks tend to generate the desired nominal depreciation and a subsequent decrease in imports, but they have counterfactual implications for the current account and the volume of credit, as consumers would smooth the temporary decrease in income through an increase in externally financed credit and a higher current account deficit. Meanwhile, the decrease in banks' risk appetite helps match the current account reversal and the contraction in credit but by itself would result in an appreciation of the currency, as relative demand for foreign goods would decrease. It is only by combining the three shocks that the model can reproduce the stylized facts.

Third, our modelling exercise shows that developments in the banking sector were an important part of the transmission of the crisis to the domestic economy. In our model, the contraction in credit induced by banks is required to generate the right current account reversal, while its impact on aggregate demand helps generate the decline in inflation observed during the crisis. The increase in lending premia is also helpful to understand the impact on aggregate demand, although by itself it would not generate a current account reversal. Moreover, banks demand for liquid and safe assets helped shape the monetary policy stance, given the money-targeting regime in place.

Finally, our model shows that the 'stop and go' policy response was counter-productive, in that it may have contributed initially to the contraction in aggregate demand. A more accommodating policy would have helped stabilize the economy earlier, albeit at the cost of higher nominal depreciation and inflation. While the effect would have been limited in absolute terms, given the magnitude of the real shocks hitting the economy, such a policy would have reduced the decline in private spending in 2009 by 3 to 6 per cent, depending on the specification. Policy rules that respond to various developments in the banking system (changes in the growth rate of credit or deposits) would have also helped stabilize the economy.

In light of the last result, we also discuss the determinants of the initial 'stop' response of monetary policy. We find that the policy response appears to have been driven by 'rear-view' or 'side-view' issues, not all of them directly related to the crisis. First, authorities were concerned with inflationary pressures at the time, mostly associated with the food and fuel price shock of 2007 and early 2008. Second, authorities may have also been responding to the large nominal depreciation induced by the crisis. Third, authorities may have been reluctant to loosen policy at a time of incipient increases in measures of 'excess liquidity'. Policy-makers were also likely influenced by the overshooting of reserve money targets during 2008, which may have led to a view that monetary policy was loose.

Our chapter is related to the large and growing literature on the impact of the recent financial crisis.[4] Relative to previous work on the credit channel, which focused on the role of borrowers' financial conditions on the amplification of

---

[4] Papers on the overall impact of the crisis in low-income counties include IMF (2009b) and Berg et al. (2010).

shocks, recent work has emphasized developments in the financial system itself as the source of the crisis.[5] Our work has elements of both, giving importance to both systemic and counterparty-specific risks. Unlike most of these recent contributions, however, we limit ourselves to a relatively simple treatment of the banking sector in an open economy, since our goal is to provide a coherent story for Zambia's experience during the crisis.

Our chapter is also related to the literature on financial crises in emerging markets, especially on the role of monetary policy.[6] We differ in that our focus is on a combination of external shocks—rather than just the current account reversal—and we pay special attention to developments in the banking/monetary system. Also, the relatively low degree of financial dollarization in Zambia (less than 30 per cent of loans and deposits) allows us to abstract from currency mismatches—a central theme in that literature. Finally, our work is also related to Agenor and Montiel (2006, 2008) who emphasize—in a static small open economy framework—the role of the domestic banking system in monetary policy in developing countries.

The chapter is organized as follows. Section 2 briefly reviews relevant aspects of the structure of the Zambian economy and sets the stage. Section 3 introduces the structure of the model and the shocks we consider. Section 4 discusses the Zambia data and the calibration, and applies the model to Zambia under the actual path of monetary policy and under alternative policy responses. Section 5 discusses the factors behind the initial monetary policy response. Section 6 derives some policy implications for low-income countries and concludes.

2 THE ECONOMY OF ZAMBIA AND THE GLOBAL FINANCIAL CRISIS

Zambia is in many ways a typical low-income country and faced a typical set of shocks, for such countries, during the global financial crisis.[7] It exports mainly commodities, mostly copper. It is relatively—and typically—closed to trade, aid-dependent, and rural (Table 17.1). Agriculture, mining, manufacturing, and construction each make up roughly a tenth of GDP, again broadly like other low-income countries (Figure 17.1). Employment is much more skewed towards agriculture at about 70 per cent of the total, reflecting the typically large agriculture productivity gap.[8]

---

[5] The former literature was built on the seminal contributions of Bernanke, Gertler, and Gilchrist (1999) and Kiyotaki and Moore (1997). New work on financial intermediation includes Goodfriend and McCallum (2007), Christiano, Motto, and Rostagno (2010), Curdia and Woodford (2009), Adrian and Shin (2011), and Gertler and Kiyotaki (2011). See Woodford (2010) for a simple exposition.

[6] The seminal paper is by Calvo (1998). Other contributions include Aghion, Bacchetta, and Banerjee (2001), Christiano, Gust, and Roldos (2004), Chari, Kehoe, and McGrattan (2005), Mendoza (2006), Calvo, Izquierdo, and Talvi (2006), among many others.

[7] Indeed, we chose to study Zambia not because of its idiosyncrasies but because of a timely request from the IMF country team.

[8] See Gollin, Lagakos, and Waugh (2014).

Table 17.1. Selected Economic Indicators

Groups	Exports	Imports	Aid	Rural Population	Commodity Exports
	(% of GDP)	(% of GDP)	(% of GDP)	(% of Total)	(% of Exports)
Zambia	46.0	37.0	4.8	60.8	89.5
Kenya	29.1	46.0	9.8	76.0	60.9
Uganda	23.7	34.5	9.9	84.4	62.6
Tanzania	31.1	50.2	10.3	73.3	73.3
Rwanda	13.4	32.5	19.7	80.9	89.0
Low-Income Countries	28.3	48.4	13.1	69.2	64.0
Emerging Economies	42.2	41.4	1.8	34.5	27.9
Advanced Economies	65.5	61.0	0.0	20.5	19.5

Data are for 2011, except for Kenya (2010). Commodity exports include food, agricultural raw materials, and ore and minerals.

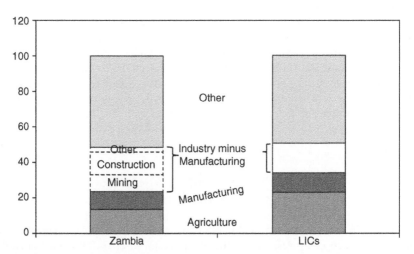

Figure 17.1. GDP Composition by Sector, 2011
Source: WDI and dxTime database.

Its financial sector contains a number of features of particular importance for the transmission mechanism of external financial shocks and monetary policy, again typical of most low-income countries. The financial sector is underdeveloped and fairly concentrated, with foreign-owned banks playing the central role. It is moderately dollarized, and the capital account is fairly open (Table 17.2).

Its monetary policy framework is also fairly representative of many low-income countries, particularly in sub-Saharan Africa. The Bank of Zambia targets monetary aggregates under a managed floating exchange rate regime. Perhaps somewhat more unusually, its float is quite 'pure', with the central bank engaging minimal foreign exchange intervention (at least during the period in question).

Like many such countries, including in sub-Saharan Africa, Zambia has enjoyed strong growth for many years, with real per capita growth averaging about 2.3 per cent during 2000–07, compared to an average of 2.7 per cent for low-income countries.

Table 17.2. Financial Depth Indicators

Groups	Domestic Credit to Private Sector (% of GDP)	Private Bank Credit (% of GDP)	5-Bank Asset Concentration (%) (% of GDP)	Stocks Traded Total Value (% of GDP)	Credit to Government	Dollarization	Chinn-Ito Financial Openness Index
Zambia	12.3	10.9	81.7	0.5	13.7	31.7	2.5
Kenya	38.1	33.6	60.5	2.6	13.7	10.8	1.1
Uganda	17.9	13.8	73.6	0.1	4.6	21.8	2.5
Tanzania	17.8	15.8	67.6	0.1	7.3	20.3	−1.2
Rwanda	16.9	13.2	100.0	n.a.	1.1	20.0	−0.9
Low-Income Countries	19.6	18.8	80.0	4.9	7.2	12.8	−0.4
Emerging Economies	60.9	49.1	69.6	26.6	12.0	4.0	0.3
Advanced Economies	145.3	133.7	84.4	70.2	17.3	0.5	2.2

Data are for 2011, except for Kenya (2010). Commodity exports include food, agricultural raw materials, and ore and minerals.

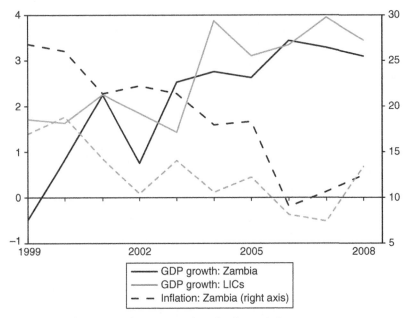

Figure 17.2. Real Per Capital GDP Growth and inflation (%)
Source: WDI.

Zambia also had reasonable—and typical—success with inflation stabilization, with inflation coming down from 76 per cent during 1990–99 to 18 per cent during 2000–07 (Figure 17.2).

The global financial crisis hit countries such as Zambia fairly hard along several dimensions, with large declines in terms of trade as commodity prices collapsed

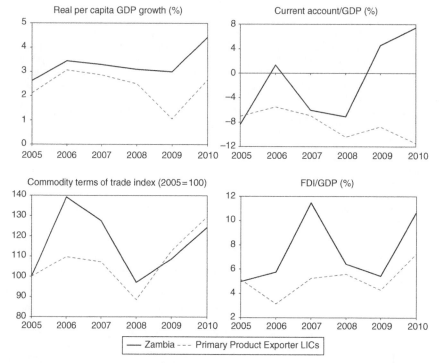

Figure 17.3. Zambia During the Crisis
Source: WDI.

and the sharp increase in global risk aversion and reductions in capital inflows (Figure 17.3). With these shocks, the real exchange rate depreciated sharply, while inflation—already high with the rise in food and fuel prices in 2008—ticked up. According to official GDP statistics, Zambia had no noticeable dip in growth during the 2008–09 period, quite unusually for sub-Saharan African LICs, and a point to which we return below.

After detailing the model structure in the next section, we will confront the data much more closely in Section 3 to understand these events and in particular the role of monetary policy.

3 CORE MODEL STRUCTURE

The model is made up of the following six blocks: households, firms, the banking system, the monetary authority, the government, and the rest of the world. The flow chart in Figure 17.4 visualizes the links and feedback relations between these blocks.

For each block we present the equations that describe behaviour. See Appendix A in Baldini et al. (2015) for a derivation from utility and profit maximization. Note that in some cases we relax some of the restrictions imposed by optimization

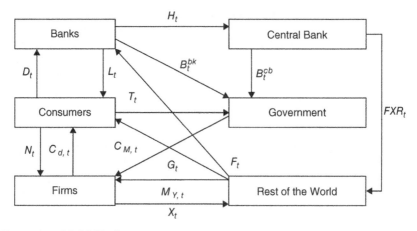

Figure 17.4. Model Blocks

to allow for greater flexibility in the dynamics of the model. This greater flexibility helps match the specific path of real macro and financial variables during the crisis, without forsaking the logic of first principles or diluting the mechanisms of interest.[9]

3.1 Households

Our modelling of households has the following features. First, households' intertemporal decisions are influenced by the domestic lending rate (R_t^L), reflecting the dominance of banks in financial systems in LICs. Second, consumers may be constrained in their ability to borrow at the lending rate offered by banks. These features are reflected in our Euler equation for consumption:

$$\lambda_t = E_t \left[\lambda_{t+1} \frac{\beta R_{L,t}}{\pi_{c,t+1}} \right] + u_{F,1,t}, \tag{1}$$

where $\pi_{c,t}$ is CPI inflation, λ_t is the marginal value of wealth, and $u_{F,1,t}$ is the value of the multiplier associated with the borrowing constraint.[10] The marginal value of consumption is given by:

$$\lambda_t = \frac{1}{(C_t - \chi C_{t-1})}.$$

The parameter χ measures the degree of backward-looking behaviour (or habit formation). We assume total consumption is spent on domestic goods and

---

[9] See Erceg, Guerrieri, and Gust (2006) for a discussion of the restrictions implied by fully micro-founded models and their implications for matching short-run properties of the data.

[10] See Mendoza (2006).

imports following a Leontieff specification, which implies the following demand for domestic goods: $C_{d,t} = \omega C_t$. This specification captures the view that in low-income countries imports are not close substitutes with domestically produced goods. The CPI is a weighted sum of import and domestic prices: $P_{c,t} = \omega P_{d,t} + (1 - \omega) P_{M,t}$. The demand for imports is also potentially affected by a borrowing constraint:

$$C_{M,t} = (1 - \omega) C_t - u_{F,2,t}, \tag{2}$$

with $u_{F,2,t}$ denoting the marginal value of the constraint.[11] This restriction allows us to emphasize the impact of a financial shock on the demand for imports rather than on overall consumption (more on this below). Financing for import consumption requires lenders' acceptance of additional foreign currency exposure. It is plausible that banks may be especially unwilling to finance such exposure during the crisis.[12]

Consumers demand deposits from banks, which earn interest at the rate $R_{D,t}$. The demand for real deposits is given implicitly by the following function:

$$\frac{R_{L,t}}{R_{D,t}} = D\left(C_t, C_{t-1}, \frac{D_t}{P_{c,t}}\right), \tag{3}$$

where $D(*, *, *)$ is continuously differentiable and homogeneous of order zero, with $D_i > 0$ for $i = 1, 2$ and $D_3 < 0$. Demand for real deposits depends on consumption and the ratio of lending rates and deposit rates; lagged consumption is introduced to generate sluggishness in the demand for deposits.

The supply of labour by consumers is subject to nominal wage rigidities. This results in a Phillips curve for nominal wage inflation ($\pi_{W,t} = \frac{W_t}{W_{t-1}}$), which depends on future and past wage growth and deviations between the marginal disutility of labour—which is constant—and the marginal value of real wages:

$$log\left(\frac{\pi_{W,t}}{\pi_{W,t-1}}\right) = \beta log\left(\frac{E[\pi_{W,t+1}]}{\pi_{W,t}}\right) + \xi_w\left(\frac{1}{\frac{W_t}{P_{c,t}}\lambda_t} - 1\right). \tag{4}$$

3.2 Firms

There are two types of firms in the economy: those that produce for domestic consumption and firms that produce export goods for the world market.

---

[11] This constraint can be microfounded by assuming that consumers pay for imports at the beginning of the period, before receiving their labour and interest income, and that such lending is subject to a borrowing constraint that may fluctuate over time. While the rate at which consumers borrow within the period would also show up in the consumer price index, we assume such rate is equal to zero.

[12] We do not model issues related to currency risk. Efforts to microfound this risk might be instructive but are outside the scope of this chapter.

3.2.1 Domestic Firms

Domestic firms produce consumption goods using labour, capital—the stock of which has been fixed to 1—and imported inputs $M_{Y,t}$:

$$Y_t = N_{Y,t}^{\gamma_N} M_{Y,t}^{\gamma_M}. \tag{5}$$

Cost minimization leads to the following equations for factor demand:

$$\gamma_N P_{Y,t} Y_t = W_t N_{Y,t} F\left(\frac{N_{Y,t}}{M_{Y,t}}, \frac{N_{Y,t-1}}{M_{Y,t-1}}, E_t\left[\frac{N_{Y,t+1}}{M_{Y,t+1}}\right]\right), \tag{6}$$

$$\gamma_M P_{Y,t} Y_t = P_{M,t} M_{Y,t} F\left(\frac{N_{Y,t}}{M_{Y,t}}, \frac{N_{Y,t-1}}{M_{Y,t-1}}, E_t\left[\frac{N_{Y,t+1}}{M_{Y,t+1}}\right]\right), \tag{7}$$

$$(1 - \gamma_N - \gamma_M) P_{Y,t} Y_t = Q_t, \tag{8}$$

where $W_t, P_{M,t}$, and Q_t are factor costs and $P_{Y,t}$ is the sector's nominal marginal cost. The function $F(*, *, *)$ introduces sluggish adjustment in the demand for labour and imported inputs in response to changes in (relative) factor prices; it is introduced to improve the empirical properties of the model.

Domestic inflation $\pi_{d,t} = \frac{P_{d,t}}{P_{d,t-1}}$ is given by a hybrid Phillips curve:

$$\log\left(\frac{\pi_{d,t}}{\pi_{d,t-1}}\right) = \beta \log\left(\frac{E_t[\pi_{d,t+1}]}{\pi_{d,t}}\right) + \xi_c\left(\frac{P_{Y,t}}{P_{d,t}} - 1\right). \tag{9}$$

Finally, the nominal value of capital $P_{K,t}$, which as we will see later matters for risk premia in the banking sector, is given by a standard forward-looking asset pricing equation:

$$P_{K,t} = \sigma_K E_t\left[\frac{1}{R_{L,t}}\left(Q_{t+1} + (1 - \delta)P_{K,t+1}\right)\right] + (1 - \sigma_K)P_{K,t-1}, \tag{10}$$

where δ is the depreciation rate for physical capital and σ_K is the degree of forward-looking behaviour in the pricing of capital.

3.2.2 Exporting Firms

Exporting firms use domestic and imported inputs. They take prices for their output as given by world markets $(P_{X,t})$. Supply of exports is given by the ratio between the price of exports and the marginal cost of firms in that sector, subject to adjustment costs:

$$\frac{P_{x,t}}{aP_{Y,t} + (1 - a)P_{m,t}} = 1 + \psi_X \log\left(\frac{X_t}{X_{t-1}}\right) - \beta\psi_X \log\left(\frac{E_t[X_{t+1}]}{X_t}\right), \tag{11}$$

where a is the share of domestic goods in the production of traded goods. This parsimonious specification helps capture a low elasticity of exports to relative prices, given an inelastic supply of factors and limited mobility across sectors. The price of exports $P_{X,t}$ is subject to shocks to the terms of trade T_t:

$$P_{x,t} = P_{M,t}T_t = S_t P_{w,t}T_t, \ln T_t = \ln T_{t-1} + u_{T,t}, \tag{12}$$

where S is the nominal exchange rate.

3.3 The Banking Sector

We assume financial intermediation is carried out by a perfectly competitive banking system, which consists of wholesale and retail branches. At the wholesale level the representative bank's balance sheet is the following:

$$L_t + H_t + B_{bk,t} = D_t + F_t. \tag{13}$$

Banks' liabilities consist of deposits by residents D_t and foreign debt F_t—denominated in foreign currency but measured here in local currency. Assets consist of loans L_t, government bonds $B_{bk,t}$, and reserves at the central bank H_t, which earn no interest but help banks manage liquidity needs associated with deposits.

Profit maximization by banks leads to several arbitrage conditions. First, arbitrage between local currency returns on domestic and foreign bonds, $R_{B,t}$ and R_t, respectively, lead to the following relation:

$$R_{B,t} = R_t, \tag{14}$$

where R_t is given by the uncovered interest parity with world interest rates plus a potential shock to the country risk premium:

$$R_t = R_t^* E_t \left[\frac{S_{t+1}}{S_t} \right] + u_{R,t}. \tag{15}$$

Arbitrage between (net) returns on loans and other assets lead to the following relation between wholesale lending rates $R_{L,t}^*$ and interest rates on government bonds:

$$R_{L,t}^* = R_{B,t} + u_{F,3,t}, \tag{16}$$

where we have included an exogenous component to the risk premium on loans ($u_{F,3,t}$). Note that wholesale lending rates are not directly relevant for private sector decisions.

Finally, liquidity needs to manage deposit results in the following implicit demand for H:

$$R_{B,t} = H(D_t, H_t) + u_{F,4,t}, \tag{17}$$

where $H(*, *)$ is continuously differentiable and homogeneous of degree zero, with $H_1 > 0$ and $H_2 < 0$. Banks demand for liquidity is also subject to a shock $u_{F,4,t}$. As a result of these liquidity needs there is a negative premium on the interest rate on deposits:

$$R_{D,t} = R_t - \Lambda \left(\frac{D_t}{H_t} \right), \tag{18}$$

with $\Lambda_1 < 0$.

At the retail level, branches receive funding from wholesale branches and extend credit to households with some degree of monopoly power.[13] Retail lending is risky and rates are subject to adjustment costs, all of which results in the following pricing equation for loans:

$$log(R_{L,t}/R_{L,t-1}) = \beta log(E_t[R_{L,t+1}]/R_{L,t}) + \xi_R log\left(R_{L,t}(1 - g_t)/R_{L,t}^*\right),$$

where g_t is given by:

$$g_t = g_1\left(\frac{R_{L,t}L_t}{E_t[P_{k,t+1}]} - \frac{\bar{R}_L L}{\bar{P}_k}\right), \tag{19}$$

and a $(\bar{*})$ on top of a variable denotes its steady state value. Three factors affect the risk premium on lending rates. The first factor is the external finance premium g_t. It is usually micro-founded by assuming that returns on loans are risky, reflecting idiosyncratic risk on the borrowers part, which is costly for banks to verify and requires a compensating premium. This informational asymmetry is greatly reduced if borrowers can provide their own funds (capital in this case) to finance part of their project, which is why lowering the ratio of gross repayments to the value of capital reduces the premium. The second factor is the exogenous component $u_{F,3,t}$ in equation (16). Finally the dynamic path of the lending rate is also affected by the adjustment costs at the retail level.

Beyond the arbitrage conditions between different interest rates, we also allow for the possibility that banks may ration borrowers at the prevailing lending rate. The rationing is captured by the shocks $u_{F,1,t}$ and $u_{F,2,t}$. While we do not model the rationing formally, we believe there are reasons why banks may be reluctant to raise interest rates sufficiently to eliminate excess demand for loans, because of adverse selection (as in Stiglitz and Weiss, 1981), costly state verification (as in Williamson, 1987), or moral hazard (as in Bester and Hellwig, 1987).

We model a decrease in banks' appetite for risk as a simultaneous increase in shocks $u_{F,i,t}$, for $i=1,\ldots,4$. As a result of higher aversion, banks simultaneously increase the premium on lending rates ($u_{F,3,t}$ in equation (16)), ration their lending to the domestic private sector, including import finance (shocks $u_{F,1,t}$ and $u_{F,2,t}$ in equations (1) and (2), respectively), and increase their demand for liquidity ($u_{F,4,t}$ in equation (17)). This simultaneity justifies treating these proximate shocks as coming from one single shock—the increase in banks' appetite for risk, which we denote $u_{F,t}$. We impose the following normalization:

$$u_{F,1,t} = u_{F,t}; u_{F,2,t} = \mu_2 u_{F,t}; u_{F,3,t} = \mu_3 u_{F,t}; u_{F,4,t} = \mu_4 u_{F,t}, \tag{20}$$

where the μ_is are chosen to improve the fit of the model.

---

[13] The modelling choice that banks lend to retail is partly practical and partly empirical. Because there are few reliable data on investment, we have not incorporated that variable and as a result the simplification involved in assuming lending goes to households, costs little. And in fact, 46 per cent of outstanding bank lending from the formal financial sector in 2008 went directly to households (Bank of Zambia, 2011). In addition, according to survey data, credit from non-bank and informal financial institutions to individuals is substantially higher than formal bank credit, consistent with the view that some of the bank lending to enterprises may involve on-lending to individuals (Finscope Zambia, 2010).

3.4 Monetary Authority

We allow for different options regarding how the monetary authority operates, i.e., what variables are targeted by the central bank, and what instruments—or combinations of instruments—are used. We allow for such flexibility in this block of the model in order to help account for systematic differences between policy choices in LICs and advanced economies, and to compare among various policy rules.

Here are the policy rules we model:

- A reserve money growth rule:

$$\frac{H_t}{H_{t-1}} = 1 - \kappa_{\pi,H}(E_t[\pi_{c,t+1}] - 1) - \kappa_{D,H}\left(\frac{D_t}{D_{t-1}} - 1\right) - \kappa_{L,H}\left(\frac{L_t}{L_{t-1}} - 1\right) - u_{M,t}.$$

The reserve money growth rule nests various specifications: (i) an inflation targeting regime implemented using reserve money growth as the policy instrument ($\kappa_{D,H} = \kappa_{L,H} = 0$, $\kappa_{\pi,H} > 0$); (ii) a constant money growth rule ($\kappa_{D,H} = \kappa_{L,H} = \kappa_{\pi,H} = 0$); (iii) a rule that combines inflation targeting with broad money targeting ($\kappa_{D,H} > 0$, $\kappa_{\pi,H} > 0$); (iv) a rule that targets credit growth ($\kappa_{L,H} > 0$). Note that rule (iii) is consistent with current practice in some LICs, where broad money is often an intermediate target whereas reserve money serves as an operational target.

- Standard Taylor rule with the interest rate on government bonds being the main policy instrument:

$$R_{B,t} = \rho_R R_{B,t-1} + (1 - \rho_R)\left(\bar{R}_B + \kappa_\pi(E_t[\pi_{c,t+1}] - 1)\right) + u_{M,t}.$$

Note that in both of types of rules we abstract from targeting the output gap since this variable is difficult to assess in low-income countries, with quarterly GDP often unavailable. Without loss of generality, our policy rules imply a zero inflation target: when comparing the model with the data we add a constant term—reflecting the authority's implicit inflation target—to the inflation dynamics of the model. Depending on the rule, a tightening of monetary policy can be modelled as a positive shock $u_{M,t}$ to the policy rate/short-term T-bill rate $R_{B,t}$ or a liquidity withdrawal $-u_{M,t}$ on H_t.

We also keep track of the central bank balance sheet:

$$B_{cb,t} = H_t + F_t, \tag{21}$$

where $B_{cb,t}$ denotes the central bank's holdings of government debt and F_t are the central bank's international reserves (measured in local currency). In this chapter we set F_t to zero, since intervention in the foreign exchange market did not play an important role in Zambia during the global crisis. Regardless of the policy regime, we assume the central bank implements policy by varying $B_{cb,t}$. Finally we define a measure of relative or 'excess' liquidity in the banking system, which is given by the inverse of the money multiplier:

$$EL_t = \frac{H_t}{D_t}. \tag{22}$$

3.5 The Government

The government taxes economic agents, spends on a basket of goods similar to those of consumers, issues debt, and pays interest. Its budget constraint is given by:

$$P_{c,t}G_t = T_t + B_t - B_{t-1} - R_{B,t-1}B_{bk,t}, \tag{23}$$

where G_t is real government spending, T_t is the nominal tax revenue, and B_t is the total stock of government debt ($B_t = B_{bk,t} + B_{cb,t}$). We assume the government only pays interest on debt held by commercial banks. Consistent with the tax structure in many low-income countries, where import duties make a large share of government revenue, we assume that tax revenue (in per cent of nominal GDP) is sensitive to the value of imports:

$$\frac{T_t}{Y_t^N} = \frac{T}{Y^N} + \phi\left(\frac{P_{M,t}M_t}{Y_t^N} - \frac{P_M M}{Y^N}\right) \tag{24}$$

Y_t^N is the level of nominal GDP and ϕ measures the sensitivity of tax revenues to imports.

Government debt is anchored by the following spending rule:

$$\frac{P_{c,t}G_t}{Y_t^N} = \rho_G \frac{P_{c,t-1}G_{t-1}}{Y_{t-1}^N} + (1 - \rho_G)\left(\frac{P_c G}{Y^N} - \tau_G\left(\frac{B_{bk,t}}{Y_t^N} - \frac{B_{bk}}{Y^N}\right)\right). \tag{25}$$

This rule ensures that government debt outstanding converges to a given long-run level $\frac{B^{bk}}{Y^N}$. The parameter ρ_G measures the sluggishness in real government spending (in per cent of GDP), while τ_G—together with ρ_G—measures the speed of adjustment to reduce debt levels.[14]

Note that the country's resource constraint requires $Y_t = X_t + C_{d,t} + \omega G_t$, while nominal GDP is defined as $Y_t^N = P_{c,t}(C_{d,t} + G_t) + P_{X,t}X_t - P_{M,t}M_t$ (with $M_t = C_{M,t} + M_{Y,t} + (1 - \omega)G_t$).

3.6 Relationship with the Rest of the World

We close our model by keeping track of the country's balance of payments:

$$F_t = R_{t-1}^* \frac{S_t}{S_{t-1}} F_{t-1} - (P_{x,t}X_t - P_{M,t}M_t). \tag{26}$$

4 APPLYING THE MODEL TO ZAMBIA

Having introduced the core structure of the model, we now apply it to Zambia. In this section we discuss the data, calibration, the characterization of the crisis, and the simulation results.

---

[14] Our modelling of fiscal and monetary policy assumes lack of fiscal dominance, i.e., monetary policy is active while fiscal policy is passive. See Baldini and Poplawski-Ribeiro (2011) for an assessment of fiscal dominance in sub-Saharan Africa.

4.1 The Zambia Dataset

We collected data for fifteen quarterly macroeconomic and financial variables.[15] On the external sector the data includes the terms of trade, imports, the current account, and the nominal exchange rate. Data on the banking/monetary sector includes reserve and broad money, credit to the private sector by the banking system, interest rates on treasury bills, and lending rates. As in our model, we use the ratio of reserve money to broad money to assess liquidity in the banking sector, rather than the measure of liquidity used by the authorities—banks' reserves in excess of those needed to satisfy regulatory requirements.[16] On the fiscal side, we collected data on total revenues, spending, and the stock of government debt. On the real sector side, we have quarterly data on GDP, interpolated from annual data.

We present the data as follows. About half of the variables (terms of trade, real credit to the private and public sector, real imports, real GDP growth, and excess liquidity) are expressed as percentage deviations from a deterministic trend or constant, which we calculate using pre-crisis data for each variable. Nominal variables are expressed in percentage points—Zambia's inflation target during this period is assumed to be 10 per cent. Finally, to help understand the magnitude of the macroeconomic adjustment, government revenues, government spending, and the current account are measured in per cent of GDP.

4.2 Calibration and Functional Forms

Simulating the model requires specifying functional forms for functions D, F, H, and Λ. Consistent with the optimization in Appendix A in Baldini et al. (2015), the functional forms are as follows:

$$D\left(C_t, C_{t-1}, \frac{D_t}{P_{c,t}}\right) = c_1 \frac{C_t^{\varrho_1} C_{t-1}^{\varrho_2} \bar{C}^{1-\varrho_1-\varrho_2}}{D_t/P_{c,t}} \left(\log\left(\frac{C_t^{\varrho_1} C_{t-1}^{\varrho_2} \bar{C}^{1-\varrho_1-\varrho_2}}{D_t/P_{c,t}}\right) - c_o\right),$$

$$H(D_t, H_t) = \frac{1}{\beta} + h_1 \frac{D_t}{H_t}\left(\log\left(\frac{D_t}{H_t}\right) - h_o\right),$$

$$\Lambda\left(\frac{D_t}{H_t}\right) = h_1\left(\log\left(\frac{D_t}{H_t}\right) - h_o\right),$$

$$F\left(\frac{N_{Y,t}}{M_{Y,t}}, \frac{N_{Y,t-1}}{M_{Y,t-1}}, E_t\left[\frac{N_{Y,t+1}}{M_{Y,t+1}}\right]\right) = 1 + \frac{\psi_y}{\gamma_N}\left(\log\left(\frac{N_{Y,t}}{M_{Y,t}} \middle/ \frac{N_{Y,t-1}}{M_{Y,t-1}}\right)\right.$$
$$\left. - \frac{\beta\psi_y}{\gamma_N}\left(\log\left(E_t\left[\frac{N_{Y,t+1}}{M_{Y,t+1}}\right] \middle/ \frac{N_{Y,t}}{M_{Y,t}}\right)\right).$$

---

[15] See Appendix 17A for a description of the data.

[16] This choice is inconsequential: the correlation between the inverse of the money multiplier and the authorities' measure of excess liquidity, at the monthly frequency, was 0.92 during 2008–10.

Table 17.3. Calibration of Model Parameters and Steady State Ratios

Households			
Parameter	Value	Parameter	Value
β	$0.97^{1/4}$	χ	0.3
ψ_c	0	ω	0.98
ξ_w	0.02	c_1	1
ϱ_1	0.2	ϱ_2	0.2
$\bar{P}_C C/\bar{D}$	1		

Firms			
γ_N	0.50	γ_M	0.20
δ	0.02	α	0.50
ξ_c	0.03	σ_K	1
ψ_X	60	ψ_y	3

Banks			
g_1	0.005	h_1	0.02
$\bar{D}/\bar{H}$	3.49	$\bar{F}/\bar{Y}^N$	0.60
μ_2	0.25	μ_3	0.12
μ_4	0.045	ξ_R	0.06

Monetary Authority			
$\kappa_{\pi,H}$	1.5	$\kappa_{D,H}$	0
ρ_H	0		

The Government			
ϕ	0.12	τ_G	0.1
ρ_G	0.95	$\bar{T}/\bar{Y}^N$	0.23
$\bar{P}_C G/\bar{Y}^N$	0.22	$\bar{B}^{bk}/\bar{Y}^N$	0.60

Regarding calibration, Table 17.3 contains all parameter values and key steady state ratios, organized by economic agent. Choosing parameter values for Zambia was a difficult exercise, and our calibration is tentative. To our knowledge, there has been little empirical work—either micro-level studies or econometric estimates of macro models—that would help inform the calibration; more work is clearly needed in this area. Our approach was the following:

- All the relevant steady state ratios ($\bar{P}_C C/\bar{D}$, $\bar{D}/\bar{H}$, $\bar{F}/\bar{Y}^N$, $\bar{T}/\bar{Y}^N$, $\bar{P}_C G/\bar{Y}^N$, $\bar{B}^{bk}/\bar{Y}^N$) are calibrated to the Zambian economy. Parameters γ_M, ω and α are also chosen to replicate the degree of openness of the economy.

- Several parameters (χ, ξ_w, s, γ_M and ξ_c) are set in accordance with recent empirical work on African countries (Chapters 8 and 12).

- Some parameters (β, δ, σ_K, ψ_y and ξ_R), for which there is no Zambia—or LIC—specific data, are set to standard values in the literature.

- We set g_1 to zero to explicitly remove the financial accelerator from the analysis. This transmission channel was not helping match the dynamics of the crisis. Since we believe it may be relevant in other situations and for other countries, we leave it in the model for future use.[17]

- The value of ψ_X reflects our prior that real exports in Zambia are likely to be fairly unresponsive to movements in the real exchange rate, mainly because copper exports represent 75 per cent of total exports.

- We choose the money growth specification for monetary policy. In our baseline we assume monetary authorities do not respond to broad money or loan growth, which is consistent with the response during the crisis. We relax that assumption in our sensitivity analysis. We have little to go on in calibrating the parameters of this rule, in part motivating the sensitivity analysis. Our view is that it is in fact difficult to characterize Zambian monetary policy as being mainly rule-based, as reflected in the discussion below and in the importance of monetary policy shocks in explaining its evolution. However, we estimated a slightly simplified version of the reaction function using single-equation GMM. From equations (18) and (20), we can drive a specification:

$$R_t = R_{t-1} + h_1 log(D_t/D_{t-1}) - h_1 \kappa_{\pi,H}(\pi_{c,t+1} - \bar{\pi}) + u_{M,t} + \epsilon_t - \epsilon_{t-1}$$

where h_1 is the inverse of the interest semi-elasticity of demand for reserves H and ϵ_t is an assumed shock to demand for reserves added to equation (18) for estimation purposes. Our point estimate for h_1 is 0.159 (HAC standard error of 0.028) and for the coefficient on expected inflation of 0.158 (0.028), for an estimated value of $kappa_{\pi,H}$ of 1.0. This is insignificantly different from the calibrated value of 1.5.[18]

- On the government side, we choose ϕ, τ_G, and ρ_G to broadly reproduce the path of fiscal variables during the crisis.

- The remaining parameters are chosen to improve the fit of the model. On the consumers' side this applies to ϱ_1 and ϱ_2 (parameters that affect the income elasticity of broad money demand). On the banks side, the parameters chosen this way are ι (related to the interest elasticity of reserve money demand), μ_2, μ_3, and μ_4 (related to the shock to banks' appetite for risk). Note that ϱ_1, ϱ_2, and ι help shape the path of broad and narrow money during the crisis but do not alter the sign of the response. We discuss the choice of μ_i's in subsection F.

---

[17] In an earlier specification of our model we attempted to reproduce the crisis without the banking shock but with an active financial accelerator. This specification could generate the observed increase in lending rates but at the cost of a counterfactual increase in the current account deficit and an increase in private-sector loans. The increase in loans was required for the premium to increase endogenously, as the model could not generate a sufficient decrease in the price of domestic capital (an alternative way of generating an increase in the premium). For this reason we decided to focus on an exogenous shock to the banking sector instead.

[18] We allowed the coefficient on the lagged interest rate to differ from 1, and indeed it was estimated to be 0.87. With only forty-five observations and the restrictive identifying assumptions required, these results need to be taken with a grain of salt. However, it is reassuring that the specification passes the usual Hansen overidentification test and weak instrument tests, and that the results are consistent with the calibration. These results are available on request.

As can be seen from our calibration of the last set of parameters, our approach differs somewhat from a pure calibration exercise. In particular, we use the information derived from fitting the model to the data to improve our choice of the last group of parameters, some of which do not have a specific micro-foundation to support them. This approach could be defined as informal/partial estimation. We believe our approach is justified by the purpose of our model, which is to serve as a data-consistent story-telling device.

4.3 Overview of Shocks and the Transmission Mechanism

Before analysing Zambia's experience during the crisis, we briefly present impulse responses of key model variables to each of the four shocks in our model. This will help illustrate the underlying transmission channels. Figure 17.5 summarizes the model's response to a terms of trade improvement of 20 per cent and to a loosening of monetary policy expressed as an increase in the growth rate of reserve money by 10 per cent, respectively. Both shocks lead to a temporary

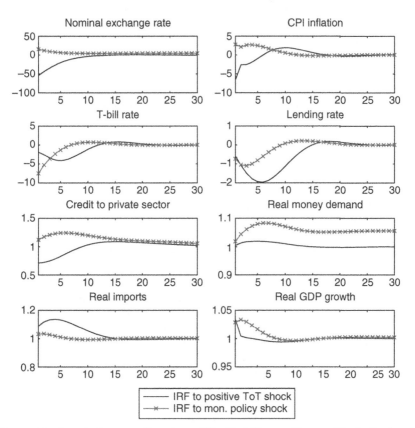

Figure 17.5. Impulse Response Functions of Key Variables to a Terms of Trade Shock and a Monetary Policy Shock

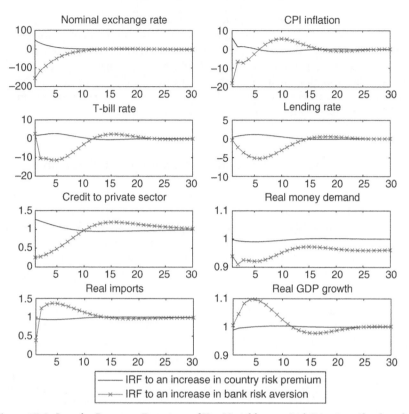

Figure 17.6. Impulse Response Functions of Key Variables to a Risk Premium Shock and a Banking Shock

increase in domestic demand and output, as is shown in the path of real imports, money demand, and GDP growth. They differ in terms of their effect on inflation: the terms of trade improvement appreciates the exchange rate and lowers inflation, while the monetary loosening leads to higher inflation and nominal depreciation. The effects of the two shocks are also qualitatively different for the volume of credit to the private sector. While the policy loosening encourages higher borrowing and an increase in real credit, the terms of trade improvement results in a decrease in the volume of private credit, reflecting consumption smoothing.

Figure 17.6 summarizes the impulse response functions to the two risk shocks in the model: a 10 percentage-point increase in the shock to the country-wide risk premium u_R, and a shock to the banking sector's risk appetite u_F, such that— all else equal—the premium on the 'notional' lending rate would increase by 5 percentage points. The increase in the country premium leads to a nominal depreciation, with upward pressure on inflation and an ensuing increase in policy and lending rates, which in turn leads to a contraction in domestic demand and output. The banking shock, on the other hand, leads to a squeeze in credit and a sharp fall in real imports. The fall in domestic demand triggers disinflation, lowers marginal costs for exporters and together with the drop in imports, improves the current account and contributes to higher GDP.[19] Finally, the shock to banks' risk appetite would—by itself—generate a nominal and real appreciation, as the demand for imports would fall.

Overall, the transmission channels operate as one would expect from a model of this type, although it must be emphasized that some of the shocks are pushing key variables (such as exchange rates and the current account) in opposite directions. The interesting question for the remainder of the chapter is whether the model can provide us with explanations to our case study of Zambia, given the particular constellation of shocks and policy responses the country faced during the crisis.

4.4 Replicating the Crisis

Having analysed the impact of each shock separately, we now combine them together to mimic the impact of the crisis. As mentioned earlier, the aim here is to replicate Zambia's external environment during this period. Our approach is as follows. We set the path of the terms of trade shock $u_{T,t}$ and the risk premium shock $u_{Rf,t}$ such that the model's terms of trade and nominal exchange rate exactly replicate their counterparts in the data from 2008:Q4 to 2010:Q2.

Regarding the shock to the banks' risk appetite $u_{F,t}$, we set their path so as to match the current account from 2008:Q4 to 2009:Q4. We focus on the mapping between the current account and banks' appetite for risk for the following reasons. Given the structure of the banking sector in the model (all of the country's financing including foreign borrowing goes through the banking sector), this shock has direct implications for the current account behaviour. This linkage is consistent with the literature on sudden stops, where the external shock enters the model in the same way as our shock $\mu_{F,1,t}$ in equation (1).[20] In addition, the mapping between the banking shock and the current account reversal is also consistent with the fact that Zambia's banking system is largely foreign-owned, so that a change in banks' attitude toward domestic loans would likely be reflected in capital flight.[21]

Regarding monetary policy, we set the path of shocks $u_{M,t}$, such that the model replicates the observed path of the ninety-one-day T-bill rate in Zambia during the same period. As will become evident later, we believe the behaviour of monetary authorities cannot be characterized by a systematic rule but rather as a sequence of discretionary policy measures. The use of shocks to mimic the policy response is therefore more appropriate. Finally, to ensure consistency with the standard analysis of impulse responses in this type of models, we assume the path of shocks is fully anticipated at the beginning of our simulations (which corresponds to 2008Q3 in the data).

---

[19] The expansion in GDP observed for the shock to u_F is a common finding in models of sudden stops, which also involve shocks to a binding collateral constraint as in equation (1). See Chari, Kehoe, and McGrattan (2005).

[20] See Christiano, Gust, and Roldos (2004) and Chari, Kehoe, and McGrattan (2005), among others.

[21] It is possible, however, that the contraction in credit might have been due to domestic considerations unrelated to—but coincident with—capital outflows. In this case there would be two different shocks, one accounting for the capital outflows and the other for the contraction in credit.

The mapping between shocks and selected variables warrants some discussion. We use the IRIS toolbox, developed by one of our co-authors, to implement this mapping. The procedure requires (i) solving the linear approximation of the model using standard rational-expectations techniques, under the assumption that all shocks are anticipated at the beginning of the simulation; (ii) inverting the VAR representation of the model's solution to recast the shocks as linear functions of the model variables (including leads and lags); and (iii) backing out the sequence of shocks that is necessary to reproduce the path of selected variables. The IRIS toolbox contains built-in functions to carry out this procedure.

4.5 Baseline Results

Conditional on the four 'hard-tuned' variables above, we simulate the model's response and compare the remaining model variables with their counterparts in the data. The starting point of the data and the model is the same in most cases, except for inflation and the growth rate of reserve money, for which the model's starting point is the pre-crisis average. By doing so, we are assuming that the economy was broadly at trend before the crisis hit. We return to the pre-crisis behaviour of inflation in the last section.

First, we characterize the evolution of the key observed variables during the crisis, starting in 2008-IV (Figure 17.7). Along with the terms of trade deterioration we observe an immediate depreciation of the nominal exchange rate S. The exchange rate depreciation feeds initially into higher inflation. The current account reversal is in the order of 20 percentage points of quarterly GDP, reflecting the exit of foreign investors. The capital flight is associated with a large contraction in the volume of credit issued by the domestic banking system and an increase in lending rates, which prevents private agents from borrowing abroad to smooth out the effects of the crisis. Aggregate demand contracts significantly as a result of the credit crunch and inflation subsequently declines, while real deposits in the banking sector decrease by over 15 per cent.[22] Note that the behaviour of GDP, which has been interpolated to generate quarterly series, is not consistent with the overall macroeconomic picture. The fiscal outcome worsens—especially revenues—and the outstanding stock of government debt increases by about 20 per cent.

In this context the initial monetary policy response can be characterized as contractionary. Interest rates on treasury bills increase by about 400 basis points between July 2008 and July 2009. This is associated with a decrease in the growth rate of the monetary base and contributes to the contraction of broad money and the increase in lending rates.

Starting in July 2009, however, there is a reversal in the monetary stance in response to the slowdown. Liquidity is injected into the banking system (H increases) above the pre-crisis level and the T-bill rate drops sharply, by about 1,300 basis points by July 2010. This loosening policy drives down the lending rate

---

[22] Part of the decline in inflation could be accounted for by the fall in the international prices of food and fuel in the second half of 2008. We do not account for such effects here.

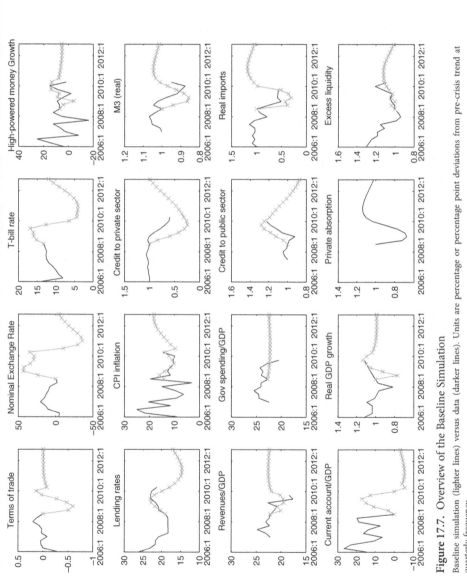

Figure 17.7. Overview of the Baseline Simulation

Baseline simulation (lighter lines) versus data (darker lines). Units are percentage or percentage point deviations from pre-crisis trend at quarterly frequency.

and brings aggregate demand slowly back towards the baseline level. The monetary loosening coincides with a recovery of the terms of trade which appreciates the exchange rate, lowers inflation, and supports the recovery in demand.

How do the model's predictions compare with the data? In general, the model performs well qualitatively and comes close to the data for the lending rate, inflation rate and import demand. For the other variables, the model predicts correctly the direction, although the magnitudes are, as can be expected, not always closely matched. For example, in the model, credit to the private sector contracts faster and stronger than in the data, as is also the case with real money demand, while credit to the government is predicted to surge faster than in the data. The fiscal variables (revenues and spending as share of GDP) are slightly more volatile in the data than the model predicts. Clearly, the model cannot account for all sources of rigidities or policies that may shape the path of the economy. There are more sources of government and private credit funding, such as aid donors, non-banks etc., which may generate either additional volatility or delays in some of the macro responses that the model does not capture.

Regarding GDP growth, however, the model's predictions are completely at odds with the annual GDP data: the model predicts a large contraction in GDP while the data indicate no such contraction. A first consideration is that the only available data are annual, while the contraction in the model takes place at the end of 2008 and beginning of 2009. An estimate of the quarterly output gap extracted from available quarterly data produces a recession whose timing is quite similar to that of the simulation (Figure 17.8).

The magnitude of the recession is still much smaller in the data, however. A partial explanation could be the very poor data quality of Zambian real GDP data, probably even more than other Zambian data used here.[23] That there may be something wrong with the Zambian data in this regard, in broad terms, is suggested by the fact that in general primary product-exporting LICs experienced substantial growth slowdowns in 2009 (Figure 17.3).

Zambia also benefited from some large positive supply shocks during the period in question. First, thanks to good weather, the harvest was unusually large in 2008 and 2009, such that real agricultural output grew by 2.6 per cent in 2008 and 7.2 per cent in 2009, compared to an average of 1.6 per cent over 2002–2007. Second, as new mining capacity came on stream during 2009, reflecting the lagged effect of high FDI over preceding years, real GDP in mining grew by 20.2 per cent in 2009 (despite substantial anecdotal evidence that low copper prices drove temporary mine closures during late 2008 and early 2009). Output excluding mining and agriculture grew substantially slower in 2008 and 2009 than in previous years (Figure 17.9).

Finally, and more speculatively, FDI collapsed from a sharp peak of 12 per cent of GDP in 2007 to 6 per cent in 2008 and 5 per cent in 2009. This is not

---

[23] 'There is a high degree of uncertainty attached to estimates of the level and growth rate of real GDP' (IMF, 2014: p. 10). The only available series for this period uses 1994 as the benchmark year to estimate GDP from the supply side. Especially for services and construction, no appropriate indicators exist. On the expenditure side, no reliable indicators of household consumption exist. The above quarterly series does not address most of these weaknesses, because the Chow-Lin method used to estimate the quarterly output gap tracks the available annual data.

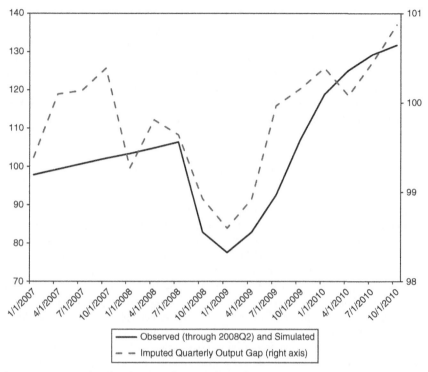

Figure 17.8. Simulated and Imputed Quarterly Real GDP

Imputed Quarterly GDP is based on a factor-augmented VAR using 12 available quarterly series (exports, imports, terms of trade, industrial production (IP) in mining, manufacturing, electricity, CPI inflation, base money, broad money, credit to the private sector, the ninety-one-day T-bill rate, and the bilateral (dollar) nominal exchange rate). We apply Chow-Lin distribution methods to estimate quarterly GDP based on official annual GDP data and the three principle factors, then apply a band-pass filter to extract the cyclical component (details available on request).

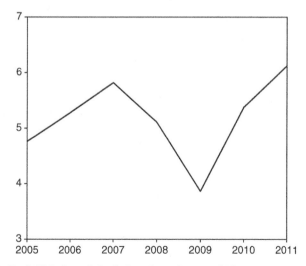

Figure 17.9. Real GDP Growth Excluding Agriculture and Mining

Source: dxTime.

explicitly modelled. It is reasonable to expect, however, that much of this FDI financed imports of intermediate investment goods. By abstracting from this factor, the model requires that the fall in imports be associated with a similar fall in consumption of domestic goods, given the utility function. In fact, though, some of this import decline may have been a direct result of the decline in FDI and hence had less implication for domestic activity. An extension to consider FDI explicitly might be useful, though calibration would place strong demands on weak investment data.

4.5.1 A Digression on Fiscal Policy

Beyond its quantitative properties, the model also illustrates how fiscal policy affects the transmission of external shocks. As mentioned earlier, the fiscal outlook worsened as a result of the global crisis, and public debt increased. In normal circumstances, holding everything else constant, such an increase in debt would have been financed in part by capital inflows and in part by a crowding out of private sector credit and an increase in interest rates. In this case, however, the increase in debt coincides with a large decrease in private sector credit and a reversal of capital flows. While these two factors are pushing in opposite directions, the net effect more than outweighs the effects of fiscal policy. Holding reserve money growth constant, the T-bill rate would have decreased. However, for a given current account path, higher government debt would have resulted in an additional decline in private sector credit. Note that the impact on aggregate demand from stable government spending (financed by debt) is positive.

4.6 Shock Decomposition

It is helpful to analyse how the different shocks contributed to each variable's dynamics.[24] Figure 17.10 presents the path of all three external shocks. The initial path of all three shocks is consistent with the above narrative: there is an increase in banks' risk aversion (positive u_F) through the first five quarters, a deterioration in the terms of trade (negative u_T) that recovers by the end of 2009, and an increase in the country-risk premium from 2009 to 2010Q2 (positive u_R).[25]

Figure 17.11 presents the shock decomposition for three nominal variables: the nominal exchange rate, the lending rate, and the inflation rate. One striking observation is that the shocks are generating opposing effects on the dynamics of these variables. The terms of trade and external risk premium shocks (u_T, u_R)

---

[24] The IRIS toolbox can carry out this type of exercise.

[25] The initial drop in u_R results from the forward-looking behaviour of the exchange rate and is necessary to maintain consistency of the observed exchange rate with the UIP condition. Note that the size of the shocks is consistent with the magnitude of the event, e.g., the initial shock to the terms of trade corresponds to a 50 per cent decline. The shock to the financial system, holding all else equal, implies a 20% decline in quarterly consumption. Although it is difficult to compare across models, the shocks are larger in magnitude than shocks found in the sudden stop literature, e.g., Mendoza (2010).

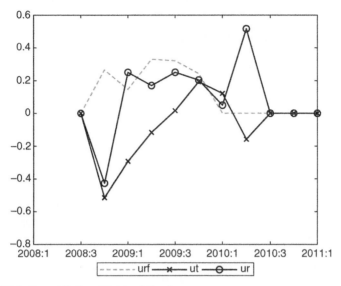

Figure 17.10. Tuned Paths of External Shocks

Tuned path of the banking/financial shock (uf), the terms of trade shock (ut), and the country risk premium shock (ur). Units are percentage deviations from pre-crisis steady state at quarterly frequency.

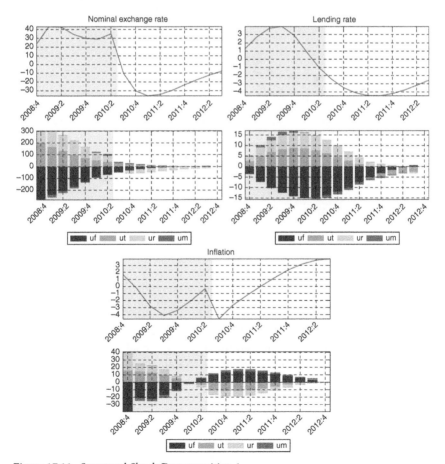

Figure 17.11. Structural Shock Decomposition 1

Baseline simulation paths for selected price variables and their decomposition to four structural shocks of the model. Units are percentage point deviations from pre-crisis trend at quarterly frequency.

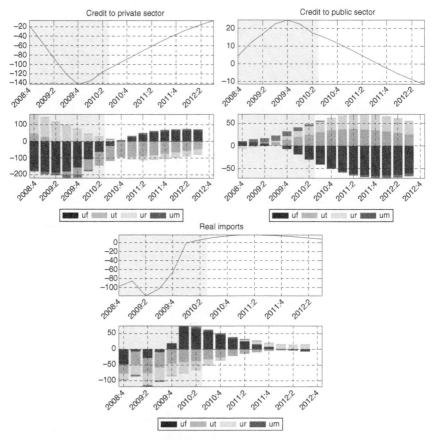

Figure 17.12. Structural Shock Decomposition 2

Baseline simulation paths for selected quantity variables and their decomposition to four structural shocks of the model. Units are percentage point deviations from pre-crisis trend at quarterly frequency.

are generating pressures for nominal exchange rates to depreciate and lending rates and inflation to increase, while the banking sector shock (u_F) is having the opposite effect.

More importantly, the banking shock plays an important role in the transmission of the crisis. This reflects the dominant role of the banking sector in our model. The decrease in banks' risk appetite in the period up to the end of 2009 exerts a downward pressure on inflation and the exchange rate, as it generates a decline in consumption, including for imports. The overall effect of the banking shock on lending rates is negative, despite the appearance of the shock in equation (16): as the shock makes private demand contract and inflation fall, the endogenous response of monetary policy—combined with a contraction in the demand for money—makes T-bill (and lending) rates fall.

Figure 17.12 shows the shock decomposition for the volume of credit to the private sector, credit to the public sector and real imports. The figure reveals how strongly the credit rationing of banks affected the contraction in lending and import demand. In the absence of the banking shock, the other two shocks would have resulted in an increase in lending for smoothing purposes. In the case of government debt, all shocks are initially contributing to its increase.

Finally, note that the tightening of monetary policy exacerbates the negative impact of the shocks in the initial quarters. The lending rate is further increased, private credit is further reduced and demand (see imports) contracts slightly more given this tightening policy. However, relative to the contribution of the external and financial shocks triggered by the crisis, the impact of policy is far less decisive for the evolution of demand and economic activity. This reflects the severity and sheer magnitude of the exogenous shocks that hit the economy during this episode. In the following section, the role of monetary policy is discussed in detail.

Having described the performance of the model and how each shock contributed to the path of key variables, we can now justify our choice for the weights on the different components of the bank risk shock (the μ_is). As can be seen from the shock decomposition exercise, the greatest impact of the bank risk shock is on credit volumes. This makes it natural to normalize the shock to consumers' borrowing constraint ($u_{F,1,t}$) and guided our calibration of the overall bank shock itself ($u_{F,t}$). The choice of $\mu_{F,2}$ is guided by the observation that ($u_{F,1,t}$) is highly contractionary, as it has large effects on aggregate demand. Shocks to import financing ($u_{F,2,t}$) do not have such large effects; a substantial weight on ($u_{F,2,t}$) is thus helpful in matching the large current account reversal absent a notable output decline. The increase in lending spreads helps calibrate $u_{F,3,t}$—absent such a shock, lending spreads would not increase. Finally, $u_{F,4,t}$ helps track the behaviour of reserve money. In its absence the model would require an implausibly large contraction in reserve money to replicate the path of the T-bill rate.

4.7 The Role of the Monetary Policy Response: Shock Counterfactuals

Recall that the monetary policy rule is specified in terms of the growth rate of reserve money, reproduced here for convenience:

$$\frac{H_t}{H_{t-1}} = 1 - \kappa_{\pi,H}(\pi_{c,t+1} - 1) - \kappa_{D,H}\left(\frac{D_t}{D_{t-1}} - 1\right) - \kappa_{L,H}\left(\frac{L_t}{L_{t-1}} - 1\right) - u_{M,t},$$

with discretionary deviations from the rule captured by the shock process $u_{M,t}$.

Figure 17.13 displays the decomposition of the dynamics of reserve money growth, the T-bill rate, and real broad money. Not surprisingly, the monetary shock accounts for most of the movements in reserve money growth and the T-bill rate. In other words, fluctuations in monetary policy are directly responsible for the behaviour of two key nominal variables (short rates and reserve money growth). This is not true of real money variables: most of the variance of real broad money balances is accounted for by the real shocks.

To assess the role of policy, we first simulate the model without policy shocks. Figure 17.14 compares the model dynamics with and without policy shocks. In contrast with the previous stop and go pattern, reserve money growth is now mostly flat. Given the contraction in demand for broad money, this results in an initial decline in the T-bill rate, which amplifies the nominal depreciation and

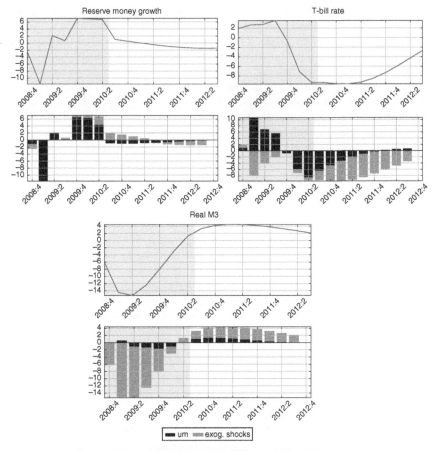

Figure 17.13. Structural Shock Decomposition: Monetary Variables

Baseline simulation paths for the monetary variables (reserve money growth, T-bill rate, broad money) and their decomposition to monetary policy shock (um) and exogenous (real) shocks (exog. shocks). Units are percentage point deviations from pre-crisis trend at quarterly frequency.

raises inflation. At the same time, the increase in the lending rate is not as large, as liquidity is more abundant than under baseline. Another clear effect of the neutral monetary policy is the dampening of the increase in outstanding public debt since the lower T-bill rate implies lower debt servicing costs.

In terms of real variables, the effect of the accommodating policy stance appears to be limited. The contraction on import demand is slightly smaller, as is the contraction in credit to the private sector. A closer look reveals sizable effects, however. Table 17.4 summarizes the relative performance of alternative policy responses, relative to the baseline, along a number of dimensions. The average difference between private spending (C_t) under 'stop and go' and under the more neutral stance, over the period 2009:I to 2009:IV, is 2.8 per cent of steady state spending. During the same period the model predicts a moderately higher inflation—3 percentage points higher—although in line with Zambia's implied

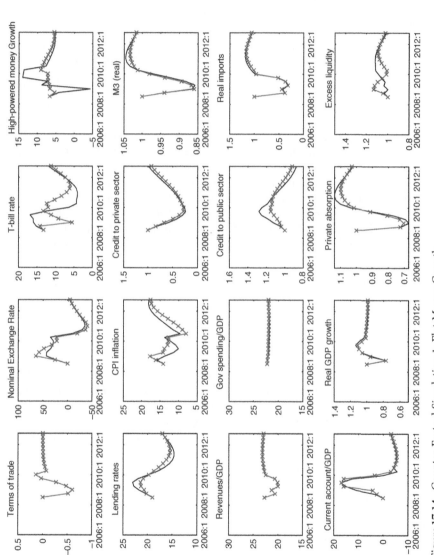

Figure 17.14. Counter-Factual Simulation 1: Flat Money Growth

Baseline simulation (darker lines) versus counter-factual (lighter lines). Units are percentage or percentage point deviations from pre-crisis trend at quarterly frequency.

Table 17.4. Model Performance Across Alternative Monetary Policy Responses

Monetary Policy	Neutral	Loose	Broad Money	Credit Growth	Taylor Rule
			Targeting	Targeting	
Private Spending	2.8	5.4	3.4	5.5	4.1
Inflation	3.0	6.2	3.3	7.3	6.1
Nominal Depreciation	12.4	24.0	14.7	31.8	29.6

Each row indicates the average difference between the alternative monetary policy regime and the baseline, in per cent of that variable's steady state value, in 2009.

inflation target of 10 per cent, while the nominal exchange rate would have been 12 per cent more depreciated.

Figure 17.15 displays simulation results if monetary policy had actually been loosened, i.e., money growth higher than average during 2009:I to 2009:IV. The inflationary effects are now larger (see also Table 17.4). Inflation is now 6 percentage points higher than under the baseline, while the nominal exchange rate is 24 per cent more depreciated. However, the model predicts lending rates would have stayed flat and private spending would have been 5.4 per cent higher. One important observation is that, given the steady state value of the T-bill nominal interest rate, there is a lot of room for interest rates to fall—1,300 basis points—without hitting the zero lower bound. In this scenario monetary policy comes very close to hitting the zero bound but stays above it.

4.8 The Role of the Monetary Policy Response: Rule Counterfactuals

We now explore the performance of the model under three alternative policy rules. In the first case, the authorities continue to implement an inflation-targeting regime by setting targets for reserve money growth, but they also respond to deviations in broad money growth from its long-run value ($\kappa_{D,H} = 0.5$). In the second case, we assume the authorities target the growth rate of loans rather than the growth rate of deposits ($\kappa_{L,H} = 0.3$). In the third case, we assume the authorities follow the interest rate rule:

$$R_{B,t} = \rho_R R_{B,t-1} + (1 - \rho_R)\left(\bar{R}_B + \kappa_\pi(\pi_{c,t+1} - 1)\right) + u_{M,t},$$

with $\rho_R = 0.5$ and $\kappa_\pi = 3$.

The results are summarized in Table 17.4. All three rules would have improved the country's private spending performance, although again at the cost of higher inflation and nominal depreciation. The conclusion from this exercise is that policymakers were confronted to a trade-off: while a loser policy would have helped weather the external shocks, the country would have faced somewhat higher inflation as a result. This reflects the nature of the 'global crisis' shock, which does not easily lend itself to an aggressive monetary policy response. In this case there is no 'divine coincidence' (Blanchard and Gali, 2007).

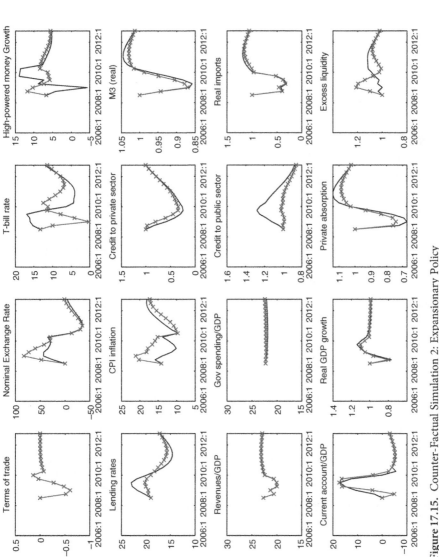

Figure 17.15. Counter-Factual Simulation 2: Expansionary Policy

Baseline simulation (darker lines) versus counter-factual (lighter lines). Units are percentage or percentage point deviations from pre-crisis trend at quarterly frequency.

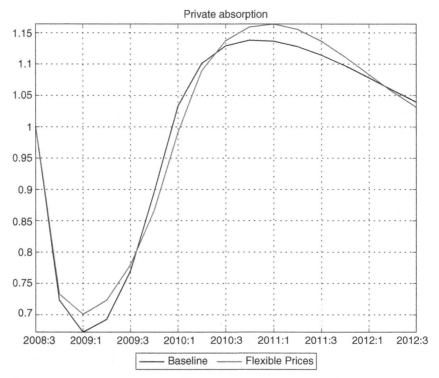

Figure 17.16. Counter-Factual Simulation 3: the Role of Nominal Rigidities

Baseline simulation (blue) versus flexible price simulation (green). Units are percentage or percentage point deviations from pre-crisis trend at quarterly frequency.

4.9 The Role of the Nominal Rigidities

The assessment that monetary policy played a role during the crisis is closely related to the inclusion of nominal rigidities in our model, reflected in parameters ξ_c and ξ_w. As is well known, the latter feature is what allows monetary policy to have real effects in DSGEs. In addition to the shocks-based analysis and the impact of various policy rules, an alternative exercise to measure the importance (and the limits) of monetary policy is to compare the results of the model under sticky and flexible prices, in which case monetary policy is irrelevant for the real effects of the crisis.[26] We therefore compare the baseline simulation with the flexible-price version of our model ($\xi_c = \xi_w = \infty$). For the sake of brevity we limit the comparison to consumption, which is presented in Figure 17.16.

This exercise is in line with our previous finding. On the one hand, the presence of nominal rigidities in the baseline results in a decrease in consumption that is larger than the decline in consumption under flexible prices. This confirms our initial assessment that the initial tightness of monetary policy aggravated the impact of the crisis. On the other hand, the decrease in consumption is broadly

---

[26] We are grateful to Andy Levin for suggesting this approach.

similar across the two cases, which confirms that real (non-monetary) factors were the main factors behind the crisis.

5 UNDERSTANDING THE INITIAL MONETARY POLICY RESPONSE

In this section we analyse the motivation behind the initial policy response. We start by looking at the behaviour of policy before mid-2008 (see Figure 17.17). Interest rates were broadly constant prior to the crisis but then began to increase steadily around or possibly a few months before the onset of the crisis. What factors can account for such behaviour?

We can divide the factors depending on when they occurred. Following the metaphor from the introduction, we distinguish between 'rear-view' factors and 'side-view' factors. The former refer to factors that, while having occurred in the past, were still influencing policy; the latter refer to factors that were occurring at the time of the policy decision.

The first 'rear-view' factor is inflation itself. When simulating the model and confronting it to the data, we made the simplifying assumption that the economy was starting from steady state. As we mentioned earlier, this assumption was more or less valid for most variables in our sample, with the notable exception of inflation. Figure 17.17, top right corner, shows the monthly behaviour of

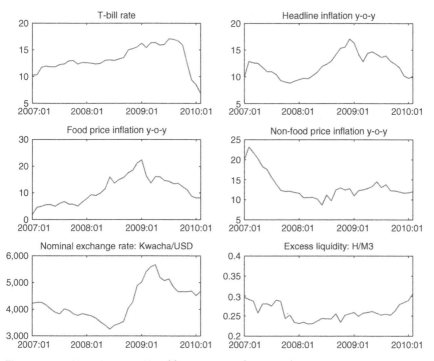

Figure 17.17. Key Monetary Variables Prior to and During the Crisis

year-on-year inflation since 2006. As is clearly visible, inflation had begun increasing steadily since end-2007, going from 8.9 to 16.6 per cent by December 2008. The increase is mostly accounted for by food prices, which had gone from close to 0 to 21 per cent between end-2006 and end-2008. Note that non-food inflation was falling throughout most of 2008.

It was well understood at the time that food inflation was driven by the ongoing global food and fuel shocks of 2007–08, during which the price of most commodities doubled or tripled in a few months. While the policy adage is to allow for first-round (direct) effects of such shocks and to prevent second-round (indirect) effects, there was a concern at the time that inflation risked losing its anchor and that a policy tightening was needed.[27]

An additional and related 'rear-view' factor was the consistent miss of reserve money targets during 2009. Table 17.5 displays the targets and the actual levels of reserve money.[28] The misses reflected an intentional accommodation of the surge in demand for nominal balances as a result of higher inflation, and were interpreted at the time as indicating neutral policy. However, the gradual increase of T-bill rates during 2008 suggests policy was not as accommodative as the target misses suggested.

The combination of target misses and high inflation in 2008 led to an effort to (further) tighten policy in 2009. This can be seen by looking at the targets set—at the end of 2008—for reserve money growth in mid-2009 (see Table 17.5), which were lower than end-2008 values.[29] The targets were subsequently revised midway through 2009, coinciding with the large fall of T-bill rates. It is worth noting that

Table 17.5. Money Targets in Zambia (2008–2009), in bn of Kwacha

	Target	Rev. target	Actual
2008Q2	2522		2535
2008Q3	2655		2755
2008Q4	2789		3221
2009Q2	3151		3247
2009Q3	3333		3276
2009Q4	3661	3821	3658

Source: IMF Staff Reports.

[27] 'In the second half of 2008, the monetary policy objective will be to achieve the end-year inflation target of 7.0% [from 12.1% in the 12 months through June 2008]. However, a number of factors pose challenges to the achievement of the inflation objective and money supply targets. These challenges include the cost-push effects of expected higher prices of oil on the world market; expected increases in utility charges; continued electricity outages; and the rise in world food prices.' (Bank of Zambia, 2008). See also IMF (2009a, 2010).

[28] These targets were set in the context of the Fund-supported Policy Reduction and Growth Facility arrangement. Targets for 2008 were set in early 2008, targets for 2009 were set in early 2009, with a revision mid-2009. See IMF (2009a).

[29] 'The primary objective of monetary policy in the first half of 2009 is to achieve an end-year inflation target of 10.0% at end-December 2009 [from 17% at end-December 2008] . . . To achieve this objective, the Bank of Zambia will implement appropriate monetary policy to ensure that reserve money and consequently broad money remain within their programmed path in order to dampen inflationary pressure' (Bank of Zambia, 2009).

the targets were missed in the opposite direction in the second half of 2009, suggesting the authorities did not anticipate the crisis-induced decline in demand for reserve money during that period.

In terms of 'side-view' factors, we believe the nominal depreciation—and the associated capital flight—may have made the authorities reluctant to loosen policy sooner. Indeed, during the second half of 2008, the nominal exchange rate had depreciated by 50 per cent, and foreign direct and portfolio investments had fallen by more than 30 per cent. As predicted by our model, a loosening would have accelerated capital flight and amplified the nominal depreciation, the prospects of which were likely to concern the authorities.

Finally, an additional 'side-view' consideration may have been the reluctance to provide the banking sector with additional liquidity as the banking system appeared to have ample liquidity. As Figure 17.17 indicates, the ratio of reserve money to broad money had been increasing since the end of 2007, by about 20 per cent by end-2008, which may have reinforced the perception that monetary policy was loose. In our model, such dynamics were driven instead by the fall in broad money and the increase in liquidity demand by banks, which indicates policy was actually tight instead.

6 CONCLUSION

We have shown that a DSGE model, fitted to the specifics of a low-income country, provides a reasonable characterization of Zambia's performance during the crisis. We believe our framework is well-suited for confronting the model with data and for making forecasts conditional on various policy scenarios.

Our analysis yields several lessons for policymakers in low-income countries. First, monetary policy should be forward-looking and respond to current or expected shocks, instead of responding to the current inflationary effects of past shocks. Such a strategy of 'driving by looking through the rear-view mirror' exposes the central bank to potentially large policy mistakes that need to be reversed later, further contributing to economic instability. Second, central banks should avoid paying excessive attention to banks' liquidity—or reserve money—as the exclusive indicator of the monetary policy stance—a common practice in sub-Saharan Africa. Rather than loose monetary policy, the build-up of liquidity may reflect growing risk aversion in the banking system. More generally, central banks in the region need to monitor overall developments in the banking system, including credit volumes and interest rate premia, in order to gauge the right policy stance. These lessons are well understood in developed and emerging market countries, but they have yet to take hold in low-income countries.

While reserve money targeting remains a common practice in sub-Saharan Africa, the flexibility with which it is implemented can help avoid potential policy mistakes. In addition, as central banks in the region move toward incorporating additional elements of inflation targeting in their frameworks—with its emphasis on the inflation forecast, greater policy clarity, less reliance on monetary aggregates, and a greater role for short-term rates—the response to large unexpected events should improve.

Our model has also shown, however, that—at present—monetary policy in LICs may be limited in its ability to offset large external shocks. These shocks—worsening in the terms of trades, increases in risk premia—confront policymakers with unpleasant trade-offs between output and inflation. Our results also show, however, that monetary policy errors can add to the volatility. More generally, a systematic forward-looking policy response can enhance credibility and anchor expectations in a way that should reduce over time these unpleasant trade-offs.

From an analytical perspective, we have found it important to model the crisis as a combination of shocks. In particular, we have found that the inclusion of the shock to the banking sector—itself a collection of shocks to various aspects of the banks' profit maximization conditions—greatly improves the quantitative performance of the model. Further analysis of the mechanisms underlying these shocks is a fruitful topic for further research. Explicit treatment of FDI may also be important for some purposes.

Our framework has abstracted from other key aspects of central bank policy in low-income countries, most notably the direct intervention in foreign exchange markets. In related work, Chapter 13 analyses the interaction of monetary policy rules with rules describing foreign exchange rate interventions. We have also abstained from analysing in greater detail the challenges posed by fiscal policy in the implementation of monetary policy, even though our model explicitly incorporates the fiscal sector. Chapter 12 explores the interaction of fiscal and monetary policy in the context of aid shocks, but more work is needed in this area.

APPENDIX 17A: QUARTERLY MACROECONOMIC AND FINANCIAL VARIABLES

Description	Source	Seasonally adjusted	Frequency	Comments
Broad Money/ Deposits (M3)	IFS/Bank of Zambia	x	Monthly	Aggregated to quarterly frequency (averaging)
Reserve money (M1)	IFS/Bank of Zambia	x	Monthly	Aggregated to quarterly frequency (averaging)
Commercial lending rates	Bank of Zambia		Monthly	Aggregated to quarterly frequency (averaging)
Headline CPI	IFS/Bank of Zambia	x	Monthly	Aggregated to quarterly frequency (averaging)
CPI—Non-food	IFS/Bank of Zambia	x	Monthly	Aggregated to quarterly frequency (averaging)
CPI—Food	IFS/Bank of Zambia	x	Monthly	Aggregated to quarterly frequency (averaging)
Exchange rate Kwacha per USD	IFS	x	Monthly	Aggregated to quarterly frequency (averaging)
US import price index	IFS	x	Monthly	Aggregated to quarterly frequency (averaging)
Net claims on private sector by banks	IFS/Bank of Zambia	x	Monthly	Aggregated to quarterly frequency (averaging)
Stock of outstanding domestic debt	Bank of Zambia	x	Monthly	Aggregated to quarterly frequency (averaging)

Revenues and grants	IMF staff/Zambian Authorities (MOF)	x	Monthly	Aggregated to quarterly frequency (averaging)
Total exports	IMF staff/ Zambian Authorities (MOF)	x	Monthly	Aggregated to quarterly frequency (averaging)
90-day Treasury bill rate	IFS		Monthly	Aggregated to quarterly frequency (averaging)
Deposit rate	IMF Staff/Bank of Zambia		Monthly	Aggregated to quarterly frequency (averaging)
Price of copper (USD per metric tonne)	London Metal Exchange (LME)	x	Monthly	Aggregated to quarterly frequency (averaging)
Nominal imports— Goods and services (millions, USD)	Bank of Zambia		Quarterly	
Current account (millions, USD)	Bank of Zambia		Quarterly	
GDP at constant prices	IFS		Yearly	Interpolated to quarterly frequency (quadratic interpolation)
GDP at current prices	IFS		Yearly	Interpolated to quarterly frequency (quadratic interpolation)
GDP at current prices (USD)	IFS		Yearly	Interpolated to quarterly frequency (quadratic interpolation)

REFERENCES

Adrian, T., and H. S. Shin (2011). Financial Intermediation and Monetary Economics, in B. Friedman and M. Woodford (Eds.) *Handbook of Monetary Economics*. Amsterdam: North Holland.

Agenor, P.-R., and P. Montiel (2006). *Credit Market Imperfections and the Monetary Transmission Mechanism. Part I: Fixed Exchange Rates*. The School of Economics Discussion Paper Series 0628. Manchester: The University of Manchester.

Agenor, P.-R., and P. Montiel (2008). Monetary Policy Analysis in a Small Open Credit-Based Economy. *Open Economies Review*, 19(4), 423–55.

Aghion, P., P. Bacchetta, and A. Banerjee (2001). Currency Crises and Monetary Policy in an Economy with Credit Constraints. *European Economic Review*, 45, 1121–50.

Baldini, A., and M. Poplawski-Ribeiro (2011). Fiscal and Monetary Determinants of Inflation in Low-Income Countries: Theory and Evidence from Sub-Saharan Africa. *Journal of African Economies*, 20(3), 419–62.

Baldini, A., J. Benes, A. Berg, M. Dao and R. Portillo (2015). Monetary Policy in Low-Income Countries in the Face of the Global Crisis: A Structural Analysis. *Pacific Economic Review*, 20(1), 149–92.

Bank of Zambia (2008). Bank of Zambia Monetary Policy Statement July–December 2008, available at http://www.boz.zm.

Bank of Zambia (2009). Bank of Zambia Monetary Policy Statement January–June 2009.

Bank of Zambia (2011). Financial and Other Statistics 2011, available at http://www.boz.zm.

Berg, A., C. Papageorgiou, C. Pattillo, and N. Spatafora (2010). *The End of an Era? The Medium- and Long-Term Effects of the Global Crisis on Growth in Low-Income Countries*. IMF Working Paper 10/205.

Bernanke, B., M. Gertler, and S. Gilchrist (1999). The Financial Accelerator in a Quantitative Business Cycle Framework,' in J. Taylor and M. Woodford (Eds.), *Handbook of Macroeconomics*. Amsterdam: North Holland.

Bester, H., and M. Hellwig (1987). Moral Hazard and Equilibrium Credit Rationing: An Overview of the Issues, in G. Bamberg and K. Spremann (Eds.), *Agency Theory, Information and Incentives*. Berlin: Springer-Verlag.

Blanchard, O., and J. Gali (2007). Real Wage Rigidities and the New-Keynesian Model. *Journal of Money, Credit, and Banking*, 39(1), 35–65.

Calvo, G. (1998). Capital Flows and Capital-Market Crises: The Simple Economics of Sudden Stops, *Journal of Applied Economics*, 1(1), 35–54.

Calvo, G., A. Izquierdo, and E. Talvi (2006). Sudden Stops and Phoenix Miracles in Emerging Markets. *American Economic Review Papers and Proceedings*, 96(2), 405–10.

Chari, V. V., P. J. Kehoe, and E. R. McGrattan (2005). Sudden Stops and Output Drops. *American Economic Review Papers and Proceedings*, 95(2), 381–7.

Christiano, L., C. Gust, and J. Roldos (2004). Monetary Policy in a Financial Crisis. *Journal of Economic Theory*, 119, 64–103.

Christiano, L., R. Motto, and M. Rostagno (2010). *Financial Factors in Economic Fluctuations*. European Central Bank Working Paper 1192.

Curdia, V., and M. Woodford (2009). Credit Frictions and Optimal Monetary Policy. Unpublished manuscript, Columbia University.

Erceg, C., L. Guerrieri, and C. Gust (2006). SIGMA: A New Open Economy Model for Policy Analysis, *International Journal of Central Banking*, 2(1) 1–49.

Finscope Zambia (2010). Finscope Zambia 2009: Final Report, available at https://www.datafirst.uct.ac.za/dataportal/index.php/catalog/618/download/9002.

Gertler, M., and N. Kiyotaki (2011). Financial Intermediation and Credit Policy in Business Cycle Analysis, in B. Friedman and M. Woodford (Eds.), *Handbook of Monetary Economics*. Amsterdam: North Holland.

Gollin, D., D. Lagakos, and M. Waugh (2014). The Agricultural Productivity Gap. *Quarterly Journal of Economics*, 129(2), 939–93.

Goodfriend, M., and B. T. McCallum (2007). Banking and Interest Rates in Monetary Policy Analysis. *Journal of Monetary Economics*, 54(5), 1480–1507.

IMF (2008). Monetary and Exchange Rate Policies in Sub-Saharan Africa, in *Regional Economic Outlook, Sub-Saharan Africa*, Chapter 2. Washington, DC: IMF.

IMF (2009a). *Zambia: First and Second Reviews of the Three-Year Arrangement Under the Poverty Reduction and Growth Facility*. IMF Country Report No. 09/188. Washington, DC: IMF.

IMF (2009b). *The Implications of the Global Financial Crisis for Low-Income Countries*. Washington, DC: IMF.

IMF (2010). *Zambia: Fourth Review Under the Extended Credit Facility*. IMF Country Report No. 10/208. Washington, DC: IMF.

IMF (2014). *Zambia: Staff Report for the 2013 Article IV Consultation-Informational Annex*. IMF Country Report No. 14/5. Washington, DC: IMF.

Kiyotaki, N. and J. Moore (1997). Credit Cycles. *Journal of Political Economy*, 105, 211–48.

Mendoza, E. (2006). *Lessons from the Debt-Deflation Theory of Sudden Stops*. NBER Working Paper 11966.

Mendoza, E. (2010). Sudden Stops, Financial Crises, and Leverage. *American Economic Review*, 100, 1941–66.

Stiglitz, J. and A. Weiss (1981). Credit Rationing in Markets with Imperfect Information. *American Economic Review*, 73(5), 393–410.

Williamson, S. (1987). Costly Monitoring, Loan Contracts, and Equilibrium Credit Rationing. *Quarterly Journal of Economics*, 102(1), 135–45.

Woodford, M. (2010). Financial Intermediation and Macroeconomic Analysis. *Journal of Economic Perpectives*, 24(4), 21–44.

18

Introducing a Semi-Structural Macroeconomic Model for Rwanda

Luisa Charry, Pranav Gupta, and Vimal Thakoor

1 INTRODUCTION

After facing some challenges in the conduct of monetary policy and to further legitimize their commitment to a low and stable inflation, central banks of the East African Community (EAC) have embarked on gradually updating their monetary policy frameworks. The main changes include allowing greater exchange rate flexibility, enhancing the role of policy rates in signalling the policy stance, announcing inflation targets, and introducing forward-looking elements in policy formulation and communication strategies. As part of this process, efforts have also been undertaken to better understand the transmission channels of monetary policy to real economic activity and prices. This chapter contributes to this effort.

The National Bank of Rwanda (NBR) has been working on strengthening its monetary policy framework. One of the dimensions through which understanding of the transmission mechanism can be enhanced is through the introduction of a semi-structural macroeconomic model that links the monetary policy stance to economic activity and inflation. Such a model can then be integrated into a wider set of processes and tools (a Forecasting and Policy Analysis System, FPAS) to prepare coherent macroeconomic forecasts, perform scenario analysis, and inform the monetary policy formulation process.

As in other chapters of this book, the model introduced here is a rational-expectations New Keynesian model, similar to models used in central banks around the world. The model consists of four basic behavioural equations: an IS curve (aggregate demand), which relates monetary policy and real economic activity; a set of Phillips curves (aggregate supply) that link economic activity and inflation; a monetary policy rule that describes the response of the central bank to deviations of inflation from the target and the phase of economic activity.

A key feature of the model in this chapter is the introduction of a modified uncovered interest parity condition (UIP), which describes exchange rate dynamics. This modification to the UIP condition seeks to capture key structural features of Rwanda's economy and policy framework, such as the rather closed nature of the capital account, its shallow and underdeveloped financial system, and the existence of dual targets on both inflation and the nominal exchange rate.

The model is calibrated to reflect a set of stylized facts of the Rwandan economy, especially the heavy reliance of monetary policy on a stable exchange rate. A filtration of the last ten years of observed data through the model allows us to determine the contribution of various factors to inflation dynamics and its deviations from the inflation target of 5 per cent. In particular, we are able to dissect the contribution of food and oil prices to inflation. Our results, consistent with evidence for other countries in the region, suggest that food and oil price shocks have accounted for the bulk of inflation dynamics in Rwanda, particularly in 2008 and 2011. Fluctuations in food prices have the greatest impact on inflation, while the impact of inflation from international oil price changes is somewhat lower. This can be explained by the fact that there is only partial pass-through from international prices to the domestic pump price structure, which is administratively updated on a regular basis to mitigate their impact.

The filtration exercise also enables us to show that there have been periods when the monetary policy stance has been more accommodative than warranted, most significantly in 2008 and 2011, and this in turn has contributed to inflation deviating from its target. In 2008 monetary policy was significantly looser than required, given the inflationary developments. In 2011, while policy was looser for a longer duration, the magnitude was smaller compared to 2008. We also disentangle the contribution of the exchange rate to inflation. We find that exchange rate developments were a significant contributor to inflation in 2008 and the second half of 2012, when the exchange rate depreciated in response to a suspension of foreign aid flows and reduced reserve buffers. The impact was, however, mitigated by favourable food price developments. The model thus enables a clear identification of the factors contributing to inflation, both from domestic and external factors, as well as those that are policy induced. Furthermore, the exercise shows that properly tailored structural models can provide useful insights even when the data are noisy or scarce, financial markets underdeveloped, and regimes changing. The rest of this chapter is organized as follows. Section 2 presents an overview of the Rwandan economy and the implementation of monetary policy. The model, and the results of the filtering and forecasting exercises are presented in Section 3. Section 4 discusses the authorities' conduct of monetary policy in light of the findings from the model. Section 5 concludes.

2 AN OVERVIEW OF RWANDA'S ECONOMY AND MONETARY POLICY REGIME

Rwanda's economy has come a long way over the past two decades. Judicious economic policies, coupled with ample donor support, have allowed the economy to sustain a real annual growth of around 8 per cent over the past decade. The sectors that have contributed most to growth are agriculture and services. Targeted policies and improving productivity have increased the contribution of the agricultural sector, which accounts for 30 per cent of GDP and 70 per cent of employment (National Institute of Statistics of Rwanda).

The construction and services sectors have also sustained growth, reflecting high public investment and a deliberate policy to stimulate private sector credit growth. While achieved from an initial low base, this sustained growth has enabled the country to make significant inroads in the fight against poverty, as real GDP per capita increased from around US$200 in 2001 to US$660 in 2013. Foreign grants have traditionally been a major component of budgetary resources but are on the decline (about 10 per cent of GDP, or nearly 40 per cent of the budget). Since 2012, when major donors suspended aid flows, the authorities have been discussing options to further reduce Rwanda's aid reliance and foster greater domestic revenue mobilization. The narrow export base is dominated by low-value products like coffee and tea. Mineral exports are increasing, although the sector is not yet operating at full potential. Despite exhibiting strong *Doing Business* indicators, FDI flows have yet to materialize on a significant scale. Debt relief coupled with prudent fiscal policies have contained external debt to under 25 per cent of GDP. In 2013, Rwanda tapped the international capital markets for the first time in its history, with the issuance of a US$400 million Eurobond.

The objectives of the NBR include maintaining inflation in single digits while supporting growth. Accordingly, the NBR targets an inflation rate of 5 per cent. Monetary policy has been formulated in the context of challenging, and at times difficult, domestic and external environments. In particular, food and oil price shocks have played an important role in inflation dynamics. Also, the economy has been subject to significant demand shocks stemming from the global financial crisis in 2009. The suspension of aid flows in 2012 and reduced reserve buffers have added an additional dimension to the policy formulation challenges.

Inflation, while volatile, has been contained in single digits (Figure 18.1). Food and fuel prices are substantial components of headline inflation—food accounts for 35 per cent of the CPI in Rwanda. About 85 per cent of the food basket is sourced locally, while the rest is imported. As a country that relies heavily on imported oil, Rwandan inflation is also exposed to changes in international fuel prices, albeit the impact is somewhat limited as local fuel prices are subject to administrative controls. In the CPI statistics, fuel is included in the transportation component, which accounts for 12 per cent of the basket.

The NBR conducts policy in the context of a flexible monetary targeting framework, with reserve money used as the operational target and broad money (M3) as an intermediate target. An array of instruments is used to manage liquidity, including reserve requirements, open market operations, standing facilities, and foreign exchange operations. The NBR has also increasingly relied on its policy rate—the Key Repo Rate (KRR)—to signal its monetary policy stance. Since the introduction of the KRR in 2008, the NBR conducts repo transactions with commercial banks to navigate interbank rates in a corridor around the KRR. However, the coexistence of both quantity and price targets has, on occasions, led to inconsistent signalling of the policy stance.[1]

---

[1] For example, in late 2008 and in response to a liquidity squeeze, the NBR lowered reserve requirements and introduced new credit facilities for commercial banks. However, at the same time, the NBR increased the KRR, to promote deposits.

Monetary Policy in Sub-Saharan Africa

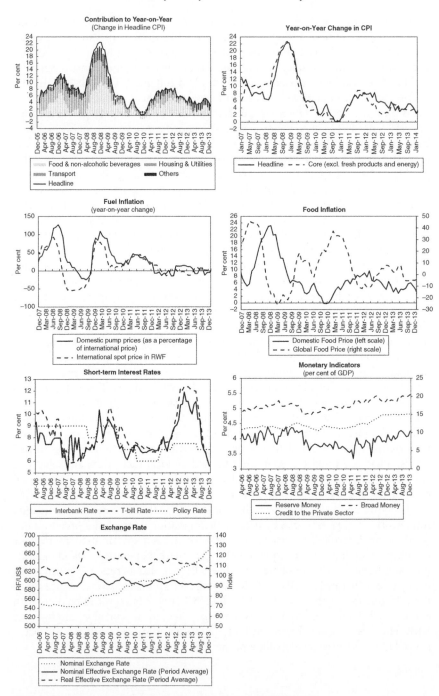

Figure 18.1. Rwanda: Selected Economic Indicators, 2006–2013

Source: IMF staff based on authorities' data.

Monetary policy implementation remains challenging. Reserve money targets often overshoot the target during quarters, even if end quarter targets are met.[2] However, these target misses have not translated into higher inflation. A gradual shift to a quarterly average for reserve money, within a band, has recently provided the authorities greater flexibility in the conduct of their monetary policy operations. However, the slow or non-response of the KRR to changing monetary conditions and market developments has undermined its signalling role and its effectiveness in the transmission mechanism. In early 2013, the divergences between the KRR and the interbank rate widened. Hence, the authorities have had at times needed to have recourse to moral suasion to affect market rates, or take administrative measures—for example, by not fully passing through international oil price changes—to contain inflation.

The NBR has been taking measures to improve the transmission of monetary policy and ensure greater relevance for the policy rate. To better absorb liquidity, the NBR has started issuing longer-term instruments and has reactivated the secondary market to support the development of an active interbank market. The NBR is also bolstering its communication strategy with market participants to promote a better understanding of monetary policy decisions and to guide expectations formation. The recent publication of the quarterly inflation report goes in this direction.

The Rwandan authorities have traditionally favoured a stable exchange rate. The NBR has intervened regularly to maintain the currency within a narrow band of the official rate. However, the determination of the market exchange rate suffers from some structural issues. The interbank market remains shallow, dominated by the central bank. To foster greater exchange rate flexibility, the authorities introduced an exchange rate corridor system in March 2010 and committed to intervening in the market only to smoothen out temporary volatility. Following the aid shock in 2012, and in a bid to preserve reserve levels and contain pressures in the forex market, the NBR has allowed greater exchange rate flexibility. The currency has depreciated by about 12 per cent since then. Rwanda's de facto exchange rate classification has since been revised from crawl-like to other managed arrangement. The de jure exchange rate arrangement is classified as floating (IMF, 2013).

3 THE MODEL: OUTLINE, CALIBRATION, FILTERING, AND FORECAST EXERCISE

3.1 The Model

The model consists of four blocks: aggregate demand, aggregate supply, links with the rest of the world through arbitrage conditions, and a monetary policy rule.

---

[2] However, ample flexibility has been observed, as when in June 2011, the NBR allowed some banks to miss the mandatory reserve requirement levels without the required penalties to meet the reserve money target. This is tantamount to implicitly relaxing the reserve requirement, implying a further loosening of monetary policy.

In terms of general notation, for any given variable x, a bar ($\bar{x}$) denotes that variable's trend or long-run value, and a gap term added to the variable ($xgap$) denotes deviations from trend. The model is specified for quarterly frequencies, a delta (Δ) in front of the variable indicates, except for inflation rates which are denoted by π and correspond to quarter over quarter annualized seasonally adjusted changes. Finally, an asterisk * denotes a foreign variable and ss sub-indexes stand for steady state values.[3] Behavioural equations also include auto-regressive components to better match the properties of the data.

3.1.1 Aggregate Demand

Equation 1 describes the behaviour of deviations of output from trend (the output gap), where $ygap$ is the output gap, $rmci$ is the real monetary conditions index (an overall indicator of the monetary policy stance, which is a weighted average of the deviation of the real interest rate and real exchange rate from their trends), $ygap^*$ is the US output gap, $rgap$ is the real interest rate gap, and $zgap$ is the real exchange rate gap.[4] ϵ_t^{ygap} represents a shock or innovation to domestic aggregate demand which picks up non-modelled effects. The real interest rate is the ex ante interbank rate deflated by headline inflation.

$$ygap_t = \beta_1 ygap_{t-1} - \beta_2 rmci_{t-1} + \beta_3 ygap_t^* + \epsilon_t^{ygap} \tag{1}$$

$$rmci_t = (1 - \beta_4)rgap_t - \beta_4 zgap_t \tag{2}$$

3.1.2 Aggregate Supply

To better capture the effects of supply shocks on inflation dynamics and the conduct of monetary policy, we introduce behavioural processes for core, food, and fuel inflation. Core inflation (π^{core}) dynamics evolve according to Equation 3. Here, the lagged term in the Phillips curve captures the backward-looking expectations of agents based on learning, imperfect credibility of the central banks, or indexation. $E_t \pi_t$ stands for headline inflation expectations and is defined as a function of lagged and future inflation.[5] rmc denotes the real marginal costs, given by a weighted average of the real exchange rate gap ($zgap$) and the output gap ($ygap$). The real exchange gap reflects the effect of imported goods' prices on inflation while the output gap captures excess aggregate demand pressures. Once again, ϵ^{core} stands for shocks coming from excluded factors.

$$\pi_t^{core} = \lambda_1 \pi_{t-1}^{core} + (1 - \lambda_1)E_t \pi_t + \lambda_2 rmc_t + \epsilon_t^{core} \tag{3}$$

---

[3] For simplicity, we use US variables to proxy for the rest of the world.

[4] The nominal exchange rate is defined as units of domestic currency (Rwandan Franc) per US dollar. The real exchange rate is a bilateral rate vis-à-vis the US dollar.

[5] This specification allows us to capture potential 'second-round' effects of supply shocks on core inflation.

$$E_t \pi_t = a\pi_{t-1} + (1 - a)\pi_{t+1} \tag{4}$$

$$rmc_t = \theta(zgap_t) + (1 - \theta)ygap_t \tag{5}$$

Food inflation dynamics (π^{food}), in turn, are represented by Equation 6. Similar to core inflation, food inflation is explained by its past level, inflation expectations, and excess aggregate demand pressures. Additionally, the $\hat{\varphi}food$ term captures price pressures arising from changes in international food prices (π^{food*}) relative to domestic food prices. Here Δs stands for changes in the nominal exchange rate and $\Delta \bar{z}_t$ denotes changes in the trend value of the real exchange rate, and ϵ^{food} is a perturbation term.

$$\pi_t^{food} = \lambda_3 \pi_{t-1}^{food} + (1 - \lambda_3)E_t\pi_t + \lambda_4\hat{\varphi}food_t + \lambda_5 ygap_t + \epsilon_t^{food} \tag{6}$$

$$\hat{\varphi}food_t = (\Delta s_t + \pi_t^{food*} - \pi_t^{food} - \Delta\bar{z}_t)/4 \tag{7}$$

The specification for oil inflation (π^{oil}) has a similar structure as the one for core and food inflation (Equation 8).

$$\pi_t^{oil} = \lambda_6 \pi_{t-1}^{oil} + \lambda_7 E_t\pi_t + (1 - \lambda_6 - \lambda_7)(\pi_t^{oil*} + \Delta s_t - \Delta\bar{z}_t) + \epsilon_t^{oil} \tag{8}$$

Finally, headline inflation is defined as the weighted average of core, food, and oil (Equation 9).

$$\pi_t = w_1\pi_t^{core} + w_2\pi_t^{food} + (1 - w_1 - w_2)\pi_t^{oil} \tag{9}$$

3.1.3 Exchange Rate Determination

The block that models the links with the rest of the world is comprised by a set of arbitrage conditions. We introduce a modified uncovered interest rate parity condition to simulate nominal exchange rate dynamics in Rwanda (Equation 10), where s_t is the nominal exchange rate, s_t^T is the target exchange rate, i and i^* are the Rwandan interbank rate and the US Federal Funds rate, and ρ is a risk premium. The parameter η controls the degree of flexibility of the nominal exchange rate and/or deviations from uncovered interest parity.[6] We also assume that the rate of crawl (Δs_t^T) is such that in the long run the target exchange rate is determined by relative purchasing power parity adjusting for trends in the real exchange rate. This, in turn, implies that efforts by the central bank to manage the exchange rate have to be consistent with the inflation objective.[7] This process is represented by Equation 12, where $\bar{\pi}$ stands for the domestic inflation target, $\bar{\pi}^*$ is the US inflation rate, and $\Delta\bar{z}$ is the change in the equilibrium real exchange rate.

---

[6] See Benes, Hurnik, and Vavra (2008) for alternative ways to model exchange rate dynamics in the context of managed exchange rate regimes.

[7] Modifications to the central bank's exchange rate policy can be captured either through changes in parameter η, changes in σ_1 or, changes in the rate of crawl.

$$s_t = \eta_1 s_t^T + (1 - \eta_1)(s_{t+1} - (i_t - i_t^* - \rho_t)/4) + \epsilon_t^s \qquad (10)$$

$$s_t^T = s_{t-1}^T + \Delta s_t^T/4 \qquad (11)$$

$$\Delta s_t^T = \sigma_1 \Delta s_{t-1}^T + (1 - \sigma_1)(\bar{\pi}_t - \bar{\pi}_t^* + \Delta \bar{z}_t) + \epsilon_t^{\Delta s^T} \qquad (12)$$

The modification to the UIP condition is very general, but by allowing for a parameter ($\sigma 1$) to capture the degree of capital mobility and the response of the exchange rate to monetary policy, the model is better able to fit the data. It also permits us to better characterize the policy framework in place in Rwanda, typified by active exchange rate management through the use of unconventional instruments (interventions, moral suasion, etc.) and where dual nominal anchors coexist. This setting can be used to characterize the policy frameworks of other frontier markets in the region. Other issues that arise from this adaptation, such as the relationship between international reserve stocks and the risk premium, or the two-instrument/two-target problem more generally are not incorporated.[8]

3.1.4 Interest Rate Policy Rule

We close the model by introducing a monetary policy reaction function, according to which the central bank sets the interest rate in response to deviations of the one-year ahead inflation forecast from the inflation target and the output gap (Equation 13).[9] Here $\bar{i}$ is the long-run (neutral) nominal interest rate, $\pi 4$ is year-on-year (YoY) inflation rate, $\bar{r}$ is the neutral real interest rate, and ϵ^i is an error term that can be interpreted as a measure of the unsystematic component of monetary policy.

$$i_t = \tau_1 i_{t-1} + (1 - \tau_1)(\bar{i}_t + \tau_2(\pi 4_{t+4} - \bar{\pi}_{t+4}) + \tau_3 ygap_t) + \epsilon_t^i \qquad (13)$$

$$\bar{i}_t = \bar{r}_t + \bar{\pi}_{t+4} \qquad (14)$$

We also specify a stochastic process for the inflation target (Equation 15), which allows us to simulate different disinflation paths.

$$\bar{\pi}_t = \tau_4 \bar{\pi}_{t-1} + (1 - \tau_4)\pi^{ss} + \epsilon_t^{\bar{\pi}} \qquad (15)$$

3.1.5 Long-Run Trends

The long-run values of the real interest rate, the change in potential output and the real exchange rate are assumed to follow a simple first order autoregressive process given by:

---

[8] See, for example, Chapter 13, and Ostry, Ghosh, and Chamon (2012).

[9] We use the overnight interbank rate as a proxy for the stance of monetary policy in Rwanda. An increase of the interbank rate is interpreted as a tightening of monetary policy whereas a decrease reflects a loosening of policy.

$$\bar{r}_t = \psi_1 \bar{r}_{t-1} + (1 - \psi_1)\bar{r}_{ss} + \epsilon_t^{\bar{r}} \tag{16}$$

$$\Delta\bar{y}_t = \psi_2 \Delta\bar{y}_{t-1} + (1 - \psi_2)\Delta y_{ss} + \epsilon_t^{\Delta\bar{y}} \tag{17}$$

$$\Delta\bar{z}_t = \psi_3 \Delta\bar{z}_{t-1} + (1 - \psi_3)\Delta z_{ss} + \epsilon_t^{\Delta\bar{z}} \tag{18}$$

where $\Delta\bar{y}_{ss}$, $\Delta\bar{z}_{ss}$ and $\bar{r}_{ss}$ are the steady state values of potential output growth, the change in the real exchange rate, and the real interest rate, respectively.

3.1.6 Foreign Block

The dynamics of our model are completed by adding a simple rest of the world block, which we proxy with US variables. The block is comprised by a foreign output gap equation ($ygap^*$), an autoregressive process for the foreign neutral real interest rate ($\bar{r}^*$) and headline inflation (π^*), and a nominal interest rate policy rule (i^*).

$$ygap_t^* = a_1 ygap_{t-1}^* + \epsilon_t^{ygap^*} \tag{19}$$

$$\bar{r}_t^* = a_2 \bar{r}_{t-1}^* + (1 - a_2)\bar{r}_{ss}^* + \epsilon_t^{\bar{r}^*} \tag{20}$$

$$i_t^* = a_3 i_{t-1}^* + (1 - a_3)(\bar{r}_{t-1}^* + \pi_{ss}^* + a_4(\pi_{t+4}^* - \pi_{ss}^*)) + \epsilon_t^{i^*} \tag{21}$$

$$\pi_t^* = a_5 \pi_{t-1}^* + (1 - a_5)\pi_{ss}^* + \epsilon_t^{\pi^*} \tag{22}$$

3.2 Data and Calibration

The complete dataset along with the sources is described in Table 18.1. The database spans from 2003Q1 to 2013Q3.[10] The disaggregation of inflation into core, food, and oil follows the National Institute of Statistics all-urban consumer price index. The weight for food and non-alcoholic beverages in the overall CPI basket is 35.4 per cent, whereas the weight for oil (transport) is 11.9 per cent. Core CPI is calculated by excluding food and oil CPI from the overall CPI index. The international oil and food price indexes are those of the World Economic Outlook (WEO).

The GDP and CPI series are seasonally adjusted using the X12-ARIMA filter. The quarterly GDP data is also smoothened using the Hodrick-Prescott (HP) filter, using a smoothing parameter of 0.5. This de-trending of the series seeks to

---

[10] Monthly series are averaged to quarterly frequencies.

Table 18.1. Data Series

Variable	Description	Source
s	Exchange rate (Franc/USD)	NBR
i	Interbank rate	NBR
y	Quarterly GDP	IMF (IFS)
CPI	Quarterly CPI (headline)	NISR
CPI^{oil}	Quarterly CPI (oil)	NISR
CPI^{food}	Quarterly CPI (food)	NISR
ΔP_{oil}^{world}	International oil prices	IMF (WEO)
ΔP_{food}^{world}	International food prices index	IMF (WEO)
CPI^*	US CPI	IMF (IFS/WEO)
i^*	US Federal Funds rate	IMF (IFS/WEO)
$ygap^*$	US output gap	IMF (IFS/WEO)

Note: compilation of quarterly GDP: for 2006 and afterwards, the IMF's annual GDP series
is converted to a quarterly frequency using the authorities' quarterly GDP estimates. For
the earlier period, quarterly weights computed from the authorities' quarterly GDP estimates
for 2006–11 are applied to the IMF's annual series.
NISR: National Institute of Statistics for Rwanda
NBR: National Bank of Rwanda
WEO: World Economic Outlook
IMF: International Monetary Fund
IFS: International Financial Statistics

remove some of the volatility associated with supply shocks, which are difficult to
model in structural terms.

The model parameters are calibrated to match the broad properties of the data,
following basic economic principles and how sensible the properties of the
resulting model look (Table 18.2).[11] The steady state values of the real interest
rate, output growth, and the real exchange rate change correspond to the average
of the last six years. The inflation target is consistent with the target of the NBR of
5 per cent. To check the consistency of our choice of parameters, we estimate the
sacrifice ratio obtained from the model and match it with the sacrifice ratio calculated from the observed data for the disinflationary period of 2008Q2–2010Q3,
following Ball (1994). The observed sacrifice ratio (amount of output that must be
forgone to achieve a given permanent reduction in inflation) turns out to be 2.0 for
headline inflation, while the model's sacrifice ratio stands at 1.8.

Figures 18.2–18.4 present a set of the model impulse response plots that
illustrate its basic properties.[12] A positive aggregate demand shock ($e^{ygap} = 1$)
translates into increases in core, food, and oil inflation by 0.55 per cent, 0.4, and
0.35 per cent (all presented on a quarter on quarter basis), respectively. The
central bank then responds by tightening monetary policy and increasing the
interest rate. Inflation returns back to target as the exchange rate appreciates and a
negative output gap opens up. Figure 18.3 presents the responses to supply shocks

---

[11] See Berg, Karam, and Laxton (2006) and Chapter 15 for guidelines on calibrating this class of
model in low-income economies.

[12] In all cases, these correspond to responses to a temporary 1 per cent increase during one quarter
in the shock term. The results are presented in deviations from steady state values.

Table 18.2. Calibration

Parameter	Description	Value
	Output Gap Equation	
β_1	AR(1) parameter	0.69
β_2	Coefficient on real monetary conditions (*rmci*)	0.47
β_3	Coefficient on the foreign output gap	0.05
β_4	Weight of the real exchange rate gap in *rmci*	0.30
	Core Inflation Equation	
λ_1	AR(1) parameter	0.65
λ_2	Coefficient on real marginal costs (*rmc*)	0.51
Θ	Weight of the real exchange rate gap in *rmc*	0.20
α	AR(1) in inflation expectations process	0.50
	Food Inflation Equation	
λ_3	AR(1) parameter	0.35
λ_4	Coefficient on international food price pressures	0.17
λ_5	Coefficient on the output gap	0.06
	Oil Inflation Equation	
λ_6	AR(1) parameter	0.35
λ_7	Coefficient on inflation expectations	0.57
	Headline Inflation	
w_1	Core inflation weight	0.53
w_2	Food inflation weight	0.36
	Exchange Rate Rule	
$\eta 1$	Coefficient on the target exchange rate	0.95
σ_1	AR(1) parameter	0.80
	Monetary Policy Rule	
τ_1	Smoothing parameter	0.45
τ_2	Coefficient on inflation forecast deviation from target	2.10
τ_3	Coefficient on the output gap	0.90
τ_4	AR(1) parameter in the inflation target process	0.50
	Trends	
ψ_1	Persistence, long-run real interest rate	0.45
ψ_2	Persistence, long-run output growth	0.38
ψ_3	Persistence, long-run real exchange rate	0.55
	Foreign Block	
$a1$	Persistence in output gap	0.80
$a2$	Persistence, real interest rate trend	0.50
$a3$	Smoothening parameter in US Taylor rule	0.80
$a4$	Coefficient on expected inflation deviation from target	3.50
$a5$	AR(1) parameter	0.30
	Steady state/long-run values	
$\bar{r}_{ss}$	Long-run real interest rate	3.50
$\Delta\bar{y}_{ss}$	Long-run output growth rate	7.50
$\Delta\bar{z}_{ss}$	Long-run real exchange rate change	−1.00
$\bar{\pi}$	Inflation target	5.00
$\bar{r}^{*}_{ss}$	Foreign long-run real interest rate	0.50
$\bar{\pi}$	Foreign inflation target	2.00
	Standard deviation of shocks	
ϵ^{ygap}	Output gap shock	0.15
ϵ^{core}	Core inflation shock	0.50
ϵ^{food}	Food inflation shock	1.50
ϵ^{oil}	Oil inflation shock	1.50
ϵ^{i}	Monetary policy rule shock	0.60
ϵ^{π}	Inflation target shock	3.20
ϵ^{s}	Uncovered interest rate parity shock	0.60
$\epsilon^{\Delta s^{T}}$	Exchange rate target shock	1.50
$\epsilon^{\bar{r}}$	Long-run real interest rate shock	0.20

(continued)

Table 18.2. Continued

Parameter	Description	Value
$\epsilon^{\Delta\bar{y}}$	Long-run output growth shock	0.27
$\epsilon^{\Delta\bar{z}}$	Long-run real exchange rate shock	0.36
ϵ^{ygap*}	Foreign output gap shock	0.25
$\epsilon^{\bar{r}*}$	Foreign long-run real interest rate shock	0.75
ϵ^{i*}	Foreign interest rate shock	0.45
$\epsilon^{\pi*}$	Foreign inflation shock	1.30
ϵ^{woil}	World oil prices shock	1.50
ϵ^{wfood}	World food prices shock	1.50

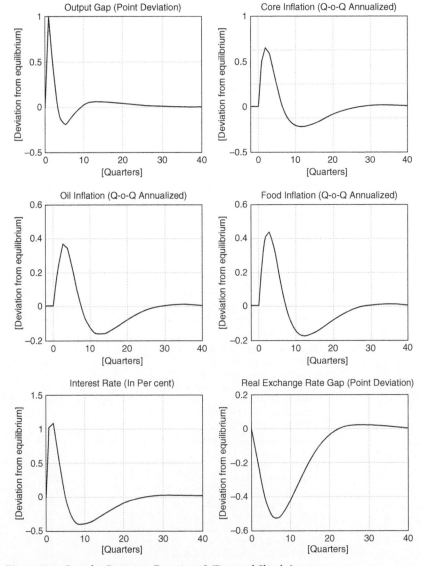

Figure 18.2. Impulse Response Functions I (Demand Shocks)

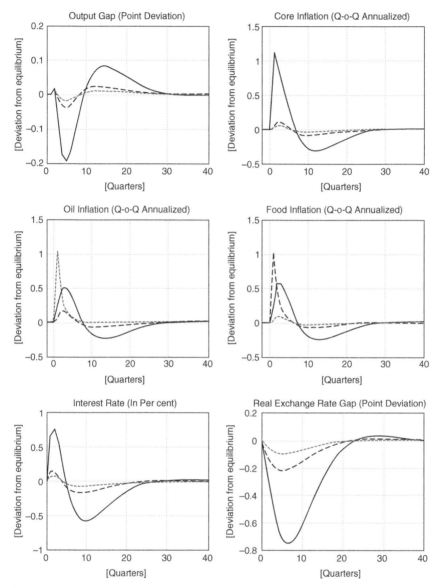

Figure 18.3. Impulse Response Functions II. Supply Shocks: Core (solid line), Food (long-dashed line), and Fule (short-dashed line)

to core ($\epsilon^{core} = 1$), food ($\epsilon^{food} = 1$), and oil ($\epsilon^{oil} = 1$) inflation. In all three cases, the central bank responds by tightening policy, but less so in the case of shocks to food and oil inflation. Accordingly, in all cases tighter policy leads to a negative (even though small) output gap and an appreciation of the exchange rate. Figure 18.4 presents responses to an interest rate shock.

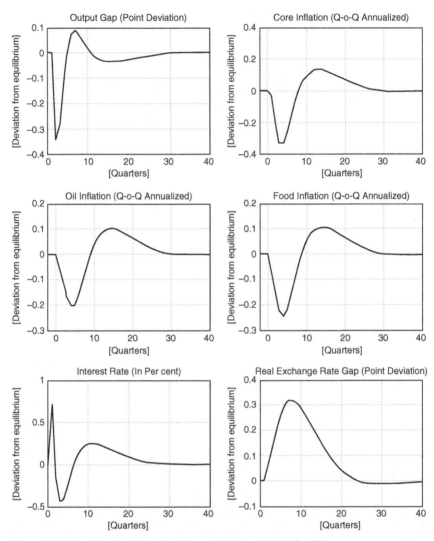

Figure 18.4. Impulse Response Functions III (Interest Rate Shock)

4 FILTERING RWANDAN DATA THROUGH THE MODEL

Written in its state-space form, the model allows for the unobserved variables (state variables) to be estimated with the Kalman filter.[13] Figures 18.5–18.7 present the trend and gap components of the real exchange rate (z_t), the real interest rate (rr_t), and output (y_t), respectively. The estimate of the output gap

[13] In our case, the set of unobserved states includes the gap (deviations from trend) components. The filtering exercise covers the period from 2008 onwards.

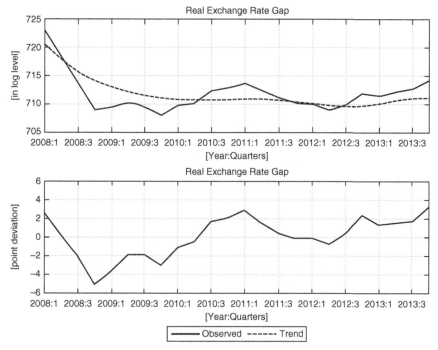

Figure 18.5. Real Exchange Rate Trend and Gap

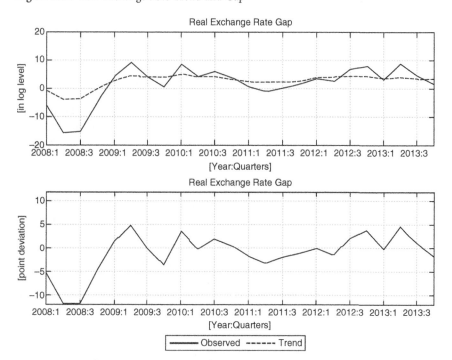

Figure 18.6. Real Interest Rate Trend and Gap

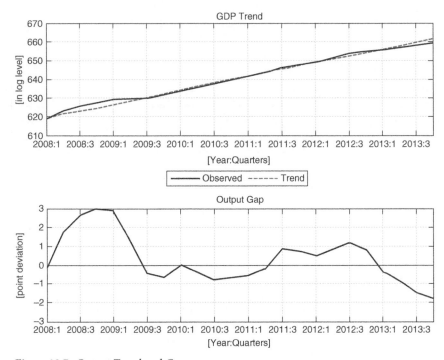

Figure 18.7. Output Trend and Gap

permits to identify a complete business cycle between 2008H1 and 2011H1, and a second one unfolding after 2011H2. The model captures well the negative effects of the global financial crisis on output, and the subsequent expansion on the back of more accommodative policies, as indicated by a negative real interest rate gap. The negative effect of the 2012 aid shock on economic activity is also evident, with the opening up of a negative output gap (of about 2 per cent of GDP in 2013). The real depreciation triggered by this episode and the consequent tightening of monetary policy (as signalled by higher real interest rates) is also well captured by the model.[14]

The model also allows us to decompose the observed data into the different structural shocks hitting the economy. The results (Figures 18.8–18.12) indicate that exchange rate shocks play an important role in inflation dynamics all throughout the period under consideration. Likewise, supply shocks in the food sector (and less so in the oil sector) seem to play a large role. Core inflation dynamics, on the other hand, seem to be dominated by exchange rate shocks, monetary policy shocks, and supply shocks. The systematic nature of monetary policy shocks in the determination of core inflation, particularly since 2010 could either indicate that there is an additional element to include in the model's

---

[14] The higher real depreciation after the aid shock was achieved through an upward adjustment in the rate of crawl by the central bank.

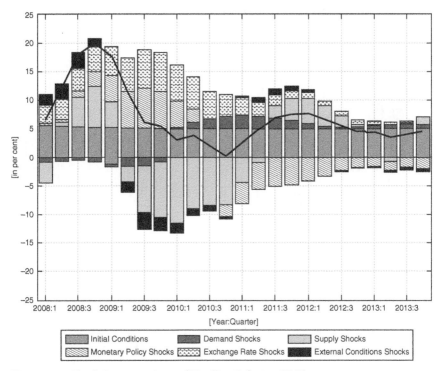

Figure 18.8. Shock Decomposition of Headline Inflation (YoY)

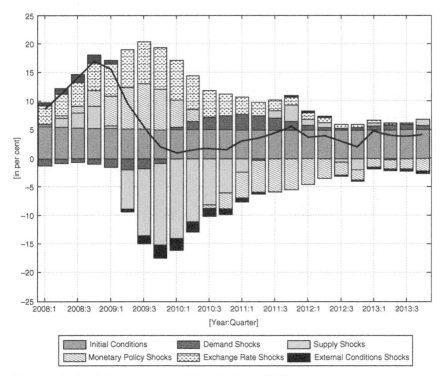

Figure 18.9. Shock Decomposition of Core Inflation (YoY)

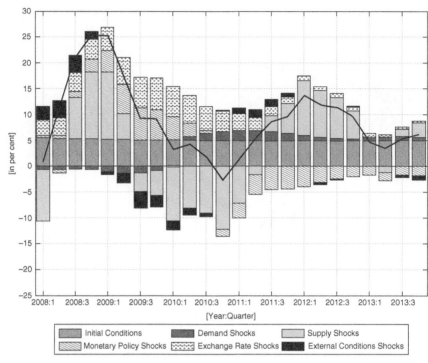

Figure 18.10. Shock Decomposition of Food Inflation (YoY)

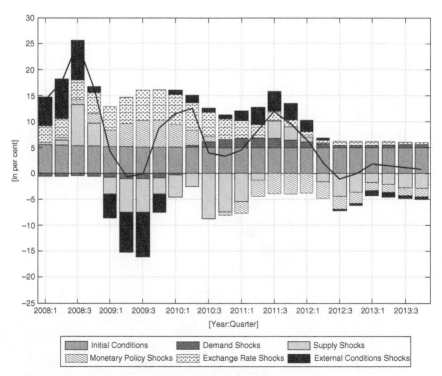

Figure 18.11. Shock Decomposition of Oil Inflation (YoY)

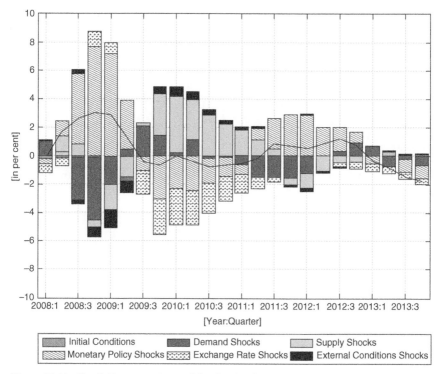

Figure 18.12. Shock Decomposition of the Output Gap

monetary policy rule (such as the role played by monetary aggregates), or that there are in fact areas of improvement in the way monetary policy is currently conducted to better anchor inflation expectations.

4.1 Forecast

One way of assessing the reliability of the model is by evaluating its in-sample forecasting capabilities. We also present an out-of-sample forecast to showcase the usefulness of the tool to conduct policy analysis in a forward-looking context.

4.1.1 In-Sample Forecast

In-sample forecasts are generated on a quarterly basis, for the period 2007Q4–2013Q4. We assume an equilibrium real exchange rate appreciation of 1 per cent, with inflation converging to a target of 5 per cent. For this exercise, the in-sample variables of the rest of the world block and the world oil and food prices are exogenous and equal to their observed values (the trajectories of the external variables and world food and oil prices are shown in Figure 18.13).

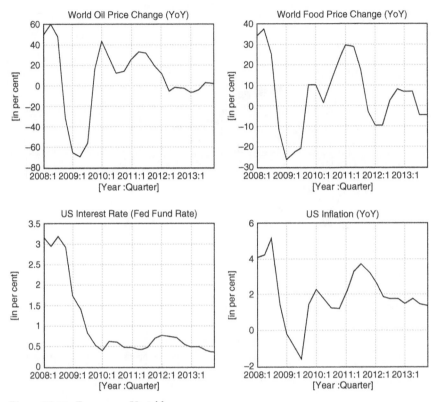

Figure 18.13. Exogenous Variables

The forecasts are shown in Figure 18.14. The model predicts the disinflation of 2009 fairly well; however, it underestimates the magnitude of the inflationary pressures in 2010. The model does tend to closely track inflation in 2011 and after 2012, also helped by the fact that inflation was less volatile than in the previous years. All in all, the results suggest that the model is broadly satisfactory, particularly at short horizons. However, its performance is somewhat less reliable in the presence of large exogenous shocks, as in 2008. Nevertheless, a comparison of the in-sample model forecasts with those of a simple random walk model shows that the model outperforms the random walk model, especially at longer horizons

4.1.2 *Out-of-Sample Forecast*

The main outputs of the out-of-sample forecast, starting from 2014Q1l are presented in Figure 18.15. This is in a context where the aid situation has normalized with the return of donors, but near term growth has slowed down, with 2014 growth projected at 6 per cent, while we estimate potential GDP growth to stand at 7 per cent. The economy is thus operating below its potential, and the

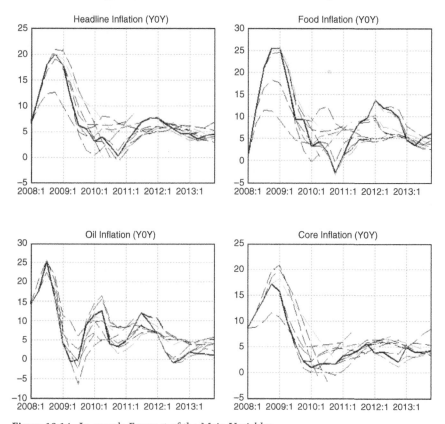

Figure 18.14. In-sample Forecast of the Main Variables

negative output gap (2 per cent of GDP at the start of the simulation) is not expected to close until the first half of 2015. The exchange rate pressures noticed at the peak of the aid shock have subsided significantly. The Rwandan franc depreciated by nearly 12 per cent between January 2012 and December 2013, but the pace of depreciation slowed in the first quarter of 2014, reflecting both the slowdown in economic activity and resulting decline in demand for imports as well as a return of donor flows. The premium between the official and market exchange rates is now below the ordinary 2 per cent. On the external front, the main change we anticipate over the forecast horizon is a normalization of US interest rates as after 2015. Commodity prices are expected to remain relatively stable over the period.

Bearing in mind these conditions, the baseline forecast suggests that headline inflation will remain within a range of 3 to 5 per cent in 2014, and the NBR's current monetary policy stance can be considered as appropriate. However, should growth weaken further there may be room to ease monetary conditions to spur economic activity.

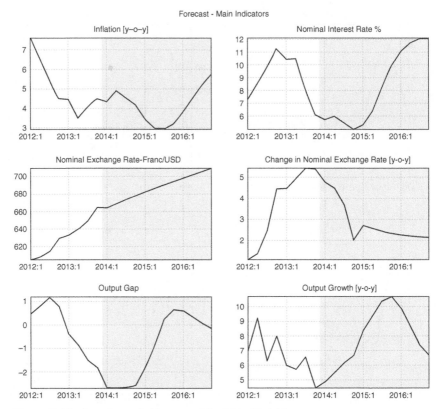

Figure 18.15. Out-of-sample Forecast of the Main Variables

5 CONCLUSIONS

The policy decision-making process by the NBR's monetary policy committee is currently anchored on an analysis of mostly backward-looking indicators, which at times are available after a considerable lag. This has occasionally hindered the NBR's response to economic developments, resulting in an expansionary policy being maintained despite rising inflationary pressures. Hence, the recent efforts by the NBR in developing tools to enhance its policy analysis apparatus, by introducing and FPAS, represent a step in the right direction. Models like the one presented here provide a framework within which to analyse monetary policy in a systematic and forward-looking way, which is the reason why they usually stand at the centre of such systems.

The use of the model allows us to show the key contributors to inflation in Rwanda, placing special emphasis on tracing the effects of food and oil price developments, as well as the nature of the exchange rate regime. For the period under consideration, exchange rate and supply shocks have played an important role in inflation dynamics. The results also suggest that monetary policy shocks have contributed to macroeconomic developments.

The NBR is considering adopting an inflation targeting regime and has been working to introduce the different elements of such a framework. Improving the policy decision-making processes by introducing forward-looking analytical tools so as to better gauge the response of the economy to policy changes is also likely to translate into superior policy and macroeconomic outcomes. This chapter is a contribution in that direction. However, in putting together the model in this chapter we have had to abstract from many of the complexities of the actual operating and policy framework in Rwanda, notably the complex and interrelated roles of money aggregates, the policy interest rate, and the exchange rate. Further progress in clarifying the instruments and objectives of the central bank will make this process more successful. It will also enable the execution of a clear and transparent communication strategy and more broadly enhance the credibility of the central bank.

REFERENCES

Ball, L. (1994). What Determines the Sacrifice Ratio? In N. Gregory Mankiw (Ed.). *Monetary Policy* (pp. 155–93). Chicago: The University of Chicago Press.

Benes, J., Hurnik, J., and Vavra. D. (2008). Exchange Rate Management and Inflation Targeting: Modeling the Exchange Rate in Reduced-Form New Keynesian Models. *Czech Journal of Economics and Finance*, 58, 3–4.

Berg, A., Karam, P., and Laxton, D. (2006). *Practical Model-Based Monetary Policy Analysis—A How-To Guide*. IMF Working Paper 06/81. Washington, DC: International Monetary Fund.

International Monetary Fund. (2013). *Annual Report on Exchange Arrangements and Exchange Restrictions*. Washington, DC: International Monetary Fund.

Ostry, J. D., Ghosh, A. R., and Chamon. M. (2012). *Two Targets, Two Instruments: Monetary and Exchange Rate Policies in Emerging Market Economies*. Staff Discussion Notes 12/01. Washington, DC: International Monetary Fund.

19

Inflation Forecast Targeting in a Low-Income Country

The Case of Ghana

Ali Alichi, Marshall Mills, Douglas Laxton, and Hans Weisfeld

1 INTRODUCTION

Over the past two decades, numerous monetary authorities have used inflation targeting to solve a chronic inflation problem.[1,2] They announced numerical inflation reduction targets for the medium-term, and in some cases a long-run target, which may be interpreted as a price stability objective.

Although, in the end, most of these countries achieved the goal they sought, the disinflation phase was often uneven, with inflation outcomes outside the target range. Roger and Stone (2005) found that the frequency of outcomes outside the range for countries with inflation targets was 60 per cent. In retrospect, monetary policy in some cases responded too vigorously to these deviations in an attempt to get inflation quickly back to the target.

Indeed, early IT strategy put heavy emphasis on achieving annual reductions in the inflation rate on schedule, as a way to establish central bank commitment to price stability. This was an essential objective because monetary policy credibility had been badly eroded by high and persistent inflation, such as the Great Inflation of the 1970s and 1980s. Policymakers were also aware of the credibility problem implied by the theory of time-inconsistency in monetary policy. While this theory holds that short-run political time horizons create the time-inconsistency, the proposed solutions, e.g. by Barro and Gordon (1984) and Rogoff (1985), recommend that policymakers take a longer-run view. In practice, the focus on hitting short-run targets soon ran into difficulties, largely because of lags in the policy

---

[1] This chapter is a slightly revised version of IMF (2008). See also Alichi et al. (2010). Though there have been some significant changes to Ghana's inflation targeting framework since then, the analysis presented here remains informative for thinking about the ongoing (and recurrent) disinflation challenge in that country.

[2] Examples of countries that have introduced inflation-reduction targets are Brazil, Canada, Chile, Colombia, Czech Republic, Hungary, Israel, Korea, Mexico, New Zealand, Peru, Poland, and the United Kingdom (Mishkin and Schmidt-Hebbel, 2001, Table 2).

transmission mechanism. The effects of forceful policy reactions would stretch beyond their intended short-run purpose, pushing inflation to the other side of the target range and requiring actions to reverse it.

A lesson from this experience is that a modern approach to IT—which can be described as inflation forecast targeting (IFT)—should be more flexible and forward-looking as well as providing better communication. Credibility is not helped by policy actions that attempt to keep inflation within a target range every single year. Experience has shown that common shocks can be so large that such a goal may not be feasible, let alone desirable. Moreover, the objective of short-run output stability may influence policy actions, without harming credibility, as long as this influence is unbiased over time. A central bank can strengthen its credibility by openly focusing its policy on more than just hitting annual targets, recognizing that its actions involve short-run trade-offs and being mindful of undesired effects on output and employment. IFT instead emphasizes longer-term results, the framework committing monetary policy to a low-inflation goal, and accountability and transparent communications. Under IFT, central banks publish regular monetary policy reports that contain their forecast for inflation, associated macroeconomic variables, and at least a qualitative indication of the likely course of the policy interest rate; some have gone so far as to publish an explicit forecast for the policy interest rate.[3] Each of the elements of the flexible approach requires that the policymakers have realistic, coherent models of the monetary policy process, from policy instruments to objectives.

While Ghana is one of several emerging market economies to adopt IT, it may be the first low-income country to have done so (IMF, 2008b). An important consideration for adopting an IT regime was that the existing framework, which was based on targeting monetary aggregates, proved to be increasingly infeasible as the demand for money changed rapidly in the wake of major structural transformation.

As a small, open low-income economy, Ghana faces several major challenges in its conduct of disinflation policy:

- It is highly vulnerable to supply shocks.
- Deviations from inflation targets tend to be larger during disinflation than with stable low targets.
- Inflation expectations can be volatile and based on past experience.
- The technical capacity of Bank of Ghana (BoG) is incipient, though still evolving.

Despite these challenges, the IFT approach can effectively deliver a program of inflation reduction for Ghana while limiting output loss.

To support this approach, we construct a model-based framework for disinflation under IT with the following features:

- It explicitly models inflation expectation dynamics. Inflation expectations and policy responses depend on policy credibility.
- It replaces the Taylor rule for interest rate setting with a time invariant objective function.

---

[3] Examples are the Reserve Bank of New Zealand, the Norges Bank, the Riksbank, and the Czech National Bank.

- It avoids the shortcomings of inadequate communication strategies.
- It generates plausible results for responding to shocks.

This approach offers responses to the questions facing any central bank thinking of disinflation:

- What is an appropriate pace of disinflation?
- Should a long-run target be announced?
- Should the disinflation targets be revised following a shock? What sort of flexibility is appropriate in the execution of policy?

2 INFLATION TRENDS IN GHANA THROUGH 2007

Ghana has historically experienced volatile and often high inflation rates (Figure 19.1). Ghana's economy suffered bouts of high inflation in 1999–2000 and 2002–03, which were related to external shocks, unsustainable macroeconomic policies and exchange rate depreciation. A period of disinflation began in 2004 that brought inflation down to near 10 per cent in 2006, where it roughly stabilized until late 2007.

The BoG formally adopted IT in May 2007 after three years of informal IT management. It has been building the main institutional, analytical, and communications elements of this framework since 2002. With the enactment of the 2002 Bank of Ghana Act, the BoG had in place all of the key institutional components of modern central banking, especially independence and a statutory mission of price stability. In addition, central bank credit to the government each year is limited by law to 10 per cent of total revenue collected that year, but in practice the government has not resorted to any central bank financing for the last several years. The target range for CPI inflation is set jointly by the government and the BoG as part of the budget. Staff describe the current regime as 'inflation-targeting

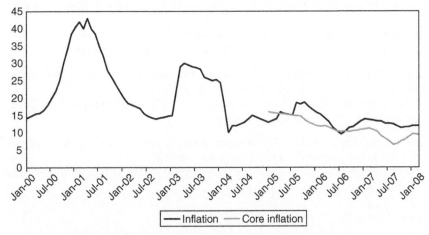

Figure 19.1. Ghana: CPI Inflation, 2000–2008 (Per cent year-on-year)

lite', because exchange rate stability is an important secondary objective and because operational transparency has not developed sufficiently to classify it as a fully fledged IT regime.

When the BoG formally launched IT, it established a large measure of goal transparency, aiming for disinflation over three years to achieve stability around 5 per cent, with a range of ±1 per cent. It also announced a fairly straight-line path of intermediate inflation targets to get to 5 per cent. In support of IT, the BoG has also developed a forecasting model and a detailed communication strategy. After each Monetary Policy Committee (MPC) meeting (every other month), it issues a press release and holds a press conference, chaired by the BoG Governor, at which it explains its decision. A detailed monetary policy report is then published.

In October 2007, inflation started to pick up again due to both demand shocks (from an expansionary fiscal policy and strong private sector credit growth) and supply shocks (from higher international fuel and food prices). The BoG has noted that core CPI inflation—which excludes energy and utilities—has been lower than the headline but has also begun to rise. In response, the BoG has raised the policy rate by a cumulative 350 basis points since November 2007. These inflation developments have posed an early challenge for the IT regime. The current straight-line disinflation path and communication strategy seem too rigid to respond well. As a result, the BoG credibility that was built up over the last four to five years may be at risk.

3 STANDARD MODEL

In the standard New Keynesian model in use at the Fund for several countries, the central bank sets an inflation target path dependent on current inflation and its long-run inflation objective and employs a Taylor-type rule to determine the policy (interest) rate, subject to the following behavioural equations:

- an output gap equation (actual minus potential output—a gauge of excess demand—as a function of the interest rate, the exchange rate, and external demand);
- an inflation rate equation (an expectations-augmented Phillips curve); and
- an exchange rate equation (a relation embodying uncovered interest parity, a variable risk premium, and long-run purchasing power parity).

In the standard model, the central bank's credibility is proxied by a parameter and is captured to some extent by the degree to which households form inflation expectations in a forward-looking rather than a backward-looking fashion. The standard model works reasonably well for countries that have already achieved low inflation rates, even though there is evidence that shows that a well-managed IT framework will over time strengthen central bank credibility.[4] However, it is less appropriate for Ghana because during disinflation periods credibility is likely to change over time, which is not endogenously captured in the standard model.

---

[4] See for example Kamenik et al. (2008) and International Monetary Fund (2006).

4 MODEL FOR DISINFLATION UNDER INFLATION FORECAST TARGETING

Our framework adds to the standard model three novel features relevant to a policy of inflation reduction:[5]

- An endogenous credibility process. Starting from a situation in which agents initially expect inflation to remain high, policymakers may build credibility over time by providing a sufficient track record that anchors inflation to the target.

- A monetary policy loss function that recognizes costs of fluctuations in output and interest rates, as well as costs of deviations of inflation from target—in place of a conventional interest rate reaction function for the policy interest rate. The advantage of the loss function approach over reaction functions is that the responsiveness of interest rates will change automatically over time and will be more aggressive in responding to shocks when credibility is low.

- A non-linear Phillips curve. In practical terms, this means that the relationship of inflation and output gap depends on how big the output gap is. For very high output gap cases (high excess demand), small increases in output gap will translate into big increases in inflation. However, for reasonably low levels of excess demand, the relationship could be closer to a linear one. A non-linear Phillips curve serves to generate a number of important predictions and policy implications that are missing from linear models that presume high levels of policy credibility. First, the model suggests that it can be easier to lose credibility than it is to regain once lost, as it takes time and a period of significant slack in the economy to re-anchor inflation expectations. Second, this formulation strongly favours gradualism to prevent unnecessary cumulative output losses associated with disinflation.

Our simulation results based on this model suggest that monetary policy should enable the BoG to reduce inflation while limiting output losses. The model is calibrated on the basis of a wide range of international experience and is frequently refined using a continuing iterative feedback process. Note that these results are simply indicative; they do not constitute staff recommendations, but are merely one of several inputs into staff assessments.[6] Model results should always serve as only one of several inputs into decision-making by monetary policymakers.

5 SIMULATION RESULTS: DYNAMIC RESPONSES TO SHOCKS

We first study disinflation under imperfect and perfect credibility in the absence of shocks. Thereafter, we introduce supply and demand shocks and study both the policy reaction and the paths of all other economic variables.

---

[5] For details of the two models, see Appendices A and B, and Alichi et al. (2010).

[6] The model was formulated in close cooperation with the authorities but is the sole responsibility of IMF staff; it does not reflect the conclusions of BoG analysis.

5.1 Baseline—Disinflation under Imperfect Credibility

In the extended model, credibility is imperfect in the sense that people do not have full confidence that the central bank will achieve its announced objectives, and may not even believe that the bank will try to achieve them. In forming expectations of inflation, they give considerable weight to the recent history of inflation and to the risk that policymakers might have a covert high-inflation agenda. Monetary policy is assumed, however, to have some credibility: in the process of forming expectations; we set the initial weights at 0.4 on the announced low-inflation policy, and at 0.6 on the alternative possibility of a high-inflation policy. Furthermore, the central bank can earn an increased stock of credibility—moving the low-inflation weight towards unity—only by delivering an actual drop in inflation toward the official objective.

Monetary policy in the model follows a loss-minimizing strategy to get to the assumed ultimate inflation target of 5 per cent. We posit initial conditions similar to those prevailing in Ghana in the second quarter of 2008. The economy is experiencing excess demand pressures and has suffered an external price shock: inflation is high; growing fiscal deficits and easy monetary conditions are stimulating further inflation. In numerical terms, to start the model simulations we set the 2008 Q2 rate of inflation at 15.3 per cent, the annual output gap (excess demand) at 0.5 per cent; and the short-term rate of interest controlled by the central bank at 16 per cent.[7] The initial real interest rate is below 1 per cent, and hence much less than the assumed natural equilibrium rate of about 3 per cent. We suppose that the central bank announces an ultimate target for the inflation rate of 5 per cent in 2008 Q3 and immediately starts implementing the loss-minimizing policy to this end.

The charts in Figure 19.2 show the simulated disinflation path. Given the level of inflation expectations at the outset and lags in the expectations process, the central bank has to raise the policy rate substantially to achieve the desired increase in the real interest rate. Optimal policy in the model—in the sense of achieving targeted disinflation with minimum loss in output—involves raising the interest rate to 19.6 per cent in 2008 Q3, and to a peak of 20 per cent in 2008 Q4.

This has an immediate impact on the nominal price of foreign exchange: the domestic currency appreciates against the US dollar. This combined with the higher domestic inflation rate compared to the United States implies that the real exchange rate appreciates by 12 per cent. The increased interest rate and reduced real price of foreign exchange (real appreciation of the domestic currency) both reduce demand for domestic output. This eliminates excess demand: the annual output gap declines from a +0.5 per cent to −1.5 per cent (indicating excess capacity) by 2008 Q4, and to a trough of −3.9 per cent in 2009 Q4. This excess capacity represents the short-run output sacrifice required for disinflation in the model.

Low credibility results in upward-biased expectations. During the inflation-reduction phase people expect a higher inflation rate than monetary policy actually delivers. Since expectations have a direct effect on actual inflation in the Phillips curve, monetary policy has to be tighter than if people had 100 per cent

---

[7] This was end-April 2008 inflation (year-on-year).

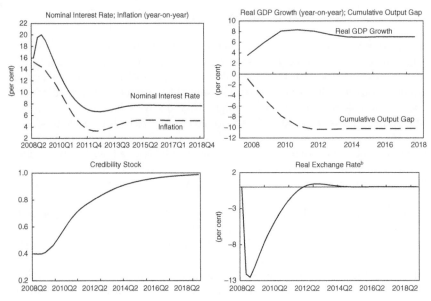

Figure 19.2. Ghana: Baseline IT, 2008–2018[a]

[a] All variables are quarterly, except for Real GDP growth, which is annual because quarterly GDP data are not reported in Ghana.
[b] Increase represents depreciation of the cedi.

Source: IMF staff calculations.

confidence in the objectives, and the loss of output and employment is greater. Thus, low credibility worsens the short-run inflation-output trade-off.

Excess productive capacity does reduce the rate of inflation though. In response, the public gradually revises downwards its expectations of future inflation and gives increased weight to the announced 5 per cent target. By mid-2011 actual inflation reaches this rate. Thus, monetary policy reduces the inflation rate by 10 percentage points over three years, an average reduction of just above 3⅓ per cent per year. The corresponding sacrifice ratio (the cumulative output loss divided by the inflation reduction) is just below one. By historical standards, despite the initial moderate credibility, this would represent a fairly rapid low-cost disinflation (Roger and Stone, 2005).

By 2014 the economy would be almost on its full long-run equilibrium path (barring new shocks). The stock of credibility is close to unity and the output gap is virtually zero. The real exchange rate stabilizes at its initial equilibrium value, but the nominal exchange rate continues to rise, reflecting the domestic-US inflation differential.

5.2 Disinflation under Perfect Credibility

This sub-section repeats the baseline but it assumes that the public has full confidence from the outset in the target announced by the central bank. This assumption implies the fastest path of disinflation consistent with loss minimization. The results show inflation declining to the 5 per cent range just six quarters after the announced

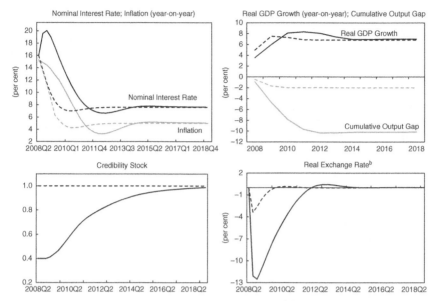

Figure 19.3. Ghana: Baseline with Full Credibility, 2008–2018[a]

Dotted = Full credibility; Solid = Endogenous credibility
[a] All variables are quarterly, except for Real GDP growth, which is annual because quarterly GDP data are not reported in Ghana.
[b] Increase represents depreciation of the cedi.
Source: IMF staff calculations.

policy takes effect (Figure 19.3). The reduction in expected inflation itself raises the real interest rate above the natural rate without an increase in the nominal rate. Indeed, the nominal rate declines through the disinflation phase, as the inflation premium goes down. The sacrifice ratio over the six-quarter inflation-reduction period is less than 0.1—almost negligible.

5.2.1 Supply Shock

The first experiment here is a significant increase in the rate of inflation caused by an increase in world energy and food prices, which calls for a strong policy response. A stagflationary supply shock of this type clearly presents a very difficult problem for monetary policy in the absence of well-anchored inflation expectations. Policy has to guard against an inflationary spiral as the short-run increase in inflation may cause people to expect higher inflation in the future and to lose confidence in the announced 5 per cent objective. The loss-minimizing policy calls for considerable and repeated increases in the interest rate—by 450 basis points over eight quarters—relative to the baseline (Figure 19.4). In levels, the interest rate peaks at 24 per cent in 2008 Q4. This reaction, and the large, though short-lived, appreciation of the exchange rate that accompanies it, does not prevent a prolonged divergence of inflation from target. Twelve quarters after the shock, inflation is still 3 percentage points above the baseline rate. The reasons for this

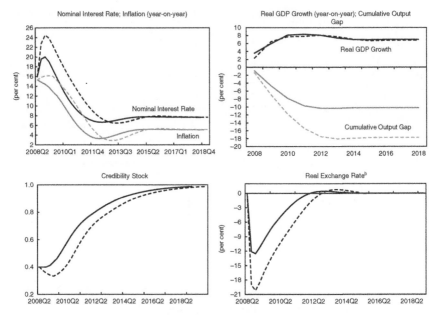

Figure 19.4. Ghana: Negative Supply Shock, 2008–2018[a]

Dotted = Negative shock; Solid = Baseline

[a] All variables are quarterly, except for Real GDP growth, which is annual because quarterly GDP data are not reported in Ghana.

[b] Increase represents depreciation of the cedi.

Source: IMF staff calculations.

are (i) the lagged response of the output gap to the interest rate and exchange rate; and (ii) the adverse, self-reinforcing, impact of the increase in inflation on expectations and credibility.

The second experiment considers a supply shock of the opposite sign, against which BoG does not have to raise the interest rate as much to contain inflationary pressures (Figure 19.5). The inflation does fall below the baseline for an extended period, but this is in line with the announced policy objective, and boosts the stock of credibility. The potential size and duration of the effects of supply shocks on the inflation rate, even when a policy provides appropriate resistance, is a major reason for avoiding rigid adherence to short-run target ranges during the disinflation process.

With full credibility, the central bank raises the interest rate, relative to baseline, by less than 100 basis points.[8] The real price of foreign exchange shows a small, brief increase. The modest tightening, resulting in a small negative output gap, is sufficient to keep inflation close to 5 per cent, because public expectations of inflation are anchored firmly to the target. This result is in line with the experience of the past two decades in countries that have moved from high inflation to stable low inflation. In the 1970s and 1980s, unstable expectations transformed

---

[8] This was end-April 2008 inflation (year-on-year).

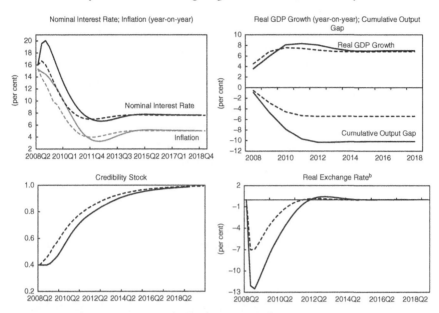

Figure 19.5. Ghana: Positive Supply Shock, 2008–2018[a]

Dotted = Positive supply shock; Solid = Baseline
[a] All variables are quarterly, except for Real GDP growth, which is annual because quarterly GDP data are not reported in Ghana.
[b] Increase represents depreciation of the cedi.

Source: IMF staff calculations.

shocks that under good monetary policy regimes should only have price-level implications—e.g. energy price increases and currency depreciations—into inflation spirals. Monetary policy contained the problem eventually, but only with very tight monetary policies, and at the cost of a substantial output loss. Since the early 1990s, however, many central banks have re-established low-inflation and monetary policy credibility. The public now has confidence that the low-inflation policy objective will prevail, even after substantial price shocks. This in some cases has virtually eliminated the second- and third- round effects of such shocks on the price level. A beneficial supply shock where there is full monetary policy credibility has symmetric implications to the adverse shock (results not reported). The non-symmetries during the process of inflation-reduction and credibility-building are no longer present.

5.2.2 Demand Shock

The results for the expansionary shock, e.g., a change in government spending equivalent to 0.5 per cent of GDP (not reported) are similar to, but more pronounced than the baseline (not reported). This is because the baseline also was a situation of excess demand in the economy. For the expansionary shock, the appropriate policy reaction is a prompt sharp change in the interest rate, and hence in the exchange rate. Firm interest rate reaction effectively mitigates the impact on the goal variables, output and inflation. The contractionary shock requires a slightly more moderate policy reaction. One reason for the asymmetry between the effects of the two shocks is that in the case of the expansionary shock, unlike the contractionary one, the central bank has to offset the potential weakening of credibility. In effect, the drop in demand in the second experiment does some of the disinflationary work for monetary policy.

5.2.3 Costs of Delaying Interest Rate Increase under Imperfect Credibility

Our simulations show that if policymakers delay their response shocks, serious inflationary consequences will follow. Suppose policymakers announce a 5 per cent inflation target in 2008 Q3, but put off the required large interest rate increases until 2009 Q2 out of concern to maintain the level of output. The simulated response shows serious inflationary consequences (Figure 19.6). For several years the deviation between the inflation and the baseline rate widens—to over 5 per cent in 2011. The inflation rate would rise from about 15 per cent currently and remain in double digits until 2011. After an initial hesitation, the interest rate has to play catch-up, and eventually rise far above the baseline—to above 25 per cent in 2009 Q4. From a historical perspective, this would not be

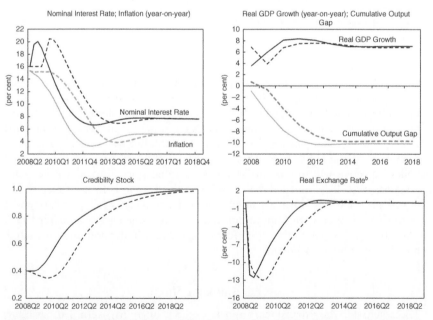

Figure 19.6. Ghana: Positive Demand Shock with Delayed Policy Response, 2008–2018[a]

Dotted = Positive demand shock; Solid = Baseline
[a] All variables are quarterly, except for Real GDP growth, which is annual because quarterly GDP data are not reported in Ghana.
[b] Increase represents depreciation of the cedi.

Source: IMF staff calculations.

unprecedented—e.g., in the early 1980s the US Federal Reserve and the Bank of Canada had to raise short-term interest rates above 20 per cent to stop double-digit inflation. Short-run low interest rate policy, in the face of inflation, eventually turns into a high interest rate policy.

An erosion of credibility is, not surprisingly, a large part of the problem. The stock of credibility declines as the inflation rate fails to decline. Relative to baseline, the simulated loss in the stock of credibility has significant implications. The delay in raising the interest rate does keep demand high in the short run—excess demand intensifies for several quarters. But disinflation requires that a negative output gap eventually open up, and after two years, the gap is wider than in the baseline. Thus, the cost of the monetary policy delay is several years of stagflation.

5.3 Recommendations for Ghana

To respond to Ghana's current challenges for disinflation, the BoG could shift to a more flexible IT regime presented above as IFT, drawing on a model like the one described. As noted, Ghana's challenges are far from unique—IT often encounters problems in the disinflation phase. To respond to these difficulties, IFT is more forward-looking and flexible than the earlier form of IT; indeed, the inflation forecast should be used as an ideal intermediate target in these circumstances. Clearly, a solid forecasting model is an essential element of this approach, and the model presented above could provide a good starting point.

This approach stresses that the key to credibility lies not in hitting precise short-run targets but in a consistent record of policy actions that get the inflation rate back on target within two or three years—a critical difference that applies well to Ghana currently. Figure 19.7 contrasts a traditional 'straight-line hard target' approach to disinflation with a more flexible and modern IFT approach. The optimal path in the baseline scenario differs from the linear path (due to lags and concerns over output losses), and in the event of shocks, the optimal path diverges even further from the linear path. These divergences need not necessarily weaken credibility; a large body of evidence on IT—in countries with widely differing features and initial conditions—indicates that long-term expectations do gravitate over time to the low-inflation targets pursued by a committed monetary policy (which eventually earns strong credibility), despite short-term deviations.

Transparent communications are essential to build credibility in this flexible approach. Transparency is needed with respect both to policy objectives and to the way in which current policy actions are intended to achieve them—operational transparency. Ghana already has an element of goal transparency (the medium-term target of 5 per cent inflation), but could greatly strengthen its operational transparency. Doing so requires that the monetary policymakers have realistic, coherent models of the monetary policy process, from policy instruments to objectives, which they communicate openly.

In particular, the BoG can consider two new steps to strengthen communication:

- publish its forecasts for inflation, the output gap, and the policy rate after each MPC meeting. These forecasts would be revised after each meeting,

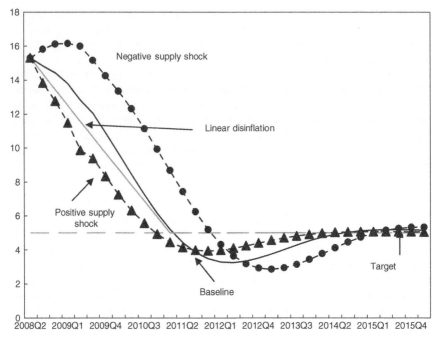

Figure 19.7. Ghana: Linear versus Optimal Disinflation[a] 2008–2015 (year-on-year, per cent)

[a] The optimal disinflation paths are as follows: Baseline (no shocks), Positive supply shock (of 0.5 per cent of GDP), and Negative supply shock (of −0.5 per cent of GDP).

Source: IMF staff calculations.

creating a continuous flow of information about the BoG's reactions to developments; and

- explain ex ante how it would react to different shocks (as in Figure 19.7), providing further transparency and predictability. Indeed, by 'tying its own hands' in advance, the BoG may even insulate itself more from political influence.

Operational transparency magnifies the impact of the central bank's policy on expectations, which in turn reinforces its effectiveness. The Norges Bank has adopted this communication strategy with considerable success. It publishes model-consistent fan charts for all these forecasts, along with examples in the form of risk assessments explaining how it is likely to respond to future shocks. Market participants have begun to anticipate its policy moves, effectively enlisting them as allies in the monetary policy process. This anticipation can be seen in the muted reaction of market interest rates to MPC announcements after this policy was adopted. The impact of shifting to this approach could be enhanced considerably by publishing a policy paper explaining the new approach and including how it would likely react to different future shocks.

6 CONCLUSIONS

In adopting IT while still a low-income emerging-market economy, Ghana has been a trail-blazer. Its recent adverse inflation developments are reason not to abandon IT, but to improve the framework by adopting a more flexible and forward-looking approach to IT.

To support this approach, this paper presents a model that recognizes the difficulties facing Ghana, among them less than perfect credibility of announcements of inflation reduction and policymaker aversion both to movements of output from its potential level and to variability in the interest rate. The model emphasizes the importance of the BoG building credibility over time through consistent pursuit of a low-inflation goal. The nominal anchor is the ultimate target for low inflation; from this foundation, and for given initial conditions, a sequence of short-run inflation-forecast targets may be derived. A loss-minimizing monetary policy would not be locked into a rigid predetermined path of inflation reduction with fixed near-term targets.

The model simulations bear out some intuitive lessons about how monetary policy needs to react in response to shocks during disinflation. The effects of supply shocks on inflation can be large and of significant duration, even with an appropriate policy response—this is a reason to avoid rigid non-credible commitments to short-term inflation-reduction targets. Even so, the BoG must be prepared to raise interest rates to a level that dampens demand and visibley reduce in inflation. Any delay in responding (e.g., out of concern for near-term output losses) damages credibility, ultimately bringing on higher inflation and more prolonged output losses (in a word, stagflation).

The key to transparency and communications in this approach is 'saying what you do and doing what you say'. By providing the public with its forecasts for inflation, output gap, and policy rates, the BoG could better shape expectations despite recent rises in inflation. Explaining ex ante how the BoG would react to different shocks would help market participants anticipate policy moves.

There are many aspects of this model that could be considered for other emerging low-income economies that wish to enhance their monetary policy framework, including incorporation of credibility as an endogenous variable and enhancing the operational transparency and communication strategy of the central bank. These could be useful not only for countries considering a move to IT but also for countries which wish to introduce a more formal and credible commitment to low inflation generally.

APPENDIX 19A: THE STANDARD MODEL

The standard model, presented in Berg, Karam, and Laxton (2006a, b), has four behavioural equations, which feature variables both in terms of deviations from equilibrium values, i.e., as gaps, and in levels:[9]

---

[9] This appendix draws on Alichi et al. (2010).

- Output gap equation
  The output gap equation is an IS curve that relates the output gap to expected and past output gaps, the real interest rate gap, the real exchange rate gap, and the foreign output gap:

$$ygap_t = \beta_{ld}ygap_{t+1} + \beta_{lag}ygap_{t-1} - \beta_{RRgap}RRgap_{t-1}$$
$$+ \beta_{zgap}zgap_{t-1} + \beta_{USygap}ygap_t^{US} + \epsilon_t^{ygap},$$

- where $ygap$ is the output gap, $RRgap$ is the real interest rate gap in percentage points, $zgap$ is the real exchange rate (measured so an increase is a depreciation, in percentage points), and $ygap^{US}$ is the foreign output gap. The output gap is measured as the deviation, in percentage points, of actual output from a measure of the trend or equilibrium level of GDP (a positive number indicates that output is above trend). Economic agents are assumed to know the model and have rational expectations.

- Phillips Curve
  The Phillips curve relates inflation to past and expected inflation, the output gap, the exchange rate, and possibly key world market prices such as oil prices; the Phillips-curve equation may be split into two, one for overall inflation and one for core inflation:

$$\pi_t = a_{\pi ld}\pi 4_{t+4} + (1 - a_{\pi ld})\pi 4_{t-1} + a_{ygap}ygap_{t-1} + a_z[z_t - z_{t-1}] + \epsilon_t^{\pi},$$

where π is the annualized month-on-month inflation rate, $\pi 4$ is the four-quarter change in the CPI, and z is the real exchange rate.

- Taylor Rule
  The variant of the Taylor rule chosen here determines the policy interest rate as a function of the output gap and expected inflation:

$$RS_t = \gamma_{RSlag}RS_{t-1} + (1 - \gamma_{RSLAG}) * (RR_t^* + \pi 4_t + \gamma_{\pi}[\pi 4_{t+4} - \pi_{t+4}^*]$$
$$+ \gamma_{ygap}ygap_t) + \epsilon_t^{RS},$$

where RS is the monetary authorities' nominal interest rate and $*$ denotes equilibrium values.

- Exchange Rate Equation

The exchange rate equation imposes uncovered interest parity (IP), an arbitrage condition that says that real interest rates (on investments in different currencies) will be equalized across countries, up to a country risk premium. A real exchange rate definition is used to write the conventional IP condition as a real IP condition as follows:

$$z_t = \delta_z z_{t+1} + (1 - \delta_z) z_{t-1} - [RR_t - RR_t^{US} - \rho_t^*]/4 + \epsilon_t^z,$$

where RR^{US} is the foreign real interest rate and ρ^* is the equilibrium risk premium. The first two terms on the right hand capture agents' real exchange rate expectations.

Equilibrium values are determined on the supply side. To preserve simplicity, the supply-side variables are assumed to follow simple stochastic processes not shown here for brevity. In practice this means that the analyst must make assumptions about equilibrium values, based on a variety of sources, including judgemental estimates or econometric analyses.

APPENDIX 19B: THE MODEL

Our model of inflation with endogenous credibility has the following main components:

- Inflation equation—an expectations-augmented Phillips curve.
- Expectations process and credibility.
- Non-linear output gap effect.
- Output gap equation.
- Exchange rate-real interest rate parity equation.
- Monetary policy loss function.

We explain each of these components below.

Inflation Equation—An Expectations-Augmented Phillips Curve

The inflation equation is as follows:

$$\pi_t = \lambda_1 * \pi 4_t^e + (1 - \lambda_1) * \pi 4_{t-1} + \lambda_2 * \left(\frac{y_{t-1}}{y_{max} - y_{t-1}} y_{max}\right) + \lambda_3 * \Delta z_t + \epsilon_t^\pi$$

where, $\pi 4_t^e$ and $\pi 4_{t-1}$ are the forward-looking and backward-looking components of inflation, y_{t-1} is the output gap in period $t - 1$, y_{max} is the maximum output gap possible. z (in logs) is the real exchange rate (measured so an increase is a depreciation, in percentage points), and Δz_t is changes in real exchange rate (z_t) from last period's level (z_{t-1}). λ_1, λ_2, and λ_3 are model parameters and ϵ_t^π is the supply shock.

The terms in the equation, from left to right, represent:

- backward- and forward-looking components to the expectations process—with an endogenous credibility stock in the forward-looking component $\lambda_1*\pi 4_t^e + (1 - \lambda_1)*\pi 4_{t-1}$ where, $\pi 4_t = \frac{1}{4}\sum_{i=1}^4 \pi_{t+i}$ and $\pi 4_t = \frac{1}{4}\sum_{i=1}^4 \pi_{t-i}$. We will characterize how inflation expectations—$\pi 4_t^e$—are formed in the next sub-section.
- non-linear output gap effect ($\lambda_2*(\frac{y_{t-1}}{y_{max}-y_{t-1}} y_{max})$).
- exchange rate pass-through ($\lambda_3*\Delta z_t$).

In line with the evidence, the equation contains a mechanism that changes the formation of expectations from a drifting, backward-looking, process to one which is anchored by the low-inflation target.

Expectations Process and Credibility

Inflation expectations are formed as follows:

$$\pi 4_t^e = \gamma_t * \pi 4_{t+4} + (1 - \gamma_t) * \pi 4_{t-1} + b_t + \epsilon_t^{\pi^e}$$

The first two terms in the equation for expected inflation comprise a weighted average of a model—consistent forecast of the four-quarter inflation rate (forward-looking component) and the inflation rate observed last quarter (backward-looking component). The weight on the forward-looking component, γ_t, evolves between 0 (no credibility) and 1 (full credibility)—and is therefore a measure of the stock of credibility.

We use these scenarios to define a credibility coefficient. In order to define the evolution of the credibility stock, we postulate that the public sees a possibility for one of two inflation regimes—'L' and 'H', for 'Low' and 'High' inflation. In the 'L' scenario, inflation would converge to the announced inflation target of π_t^{*}[10]. The 'H' scenario corresponds to a

[10] The inflation target is defined as the mid-point of the targeting range.

suspicion in the public mind that monetary policy might deliver an inflation rate much higher than the announced target—we suppose that rate to be very high, say 40 per cent. Under the H scenario, inflation would converge to 40 per cent. We use these scenarios to define a credibility coefficient:

$$\eta_t = \frac{\left(\pi 4_t^H - \pi 4_t\right)^2}{\left(\pi 4_t^H - \pi 4_t\right)^2 + \left(\pi 4_t^L - \pi 4_t\right)^2}.$$

The coefficient η_t gauges the extent to which inflation outcomes are seen as consistent with the 'Low' inflation scenario. Consider two extreme cases:[11] in the 'L' case, inflation converges gradually to the inflation target and η_t converges to 1, since the term $\left(\pi 4_t^L - \pi 4_t\right)$ in the denominator of the equation above equals 0;[12] in the 'H' case on the other hand, η_t equals 0, implying complete lack of credibility. Credibility is lost—people give increased weight to a suspected high inflation scenario—if inflation outcomes are above the announced target.[13] The credibility stock (γ_t) then evolves in the following autoregressive form:

$$\gamma_t = \rho * \gamma_{t-1} + (1 - \rho) * \eta_{t-1} + \epsilon_t^{\gamma}.$$

An increase in η_t results in a rise in the weight of the forward-looking component of expectations. This ties inflation more tightly to the target, such that the central bank has to do less in response to shocks and that convergence to the target rate is faster. Disturbance term ϵ_t^{γ} represents a shock to central bank credibility, which may be positive or negative.

b_t, the inflation expectations 'bias' is simply defined as a proportion of the deviation of a weighted average of hypothetical inflation expectations from the inflation target, where the weights reflect the credibility stock (γ_t):

$$b_t = 0.2 * \left(\gamma_t * \pi 4_t^{e,L} + (1 - \gamma_t) * \pi 4_t^{e,H} + \pi_t^*\right).$$

Based on this equation, as credibility approaches unity, the bias converges to zero, since $\pi 4_t^{e,L}$ will tend to converge to the inflation target.

Under the no credibility scenario $(\gamma_t = 0)$, the inflation bias is positive and is proportional to the difference between the high hypothetical inflation expectations and the target.[14]

Non-linear Output Gap

Empirical evidence suggests that the output gap effect on inflation is non-linear (e.g. Debelle and Laxton, 1997). In the Phillips curve we introduced an exponentially increasing impact on inflation, as follows: $\lambda_2 * \left(\frac{y_{t-1}}{y_{max} - y_{t-1}} y_{max}\right)$.

The parameter λ_2 captures the marginal effect of inflation for small values of the output gap. This term implies that output gap cannot exceed a maximum value of y_{max}. We set y_{max} equal to 5 per cent in the model simulations. Thus, as the gap approaches 5 per cent, it has a diverging positive effect on the inflation rate (see Figure B.1). This puts a limit on the

[11] We can think of inflation as specified in equations 6 and 7 to evolve according to a first-order, stationary autoregressive process, reverting in the long run to a targeted level of inflation in the 'L' case and 10.8% in the 'H' case. The parameter values on lagged inflation are indicative of the rate of convergence to the steady state, with high persistence values implying a longer time to converge.

[12] This term is the expectation error of the low hypothetical inflation expectation.

[13] The convergence rate parameter of the credibility stock was calibrated to 0.7, i.e., it takes 1.5–2.0 years for credibility to rebuild from some below-full level of initial credibility.

[14] Clear evidence of inflation bias stemming from a credibility problem is seen in the behavior of the inflation premium in the UK bond market before 1997.

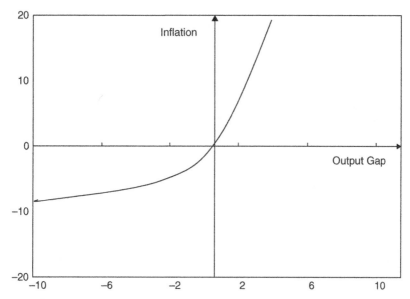

Figure 19B.1. Non-linear Phillips Curve, an Example

Inflation (per cent); Output Gap (per cent of GDP)

Source: IMF staff calculations.

extent to which expansion of demand can stimulate an increase in output: at y_{max}, increases in demand result only in increasing inflation. Because of the non-linearity, an economy operating with an output gap near the maximum will subsequently have to incur long periods of negative output gaps to restore the desired inflation rate.

Output Gap Equation

Domestic output depends on the real interest rate, the real exchange rate, and demand in the rest of the world, represented by the United States.[15]

The equation is written in terms of deviations from equilibrium values. The output gap is the deviation, in percentage points, of actual output from a measure of the trend or equilibrium level of GDP (a positive number indicates that output is above trend). It is a function of the gap between the actual real interest rate and its equilibrium value, the real exchange rate gap, and the US output gap. Dynamics are added through the influence of past and future domestic output gaps, and lagged reactions to the interest rate and exchange rate:

$$y_t = \beta_1 * y_{t-1} + \beta_2 * y_{t+1} - \beta_3 * (rr_{t-1} - \overline{rr}) + \beta_4 * (z_{t-1} - \bar{z}) + \beta_5 * y_t^{US} + \epsilon_t^y.$$

[15] Representations such as this one are usually motivated with a first-order condition consistent with optimizing consumers with habit formation. See Smets and Wouters (2003) or Laxton and Pesenti (2003) for a linearized version of the Euler equation for consumption that depends on lagged and expected consumption, real interest rates, and a habit-persistence parameter. However, habit-persistence alone cannot account for a very large weight on the lagged output gap, which is resolved in DSGE models by adding investment to the model and significant adjustment costs associated with changing the levels of investment.

where rr is the real interest rate in percentage points, y_t^{US} is the U.S. output gap, and '-' denotes the equilibrium value of a variable. The term ϵ_t^y represents a demand shock.

Exchange Rate-Real Interest Rate Parity Equation

We assume real uncovered interest parity (IP) holds, up to a country risk premium. The expected increase in the exchange rate is equal to the domestic-foreign interest differential plus the risk premium. The equation for the current exchange rate equation may thus be written (in logs) as:

$$[rr_t - rr_t^{US} - \delta]/4 = (z_{t+1}^e - z_t) + \overline{rr} + \overline{rr}_t^{US} + \epsilon_t^z$$

where, rr_t^{US} is the US real interest rate and δ is the equilibrium risk premium.

Expectations for the exchange rate are a weighted average of a forward-looking, model-consistent component, and a backward-looking component:

$$z_t^e = \varphi * z_{t+1} + (1 - \varphi) * z_{t-1}.$$

Portfolio preference shocks, e.g. exchange market disturbances, which can be large for emerging market economies, are in the term ϵ_t^z.

Monetary Policy Loss Function

Under IT, almost by definition, the monetary policy loss function attaches a high cost to deviations of inflation from target. In the short run, monetary actions also affect interest rates and output, and policymakers are averse to fluctuations in output from potential and to variability of the interest rate from one period to the next. Aiming to keep output at its potential level—i.e. minimizing the amplitude of the business cycle—has an obvious justification since this is a fundamental objective of macroeconomic policy.

Aversion to interest rate variability, which is evident in the widely observed practice of central banks to adjust interest rates only gradually in response to changes in conditions, has a more technical rationale. Whereas the policy interest rate controlled by the central bank is a very short-term rate, the market interest rates that affect spending and output are not so short-term. Effective transmission of policy actions requires that these market rates respond predictably, in line with movements in the policy rate. With low variability in the policy rate, financial markets can project that a change this quarter will have some duration in the quarters ahead. Longer-term rates, which incorporate expectations of the future policy rate, then respond relatively strongly to policy actions.[16]

High quarter-to-quarter variability in the policy rate, on the other hand, reduces its impact on relevant market rates, and weakens the effectiveness transmission.

With these considerations in mind, the loss function in the model cumulates a weighted sum of:

- squared deviations from the inflation target
- squared output gaps, and
- squared one-quarter changes in the policy interest rate

$$Loss_t = \sum_{t=1}^{\infty} v^t [\omega_1 * (\pi 4_t - \pi^*)^2 + \omega_2 * y_t^2 + \omega_3 * (rs_t - rs_{t-1})^2].$$

---

[16] On these lines, Woodford (2003) argues that a strategy of gradual interest adjustment may be optimal.

The weights (ω_i) embody the costs policymakers attach to each of these items. The discount factor is denoted by v. Monetary policy minimizes this loss function, subject to the constraints imposed by the structure of the model. Monetary policy has choices with respect to the path towards the inflation target. This may be fast, if the cost of misses is high relative to the costs of output and interest rate instability. Or it may be slow, if the cost of targeting errors is relatively low.

The quadratic loss function implies symmetric aversion to overshoots and undershoots with respect to the inflation target. One might argue that policymakers' preferences would not be symmetric under a program of inflation reduction. They might regard an undershoot as a benign, though unexpectedly rapid, approach to the low-inflation objective, but an overshoot as a serious threat to the program. Despite the symmetric loss function, the full model does not imply symmetric policy responses. For example, endogenous credibility encourages a stronger interest rate response to overshoots than to undershoots.

REFERENCES

Alichi, A., Laxton, D., Dagher, J., Clinton, K., Mills, M., and Kamenik, O. (2010). *A Model for Full-Fledged Inflation Targeting and Application to Ghana.* IMF Working Paper 10/25. Washington, DC: International Monetary Fund.

Barro, R. and Gordon, D. (1983). A Positive Theory of Monetary Policy in a Natural Rate Model. *Journal of Political Economy*, 91(4), 589–610.

Berg, A., Karam, P., and Laxton, D. (2006a). *A Practical Model-Based Approach to Monetary Policy Analysis: Overview.* IMF Working Paper 06/80. Washington, DC: International Monetary Fund.

Berg, A., Karam, P., and Laxton, D. (2006b). *A Practical Model-Based Approach to Monetary Policy Analysis: A How-To Guide.* IMF Working Paper 06/81. Washington, DC: International Monetary Fund.

Debelle, G., and D. Laxton (1997). Is the Phillips Curve Really a Curve? Some Evidence for Canada, the United Kingdom, and the United States. *IMF Staff Papers,* 44(2) 249–82.

International Monetary Fund (2006). Country Report No. 06/229. Washington, DC: International Monetary Fund, pp. 12–17.

International Monetary Fund. (2008a). *Ghana: Selected Issues.* Washington, DC: International Monetary Fund.

International Monetary Fund. (2008b). *Regional Economic Outlook, Sub-Saharan Africa.* Washington, DC: International Monetary Fund.

Kamenik, O., Kiem, H., Klyuev, V., and Laxton, D. (2008). *Why is Canada's Price Level So Predictable?* IMF Working Paper 08/25. Washington, DC: International Monetary Fund.

Laxton, D. and Pesenti, P. (2003, July). Monetary Polciy Rules for Small, Open, Emerging Economies. *Journal of Monetary Economics*, 50, 1109–46.

Mishkin, F. and K. Schmidt-Hebbel. (2001). *One Decade of Inflation Targeting in the World: What Do We Know and What Do We Need to Know?* NBER Working Papers 8397. National Bureau of Economic Research.

Roger, S. and Stone, M. (2005). *On Target?: The International Experience with Achieving Inflation Targets.* IMF Working Paper 05/163. Washington, DC: International Monetary Fund.

Rogoff, K. (1985). The Optimal Degree of Commitment to an Intermediate Monetary Target. *The Quarterly Journal of Economics*, 100(4), 1169–89.

Smets, F. and Wouters, R. (2003). An Estimated Stochastic Dynamic General Equilibrium Model of the Euro Area. *Journal of European Economics,* 49, 947–81.

Woodford, M. (2003). Optimal Monetary Policy Inertia. *Review of Economic Studies*, 70, 86–8.

20

A Structural Analysis of the Determinants
of Inflation in the CEMAC Region

Rafael Portillo

1 INTRODUCTION

In this chapter[1] we aim to identify the main determinants of inflation in the Communauté Economique et Monétaire de l'Afrique Centrale (CEMAC) and the transmission channels involved. The CEMAC is a monetary union comprising six countries in Central Africa (Cameroon, Congo, Gabon, Equatorial Guinea, the Central African Republic, and Chad), with monetary policy run at the regional level by the Banque des Etats de l'Afrique Centrale (BEAC), and with the local currency (the CFA franc) fixed to the euro.[2] Our focus is on the region as a whole rather than on the individual countries.

We are particularly interested in the role of fiscal policy in inflation dynamics. Oil is the largest export sector in the CEMAC, and a large share of oil revenues accrues to the national governments.[3] Fluctuations in oil revenues can therefore lead to sizeable changes in the fiscal stance, aggregate demand, and inflation. Movements in the latter variable also play an important role in external adjustment. This is because oil windfalls and the associated fiscal policy response affect the equilibrium real exchange rate, but under a fixed exchange rate this can only be achieved through changes in inflation. This dual nature of inflation is a key part of the macro policy challenge in pegs, and the CEMAC is no exception.

Our analysis consists of two parts. First, we use a semi-structural VAR analysis to identify the sources of inflation empirically. Second, we develop a dynamic stochastic general equilibrium model to analyse the channels through which oil-revenue-driven fiscal policy propagates in the region. We find that fiscal shocks—measured as changes in the non-oil fiscal stance—have been an important source

---

[1] This chapter is a considerably revised version of IMF (2008).

[2] There are two monetary unions in Africa with their currency fixed to the euro, the second being l'Union Economique et Monétaire Ouest-Africaine (UEOMA), which comprises eight West-African countries: Benin, Burkina-Faso, Guinea-Bissau, Cote d'Ivoire, Mali, Niger, Senegal, and Togo.

[3] All countries in the CEMAC region export oil, with the exception of the Central African Republic (its main export commodity is diamonds). An important issue for the region is the expected depletion of oil reserves over the next two to three decades, which raises a number of macro challenges but is outside the scope of this chapter.

of inflation, accounting for about 20 per cent of inflation volatility over the last ten years. In addition, passive monetary accommodation plays an important role in the propagation of fiscal shocks. This is not because of direct monetary financing or fiscal dominance more generally. Instead, fiscal expansions in commodity exporters are associated with improvements in the balance of payments, which also result in endogenous, unsterilized increases in reserve accumulation under the fixed exchange rate, and a corresponding monetary accommodation. By allowing inflation to increase, monetary policy helps deliver the real appreciation mentioned above.

We also use the model to study the implications of a more active monetary policy, in which case the central bank balance sheet would no longer expand endogenously in response to an oil-driven fiscal expansion. Under a peg, the latter policy is only possible if the capital account is closed, which is a strong but somewhat plausible assumption for the CEMAC region. An active monetary policy would be associated with greater (sterilized) reserve accumulation, which would help contain equilibrium appreciation pressures and therefore the pressures on inflation. The cost is that the private sector would be crowded out to create the necessary savings to support higher reserves. The policy lesson is that attempting to use monetary policy to contain inflation under a peg has important drawbacks, which further highlights the importance of prudent fiscal policy for macro and price stability in these regimes.

The chapter is organized as follows: Section 2 presents some visual evidence regarding the link between fiscal policy (and other variables) and inflation. Section 3 presents results from a VAR-based approach. Section 4 presents the DSGE model, while Section 5 presents model-based simulation results. Section 6 concludes.

2 STRUCTURAL DETERMINANTS OF INFLATION IN THE CEMAC REGION: THE USUAL SUSPECTS

The structural analysis of inflation requires the identification of the main shocks that may affect the price level, as well as the channels through which these shocks operate. A list of potential candidates includes fiscal policy, monetary policy, imported inflation, domestic supply shocks, and changes in regulated prices. While they are all likely to be important in accounting for price fluctuations at any given quarter, this chapter does not address the issue of regulated prices. Each of the remaining shocks is discussed below.

2.1 Fiscal Policy

As discussed above, oil-driven fiscal policy may be an important source of aggregate demand. This is especially the case if government spending is concentrated primarily on local goods and services. To identify the fiscal impulse in oil-rich economies requires that oil revenue be excluded from the measure of the

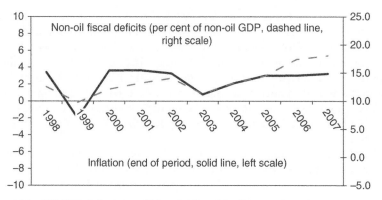

Figure 20.1. CEMAC: Inflation and Non-Oil Fiscal Deficits 1998–2008

fiscal stance. The resulting non-oil fiscal balance for the entire region, defined here as the sum of non-oil deficits over the sum of non-oil GDP for each country is presented in Figure 20.1 along with end of period inflation for the entire region.[4]

There is a clear link between these two variables at annual frequency. However, there is the risk that the positive relationship may be driven by a third variable. For example, if the real depreciation of the CFA franc is positively correlated with inflation (which is the case, as will be shown later), then the co movement in Figure 20.1 could be driven by public expenditure items that are sensitive to exchange rate fluctuations, such as interest payments on external debt, or expenditure items concentrated on imported goods, such as capital expenditures. Since these items should not lead to an increase in demand pressures, the measure of the fiscal stance is further refined by removing these components.[5] Figure 20.2 shows the time series for this alternative measure.

The co movement between the fiscal stance and inflation is now higher than before: the correlation is 0.83. In order to understand where this co-movement is coming from, we explore the link between the fiscal stance and other variables. First, the fiscal stance is also correlated with non-oil GDP growth (Figure 20.3), which suggests that the fiscal stance has a considerable impact on aggregate demand.

In addition, the region's fiscal stance is also closely correlated with average money growth.[6] Figure 20.4 displays the co movement between the fiscal stance and money growth, measured both in terms of money and in terms of non-oil GDP.

---

[4] Inflation numbers for the CEMAC region are constructed as a PPP-weighted geometric average of member countries' inflation.

[5] There is a break in the series in 2002. This may reflect a change in the classification of spending or revenue items. However, the comovement between the series pre-break with the variables of interest (money growth, inflation, non-oil growth) is as strong—at least visually—as it is post-break, albeit a different level. For the purpose of the analysis, we correct the pre-break series with the difference in levels pre- and post-2002.

[6] We define average money growth as the average of the end of period money growth over four quarters.

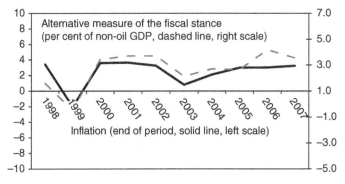

Figure 20.2. CEMAC: Inflation and the Fiscal Stance 1998–2008

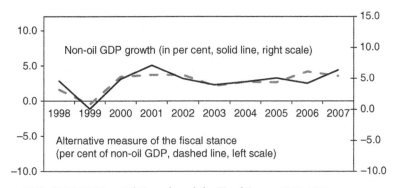

Figure 20.3. CEMAC: Non-Oil Growth and the Fiscal Stance 1998–2008

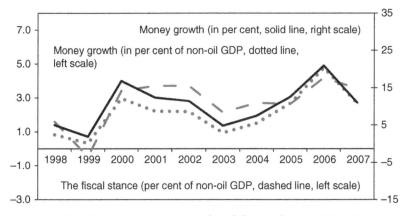

Figure 20.4. CEMAC: Average Money Growth and the Fiscal Stance 1998–2008

Two features of the relationship are worth emphasizing. First, there is a strong co movement between money growth and the fiscal stance: the correlation is 0.83. Second, the magnitude of the changes in broad money, measured as a fraction of non-oil GDP, is similar to the magnitude of the fiscal stance. This relation does not operate through the standard concept of fiscal dominance, which would interpret such relations as driven by direct monetary financing of the deficit. Indeed, the comovement between the fiscal stance and growth in net credit to the government during this period is −0.37. Instead, this comovement is the result of higher government spending out of oil revenue, which is associated with greater reserve accumulation and monetary policy accommodation. This mechanism will be explored in our model.

2.2 Monetary Policy

In principle, under a fixed exchange rate regime (fixed to the euro in this case), monetary policy is not autonomous. Capital mobility implies that the domestic short-term interest rate is determined by the rate in the euro plus the risk premium associated with that country or group of countries. Moreover, the stock of money is determined by the liquidity needs of economic agents and the inflows of foreign capital to finance purchases of local assets and goods. In the CEMAC region, however, there is de facto limited mobility of capital, which provides some degree of independence for monetary policy and implies that the short-term interest rate may deviate from the euro rate, or more generally that monetary policy shocks may be a source of inflation pressures. In practice, however, monetary policy is mostly passive, in that the policy stance reflects endogenous changes in money demand and in the balance of payments, often as a result of fiscal policy developments. For this reason, we do not consider monetary policy shocks, i.e., exogenous changes in the policy stance, as a likely candidate for driving inflation. However, it also implies that endogenous changes in monetary policy can play an important role in inflation dynamics. Note that we will also consider the implications of a more active monetary policy with the use of the DSGE model.

2.3 Imported Inflation

Imported inflation is another likely candidate that can help account for fluctuations in prices. Figure 20.5 displays imported inflation, measured as an import-weighted index of inflation in the CEMAC's main trade partners multiplied by their nominal exchange rate vis-à-vis the CFA franc:

From Figure 20.5, imported inflation leads domestic inflation by two or three quarters. It can therefore help predict domestic prices at a relatively high frequency.

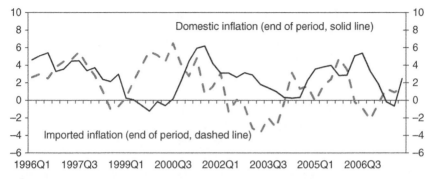

Figure 20.5. CEMAC: Domestic and Imported Inflation 1996:1–2007:4

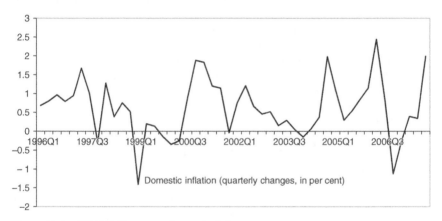

Figure 20.6. CEMAC: Domestic Quarterly Inflation 1996:1–2007:4

2.4 Domestic Supply Shocks

Finally, inflation displays large one time changes from one quarter to the next, as shown in Figure 20.6.

While some of these quarterly changes reflect the lower frequency fluctuations in the fiscal stance, part or most of this high-frequency variation is likely due to domestic supply shocks, such as changes in domestic agricultural production. Indeed, the low average inflation observed in 2007 is attributed in part to agricultural developments in Chad. These high-frequency changes could also reflect changes in regulated prices and/or measurement error, which is an important issue in the region. However, we will not dwell on those issues for the purposes of this analysis.

The previous analysis has indicated that there are three major likely candidates for understanding inflation developments in the region: fiscal policy shocks, shocks to imported inflation, and domestic supply shocks. It is important to identify the contribution that each one of these shocks has made to the overall variance of inflation. We estimate such contribution with a semi-structural VAR for the CEMAC economy, presented below. Secondly, we compare those results with a DSGE model, with an emphasis on the fiscal shock.

3 ASSESSMENT OF STRUCTURAL SHOCKS WITH A SEMI-STRUCTURAL VAR

In light of the evidence presented in Section 2, we estimate a vector auto regression (VAR) with two lags and five variables: imported inflation, the fiscal stance, non-oil GDP growth, money growth, and inflation. We make the following identifying assumptions. First, we assume that imported inflation is exogenous relative to the other variables. Second, we identify fiscal shocks by assuming that these respond contemporaneously to shocks in imported inflation only.[7] Third, we interpret domestic supply shocks as unexpected changes in inflation that are orthogonal to contemporaneous movements in all other variables. This identification scheme seems plausible but, as with all VAR identification schemes, is not without drawbacks. For example, it may lead to a downward bias in the estimated contribution of supply shocks to overall inflation.[8]

We first present the variance decomposition of all variables by type of shocks in Table 20.1. Since the VAR is only semi-structural, the contribution of the three shocks need not add up to one. Imported inflation accounts for about 36 per cent of the volatility of inflation, while shocks to the fiscal stance account for about 20 per cent and domestic supply shocks explain an additional 16 per cent. Fiscal shocks also account for a sizeable fraction of the volatility of money growth, consistent with Figure 20.3. The variance decomposition only provides the

Table 20.1. CEMAC: Variance Decomposition by Type of Structural Shock

	Fiscal shocks	Shocks to imported inflation	Domestic supply shocks
	Share of total volatility (in per cent)		
Inflation	18.23	36.25	15.9
Money growth	27.71	57.35	0.42
Non-oil GDP growth	30.51	36.25	9.4
Fiscal stance	37.29	42.33	5.3
Imported inflation	0	100	0

Source: Staff calculations

---

[7] The use of VARs to identify exogenous changes in fiscal policy and trace their effects through the economy starts with Blanchard and Perotti (2002). Alternative measures rely on a narrative approach to identification, such as in Ramey and Shapiro (1998).

[8] The VAR is estimated with quarterly data for the period 1998 Q1–2007 Q4; the annual statistics for the fiscal stance and non-oil GDP growth are interpolated to create quarterly time series.

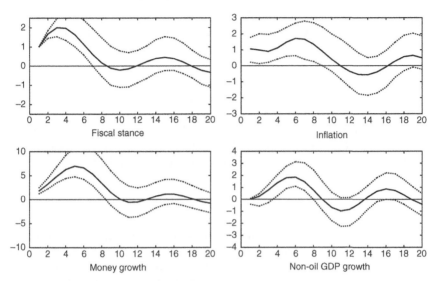

Figure 20.7. CEMAC: Impulse Response Functions Following a 1 Per Cent Increase in the Fiscal Stance, Based on VAR Estimates

contribution of fiscal shocks, rather than the contribution of the fiscal stance itself. Indeed, part of the contribution of higher import prices to inflation may be operating through an endogenous response in the fiscal stance: higher imported inflation, if it represents an appreciation of the dollar, may fuel an expansionary fiscal response since oil revenues are increasing in FCFA. The large role of imported inflation in the VAR may thus be explained in part by the fiscal expansion that may follow, and the share of money growth volatility that is accounted by the latter attests to that hypothesis.

Figure 20.7 presents the impulse response function for all variables (except imported inflation, which by assumption is exogenous) following a one percentage point increase in our measure of the fiscal stance, with the tenth and ninetieth percentiles of their distribution.[9] Inflation increases by as much as 1.7 per cent after five quarters, while money growth increases by almost 7 per cent and non-oil GDP increases by about 1.5 per cent. These estimates are in line with the comovement we observed in previous graphs and suggest that the non-oil fiscal stance is an important source of aggregate demand in the region.

We now describe a macroeconomic model that can help us rationalize the evidence just presented.

4 THE MODEL

The DSGE model is a simplified version of the model in Chapter 12. The model has been extended by introducing habit formation in utility and backward-looking

---

[9] Confidence intervals were derived using the bootstrap procedure described in Kilian (1998).

indexation in the Phillips curve. This section briefly presents the equations of the model in log-linearized form (i.e., in percentage deviations from the steady state), organized by economic agent.[10]

4.1 Consumers

Every quarter, the representative consumer chooses an inter-temporal path for consumption (C_t), demands financial assets and money, and makes labour supply decisions. Consumption decisions are given by the now-standard forward-looking IS equation:

$$C_t = \frac{1}{1+h} E_t C_{t+1} + \frac{h}{1+h} C_{t-1} - \frac{1-h}{1+h} \sigma^{-1}(R_t - E_t \pi_{t+1})$$

where R_t is the short-term nominal interest rate and $E_t\pi_{t+1}$ is the expected quarterly inflation rate. The parameter h denotes the degree of habit formation in consumption, while σ is the relative risk aversion coefficient. Consumers also choose how to allocate consumption between three types of goods: non-traded goods and services (C_t^N), domestic agricultural products (C_t^{NF}), and imported goods (IMP_t). Demand for each is as follows:

$$C_t^N = \chi p_t^N + C_t$$

$$C_t^{NF} = \chi p_t^{NF} + C_t$$

$$IMP_t = \chi p_t^{IMP} + C_t.$$

Demand depends on the prices of each type of good relative to the overall CPI: p_t^N, p_t^{IMP}, and p_t^{NF}.[11] The parameter χ refers to the price elasticity of demand. We assume that the law of one price holds, which implies $p_t^{IMP} = s_t$, where s_t (S_t) is the real (nominal) exchange rate $(s_t = s_{t-1} + S_t - S_{t-1} - \pi_t)$.

The allocation of consumption across goods leads to the following equation for inflation (as deviation from steady state inflation, which equals zero):

$$\pi_t = n_1 \pi_t^N + n_2 \pi_t^{NF} + (1 - n_1 - n_2)\pi_t^{IMP}.$$

Imported inflation is set to zero for simplicity $(\pi_t^{IMP} = 0)$. Regarding financial assets, consumers choose between domestic and foreign assets $(b_t$ and $b_t^*)$, subject to a portfolio adjustment cost—measured in terms of changes in holdings of foreign assets—that prevents uncovered interest rate parity from holding in the model. This leads to the following relation between domestic interest rates R_t and the expected rate of depreciation of the nominal exchange rate $(S_{t+1} - S_t)$:

$$R_t = -\phi b_t^* + E_t(S_{t+1} - S_t).$$

---

[10] For an introduction to DSGE models, see Gali and Gertler (2007) in the case of a closed economy and Gali and Monacelli (2005) in the case of a small open economy.

[11] Relative prices are related to inflation measures as follows: $p_t^i = p_{t-1}^i - \pi_t + \pi_t^i$, for $i = N, NF, IMP$.

The portfolio adjustment cost, given by the coefficient ϕ, is a proxy for the degree of capital mobility in the model. Demand for real money balances is as follows:

$$m_t = M_t - P_t = \frac{\sigma}{1-h}C_t - \frac{\sigma h}{1-h}C_{t-1} - \gamma R_t.$$

Finally, labour supply (L_t) is given by a Frisch-type equation derived from utility maximization:

$$\frac{1}{\eta}L_t = w_t - \frac{\sigma}{1-h}C_t + \frac{\sigma h}{1-h}C_{t-1}.$$

4.2 Firms

There are two local non-oil sectors in the economy: the non-traded sector and domestic agriculture. Firms in the non-traded sector produce goods using local labour: $Y_t^N = aL_t^N$. Firms have some degree of market power and set the prices at which they sell their products. Price setting is also subject to nominal rigidities, as well as some degree of indexation to past prices, all of which leads to a hybrid Phillips curve for non-traded goods inflation π_t^N:

$$\pi_t^N = \rho_\pi E_t \pi_{t+1}^N + (1-\rho_\pi)\pi_{t-1}^N + \kappa_\pi(mc_t^N - p_t^N).$$

Non-traded inflation increases if real marginal costs increase relative to real prices in the sector. Real marginal costs are given by:

$$mc_t^N = w_t - (1-a)L_t^N.$$

Finally, production of local agricultural goods is assumed as exogenous and set to zero $Y_t^{NF} = 0$. Non-oil GDP is given by the sum of these two sectors, weighted by their steady state shares:

$$Y_t = \lambda_N Y_t^N + (1-\lambda_N)Y_t^{NF}.$$

4.3 The Government

To simplify, we assume that the government's sole source of revenue comes from oil, which is modelled as an exogenous flow of foreign resources. In addition, we assume that all government spending is focused on the non-tradable sector. The government's inter-temporal budget constraint is the following (θ_X refers to the steady state level of variable X in per cent on non-oil GDP):

$$\theta_G(p_t^N + G_t) = \theta_{OIL}(s_t + OIL_t) + \theta_b(b_t - b_{t-1} + \pi_t)$$
$$-\theta_{bc}(\beta^{-1} - 1)(bc_{t-1} - \pi_t).$$

An increase in oil revenue will lead to an increase in government spending (G_t), all else equal. In addition, a real appreciation of the currency ($s_t \downarrow$) and/or an increase in the relative price of non-tradable ($p_t^N \uparrow$) will reduce the purchasing power of oil revenues and will lead to a decline in real government spending.

The variable b_t denotes deviations in real debt from its steady state value. bc_t denotes the log-level of real debt that is held by private agents, on which the government pays real interest rate $\beta^{-1} - 1$ (at steady state).[12] We assume that the government perfectly targets a constant level of real debt, which implies $b_t = 0$.

Oil revenues follow an exogenous AR(1) process:

$$OIL_t = \rho_{OIL} OIL_{t-1} + u_t^{OIL}.$$

We also define the non-oil fiscal balance as a percentage of non-oil GDP as $gy = p_t^N + G_t - Y_t$.

4.4 The Central Bank

In real terms, changes in the central bank balance sheet are given by:

$$\theta_m(m_t - m_{t-1} - \pi_t) = \theta_{bcb}(bcb_t - bcb_{t-1} - \pi_t) + \theta_{RR}(RR_t^* - RR_{t-1}^*)$$

where bcb_t refers to the central bank's holdings of government debt and RR_t^* is the level of international reserves. Reserve accumulation is as follows:

$$RR_t^* = \omega_S(S_t - S_{t-1}).$$

Reserve accumulation depends on the degree of exchange rate targeting. In the case of a fixed exchange rate regime such as the CEMAC's, ω_S is calibrated to be infinitely large, which implies $S_t = S_{t-1} = \bar{S} = 0$.

With regards to monetary policy, we assume that the size of the central bank balance sheet (and therefore the stance of policy to some extent) is determined by the endogenous accumulation of international reserves. This is implemented by setting the level of the central bank's net domestic assets to be constant in nominal terms, which implies the following process for the real level of domestic assets (in logs):

$$bcb_t = bcb_{t-1} - \pi_t.$$

Such an exogenous rule is consistent with monetary policy implementation in the CEMAC region, which as we discussed earlier is mostly passive.

4.5 Market Equilibrium Conditions

Closing the model requires ensuring that markets clear. There are three equilibrium conditions and one resource constraint (or external balance condition) that must hold at every period. First the labour market must clear:

$$L_t = L_t^N.$$

[12] The remaining stock of government debt is held by the central bank, such that: $\theta_b b_t = \theta_{bc} bc_t + \theta_{bcb} bcb_t$.

Second, the non-traded goods market and the market for locally produced agricultural products must also clear:

$$\lambda_N Y_t^N = n_1 \theta_c C_t^N + \theta_G G_t^N$$
$$Y_t^{NF} = C_t^{NF}.$$

Finally, external balance requires that imports be financed by: (i) oil revenues (OIL_t), (ii) drawing down on private sector foreign assets (b_t^*), or (iii) drawing down on international reserves (RR_t^*). This yields:

$$\theta_{IMP}(IMP_t + p_t^{IMP}) = \theta_{OIL}(OIL_t + s_t) - \theta_{b^*}\left(b_t^* - \beta^{-1}b_{t-1}^* + (1 - \beta^{-1})s_t\right)$$
$$-\theta_{RR}(RR_t^* - RR_{t-1}^*).$$

5 CALIBRATION AND SIMULATION RESULTS

The model has twenty-four parameters, of which four are imposed by steady state identities $(\theta_{bcb}, \theta_b, \theta_{OIL}, \theta_{IMP})$. Seven parameters $(\theta_G, \theta_{bc}, \theta_m, \theta_{RR}, \lambda_N, n_1, n_2)$ are based on broad features of the CEMAC region. Calibration is presented in Table 20.2. The portfolio adjustment cost (ϕ) and the degree of exchange rate targeting via reserves (ω_S) are set 'infinitely high' (10^5) to replicate a closed capital account and a fixed exchange rate regime, respectively. The country's steady state private net foreign asset position (θ_{b_*}) was set to zero for simplicity. The habit parameter (h) and the backward-looking term in the Phillips curve (ρ_π) were chosen to generate plausible inflation dynamics in the model, while the choice of parameters (a, β, η, γ) follows standard practice in the DSGE literature. The risk aversion coefficient (σ), the elasticity of inflation to real marginal costs (κ_π), and the elasticity of substitution across types of goods (χ) reflect our priors that in developing countries: (i) aggregate demand is not very sensitive to changes in financial conditions, (ii) inflation is moderately sensitive to movements in output, and (iii) there is limited substitutability between imports and domestic goods. Finally the persistence of oil revenues (ρ_{OIL}) is consistent with the prolonged, though ultimately temporary, nature of fluctuations in oil revenues.

Table 20.2. Calibration

h	0.90	a	0.6000	θ_G	0.15
σ	5.00	ρ_π	0.1000	θ_{OIL}	0.149
χ	1.10	κ_π	0.0500	θ_B	0.15
n_1	0.35	λ_N	0.5000	θ_{BC}	0.1
n_2	0.50	ρ_{OIL}	0.9000	θ_{BCB}	0.05
ϕ	10^5	β	0.9900	θ_{IMP}	0.15
γ	-1.50	ω_S	10^5	θ_M	0.15
η	0.50	θ_{b^*}	0.01	θ_{RR}	0.1

Figure 20.8 presents the impulse response functions in the model following a one percentage point increase in the fiscal stance, driven by higher oil revenues ($u_t^{OIL} > 0$). The paths are similar to those found in the VAR, except that the responses display less persistence and the growth rate of money is smaller. This relatively good match between data and model supports using the model to study the channels of transmission of fiscal policy and the interaction with monetary policy, which we do next.

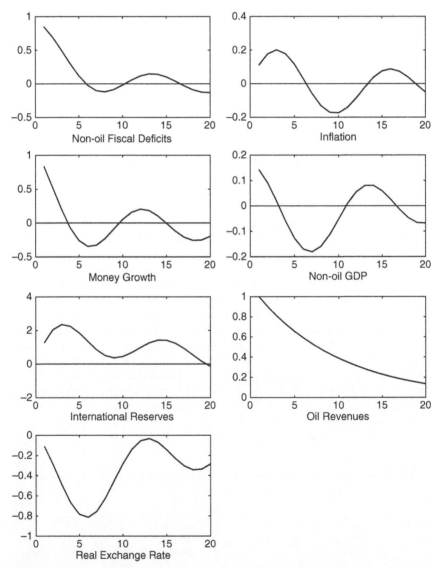

Figure 20.8. Impulse Response Functions Following a 1 Per cent Increase in the Fiscal Stance, Model Simulations

5.1 The Impact of Fiscal Shocks in the DSGE

Here we elaborate on the impact of an increase in the non-oil fiscal deficit according to the model. When the government receives the additional oil income, and before the fiscal stance is changed, it is typically the case that the additional external revenue is deposited at the central bank. International reserves increase by the amount of the oil revenue, while net domestic assets of the central bank decrease, as government deposits are now higher.

As the government proceeds to spend this additional revenue, there is both a demand and a liquidity dimension to the spending. On the real side, provided it focuses on the non-traded sector, an increase in government spending will increase the demand for these goods, causing an increase in non-traded production and incipient inflationary pressures. The increase in the price of non-traded goods, i.e., the real appreciation, will lead consumers to substitute those goods for imports, which will help absorb part of the additional external revenues.

On the liquidity side, the drawing down of government deposits to finance the higher spending will lead a monetary injection. Under the assumption that monetary policy is passive, there is no offsetting operation to undo the effect on the monetary base. This monetary injection accommodates the increase in non-traded goods inflation described earlier. On the other hand, the increase in imports partially offsets the monetary expansion as it draws on the additional international reserves that were initially accumulated. Of course, ultimately what matters for the stance of policy is the level of nominal and real interest rates, which would be expected to decrease following the monetary expansion. However, interest rates are also affected by the increase in money demand. The stronger the increase in money demand, due to the expansion in nominal economic activity, the smaller the decrease in nominal and real interest rates.[13] The latter effect helps dampen the inflationary pressures to some extent.

The end result from these various interactions is an expansion in activity, a temporarily higher inflation rate, a more appreciated real exchange, a decline in real interest rates though not necessarily nominal rates, an endogenous expansion in the size of the central bank balance sheet, and an increase in international reserves.

5.2 Active Versus Passive Monetary Policy

Is there a role for a more active monetary policy in this context? First, much depends on the degree of international capital mobility. Under our assumption of a perfectly closed capital account, there is scope for great monetary policy activism, since domestic interest rates are not pinned down by uncovered interest rate parity. We explore such activism by replacing the zero nominal growth rule for the central bank's net domestic asset ($bcb_t = bcb_{t-1} - \pi_t$) with a rule specifying zero growth for nominal money balances:

---

[13] An increase in the nominal interest rate is also possible, though the increase in inflation makes real interest rate increases less likely.

$$m_t = m_{t-1} - \pi_t.$$

The above rule implies that any monetary expansion resulting from the accumulation of reserves and drawing down of government deposits will be sterilized by selling part of the central bank's stock of government bonds ($bcb_t \downarrow$).[14] Figure 20.9 compares the macroeconomic effect of fiscal expansions under these two rules.

By preventing the monetary base from expanding, the central bank is containing aggregate demand pressures in the economy, which is reflected in the smaller increase in inflation and smaller real appreciation, even though the fiscal expansion is broadly the same.[15] A tighter control of aggregate demand leads to a decrease in private absorption and reduces the increase in imports, which implies a larger share of the additional oil revenue is accumulated as reserves. The latter is also consistent with a smaller real appreciation. The tighter monetary policy stance is reflected in higher real interest rates, compared with the passive case (at least over the first eight quarters).

5.3 Discussion

Does the above simulation suggest the central bank should be more active, or as active as is allowed by the degree of international capital mobility? Although it would appear that a tighter policy would be consistent with the price stability mandate, the reality is more complex. This is because an active monetary policy in this environment (peg and limited capital account) has real effects which go beyond the standard role of nominal aggregate demand management. In particular, the sterilized accumulation of reserves is affecting the degree of economy-wide absorption of the additional oil revenue, and comes at the cost of crowding out the private sector, in a context in which much needed additional external resources are becoming available to the country's development. It is unlikely that the costs from preventing the private sector from accessing those resources would be warranted by the benefits from price stability. This further points to the dual role of inflation in countries with fixed exchange rates that we have stressed throughout this chapter.

The above discussion does not imply that there is little merit in accumulating reserves, or sovereign assets more generally, when there are external windfalls such as higher oil revenues. Nor does it imply that there is little to gain from greater macro and price stability in pegs. However, these objectives are best achieved by making fiscal policy less pro-cyclical, and by tying the accumulation of external assets to public savings (and explicit rules for the latter), as is the case for example with sovereign wealth and macro stabilization funds.[16]

---

[14] If the capital account is perfectly open, then efforts to sterilize the accumulation of reserves would result in large capital inflows, by adding incipient pressures on domestic interest rates, and further reserve accumulation. The central bank may stop sterilizing if the stock of reserves (and the associated sterilization costs) becomes too large.

[15] On the margin, the smaller real appreciation when monetary policy is active makes the (real) fiscal expansion larger.

[16] See for example, Chapter 12 and Berg et al. (2013).

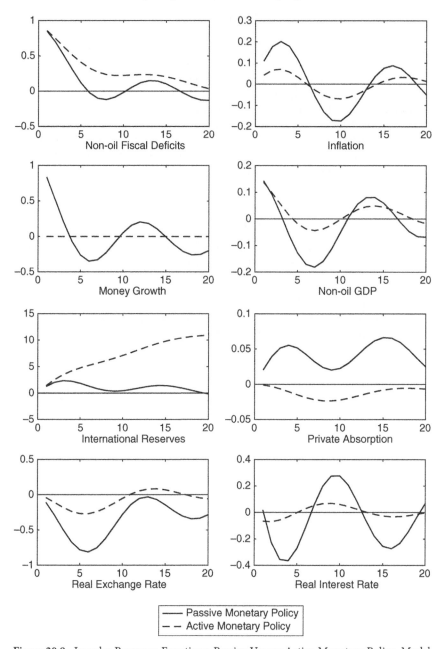

Figure 20.9. Impulse Response Functions, Passive Versus Active Monetary Policy, Model Simulations

6 CONCLUSION

The results presented in this chapter have highlighted the role of the fiscal stance in driving inflation in resource-rich countries with fixed exchange rates. The chapter has also presented a general equilibrium model to understand the channels through which fiscal policy affects inflation under a peg, and the role of passive versus active monetary policy rules.

From a policy perspective, the framework presented here could be useful for the BEAC when assessing its policy options. In particular, it could simulate alternative paths for the economy under alternative fiscal policy responses, as well as under different monetary policy arrangements.

REFERENCES

Berg, A., Portillo, R., Yang, S. C., and Zanna, L. F. (2013). Public Investment in Resource-Abundant Developing Countries. *IMF Economic Review*, 61(1), 92–129.

Blanchard, O., Perotti, R. (2002). An Empirical Characterization of the Dynamic Effects of Changes in Government Spending and Taxes on Output. *Quarterly Journal of Economics*, 117(4), 1329–68.

Gali, J. and Gertler, M. (2007). Macroeconomic Modelling for Monetary Policy Evaluation. *Journal of Economic Perspectives*, 21(4), 3–24.

Gali, J. and Monacelli, T. (2005). Monetary Policy and Exchange Rate Volatility in a Small Open Economy. *Review of Economic Studies*, 72, 707–34.

International Monetary Fund. (2008). *Central African Economic and Monetary Community: Selected Issues Paper*. IMF Country Report 08/254. Washington, DC: International Monetary Fund.

Kilian, L. (1998). Small Sample Confidence Intervals for Impulse Response Functions. *Review of Economics and Statistics*, 80(2), 218–30.

Ramey, V. and Shapiro, M. (1998). Proceedings from Carnegie-Rochester Conference Series on Public Policy 48: *Costly Capital Reallocation and the Effects of Government Spending*. North-Holland: NBER.

Index

Printed and bound by CPI Group (UK) Ltd, Croydon, CR0 4YY